ART NOUVEAU ARCHITECTURE

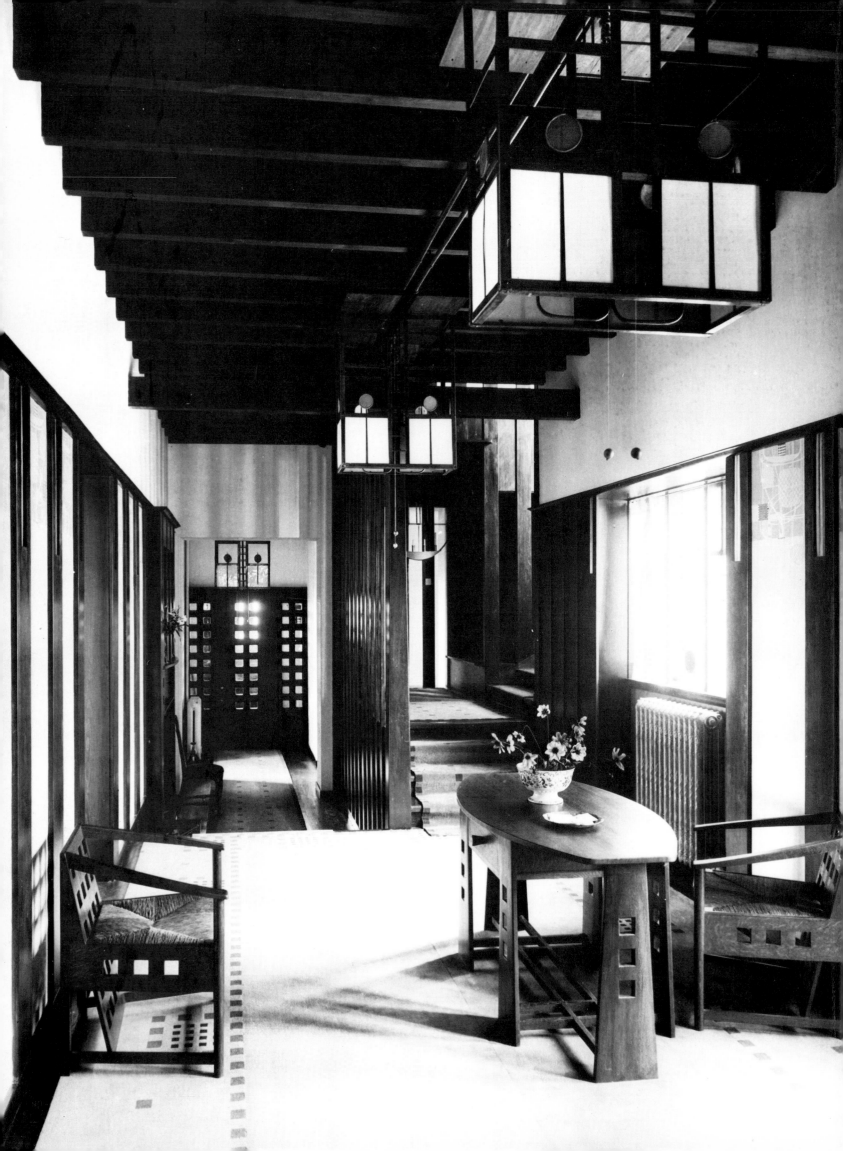

ART NOUVEAU ARCHITECTURE

Edited by Frank Russell

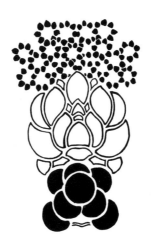

ACADEMY EDITIONS·LONDON

Front cover
HORTA *Maison and atelier Horta* Brussels 1898–1900, detail of rooflight above main staircase (photograph Le Berrurier)

Front flap
OLBRICH *Ernst Ludwig Haus* Darmstadt 1899, entrance detail (photograph Benton)

Back cover
WAGNER *Second Villa Wagner* Vienna 1912-13, entrance detail (photograph Godoli)

Back flap
MACKINTOSH *Glasgow School of Art* Glasgow 1896-1909, staircase (photograph Goulancourt)

Frontispiece
MACKINTOSH *Hill House* Helensburgh 1902-03, hallway (photograph Lemere)

This edition published in 1983 by
Bibliophile Books, 33 Maiden Lane, London, WC2E 7JS.

First published in Great Britain in 1979 by
Academy Editions 7/8 Holland Street London W8

First paperback edition 1983

ISBN 0 85670 136 X

Printed and bound in Hong Kong

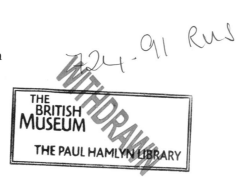

CONTENTS

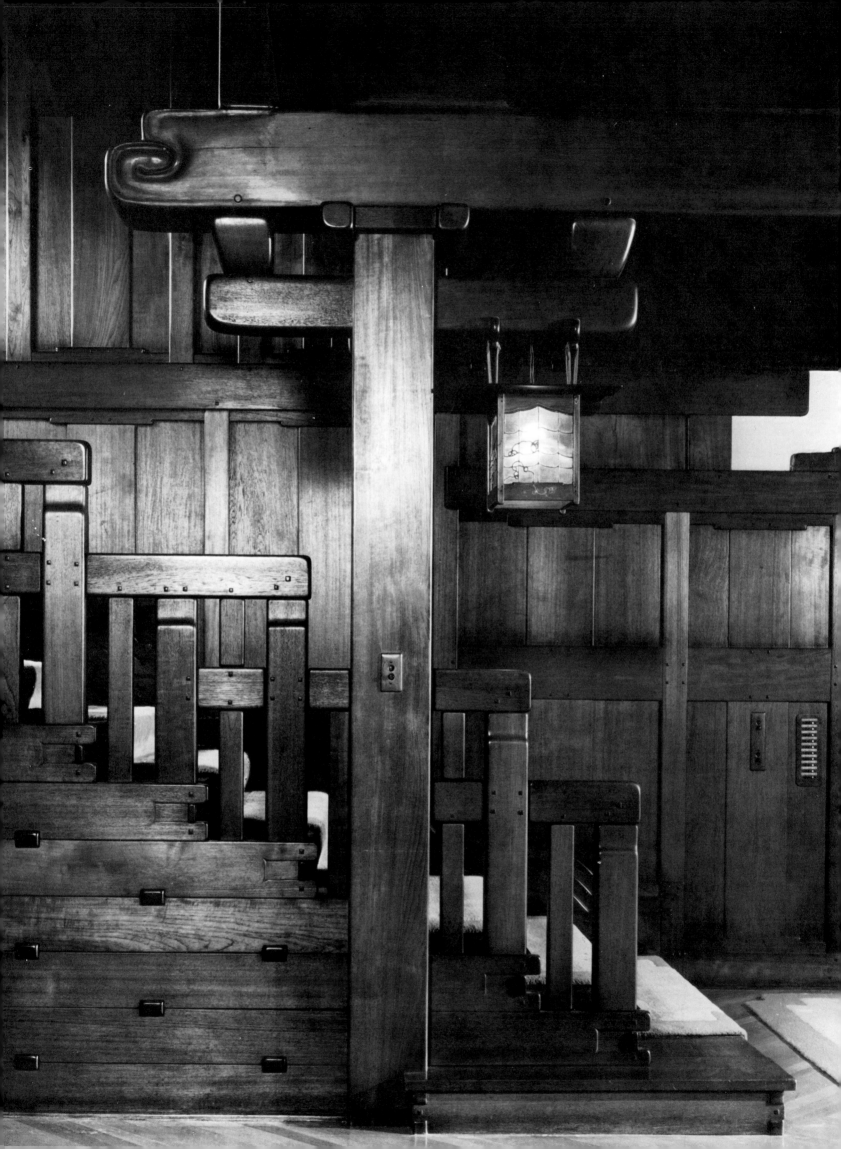

FOREWORD

Only recently has Art Nouveau architecture ceased to be regarded as a retrogressive interlude between historicism and the Modern Movement, and this largely as a result of the re-evaluation of the role and importance of ornamentation in architecture. This book, the result of over five years of collective research, has arisen in response to the need for an international survey of the work carried out immediately before and after the turn of the century. The period 1895 to 1905 was one of great inventiveness and variety, giving rise to both the curvilinear style seen in the work of Horta and Guimard and the rectilinear style of Mackintosh and Hoffmann which heralded the modern preoccupation with geometry. The term Art Nouveau is here used to describe both idioms. It was a period which also coincided with the culmination – and inception – of the careers of a number of celebrated masters: Mackintosh, Gaudí, Horta, Guimard, Berlage, Jeanneret, Behrens, D'Aronco, Kotěra, Olbrich, Hoffmann, Wagner, Sullivan, Wright; the roll-call of practitioners speaks for itself. These and other architects who designed in an Art Nouveau manner built not only private houses for wealthy entrepreneurs but also schools, hospitals, civic centres, theatres and churches. It is to be hoped that this cultural legacy is recognised before more of the recent planning insanities witnessed in Brussels, Paris and other centres are repeated, and that the example set by the Amigos de Gaudí in Barcelona and the Prague Symposium of 1971 is followed and the best of Art Nouveau architecture preserved.

Contained in the following pages is a survey of Art Nouveau architecture in all the principal Western countries, set against a discussion of the current ideological and social background. Even in a book of this scope, however, many interesting examples to be found elsewhere – in Moscow, Kracow and even Istanbul – have had to be omitted. For practical purposes the work of a particular architect will usually be found under the country in which it was executed, and indeed the international character of the movement can be seen by the numerous cases of architects who received commissions abroad.

It is in the nature of the subject that the illustrations play an important part, and wherever possible contemporary photographs have been used. Photography has been specially commissioned in a number of cases where a building has been maintained in its original condition. Photographers are credited individually, archival sources may be found in the appendix; all other photographs are from the Academy Editions archives. Original plans and elevations have been redrawn for clarity, and thanks go to Ian Latham for the Olbrich drawings and to John Read for all others. In addition thanks go to Adrian Bertolucci (Austria), Eve Horwitz (Belgium), Richard Padovan (Italy) and Vicky Wilson (Introduction, France) for translations. Thanks above all go to the contributors for their collaboration and patience. This book was originally conceived by the publisher Dr Andreas Papadakis, whose constant enthusiasm and encouragement have been invaluable.

Opposite
GREENE & GREENE *Robert R. Blacker house*
Pasadena 1907, entrance hall staircase (photograph Rand)

Frank Russell
London, 1979

7

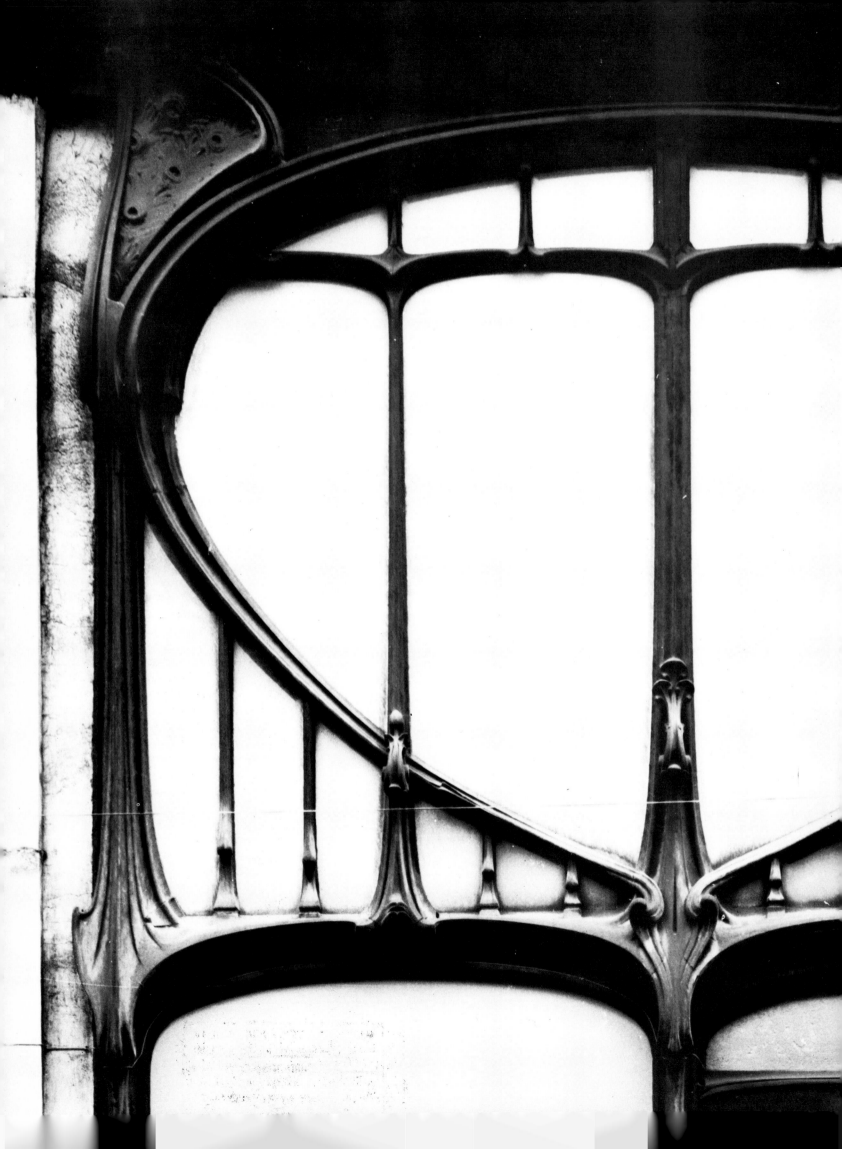

INTRODUCTION

Roger-Henri Guerrand

In the second volume of his *Entretiens sur l'Architecture* which first appeared in 1872, Viollet-le-Duc advocated a 'sinewy' style of architecture, to be achieved by the use of metal, which would allow a lighter structure. A prototype of this style had already been in existence for twenty years – Sir Joseph Paxton's Crystal Palace. One could also add the Menier factory, built at Noisiel between 1871 and 1872 by J. Saulnier, an architect who had not been trained by the Ecole des Beaux-Arts. In the middle of Paris on the rue de Sèvres in 1878, L. C. Boileau erected a building for the shop 'Au bon marché' in collaboration with the engineer Eiffel – a simple metal cage in which each upright and crosspiece constituted an essential part of the whole. But Aristide Boucicaut, who was on the point of revolutionising the principles of mass-distribution, wanted to dazzle his customers with a display of palatial luxury – inside, Boileau was forced to install a proliferation of bronzes, stuccos and re-mounted canvases.

It would be easy to cite other equally convincing examples, both in France and abroad. It was imperative that iron should make an impression in a century during which its production in the industrial West broke new records each year. J. K. Huysmans, a shrewd observer of contemporary life, wrote in his work *L'Art Moderne* in 1879: 'It is easy for us today to recognise a well-defined evolution in the fields of literature and painting; it is just as easy for us to gauge what the modern conception of architecture will be. The monuments are there for all to see: the architects and engineers who built the Gare du Nord, les Halles, the cattle market of la Villette and the new hippodrome have created a new art, just as noble as the old, but an art which is contemporary from top to bottom, which has almost excluded wood and the raw materials supplied by the earth to take from the factories and foundries the power and lightness of their furnaces.'

At the Paris Universal Exhibition of 1889 some fine minds saw the 'Galerie des Machines', designed by Ferdinand Dutert in collaboration with the engineer Contamin, as a continuation of the style of the Crystal Palace. An irreversible trend was to be set in motion which would wipe out the degenerate neo-classicism of the Ecole des Beaux-Arts. For the School had regarded itself as an inviolable temple to classicism since M. Ingres, in his reply to the statement which preceded the attempted reform of Napoleon III, had dismissed Industry with the words: 'Let it stay where it belongs, and not come and settle on the steps of our School, true temple of Apollo, dedicated only to the art of Greece and Rome!'

No-one dared to attack Dutert – one of the most brilliant members of the Ecole des Beaux-Arts, winner of the Grand Prix de Rome in 1869 and an eminent archaeologist – but the ignoble tower of the engineer Eiffel provided an easy target for fiery criticism, and a solemn protest was sent to Alphand, organiser of the exhibition, by a committee of artists which included Garnier and Vaudremer: 'Is then the city of Paris to associate herself with the eccentric and mercantile ideas of a machine manufacturer, to dishonour herself and irreparably spoil her beauty? For the Eiffel Tower, which even commercial America would not want, is, make no mistake about it, a dishonour to Paris.'

An outburst of such self-righteous indignation is characteristic of the architect of the Paris Opéra, and provides a remarkable example of a group of professionals in the process of self-organisation, for Garnier was to become the president of their 'Société centrale'. We know that Garnier and his collaborators travelled around Europe to study the lay-out of the principal Opera houses then in existence, and yet the Paris Opéra has no innovative features, except perhaps its dimensions and its orgy of polychromatic decoration. But Garnier never thought of trying to conceal his plagiarisms: he displays them all openly with a sincerity which disarms the critic. After the harsh, pure neo-classicism of the first half of the nineteenth century, the age of eclecticism, of the bourgeois curio collector's favourite antique shop had arrived.

A man of lower-class origins – an insignificant Parisian from the rue Mouffetard – Garnier was fascinated by the middle-class society of his time, paying it homage in the main staircase of the Opéra (for the theatre was for a long time merely a fashionable parade ground). Viollet-le-Duc was the only one to reproach him for sacrificing his auditorium to this show of virtuosity which, apart from its dimensions, lacked even the merit of being original. Garnier was infatuated by the charm of the picturesque to the point of absurdity (he protested against Haussmann's orders for the resurfacing of facades and was a great supporter of the corbelling in the streets of the city), and tended to sacrifice everything to the most flashy effect possible. For proof, there is no need to look further than the Opéra itself, where he decided on principle that it would be impossible to build an auditorium in which the stage would be visible from every seat (the Opéra contains 318 'blind' seats and 120 which are 'monocular', according to R. Lieberman) and was reluctant to give up his chandelier despite the fact that a system of concealed lighting had already been perfected and was in use at the Châtelet and the Théâtre Lyrique: 'Without this prominent, salient feature, the vista would look cold and bare, the auditorium empty and monotonous, like a plain without trees, a sea without ships.'

Another consequence of the unhealthy romanticism in which Garnier revelled was his contempt for iron. A victim of the teaching of a school to which he owed his rise in society, Garnier confirmed himself as a supporter of the wall: 'When it is necessary to enclose and encompass, when it is necessary to build a wall, iron will be rejected as incompatible with solidity. As solidity, and thus walls, are the basic, imperative elements of the art of architecture, we will have to return to the materials which suit their requirements.'

Garnier was thus to become a stubborn opponent of Eiffel and those of his colleagues seduced by the attractions of metal. In 1886, when the plans for the Paris underground seemed almost complete, Garnier wrote to the Minister of Public Works: 'The underground, in the eyes of the majority of Parisians, will be inexcusable unless it totally rejects any industrial characteristics and becomes a true work of art. Paris must not turn into a factory; she must remain a museum. Do not therefore be afraid to cast aside latticed beams and steel frames; recall stone and marble, bronze, sculptures and triumphal columns.' The policy of the Moscow underground under Stalin . . .

Garnier was a typical sample of the products of the Ecole des Beaux-Arts in Paris. Dangerous even by his example, he luckily took no part in the training of architectural students. The latter, however, were placed in excellent hands after the birth of the Third Republic – those of Julien Guadet, the true master of French architecture throughout the last quarter of the nineteenth century. A pupil of the School at the time of Napoleon III's attempted reform in 1863, Guadet headed the opposition against Viollet-le-Duc. Although he built very little, his work *Eléments et théorie de l'architecture*, of some 2,700 pages in length, was the Bible of the rue Bonaparte for many decades.

It is Guadet who was chiefly responsible for the lack of serious training given to pupils at the Ecole des Beaux-Arts during a period when the manufacture of new materials such as iron and concrete heralded a revolution in the art of building. His inauspicious actions – already denounced by Anatole de Baudot, himself a faithful disciple of Viollet-le-Duc – held back the evolution of the School for half a century. Hypocritically benign (he liked to talk of our school as a prime example of 'friendly education', where the teacher must respect the pupil's personality), Guadet was in fact a convinced elitist: he would have liked to have seen the technical side of architecture (mathematics, surveying, legislation etc.) confined to colleges entrusted with the selection of pupils gifted for 'le Beau'. To these alone would the School be prepared to impart an education centred on preparation for the Concours de Rome.

In this promotion of 'Beauty', it was naturally necessary to proscribe the 'Useful'. It was to the Acropolis, not to the Palais de l'Industrie, that the professors took their pupils. Iron became a symbol of materialism (for since the Second Empire there had been a return by the middle classes to 'spiritual values' and Catholicism), and engineers were seen as an obvious incarnation of its adherents. They were also suspected of socialism because of the close contact they maintained with the workers. These technicians showed themselves incapable of drawing up aesthetically pleasing plans, and also lacked all sense of symmetry, that key concept of French architecture.

The results of this way of teaching can still be seen almost in their entirety today, and constitute an awesome museum of impotence. We may admire the castle of Chantilly by Honoré Daumet, winner of the Grand Prix in 1885 – a subtle anthology of Philibert Delorme and a pillage of various documents published on the Renaissance, the result of which was unanimously considered to be a work of genius. Or perhaps we might prefer the work of Jean-Louis Pascal, winner of the Grand Prix in 1866, a master of imitation who paraphrased the style of Louis XIII in his Bibliothèque Nationale. The next generation was to introduce the note of eroticism which these somewhat dry chapters, lifted from a stylistic textbook, lacked. The 'spirit' of the painting of Bouguereau, Cabanel and Gervex was to pass into architecture, which from then on began to use callipygous nudes. The most depraved of these pornographers, apart from Victor Laloux, winner of the Grand Prix in 1878, who covered the Town Hall of Tours in Atlases and reclining nymphs, seems to be Paul-Henri Nénot, winner of the Grand Prix in 1877. On his return from Rome, he was entrusted with the construction of the new Sorbonne – an austere building if ever there was one, but with a delectable surprise for the well-informed erotomaniac displayed boldly and doubtlessly with sacrilegious intent in the holy of holies, the 'salle des thèses', the famous Louis Liard lecture theatre. From the four corners of the ceiling hang ample breasts covered in scales, with artistically bared pink nipples . . .

★　　★　　★

The irreparable damage caused by the rue Bonaparte was not confined to France, for the School accepted many foreign students, particularly Americans. American students zealously took the sound doctrines they had learned back home, and were able to make a name for themselves with works which were directly descended from French soil. Richard Morris Hunt, who entered the School in 1846, was the favourite pupil of Lefuel, with whom he worked for several years at the Louvre. On his return to America, he soon became a specialist in Renaissance style homes for multi-millionaires: the Vanderbilt residence, on Fifth Avenue, New York had a fine heritage. Henry Hobson Richardson, who entered the School in 1860 and was a pupil of André, stayed in Paris for six years and numbered among the collaborators of Labrouste. It was Richardson who introduced the Romanesque of Auvergne to America, and the undisputed masterpiece in this style will always be the Boston Trinity (1872-77), in red sandstone. This honest, craftsman's reproduction was to fascinate American architects for at least twenty years, and they continued to build villas and farms in a modernised Romanesque manner. But Richardson was not a man of just one style – he built the New York State Capitol in Albany as a replica of the Hôtel de Ville in Paris. One day, Grace descended upon him. He came to Chicago and built, in ashlar, blocks of flats which, in their strictly functional character, were inconsistent with the sacred principles of the Ecole des Beaux-Arts and thus prepared the way for the advent of the sky scraper.

The new age began with the works of William Le Baron Jenney, himself a true engineer, trained at the Ecole Centrale des Arts et Manufactures de Paris, where he received his diploma in 1856. Sullivan, a former pupil of Vaudremer (la Santé prison and the church of Saint-Pierre in Montrouge) was to bring the new trend to a point of perfection, and during the 1890s it seemed legitimate to think that America would become the melting pot for types of architecture unknown in Europe. This was, however, without reckoning on the untapped strength of academicism and its followers. An act of Congress authorised the staging of an international exhibition in Chicago to coincide with the four hundredth anniversary of the discovery of America by Columbus. A vast site – three times larger than that of the Paris Exhibition of 1889 – was reserved on the lakeside. The ten most famous American architects were each commissioned to construct a pavilion. The Horticultural Building was assigned to Jenney and the Transportation Building to Sullivan.

The young architect hoped that this exhibition would be a landmark in the history of world architecture, but he had underestimated his adversaries. One of those responsible for the totality of the project, in the Italian Renaissance style which was finally adopted, was none other than Richard Hunt. As a result, the machine pavilion looked like a church, with two bell towers and a peristyle. Venetian gondoliers were imported, and the emigrants found themselves back amidst the décor of good old Europe. Sullivan, however, felt that this antiquarian masquerade marked the death of architecture in a land of liberty and democracy which prided itself on its imagination, its spirit of enterprise and its progressive attitude: '. . . and thus ever works the pallid academic mind, denying the real, exalting the fictitious and the false . . . The damage wrought by the World's Fair will last for half a century from its date, if not longer.'

This prophecy was to come true. Until the arrival of the German architects Gropius and Mies van der Rohe, driven from Germany by Nazism, America was dominated by a retrograde movement which was to efface almost all the achievements of the precursors of the nineteenth century. American students continued to enroll at the Ecole des Beaux-Arts in Paris: after the First World War, the average number of American candidates at the entrance examination was fifteen, as against sixty French applicants. As Jacques Gréber wrote in 1920, in a work whose title is in itself a masterpiece:[1] 'Young American architects come to Paris to learn drawing, composition and to formulate their taste at our Ecole des Beaux-Arts. They complete their visual education, and acquire a little of our instinct for harmony and of our creative sensibility while travelling through the ancient regions of our land where they breathe in the atmosphere of the past along with our air and climate.' Which shows that, as far as the 'cultured' Frenchman was concerned, the Chicago School never existed. Louis Gillet, a member of the Académie Française, mentions Sullivan in the passage dealing with religious architecture in the U.S.A. in volume VIII of André Michel's famous *Histoire de l'Art* (1928-29), and puts him on the same footing as Goodhue, a specialist in neo-Gothic. More recently, neither Pierre Lavedan in his *Histoire de l'Art* nor the compilers of the *Grand Larousse Encyclopédique* even mention the Chicago School.

And so, in the industrial society of the nineteenth century, as was already the case in painting, no artist would set to work without the shelter of a cultural patronage, and it became necessary to give 'classical' guarantees at every step. Gottfried Semper was right when he noted in his work *Der Stil* (1860): 'Our towns are mosaics of buildings from every country and every age, to the extent that in the end we will no longer know to which century we belong.' When this perspicacious architect tackled a building such as the Dresden Opera, however, he had no hesitation in conceiving it in the style of the early Renaissance. When his work was destroyed by fire in 1869, Semper rebuilt it in a late Renaissance style. The building was again destroyed by bombs in February 1945, and after twenty-five years of deliberation, the East Germans finally decided to rebuild it exactly as it had been originally. This time, could one speak of 'modernised' Renaissance?

In Great Britain, which was at the time increasingly open to exoticism, different styles from all over the world appeared on the streets, from Chinese pagodas to Egyptian temples, and from Indian palaces to pure Gothic constructions. Between 1840 and 1852 Charles Barry and Auguste Pugin built the Houses of Parliament, a mad pastiche which was soon to become a paradigm. Steindl drew his inspiration for the Parliament in Budapest from it, while the Stock Exchange at Anvers, built in iron, is also clothed in neo-Gothic forms. In the young kingdom of Belgium, Joseph Polaert was seized by a wave of Hellenic excess, and designed his Palace of Justice as a fantastic arrangement of oriental intrigues. Lost among this mish-mash of increasingly insane collages, the Hungarians broke all bounds. In his Palais de la Redoute, Feszl combined decorative elements taken from the facades of the Romanesque churches in Poitou with motifs found in the trimmings of his compatriots' national costumes. And as for Lechner, his pupil, he was to weave variations on the

Granada Alhambra.

The exhibition of 1900 seemed to sanctify the triumph of the pasticheurs, marking a clear regression from that of 1889, which had had the audacity to present iron in all its nudity. The exhibition was simply a fairy-tale palace, created by a bourgeois class seized by a fever of colonial exoticism. 'Provincial observers are astonished', wrote one chronicler, 'to see rising up before their dazzled eyes more minarets than around the Golden Horn, more cupolas than at Odeypour, more gopuras and stone lattice-work than at Kombakoroum or Chillambaram.' This delirium was stamped with the highest possible guarantee: that of the venerated master, Julien Guadet himself. As Paris was situated in the centre of a clay basin, it seemed logical to clothe the iron skeletons in clay. 'Just as the theatre gives us an impression of the monumental by using the illusion of perspective,' wrote Guadet, 'so plaster décor can give us this impression in relief by using the illusion of substance.'

Only three buildings have survived from the extraordinary collective orgasm of the Universal Exhibition of 1900. The single metal arch of the Alexandre III bridge, the work of two engineers Resal and Alby, was alone worthy of the 'seal of architectural art', granted by Cassien-Bernard and Cousin, who surpassed themselves with their pylons and obelisks. The commission for the Grand Palais was shared between three associates who cased the metal entrance hall in stone, a process for which Baltard had already furnished the sublime example at Saint-Augustin. The favourite style was the gigantesque of Baalbeck, cross-bred with classical references. Charles Girault, winner of the Grand Prix in 1880, made an impression as a specialist in modern Louis XVI. He was an easy winner of the competition for the Petit Palais, and this charming building was such a success that it prompted Léopold of Belgium to entrust other important works to its architect . . .

*   *   *

The academicians thought the fight was over. The French innovators were no longer supported by *Le Figaro*: 'We are not as neurotic, as hallucinated, such smokers of opium as we appear', wrote one editor. 'The modern style is a degenerate attitude which we have assumed, just as one sometimes sees respectable women plaster their fresh skin with outrageous make-up and affect loose manners only to frustrate immediately the hopes they have aroused.'

Luckily, the rot went a lot deeper than the casual observer might have suspected. During the exhibition of 1900, the International Congress of Architects sat for the fifth time, and Professor Johannes Otzen, from the Academy of Arts in Berlin, read an astonishing paper. In the presence of Emile Trélat, Director of the Ecole Spéciale d'Architecture in Paris, who had just divulged to his colleagues the profound aesthetic emotion which gripped him when he confronted the Alexandre III bridge, the German architect condemned eclecticism and praised the efforts of modern artists in their fight against the academic mainstream.

A fifty-year-old struggle was coming to a close – the Comte de Laborde, Ruskin and Viollet-le-Duc had not preached to deaf ears. From that moment onwards, their names were invoked everywhere as the liberators of art. Despite the contradictions in their ideas, they deserve praise for being the only ones to have tried to overcome the Art-Industry paradox, the key problem of their time. An art suitable for democratic countries was now given a chance to develop, transforming streets, houses and everyday objects. The dream of Viollet-le-Duc could, perhaps, be realised: 'The arts can only establish themselves, develop and make progress in the living heart of the nation; they need, in other words, to circulate with its blood, with its passions, and to reflect its aspirations.' The Art Nouveau Revolution was to smash the columns of the temple and drive the 'true friends of the Parthenon' – those who would feel it a dishonour not to resort to pseudo-Doric columns to support the superstructure of the Paris underground – back to their archaeological studies. For the first time the vicissitudes of these historical events, hitherto carefully cloaked in silence, may be fully appreciated. We will now know the problems which the pioneers had to overcome, and will thus have a better understanding of the richness of 1900.

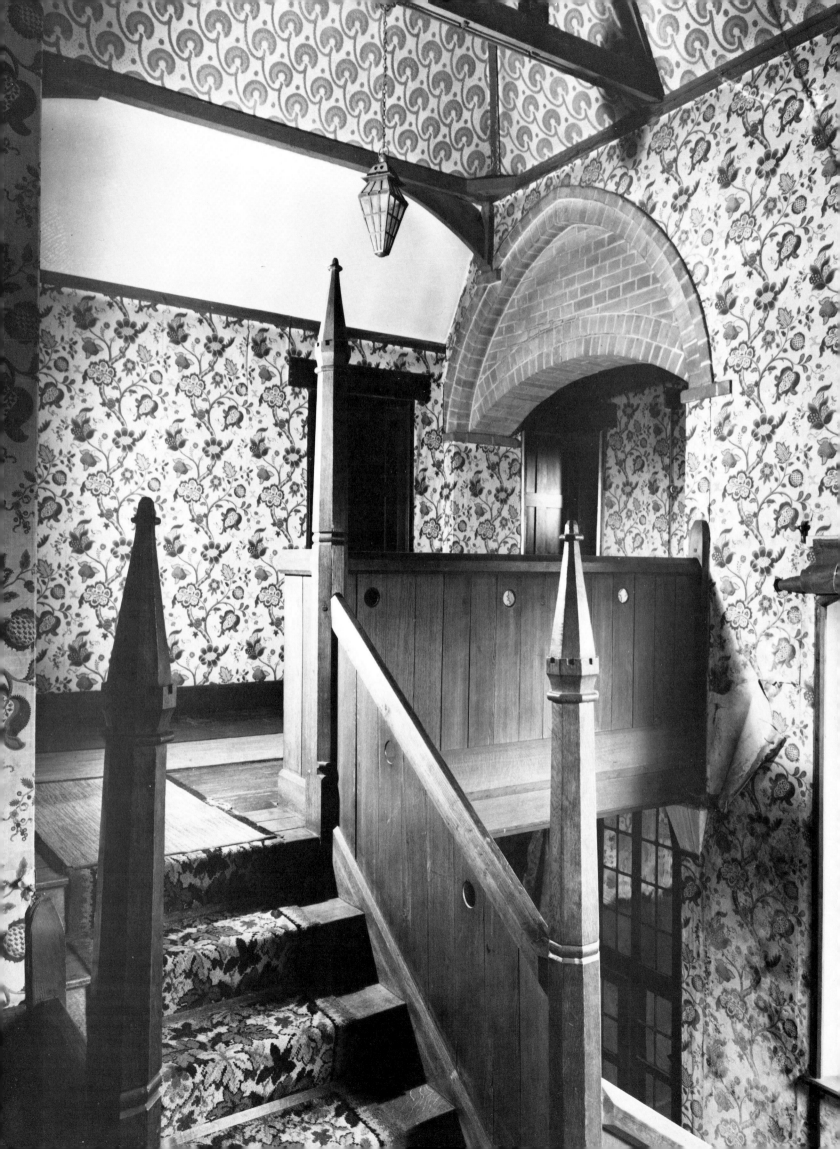

1. GREAT BRITAIN
Arts and Crafts and Art Nouveau

Tim Benton

It is highly debatable whether there is any architecture in Britain which can be helpfully described as Art Nouveau, if we intend to centre our definition of the style around the work of men like Horta, Guimard or van de Velde. But it is undeniable that many of the sources of the continental movement are to be found in Britain – the writings of Pugin, Ruskin, Morris and Walter Crane, the graphic work of Beardsley or Mackmurdo, the fabric and wallpaper designs of Voysey and many others. From a theoretical point of view, Art Nouveau was simply an offshoot of the British Arts and Crafts Movement, stiffened by a range of rationalist writing such as that of Viollet-le-Duc. And many of the formal devices of Art Nouveau derive from the same search for new forms in nature which prompted the British designers. But in the field of architecture, British architects stopped short of anything truly comparable to what took place in Brussels, Nancy or Paris. To understand why this is so, we must look first at the underlying differences between Britain and the continent in the field of design, despite the apparent similarities, and secondly at the very different architectural tradition to which British Arts and Crafts architecture belongs.

The general British distaste for continental stylistic experiments is well documented: '"It is most interesting to see the results of the Parisian movement towards English decorative art", said the Lay Figure as it took what it fondly believed to be a very French déjeuner with its friends, outside a café in the "Boul' Mich", as students have come to call that busy thoroughfare . . . "Yet I prefer English decoration on the whole", said the man with the Liberty tie. "These rival attempts are full of style and fancy, better, or at least more daring in colour; but they miss the true inwardness of our own work".' (*The Studio*, V, 1895, p. XVI.) From the Arts and Crafts standpoint publicised by *The Studio*, progress should be judged in terms of sincerity and spiritual commitment. Style itself is a dubious quality, too often bought at the price of integrity. To the French, of course, British design was too meagre: 'English furniture, which for fifteen years or so has been having the kind of success which good manners requires us to accord to all foreign work, has not been imitated except in certain German towns. Perhaps the English have had the merit of taking taste back to simple forms based on construction, but the notions of comfort which these pieces satisfy appear to be restricted to the requirements of the bathroom or dressing room. The abuse of spindly forms does not evoke that feeling of *bien-être* which the fine French furniture of the seventeenth and eighteenth centuries inspires in us.' (Lucien Magne, in *Art et Décoration*, 1898, p. 88.)

This contrast really identifies the essential difference between Art Nouveau and Arts and Crafts thinking. In European eyes, Art Nouveau was an attempt to create a fully formed style – a new visual language capable of complete expressive deployment, like the styles of the past. For an architect like Lucien Magne, steeped in the rationalist tradition of Viollet-le-Duc, style was something which the individual should form by a re-analysis of his art, generation by generation. 'Style is the particular interpretation each period makes of the

1.1 WEBB *Red house* Bexley 1859-60, staircase

15

decorative elements which the artist finds in nature.' (Lucien Magne, from his Course on Architecture, *Revue des Arts Décoratifs*, XXII, 1902, p. 10.) The Egyptians looked at nature in a certain way, mediaeval Frenchmen in another; both were conditioned by the differences in society and ideology which differentiated them. The modern architect's job is to analyse his age and adapt his style to conform with what he has learnt. British Arts and Crafts thinking, however, distrusted style altogether. A characteristically Ruskinian definition of art was given on the occasion of the 1897 Arts and Crafts Exhibiting Society's show: 'I have defined the function of art: it is the setting in order the house of mankind. I now define the future of art; it is the setting in order the house of mankind in exalted consciousness of the environment amid which it is placed . . . Art is . . . primarily and chiefly, and always, the doing a right thing well in the spirit of an artist who loves the just, the seemly, the beautiful . . .' (T. J. Cobden Sanderson, 'Of Art and Life', Arts and Crafts Exhibiting Society lectures, 1897.) This 'exalted consciousness' looked askance at any flashy attempts at creating a new style. As we shall see when discussing individual architects, British Arts and Crafts men had particular difficulties in dealing with the problem of originality. And this accounts, in part, for their hostility to European Art Nouveau in virtually all its forms.

The clearest expression of this insularity followed from George Donaldson's donation of a large collection of Art Nouveau pieces (exhibited in the 1900 Exhibition in Paris) to the South Kensington Museum. In 1901, he described his rather pragmatic reasons for wanting to present British designers with these examples: 'In those eleven years [since the 1889 exhibition] there had sprung up a quite astounding expansion and development in the production of artistic furniture on fresh lines and denominated "New Art". I saw that this, far from being the result of accidental, isolated or local efforts, was a very active artistic evolution which had spread over the countries of the continent, and which gave unmistakeable evidence of enormous mercantile advantage to its producers.' (George Donaldson, letter to the *Magazine of Art*, 1901, p. 466.) Donaldson had served on international furniture juries since 1867. The response was immediate. *The Studio* published a short notice entitled 'Pillory' describing the furniture as 'pretentious trash', 'wretched in design and construction', the 'rinsings of the dish, the after-effects of the fantastic malady'.

Walter Crane and three other leading architects and designers wrote to *The Times* in a similar vein. One of the signatories of the letter, T. G. Jackson, summed up both the letter and the general British Arts and Crafts view of Art Nouveau in a symposium in 1904: 'We explained that the main motive of the designs was a conscious striving after novelty and eccentricity, which is the basest of all motives in Art; that the forms of the objects, instead of expressing and illustrating the lines of the construction, obscured and ignored them . . . and that there was throughout a fidgety, vulgar obtrusiveness quite destructive of all dignity and repose . . . The propaganda, however, has done its mischievous work, and "The Squirm" is now the fashionable element in design.' (From 'L'Art Nouveau: What it is and what is thought of it', *Magazine of Art*, N.S. II, 1904, p. 210.) This symposium in the *Magazine of Art* provided the opportunity for virtually all the leading British designers and architects to line up against Art Nouveau. Alfred Gilbert, whose sculptural style came as close as anything in Britain to the curvilinear richness of van de Velde, mocked it: 'L'Art Nouveau, forsooth! Absolute nonsense! It belongs to the young lady's seminary and the "duffer's" paradise.' (*Ibid.*) And Walter Crane pinpointed the Arts and Crafts distrust of anything successful at a commercial level: 'One rather unfortunate sign was the readiness with which its characteristic forms seemed to lend themselves to exploitation by commercialism. A certain decorative rhetoric in form and line has already been so oft repeated and so constantly reappears in nearly every kind of design, that we are already weary, and any impression of novelty has completely worn off.' (*Ibid.*) Although Crane was addressing his remarks to the work exhibited in the Turin Exhibition of 1902, where he was the English representative, the same comments were frequently made about the popularisation of the style in the department stores, even in Liberty's, which offended the scruples of Arts and Crafts designers. The logical consequence of this idealistic and impractical approach was that men like C. R. Ashbee, who had founded the Guild of Handicraft in 1888 to carry out Arts and Crafts work, felt it necessary to take

Opposite
MACKINTOSH *Glasgow School of Art* Glasgow 1896-1909, library (photograph Goulancourt)

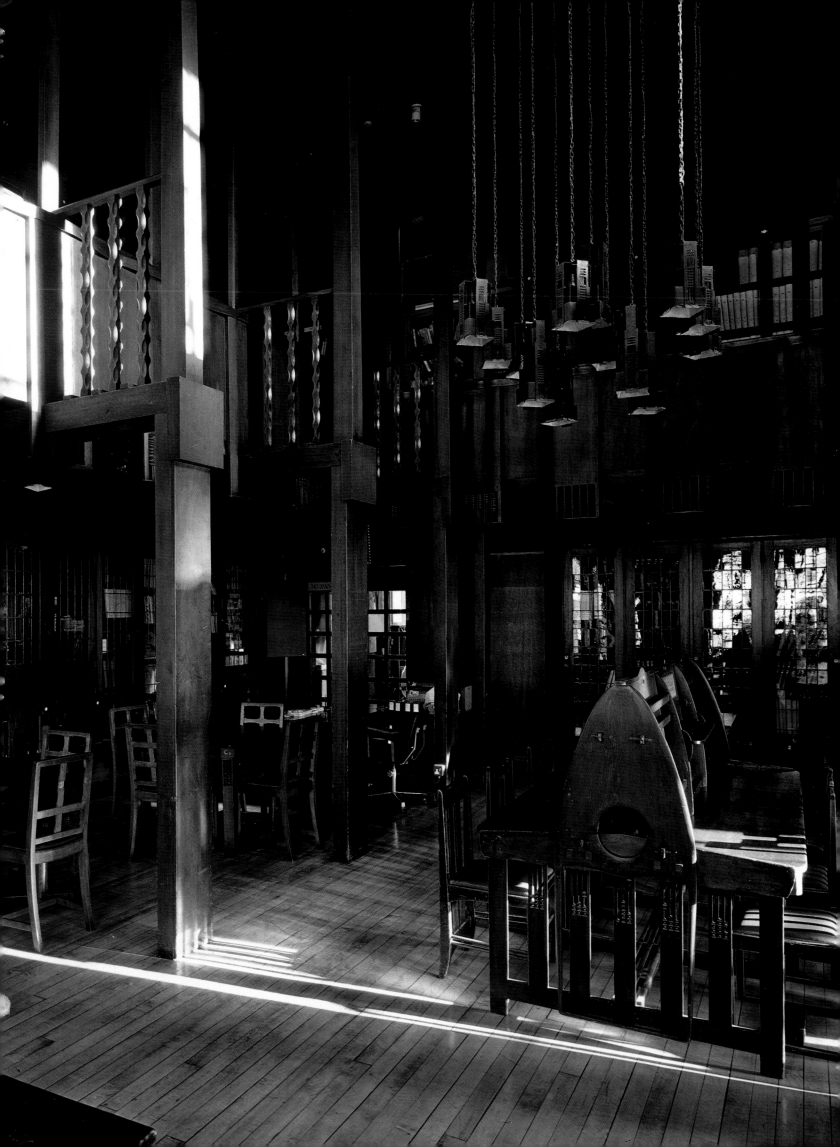

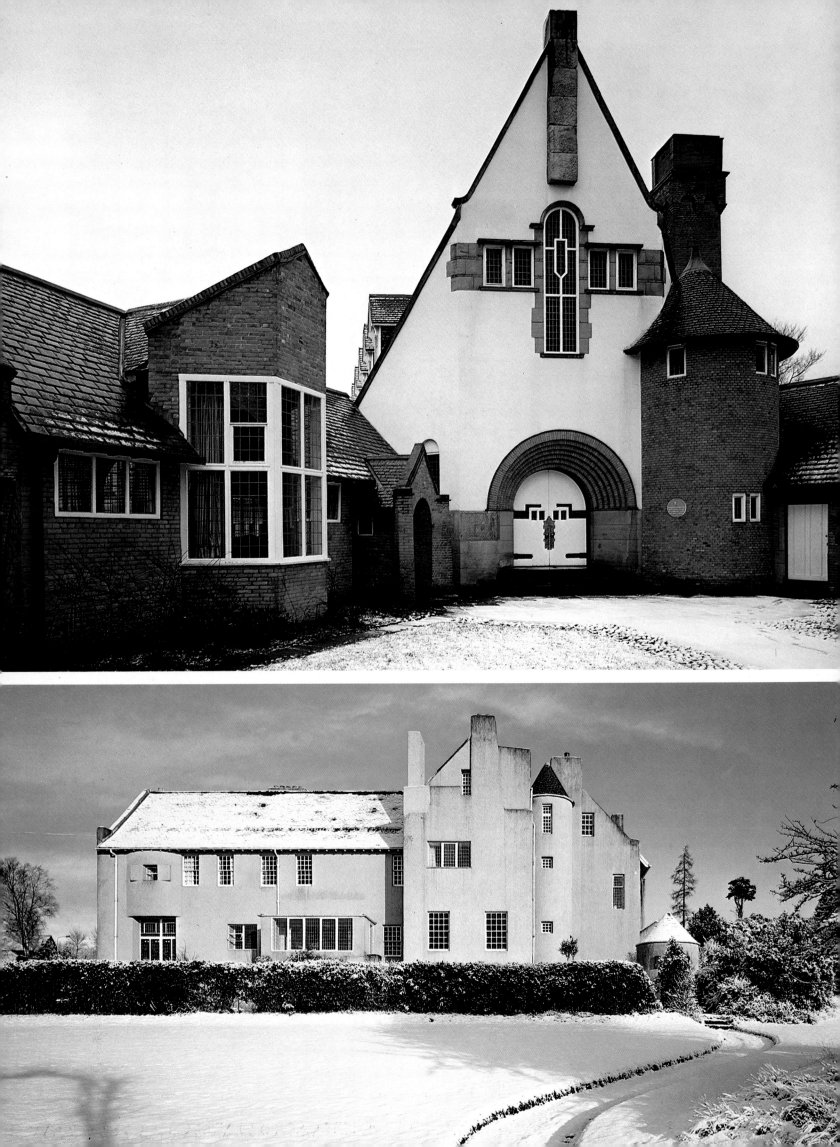

his whole group out of the East end of London and risk economic disaster in the Cotswold village of Chipping Campden. This move, made in 1902 as disillusion with the exploitation of Arts and Crafts ideas in London was growing, is as symptomatic of the decline of the movement as the actual economic collapse of the Guild in 1908.

In architecture, as well as design, the Arts and Crafts Movement began to suffer loss of confidence by the turn of the century. To understand this decline, as well as the architectural context of the movement, we must briefly go back to the Battle of the Styles and the heyday of high-principled neo-Gothic Revival.

The central strand of Gothic Revivalism, represented by Pugin, the Ecclesiological Society, Butterfield, Street and others had striven to combine the highest possible respect for the spirit of Gothic architecture with a flexible and innovative approach to problem-solving in architectural design. Gothic architecture was more than a style, it was an approach to building and society which centred itself on ideas of propriety, structural logic, craftsmanship and a method of planning which expressed separate parts of buildings as clearly as possible. Steeped in the ethical conviction that the highest achievement of architecture could only flow from an honest or natural, rather than a contrived, mastery of these designing procedures, Gothic Revival architects saw the possibility of creating new forms and a new architecture relevant to the age only with great difficulty. Butterfield (1814-1900) and Street (1824-81) were brilliant exponents of this phase of the Revival because they believed so strongly in the 'spirit of Gothic' that they were prepared to break any merely archaeological rules in order to respond honestly and deeply to the problem presented by each commission. Direct heirs to this high tradition were Philip Webb (1831-1915) and his great admirer and biographer William Lethaby.

But many architects sympathetic to the principles of the Gothic Revival, such as T. G. Jackson, Richard Norman Shaw or Ernest George, found these sympathies losing their purist cutting edge as fame and fortune came their way. Shaw, in particular, was too brilliant and inventive a designer to be restrained within the rigid disciplines of pure Gothic Revival theory. Shaw was always ready to aim at spectacular picturesque effects, rather than working out every design with the rigorous logic his senior draughtsman, William Lethaby, would have wished. Jackson turned to various forms of Elizabethan and Jacobean architecture, as did Ernest George and his partner Peto. And the work of these architects, as well as that of Eden Nesfield and George Devey, moved further and further towards classicism as they experimented with Dutch and English seventeenth-century styles. It was the emergence in the late 1860s of this Queen Anne style, of which Shaw became the undisputed master, which eroded the last unity within the Gothic Revival camp. It was precisely because the Queen Anne style emerged within the bosom of the Gothic Revival circle that its impact was so great. Apologists for the new style, like J. J. Stevenson, felt able to stretch Puginian theory to embrace the supposedly English (though in origin Dutch) quality of Queen Anne and Georgian architecture: 'The style in all its forms has the merit of truthfulness; it is the outcome of our common modern wants picturesquely expressed. In its mode of working and details it is the common vernacular style in which the British workman has been apprenticed, with some new life from Gothic added.' (J. J. Stevenson, 'On the Recent Reaction of Taste in English Architecture', *Builder*, 1874.)

A greater degree of eclecticism began to pervade the whole architectural profession, beginning with T. G. Jackson's and Ernest George's variations on English Renaissance and leading in the end to the classical resurgence known as Edwardian Baroque and the Georgian Revival. With two great country houses, Bryanston (1890) and Chesters (1891), Shaw himself slipped over into the fully fledged Grand Manner. And architects like John Belcher and Sir Aston Webb began to attract public attention for important public commissions, with their free interpretations of late Renaissance and Baroque mixed with Arts and Crafts touches.

The last quarter of the nineteenth century was a period of great inventiveness and diversity, as almost every architect attempted to work out his own 'mix' of architectural language consistent with some view of architectural 'honesty' and appropriateness. Men like Belcher, Jackson, George and Beresford Pite were reluctant to abandon the belief in the 'spirit of Gothic' which had

Opposite above
WOOD *First Church of Christ Scientist* Manchester 1903-08 (photograph Goulancourt)

Opposite below
MACKINTOSH *Hill House* Helensburgh 1902-03 (photograph Goulancourt)

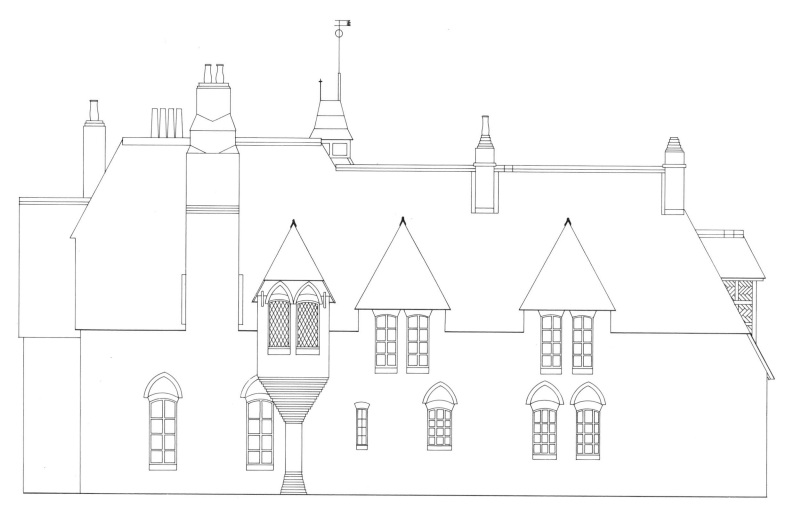

nourished their earlier commitment to the Gothic Revival. They managed to do so by abstracting Puginian theory step by step: 'Theoretically, our definition of it [the spirit of Gothic], will come simply to this – "The practice of architecture in Great Britain according to true and natural principles".' (T. G. Jackson, *Modern Gothic Architecture*, 1873.) The common denominator between all this eclectic activity was the search for a national 'free' style which could be seen to be more practical and monumental than Gothic, but which would somehow retain the high minded attitude to materials, construction, planning and the unity of the arts.

The Arts and Crafts Movement grew up in the heart of the Gothic Revival, and can be seen as a sort of rump of 'pure' Gothic feeling while all around were sliding into classicism and eclecticism. Arts and Crafts theory followed on directly from that of the Gothic Revival, with the addition of a more determined approach to the crafts, as outlined by Morris, following Ruskin. Not everyone accepted Morris's brand of utopian socialism, but many leading members, such as Walter Crane and William Lethaby, were committed socialists. The Movement began among the members of the Pre-Raphaelite Brotherhood, and it was the building and decorating of Morris's house (1859-60), designed by Philip Webb, which first gave a focus to Arts and Crafts ideas. And Webb and Morris, primarily through their leadership in the Society for the Protection of Ancient Buildings (founded 1877), maintained the continuity between the Gothic Revival and the Arts and Crafts Movement. But the spread of Arts and Crafts ideas only really began to gather momentum as the Gothic Revival began to hesitate and disperse – that is, in the 1880s.

Two main groups came together in 1884 to found the Art Workers' Guild, the formal centre of the Movement. A group of Norman Shaw's assistants had been meeting in 1883 as the St George's Guild, and they invited their friends, and a group of designers (known as The Fifteen) led by L. F. Day to come together and form a unified group. Founder members were, therefore, Lethaby, E. S. Prior, Ernest Newton and Mervyn Macartney (the architects)

1.2 WEBB *Red house* Bexley 1859-60, elevation (from the original drawing)

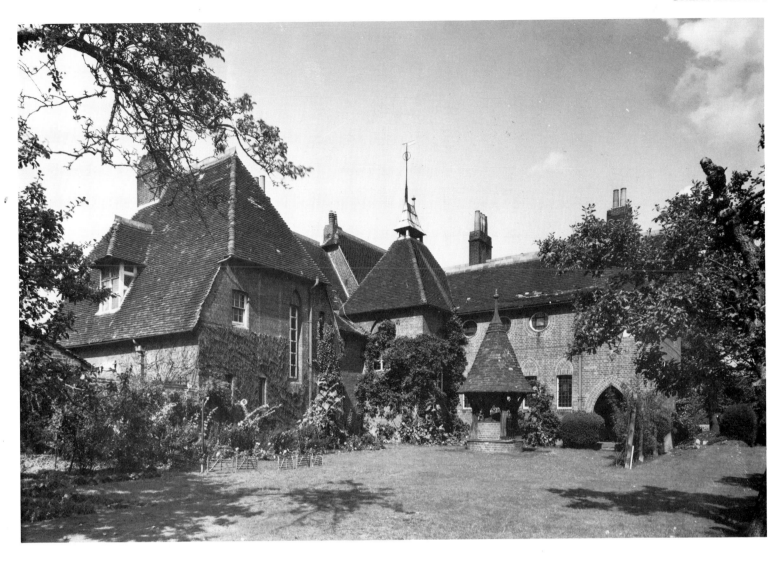

1.3 WEBB *Red house*, exterior view

and Day, Walter Crane and a number of other designers. Most of the architects also attended SPAB meetings, and it was here that the characteristic features of Arts and Crafts theory were worked out. Webb and Lethaby both had an 'objective' approach to history, unlike the highly partisan view of earlier Gothic Revivalists. The periods of the past should be studied for what they can teach us, regardless of whether we happen to approve of the architectural style of the time. Philip Webb pursued a brilliant but baffling policy of eclecticism in his own work, submitting every device he came across in past work to the scrutiny of his own highly rationalist analysis. Anything is worth using if it reveals an interesting use of materials, a positive approach to the expression of structure and is consistent with the whole and its surroundings. Lethaby continued on the same road, being a historian of Byzantine as well as Gothic architecture and responsive to the best in all periods of architecture. But in theory he advocated an increasingly a-stylar approach, basing his hopes on the lessons of vernacular building: 'In days when the great styles of the world, Egyptian, Greek, Gothic, were being wrought, the "style" was the *natural* manner of doing work. If only we could centre our energies in doing work well, strongly, lastingly, carefully, simply *well*, then at once *true* style, *the nature of things showing through workmanship*, would certainly be present. In un-consciousness would come that agreement which is the essential condition of style.' (*Architectural Review*, Vol. 16, 1904, p. 159.) And this somewhat mystical statement is the core of Arts and Crafts theory.

The SPAB was the powerhouse of intense discussion on the theory of architecture. The Art Workers' Guild, however, began to become increasingly all-embracing in its membership. By 1889, the AWG included among its members Bentley, George, Jackson, Shaw, Belcher and Beresford Pite, all of whom were experimenting with styles as varied as Byzantine and Baroque. What held the AWG together at all was its commitment to some vague notion of 'true principles' and the promotion of craft work and the unification of the arts of sculpture, painting and architecture. But the application of these principles could stretch from Belcher and Pite's Genoese Baroque Institute of Chartered Accountants Building of 1888–93 to the more vernacular domestic work of Voysey or Prior. Most of the AWG members drifted towards a more or less classical style during the 1890s, including founder members like Mervyn Macartney or Ernest Newton, whose sophisticated, well built and planned houses set the scene for the early decades of the twentieth century.

Within the framework of ideas and personal contacts of the Art Workers' Guild and the SPAB, a body of work was produced which has enough coherence to be helpfully described as Arts and Crafts architecture. But the distinction between this and other work of the period 1880–1914 is never clear-cut, so deep-rooted were the ideas implanted by the Gothic Revival and Ruskin. Some of the architects whose work will be discussed were not members of the Art Workers' Guild – M. H. Baillie Scott or H. Fuller Clark. Edgar Wood was active in the Northern branch, but there was no formal branch in Scotland. We will not be looking at an objective cross-section of the Arts and Crafts Movement for two reasons. First, the heart of the movement remained in the field of design, which lies outside the scope of this book. Secondly, I have concentrated on those expressions of Arts and Crafts architecture which come closest to continental Art Nouveau. So I have had to omit a discussion of Ashbee's relatively small architectural output, and I have deliberately played down mainstream Arts and Crafts work by Voysey, Baillie Scott and Prior in order to draw attention to the more adventurous experiments they attempted. The selection of work illustrated, therefore, can be thought of as fin de siècle Arts and Crafts, full of that restless dissatisfaction with easy solutions but equally full of respect for the sound and modest British tradition of the main Arts and Crafts Movement.

To sum up the qualities that Arts and Crafts architecture can be said to have, and which distinguish it from other forms of 'free' style architecture of the late nineteenth century, we can list, firstly, a certain Bohemianism which sets the movement slightly apart from mainstream 'professional' activities. This Bohemianism can be seen as a legacy both of the Pre-Raphaelite days and of the Whistler-Godwin-Wilde Aesthetic movement. It was from E. W. Godwin that many of the Arts and Crafts ideas associated with the 'artistic house' derived. His Tite Street studios, notably the White house and the first project for the Frank Miles studio, with their bold and nicely judged geometric massing, influenced Mackmurdo and, via him, Voysey and Harrison Townsend. His picturesque brick manner was equally influential on MacLaren. Most of the Arts and Crafts architects and designers cultivated a certain rustic quality in their dress and manner which was derived from William Morris and his butcher-blue shirts. This arty roughness of appearance was understood in part as a tribute to the social reforming ideals of Morris, as well as to his commitment to personal involvement in practical craft work. But the Aesthetic Movement was influential in its insistence on sensitivity in the choice of colours and the use of light-toned decorative schemes, and on the belief that a man of taste and well-rounded character should express himself in all his possessions, from his clothes to his furniture and the house in which he lives. The Arts and Crafts architects carried these two kinds of Bohemian outlook, the art for art's sake and the primitive utopian socialist viewpoint, towards a new synthesis, tending towards an increasingly naive search for simplicity and innocence. The artistic life was increasingly acted out as a retreat into the fantasy world of the picture-book cottage, like a Kate Greenaway illustration. But the search for simplicity also extended to the more rigorously reformist approach of a Lethaby or a Voysey, in response to the puritanical desire to avoid any risk of contamination from eclecticism in the search for truth.

Secondly, we find an enthusiasm for vernacular building, very much supported by the SPAB approach to building methods and the use of materials. Vernacular architecture was seen not only as an object lesson in how to avoid sham ornament, but as proof that only the 'unconscious' or 'natural' method of the so-called 'anonymous' builder, the Rousseau-derived noble savage, could point the way to a twentieth-century style. Lethaby added to the vernacular builder the engineer as an example of how to do things well without artifice – producing what he described as the 'high functional beauty' of the well designed steam engine or railway bridge. But, compared to the use of iron and steel in continental Art Nouveau, British Arts and Crafts architects were

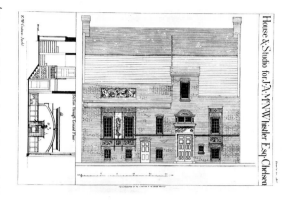

1.4 GODWIN *White house* London 1878, elevation and section through the ground floor

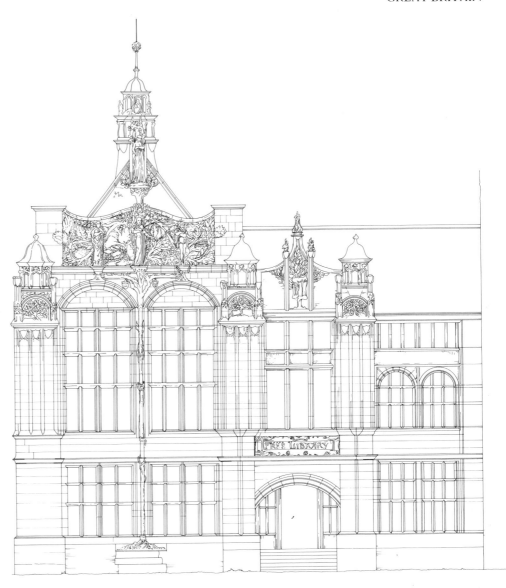

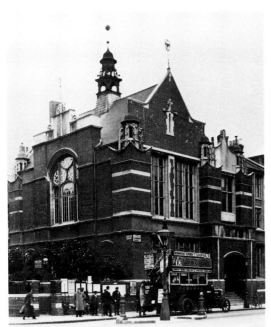

1.5-6 WILSON *Ladbroke Grove Free Library*
London 1890, exterior view (contemporary
photograph) and elevation (from the original
drawing)

relatively speaking less prepared to experiment with the new materials, and it
must be said that much of the debate about the possibilities of the new
techniques took place within the body of the professional architects rather than
on the fringes, in the Arts and Crafts Movement.

This must partly be attributed to the small domestic scale of much of the
work carried out by the Arts and Crafts men, and their greater interest in hand-
craft detailing. This is indeed the third obvious feature of Arts and Crafts
work – the belief that the architect should himself be involved in the making,
as well as the designing, of the decorative features and fixtures in his buildings.

Some buildings of this period are of interest as showing the impact of Arts
and Crafts ideas on related styles. Henry Wilson's design for the Ladbroke
Grove Free Library (1890) has been referred to as the first work of Art
Nouveau in Europe – a misleading comment based merely on some of the
brilliantly free decorative ornament which was largely omitted in construction
(1891). But the design and the building clearly reveal the time-lag between the
maturation of a fully developed style of naturalistic proto-Art Nouveau
ornamentation, which was developing in the field of design in response to
Ruskin and Morris, and the practical difficulties of finding an architectural use
for it. Similarly, a classic Arts and Crafts project (classic from the ideological
and craftsmanship point of view), was the memorial chapel for G. F. Watts
built by his wife in 1896 at Compton in Surrey. As soon as she and her husband
had moved to the country and had built their new home, Limnerslease, Mary
Watts began organising the local villagers into Arts and Crafts groups, starting
a pottery class and then setting up the workshops which would decorate the
Watts chapel. The exterior of this small neo-Byzantine Greek cross church is
covered with terra cotta tiles made by the local helpers, while the interior is
decorated all over with sumptuous coloured gesso, built up with fibre of
various kinds into swirling patterns. The style is a mixture of Celtic, Early

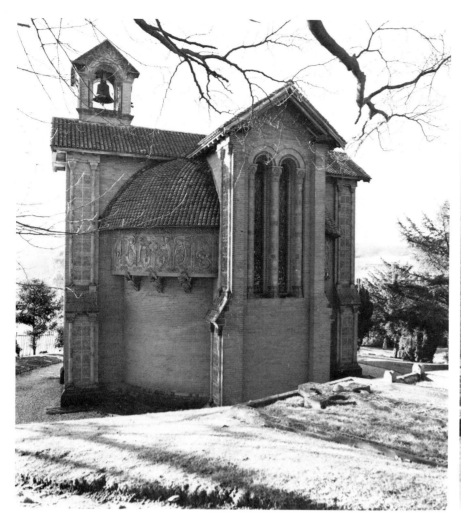
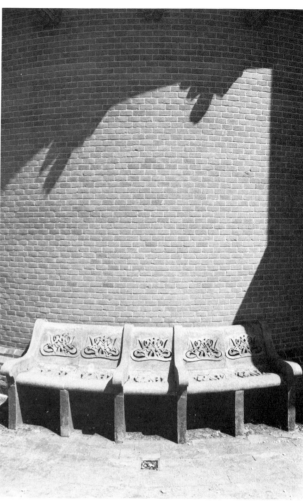

1.7-8 *Memorial chapel for G. F. Watts* Compton 1896, exterior view and detail (photographs Vonberg)

Christian and Byzantine, but the overall effect of startling individuality overrides the stylistic origins. An extraordinary elaborate allegorical programme informs all the details. This building can be seen in the context of the Celtic Revival in literature and the arts, and as a case study of an Arts and Crafts approach to decoration, but it hardly fits into any continuous development of Arts and Crafts architecture. Similarly, Messrs Edward Everards establishment in Bristol, designed by Henry Williams in 1900 and decorated with gorgeous Art Nouveau Poole pottery faience, might owe something to Charles Harrison Townsend in the little turrets flanking the facade, but is best understood as an application of two dimensional design to a facade.

Many other examples of inspired decorative treatments of relatively unexceptional buildings could be listed. One more will have to suffice here – H. Fuller Clark's converted Black Friar public house, Queen Victoria Street, London, (1905) with sculpture by Henry Poole. The exterior is decorated with stone carvings, mosaic and copper panels, while the interior includes coloured marbles, bronze reliefs, mosaic vaults and copper and brass fittings. No more perfect Arts and Crafts environment could be envisaged, with the combination of cheerful sensuality and symbolic allusions.

Although very different in approach and work, E. S. Prior (1852-1932) and William Lethaby (1857-1931), two founder members of the Art Workers' Guild, can be taken as representative of a characteristic expression of Arts and Crafts thinking. Both were more prolific as scholars and teachers than as architects. Both showed themselves capable of outstanding inventiveness in some of the architectural work which they did undertake, but curiously inconsistent when the work is taken as a whole.

Prior entered Shaw's office in 1872, at a time when Lethaby was chief draughtsman, and at the precise moment when Shaw was beginning to move over towards the Queen Anne style. Prior's early independent work, like the Red House, Harrow (1883), reveals the strong influence of Shaw's picturesque manorial style for domestic architecture. The mixture of half-timbering and Shavian bay windows, combined with the apparently wilful articulation of masses, might suggest a somewhat irreverent approach to the pure rationalism

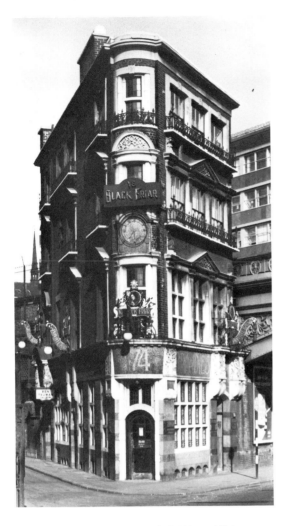

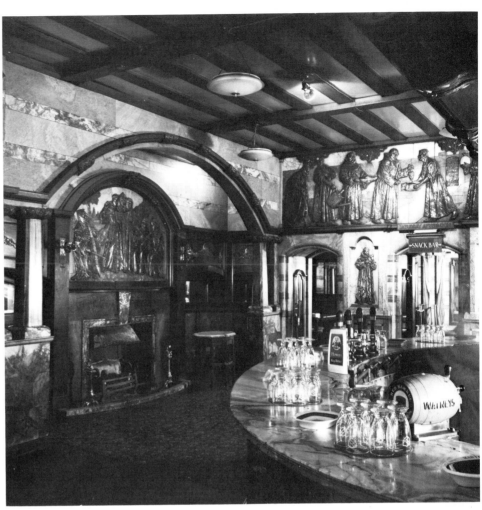

1.9-10 FULLER CLARK *Black Friar public house*
London 1905, exterior and interior

of the SPAB, where Prior was a keen disciple of Webb and Morris.

Like Lethaby, Prior set great store by vernacular building as a model for the modern architect. Nineteenth-century vanity, as he saw it, had devalued architecture by striving after effect rather than quality. Archaeology had been ransacked to save the trouble of designing new details, mechanical methods had been used to provide substitute materials in place of real ones, and fake nature had been contrived in place of a genuinely organic approach to the countryside.

'We have to take not only what does not suit us, but what is not the real thing at all – fatty compounds for butter, glucose for sugar, chemicals for beer: and just as certainly the sham house for the real building, its style a counterfeit, its construction a saleable make-believe, its carved wood a pressing from machinery, its panelling linoleum, its plaster some pulp or other, its metalwork a composition, its painted glass only paper – everything charmingly commercial and charmingly cheap . . . Wild nature must not be forced; only after long wooing and centuries of courtship will she lay her hand in man's. Let us take her as the sister of Art, with the frank admission that we make beauty for our houses and gardens by our art, for thus only is it natural for man to do.' (E. S. Prior, 'Upon House-Building in the Twentieth Century', in *Modern British Domestic Architecture and Decoration*, published by *The Studio*, 1901.) Prior combines here the typically Arts and Crafts rejection of capitalist ersatz materials with a view of nature which amounts to a virtually animist position. He went on in this article to expound his extreme views about the use of local materials and respect for the geology, climate and atmosphere of the site. His belief in the creative potential of local craftsmen led him to advocate that even a major commission such as Liverpool Cathedral would come out better if the architect restricted himself to supervising the craftsmen and selecting the materials, allowing the design to emerge from their ideas.

In 1895, Prior published a design for a country cottage on a curious splayed plan, derived from Shaw's 'X' shaped mansion, Chesters. But this delightfully simple cottage introduced a theme which, in the hands of Baillie Scott and others in Britain, and Muthesius and others in Germany, was to become something of a trademark of Arts and Crafts domestic architecture. In 1897, a house

25

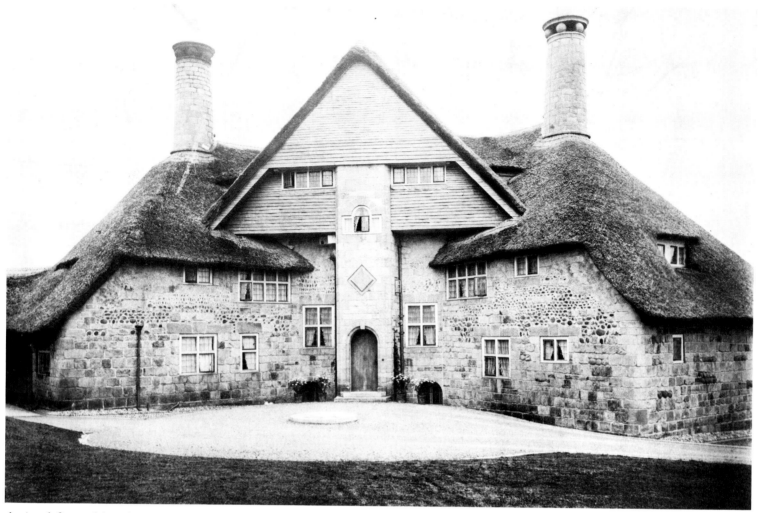

derived from this scheme (known as The Barn) was built in Exmouth, Devon. Under a monstrous thatched roof which sweeps down low on either side, walls of sandstone and beach pebbles give the impression of age-old ruins patched together. Over the front door, a clean-cut projecting tower marks the stairs, firmly capped off by a powerfully projecting gable faced in dark oak weatherboarding. The 'Model of a House' published in the *Architectural Review* two years later developed the same theme, with a rather more formal repertoire, and Home Place, Kelling, in Norfolk followed in 1904. This used a similar splayed plan, but exploited mixed materials less successfully. The overall effect was too complicated for comfort, although some semi-detached cottages for the estate achieved a more vigorous unity of expression. Prior built a few other houses in this manner, such as 'Greystones', Highcliff-on-Sea, Hampshire (1911-14), but by this time his main activities were in the literary field, having published a *History of Gothic Art in England* in 1900 and *Cathedral Builders in England* in 1905.

The young Lethaby came to London to work as Shaw's chief draughtsman in 1879. In 1889, having developed his interests in Arts and Crafts design as well as architecture, he left Shaw to work freelance, undertaking commissions for a number of architects, as draughtsman, architect and designer. During the 1890s, Lethaby carried out one or two big commissions, including Avon Tyrrell (1890) and the rather bleak house called The Hurst, 1893.

Two of his buildings show the extraordinary potency of his vision and the creative response to new materials within a wholly Arts and Crafts framework. All Saints, Brockhampton (1900), as a concrete vaulted shell covered by a thatch roof, must seem an extraordinary phenomenon to those unfamiliar with the peculiarities of Arts and Crafts thought. But every detail was intended to be seen as the product of some process of either constructional or vernacular logic. The form of the vault was dictated by statics, given the use of simple rubble walls for the exterior which prevented the use of flying buttresses. The treatment of the exterior resulted from the use of direct labour and the application of local methods – such as the traditional Hereford thatch. The furniture and lamps were designed by Lethaby himself, and the tapestries by Burne-Jones

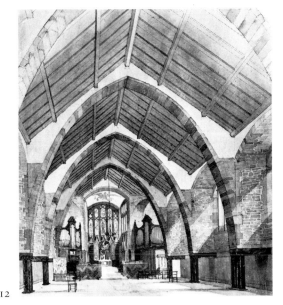

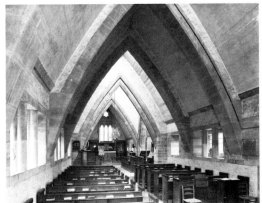

1.12

1.14

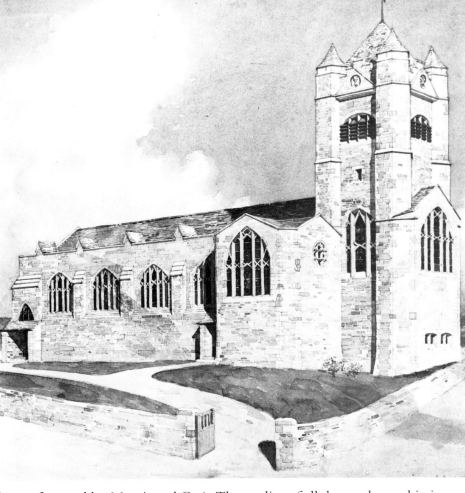

1.13

1.15

1.12-13 PRIOR *St Andrews* Roker 1904, interior and exterior perspectives

1.14-15 LETHABY *All Saints* Brockhampton 1900, interior and view from the South East

(manufactured by Morris and Co.). The quality of all the workmanship is very fine, and the building is full of curious details which show Lethaby's relentless pursuit of the unconventionally just solution. The diagonal tracery of the transept window is one such detail.

All Saints, Brockhampton can be effectively compared with E. S. Prior's masterpiece, St Andrews Roker, near Sunderland, designed in 1904, two years after the completion of Lethaby's church. There are obvious points of similarity in the interior, with the use of broad parabolic arches carrying the side thrust internally. The exterior shows a similarly radical simplification of detail, although Prior remains more faithful to the language of Gothic, however far distorted. In both buildings we find a ruthless concentration on the formal possibilities of large scale constructive elements, rather than finicky detail. In the plan, too, fresh thinking is evident, in the dramatic device of making the choir much narrower than the nave – in order to reflect the smaller space needed and to accentuate its impact – and in linking it boldly to the nave by angled arches across the crossing.

Few Arts and Crafts buildings embodied so perfectly the peculiarly British approach to structure and materials, so different from the Art Nouveau pre-occupation with iron to combine decorative and structural properties in one. A poignant expression of how British architecture might have developed, had not the classical revival and the War interrupted it, is revealed in Lethaby and Wilson's model for the Liverpool Cathedral competition of 1902. Lethaby asked a number of other Arts and Crafts believers (including F. W. Troup) to help him make this design, which was submitted in the name of Henry Wilson, normally known for his sumptuous church furnishings in a near Art Nouveau manner. It was a typically pedagogic and propagandist venture from the start – including the notion of collaborative effort which Lethaby saw as an analogy with the way mediaeval society built its cathedrals. And the bold use of reinforced concrete had its shock value too, to try to awaken interest in 'pure' building, rather than decoration and archaeological borrowing. 'Modern armoured concrete is only a higher power of the Roman system of construction. If we could sweep away our fear that it is an inartistic material, and boldly build a railway station, a museum, or a cathedral, wide and simple, amply lighted, and call in our painters to finish the walls, we might be interested in building again almost at once. This building interest must be aroused.' (William Lethaby, *Architecture*, 1912.) Needless to say, the design was unplaced, and the Gothic building eventually built, for all its virtues, marks another step towards the academicism of British architecture in the 1920s.

In taking C. F. A. Voysey (1857-1941) and M. H. Baillie Scott (1865-1945) together to represent the Arts and Crafts tradition of small scale domestic architecture, I make no attempt to cover the full extent of their work or assess the overall impact of their contribution. Both men should be seen in the context of the broad revival of vernacular house design, and their influence has been enormous, particularly in the debased forms of mass spec.-built suburban housing.

As far as our present study is concerned, however, their main interest lies in the peculiarly British image of artistic life they presented and in the important extension they gave to the Aesthetic Movement approach to interior design. Neither could be described as an Art Nouveau architect, although both made designs for all kinds of media which were Art Nouveau in feeling and influential on European Art Nouveau designers.

Voysey first tried to set himself up as an independent architect in 1883, having served nine years as apprentice and assistant to J. P. Seddon and George Devey. His first start, however, was sidetracked into the field of two dimensional design by the intervention of A. H. Mackmurdo (1851-1942), who introduced him to several manufacturers of wallpapers and carpets. Mackmurdo was a great influence on Voysey, inspiring him with the mixture of Arts and Crafts and Aesthetic views which lay behind the formation of the Century Guild (1882) and the magazine *Hobby Horse* (1884). Mackmurdo and E. W. Godwin were both in a sense architects and designers to the Aesthetic Movement, introducing a delicate tonality and Japanese influence into interior decoration and some of their buildings. Although Mackmurdo was an infinitely less capable architect than Godwin, he did carry out some exhibition designs, such as the Century Guild stand at the Liverpool International Exhibition of 1886, which proved very influential. Voysey, as well as Mackintosh and George Walton, was to copy the thin vertical members with their stylised capitals and entablatures which extend into space. And in a weird stuccoed house designed by Mackmurdo for his brother around 1887, at No. 8 Private Road, Enfield, the seed of Voysey's more disciplined rendered facades can be seen.

Voysey's second chance to build up his architectural practice came about after one of his published designs, a scheme for a cottage for himself published in *The Architect* in 1888, attracted a client, M. H. Lakin. The result was a house built at Bishops Itchington in 1889 which set Voysey on the road to a most successful domestic practice. This early design also set the pattern of virtually all his later houses, which develop only in details of planning and certain aesthetic emphases throughout his long career. The planning is simple but effective, aligning the main rooms en suite to face the sun and or view, providing elementary communication in the form of a long gallery or corridor along the entrance front, and repeating the same plan for the bedrooms on the floor above. Thin walls supported by splayed buttresses were used for economy, invariably rendered all over, but occasionally modified by half-timbering. The roof lines were kept as simple as possible, again mainly for economy, and any service suites were usually appended at right angles or to one side. Unlike Baillie Scott, Voysey rarely experimented with ingenious open spatial arrangements, and seems to have been largely uninterested in variations of ceiling level. His clients knew him as a stickler for practical detail and rigorously attentive to cost and quality of workmanship.

The house he eventually built for himself at Chorley Wood, The Orchard, sums up most of Voysey's characteristics, and shows how his work can be compared with other Arts and Crafts designers. Firstly, he was a fanatic for simplicity, to the extent of reducing to a minimum the 'rough' crafty quality of workmanship so much admired by Prior and Lethaby. The colours are unlike most Arts and Crafts hues – 'green' American slates for the roof (light grey in hue), pale green paintwork externally, contrasting with the white cement rough cast walls, grey slate floors in the public spaces inside, and carpets in the

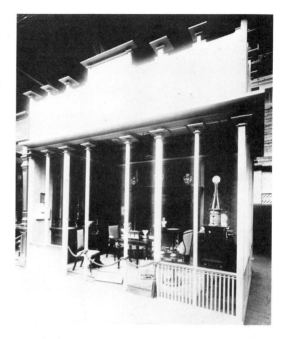

1.16 MACKMURDO *Liverpool International Exhibition* 1886, Century Guild stand (contemporary photograph)

1.17-18 VOYSEY *The Orchard* Chorley Wood
1899, elevation (from the original drawing) and
interior perspective (drawing based on a contemporary photograph)

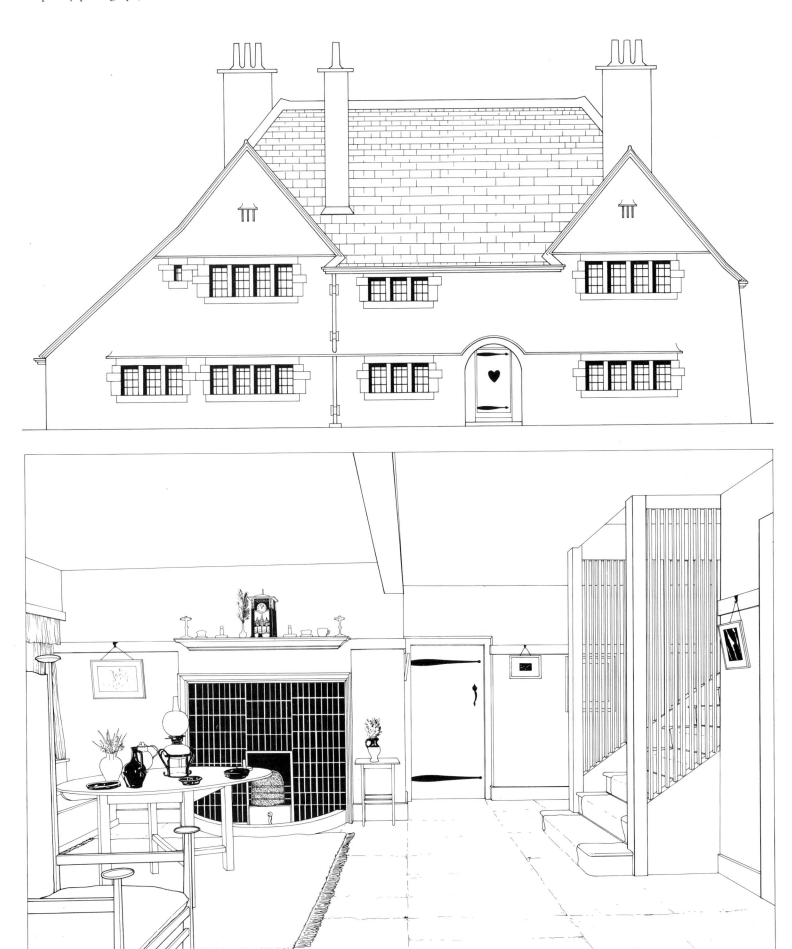

'private' rooms. The walls are purple in the hall, green in the dining room, with bright red curtains. Patterned papers are found in the other rooms, but nevertheless the overall impression is austere and somewhat naive.

Some of Voysey's houses show more invention than The Orchard, and others are more eclectic and less single-minded in their message. But it should be clear from this example why Voysey's innovations were both an example for all later suburban architecture, in the overall impression, and a dead-end in terms of detailed development. Architects like W. A. Harvey quickly took what they could from the 'Voysey look', and adapted it to the more popular needs of everyday housing – Bournville is full of such examples. But Voysey's real message was understandably too much to swallow, full of that stern moral preaching and elevated tone which runs through all his pronouncements on architecture: 'The wish to express oneself is corrupting to the soul and intoxicating to personal vanity.' (C. F. A. Voysey, 'Self-Expression in Art', *R.I.B.A. Journal*, Vol. 30, 1923, p. 211.) And yet Voysey's particular form of self-expression is unmistakable – that rather twee, childlike prettiness, with the apparently self-conscious use of recurrent motifs (large green water butts, black chimney pots, green or grey slates, heart-shaped wrought iron hinges and handles) which all have some basis in Arts and Crafts functional arguments but which eschew the heartening unpredictability of the more mature Arts and Crafts architects.

'To be simple is the end, not the beginning of design' Voysey was quoted as saying in an interview for *The Studio* in 1893, but the interviewer captured the flavour of this simplicity precisely: 'One of the most beautiful of his posses- sions – a rosy-faced lad of four, clad in a blue smock – seemed the very spirit of design in its native simplicity, and as a mere scheme of colour a thing not beaten by any of the charming patterns Mr Voysey unspread at my request.' ('An Interview with Mr. Charles F. Annesley Voysey, architect and designer', *The Studio*, I, 1893, p. 231.) And in the *Magazine of Art* Symposium of 1904, Voysey showed the puritanism which separated him from most of his con- temporaries, in Britain as well as abroad: 'Surely *L'Art Nouveau* is not worthy to be called a style. Is it not merely the work of a lot of imitators with nothing but mad eccentricity as a guide; good men, no doubt, misled into thinking that Art is a debauch of sensuous feeling, instead of the expression of human *thought* and feeling combined, and governed by reverence for something higher than human nature?' (*Magazine of Art*, Vol. 2, pp. 211-2.)

It is necessary to include Voysey in a discussion of the relationship between the British Arts and Crafts Movement and continental Art Nouveau because his work was widely published in German, French and Austrian journals and his impact was clearly felt. Baillie Scott's influence was even more direct, since he won the important international competition for the *Haus eines Kunstfreundes* announced by the German *Zeitschrift für Innendekoration* in 1900. And in 1897, Scott had been commissioned to decorate some rooms in the Palace of Darmstadt, where the Artists' Colony was to be created under Olbrich and Behrens.

Baillie Scott began his career on the Isle of Man, after training with an architect of little importance in Bath. His Red House, Douglas (1892-3) already incorporates many of the planning devices which make his work comparable in some ways to Frank Lloyd Wright's in America. Instead of aligning his rooms in rows, with a straight corridor along the back, Scott tried every possible device to make the flow of space from one to another fluid· and effective. Throughout his work, he experimented with double-height spaces in halls and living rooms, using stairs and upstairs galleries to accentuate the impact of these surprises. Sliding screens were used in many of the plans to make the room spaces adaptable to different requirements. *The Studio* gave Scott the opportunity to write a number of articles on the small suburban house or the country villa, which he later rewrote with a number of illustrations of his own work as *Houses and Gardens*, published in 1906. Unlike Voysey, who joined the Art Workers' Guild in its first year, Baillie Scott did not belong to any of the formal bodies of the Arts and Crafts Movement. Like Voysey, however, he was strikingly successful in his career until around 1910, when the supply of clients began to dry up.

Voysey was not a particularly skilful draughtsman, and relied on pro- fessional illustrators to show his houses in the architectural press. But Baillie

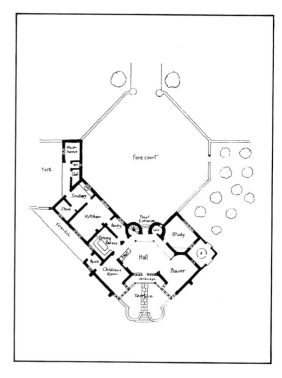

1.19 BAILLIE SCOTT *Project for a seaside house, Yellowsands* 1903, plan

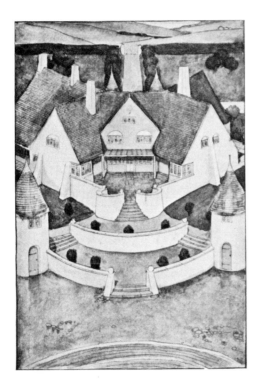
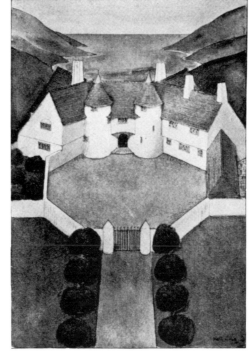
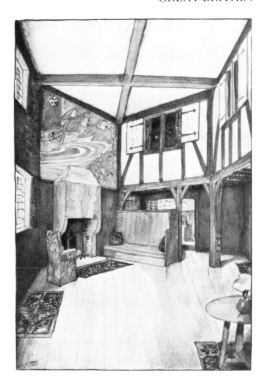

1.20-22 BAILLIE SCOTT *Project for a seaside house, Yellowsands,* sea view, road view and interior

Scott incorporated his whole domestic aesthetic in his own illustrations, in a limpid watercolour style which fully transmitted the impact of his designs. Unlike Voysey, he loved rich contrasts of texture and pattern, and preferred cosy, low lighting to the fairly stark all over effects achieved with large windows. His interiors, when he had a say in their decoration, were conceived as fairy-tale modern visions of mediaeval mansions, cut down in size but enriched with colour, pattern, textures, the use of internal brick and stone and rough, dark wood. More successfully than any of his contemporaries, Baillie Scott responded to the challenge of how to design small houses for the new middle classes in which the illusion of space and the allusion to romance was transmitted within the tenets of Arts and Crafts attitudes to materials and craftsmanship. In his use of built-in furniture and from his advocacy of new ways of using living-dining-sitting areas instead of the compartmented spaces derived from larger house-types, he also pioneered new principles. 'The house rationally planned should primarily consist of at least one good-sized apart-ment, which, containing no furniture, but that which is really required, leaves an ample floor-space at the disposal of its occupants . . . In this way, even the labourer's cottage retains its hall, which has now become the kitchen, dining room and parlour.' (M. H. Baillie Scott, *Houses and Gardens,* 1906, p. 2.) In fact, Scott's plans for semi-detached cottages for the Letchworth Cheap Cottage Exhibition of 1905, and his scheme for court houses for Hampstead Garden suburb take these principles a long way towards the modern apartment plan.

Baillie Scott's work, therefore, ranged from the small, ingeniously con-trived commission, externally very simple, to the fully fledged romanticism of projects like the winning design for the House of an Art Lover, or Yellow-sands. One of his more fantastic schemes, for Princess Marie of Romania, was constructed in rough logs half way up some living trees in the forest. Baillie Scott designed the interiors of this log cabin, illustrated as 'Le Nid', in 1898. More restrained schemes such as White Lodge, Wantage (1898) or his various schemes illustrated and discussed in *The Studio* show how persuasive his imagery was and how deep its legacy to twentieth-century suburban and country housing.

Charles Harrison Townsend (1851-1928) went into practice on his own in 1888, when he also joined the Art Workers' Guild. Compared with most of the Arts and Crafts designers and architects, his range of interests varied very widely, from modern American architecture to the early Christian churches of Ravenna. Charles's brother Horace, a journalist, had worked in Chicago and had met H. H. Richardson there. Some of his early work in Blackheath shows this Richardsonian influence most clearly, as does one of the most mature of his house designs, Cliff Towers, published in 1898. The plan of this house has some superficial similarities to the Voysey house plan, although the chunky

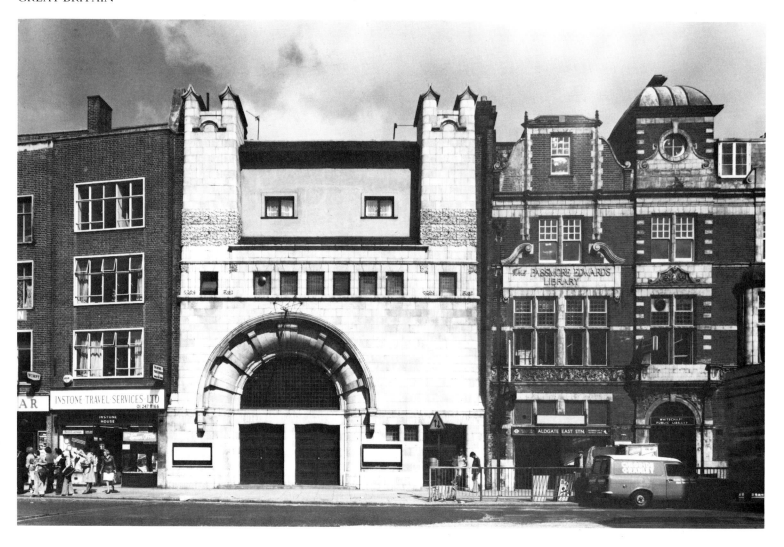

1.23 TOWNSEND *Whitechapel Art Gallery*
London 1899-1901 (photograph Goulancourt)

and massive treatment of the walls and veranda set it apart. In his description of
the project, Townsend stresses the importance of all the right Arts and Crafts
points – site, materials, convenience and so on. But the rounded walls and
battered surfaces remind one strongly of the American tradition.

Townsend comes nearest to continental Art Nouveau among the British
architects because he was able to think in more visual terms than most of his
colleagues. He rejected the Voyseyian appeal to simplicity at all costs: 'In his
building, to avoid the precedent he loathes, the man of the latest fashion cuts
out all strings and cornices, loses all the beauty and interest of their play of light
and shade, and calls the result the "simplicity of originality". It is not. It is,
instead, the *simplicity due to omission*, a negation that is a poor substitute for
invention, a cowardice pretending to be courage.' (C. H. Townsend, 'The
Value of Precedent', *The Studio*, 1894.) That Townsend was taking Philip
Webb's side, as a selective eclectic, against the Lethabite view, is confirmed in
this article by his surprising assertion: 'Better too much precedence, that is
copyism, than too little, that is Ignorance.' At the same time, however,
Townsend shared with others of his generation an impatience with real
copyism.

The Bishopsgate Institute shows the clear debt to Henry Wilson's Public
Library, Ladbroke Grove, although Townsend was able to blend the forms of
the octagonal towers, the large window and imposing central arch together
more convincingly. The composition of the whole, with the relationship of
towers and the horizontal band of ornament, has been likened to an illustration
of Brereton House, in Nash's *The Mansions of England in the Olden Time*, but
the effect, nevertheless, is quite novel.

Soon after the completion of the Institute (1894), Townsend made the first
design for the Whitechapel Art Gallery. His sister sat on the Board of Trustees
responsible for arranging exhibitions of art in the East end, and Canon Barnett
approached Charles in 1895. The first design, for a much wider frontage than
became available in the event, was a quite extraordinary composition, with a
kind of primitivist vigour which the much smaller, executed building lacked.

1.24 TOWNSEND *Whitechapel Art Gallery*
London, original design 1895

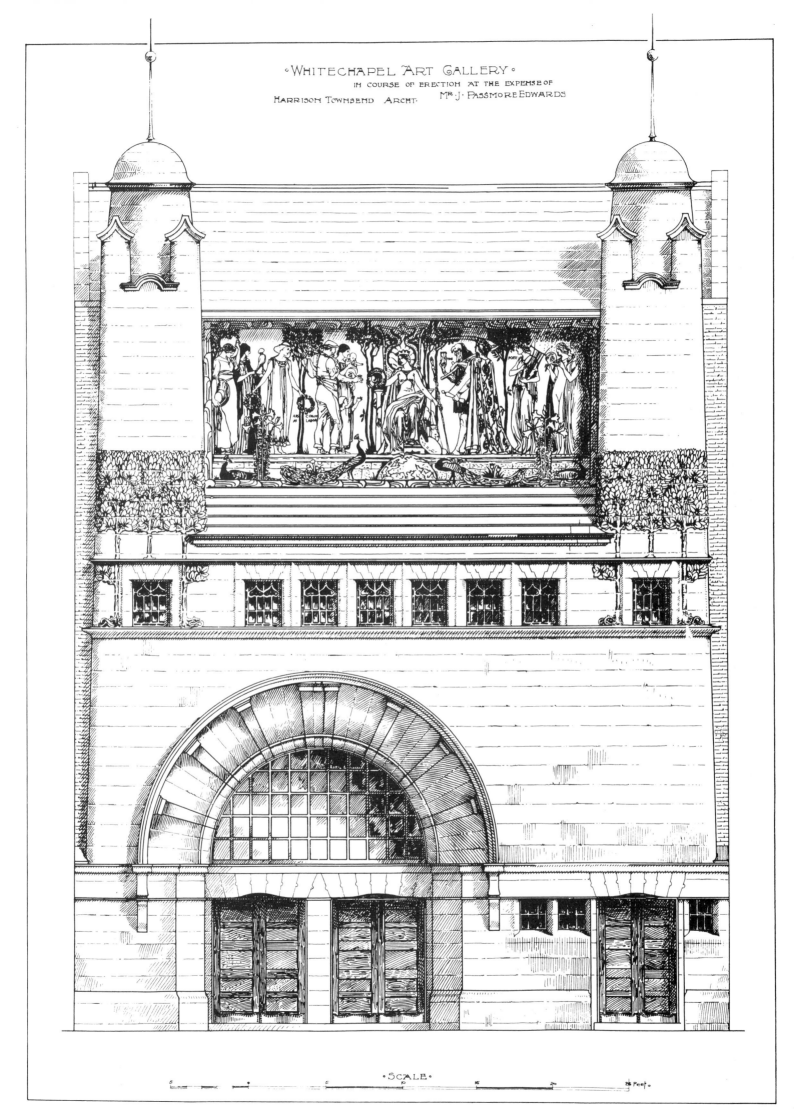

· WHITECHAPEL ART GALLERY ·
IN COURSE OF ERECTION AT THE EXPENSE OF
HARRISON TOWNSEND ARCHT·   MR J· PASSMORE EDWARDS

· SCALE ·

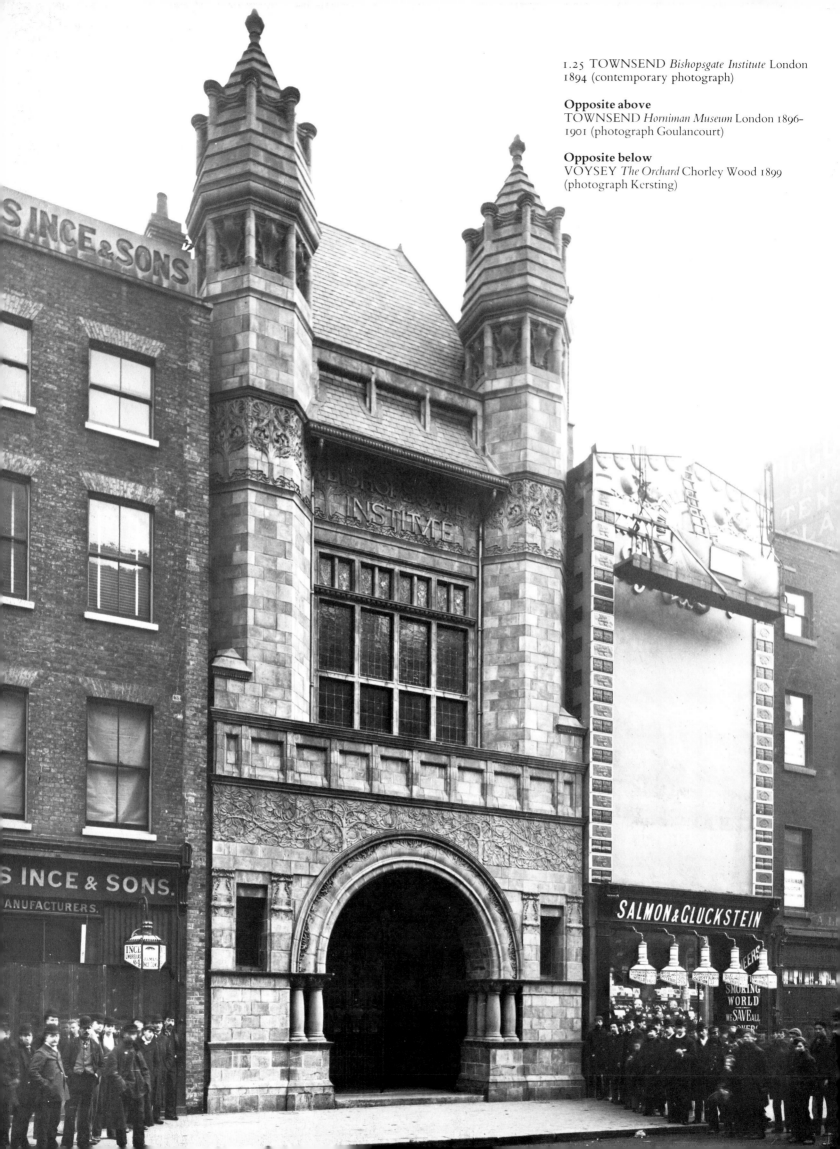

1.25 TOWNSEND *Bishopsgate Institute* London 1894 (contemporary photograph)

Opposite above
TOWNSEND *Horniman Museum* London 1896–1901 (photograph Goulancourt)

Opposite below
VOYSEY *The Orchard* Chorley Wood 1899 (photograph Kersting)

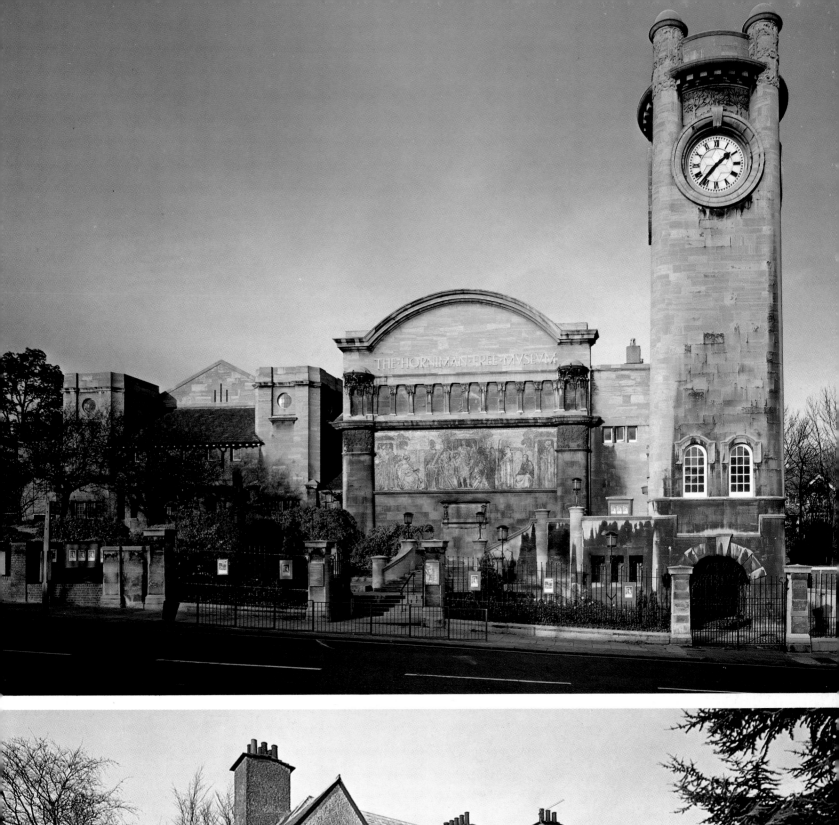
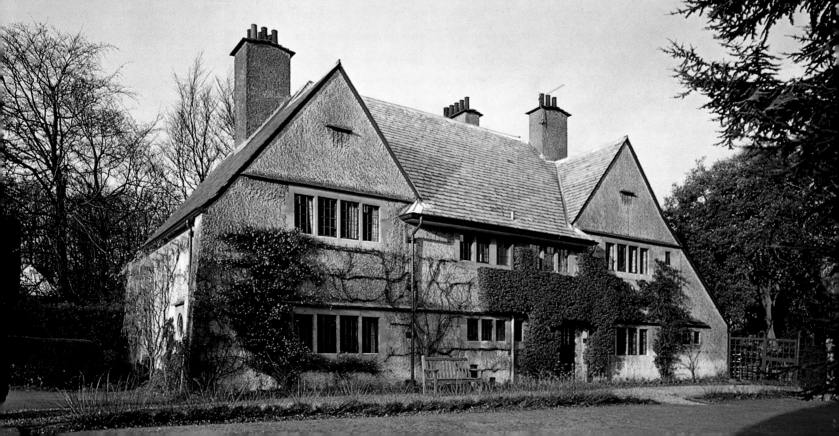

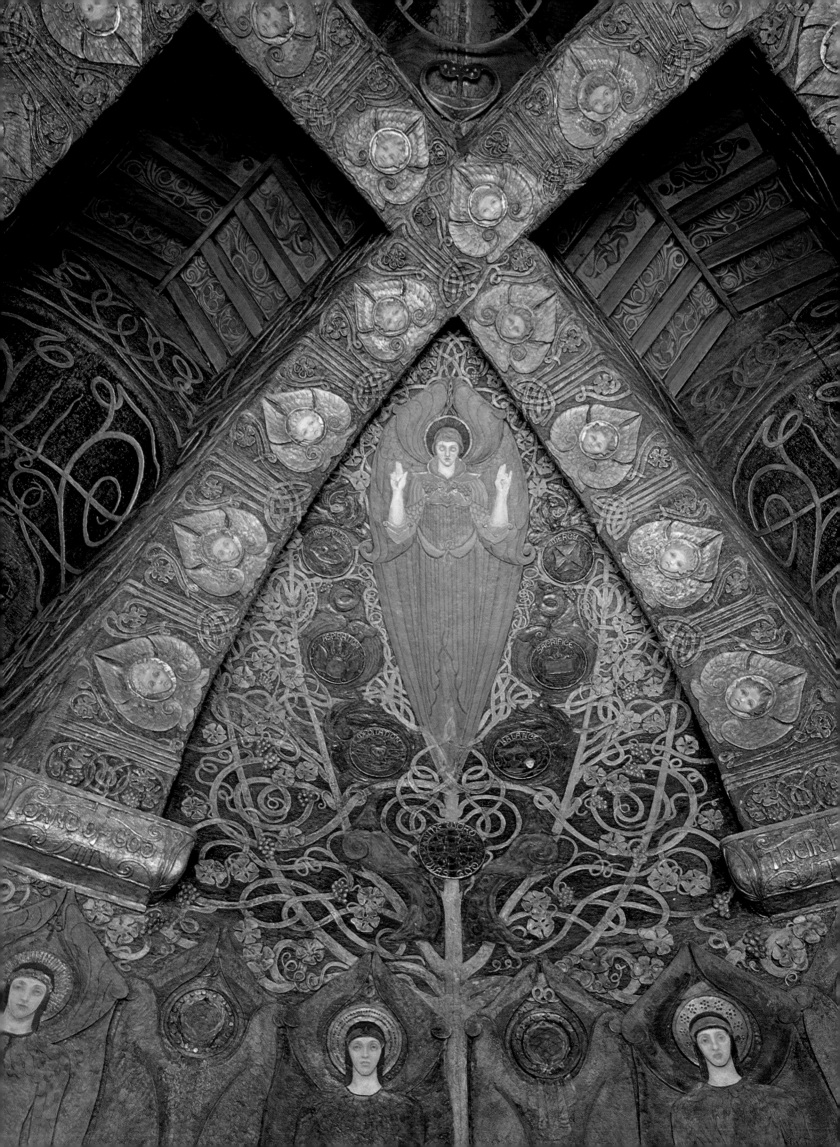

Opposite
Memorial chapel for G. F. Watts Compton 1896, detail
of interior vaulting (photograph Vonberg)

1.26–28 TOWNSEND *St Mary the Virgin* Great
Warley 1902–04, South and West elevations (from
the original drawings) and exterior view (photograph Ball)

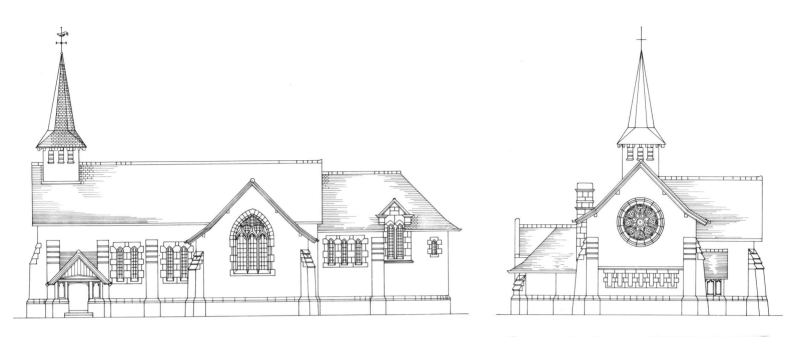

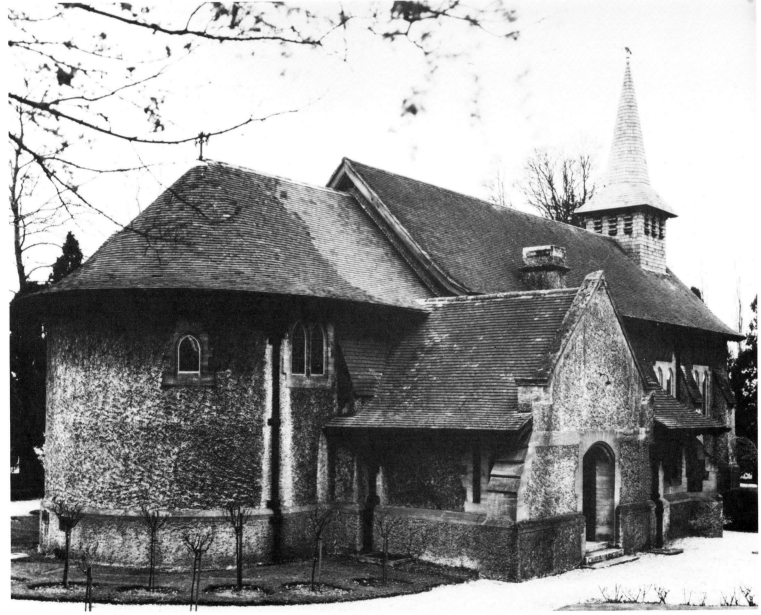

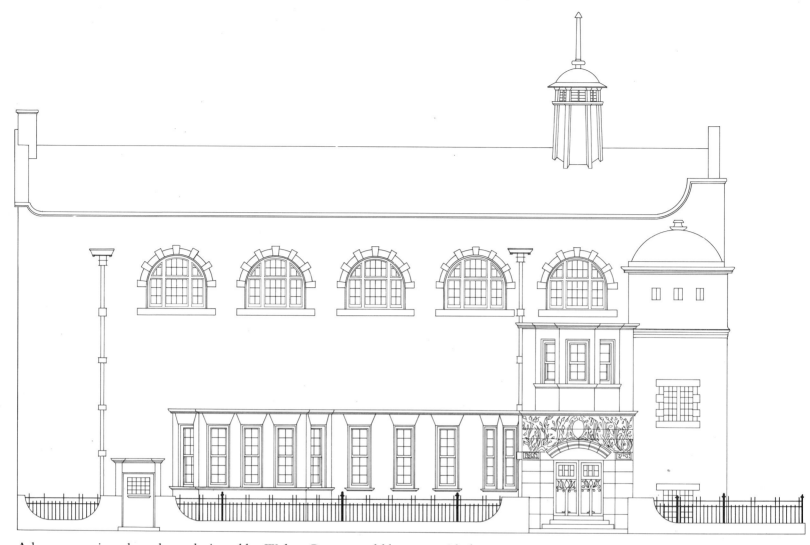

1.29 SMITH & BREWER *Passmore Edwards Settlement* London 1896-7, elevation (from the original drawing)

A large mosaic to have been designed by Walter Crane would have provided an archaic Early Christian flavour to the whole, while the massive round arches and impressive battered towers would have given the impression of a revitalised Romanesque. As built, between 1899 and 1901, with the towers reduced to minarets and the space for the mosaic left permanently blank, the Gallery impresses most by the perversity and oddity of its massive asymmetrical entrance arch. The decorative trees on the base of the towers are just like the wallpaper designed for his uncompleted Cliff Towers.

Meanwhile, another project of public utility had come along, F. J. Horniman's museum to house his collection of anthropology. Work began in 1896 and the building was completed in 1901. The breadth of the first design for the Whitechapel Art Gallery has been retained, as has one of the towers for that scheme, here set forward of the facade and acting as a fulcrum for the entrance. Behind this imposing arrangement of tower and facade, the shed to house the exhibits is arranged in two galleries with the utmost simplicity. The mosaic here was designed by another Arts and Crafts man, Robert Anning Bell. As *The Studio* remarked in its review of the building: ' . . . for Mr Horniman did not seek his architect from among the nympholepts of the old styles, who are afraid to do in "the frozen music of architecture" what Wagner and other modern composers have done with their art . . . The point of real concern to us all is this: that the architecture, whether liked or disliked, is not in the least degree an imitation, an echo of some old master's merit. It stands there at Forest Hill as a new series of frank and fearless thoughts expressed and co-ordinated in stone.'

It is worth comparing these Townsend buildings with a somewhat similar building in type and design, Smith and Brewer's Passmore Edwards Settlement in Tavistock Place, London (1896-7). Dunbar Smith and Cecil Brewer were both Art Workers' Guildsmen, with some fine Arts and Crafts domestic work to their credit. The Settlement, now known as the Mary Ward Settlement, was a typically enlightened organisation which grew out of Mrs Humphrey Ward's University Hall of 1889.

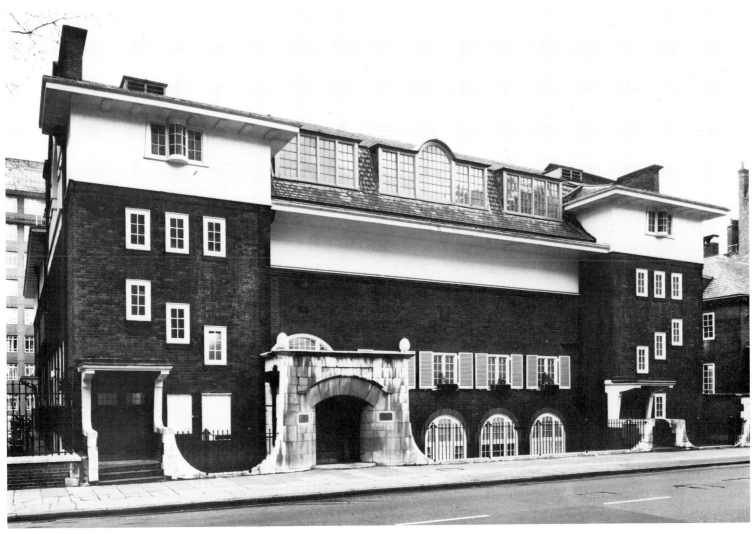

1.30 SMITH & BREWER *Passmore Edwards Settlement* (photograph Goulancourt)

The building included various dining and drawing rooms, a gymnasium, teaching rooms for discussions, a library and residential rooms in the upper floors. Inside, the furniture is simple and ingenious, including a number of folding tables which can be stored in special cupboards. The fireplaces were designed by a roll-call of Arts and Crafts designers – Lethaby, Voysey, Newton and Troup.

The exterior of the building dramatically exploits a few bold devices – sculptural portals and a long low look, achieved by leaving a strip of white wall below a deep overhang in the middle section. The same Richardsonian influences which are found in Townsend's work can also be detected here, and there is a similarity to Voysey's Hans Place flats in the curving base to the street railings. In detail, the windows are conventional enough. In the work of Smith and Brewer, this building represented only a point of transition between conventional Arts and Crafts designs and a restrained Georgian manner, not unlike Ernest Newton's work.

The last Townsend building to consider is his church and Garden of Rest at Great Warley, Essex (1902-04). Intended as a memorial to Arnold Heseltine and paid for by his brother, St Mary the Virgin presents little of radical surprise on the exterior, being a simple essay in stripped down local vernacular. The rose window, with its heart-shaped tracery invites an inspection of the interior, however, and this presents us with one of the richest and most perfect Arts and Crafts interiors in Britain. William Reynolds-Stevens undertook the gorgeous metalwork, in brass, copper, oxidised silver, pewter, and aluminium, enlivened with coloured glass, enamel and mother of pearl inlay. The floral ornamentation harks on themes of remembrance (poppies everywhere). The stained glass, by Heywood Sumner (a member of Mackmurdo's Century Guild and a brilliant designer and illustrator), has mostly been lost, through war damage. Most of the joinery was designed by Townsend, although a number of other Arts and Crafts colleagues worked on the building.

It is noteworthy that so many Arts and Crafts commissions were either domestic, commemorative or charitable in kind. The circle of sympathisers

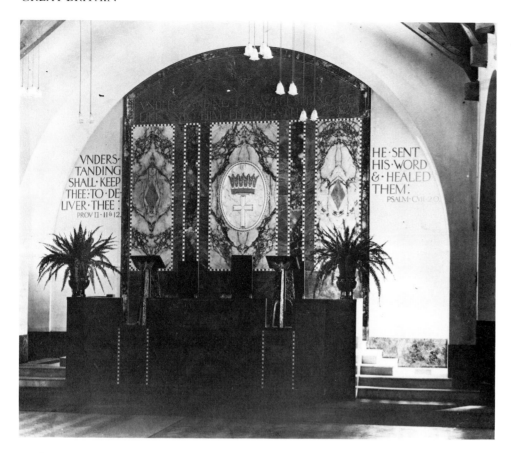

and activists remained small, if influential. By the time this church was completed, the Arts and Crafts Movement had dispersed its efforts almost to the point of dissolution, although the Art Workers' Guild and dozens of other organisations continued to preach the gospel. The difficulty was how to develop beyond the extraordinary inventiveness of the late nineteenth-century designs, without making a major step in the direction of new materials and constructional methods. So the partnership of Edgar Wood and James Henry Sellers in the Manchester area is of particular interest.

Edgar Wood (1860-1935) came from a prosperous family and was able to set up on his own as soon as he qualified in 1885. He designed a number of houses in variations on local vernacular, and was a keen Arts and Crafts man, helping to found the Northern Art Workers' Guild. A most unusual building which he designed just before Sellers joined him in 1904, was the First Church of Christ Scientist in Victoria Park, Manchester (1903-08). The plan seems to have picked up the splayed arrangement of Prior's and Baillie Scott's houses of this period. The treatment of the volumes, with their bevelled surfaces and jagged roof lines, reveals a mastery of form as well as materials. Wood was fearless in the use of windows and strips of brick to scythe through the solidity of walls, and the whole effect is as dynamic as any building of its period. In the early stages of planning, Wood tried out a number of schemes, including an octagonal plan for the main building. The final result allowed for the church to be built first, and the splayed wings of the forecourt to be added later. Wood seems to have wanted to perpetuate the octagonal geometry of the preliminary project in the details of the building as constructed.

J. Henry Sellers (1861-1954) had more of a struggle to make his way, spending a number of years working in different towns in the North of England, as assistant to very different architects. Among the skills he picked up was a mastery of architectural draughtsmanship and an interest in the possibilities of reinforced concrete for flat roof construction. In 1903, Wood met Sellers in Oldham, and they entered into partnership in 1904. It seems to have been Sellers who went back to Oldham to design the offices for Dronsfield Bros (1906-07), a firm for whom he had carried out work in one of his earlier partnerships. This extraordinary building had a flat concrete roof and walls of green glazed bricks. The arrangement of the facade can only be understood with reference to Mackintosh's Glasgow School of Art, but Sellers' classical taste has contrived an even more rigorous and disciplined work than Mackintosh's.

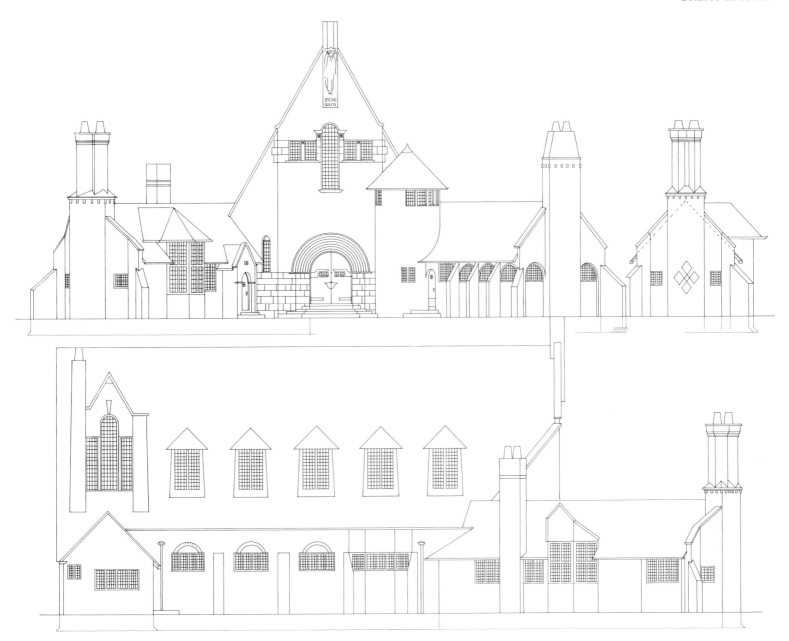

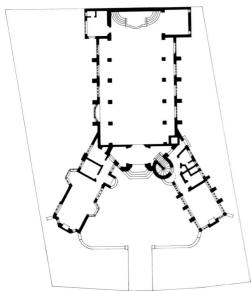

1.32-33 WOOD *First Church of Christ Scientist*, front, reading room and side elevations and plan (from the original drawings)

The partnership went on to design a number of houses using flat roofs in concrete and an austere but powerful use of straight and curved brick walls. The approach is Lethabite – a reinforced concrete flat roof frees the plan by making it independent of rectangular roof forms. Curves and other irregular plan forms were made possible, although Wood mainly used a highly axial arrangement, usually employing a curved section flanking the entrance. In 1908, Wood also experimented with coloured tiles, in chevron patterns, on some shops in Middleton. These brightly coloured tile facings occurred again over the entrance of the house he built for himself in Hale (1914-16). This house marks the border-line between Arts and Crafts thinking and the early flowering of the Modern Movement.

Meanwhile, Sellers was taking a similar road in his more classical but equally adventurous schools in Middleton – Elm Street (1908-10) and Durnford Street (1908-10). Here again, flat roofs and austere formal treatment give these buildings an ambiguous position between the advanced neo-Georgian and Early Modern Movement.

A similar combination could be found in the early work of Charles Holden, whose Central Reference Library, Bristol (1903-06) stands comparison with these and Mackintosh's buildings. Holden's Midhurst Sanatorium (1904-05), like the earlier Belgrave Hospital for Children, Kennington, were designed for his senior partner H. Percy Adams, and both buildings share a fully fledged Arts and Crafts quirkiness in the use of materials and planning arrangements, combined curiously with a classical sense of geometric internal spaces. Holden was quickly to move towards a brilliant and individual version of the classical revival which gripped all the successful architects after 1903.

Developments in Scotland remained distinct from what took place below the border despite considerable cross-fertilisation of people and ideas. Scots architects like J. J. Stevenson and James MacLaren, who worked in London but retained their Scottish connections, tended to be more influential in England than in their native land. Arts and Crafts ideas, and illustrations of Arts and Crafts buildings in magazines, had their effect in Scotland, but merged with a very strong local tradition, the so-called Scottish Baronial style, which considerably altered the flavour of the vernacular revival. With Mackintosh, furthermore, we stumble across an artist and architect of quite outstanding stature, whose reinterpretation of the forms and ideas of the English Arts and Crafts Movement went far beyond the originals in power and coherence. Mackintosh brings us closer to European developments not only through his direct links with Vienna and the Secession movement but also in his attitude to form-giving which quite consciously takes an innovatory and strikingly original approach to style. Unlike most of his English contemporaries, Mackintosh felt able to synthesise completely the new decorative freedom and the belief in constructional logic. Like the Art Nouveau architects, therefore, he was able to create buildings conceived in organic structural terms in harmony with their decoration – buildings which seem to grow naturally from a seed already charged with its formal properties.

The career of James MacLaren (1843-90) points to the connections between the English Arts and Crafts Movement and parallel developments in Scotland. Having moved to London around 1877, MacLaren was deeply influenced by E. W. Godwin and the Aesthetic Movement. His own work combined the new 'free' brick style of Godwin with reminiscences of Scottish vernacular architecture, with its asymmetrically placed stair-turrets and powerfully moulded forms.

MacLaren's private practice began around 1886, and he carried out a number of spectacular buildings in the short space before his early death four years later. Among these was a new wing to Stirling High School, including a bold Observatory Tower which applied Godwin-inspired logic to Scottish Baronial forms. The rounded corners of this tower, and the stark geometric handling of the stone detail, were to prove important for both Townsend and Mackintosh. Finally, MacLaren built a number of buildings for Sir Donald Currie's estates, notably Glenlyon house, Perthshire, which showed how the Scottish vernacular tradition, with its roughcast (harled) walls and sweeping roof-lines could form perfect material for an Arts and Crafts methodology. For MacLaren joined the Art Workers' Guild in 1886 and was an active member, absorbing the principles of vernacular revival in all its forms. That MacLaren had already discovered the picturesque quality of the harled Scottish Baronial vernacular before leaving Scotland, is shown by his drawing of Old Leckie House, Stirlingshire, drawn in 1874. There is no doubt that it was this kind of architecture which influenced the young Mackintosh.

Another Scotsman who made the move to England and whose synthesis of Scottish and English sources parallels that of Mackintosh, is the designer George Walton (1867-1933). Walton established a firm in 1888 to carry out interior design in Glasgow, within the cultural context of the 'Glasgow Boys' – a group of painters fired with an enthusiasm for Whistler and the English Aesthetic Movement. Walton was in touch with events in London through the magazines, the occasional visit, his English wife and, after 1893, his brother who moved to London in that year and who was one of the 'Glasgow Boys'.

We cannot investigate Walton's fertile career as a designer, except to note that he worked with Mackintosh on the Buchanan Street tea-rooms for Mrs Cranston and shared in the development of the Glasgow style of decorative art later dubbed the 'spook' school. Highly successful in aesthetic and economic terms, Walton had achieved an international reputation by 1897, the year in which he began to work for George Davison, an excellent photographer of the impressionist kind who was head of European Sales for Kodak. The hoardings and interiors for a large number of Kodak show-rooms all over Europe make the link between European Art Nouveau and the Glasgow school quite clear. Walton may have helped Mackintosh and The Four to think in European terms, and certainly helped them to get what limited publicity they were given in *The Studio*. Walton's work was extensively published abroad, and he carried out a number of European commissions. From 1898, Walton lived in London,

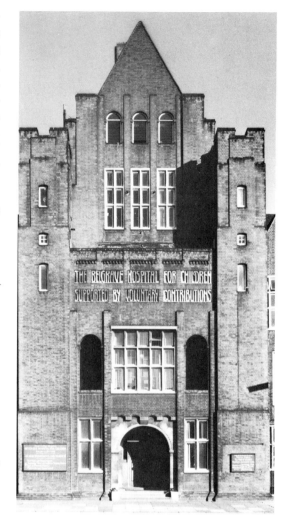

1.34 HOLDEN *Belgrave Hospital for Children* London 1903, detail of facade (photograph Goulancourt)

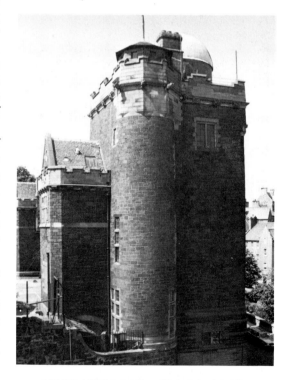

1.35 MACLAREN *Stirling High School* Stirling 1887-88, Observatory tower from the South East (photograph Mackay)

1.36-37 WALTON *Kodak show-rooms* Strand branch 1901, exterior and Brompton Road branch 1900, interior (contemporary photographs)

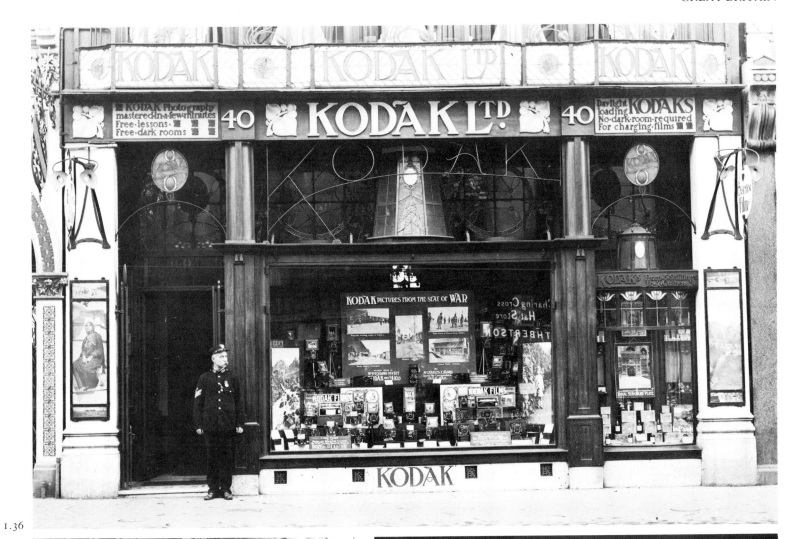

1.36

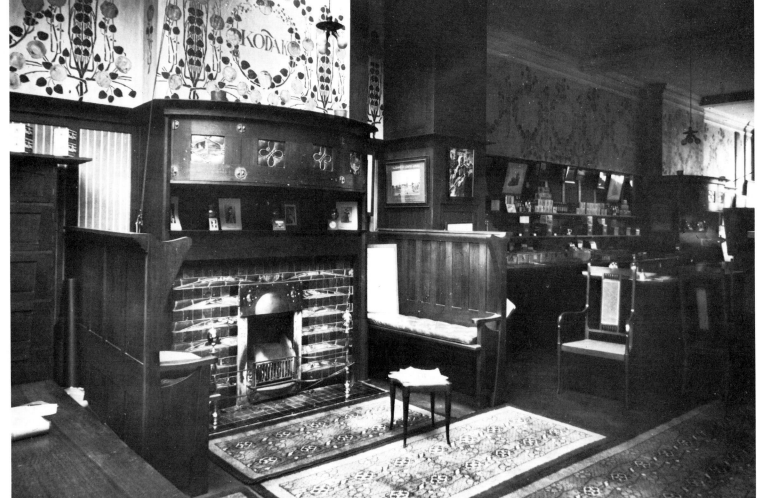

1.37

keeping up his Glasgow workshops and showroom. He carried out a few architectural commissions, mostly for the Davison family, in a neo-vernacular style picking up the character of local building methods in an approved Arts and Crafts manner.

A house for Mr Wellington at Elstree, The Leys (1901), shows how sharp Walton's perception of Lethabite rationalism could be. The interior has the high key tonality and some of the characteristic detailing of Voysey's houses, but combined with a more spacious and masculine approach. The exterior is both more symmetrical and rigorously logical than anything Voysey built, and can be compared more closely with Ernest Newton's classical facades. This house was designed at a time when Mackintosh and Walton were still in relatively close contact, and helps to explain the discipline in the younger man's subsequent houses. Walton showed how to combine sumptuous Glasgow style detailing, full of rich curvilinear forms and colour with the cool English attitude to overall form.

Recent research has shown how much more closely related the work of Charles Rennie Mackintosh (1868-1928) is to that of his contemporaries than was formerly believed. His sketching tours in Scotland and the South of England provided him with a wealth of vernacular detail which he was careful to incorporate in his own work. He learned, too, from his trips to Italy in 1891.

The architectural scene in Glasgow in which Mackintosh found his feet was subject to a number of conflicting influences. The Beaux-Arts training of John Burnet junior and the survival of the neo-classical tradition lent a cutting edge to the struggle to develop a 'free' style. The discipline of Burnet's work helped to control the Scottish Baronial revival which was always in danger of being submerged under a flood of picturesque detail. As in England, leading architects were working towards a classical revival as the new century approached, but the strength and vigour of local traditions ensured that many of the intermediary 'free' designs possessed an extraordinarily inventive quality. John A. Campbell, Burnet's partner, produced a number of important buildings in Glasgow, which helped to shape the style of Honeyman and Keppie, the firm Mackintosh joined in 1889.

Before this, Mackintosh had worked with John Hutchison, whose assistant Andrew Black carried out most of the designing work. In both offices, Mackintosh came under the influence of James Sellar's work, with its mixture of neo-Grec and Beaux-Arts styles. In his various competition projects and scholarship designs, Mackintosh worked through a representative range of contemporary Glasgow styles. The relationship between Keppie and Mackintosh appears to have been close for a number of years, until the marriage of the latter to Margaret Macdonald in 1900. Until 1896, Keppie's sister Jessie had been engaged to Mackintosh and she seems to have suffered her loss badly. Mackintosh became a partner in the firm in 1902. In 1913 he resigned, after the irregularity of his working methods had brought work in the office to a standstill.

Mackintosh began to work out his personal style in architecture around 1893, with the Glasgow Herald Building which, with the Queen Margaret College design of 1894 shows some debts to MacLaren. What prompted the radical development of these ideas towards the fully worked out forms of the Glasgow School of Art design of 1896 still remains partially obscure. Illustrations in *The British Architect* and *The Architect* must have been significant in showing Mackintosh how to simplify his designs under the influence of Lethaby and Voysey. The trips to England, with sketches of simple vernacular buildings, seem also to be significant, particularly when the latter are compared with an intriguing re-modelling of an inn in Lennoxtown (1895).

At the same time as his discovery of the English vernacular tradition Mackintosh developed the graphic and decorative style shared by Herbert MacNair and the Macdonald sisters, who arrived as students at the School of Art in 1891. The first securely dated work which carries the full spirit of the new look was *The Harvest Moon*, a drawing made in 1892 and given by Mackintosh to Keppie. The swirling forms of The Four's graphic style soon entered Mackintosh's architectural detailing. The interior design style developed by The Four was a late response to the aestheticism of Whistler and Godwin, modified by some features derived from Beardsley and Mackmurdo. Highly Bohemian in atmosphere, it was charged with that flavour of decadence

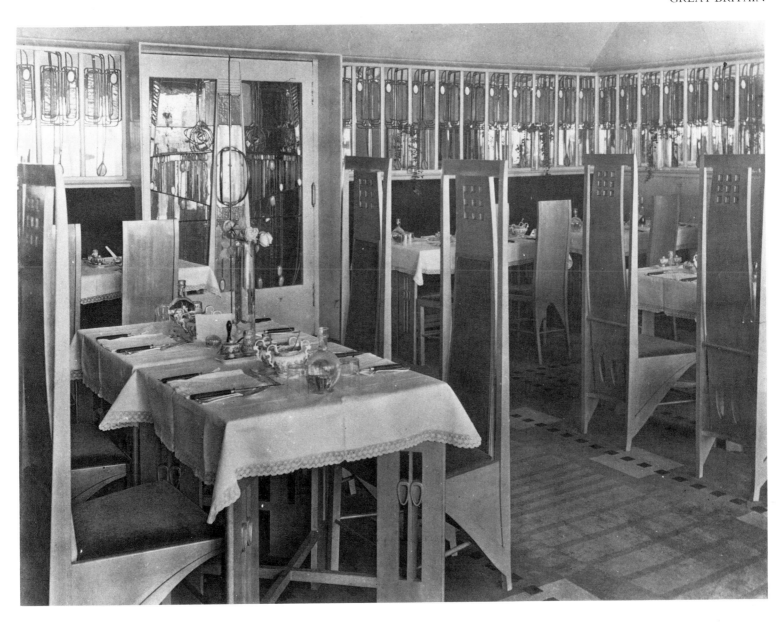

1.38 MACKINTOSH *Willow tea-rooms* Glasgow 1904, room de luxe (contemporary photograph)

appropriate to fin de siècle artistic existence.

The intensity of this Bohemian quality put off English critics and – although *The Studio* published important articles by Gleeson White on the Glasgow group of designers – reinforced English attitudes to 'originality': 'In a day when novelty is supposed to atone for any artistic revolt, we might have expected that the experiments of the Glasgow decorators would have been attractive to jaded palates. But as a rule even the most lukewarm supporter of the "things that have been" feels called upon to protest at the "things that might be", did these two young people [the Macdonald sisters] have power to work their wicked will undetected.' (Gleeson White, 'Some Glasgow Designers', *The Studio*, XI, 1897, p. 90.)

In Germany, Austria and France, however, this very originality was a matter of congratulation: 'It is now Glasgow rather than London which is likely to give modern art its new direction.' (Pascal Forthuny, 'L'Art Décoratif en Ecosse', *Revue des Arts Décoratifs*, XXII, 1902, p. 61.) Other critics, however, turned against the perversity which they saw as derived from Huysmans' *A Rebours*: 'To tell the truth, this style seems to be out of harmony with our artistic aspirations and domestic needs, and one is tempted to wonder which crazy Des Esseintes would be able to live with this kind of interior decoration.' (*Art et Décoration*, XII, 1903.) This view, in a review of the Turin Exhibition of 1902, brings us back to Walter Crane's comments on Art Nouveau cited at the beginning. The gulf between the English Arts and Crafts and the Glasgow School was as great as that separating it from continental Art Nouveau. Needless to say, however, Mackintosh did not rate Art Nouveau very highly either: 'Mackintosh didn't like *art nouveau*. He fought against it with these straight lines; these things you can see for yourself are like melted

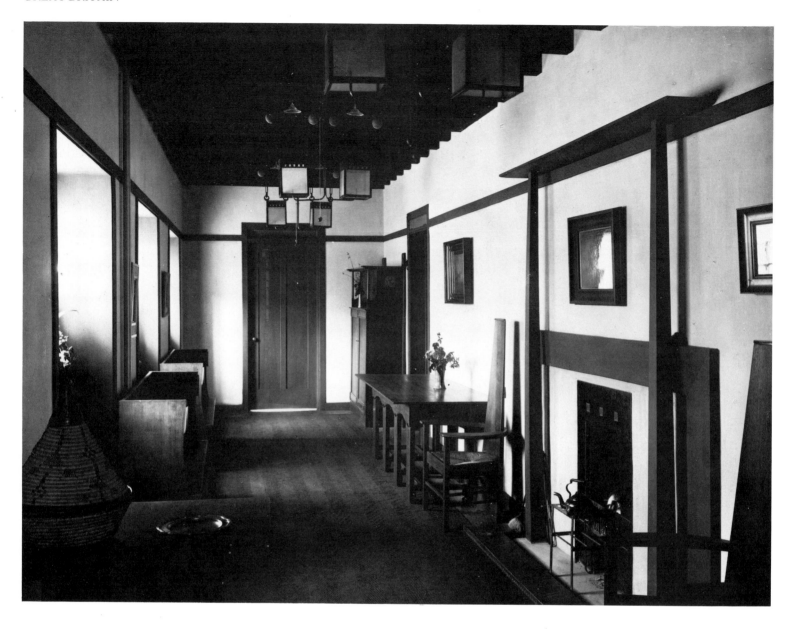

margarine . . .' (Mary Sturrock, quoted in *The Connoisseur*, 183, August 1973, p. 282.)

Despite the ready acceptance of his work in Vienna, and the mutual influences on and from Joseph Maria Olbrich and Josef Hoffmann, Mackintosh was fated to remain an outcast in Glasgow, appreciated only within a tiny artistic circle around the School of Art, and one or two clients. And when a mixture of temperament and drink forced him to leave the shelter of his partnership with Keppie, the Mackintoshs were committed to a life of almost complete obscurity in England. Recent research is revealing more details of their life in Essex and London where they established friendships and were given occasional commissions. But apart from his marvellous watercolour sketches and some wallpaper designs, Mackintosh achieved little in his last years apart from the house for W. J. Bassett-Lowke at 78 Derngate, Northampton. His fall was more complete than that of any other Arts and Crafts practitioner.

The Glasgow School of Art has an extraordinarily complicated building history, evolving as it did from the original schemes of 1896 through a number of revisions and additions until 1909, when the West wing and library were completed. Much of the character of the building depends on the continuous process of adjustment and revision as building work progressed. Mackintosh seems to have discovered the potential of the basic shape and siting of the building as he went along, increasingly impressed by Lethaby's structural rationalism. Much has been said about the sources for the great unadorned windows of the North front, the forms of the entrance with its little offset tower and recessed studio window for the Headmaster. But the end result is so definitively different from the sum of the various borrowings that these

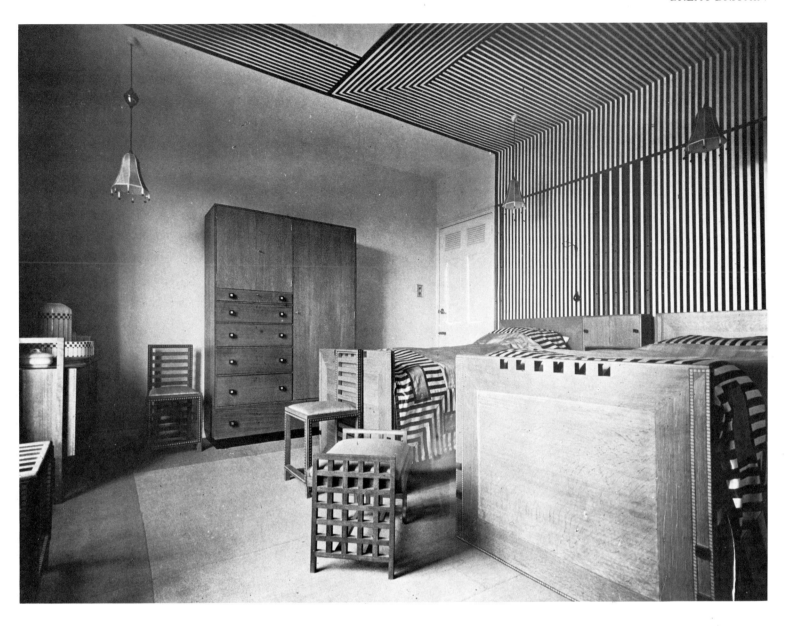

1.40 MACKINTOSH *78 Derngate* Northampton 1916-17, main bedroom (contemporary photograph)

discussions seem fruitless. It is the spatial articulation of the interior which catches the visitor unawares – the way the large, gaunt studios are deployed around the axial corridor in continually inventive ways. The masterful control of light and shade, created by natural lighting and the tonality of surface, produces a succession of surprises. The upper level of studios, in particular, is like nothing other than Gaudí in the apparently casual arrangement of parts, providing unexpected views and outlandish solutions to communication difficulties – such as the 'Hen run' tacked onto the South wall after the attic storey was added.

Any number of Mackintosh's other buildings repay detailed study, such as Windyhill, Hill House, Ruchill Church Hall, Queen's Cross Church or the Scotland Street School. One unexecuted project, however, seems to sum up his aesthetic ideas as far as domestic architecture is concerned. We have already mentioned the *Haus eines Kunstfreundes* competition in the context of the man who won it – Baillie Scott. Mackintosh's scheme was placed second and its publication, along with Scott's and Leopold Bauer's design in 1902, exerted a considerable influence on European architects and designers. A comparison between this project and Hoffmann's Palais Stoclet in Brussels is most illuminating. The plan is more fully developed than in his executed houses, where a more picturesque licence allows for service wings and a relaxed, additive process of planning. In the competition project, the service rooms are simply ignored to concentrate on a magnificent succession of spaces, from the double-height hall which connects directly with the combined music and reception rooms on one side and the dining room on the other. Less ingenious than Scott's plan, perhaps, the Mackintosh design was infinitely more impressive as an aesthetic whole. The Scottish Baronial sources are totally assimilated

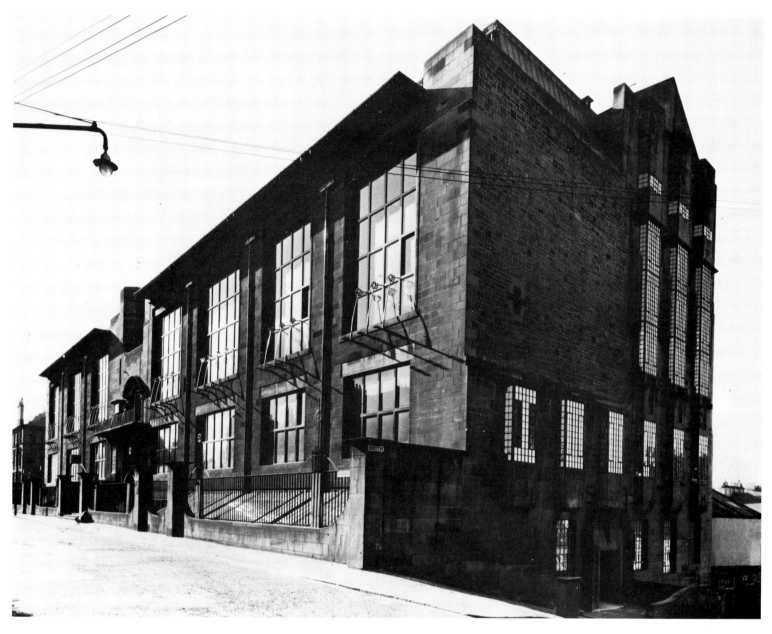

1.41 MACKINTOSH *Glasgow School of Art* Glasgow 1896-1909, view from the North West

in this design. The interiors were completely in harmony with the concentrated tension of the exterior walls. And the drawings serve to convey the brilliance of massing and the sharp articulation more forcefully than any of his executed buildings can today.

The heightened perception of Mackintosh's vision was always a little beyond what was realisable, and this is what makes him so effective an exponent of the turn of the century aesthetic trends. Whether in the form of European Art Nouveau, English Arts and Crafts, Catalan Modernismo or Viennese Secession, this spirit of creative release was essentially short-lived and transitory, seeking impossible goals and doomed to failure in the face of international classicism.

1.42-45 MACKINTOSH *Glasgow School of Art*, North and South elevations and West and East elevations of proposed alterations and extensions (from the original drawings)

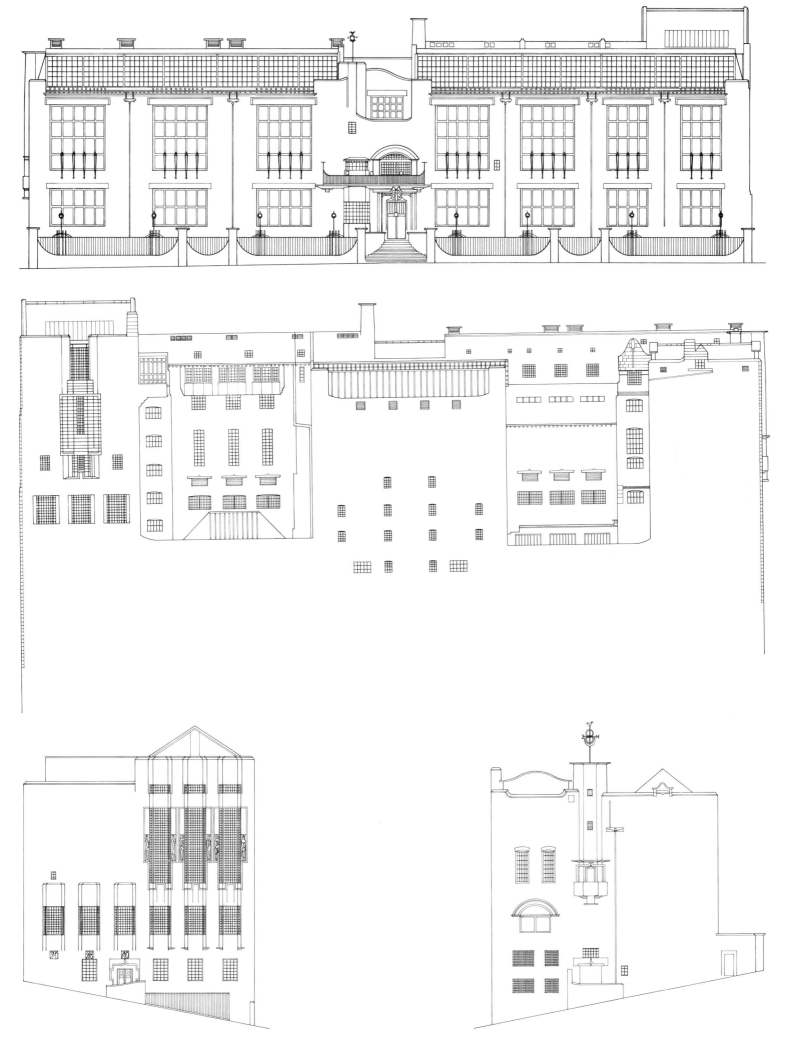

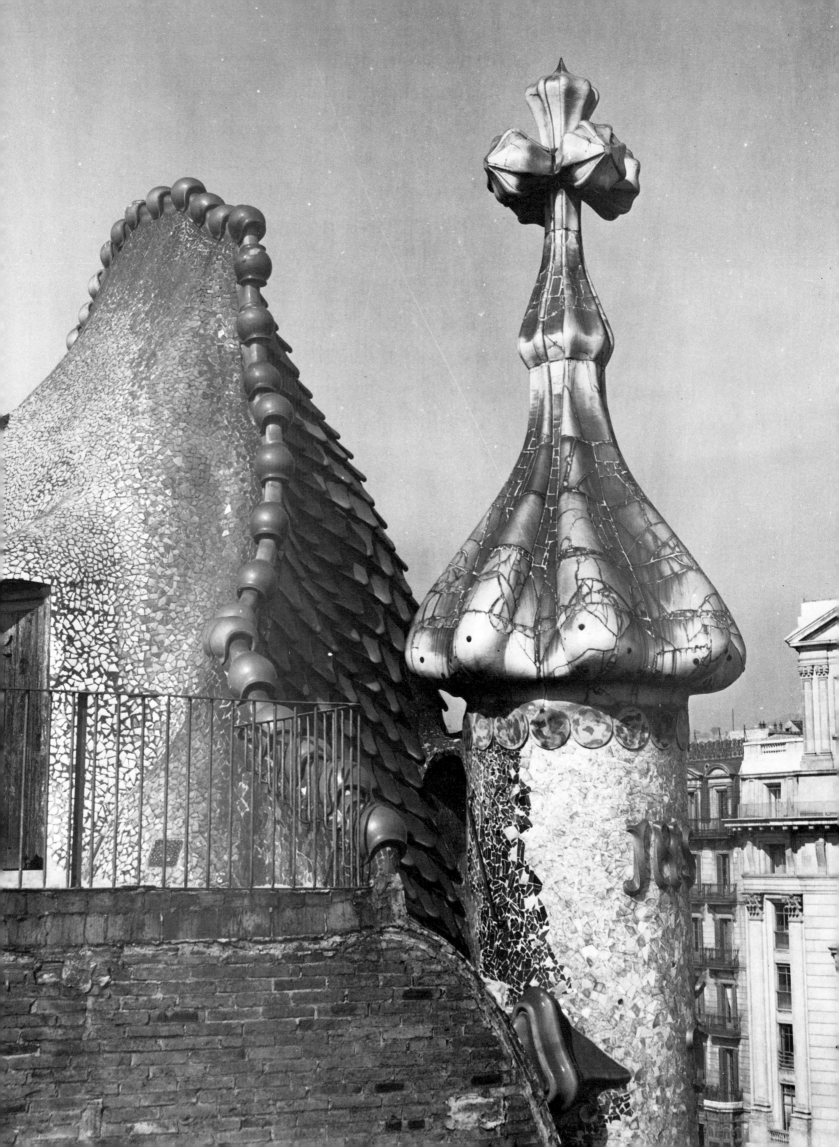

2. SPAIN
Modernismo in Catalonia

Tim Benton

A general understanding of the architecture and design of Catalan Modernismo has been hindered rather than helped by the staggering impact of the work of Antoni Gaudí i Cornet (1852-1926). Gaudí was a monster, one of those overwhelming personalities like Francesco Borromini or William Blake who appear to break free from the frame of their cultural context. The copious literature on this extraordinary man has only increased the confusion as well as the excitement caused by his work.

To Evelyn Waugh, Gaudí was a sublimely decadent slap in the face for the all too serious modernists of 1930. For Le Corbusier, who visited Barcelona in 1928 (and again in 1930) and who was introduced to the work of Gaudí by his Catalan assistant Josep Lluís Sert, the fascination lay in the mixture of purely sculptural form and structural innovation. For Salvador Dali, who met Le Corbusier there and exchanged his Surrealist viewpoint with Le Corbusier's Purist one, Gaudí was simply the exponent of 'a terrifying and comestible beauty'. The unlikely nature of this exchange could hardly be more bizarre – when Le Corbusier asked Dali for his views on modern architecture he was told, 'Architecture must be soft and hairy'. Any architect whose work is capable of such potent and evocative misinterpretation must play havoc with the niceties of historical categorisation. If it is now impossible to approach the work of Gaudí with eyes undazzled by this blaze of publicity, it is equally difficult to penetrate the corresponding gloom of the movement which nourished him and which made his work comprehensible to his contemporaries. Many people in Barcelona may have thought Gaudí mad, and said so, but they understood what motivated him exactly – his obsession with religion, his absolute dedication to Catalan nationalism, the very eccentricity and extremism he cultivated as artist and architect. Not many people could have understood what Gaudí had in mind for the Sagrada Familia, but they were intensely proud of it and showed it off to visiting dignitaries like the Papal Nuncio, Cardinal Ragonesi (1915) or the Spanish Infanta.

What linked all the works of the Catalan Modernismo was a common background in the general movement known as the Renaixensa. Since Catalonia finally lost all its independent rights to Spain at the end of the eighteenth century, a slow growth of cultural and political nationalism had begun to develop. By the 1880s, this Catalan revival had spread to all fields of linguistic, literary and artistic expression. The leading architects of Modernismo shared this nationalistic background. Lluís Domènech i Montaner (1850-1923), for example, was deeply committed to Catalan separatism, becoming the first President of the Unió Catalana and taking the chair at the epoch-making Assembly in 1892 which approved the Bases de Manresa – the statement of Catalan demands for independence. Another leading architect of the next generation, Josep Puig i Cadafalch (1867-1956), became the President of the Mancomunitat, the first united regional government of Catalonia.

The clients who supported the movement, men like Eusebio Güell i Bacigalupi (1846-1918) or the Marqués de Comillas – mostly second generation industrialists or merchants of great drive and character – shared the same

2.1 GAUDI *Casa Batlló* Barcelona 1904-06, roofscape with pinnacle

51

interests. These were people who were prepared to take great risks, financial as well as social, to show their commitment to a new order of unheard of originality and liberation. Modernism, to this newly formed aristocracy, was symbolic of the practical liberties so much desired – freedom from the domination of a Spain whose Empire overseas was to come crashing down in 1898 with the loss of Cuba, Puerto Rico and the Philippines, freedom from the dead hand of Spanish traditionalism, with its rigid caste system and distaste for commerce, freedom from the artificiality of the historical styles in architecture. The struggle to revive the Catalan language must be seen as fundamentally similar to the veneration for Catalan history and traditional arts and crafts.

Of course, the further we penetrate into fin de siècle Barcelona, the less clear the picture becomes. Politically, the Catalan nationalists formed the most heterogeneous mixture of persuasions, from the bomb-throwing anarchists who captured the headlines increasingly in the 1880s and 1890s, through a spectrum of anti-clericalists, Marxists and syndicalists, to the right wing High Church aristocrats, who formed the influential Lliga de Catalunya in 1887. Gaudí, Domènech and Puig all belonged to the last group.

Similarly, on a cultural level, a bewilderingly large number of strands have to be disentangled within the skein of Modernismo. The contributors to the magazine L'Avenç (founded in 1881) favoured a committed social stance; they were for a total transformation of society through some kind of anarchic spiritual and political whirlwind. L'Avenç was considered dangerous enough to be suspended between 1883 and 1886. More aesthetic was the group around Santiago Rusiñol, who achieved great successes with a series of *Fiestas Modernistas* at the seaside village of Sitges in 1892, 1893, 1894, 1897 and 1899. This was the world of art for art's sake, feeding off the English Aesthetes, the French Symbolists and the various Catalan and South American literary movements. Gaudí's friend the poet Juan Maragall was influenced by these trends, which he took to extremes of stylistic formalism. Many more sub-groups could be identified, and important distinctions made, but the fundamental point is that virtually every section of Barcelonan society was imbued with a generally felt urgency to see great changes and make great advances, in every field of endeavour. The great Catalan international exhibitions, such as the huge industrial exhibition of 1888 in Barcelona, demonstrated this fierce national pride to the outside world.

But if Catalonia had its very special character, with its own interests and ambitions, it would be wrong to imagine her isolated from European developments. The works of Ruskin, Goethe, Viollet-le-Duc and Richard Wagner were all translated into Catalan in the last years of the century and exerted their own influence. Because of the development of illustrated magazines as a forum for spreading artistic and architectural ideas, events in Britain, France, Belgium and Austria were closely followed in Barcelona. Close economic and cultural ties with Britain led to a particularly strong response to the graphic work of British illustrators like Beardsley. Paris exerted another kind of influence, through the spread of Bohemianism and dandyism in dress and life-style. The world of *Els Quatre Gats*, which the young Pablo Picasso frequented, was steeped in this European modernism. Many patrons like Eusebio Güell, or architects like Josep Vilaseca, travelled widely, and the books on old and new European architecture by Josep Puig i Cadafalch were well known. But although the influences flowed freely at the theoretical and stylistic level, Barcelona imposed a sea-change on all imported ideas. There is nothing here which corresponds to the 'international Art Nouveau' of Horta, Guimard and van de Velde.

The apparently paradoxical mixture of entrenched nationalism and eager internationalism makes better sense when we realise that Catalonia had always looked North for its commercial and cultural nourishment. Spain had prohibited Catalonia from sharing in the exploitation of the American colonies, and this now worked in favour of those who had been forced to develop local agriculture, textile industries and trading contacts with the industrial powers of the North. As Spain declined, Barcelona prospered, increasingly breaking its economic and cultural ties with the peninsular. The cultural consequences are well summed up by Puig in the French and Catalan introductions to the folio of his own work published in 1904: 'Thus, in urgency and haste, architectural education was improvised. Even quicker was the formation of the various

Opposite
GAUDI *Park Güell* Barcelona 1900-14, detail of entrance pavilion roof

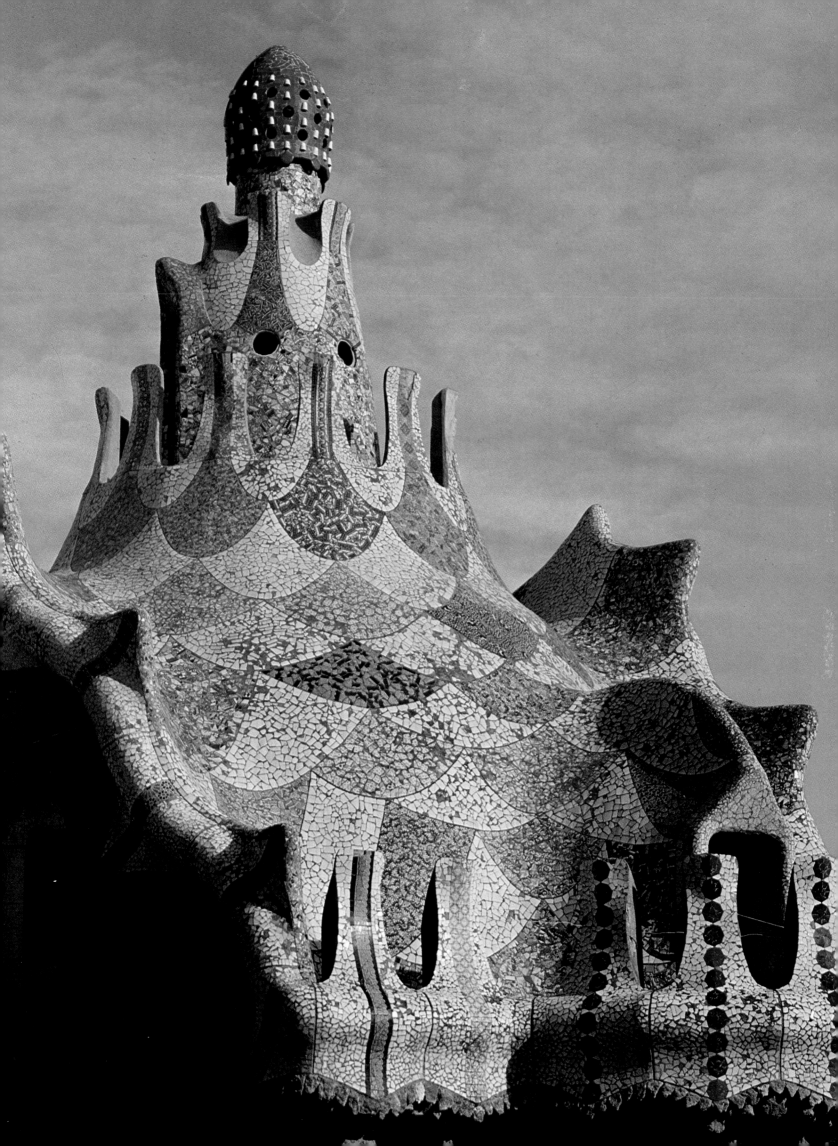

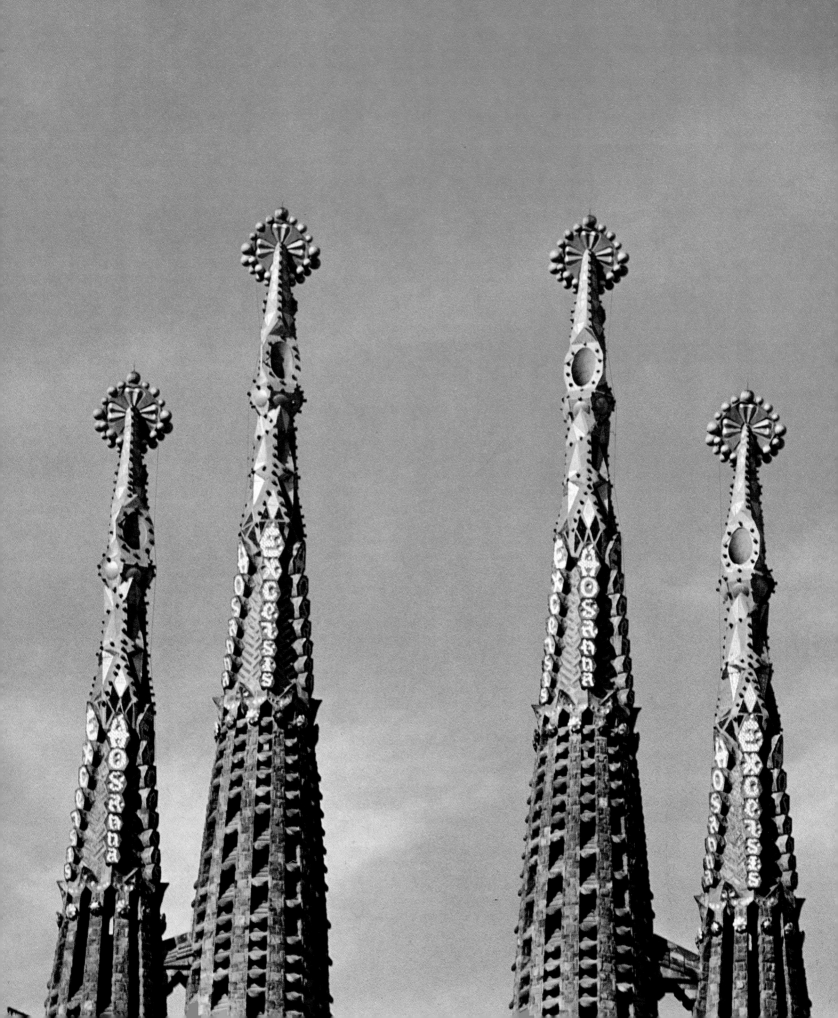

groups, with their masters and pupils, each one developing its own point of view, forming its own style. Some attempted the impossible task of reviving Romanesque architecture, others imported the French neo-Gothicism of Viollet-le-Duc, others still searching for a modern style in Germany, Austria or France, or trying to achieve architectural rationalism by expressing the nature of materials and structural logic. In all this, perhaps the most positive thing we have done is to create a modern art based on our own traditional forms, embellishing them with the beautiful properties of new materials, finding solutions to today's problems through a spirit of nationalism. We have injected into it something of the decorative exuberance of our mediaeval tradition, charged with an almost Moorish flavour and a certain vaguely oriental quality. It has been a collective labour by independent visionaries and their more conservative predecessors alike – a work of masters and disciples. All this has been helped along by a literary, social and historical Renaissance... This art which, without realising it, we have all been creating, has been more clearly understood by foreigners . . . than by ourselves.' (Josep Puig i Cadafalch, *L'Œuvre de Puig i Cadafalch Architecte*, Barcelona, 1904. My translation.)

A measure of the separateness of the Catalan cultural development known as Modernismo is that it seems to have begun earlier and ended later than in most other countries in Europe. If, like Sir Nikolaus Pevsner, we seek to define Art Nouveau stylistically in terms of the characteristically 'whiplash' curves of the Tassel House (1893), we would have to accept as typically Art Nouveau the interiors of Gaudí's Palau Güell (1886-9), or some of the details of his 'El Capricho' (1883-5), or Francesc Berenguer's Bodegas Güell (1888-90). By 1893, decorative forms in ironwork, ceramics and stained glass fully comparable in freedom of movement with anything in Paris or Brussels could be seen in a number of buildings in Barcelona. But this kind of formal analysis is sterile in the long run because it ignores the fundamentally different aesthetic quality of these forms, tinged as they were with purely local features. Alternatively, if Art Nouveau is defined more loosely, as part of the Arts and Crafts Movement and a general breaking away from 'the styles', how could we exclude from it Gaudí's Casa Vicens (1883-5) or the Café-Restaurant at the Barcelona Exhibition of 1888, designed by Domènech?

In fact, three buildings of the early 1880s seem to mark the beginnings of Catalan Modernismo. The publishing house of Montaner i Simon, built by Domènech in 1880, Josep Vilaseca's factory for the cabinet maker F. Vidal (1884) and Gaudí's Casa Vicens (1883-5). All three flow from the inventive re-elaboration of a Spanish stylistic revival known as the neo-Mudéjar, whose origins go back to the Madrid Bull Ring designed by E. Rodriguez Ayuso and L. Alvarez Capra in 1874. Characteristic of the neo-Mudéjar was the use of Moorish decorative forms and techniques – notably the use of tiled surfaces contrasted with brick construction. However significant the neo-Mudéjar style might have been as a release from academic forms and as a stimulus to revive the Catalan ceramics industries and exploit the age-old skills of the Catalan bricklayers, its influence as a style in Barcelona was short-lived, mainly because of the associations with the rest of Spain.

The generation of architects which emerged from the new School of Architecture in Barcelona in the 1870s (first Director, Elies Rogent, 1874) was taught from a strongly neo-Gothic standpoint. The strength of this mediaevalist teaching arose not only from the strong religious environment of Barcelona, but also from the importance of many of the great Catalan Gothic buildings, which seemed to express the essence of Catalan power and ingenuity during its heyday, towards the end of the Middle Ages. Spectacular feats of construction, such as the Cathedrals in Mallorca and Barcelona by Jaume Fabré, or the extension of Gerona Cathedral by Guillerm Bofill (1417), reminded the young students that the Catalan masons were the most daring in Europe. The style of Catalan Gothicism, with its exuberant foliated detail and soaring spaces, remained the dominant influence in Barcelona until the First World War, when it was challenged by the classical Noucentisme movement. But within the strict observance of the style was the seed of Modernismo, which grew from the radical teaching of Viollet-le-Duc and his followers. Many architects, such as Puig i Cadafalch, worked in both styles, using a pure Catalan Gothic interspersed with totally original Modernismo detailing. And even Gaudí respected

Opposite
GAUDI *Sagrada Familia* Barcelona 1883-   , detail of spires

the details of Catalan Gothic in the many works of restoration he undertook, including that of the Cathedral in Mallorca (1902-14).

The second volume of Viollet-le-Duc's *Entretiens* came out in 1872, just after the trauma of the Franco-Prussian war and the Commune. Gaudí borrowed a copy while still at the School of Architecture, and filled it with his notes and comments. The inspirational quality of the *Entretiens* lay in its challenge to modern architects to find radically new solutions to the problems of structure and ornament by thinking them out afresh. The best architecture, in his view, whether Greek, Roman, Gothic or modern was one in which every form had a reason, and every detail was explainable by the logic of its structure, its imitation of nature or the social conditions of the age: 'Since every part of a building or construction must have its *raison d'être*, we are unconsciously aware of every form which explains its function, just as we respond to the sight of a beautiful tree in which all the parts, from the roots which grip the earth to the very last branches which seem to seek out air and light, indicate so clearly the factors which create and sustain these great organisms.' (E. Viollet-le-Duc, *Entretiens*, I, 1863, p. 332.) This kind of organic rationalism went far beyond the mere imitation of neo-Gothic stylistic forms. In the second volume of the *Entretiens* Viollet-le-Duc devoted a great deal of space to the description of a number of imaginary designs for great buildings designed around the constructive possibilities of cast and wrought iron. Many Catalan architects picked up this theme, notably Domènech, who used exposed iron arches in his Café-Restaurant of 1888 and whose signature appeared on a student exercise by Gaudí at the School of Architecture in 1876. Domènech taught at the School and his influence was notable, particularly in this Gaudí project with its daring use of cast iron columns and decorative detail. Although Gaudí was to move away from the direct copying of Viollet-le-Duc's compositional methods, his debt to the theory and general approach of the French architect remained profound. For example, it was in the *Entretiens* that Gaudí was introduced to the problem of reinterpreting Gothic structural methods, rejecting the external flying buttress to devise internal systems of bracing and support. Viollet-le-Duc thought in terms of cast iron stanchions and wrought iron tie-rods, while Gaudí turned to the more local methods of the Catalan masons for his inspiration, but the approach was fundamentally similar. What distinguished the thought and practice of Gaudí, however, was the single-minded tenacity with which he pursued ideas beyond the point of ordinary common sense. So that what started as a response to a problem set by Viollet-le-Duc ended in the extreme solutions of his later works, when columns and walls were sharply inclined inwards to support side thrusts and the tree analogy was taken to the almost absurd lengths of the Park Güell buttresses and the nave piers of the model of the Sagrada Familia. To follow the story of Catalan Modernismo along the path towards these brilliant excesses, we must begin with the eminently reasonable work of Domènech.

Lluís Domènech i Montaner (1850-1923) qualified in 1873 and, almost immediately, won public attention with his successful competition entry, in collaboration with Josep Vilaseca, for the headquarters of the Instituciones Provinciales de Instrucción Publica. The design marked an appreciable extension of the free interpretation of the neo-Gothic style practised at the School of Architecture. Domènech followed it up with a clear statement of modernistic intent in 1878, the year in which he published an article entitled 'En busca de una arquitectura nacional' (In search of a national architecture) in the influential magazine *La Renaixensa*. Drawing together the various strands of cultural nationalism which informed the Catalan Renaixensa, he insisted that architecture must express fundamental historical developments rather than mere architectural stylisation. Any style derived from different practical and social requirements or bred from alien national characteristics should not be employed in Catalonia. Thus, although he lists the styles available to the architect of the day which he considered 'acceptable' in themselves – Romanesque, Catalan Gothic, the neo-Mudéjar – he followed Viollet-le-Duc in seeing the absurdity of employing these styles for buildings of a modern type requiring materials such as steel or cast iron. An entirely new style must be discovered: 'Let us apply openly the forms which recent experience and needs impose on us, enriching them and giving them expressive form through the inspiration of nature and from the ornamental riches offered to us by the

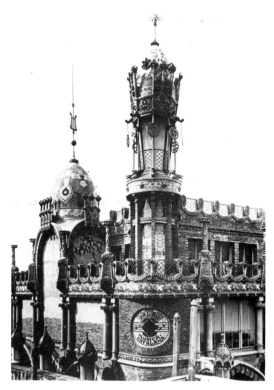

2.2 DOMENECH *Palau de la Musica Catalana* Barcelona 1905-08, facade detail showing the original iron and glass lantern surmounting the corner

2.3-4 DOMENECH *Café-Restaurant* Barcelona 1888, exterior view and interior detail showing exposed iron arches. Originally built for the 1888 Universal Exhibition, the Café-Restaurant is now a Zoological Museum

2.5-6 DOMENECH *Palau de la Musica Catalana,* auditorium and foyer

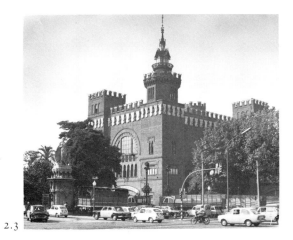

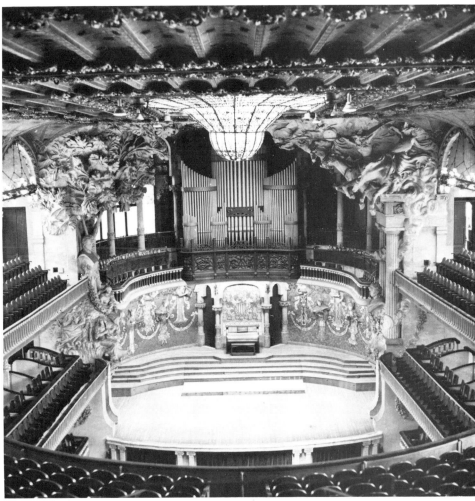

2.3

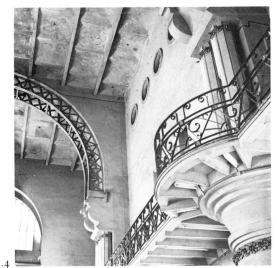

2.4

2.5

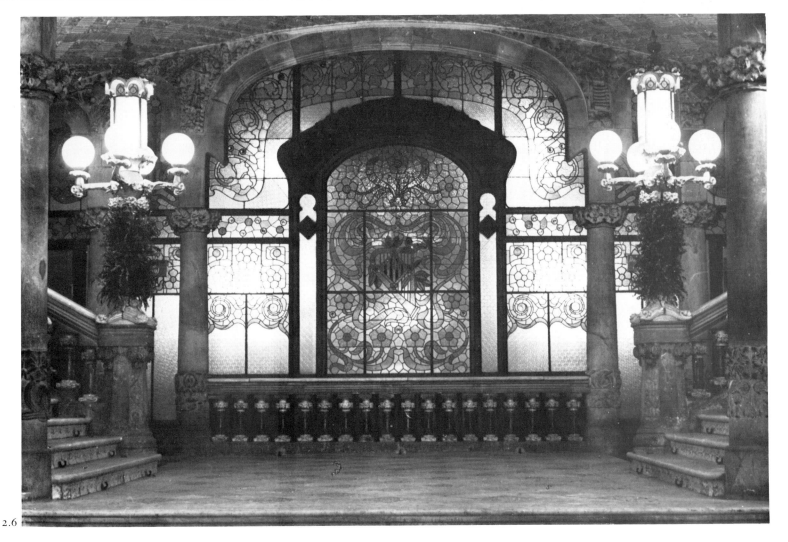

2.6

buildings of every period.' (Quoted in *Oriol Bohigas*, 1973, p. 120. My translation.)

The first buildings to show what he had in mind were the Café-Restaurant and International Hotel, both built for the 1888 Universal Exhibition in Barcelona. The Hotel has been demolished, but the Café-Restaurant has survived, converted into the Zoological Museum. It was never completed, which may give it a more stark and functional appearance than Domènech intended, but it is clear that a quite new conception of simple and clear architectural planning was being inaugurated with this building. Contrasted with the austerity of the main spaces are the refreshingly original details of stained glass, ceramics and wrought iron.

Between 1888 and 1914, when Domènech gave up architecture entirely for politics, he was extremely active, building a number of superb town houses in Barcelona. His clients were similar to those of Gaudí, including the Marqués de Comillas.

He built several buildings in Gaudí's home town of Reus in Tarragona. Perhaps his most significant buildings were the Casa Thomas (1895-8), the Casa Lleó Morera (1905) and, above all, three buildings from the end of his active career as an architect, the Palau de la Musica Catalana (1905-08), the Casa Fuster (1908-10) and the huge project which occupied him between 1902 and 1910, the Hospital de San Pablo.

The Palau de la Musica Catalana repays careful observation. To eyes unaccustomed to the architecture of Barcelona, the impression of a riot of ornament lacking any logic or control seems overwhelming. And yet the building follows exactly the exhortations of the rationalists. The structure, in brick and iron, is clearly expressed. From inside, the building turns out to be a glazed shell in which the solid walls seem to have melted away. The external display, stunning in its blaze of colour and wealth of symbolic detail, must be understood partly in terms of the elaborate eclectic ornamentation of the surrounding buildings (which require a strong response), and partly in terms of the fundamentally symbolic character of the building as an expression of Catalan cultural nationalism.

The Casa Fuster sums up not only the style of Domènech but also the main features of Barcelonan Modernismo. In overall composition, the building follows pure rationalist neo-Gothic principles – a tower at the corner to signal the building as an event, a clear differentiation between major and minor intervals in the articulation of the windows, and a picturesque and subtle overall effect. On closer inspection, we notice the forceful exaggeration of the cantilevered corner, which thrusts out over the pavement, as well as the confidence of the detailing and the mixture of distorted classical with Gothic and Art Nouveau forms. Capitals derived from Olbrich or Mackintosh come directly below cheerfully playful ionic volutes. Domènech i Montaner taught at the Barcelona School of Architecture from the 1880s and his teaching was known for its tolerance as well as for its sensitivity to new ideas.

The Hospital de San Pablo was an altogether more ambitious affair. Laid out to a plan which looks more like a city centre than a hospital, the scheme combined practical ideas based on the maximum isolation of one ward from another with planning ideas derived from the English Garden City Movement. Behind a monumental Kopfbau, with a splendid staircase and reception rooms, the complex turns into a number of self-contained pavilions each with its consulting and operating rooms. The Modernismo detailing is there in the capitals and in the free handling of the stonework, but the free eclecticism of the whole effect defies stylistic categorisation. Like so much of the best Catalan architecture of every period, stubborn originality and ambitious scale are its distinguishing features. The buildings were continued under the direction of Domènech's son.

Antoni Gaudí i Cornet (1852-1926) was born in or near the market town of Reus, in Tarragona, the son of a coppersmith. Gaudí moved to Barcelona around 1869, where his widower father and niece joined him later. Although he seems to have enjoyed company and gained access, through patrons like Eusebio Güell, to the intellectual and aristocratic elite of the city, Gaudí seems always to have been a profoundly independent person. His character was so strong that it polarised the opinions of all those who came into contact with him. Güell supported him unflinchingly, as did most of the sculptors, painters

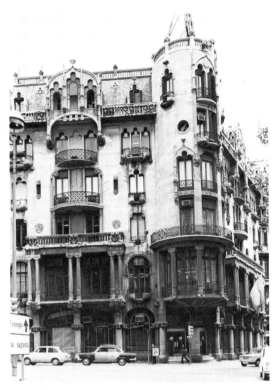

2.7-8 DOMENECH *Casa Fuster* Barcelona 1908-10, exterior and facade detail (photographs Benton)

2.9-10 DOMENECH *Hospital de San Pablo* Barcelona 1902-10, interior vaulting and main facade (photograph Benton)

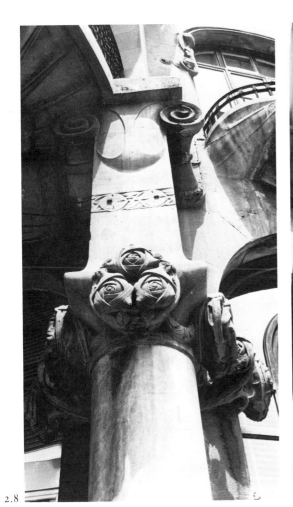

2.8

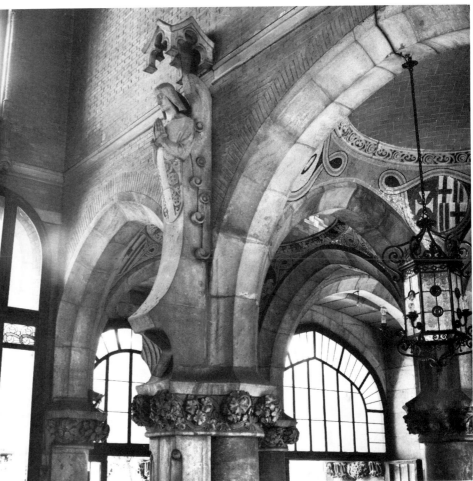

2.9

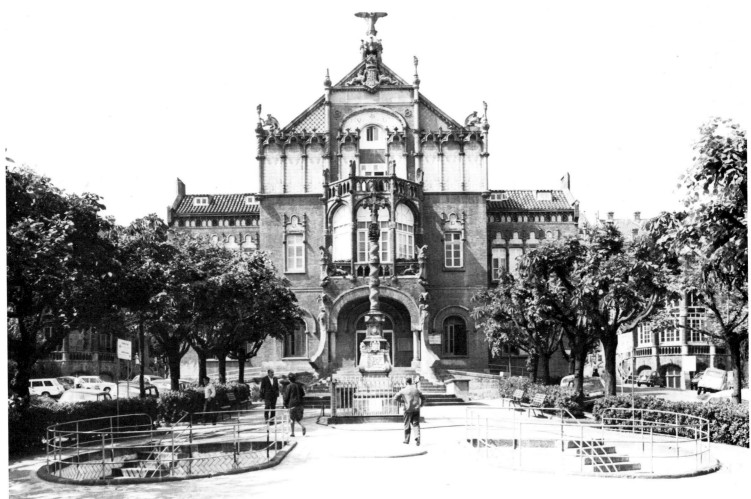

2.10

and architects who came to work for him during his life.

His initial success was due to the support of the older architects like Juan Martorell, who caused him to be given charge of the Sagrada Familia project in 1884, and to his many friends like Bishop Grau (a childhood friend from Reus) from whom Gaudí received the commission for the Bishop's Palace in Astorga.

Until 1900, Gaudí was capable of mixing a 'respectable' version of neo-Gothic and Modernismo, as in the Casa Calvet (1898-1904), with the more imaginative and excessive experiments carried out for private clients like Manuel Vicens, the Marqués de Comillas or Eusebio Güell. Picking out these more spectacular works naturally tends to give an unbalanced view of his work in this period. From around 1900 onwards, however, his work as a whole tends increasingly in the direction of free experimentation and a single-minded pursuit of his own very particular interests. Although he received his share of public scorn for buildings like the Palau Güell, his standing by 1911 was very high in Barcelona: 'Gaudí is the man most discussed both by the people of Barcelona and those visiting the city. And what more natural? He has attempted to give modern Barcelona an original architecture and this is the most audacious undertaking which the human mind can conceive. Every seven or eight centuries man produces in some corner of the globe an original architecture. Even epics are produced more frequently. In reality one ought not to discuss Gaudí as if he were just any architect. The man's talent is so dazzling that even the blind would recognise Gaudí's work by touching it. Not only has Gaudí attempted something but he has achieved it.' (Ramiro de Maetzu, 'El Arqitecto del Naturaismo' *Nueva Mundo*, Madrid, 16 March 1911, cited in E. Casanelles, 1967.) But it must also be said that by this date the effect of the very 'public' buildings in the centre of the new town of Barcelona – the Casa Batlló, the Casa Milá and the progressive stylistic exaggerations of the Sagrada Familia – began to render Gaudí more and more vulnerable to public abuse. He became increasingly bound up with the remote Colonia Güell project in the village of Santa Colomo de Cervelló, the Park Güell (both of which were doomed to fail at the outbreak of the First World War) and, especially after 1914, with the Sagrada Familia, which had progressed beyond the naturalism of the lower facade to the exuberance of the towers.

From 1910, in fact, Gaudí was becoming a recluse, saddened by the deaths of his father and closest friends – his 'right arm' Francesc Berenguer in 1914, his patron Eusebio Güell in 1918 and his trusted companion, the sculptor Lorenzo Matamala i Pinyol in 1924. The irony was that 1910 also marked the moment when Gaudí's work came to the attention of the outside world; Güell generously paid for an exhibition of Gaudí's work in Paris, which attracted a widespread, if mixed, response.

The rationalist neo-Gothic roots of Gaudí's work can be clearly seen in his student work at the School of Architecture in Barcelona. Here we find the fascination with ingenious structural solutions using cast iron columns held in tension with cable, which could almost be an illustration from the *Entretiens*.

A more typically empirical approach can be seen in the machine shed for the Obrera Mataronense (1878), an idealistic syndicalist organisation dating from 1864 which manufactured textiles and distributed the proceeds in kind among its members. Only a club house and the wooden machine shed – part of a much more ambitious plan – were actually built. The vaults of the shed are constructed of short planks bolted together in threes, forming parabolic arches braced against rafters and wall beams. From notes made around this time, it is clear that Gaudí was already preoccupied with the search for optimum structural solutions which discarded all conventional devices.

The restless search for surprising effects is clearly visible in the summer villa built for Máximo Diaz de Quijano, who had married into the Comillas family. The first Marqués de Comillas commissioned a whole colony of houses at Comillas to the designs of Martorell and Domènech i Montaner. Gaudí's contribution must be seen as a consciously playful contribution to the eclectic Gothic designs of his colleagues. The use of boldly sculptural tiles in patterns which accentuate and partly control the structural details (such as the corbels) matches the interests of Domènech, who made great efforts to search out new ceramic tile designs. The firm of Pujol i Baucis, for example, manufactured a very wide range of tiles of all kinds, for both external and interior

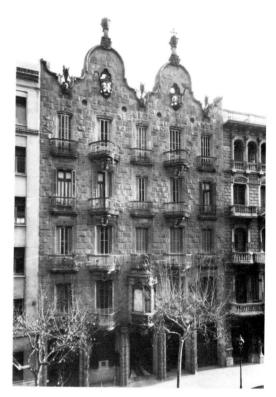

2.11 GAUDI *Casa Calvet* Barcelona 1898-1904

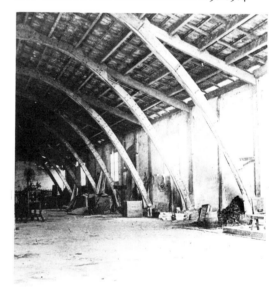

2.12 GAUDI *Machine shed for the Obrera Mataronense* Mataró 1878, interior showing wooden parabolic arches

2.13-15 GAUDI *Casa Vicens* Barcelona 1883-85, garden facade, cupola and Moorish Fumador

2.16 GAUDI *Villa for Diaz de Quijano 'El Capricho'* Comillas 1883-85

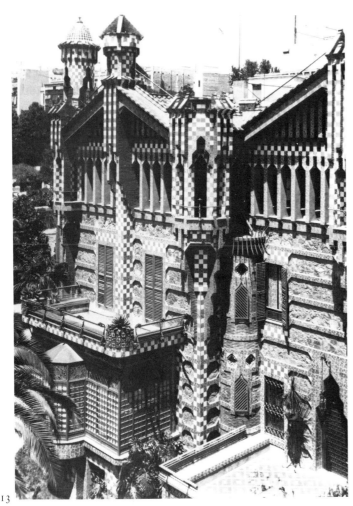

2.13

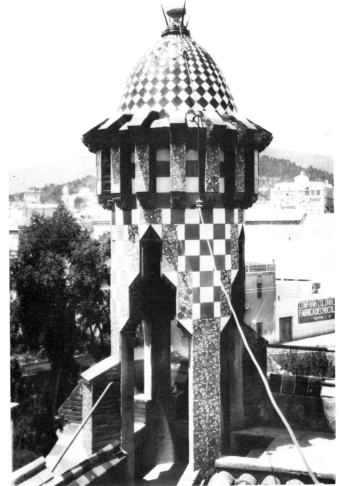

2.14

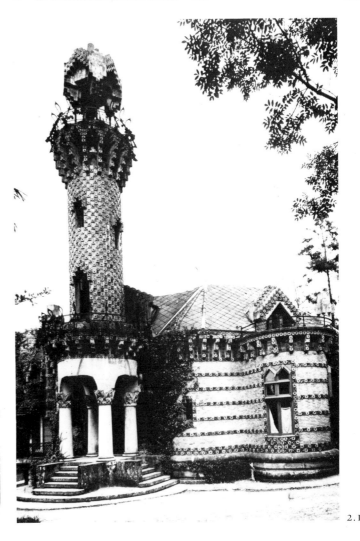

2.15

2.16

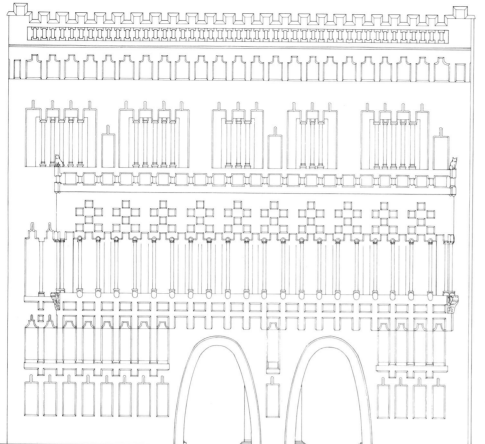

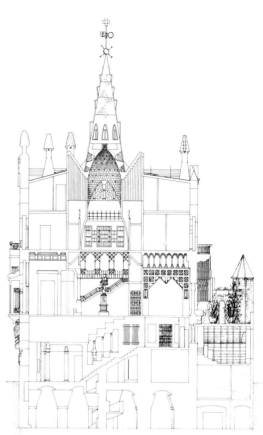

2.17-18 GAUDÍ *Palau Güell* Barcelona 1886-89, elevation and section (from the original drawings)

use, to designs by Domènech i Montaner, his assistant Galissa and Puig i Cadafalch.

Where Gaudí extends this approach is in his willingness to compose whole buildings around the decorative and modular qualities of the new tiles. The house he designed for the tile manufacturer Manuel Vicens is a product of this approach. The whole building results from the composition and play with the crisp 15 cm tiles, creating a grid into which are inserted, as it were, the soft dark panels of exposed wall surface. The building history of the house is confused, but it seems certain now that work did not begin until 1883, on a much smaller house with a large garden. In 1925, after road widening along the front, the architect De Serra Martinez extended the side of the house, making a new entrance there and erecting a new cast iron fence whose design, around 1890, seems to be attributable to Gaudí's assistant Francesc Berenguer. The neo-Mudéjar influences are most clearly expressed in the interior, particularly in the Moorish Fumador.

The first really large scale operation which Gaudí managed to carry through to its conclusion was the extension of Güell's house (1886-9). Berenguer made hundreds of preparatory drawings for Gaudí, and these are interesting in confirming the contribution Berenguer made to the structural logicality of Gaudí's style. The facade elevations stress the grid of horizontals and verticals, similar to those of the Casa Vicens, but interpreted here in ashlar instead of tile and free stone. The facade is unlike most of Gaudí's work in the severity of its handling, comparable only to those designs in Astorga and León where Gaudí was not present during construction. His more personal manner is apparent in the interior and on the roof, where the fantastic takes over. The section, prepared specially for the 1910 exhibition in Paris, shows the complex arrangement of ramps to the cellar (for the horses) and the magnificent space which, like a church, rises up through the centre of the house and links all the rooms.

To appreciate Berenguer's contribution at this period more clearly, it is worth looking at one of the projects which he carried out independently – the Bodegas Güell, Garraf. Comparisons could be made with the gatehouse for the Finca Güell in the Barcelona suburb of Las Corts, designed by Gaudí with Berenguer's collaboration. Gaudí was interested in ingenious brickwork and dramatic structural solutions, but always within the decorative possibilities of surface ornament. He covered the wall surfaces with a splendid diaper pattern,

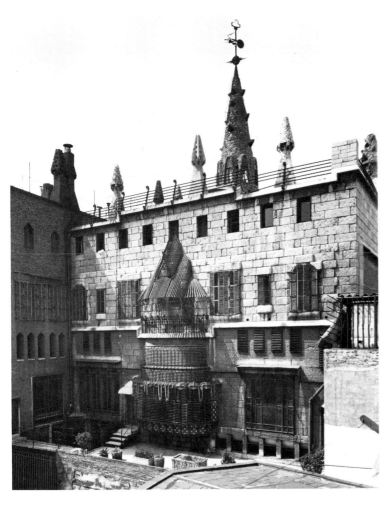

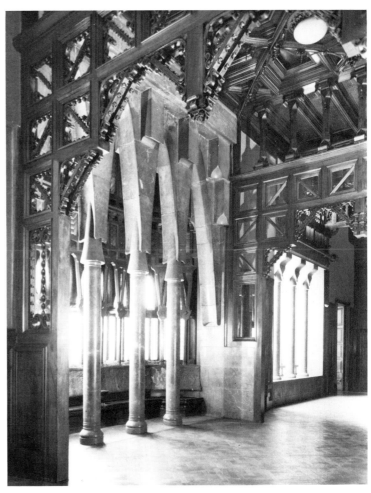

2.19-20 GAUDI *Palau Güell*, rear facade and main floor

impressed into the wet plaster, and played a number of tricks with the brick arches and edgings. By contrast, Berenguer at Garraf was after an altogether more brutal expression of stone vaulting systems. The principles of parabolic construction and leaning supports, learnt from Gaudí, are carried to more rigorous lengths here than anything which Gaudí attempted. Gaudí always looked for the complex, 'difficult' and passionate solution, as we shall see more clearly in the crypt of the Colonia Güell chapel.

Francesc Berenguer i Mestres (1866-1914), like Gaudí, was brought up in Reus where they both went to the school run by Berenguer's father. Berenguer followed Gaudí to Barcelona in 1881 where he attended the Schools of Art and Architecture. In 1887 he married and was forced to give up his studies in order to earn his living. From 1887 to 1892 he worked as assistant to Augusto Font in the mornings and helped Gaudí in the afternoons. From 1892 until his death he worked in the Architect's Department of the Barcelona borough of Gracia, under the chief architect Migel Pascal. Most of his work has been obscured by these collaborations with senior partners, although his hand can be identified in other works in Gracia. He also undertook a number of commissions free of charge for religious bodies and the youth club Centra Moral de Gracia, of which he was the President.

As for his collaboration with Gaudí, his contributions to the Finca Güell, Bellesguard (1900-02), the Crypt of the Colonia Güell (1898-1914) and much of the work on the Sagrada Familia up until his death are documented. He seems to have been responsible for most practical matters on these commissions, dealing with the workmen and handling the accounts. He was also the best architectural draughtsman in the office, preparing most of Gaudí's important presentation drawings. At Sta Coloma de Cervelló, he built a number of the ancillary buildings associated with the Colonia Güell project. His own buildings include the Mercat de la Llibertad, Valencia (1893), the Torre Matau at Llinás del Vallés (1906), the block of flats at 44 Carrer d'Or (1909) and the building for the Central Moral de Gracia (1909). His metalwork designs include the gate for the Bodegas Guell, another rather similar one for Torre Matau (now re-erected in the Park Güell) and a number of designs in the Park Güell itself.

Berenguer's contribution to Gaudí's work cannot be fully isolated, but it is important to remember that, during his lifetime, Gaudí was assured through him of a rigorously logical and disciplined point of view which helped to keep his taste for the fantastic and the curvilinear within bounds. This dialogue seems to have developed its own internal dynamic, so that it is possible to see projects such as the Casa Batlló and the Casa Milá, or the final developments of the Sagrada Familia as a sort of reaction from the discipline of Berenguer's approach, whereas the Colonia Güell chapel reflects perfectly a harmonious synthesis of two minds.

Alternatively, one can find other powerful personalities within Gaudí's office, who exerted their own influence on the master. Josep Maria Jujol i Gibert (1879-1949), for example, was a genius of invention, a man whose sensuous and spontaneous sense of sculptural form was at least as developed as Gaudí's. Gaudí once said that his one talent was knowing how to get the most out of his assistants and workmen. It would be a travesty to try to diminish his achievement by enlarging the sphere of responsibility among his collaborators, since it seems to have been Gaudí's outstanding qualities which attracted so heterogeneous and brilliant a group of architects, sculptors and artists to work with him.

Jujol's major contributions to Gaudí's work were in the fields of ceramic decoration and wrought iron work. His own architectural work was brilliantly inventive, but at times lacking in discipline. The Torre de la Creu (Torre dels Ous, 1916) was one of a number of buildings designed by Jujol in the town of Sant Joan Despí, including the Casa Negre which he continually extended and revised between 1914 and 1930. In all his work, including some of the reinforced concrete and steel designs of his later career (e.g. Casa Planells, 1923-4), we find the resolute continuation of Gaudí's curvilinear approach. Some of his designs, such as the church at Vistabella in Tarragona (1918-25) take Gaudí's structural principles further without radically responding to the new materials and conditions of the 1920s, and it must be seen as typically Catalonian that as late as 1926-9, in the design of the Montserrat Sanctuary, Jujol should have remained faithful to the forms of the Sagrada Familia and the Colonia Güell chapel. But it must be remembered that Modernismo survived as a popular style well into the 1920s, as shops such as 'El Indio', via del Carmen, Barcelona (1922) attest. Gaudí's influence was also kept alive by the work of many of his young assistants and admirers throughout the 1920s. Cèsar Martinell, for example, built a number of dramatic farm buildings and store houses of impressive size and proportions, using Gaudí's brick vaulting systems.

Some of Jujol's best work can be seen in the ceramics for the Park Güell, which Gaudí worked on between 1900 and 1914, when the project was abandoned. Laid out as a picturesque series of paths along the slope of a hill overlooking the city, the Park was originally intended as a middle-class housing development along the lines of English Garden City planning. Gaudí had the extraordinary idea of making the central feature of this scheme in the form of an open air theatre built out over the slope on classical doric columns – the covered area forming a market place. Taking Viollet-le-Duc's recommendations to their logical conclusion, Gaudí inclined the outer line of columns inwards sharply, to counteract the lateral thrusts of the hillside. In the *Entretiens,* there is a discussion of the Greek practice of very slightly inclining inwards the outer columns of the doric temple, and Viollet illustrates a drawing which exaggerates this effect. For Gaudí, however, this principle had to be taken to extremes, not only in the inclined columns, but in the free-form buttresses which support the serpentine paths which wind their way round the hillside. One of Gaudí's assistants, probably Berenguer, was instructed to work out the thrust calculations using the new descriptive geometry, and the design was recorded in one of the contemporary periodicals. The scientific rationalism of this section, and the structural thinking behind it, matches up very oddly with the weird and mysterious effect created by the buttresses themselves, and the tunnels behind them.

Similarly, we find a rich conjunction in the open air theatre itself, between the massive abutments which hold back the hillside and the delightfully naive way in which Gaudí has turned to the forms of the surrounding palm trees to articulate these supports. More and more, in his work after 1900, Gaudí was to

2.21-22 BERENGUER *Bodegas Güell* Garraf 1888-90

2.23 JUJOL *Torre de la Creu* Sant Joan Despí 1916

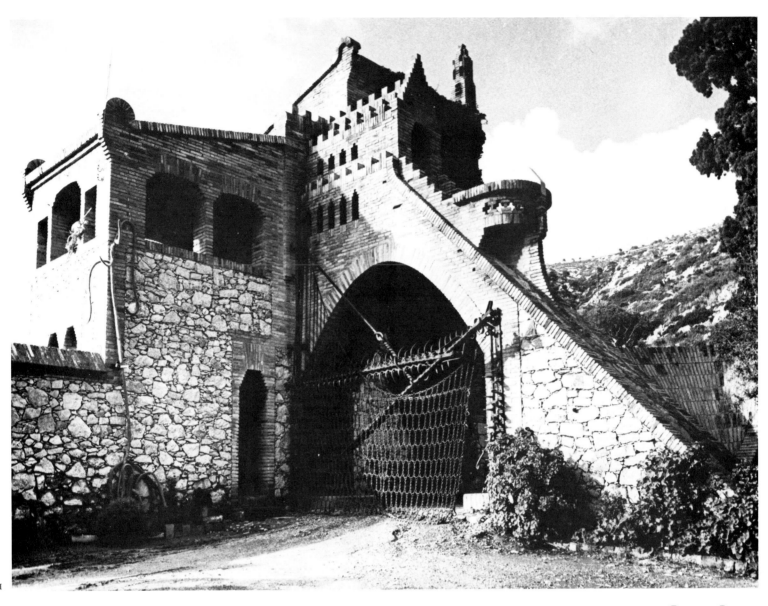

2.21

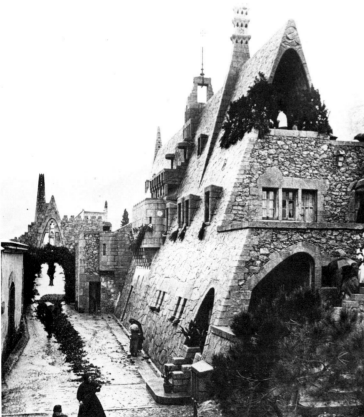

2.22

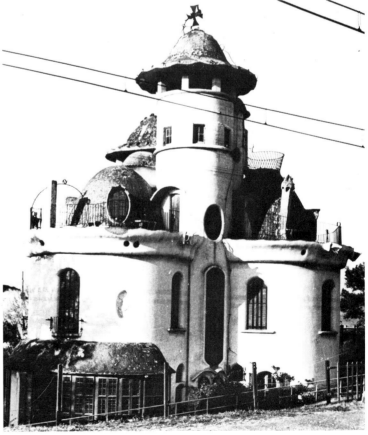

2.23

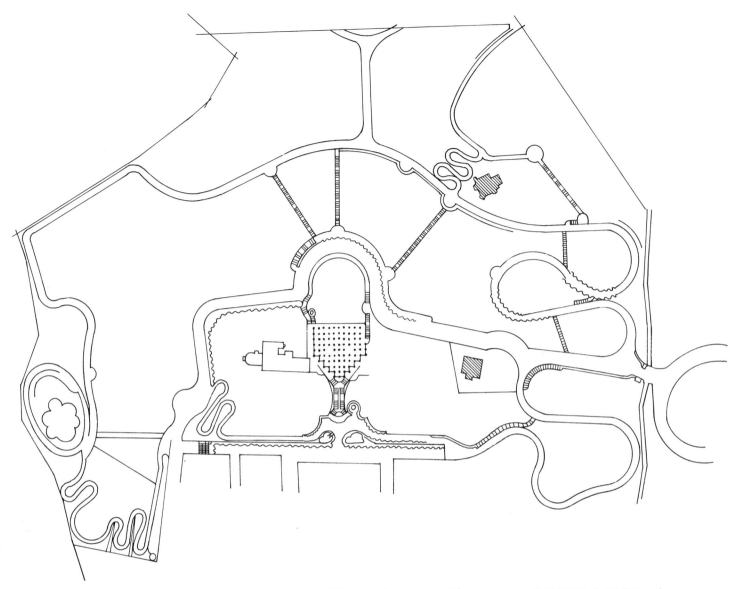

turn to the actual forms of nature to express the 'natural' laws of structure. The irony was that Gaudí could have used reinforced concrete to solve all these problems since Güell manufactured it and wanted to find new ways of using it. In fact, the roof of the market does consist of concrete beams, hidden behind the ceramic decoration.

The famous serpentine bench which runs round the raised area of the theatre was based on the profile formed by one of Gaudí's assistants lying in a bed of plaster. This 'scientific' shape was then given its rich decorative form through the ceramic work of Jujol. The contrast of cool white ceramic and brilliant colour, everywhere different and sprinkled with obscure and mysterious inscriptions, makes this bench one of the most exciting creations of the twentieth century. Jujol's more extroverted creations, the cascades lining the approach to the park, might display more virtuosity in terms of craftsmanship and invention, but belong more to the particular vocabulary of his style – there is something a little too gross about these monstrous forms dripping with water.

The Park Güell was left incomplete because the project as a whole failed to attract investors. Only three houses were built on the site and one of them, designed by Berenguer, was bought by Gaudí himself. What finally halted operations was the war, whose economic implications struck merchants like Eusebio Güell very hard. And it was the war which put an end to Güell's equally ambitious project to build a workers' colony around his factory at Sta Coloma de Cervelló. Berenguer, as we have seen, was in charge of the project as a whole, but Gaudí made some designs for the chapel of the colony, around 1898. Planning work began on the crypt of this building around 1900, but Gaudí does not seem to have taken much direct part in the operations until 1908. Typically, the project then began to take on the proportions of a major ecclesiastical commission, inextricably bound up with the Sagrada Familia

2.24-26 GAUDI *Park Güell* Barcelona 1900-14, overall plan (from the original drawing), grand plaza and cascade

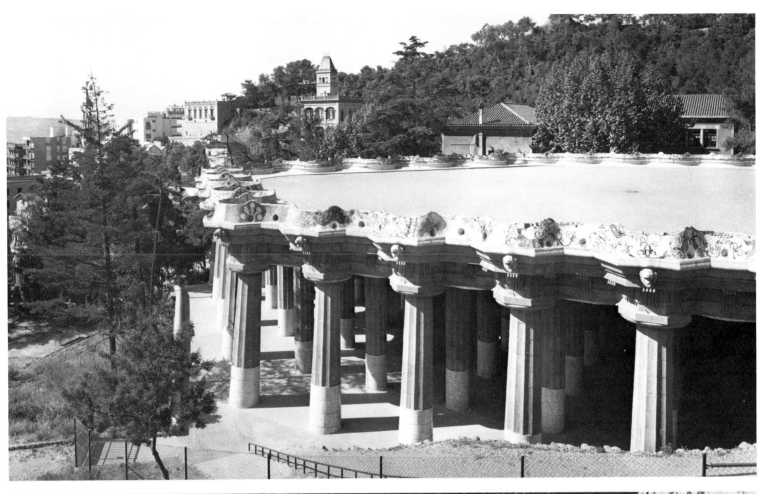

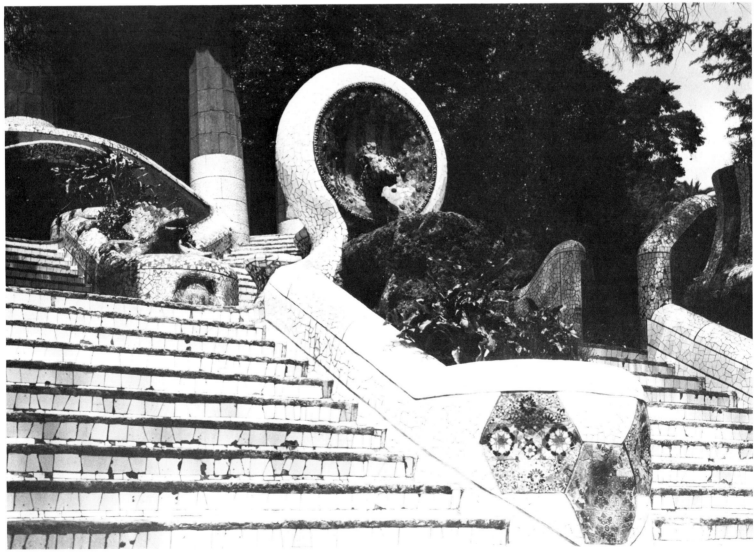

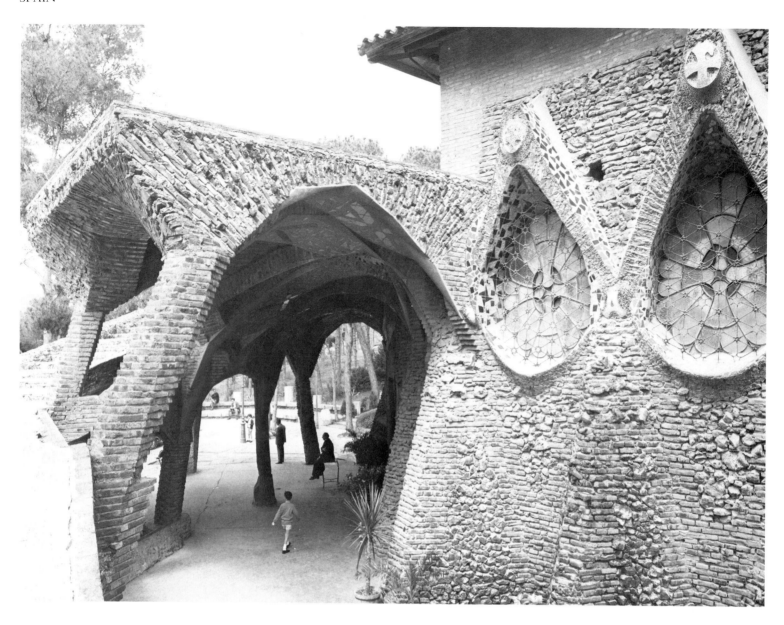

scheme. Free to plan the church as he pleased, without having to follow the neo-Gothic plan laid out by Villar for the Sagrada Familia, Gaudí turned the whole church into an exercise in his new ideas about the romantic expression of structure. The plan is irregular, following the site and making use of irregularities in the monolithic stones used for some of the columns. The techniques of the Catalan bricklayers were adapted and exaggerated, particularly in the portico, so that the entire structure takes on the natural growth of a living organism. No simple solutions were allowed – each inclined brick pier and its vault had to respond to its own position in the whole, twisting and bending to express the loads placed on it. In many ways, this is the purest of all Gaudí's works. The huge structure which should have risen over the crypt and porch was sketched by him, using an extraordinary funicular model of wires weighted with little sacks of sand. The drawings clearly show the generality of Gaudí's architectural thought by this stage. Planning was a matter of roughing out the essential movement and structural rationale of a building – the details would all follow from a painstaking revision and re-revision of every detail during construction.

By contrast, the two apartment blocks which Gaudí designed between 1904 and 1906, the Casa Batlló and the Casa Milá, must be seen as more artificial creations, lacking the pure synthesis of structure and form evident in every feature of the Park Güell and the Colonia Güell chapel. The Casa Batlló was simply a refacing job on an existing building. One of Gaudí's own drawings shows clearly what his contribution consisted of – the addition of a new facade and a new roof. The facade was designed in the most biomorphic way imaginable – a muscular surface stretched above clearly bone-like supporting members around the main first floor windows. The undulating walls are faced

2.27-29 GAUDI *Colonia Güell chapel* Sta Coloma de Cervelló 1898-1914, exterior and portico, plan (from the original drawing) and interior of the crypt

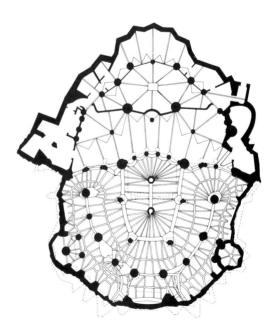

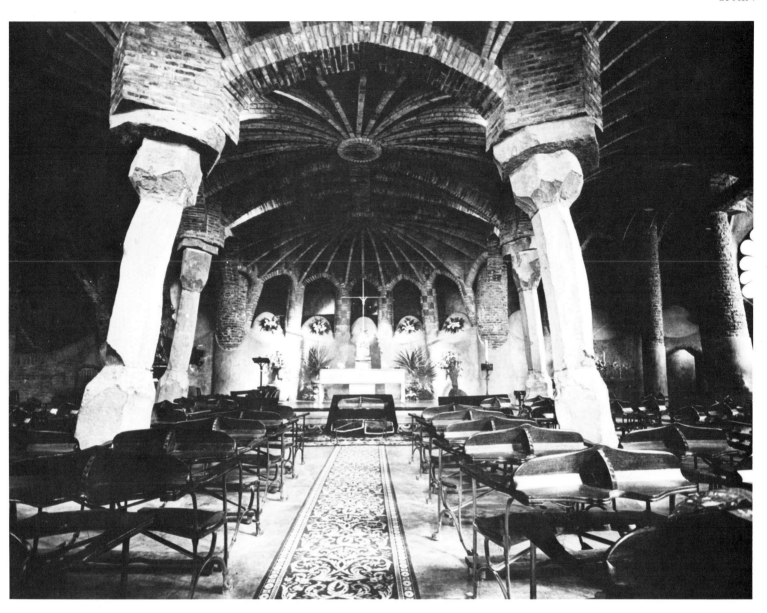

with the newly revived ceramic technique of *trencadis*, a mosaic of irregular ceramic fragments featuring specially manufactured and coloured discs. Again, Jujol seems to have been the guiding force behind the decorative work, including the ceramics and metalwork of the balconies. Some of the interiors were spectacular expressions of curvilinear Modernismo design and the light-well was most ingeniously conceived, graded in width and in the intensity of the blue tiles, so as to transmit the light down to the lower floors. The roof-scape, with its undulating domes reflecting the parabolic brick arch construction employed, shows Gaudí at his most voluptuous.

The Casa Milá seems to have developed out of the ideas in the Casa Batlló through the same process of progressive exaggeration and distortion which is the essential methodology of Gaudí's style. Free to design the whole corner block, he worked towards a completely curvilinear form, until plan and elevations responded to the same organic rhythm. Structural considerations have been left in the background. The rippling walls of massive stone blocks have no structural rationale, but have to be supported on a network of steel supports and ties. When asked to defend this building, which aroused a storm of protest, discussion and abuse, Gaudí limited himself to statements of the most general kind – the facades recall the mountains, the curves reflect the sea, there are no straight lines in nature. But the Casa Milá exhausted Gaudí's ability to sustain this kind of public debate, just as it exhausted, in a sense, his formal repertoire. He needed a rigorously disciplined restraint to his formal inventiveness, like that which a religious programme or the enforced response to a structural rationale could offer. The roof, vaulted once again in tightly stretched parabolic brick arches, provided such a constraint, and supplies some of the most emphatic elements of the building, both in the attics and on the

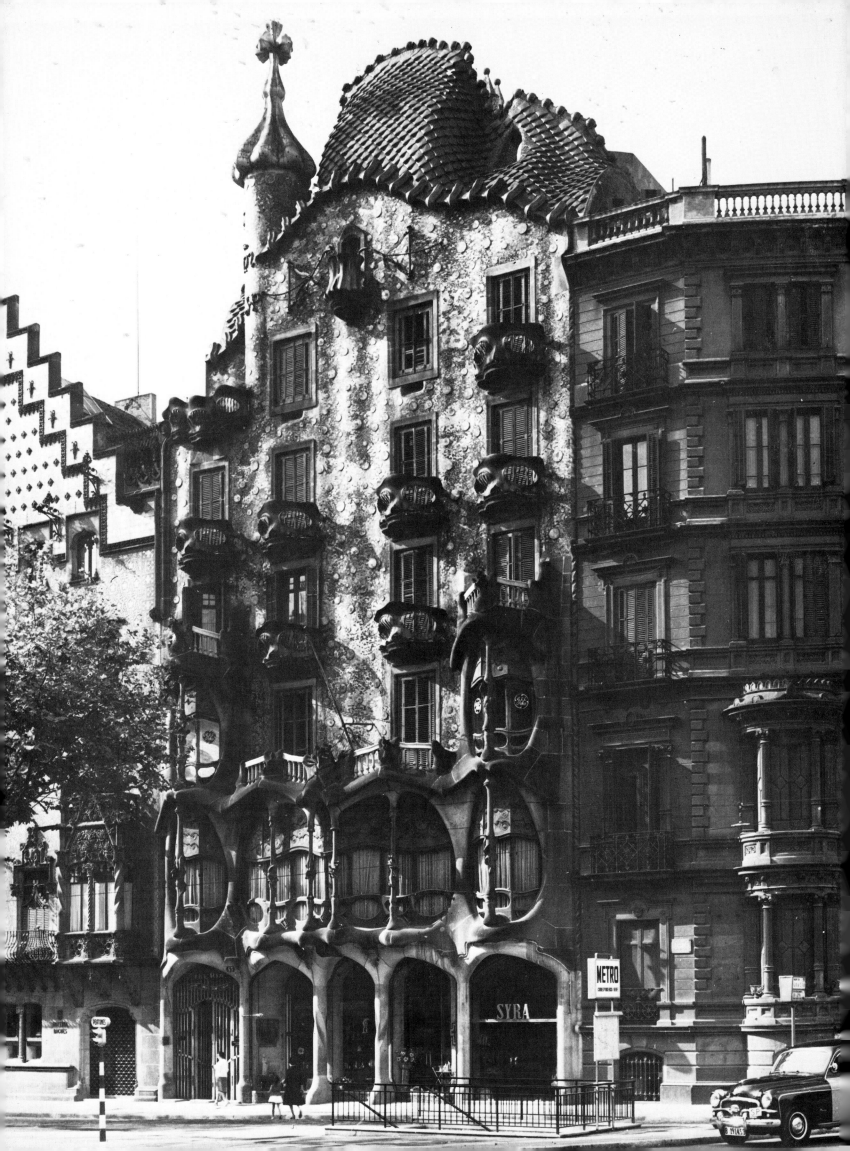

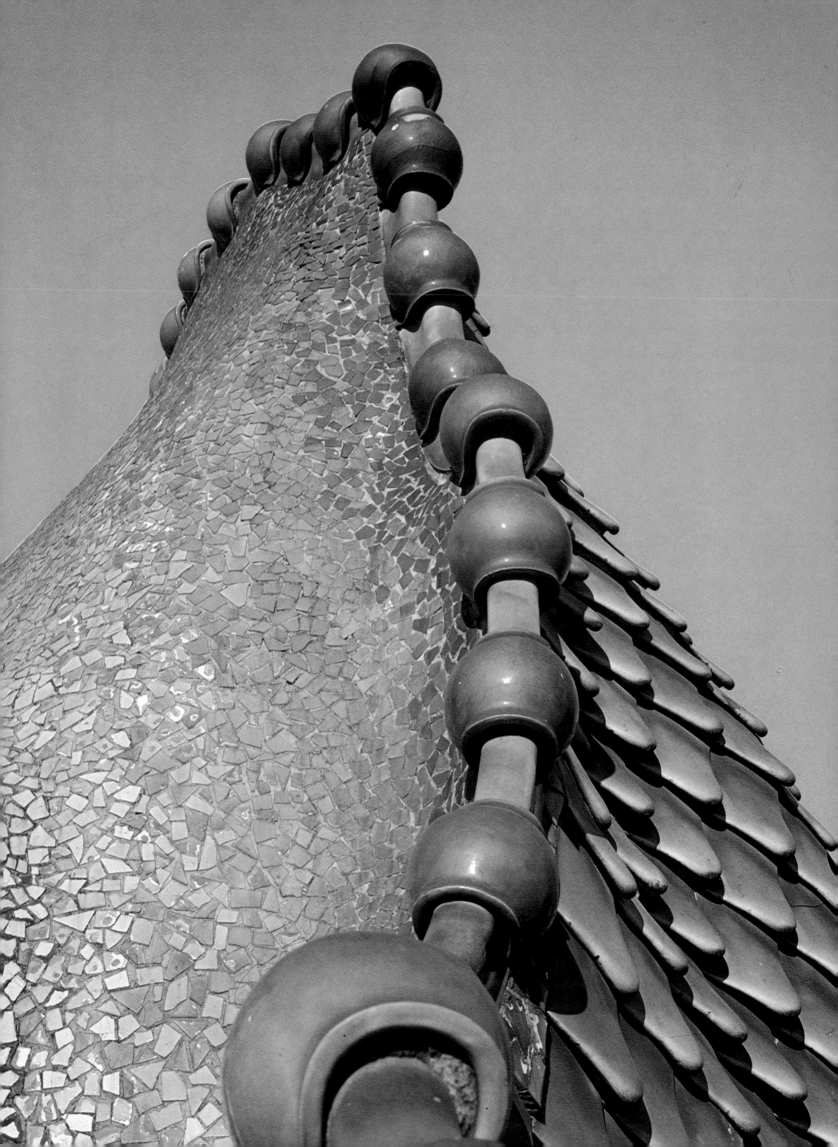

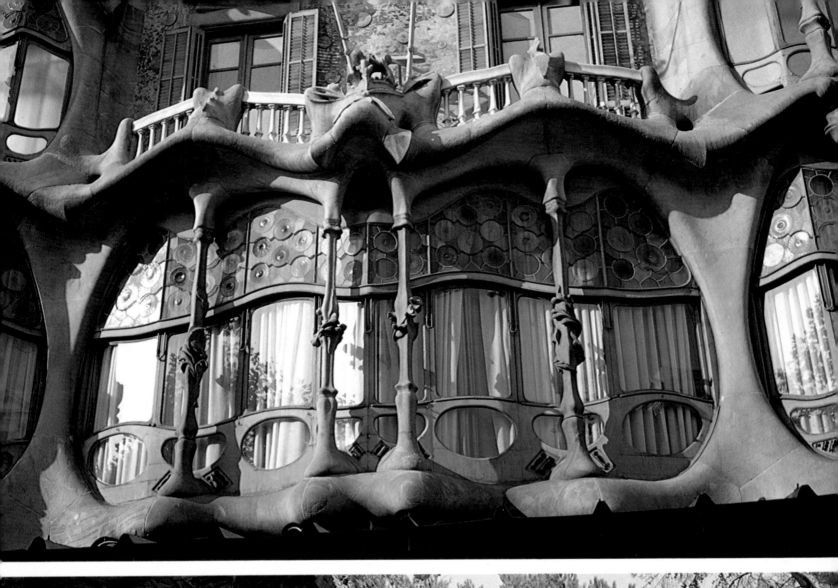

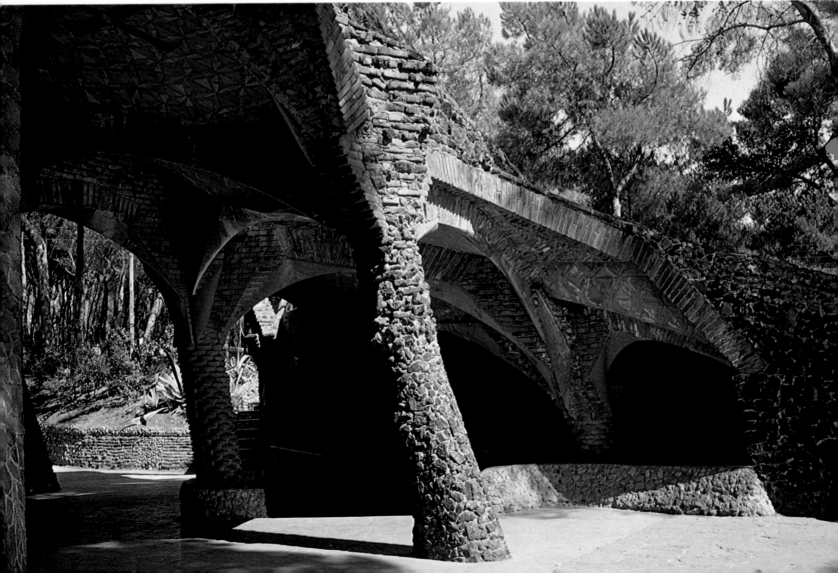

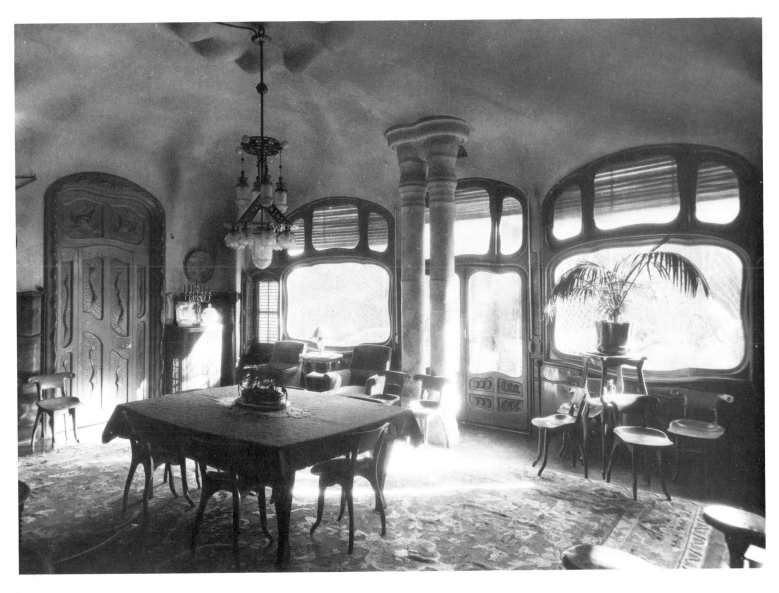

2.31 GAUDI *Casa Batlló*, dining room with furniture by Gaudí

Page 70
2.30 GAUDI *Casa Batlló* Barcelona 1904-06, facade

Page 71
GAUDI *Casa Batlló*, detail of roof

Opposite above
GAUDI *Casa Batlló*, facade detail (photograph Mooring)

Opposite below
GAUDI *Colonia Güell chapel* Sta Coloma de Cervelló 1898-1914, exterior of crypt (photograph Mooring)

rooftop itself, where the anarchic clusters of chimney were used to fantastic formal effect. Jujol's metalwork, on the balconies and in the gates, helps to enliven and quicken the heavy stone masses, but the Casa Milá as a whole needs detailed observation to overcome the initial impression of elephantine clumsiness.

The Casa Milá was Gaudí's last secular commission. By 1910, his main obsessions were the religious projects like the Colonia Güell chapel or, after 1914, the Sagrada Familia. Although Gaudí was first given authority over the construction of the Sagrada Familia in 1883, his contribution to the work of completing Villar's crypt and choir is difficult to define. It is only with the construction of the facade of the transept of the Nativity, begun in the 1890s, that Gaudí's own style comes to dominate. And the work until around 1906 seems to have been dominated by Gaudí's obsessive search for a naturalistic style of sculpture. Taking Ruskin and Goethe at more than face value, he determined to use every scientific means at his disposal, including living models, to reproduce exactly the forms of nature. His assistant Ricardo Opisso i Sala made literally hundreds of photographs of animals, natural forms and people, some of which have survived in an album. Gaudí installed a special photographic studio in his atelier at the Sagrada Familia, in which two large mirrors at right angles to each other were used as a backdrop, showing the model from three angles at once. Many of these photographs survive, so that it is possible to put the individual models' names to many of the heads and bodies carved on the facade of the Nativity. Gaudí had a fascination for the human skeleton, and made realistic and articulated models which he could use for poses. Casts were made of plants and rocks and even of still-born babies from a local hospital. The studio was littered with all these preparatory studies, along with countless maquettes and models, showing the stages of evolution of each group or figure, as it was 'corrected' for perspective distortion. Unfortunately,

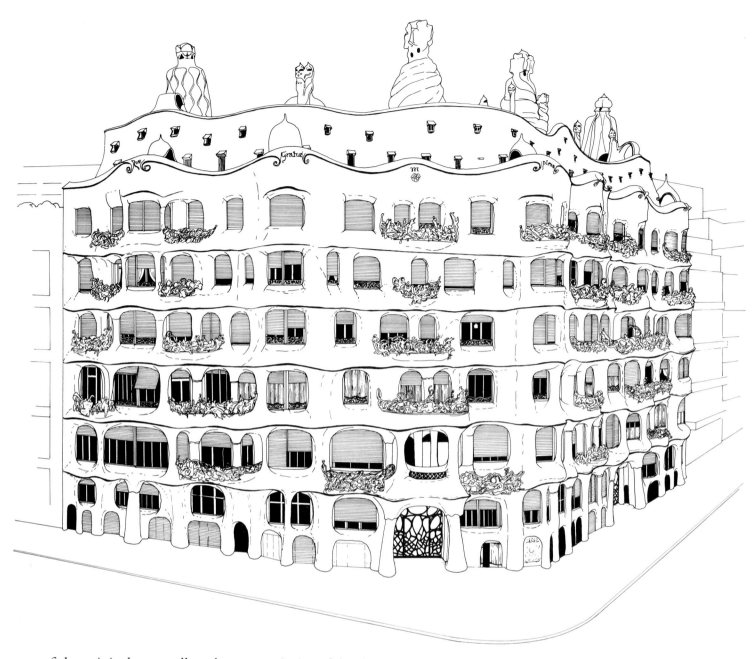

2.32-33 GAUDI *Casa Milá* Barcelona 1906-10,
undulating facade (drawing based on a
contemporary photograph) and detail of roof

most of the originals, as well as the vast majority of the drawings, were lost
during the Civil War, but a number of photographs taken between 1900 and
1926 show what was being done.

The results, in terms of what can be seen in the lower half of the facade of
the Nativity, take a lot of getting used to. In details, like the massacre of the
innocents in which the Roman soldier was based on a waiter who turned out to
have six toes on each foot, we can see the rather dry quality of the sculpture,
with the bizarre juxtaposition of different forms. The general impression,
however, is of a glutinous melting together of frond-like or wave-like forms
which ripple up the portal. In 1910, when the Gaudí exhibition in Paris was
being prepared, there was still no overall plan of the Sagrada Familia which
could be sent off. A number of assistants had to spend months trying to piece
together a picture of the whole project which could be demonstrated with
conventional plans, elevations and sections. The outline forms of the towers,
and the general effect intended had probably been fixed by around 1906. A
large model of the facade of the Nativity was sent to Paris after being coloured
by Jujol, although it was still not exactly as built. A drawing of 1915 by Juan
Rubió, an architectural assistant, still gives a very vague account of the towers.
One spire was completed just after Gaudí's death, the other three soon after.
Gaudí left a number of models for the completion of the nave and the other
two main facades. As shown in the final model, the central tower would have
been higher than St Peters in Rome. The form of the nave vaulting, yet again,
shows Gaudí's re-analysis of Gothic structural systems. He treats the piers like
tree trunks, making them lean inwards to counteract the thrust of the vaults

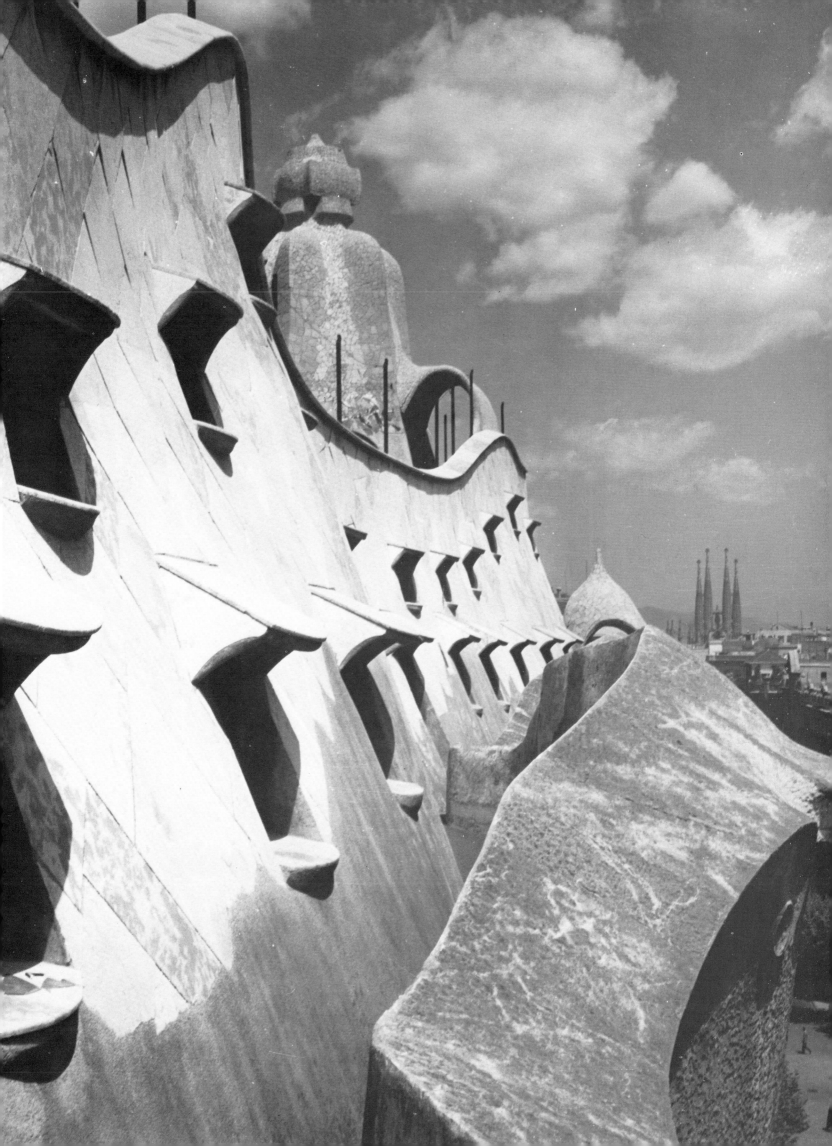

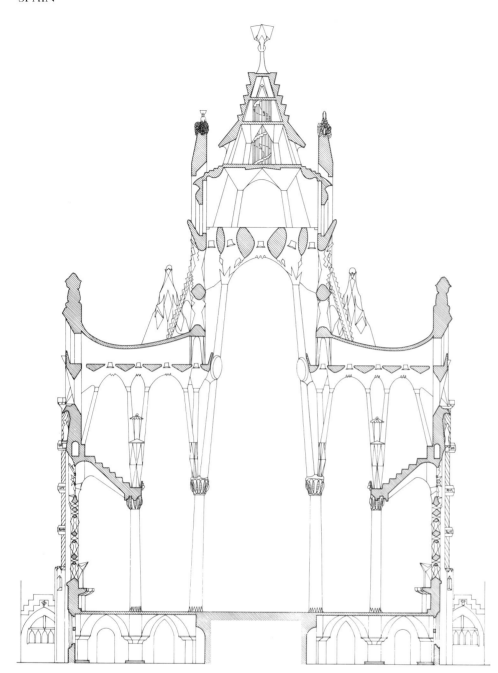

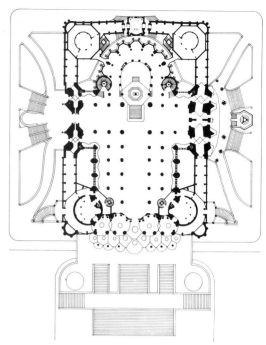

2.34-36 GAUDI *Sagrada Familia* Barcelona
1883- , section and plan (from the original
drawings) and facade of the Nativity

without the need for flying buttresses, which Gaudí referred to as crutches. The
piers split off into branches at the level of the galleries, each member taking its
share of the load.

Much of Gaudí's attention in his last years was devoted to the formal
analysis of the pinnacles crowning the facade. The towers rise like needles, and
are composed of vertical ribs held together by horizontal rings, which project
out through the slits. This terrific vertical thrust is controlled at the top by a
blaze of colour and texture. Part of the coloured display was made up of
translucent glass set into concrete, so that it would glow at night, and there
were searchlights installed in each pinnacle which would light up the central
spire, when built, and project other beams down onto the ground before the
church.

None of this has anything to do with Art Nouveau, of course, but it helps to
tie together some of the themes in European Expressionism and Constructi-
vism of the 1920s with the Naturalism and Modernismo of the lower stages of
the facade. Once again, we are reminded of the infuriating way in which the
Catalan movement refuses to fit into conventional stylistic or chronological
frameworks, standing out as a dazzling but intransigent expression of
nationalism and piety.

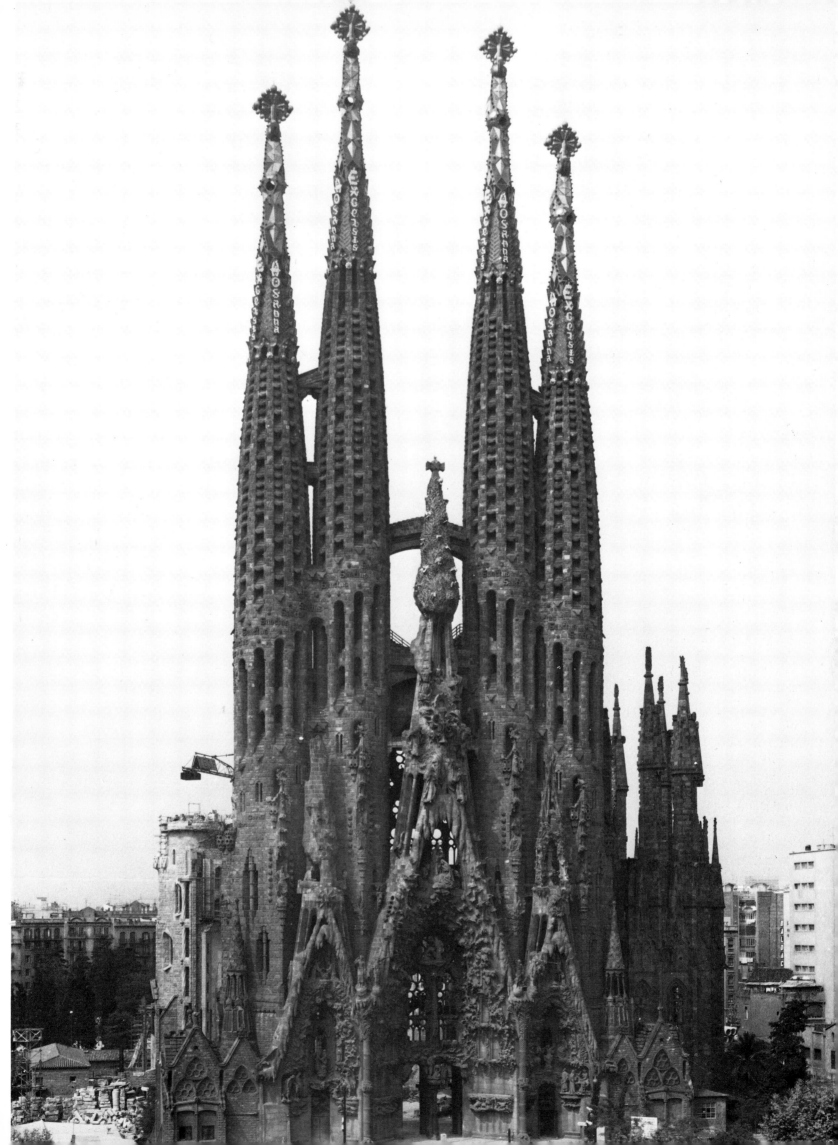

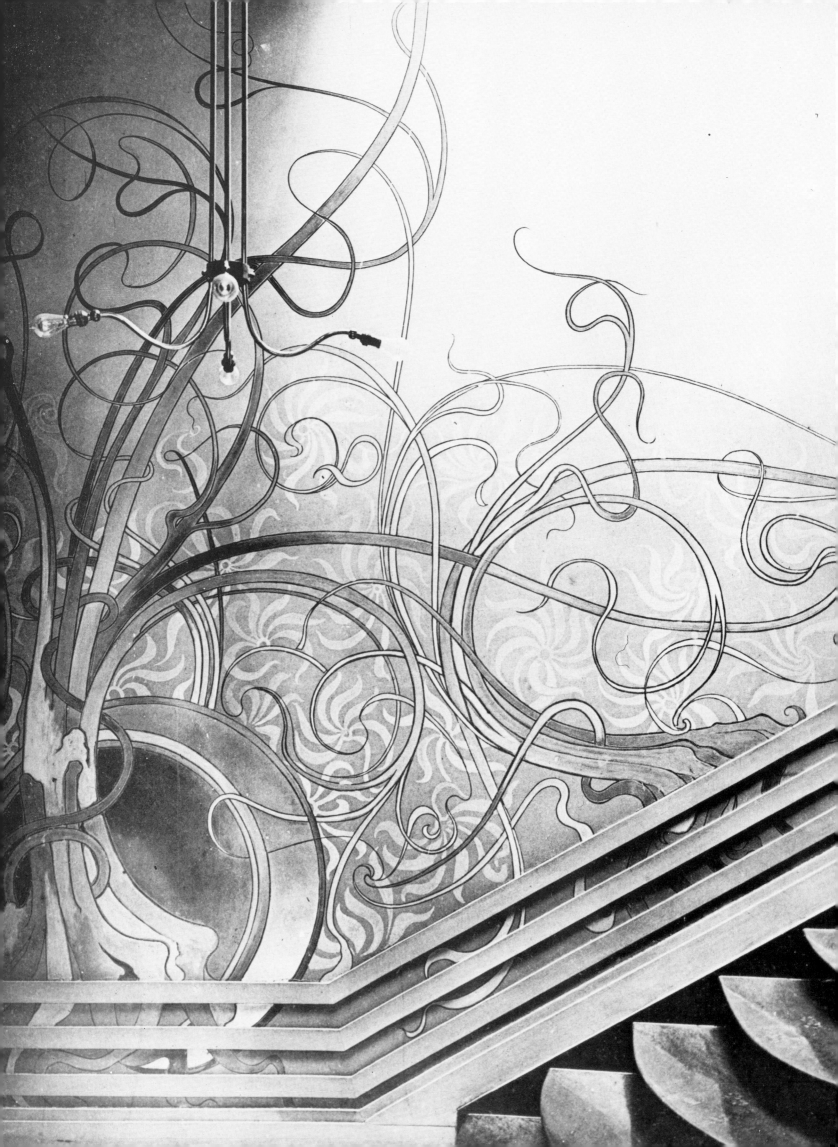

3. BELGIUM
Red steel and blue aesthetic

Maurice Culot

Normally, the need to house one's wife and the children which are expected from a marriage is not a matter for very great concern. It is exceptional for it to raise great scruples. Especially such severe scruples that they push someone who has never been involved with architecture before to build his own house.

Even more exceptional is to see someone build a house which is markedly different from the current type of house, and in finishing it, create furniture whose every component differs so strangely from what one is used to seeing!

What could possibly be the motivation for such eccentricities?

The downfall of architecture and the general corruption of taste appeared to him in a particularly repellent light. There is no doubt that a vile infection has spread its ravages over everything we see before our eyes.

It was necessary, at all costs, to protect the woman who had consented to share his life and the children who were to be born from their union.

Ugliness corrupts the soul and the mind as much as the eye.

Henry van de Velde, *La Voie Sacrée*.

In 1870, when the 'grands boulevards' were being built around the centre of Brussels on the instigation of Mayor Anspach, a disciple of Haussmann, there were only 250,000 inhabitants in the city; in 1910, a year after the death of Leopold II, the population had risen above 800,000.

In a few decades hundreds of acres of agricultural land, woods and fields had been built up into blocks of houses defined by roads. Former villages merged with one another and were absorbed into the Brussels urban area. Here the basic pattern was not street blocks as in other capitals, but small plots, even for the mansions of the upper middle classes, like the Hôtel for Mr. van Eetvelde, one of Leopold II's counsellors, built in 1895 on a long, narrow plot only nine metres wide.

This rapid population growth had as its corollary a strong measure of land speculation. When Paul Vizzavona built an apartment block in the rue du Lombard in 1909, the price of the land was about three thousand francs, as against an average of forty francs in the outer suburbs. This was accompanied by speculation in urban transport, on concessions for tramways serving the new suburbs, first horse-drawn and then, from 1892, electric.

But it was not only the price of land in the central districts which mitigated in favour of adjoining houses. The 'petite bourgeoisie' had no taste for big apartment blocks, so that the English-financed construction companies, which started building apartment blocks on the central boulevards in 1870, using French architects, rapidly went bankrupt, forcing the city of Brussels to take over the buildings.

Sander Pierron, for whom Horta built a house in 1903, which can still be seen at 157 rue de l'Aqueduc in Ixelles, wrote in 1899: 'It has only been for the last thirty years that Brussels has really merited the title of capital and has entirely stopped resembling other provincial cities. At that time, there were no premonitions of the present movement: architects were still working with heavy-handed imitations of the eighteenth century and the Empire. Specula-

3.1 HORTA *Tassel house* Brussels 1893, entrance hall (contemporary photograph)

3.2 CHAMBON *Théâtre de la Bourse* Brussels 1885, café (contemporary photograph)

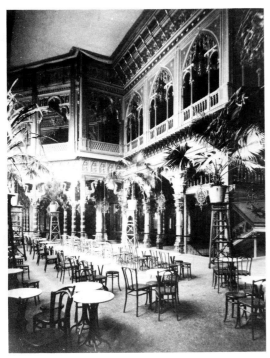

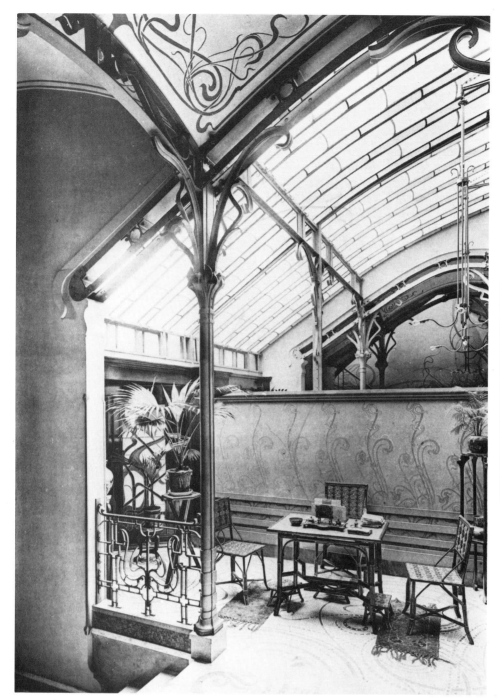

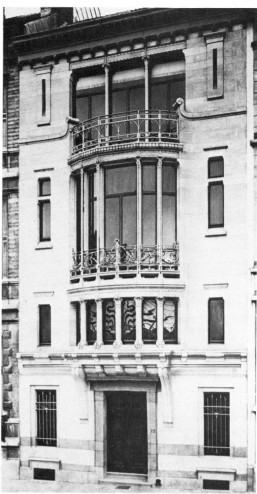

3.3-4 HORTA *Tassel house* Brussels 1893,
interior and facade (contemporary photographs)

tors who tried to "Haussmannise" the city by driving three great boulevards
through the most picturesque districts, built Parisian-style houses destined to
be occupied as apartments served by elevators. This innovation had very little
success, buildings of this kind were abandoned – even today they are largely
inhabited by foreigners – and the principle of the little house prevailed for ever
in Belgium.'[1]

New districts were thus built on the basis of private initiative, exactly the
converse of what was happening in the Netherlands during the same period,
where most of the houses were built by housing associations which did not
really appear on the Belgian scene until just before the First World War.

The construction of these new streets, avenues, squares and closes took
place within the framework of the two fundamental elements of urban
structure: on the one hand development in narrow, deep plots, and on the
other the limitations of communal building regulations. Varying from commune to commune, the latter not only controlled the maximum height of
buildings in relation to the street level, and minimum ceiling heights, but also
placed limitations on projections, balconies, plinths, cornices . . . even supervising the suitability of buildings to climatic conditions.[2] Building regulations
thus came to influence the form of houses in suggesting, for example, a
recourse to relieving arches which were eventually replaced by the solidly

Opposite and overleaf
HORTA *Maison and atelier Horta* Brussels 1898-
1900, details of staircase (photographs Le Berrurier)

Page 83 above
HORTA *Maison and atelier Horta,* interior
(photograph Le Berrurier)

Page 83 below
UNKNOWN ARCHITECT *Shop* Ghent c.1900,
detail of facade (photograph Wieser)

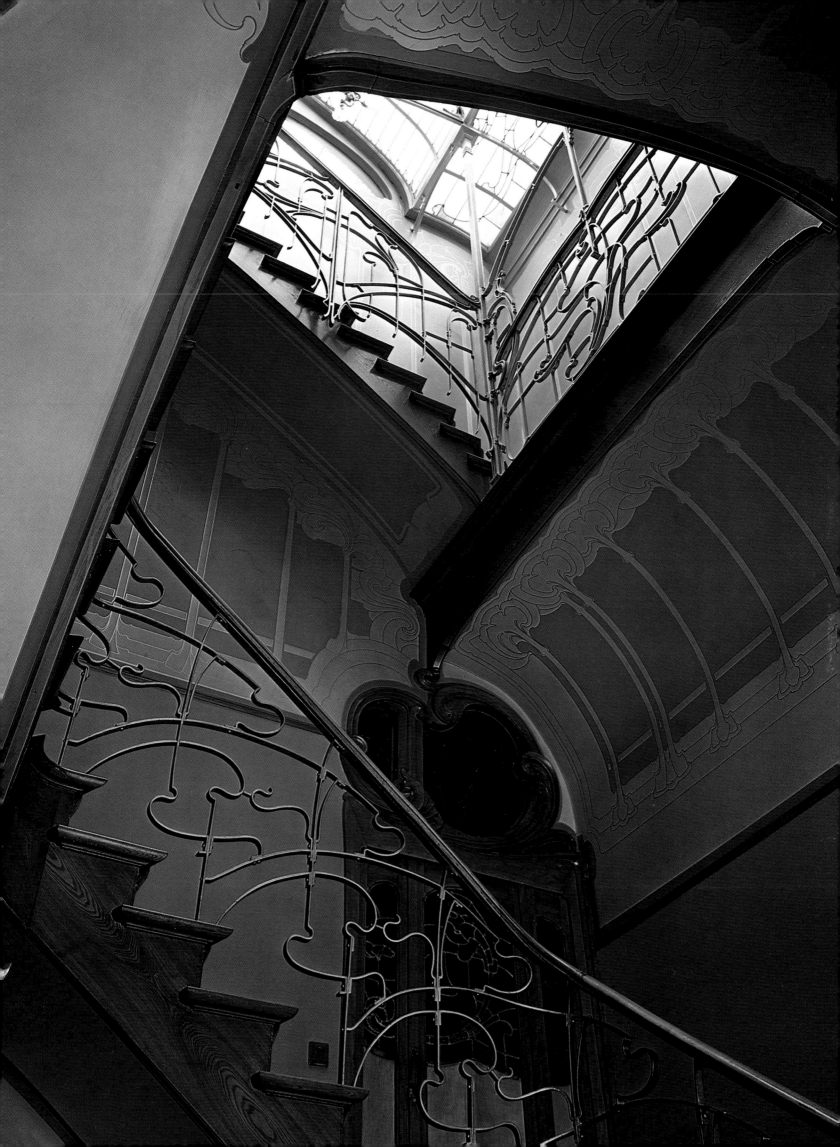

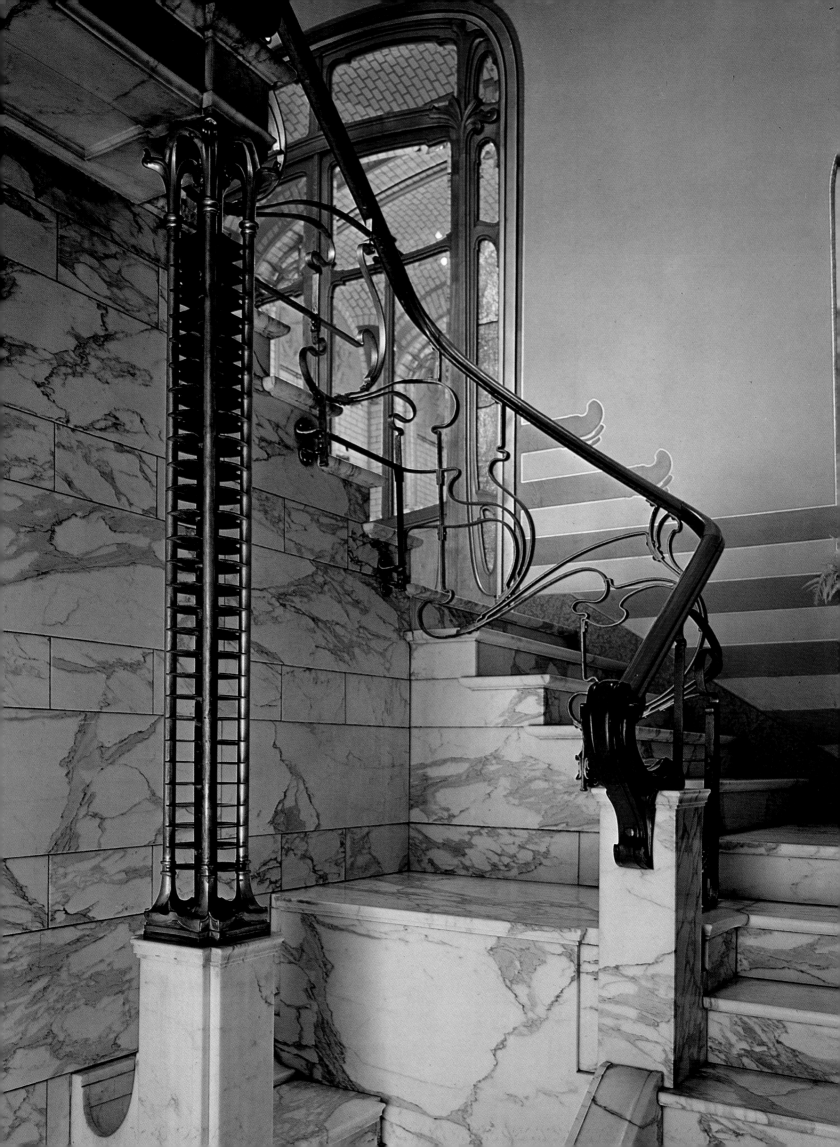

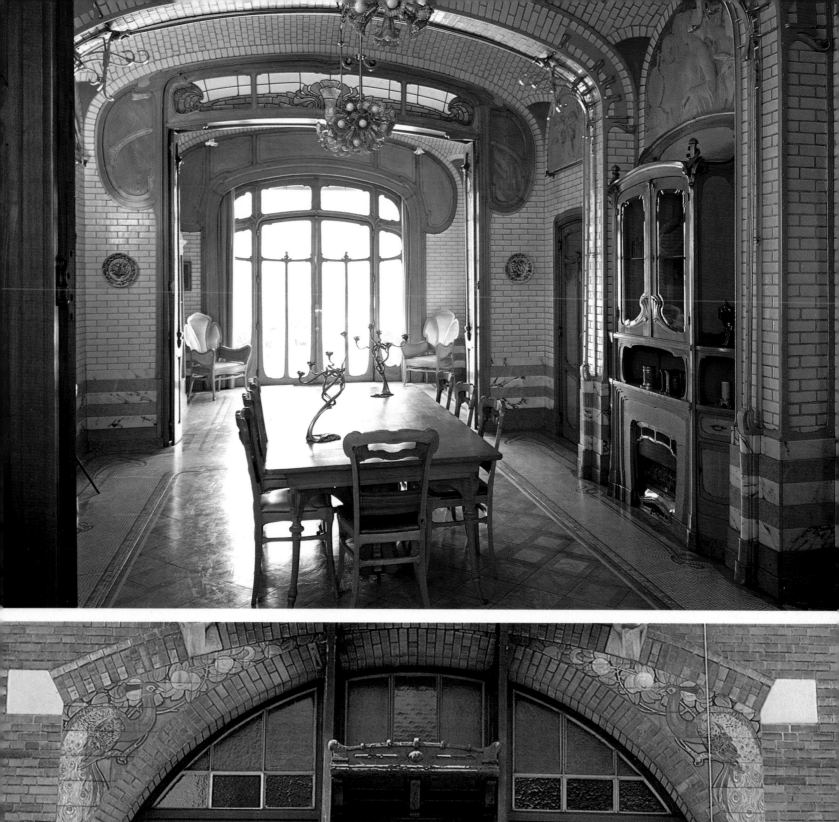
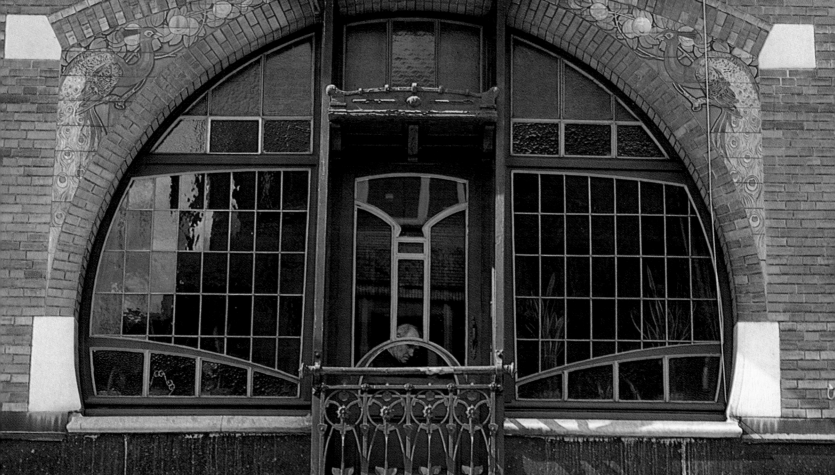

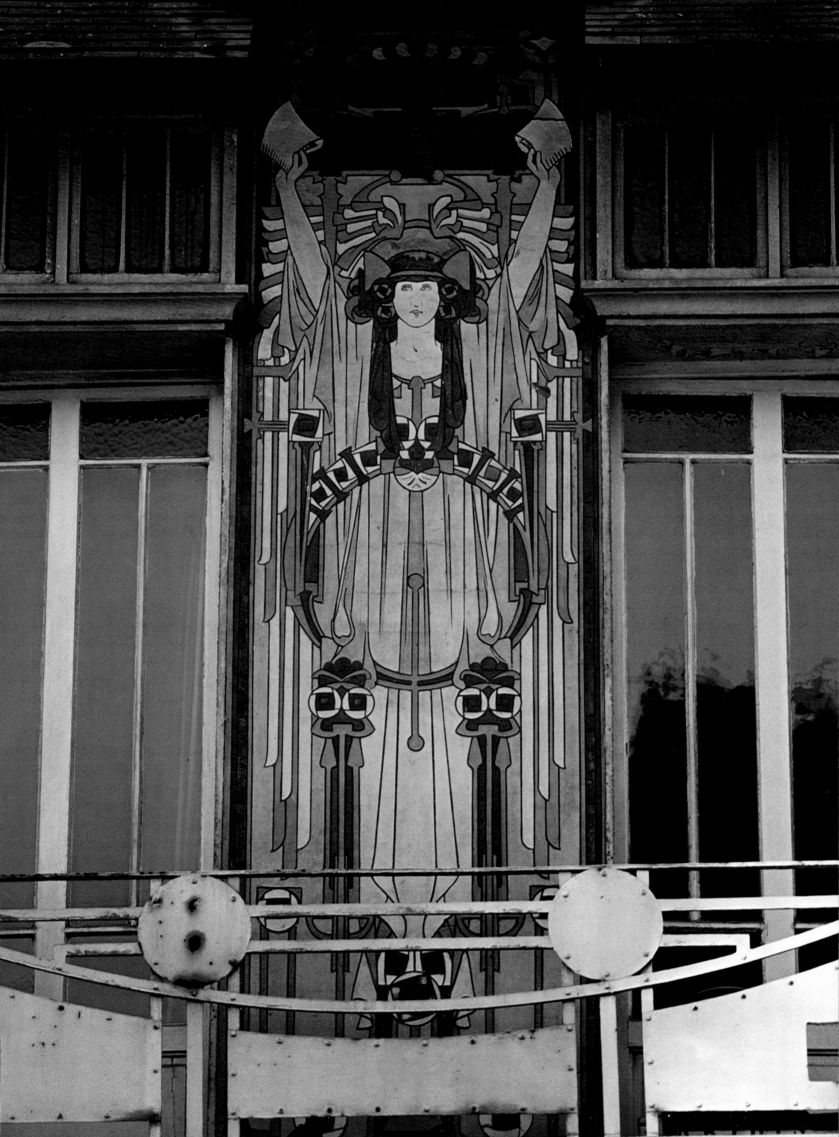

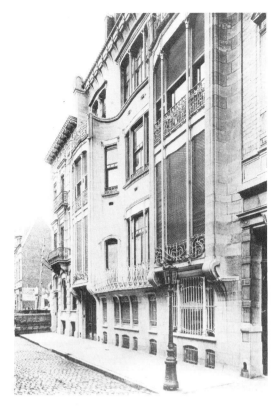

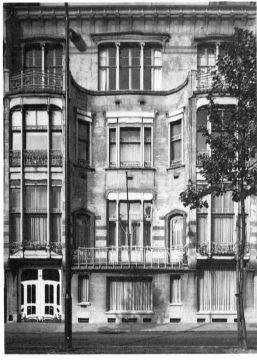

3.5-6 HORTA *Hôtel Solvay* Brussels 1894, facade before alteration (contemporary photograph) and as it is today (photograph Wieser)

Opposite
CAUCHIE *Own house* Brussels 1905, detail of caryatid (photograph Van Wynsberghe)

anchored metal bressummers of Victor Horta's A l'Innovation department stores, or Antoine Pompe's orthopaedic clinic.

But if the state of contemporary Belgian society, together with topographical, cadastral, artisanal and industrial conditions created an ideal background for the frenzied development of the street facade and sometimes even of interior volumes, in order for the new style to be greeted with such naive enthusiasm by the population – to the extent of marking the whole physiognomy of the city – a determined avant-garde had to exist who were solidly accepted and taken up by the cultural elite and the bourgeoisie.

If Art Nouveau did receive the backing of the most progressive section of the intelligentsia, it will be seen that this was caused less by creative complicity between the author of a project and an enlightened client than by solid links of friendship between young people of the same age and the same revolutionary generation, fired by a strong desire for change.

In its early years Art Nouveau was also to be a way of asserting one's membership of a progressive political family, and it could even reflect the interests of Leopold II's colonial enterprise.[3]

One has to go back to around the year 1885 to grasp the reasons which made 1892 the point of departure for a movement so irresistibly fascinating that it was to become the popular style par excellence of the twentieth century. It is in the process of social change begun some ten years earlier that we have to search for the reasons why such essentially historical landmarks in the history of art in Belgium as the house which Horta built for the engineer Tassel, the Japanese house which Paul Hankar built for himself, or the abstract design of van de Velde's wood engravings for the revue *Van Nu en Straks*, are also the point of departure for a privileged moment in popular culture.

The economic crisis which struck Europe in 1884 was particularly severe in Belgium, since the condition of the working class was worse and the density of population greater than in any other continental country. Between 1850 and 1900 the population rose from 150 to 230 per square kilometre. The Liberal government fell in 1884, and with it disappeared the regime under which the country had lived since winning independence from the Dutch in 1830. The Catholics established themselves solidly in power, and the socialists began to gain strength.

The Belgian Workers' Party (Parti Ouvrier Belge) was founded in 1885, the fruit of twenty years of effort. An awakening of class consciousness, influenced by ideas propagated at the First International, was in evidence in 1867 but did not survive the dissensions within the International and the worldwide reaction provoked by the supression of the Paris Commune. The penal code was revised in 1867, however, and workers were guaranteed the right to strike.

There were continuous economic contacts between the United States and Belgium, the latter country exporting both glass products and prefabricated metal houses. From 1870 on, the manufacture of mirrors increased considerably. Their high quality and reasonable cost opened up new possibilities for their use in architecture. Alban Chambon, who built the Théâtre de la Bourse in 1885, multiplied effects of perspective by covering the walls with mirrors. Hankar executed some surprising store windows in which the beveled edges of the polished panes fitted into woodwork cut in irregular, sinuous shapes. Horta and Saintenoy erected large department stores with wholly glassed-in facades.

On March 25th, 1886, riots broke out in the Charleroi region, and were supressed by the army with unprecedented brutality. The rank injustice of this action moved some young intellectuals to quit their social milieu and join the new Workers' Party; among them were three lawyers, Jules Destrée, Emile Vandervelde, and Max Hallet. All three eventually became intimate friends of Henry van de Velde, and it was they who persuaded the executive committee of the party to give Victor Horta the commission for the Maison du Peuple in Brussels. Max Hallet later commissioned Horta to draw the plans for his residence on the avenue Louise, and with the Antwerp socialist Camille Huysmans, was to play an important role in the creation in Brussels, in 1926, of the Institut des Arts Décoratifs which enabled Henry van de Velde to continue an educational experiment begun in Weimar at the beginning of the century.

The riots of 1886 sparked socialist action in Belgium, and from that time

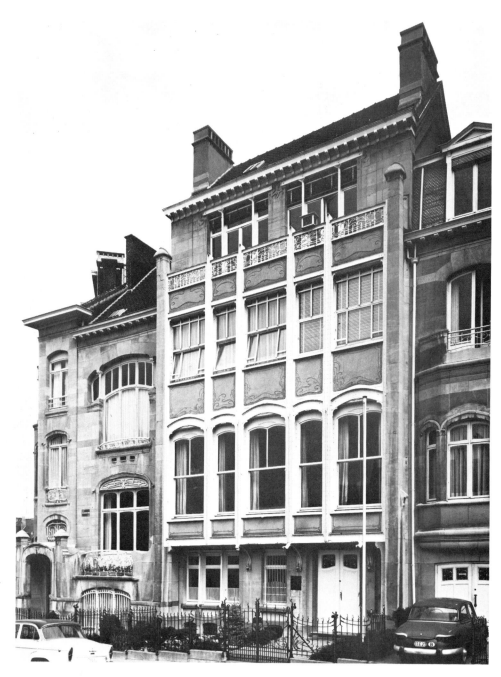

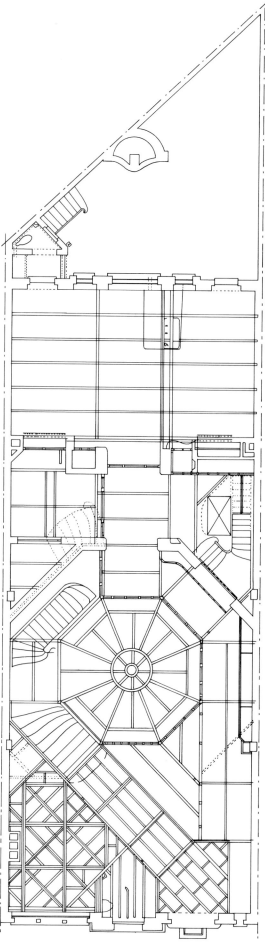

on demonstrations followed one after the other. In August 1887 13,000 miners, and in 1890 80,000 demonstrators, paraded through the streets of Brussels to demand universal suffrage. A general strike was announced, then cancelled upon receipt of promises from Parliament. Two general strikes, however, were called. The first, in 1902, was a failure because it was launched in a period of economic prosperity; it drained the strikers' relief funds without really threatening the national economy. The second, in 1903, was decisive, and forced Parliament to agree to the principle of universal suffrage – tempered, it is true, by the plural vote, which gave extra votes to the middle class electorate.

The upshot of the economic crisis of 1884 and the organisation of the forces of labour was an acceleration of industrial and financial concentration which displaced family or individual management. Stimulated principally by the Société Générale, a financial establishment created in 1822 for the purpose of providing capital to young and growing mechanised industries, the number of corporations rose from 201 in 1857 to 1,158 in 1900. Control over the business world passed into the hands of new men fired with the spirit of progress: mostly they were engineers and former colonials who had taken part in building the Congo Free State, setting up steel mills in Russia, or constructing the Peking-Hankow railway. These were the people who became Horta's most enlightened clients and had complete confidence in him – the Van Eetveldes, the Solvays, the Aubecqs, the Tassels. Intelligent and energetic, they set the

3.7-9 HORTA *Hôtel Van Eetvelde* Brussels 1897, facade, plan (from the original drawing) and interior

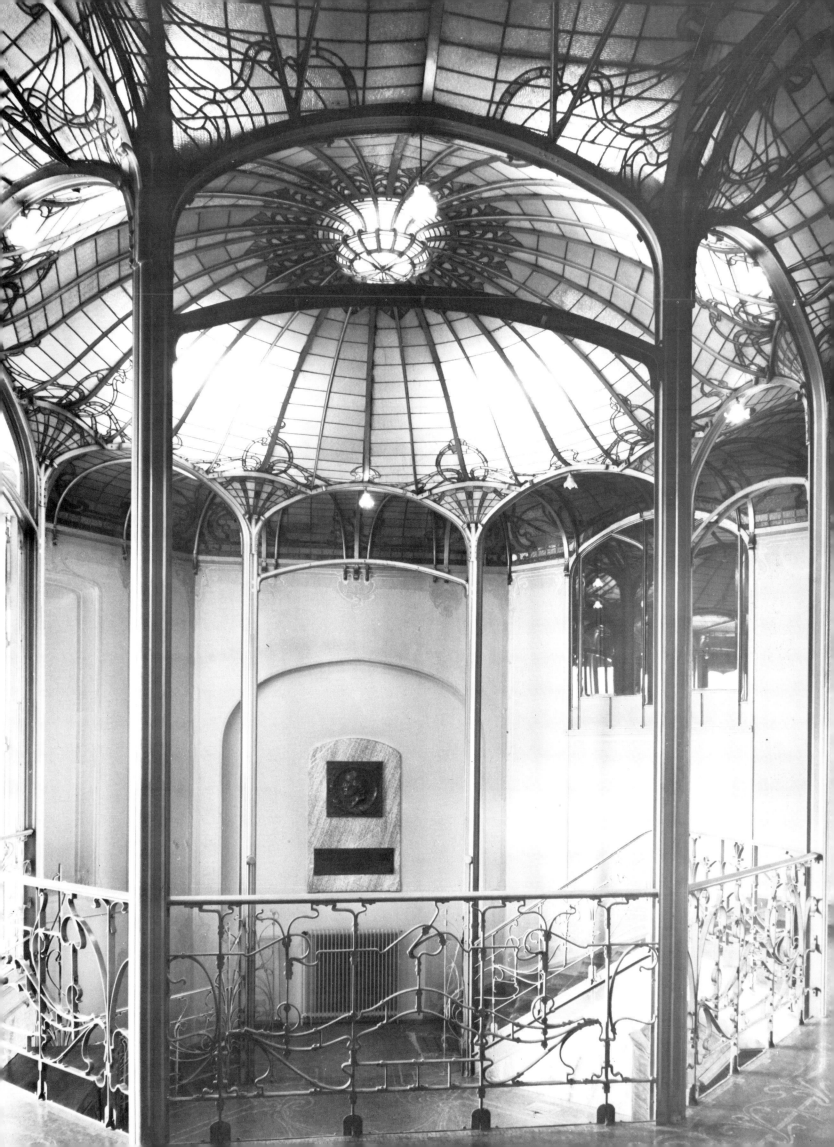

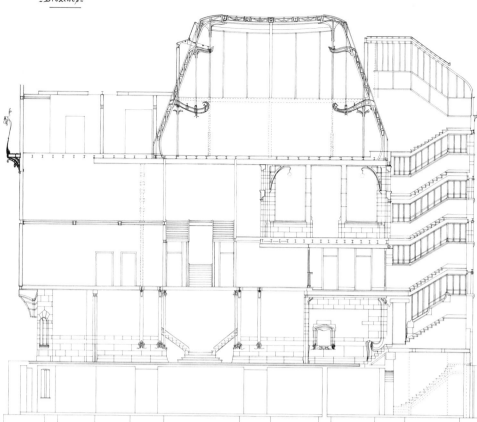

Maison du Peuple.
Bruxelles.

3.10-11 HORTA *Maison du Peuple* Brussels 1897, cross section and ground floor plan (from the original drawings)

3.12-13 HORTA *Maison du Peuple*, facade and auditorium

3.10

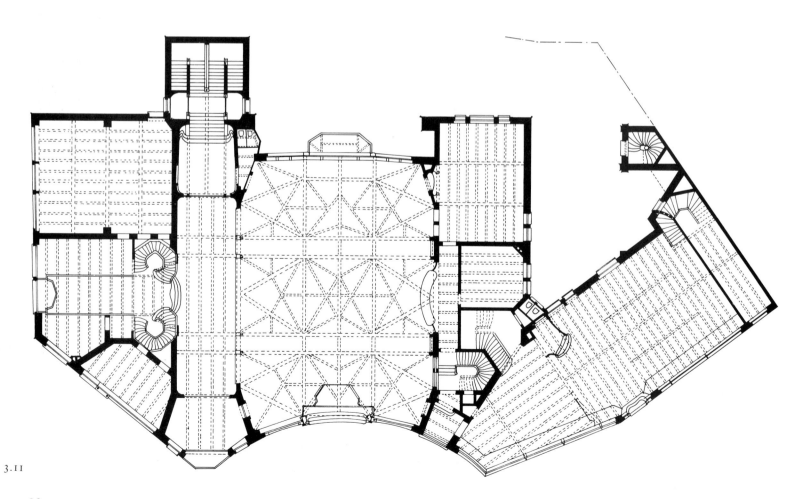

3.11

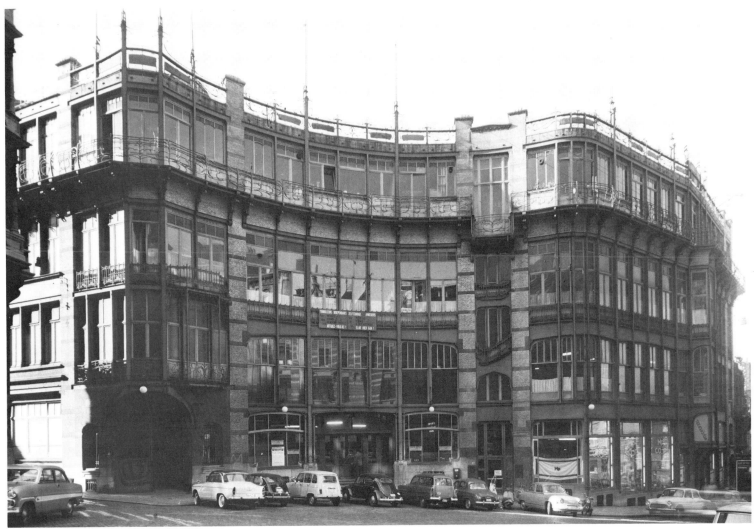

3.12

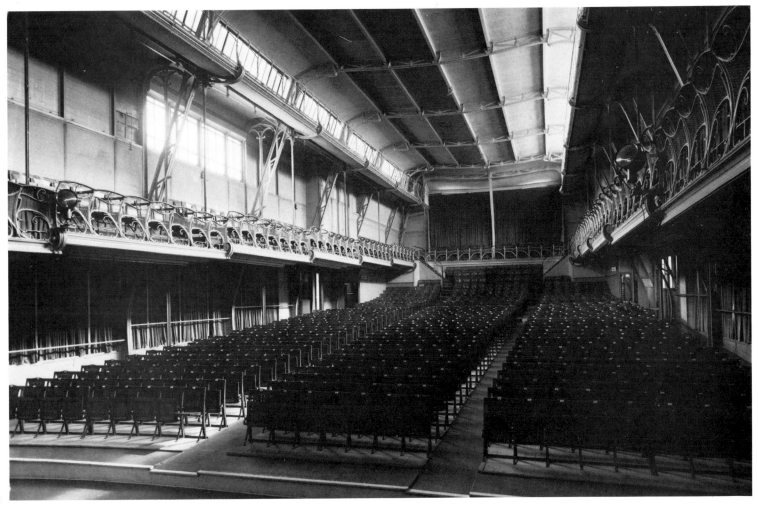

3.13

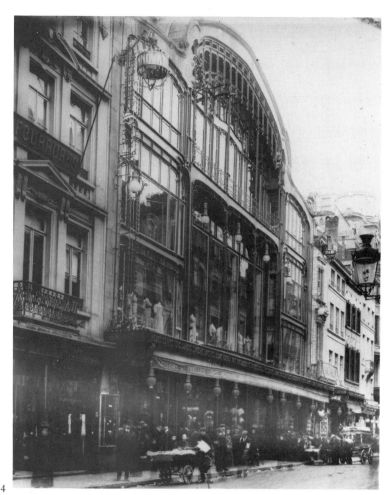

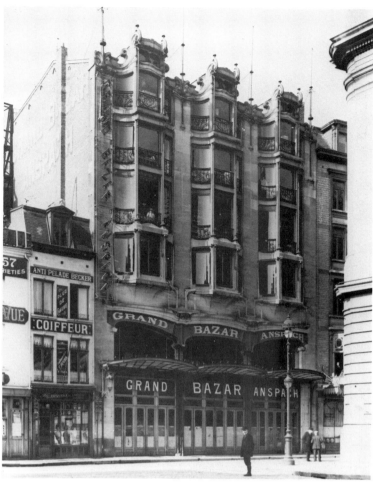

3.14

3.15

development of capitalism upon a new road. Belgium was never richer that it was on the eve of World War I: orders flowed in, and industrial activity overran the national boundaries to spread through the entire world.

When, after the riots of 1886, the directors of the Belgian Workers' Party extended a welcome to young intellectuals, deserters from the liberal middle class, they recognised that the presence of these recruits was an unexpected stroke of luck for the future of socialist action. They therefore felt no hesitancy about elevating men like Destrée, Furnémont, and Vandervelde to positions of importance, although the rank and file preferred their leaders to come from the working class rather than from the bourgeoisie. The learning, eloquence, and writings of these men brought the party a badly needed power of logic. But there was more involved than the struggle against social inequalities. The charter of the Workers' Party stated clearly that the march forward towards the society of the future was to be accompanied by intellectual as well as material transformations, and that all these developments must proceed on an equal footing and be fostered with equal care.

As things turned out, however, the field of combat was exclusively that of bettering material conditions. Cultural policy was rarely discussed, and the executive committee tacitly left it to their intellectual recruits to define the party line in that area. In the many lectures, newspaper articles, and books which the champions of the Workers' Party devoted to the problem of the relation of art to socialism, the appeal was always to the exaltation of beauty rather than to the definition of a socialist attitude in art.[4]

This attitude was justified for two reasons. The first pertained to strategy: by encouraging the proletariat to appreciate works of art, the party intended to show that socialists were not benighted barbarians who might be expected to sacrifice the nation's cultural heritage on the altar of revolution. The second reason pertained to culture itself. When they talked of art, the Destrées and Vanderveldes and Hallets were not referring to a mere abstraction, nor solely to the works of the artistic past. Implicitly they associated the notion of a progressivist art with the efforts of their artist friends – the van de Veldes, Hortas, Meuniers, Verhaerens, Maeterlincks – to free contemporary art from academicism. Here we must remember that when, in 1885 and thereabouts, some of

3.14 HORTA *A l'Innovation department store* Brussels 1901 (contemporary photograph)

3.15 HORTA *Grand Bazar Anspach* Brussels 1903 (contemporary photograph)

3.16 HORTA *A l'Innovation department store*, elevation (from the original drawing)

3.17-18 HORTA *Grand Bazar de Francfort* Frankfurt-am-Main 1903, elevations (from the original drawings)

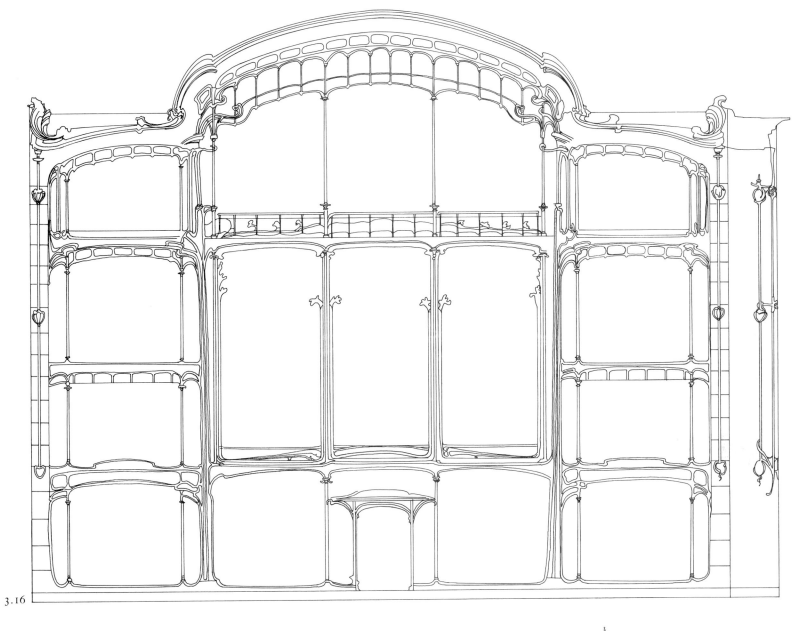

3.16

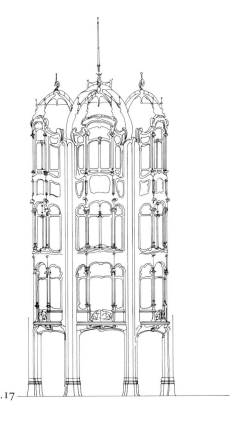

3.17

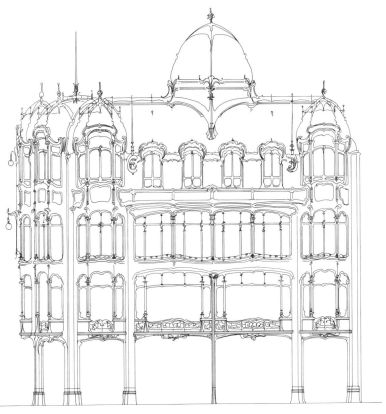

3.18

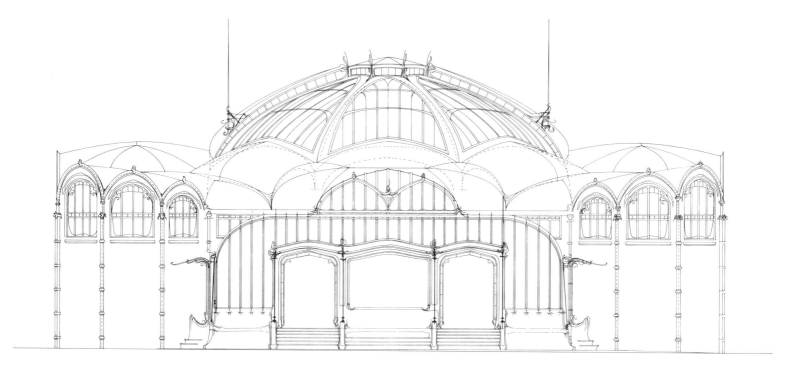

3.19 HORTA *Paris Exhibition* 1900, Congo
Pavilion elevation (from the original drawing)

the most thoughtful young intellectuals directed their interest to socialism and politics while others chose to engage in the fight for the renewal of the arts, this was not a rift but a manner of specialisation.

So it was that at the dawn of the twentieth century the aesthetic ideas of the Belgian Workers' Party rested entirely on the friendship between its young intellectual leaders and the avant-garde artists, notably those of the Groupe des Vingt, its successor La Libre Esthétique, and L'Art Moderne. And because these artists were enthusiastic about Art Nouveau, their socialist friends came out for architecture in the modern style. Thus the plans for the Maison du Peuple are Victor Horta's work, and thus Louis Bertrand, a socialist deputy mayor, saw to it that most of the public buildings in his commune – schools, swimming pool, low-cost housing – were of Art Nouveau design.[5] Although we cannot quite call Art Nouveau the official socialist style, there can be no doubt that it was given preference by the party: Henry van de Velde, for instance, was put in charge of the party's graphics, while the socialist leader Emile Vandervelde wrote in favour of the new style.[6]

However, basing an aesthetic approach on relations of friendship between the leaders of a party and a select group of artists, even if these were the most creative of their time, inevitably led to a dead end. A vibrant, forward-looking socialist aesthetic could develop only in the context of a wide, continuous, and contentious democratic debate. In fact, socialist thought on the subject petrified rapidly, the end result being a new academicism. One of the most disastrous effects of this was the indifference of socialists towards the whole problem of urban space, which, because they have failed to make it an object of thoughtful analysis, does not impress them even today as a prime field of combat for the class struggle.

From its beginnings, Art Nouveau architecture appealed to a clientele that was more open and dynamic than the 'grande bourgeoisie': engineers, lawyers, and artists were more receptive to new ideas by the very nature of their professional activities. By putting its stamp of approval on Art Nouveau, the Workers' Party confirmed and accentuated this cleavage, which found concrete expression in the Brussels street scene in a way that no one expected. Building became a medium for the expression of ideology. Freethinkers, socialists, and liberals had their buildings done in Art Nouveau style. Catholics on the other hand chose Gothic revival or Flemish Renaissance. They condemned Art Nouveau on the ground that its sinuous curves appeared to be the mark of a totally pagan lubricousness, and forbade its teaching in the architectural schools of Saint-Luc.

The extreme tension that invigorated the artistic and political avant-garde towards the end of the nineteenth century drew much of its strength from a reaction to the intellectual climate of the 1880s. In a memoir of his years as a law student Jules Destrée conveys the feeling of that climate. On his shelves

3.20–21 HORTA *Hôtel Aubecq* Brussels 1899,
facade and interior roof light (contemporary
photographs)

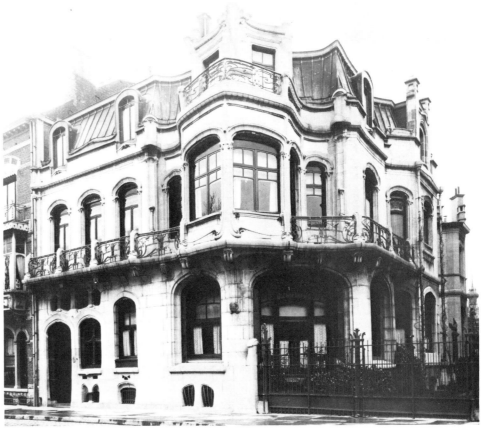

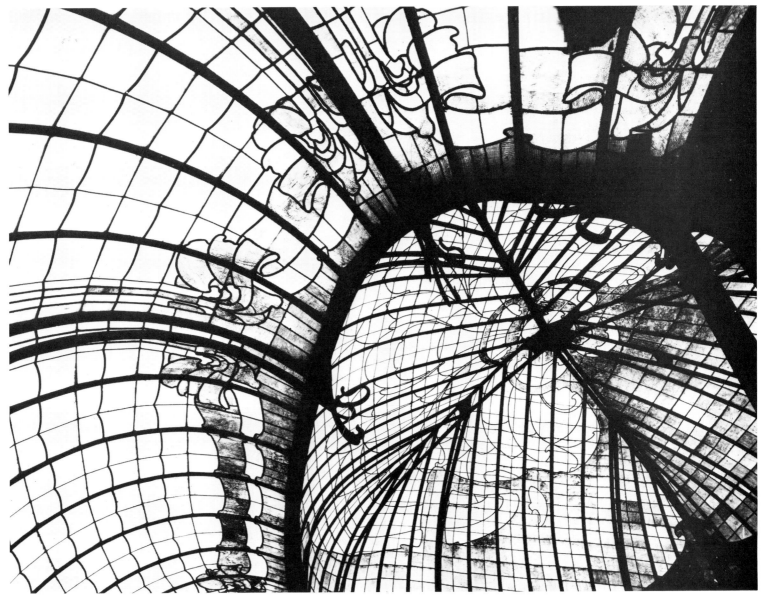

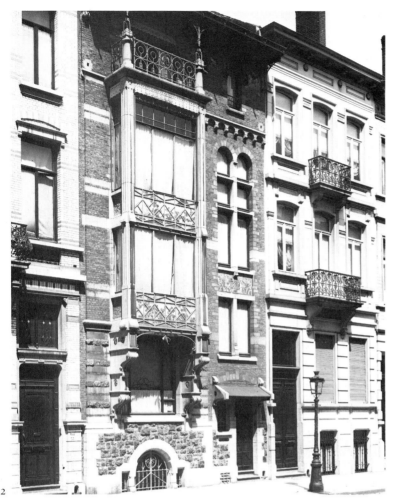

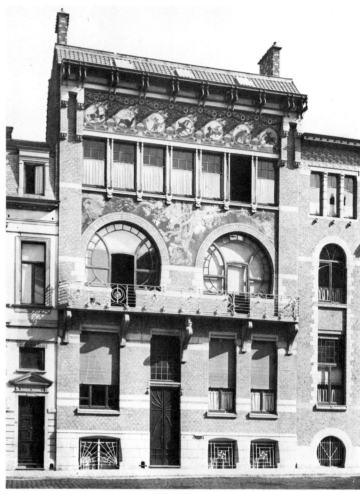

3.22

3.23

current magazines stood next to the works of Zola, Taine, and Baudelaire. A large etching by Rops hung on his wall. In the evening he went to the places then in fashion, the Vauxhall and the Eden Théâtre, as much to sit and talk as to see the show. He belonged to the Chapitrè, a small literary group which at the time was only a timid beginning, but which foreshadowed what Les Vingt, L'Art Moderne, and La Libre Esthétique were to be a few years later. The time, however, was out of joint, and it was easy to fall into the fashionable pessimism that such writers as Dostoyevsky incited.[7]

The first gust of fresh air came from the Far East, when Japanese imagery raised hopes that art could be stripped of its furbelows. Destrée, now a socialist lawyer, decorated his office walls with the same prints that Hankar the architect hung in his studio.[8] Monograms engraved by Henry van de Velde, and the wrought iron and cabinetwork of the house Hankar built for himself in 1893, reveal a graphic style clearly influenced by Japanese art.

So, in the early 1890s, two movements, one political and the other cultural, finally pierced the fog of materialism which had driven young intellectuals to take a pessimistic view of life in general. On the one hand there was socialism with its ideals and its strategy of action; on the other hand there was the budding Art Nouveau, which opposed an organic art to the revivals and laboured compositions of eclecticism.

Rarely have opinions and critical analyses on an architectural style been so divergent as those regarding Art Nouveau. A majority of the historians who wrote in the period between the two world wars, while they recognised that Art Nouveau had broken with tradition, have considered it an eccentricity, a hiatus in the evolution of architecture. Since World War II the problem has been re-examined, and more thorough analysis has thrown light on the factors that favoured the blossoming of this style. But if the ebullition of ideas characteristic of the 1880s made an ideal crucible for the shaping of a new style of architecture, by itself it does not suffice to explain a popularity so great that the face of a city like Brussels was profoundly changed in the space of less than ten years.

If the style was to flourish it needed first a suitable urban structure. Belgian cities with their communal divisions, and Brussels in particular, made such

3.22 HANKAR *Own house* Brussels 1893

3.23 HANKAR *Ciamberlani's studio* Brussels 1897 (contemporary photograph)

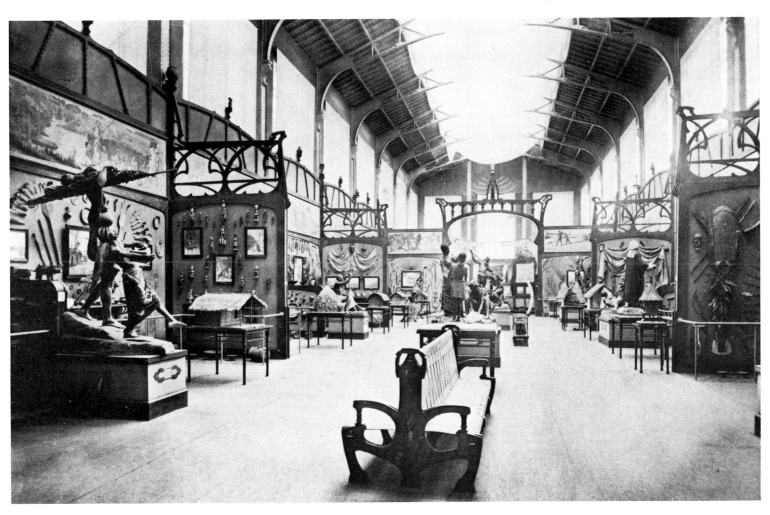

3.24 HANKAR *Brussels-Tervueren Colonial Exhibition* 1897, Ethnographical Rooms (contemporary photograph)

3.25 HANKAR & JASPAR *Project for the Théâtre Neuf* 1895, elevation (from the original drawing)

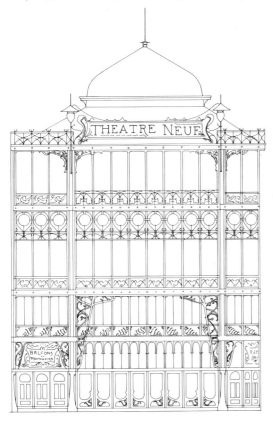

urbanisation and uniformity as was achieved in Paris practically impossible. The terrain that favoured the development of Belgian Art Nouveau architecture was the narrow building site about twenty feet wide, fronting along a street. This restriction, however, challenged the imagination: the originality of the plans of the Tassel and Van Eetvelde houses is a direct outcome of this division of land into narrow, elongated parcels. In addition to this type of site limitation, which favoured the multiplication of small properties, there was the intensely individualistic character of the householders, who, as heirs to a long tradition of communal liberties, were strongly attracted to a style that allowed so much daring and fantasy.

It was Art Nouveau's very popularity, however, that caused its rapid decline. From the point of view of building technique the style could have lasted until just before World War I, but in fact it fell into disuse shortly after 1905, and the building crafts reverted to all the 'Louis' styles in their work with iron, wood, and stone. Art Nouveau in becoming popular, moreover, reversed Horta's equation: the latter developed his elegant spaces behind relatively simple facades, while the homes of the commercial bourgeoisie were given facades in an exuberant modern style, with an interior that was often banal.

In practice their owners left the sumptuous residences built by Horta only a few years after occupying them, moved out of the city, and isolated themselves on estates laid out in the suburbs. The coming of the automobile facilitated this exodus of the rich. And as the aristocracy abandoned the city, the critics, who only the day before had extolled Art Nouveau to the skies, now began to treat it with disdain. The style died of its own popularity. Thereafter the town was given over to unbridled speculation. The aristocracy, who no longer lived there, had lost interest in preserving and adding to its beauties.

Generally speaking, historians point out relationships between the iron structures of the nineteenth century, the theories of Viollet-le-Duc, and the exposed structural elements characteristic of Art Nouveau. But, granted that Viollet-le-Duc's logic and the iron-and-glass architecture of the international exhibitions stirred the imagination of architects like Horta and Guimard, this a posteriori judgement still needs to be refined.

The nineteenth century witnessed two achievements of epic proportion: the conquest of new territories and the conquests of science. From the point of view of risks incurred, the story of the lives of the first great engineers is comparable to that of the pioneers who pressed forward into uncharted lands, and their work may even be more truly significant than the over-mythicised 'winning of the West'.

Jules Verne's engineer, a castaway on a desert island, might singlehandedly reconstruct civilisation, but the nineteenth century never confused the roles of the architect and the engineer: the former beautified the city, the latter constructed bridges, laid out railroads, put mines in working order. When Balat built the greenhouses at the château of Laeken,[9] he did not for a moment imagine that iron and glass would one day be used in so ostentatious a way for private dwellings. In fact, when he went to see the Tassel house built by Horta, a former pupil of his, he was revolted, and never forgave the younger man for having betrayed architecture by putting stained glass and bare iron in a domestic building. And when Jobard wrote, in 1847, that the *ordre métallurgique* was at hand,[10] he was not suggesting that metal be used to simplify architecture, but that the potentialities of the new material be exploited to achieve more complex architectural wonders – the sort of things that painters alone had until then dreamed up. Chambon, building his theatres in Brussels, London, and Amsterdam, was simply following Jobard's advice, using the possibilities of contemporary technology to produce palaces out of the *Thousand and One Nights*. The critics, moreover, greeted Chambon's accomplishments in the same terms Jobard had used thirty-five years earlier in his predictions.[11]

In the 1880s Brussels finally lost its neo-classical, provincial dignity, and built fairy castles in order to escape from a civilisation dominated by materialism. Everything seemed put together to create a dreamland, to ease flight into the unknown: the profusion of plants, oriental décors, star-studded cupolas, mirrors, expanses of glass, canopies, electric lights, even the curves of Thonet's chairs. . . all reminiscent of the narcotic high. Indeed people were trying drugs: in 1889, for instance, van de Velde and his friend, the poet Max Elskamp, experimented with hashish. As for the poets, they imitated Baudelaire. Iwan Gilkin's *La Nuit* was a rejoinder to *Les Fleurs du Mal,* but his descriptions are even darker; he was attacking the vices of the city, its jaded sophistication, its pessimism, and his Catholic concept of sin lent the poem a tragic mood.

The works of Chambon were designed to gratify the taste for novelty of a wealthy, carefree aristocracy. His vast metal-and-glass umbrellas, his theatres with their wide promenades and their glass-enclosed, heated foyers created an ambience which satisfied the fondness for exoticism in a completely new and grandiose way. Stained glass became the fad, succeeding the vogue for covered arcades that had raged during the first half of the century.[12] Similarly, the purpose of the greenhouses at the royal château was not so much botanical as social; they were built for the sake of prestige, to provide a place for social functions, concerts, and a pleasant promenade. So strong was the taste for glassed-in structures that a church built entirely of iron and glass was adjoined to the royal greenhouses.[13]

The thirteen years or so preceding the historic year 1893, when Victor Horta literally exploded the conventional space of the private residence, were the time when middle class social affairs also found a new environment, moving from public areas to private space. As proof that Horta's architecture represented a departure in style one need only point to the distance separating it from the eclecticism of a period which distributed styles according to the relative dignity of the rooms, from the Louis XVI boudoir to the Empire drawing room. But to talk about Horta's work as representing a break with a style of living or a forward step toward social functionalism would be an exaggeration, to say the least.

In Horta, the man of the hour, the middle class discovered an artist who knew how to provide novel, original places where people of means could live as pleasantly as possible. A significant comparison can be made between the interior arrangements in Chambon's buildings and those in Horta's private houses. The fluidity of spaces, generally recognised as one of the major characteristics of Horta's architecture, is present in the theatres Chambon built

3.26 SAINTENOY *'Old England' department store* Brussels 1899 (contemporary photograph)

3.27 SAINTENOY *81 avenue Louise* Brussels 1898 (photograph Wieser)

3.28 HAMESSE *17 place Delporte* Brussels 1907

3.29 POMPE *Dr van Neck's Clinic* Brussels 1910, facade before alteration

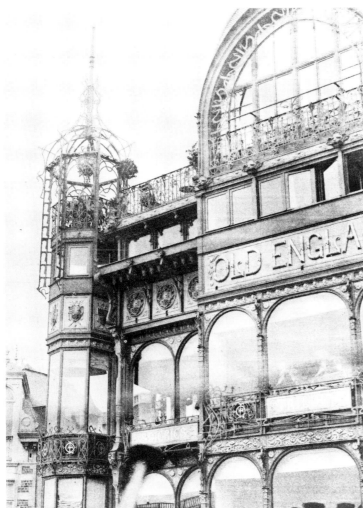

3.26

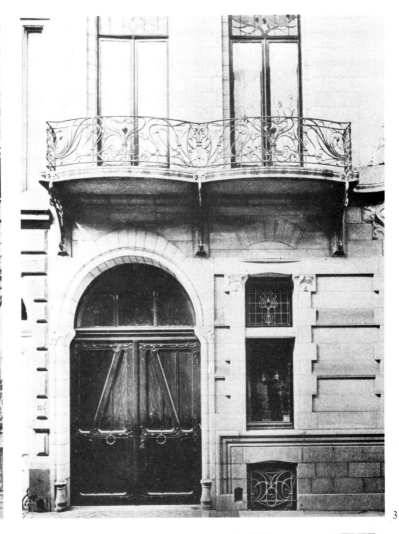

3.27

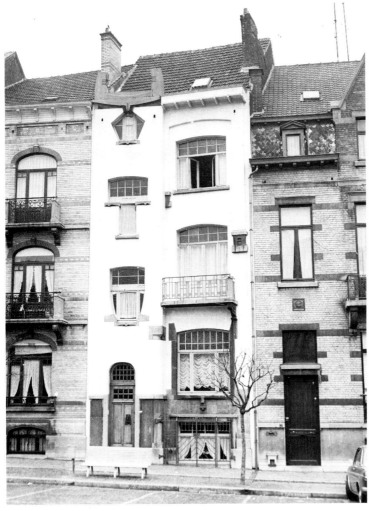

3.28

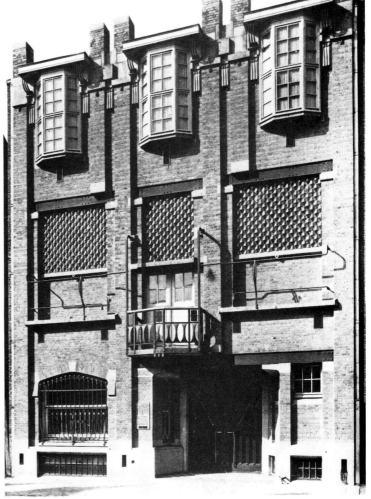

3.29

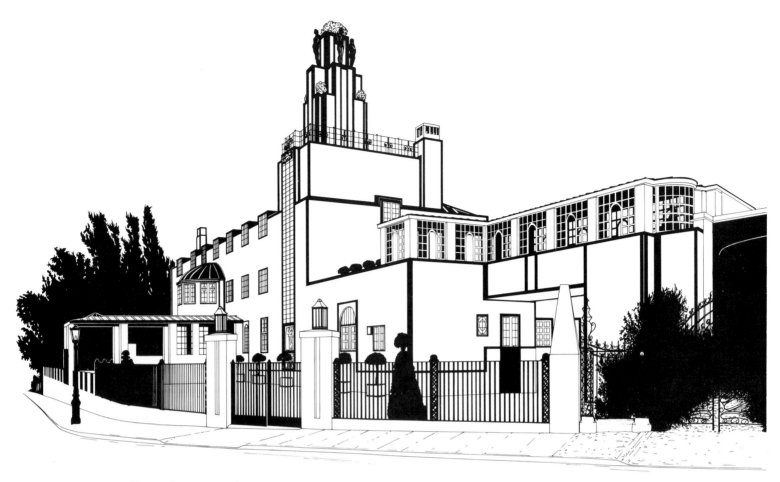

3.30-31 HOFFMANN *Palais Stoclet* Brussels
1905-11, exterior and great hall (drawings based
on contemporary photographs)

some ten years earlier, where spatial continuity unified the different floors of
the building, the monumental staircase, the auditorium and its promenades,
and the foyers prolonged by lush gardens that were covered with expanses of
glass. Plants in profusion, electric lighting, and mirrors were also arranged to
create this feeling of unity rather than to set the different areas apart.

Contemporary press descriptions of these theatres, now all demolished,
could apply quite as well to the houses Horta later built for the Solvays and the
Van Eetveldes – but with a difference. In Horta's work, garish display gave
way to refined elegance, soft gradations of paint and stained glass supplanted
blue domes studded with gold stars, marble replaced stucco, the Art Nouveau
line drove out oriental decoration; yet the same spatial fluidity was retained. If
it is true, as the Chevalier de Wouters de Bouchout held in his *L'Art Nouveau et
l'Enseignement* (1903), that stage presentations had a fundamental influence on
the taste of the worldly bourgeoisie in their choice of building styles,[14] then it
must be equally true that Chambon's sumptuous theatres had a decisive effect
in these matters.

In 1885 idlers stood around theatre entrances to see the VIPs of society, the
arts and politics, and to gawk at the ladies and their finery. After the bloody
riots of 1886, the demonstrations for universal suffrage that followed, and the
general strikes, it occurred to the wealthy that they should flaunt their riches
less openly. Social gatherings were held thereafter behind the walls of private
homes, whose entrances and exits, cloakrooms, grand staircases, and drawing
rooms had to match the appurtenances and luxury of the theatres.

Towards the end of the century, Brussels had all the contradictions of a
provincial capital cantilevered over a nation fearful of its audacities and provo-
cations. It had the contradictions of a luxury city, a banking city, a centre of
social emancipation, a flourishing arts centre, a liberal capital which did not
hesitate to invite Anarchists to camp in the Forêt de Soignes, just a few minutes
away from the prestigious avenue Louise. And yet it jibbed at ratifying
Leopold II's projects when he was taken by one of his fits of architectural or
town planning megalomania. Brussels was obstinate in its own self-confident
bourgeois individuality, stimulated by the idea of an economic revolution
which would also embody art.

This euphoria was translated by the middle classes, tradesmen and white
collar workers into the aesthetics of a flamboyant intoxication (Strauven's

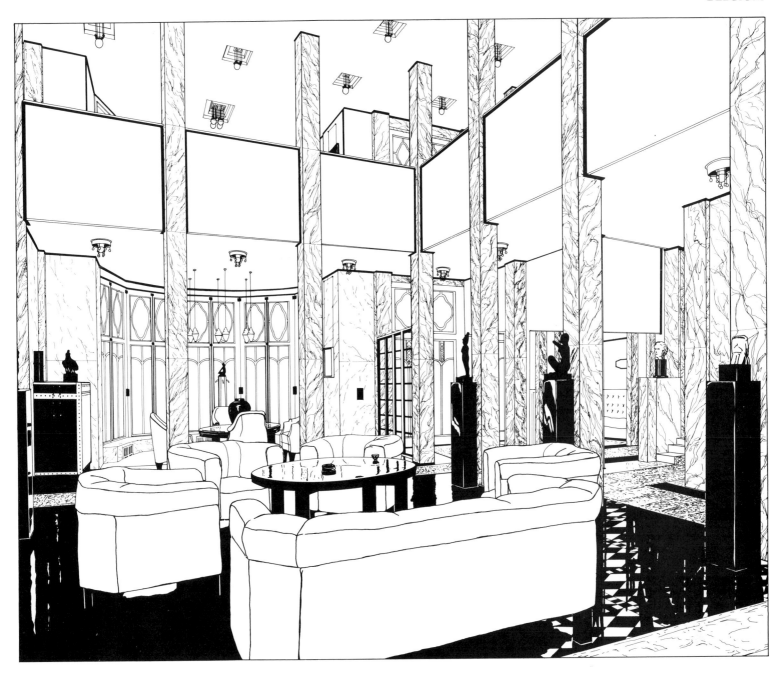

'follies' in Brussels, Deweerdt and Bascourt in Antwerp), into the poster-facades of art for everyone (the painter, Paul Cauchie's house, designed with an eye to winning the municipality's annual prize for street-art), into Leon Sneyers' geometric Viennese compositions, into Blérot's streets of repetitive Art Nouveau components. . .

The street became an electric showcase emphasising its contrast with 'bourgeois remoteness' which was to take refuge for a while longer in the cool light of Victor Horta's marble and iron palaces, a light which fell vertically through the roof so as not to disturb the calm presence of the meticulously assembled facades, where 'the external signs of richness' had been weighed out on a pharmacist's scales.

Writing his memoirs, Horta said of one of his masterpieces, the Hôtel Solvay: 'At last, a mansion *like all the others*. . . but whose interior characteristics were: an apparent metallic structure and a series of glass screens giving an extended view for evening receptions. . .'[15]

As for Henry van de Velde, he, as an artist, had long been prey to the anguish of doubt. He came to architecture by a series of detours, and because he was self-taught, he felt a crying need for reassurance. Paradoxically, he comes through clearly as a person – and an attractive one – only when seen through his blunders, misgivings and contradictions.

This painter-turned-architect was never at ease in the third dimension. And besides its heaviness, his architecture shows that it is overworked. Van de Velde's vision in space was so limited that when he was studying a project he

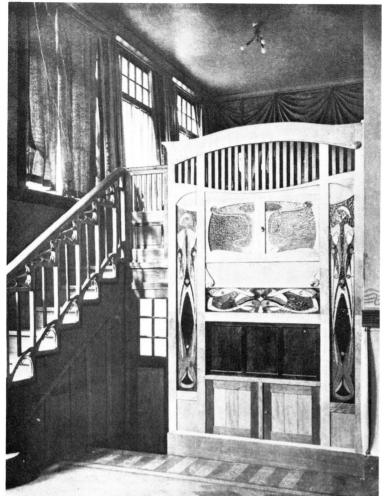

3.32

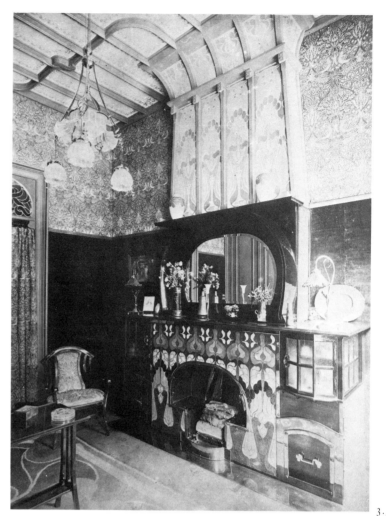

3.33

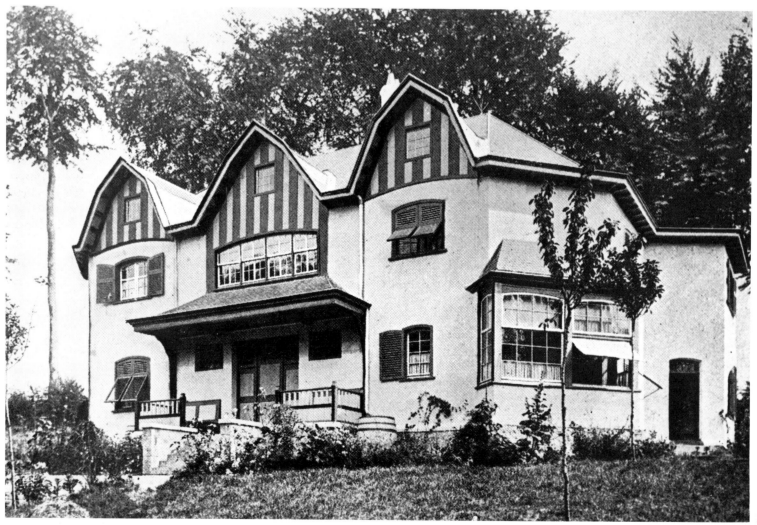

3.34

3.32 VAN DE VELDE *Hôtel Otlet* Brussels 1894, dining room (contemporary photograph)

3.33 VAN DE VELDE *Salon de M.B.* Brussels n.d. (contemporary photograph)

3.34 VAN DE VELDE *Bloemenwerf* Uccle 1895, facade with original colour scheme (contemporary photograph)

3.35 VAN DE VELDE *Bloemenwerf,* ground floor plan (from the original drawing)

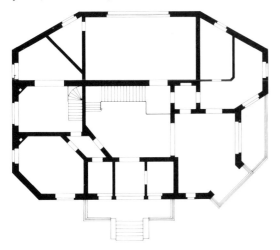

ordinarily took as his starting point a building by a colleague or one seen on a journey. But they were used only as aids to his imagination: the result was never a pastiche.

The Werkbund Theatre, built in Cologne in 1914, is a case in point. This building, which has become a classic illustration in architectural manuals, looks like the most perfect example of van de Velde's theory of line,[16] the linear dynamographic ornament *which above all represents the movement prompted by internal activity.*[17] Yet the design of this building did not result from theoretical speculation about linear ornament. On the contrary, the preliminary studies for the theatre reveal a progressive development that began with a series of sketches in the Viennese style, in the manner of Hoffmann. Step by step, van de Velde grafted his theoretical concerns upon these preliminary sketches, and when the process of assimilation was complete all traces of the sources of inspiration had practically disappeared. The disparity between his architecture and his methodological writings was a constant with van de Velde, but there was no question of a divorce between the two. Indeed, the genius of this architect is contained whole and entire in this conflict. In the last phase of his career, when van de Velde developed his theory of pure form, intellect triumphed over sentiment. The artist finally conquered his own contradictions; but the architectural result of this victory was disappointing if not mediocre.

In the city as it was in 1880 – already cut off from nature by its growth beyond the walls – Chambon had depended upon the advance of technology to recreate a 'nature' all the more exuberant and exotic because it was to provide an element of contrast to urban rigidity. Horta had mastered and directed this spirit for the use of an enlightened middle class; van de Velde strove to give the Art Nouveau line social and philosophical significance. However, while the contents, style, and typographic presentation of his *Formules de la beauté architectonique moderne* delight the mind, the formulae themselves defy any practical application. To assimilate them van de Velde would have needed an extraordinary ability to synthesize, a spatial vision which – oh, irony of fate! – Horta, his rival and arch-enemy, alone possessed.

'Do we have to wait for a social regime which we alone can create? Is it not, in the long run, more a question of sufficient existing numbers to create an atmosphere and anticipate the future?' To this hesitant affirmation which he made at the turn of the century, van de Velde gives his own reply in *Les Formules de la beauté architectonique moderne* which he published in Weimar in 1916: 'Today, this response would lack the most elementary consciousness of events. . . the world. . . could well have lost for ever its virtue of fecundity!', thus turning his back on a chapter of his life which had opened, with the statement following Lipps, that the projection of affective states in objects – in architecture – could make them participate unconsciously in human dynamism, while line[18] – Art Nouveau line – 'in the first instance represents a movement provoked by inner life'; that this line, 'considered as the adequate complement of forms conceived according to principles of rational and consecutive understanding is the image of a play of forces which we feel in all forms and in all materials'.

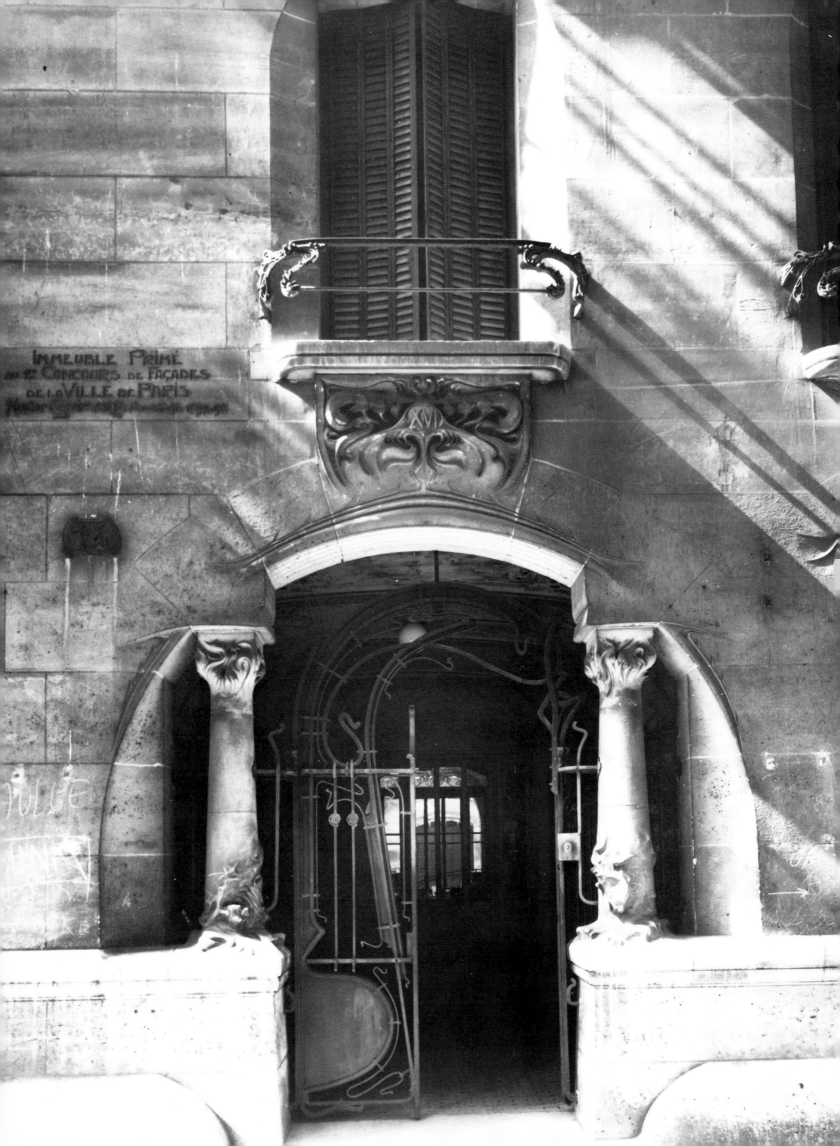

4. FRANCE

Viollet-le-Duc to Tony Garnier: the passion for rationalism

François Loyer

The history of Art Nouveau architecture in France is both straightforward and deeply disorientating, for while Guimard's debt to Viollet-le-Duc is, for example, quite obvious, a profusion of contradictory trends also appeared simultaneously at the turn of the century.

Linear histories of art written to date carefully divide artists and trends into watertight compartments which are compared without any chronological connection being established, while in reality, at a given date, totally opposed movements co-existed. Even progressionist ideology, which divides artistic production into 'historicist' or 'modernist' tendencies according to criteria which have more to do with ethics than with art, does not explain this incoherent diversity of production – a diversity which ought to be taken into consideration when drawing up a general picture of French architecture at the beginning of the twentieth century.

Recent studies have emphasised the role of the Ecole des Beaux-Arts in the diffusion of French culture, and the school's influence was particularly strong in America, especially after the Chicago World's Fair of 1893.[1] The story of the 1863 revolt is also well known because the interruption to Viollet-le-Duc's lectures led him to publish the series as the *Entretiens*.[2] But on the whole, the view we have of the academicians is totally negative, largely because of the brilliant polemicist Frantz Jourdain: their formalism is usually likened to impotence – a very unjust judgement when speaking of Charles Garnier and his pupils, who were the dominant force behind the Ecole des Beaux-Arts during the last quarter of the nineteenth century.

The important role played by the 'alternative *ateliers*' from the time of the end of the Second Empire has also been neglected. These 'alternative *ateliers*' were an extraordinary institution which arose, after the Viollet-le-Duc affair, from the students' revolt against their teachers and became an *anti-school,* with unpaid professors and pupils who covered the cost of the premises and other expenses out of their own pockets . . . The governing body of the Ecole des Beaux-Arts was finally obliged to recognise these pirate practices (which continued to exist until . . . 1968!) and, in doing so, to accept the content of the doctrines taught there, which were anti-academic and rationalist.

The 'alternative *ateliers*' played an absolutely vital role during the forty years which separated the institution of the Republic and the outbreak of the First World War, both through the message they spread among architects and by the architectural models they presented. An outlet for rationalist propaganda was also ensured by the publication of specialised magazines, including César Daly's important *Revue de l'Architecture*, and by the rationalists' position in the governing body controlling diocesan buildings attached to the Ministère des Cultes, gained thanks to the efforts of their master Viollet-le-Duc.

The rationalist theory expounded by Viollet-le-Duc was based on an honest use of materials and decoration. Leaving aside questions of style, Viollet-le-Duc proposed a perfect balance of form and ornamentation in relation to a triple rationality: technical (the sound use of materials); functional (expressed by Sullivan's famous adage 'form follows function'); and sociological (adopting methods of construction suited to the needs of the individual client, which represent one particular aspect of the function of the building). By basing art neither on a respect for a system of proportions determined by tradition, as is the case in neo-classicism, nor on an originality of 'character', as in romantic ideology, but only on what the eighteenth-century academicians termed 'expediency', the rationalists hardly offered, *a priori*, a new language: the novelty lay entirely in their methods – in the process of creation (the way in which their conception of a building evolved) rather than in its final form.

They did, however, create a new language from a plastic standpoint – derived from the French neo-Gothic of Lassus or Viollet-le-Duc and the Italian-inspired eclecticism of Ruskin. This new language was firstly one of colour, influenced by Ignace Hittorff's experiments with polychromy and the important example of Charles Garnier, whose Paris Opéra is a veritable manifesto of colour. Secondly came formal analytics: the form is the result of the accumulation of strongly expressed autonomous themes, coordinated like the complicated wheels of a machine, between which authoritative, hierarchical relationships are established.

The reasoning of this formal analytics is almost always positive: *you carry and I am carried, you assemble and I am assembled, you frame and I fill, you are used for structure and I for ornament . . .* The fundamental relationship between the various elements is a dialectical relationship based on their opposition (which enabled, in our time, Viollet-le-Duc to be taken for a structuralist!).[3] Thus, having emphasised construction, the important problem of decoration and, in this field, of ornamental symbolism, is brought to the forefront: ornament is seen not only as a means of illustrating the structure, but also as a symbolic indication of the function of the building linked, more generally, to a vision of the world based on the scientific worship of nature.

In this, the architects were not so far removed from the naturalists of the Zola school, the Symbolists in poetry and painting, the scientists of the post-Claude Bernard era or even the intellectuals, who introduced an idealised cult of Nature into their vision of history.

The meeting point of these parallel movements was undoubtedly the Gallery of Palaeontology in the Paris Museum of Natural History, built between 1874 and 1897 by Charles-Louis-Ferdinand Dutert, who also designed the 'Galerie des Machines' for the 1889 Exhibition. Dutert worked with unusual freedom, using a metallic structure[4] cased in glass to create an imposing area lit from above and surrounded by mezzanines which divide up the building, reducing it to a more human scale. The decoration is limited to the outlines of the large steel skeletons – which form an amazing symbiosis with the exhibits of skeletons of prehistoric animals – and to the repetition of an iris and fern motif in the moulded cast-iron balusters which form the banisters of the galleries and staircases.

The freedom found in Dutert's work was only possible because of the important experiments of Joseph Vaudremer, and the unorthodox way in which he split up the struggle between the carrier and the carried in the interior of his ashlar masonry – for example in the church of Saint-Pierre de Montrouge, built at the end of the Second Empire, or in the elegant Lycée Buffon (1886-89). Vaudremer, in fact, taught the American Henry Hobson Richardson, and the heavy, sober, monumental style which the latter was to develop – the result of the powerful articulation of elementary forms – was therefore not totally foreign to him.

Also important are the roles of Paul Sédille and Jean-Camille Formigé, both pioneers of steel construction and polychromatic decoration using man-made materials such as terra cotta and mosaic. Sédille's department store 'Au Printemps' was begun in 1881, and was at the time one of the most spectacular buildings in Paris – largely because of its total transparency, the use made of artificial lighting and the mosaic decoration on the panels of the balustrades, which were covered with fruit and garlands of flowers. Formigé's Palais des Beaux-Arts at the 1889 Exhibition also successfully combined steel and colour in the rich polychromy of the iron and the equally luxuriant colouring of the large clay panels, inspired by the prestigious example of Della Robbia in Florence.

The brilliant flowering of Art Nouveau in 1895 can only be understood in relation to the strength of the rationalist school in France. Many historians[5]

4.2 BIET & VALLIN *22 rue de la Commanderie* Nancy 1901-02, entrance detail (photograph Rose)

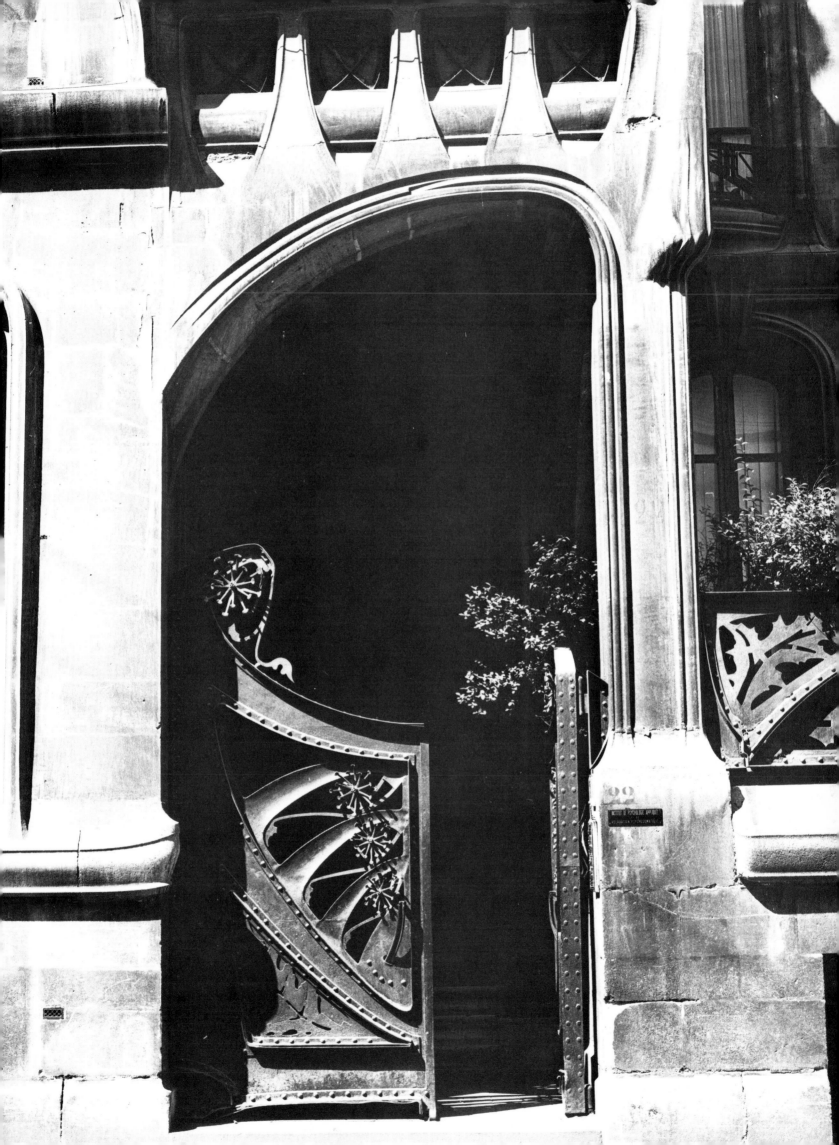

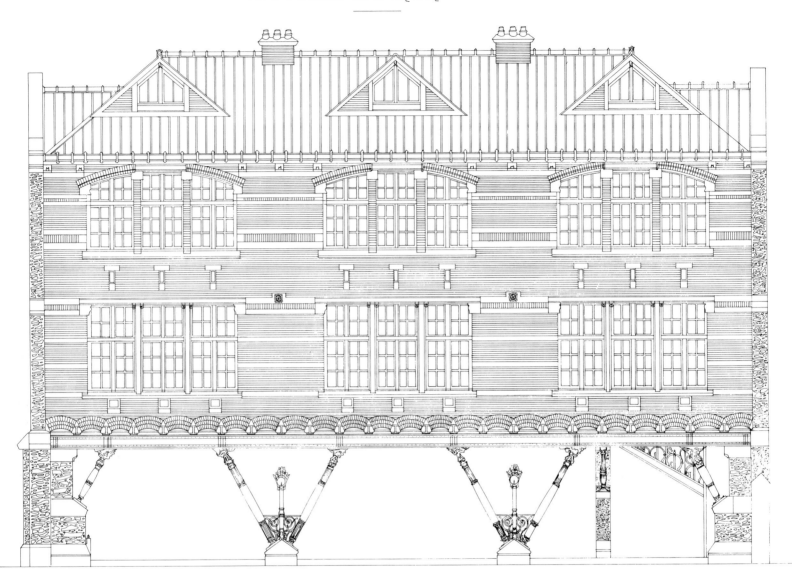

Ecole du Sacré Cœur

— Avenue de la Frillière —

Batiment des Classes

have already pointed out the premonitary role of the Comte de Laborde's statement on the London Universal Exhibition of 1851. They have also shown the similarity in developments taking place in the fields of painting, applied art and furniture and interior decorating, the latter so closely linked to architecture. I can only agree with them in speaking of the roles played by the Post-Impressionists (particularly Toulouse-Lautrec and Paul Gauguin) in emphasising the importance of line, and of the providential encounter with Japanese calligraphy, facilitated by the activities of the merchant Samuel Bing.[6] It is also necessary to take into account, as in the work of Félix Bracquemond, Emile Gallé or René Lalique, the renaissance of the object and its collusion with the world of nature or with the world of the oriental print.

The blossoming of the great decorators and cabinet-makers – Georges de Feure, Eugène Gaillard, Maurice Dufrène, Colonna, Georges Hoentschel, Louis Majorelle and Eugène Vallin – in the last years of the century was also connected with this trend. But neither Post-Impressionism, including the private experiments of Gauguin with the ceramist Ernest Chaplet from 1886[7], nor the promotion of Orientalism by the more important merchants is sufficient to explain such a sudden and mature explosion of a 'new art'.

Other explanations would be equally plausible, such as that which sees the real origin of Art Nouveau in neo-Gothic; the wallpapers of William Morris in

4.3-5 GUIMARD *Ecole du Sacré Cœur* Paris 1895, elevation (from the original drawing), exterior view (photograph Godoli) and detail of columns (photograph Sully-Jaulmes)

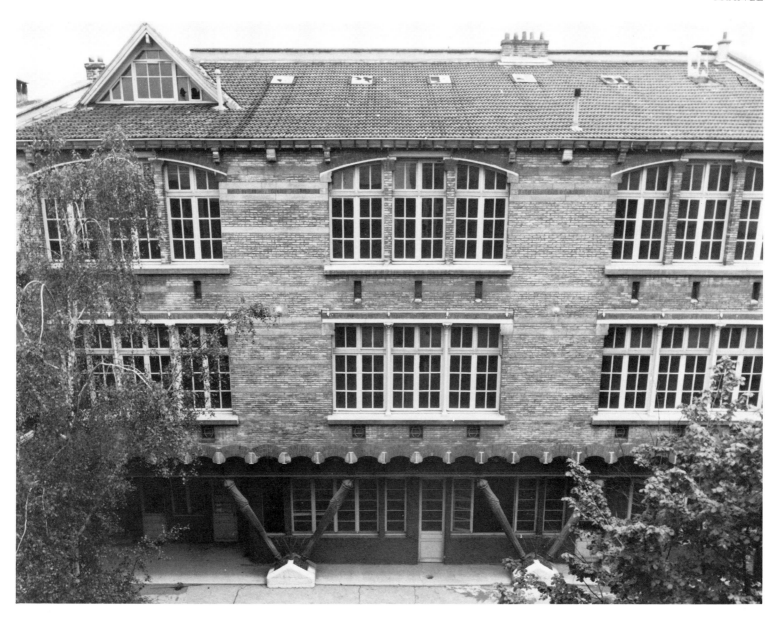

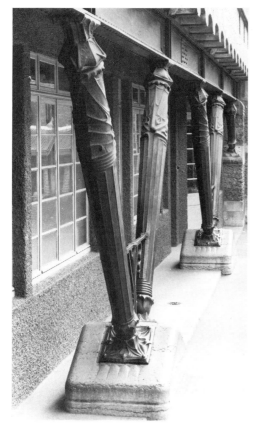

England and the interiors of Viollet-le-Duc in France (particularly at Pierre-fonds) are of no less importance, especially as neo-Gothicism and rationalism are closely related. One can see the neo-Gothic heritage both of Guimard, whose first project, the Castel Béranger, was in a Gothic style, and of the major decorators, the 'groupe des six' uniting Félix Aubert, Alexandre Charpentier, Jean Dampt, Charles Plumet and the Curator Moreau-Nélaton around Tony Selmersheim, one of the most brilliant representatives of a family of diocesan architects who worshipped neo-Gothic as if it were a religion.

The rationalist explanation, however, has the merit of avoiding any one purely formal line of approach (for example, in tracing the sources of Art Nouveau to the Post-Impressionist treatment of contour, Japanese calligraphy or the decorative aesthetics of the neo-Gothic style), by combining them all in a purely intellectual development, common to both the sciences and the arts in the last half of the nineteenth century.

Thus the explosion of Art Nouveau no longer appears as an accident of history, but rather as a conclusion. Similarly, the movement's lack of formal unity can be explained by the fact that the process of renewal was intellectual rather than plastic: the great problem at the beginning of the twentieth century was to be the search for a plastic form which corresponded to a way of thinking whose truth had never been questioned (for even the arguments of Le Corbusier during the thirties were simply a resumption of theories put forward by Viollet-le-Duc seventy-five years earlier).

Art Nouveau is a little like the search for the Holy Grail, as can be seen in the case of Guimard,[8] whose development, up to the explosion of 1895, is like a pilgrimage to various sources. A disciple of Viollet-le-Duc after his two periods of training at the Ecole des Arts Décoratifs under Charles Genuys and

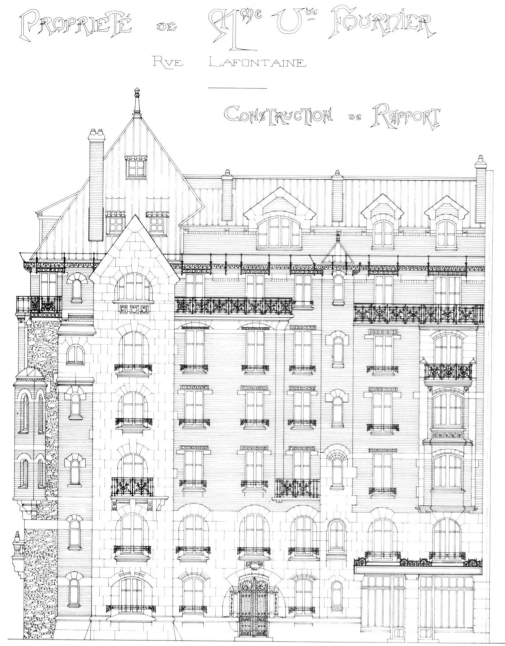

PROPRIÉTÉ DE Mme Vve FOURNIER

RUE LAFONTAINE

CONSTRUCTION DE RAPPORT

FAÇADE SUR LA RUE LAFONTAINE

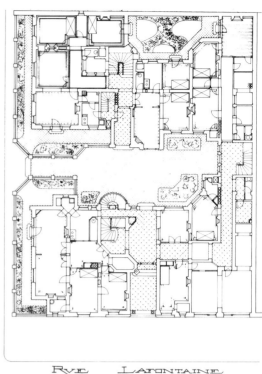

RUE LAFONTAINE

4.6-7 GUIMARD *Castel Béranger* Paris 1894-98, elevation and ground floor plan (from the original drawings)

at the Ecole des Beaux-Arts under Raulin, he soon found this precedent insufficient, and in 1894 travelled first to England and then to Belgium. His encounters with the English 'domestic revival' and Belgian Art Nouveau forced Guimard to question completely his own architectural practice: he reworked all the stylistic detail in the project for the Castel Béranger (1894-8), for which he had just requested planning permission, replacing the fine neo-Gothic graphics with a lyrical sweep of floral motifs in the style of Victor Horta.

At the time of his Ecole du Sacré-Cœur, finished in 1895, Guimard had not fundamentally transformed his means of expression: the brick construction, the huge classroom windows and the volumetric simplicity of form were all derived from schools by Vaudremer or de Baudot. On the ground floor, the famous detail of the columns with their splayed angle is in itself a signature: it is the solution advocated by Viollet-le-Duc in the *Entretiens* for a covered market, slightly altered from a structural point of view. And the decoration, which suggests by its dynamics the principle of unifying various parts (expressed in the stylistic screw-threads of the ferrules) falls well within the limits of rationalism.

In designing the Castel Béranger, Guimard only made changes to the decoration, entirely reworking the profiles of the mouldings whether in stone,

Opposite
GUIMARD *Castel Béranger*, detail of staircase (photograph Borsi)

Page 110
GUIMARD *Metro entrance Porte Dauphine* Paris 1900, type B enclosed

Page 111
4.8 GUIMARD *Castel Béranger*, exterior view (photograph Sully-Jaulmes)

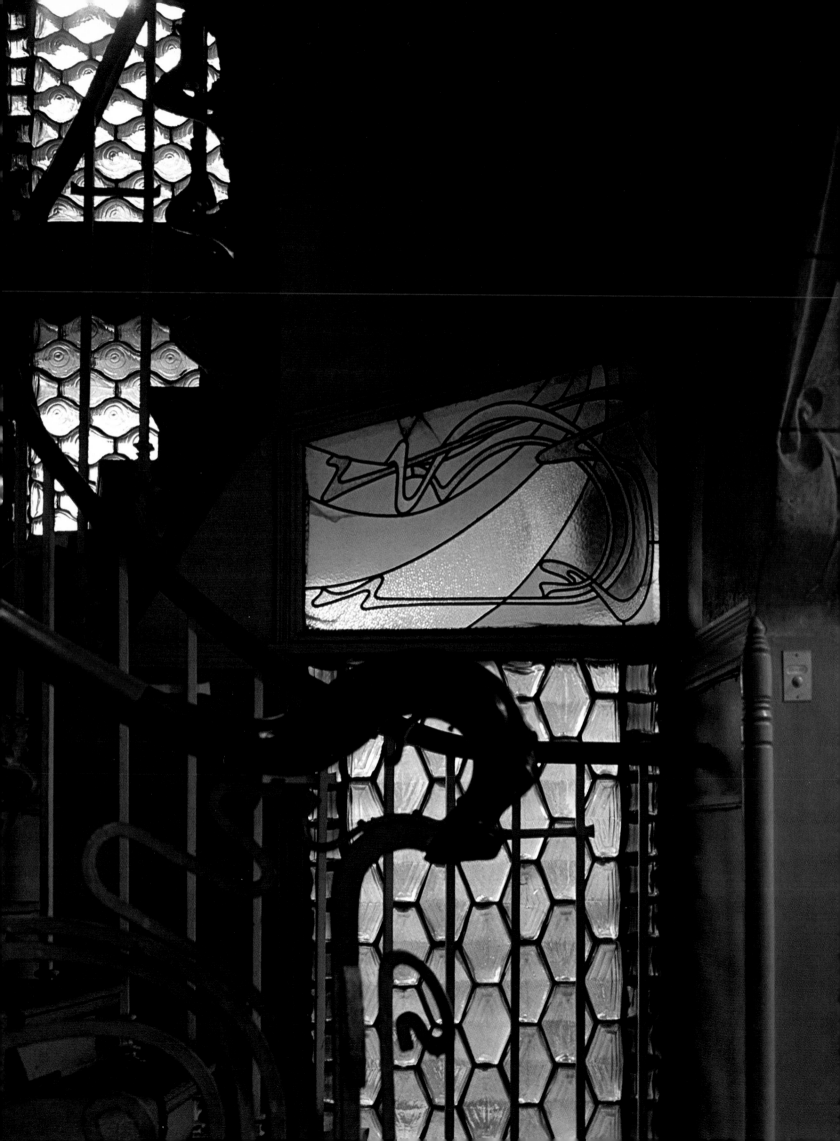

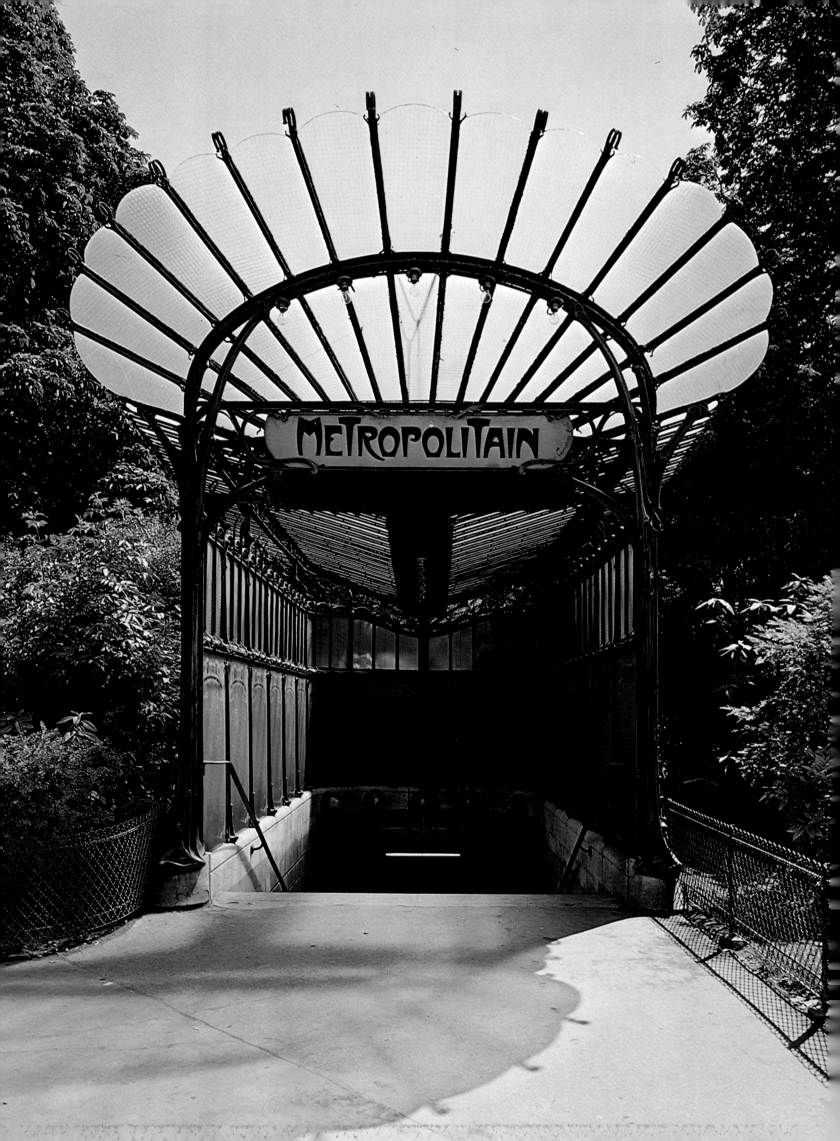

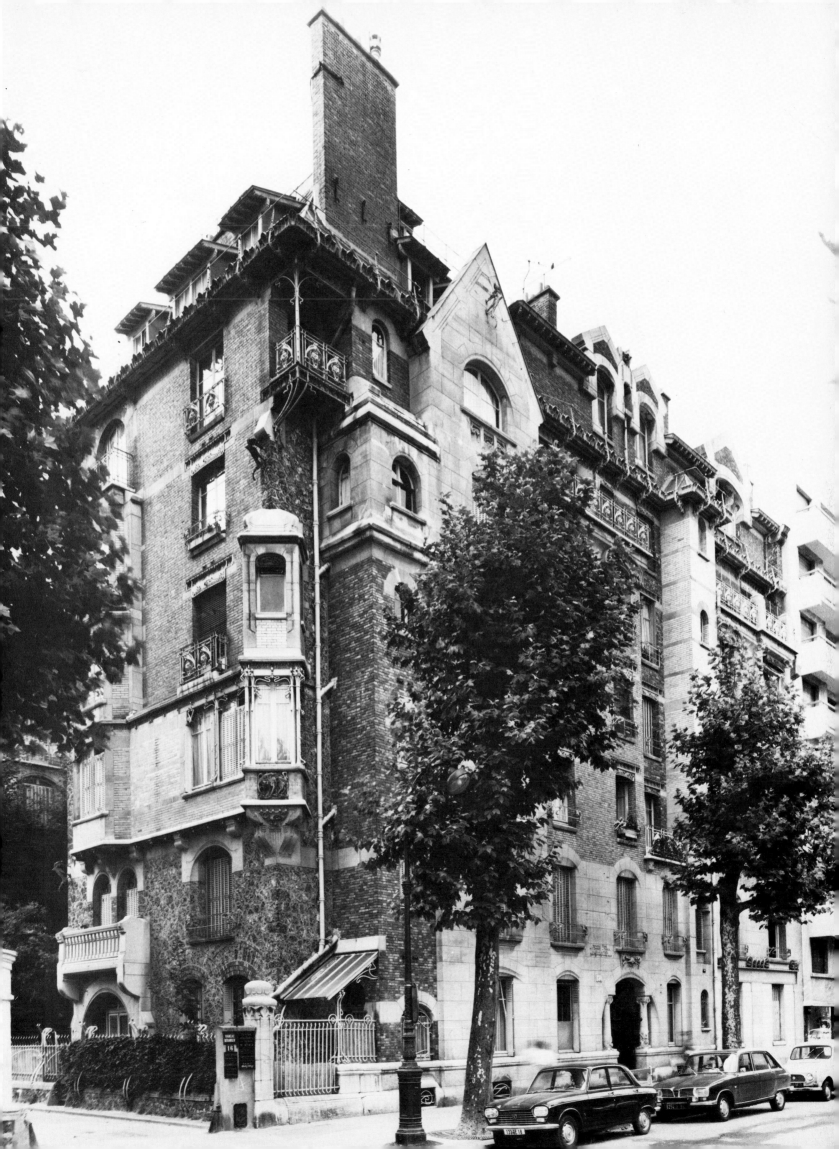

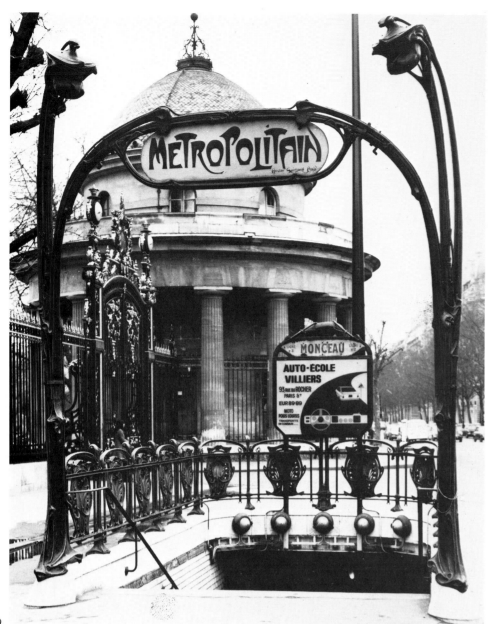

4.9

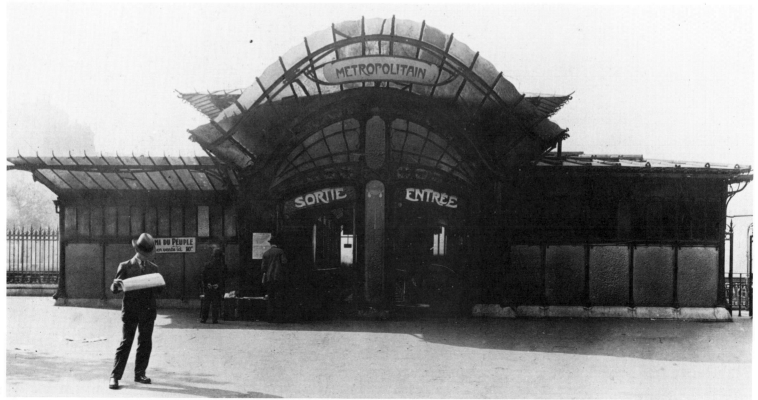

4.11

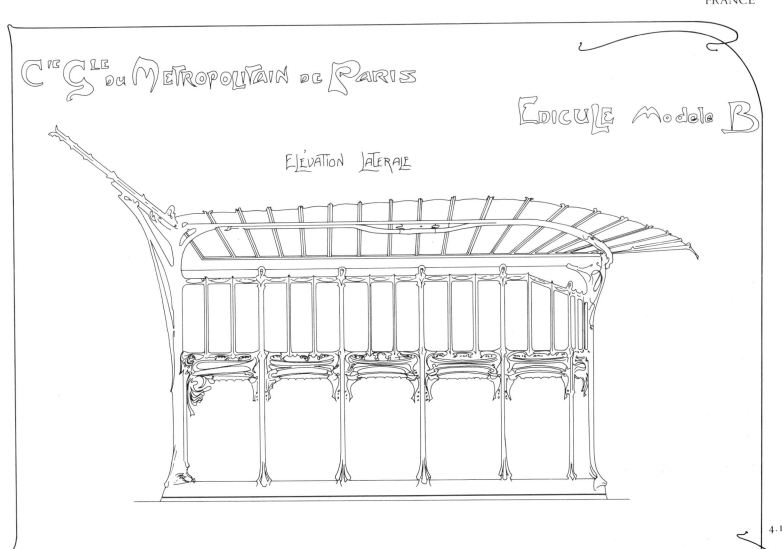

Cie Gle du Metropolitain de Paris

Edicule Modele B

Elévation Laterale

4.10

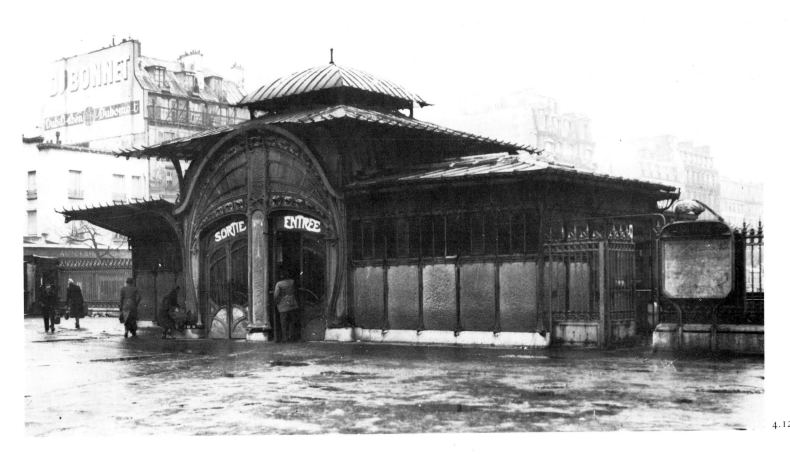

4.12

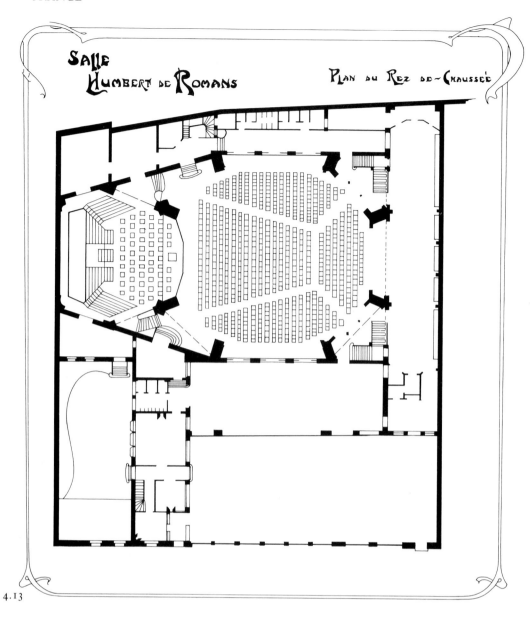

SALLE HUMBERT DE ROMANS — PLAN DU REZ DE-CHAUSSÉE

4.13

wrought iron or cast iron. Elsewhere he was to use a surprising combination of wrought iron and cast iron, whereas Belgian Art Nouveau resolutely refused the use of the latter, considering it not only as vulgar but more importantly as totally *non-plastic*, that is, without any form of its own or any individual characteristics to guide the imagination and hand of the artist. Nevertheless, it was in this field that Guimard was to realise his most startling imaginative work – the natural world suggested fantastic forms of animals or human masks, akin to those of Japanese art, of a disquieting strangeness.

The obvious ease with which Guimard worked in cast iron was soon to make him a true specialist. His work was distributed from the St-Dizier foundries in the Haute-Marne under the pleasing title of *'Fontes Artistiques pour Constructions, Fumisterie, Articles de Jardin et Sépultures, Style Guimard'* (Artistic cast iron work for Buildings, Stove-setting and Articles for gardens and tombs, in the style of Guimard).[9] It was in his entrances for the Paris underground, however, that Guimard found his most prodigious outlet. He used the principle of moulded cast iron masks which hung from a beam made up of metal sections, and created, as a sign for the entrances, an astonishing cast iron gateway, with uprights like veined stems, ending in the two large flower-like globes of the lamp posts which rise above them.

The opening of the Paris underground in 1900 constituted both a triumph for Guimard and the beginning of his disgrace in the eyes of the public – the clash between the underground entrances and certain historical monuments was no more acceptable to public opinion than the rigorous floral stylisation which is found in all his furniture. Guimard was, however, at the peak of his creative career – in the Humbert de Romans concert hall (whose plans date from 1898), he produced his most mature work. Although an obvious revival

4.13-15 GUIMARD *Humbert de Romans concert hall* Paris 1898, ground floor plan, facade elevation and section (from the original drawings)

SOCIÉTÉ ANONYME IMMOBILIÈRE DE LA RUE SAINT-DIDIER Construction d'une Salle de Musique et Patronage
FAÇADE PRINCIPALE SUR PRÉAU

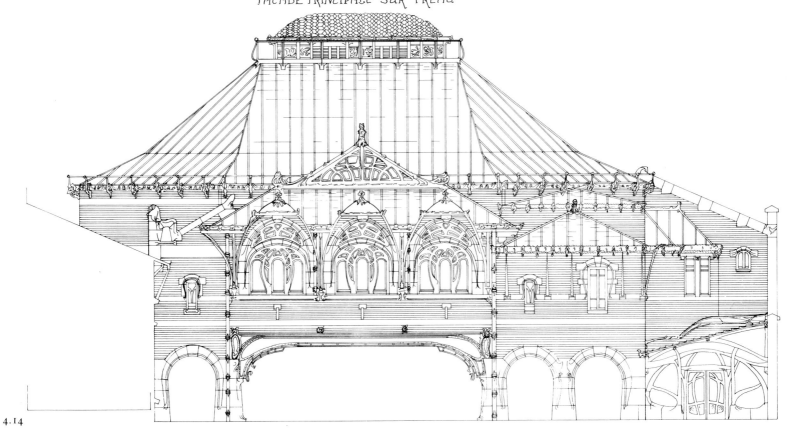

4.14

SOCIÉTÉ ANONYME IMMOBILIÈRE DE LA RUE SAINT-DIDIER Construction d'une Salle de Musique et Patronage
Coupe sur la Salle

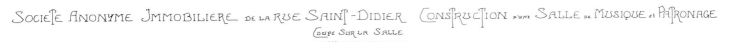

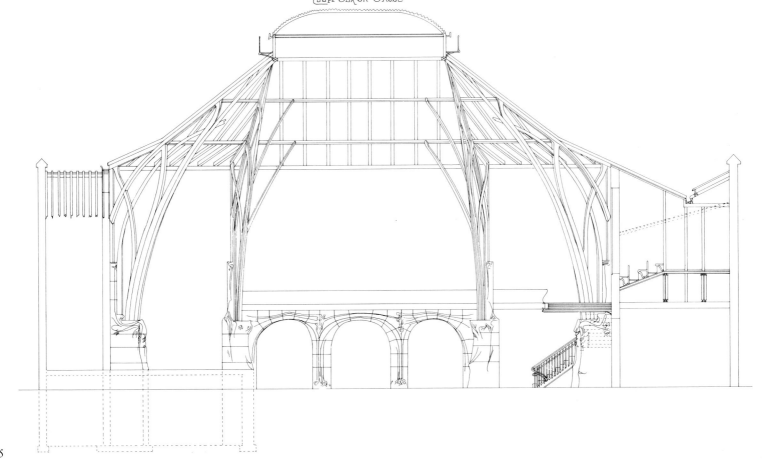

4.15

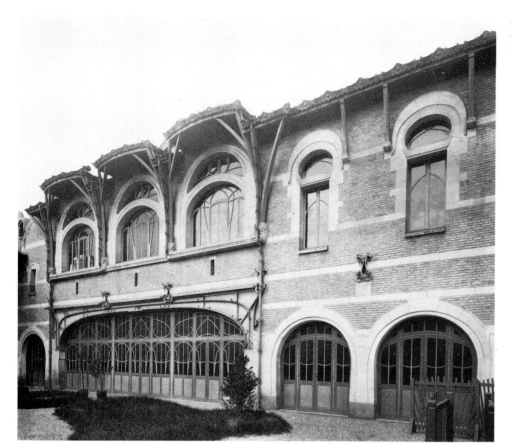

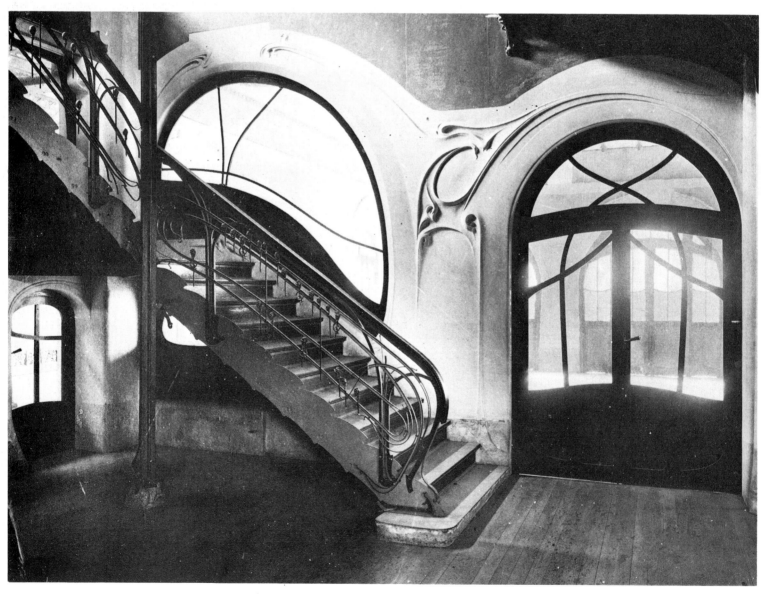

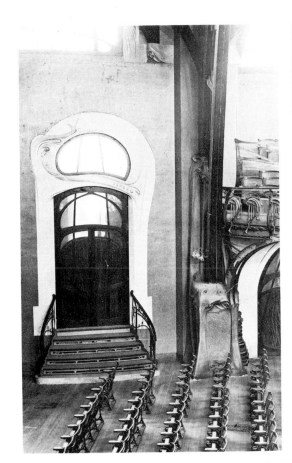

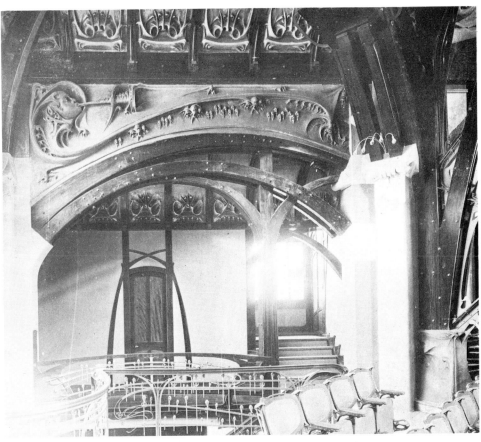

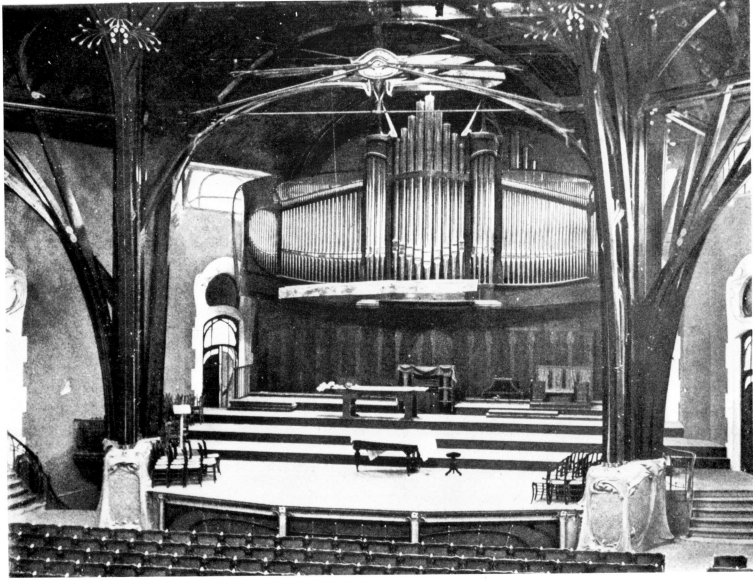

of a similar project for a concert hall published in the *Entretiens*, Guimard overcame the technical limitations connected with the use of cast iron, the only available material thirty years earlier, by constructing large oblique structures in the form of parabolas which he placed on the corners of the generating square.

Such fidelity to the aesthetics of Viollet-le-Duc, despite the formal renaissance engendered by Art Nouveau, is found even in a later work such as the Hôtel Nozal (1905), which was planned on the diagonal of a right angle in exactly the same way as a project for a hôtel in the *Entretiens*. This basic allusion did not, however, curtail the great freedom and ease Guimard showed in the manipulation of curved forms.

Nevertheless, Guimard's period of success was over, and the simple fact that both these buildings have been destroyed (the first as early as 1905!) is symptomatic of the ostracism with which his work was received for more than half a century.

Although Guimard was the most famous of the Parisian Art Nouveau architects, he was by no means the only one, and was followed very closely in reputation by his colleague Jules Lavirotte – a less coherent personality, whose picturesque, eclectic work is a living testimony to the uncertainties of Art Nouveau.[10]

In his early works, Lavirotte proved himself to be an excellent decorator of facades in an academic style – the Louis XV ornamentation of the house at 151 rue de Grenelle (1897) is a skilful transposition of rococo jewellery onto a large scale in the frames of the bays of the doors and windows and the twisted corbelling of the balconies. The same feeling is apparent in the private house at 12 rue Sédillot (1899), but this time the Louis XV is mixed with Gothic and Japanese influences through a refined use of wrought iron.

In the same year Lavirotte designed a Baroque building at 3 square Rapp, decorated with alternate rows of coloured bricks and topped by a large, almost vertical roof covered in coloured tiles (not slate as was customary in Paris). The balconies and the lintels of the bays were surrounded by lavish baked sandstone decoration. The work is not without some technical interest – it constituted one of the first applications of reinforced concrete to the roof of a building. From a purely formal standpoint, the building contains many features borrowed from early seventeenth-century Baroque, and were it not for the originality of the baked sandstone it would be very like the conventional buildings of Victor Laloux, whose monumental architecture contained similar incongruous protuberances, so typical of post-Haussmann Paris.

The brilliant picturesque of square Rapp – a combination of skill and a certain monstrosity not without charm – earned Lavirotte much respect. With his building at 29 avenue Rapp (1901), backing onto the square Rapp house, Lavirotte aroused a prodigious movement of admiration among his colleagues, winning him first prize in the competition for facades in the Ville de Paris, and a no less great feeling of stupefaction among the public.

It is true that the building – which its owner, Alexandre Bigot, wanted from the outset to be a living memorial to the glory of baked sandstone facing – seems totally incongruous in its Parisian context: only the first two floors (corresponding to the statutory sub-foundation) are in ashlar, the rest being a skeleton of reinforced concrete entirely covered in slabs of baked sandstone (which imitates an ashlar covering, but of a browny-green colour shot through with copper-coloured lights). The decoration of the doorway and the lintels on the ground floor consists of large coils of soft ferns, interlaced with women's faces and bodies. The orderly composition of the upper floors is broken by a powerful arch projected between the two bay-windows of the facade, and supporting an elegant arcaded loggia. Above, the brown tiled roof, pierced by sky-lights which seem almost late Gothic in character, accentuates the asymmetry of the building and accommodates a terrace garden. Only the floral decoration of the sub-foundation is really in an Art Nouveau style: there are also neo-Assyrian twin-headed bulls and a profusion of melting details which could be described as 'néo-gothique en saindoux'.

The building in avenue Rapp, in a conveniently situated area which was still being developed at the time, was much praised by the press and became a symbol of everything unwholesome in the Art Nouveau movement. It is true that Lavirotte, to attract attention, fully exploited the resources of the floral

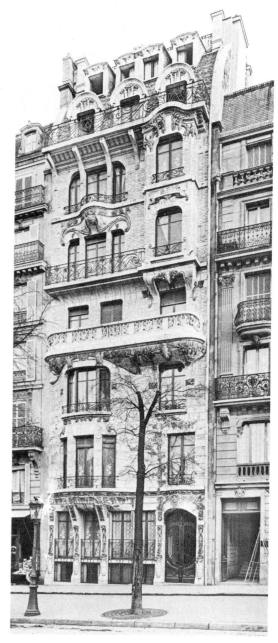

4.21 LAVIROTTE *34 avenue Wagram* Paris 1904 (contemporary photograph)

4.22 LAVIROTTE *3 square Rapp* Paris 1899 (contemporary photograph)

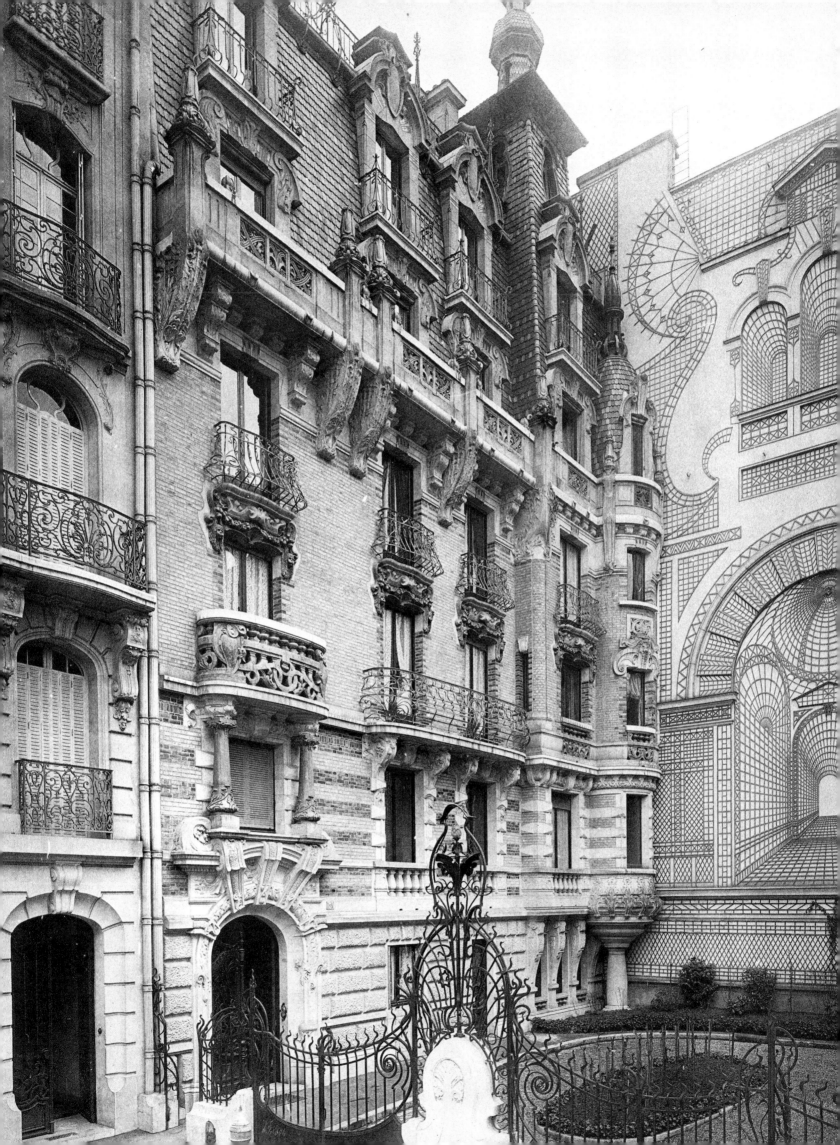

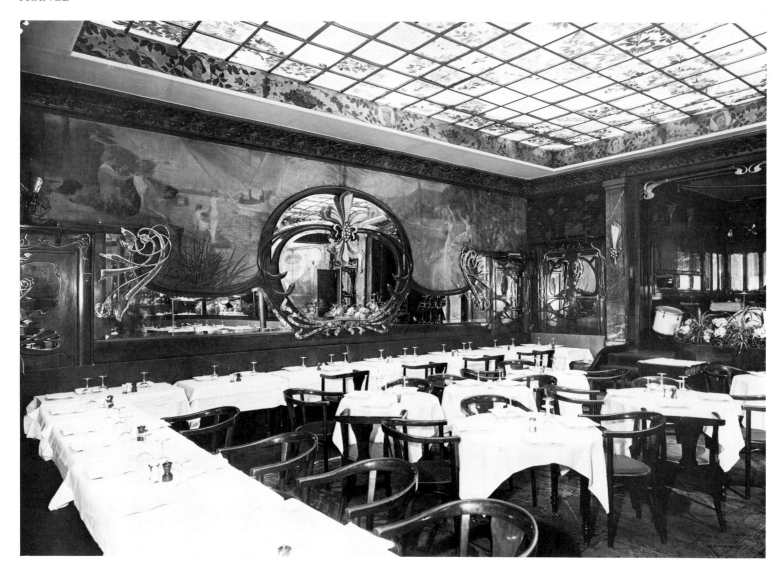

style, infusing it with a character of soft sensuality, to a point where it seems almost to drip unpleasantly. When it was a question of a conventional building, however, the same man was capable of being a lot more prudent – the floral decoration of 134 rue de Grenelle (1903) is simply a discreet endorsement of a very reassuring monumental composition in ashlar.

A little later, in 1904, Lavirotte tried a final experiment in baked sandstone for the small apartment building in avenue Wagram (now the 'Céramic Hôtel') – this time a very controlled effort, perhaps because Art Nouveau extravagances were by then out of fashion. The facade of the building is partly milky coloured sandstone, partly white brick, with rather lifeless floral decorations in the style of Louis XV offset on the ground floor by an elegant arrangement of climbing plants which coil around the bays of the doors and windows in a very realistic manner. The 'settling down' process found in Lavirotte was common to all the Art Nouveau artists (led by Guimard), and heralded the total disappearance of the movement in a final burst of floral decoration. In future, Lavirotte was to retreat even further, returning to ashlar in his building at 23 avenue de Messine (1908). The fact that he was awarded first prize in the competition for facades for the third year running (after avenue Rapp and avenue Wagram) proved that his personal development was in line with that of public opinion, now devoted to the upholding of traditional values in the decoration of facades and to a respect for a certain normality of composition – the denial of individual originality was only one of the undying cults worshipped by the urban commissioners of post-Haussmann Paris.

There were other figures who played important roles in the Paris of 1900, especially as decorators: architects like Louis Marnez who designed the restaurant 'Chez Maxim's', and continued until the 1930s to build a number of apartment buildings in the style of Louis XVI 'à la Neufforge' (that is, in a neo-classical style which strove to be bizarre in the French Piranesi-inspired tradition) or cabinet-makers like Louis Majorelle, who in 1901 was responsible

4.23 MARNEZ *'Chez Maxim's'* Paris c.1900, interior (photograph Chevojon)

4.24 SAUVAGE *Villa Majorelle* Nancy 1898–1900 (contemporary photograph)

4.25 SAUVAGE *Paris Exhibition* 1900, Loïe Fuller pavilion, final design (from the original drawing)

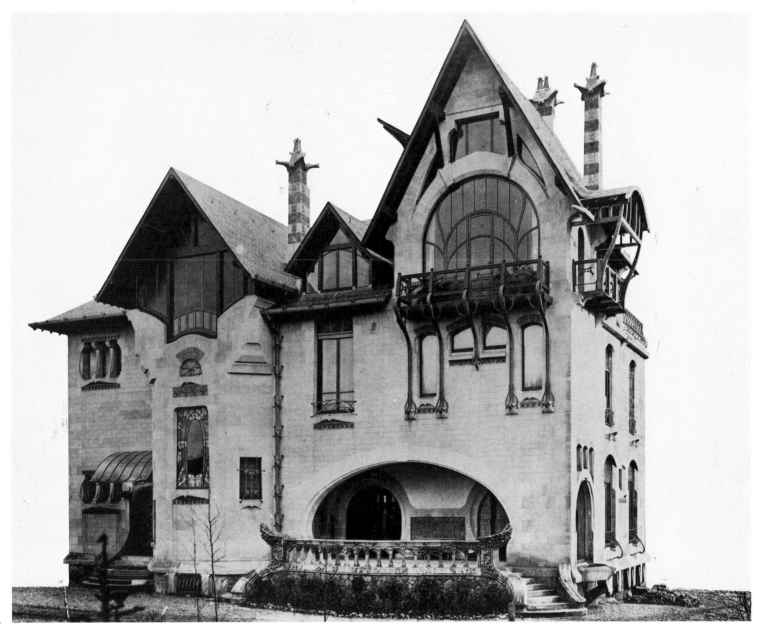

4.24

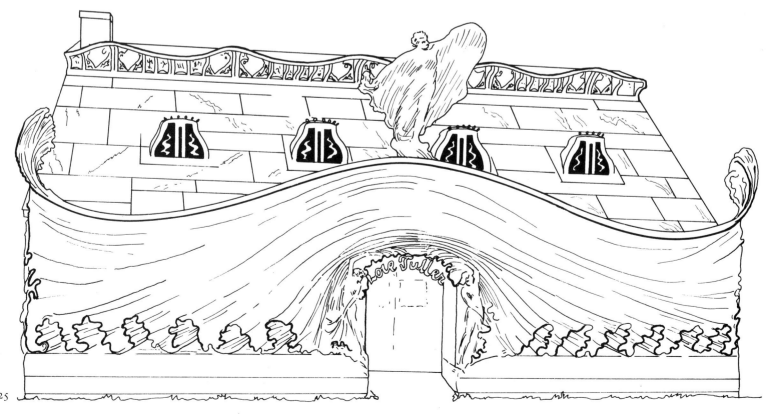

4.25

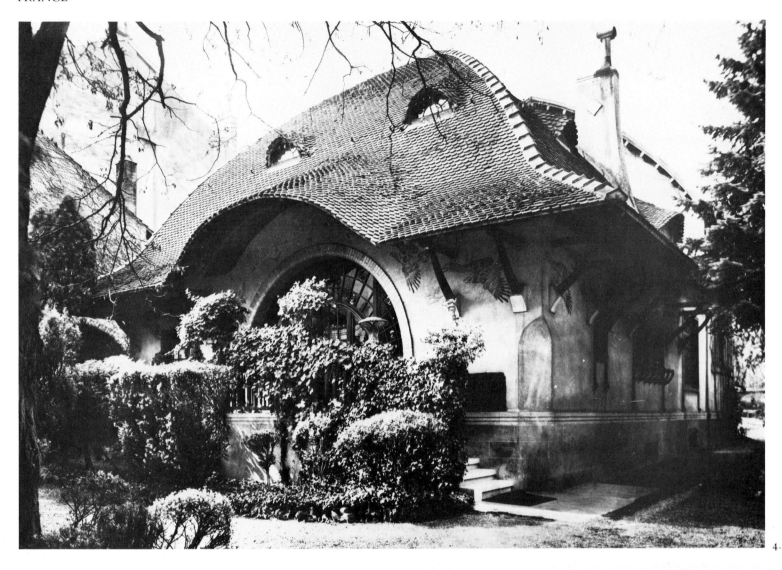

4.26

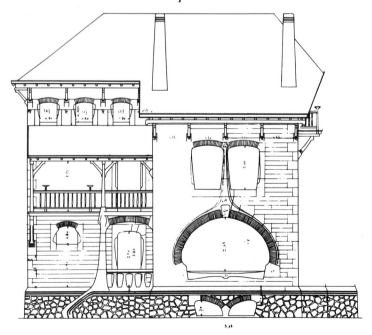

PARC DE SAURUPT.
Mr FERNBACH.
FACADE. OUEST.

ECHELLE DE 0,02 POUR 1 METRE

DRESSÉ PAR L'ARCHITECTE SOUSSIGNÉ
A NANCY LE 5 MARS 1902
E. André

4.27

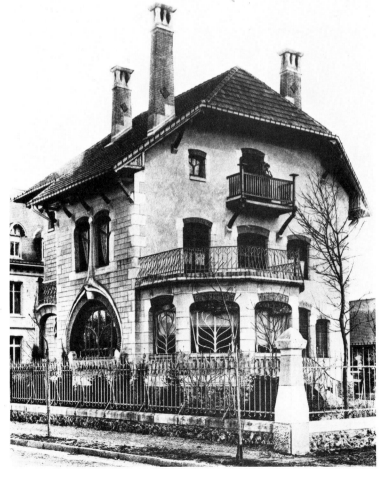

4.28

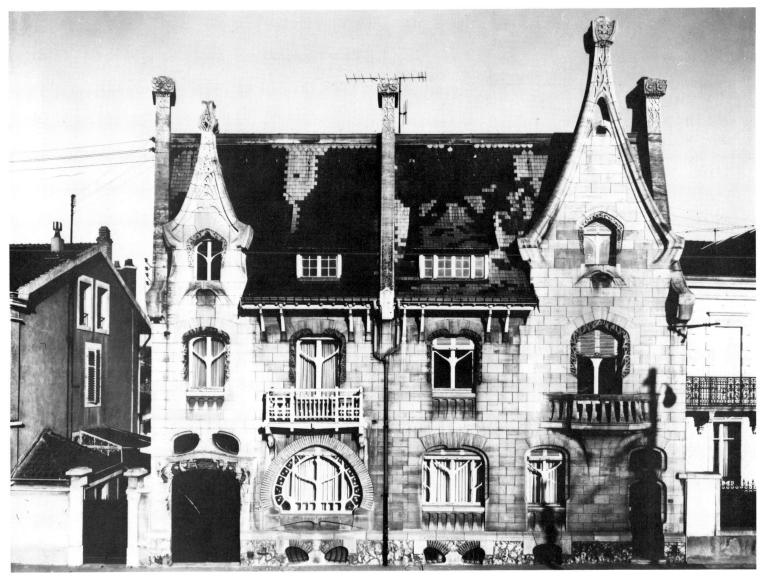

4.29 ANDRE *92-92 bis quai Claude-le-Lorrain* Nancy 1903 (photograph Rose)

4.26 ANDRE *30 avenue du Sergent-Blandan* Nancy 1903 (photograph Rose)

4.27-28 ANDRE *Villa 'Les Glycines'* Nancy 1902, elevation and exterior view (contemporary photograph)

for the admirable décor of the 'Lucas Carton' restaurant in the place de la Madeleine. Many people emulated them, and became specialists in the decoration of large Parisian restaurants such as 'Chez Jullian', 'Chez Rougeot', or 'Vagenende', spreading a commercialised style of Art Nouveau which in its most popular form provided decorative ceramic tiles for bistrots (of which charming examples can still be found in Paris), and twisted wooden shopfronts.

Majorelle was also active in his native town of Nancy, the other major centre of French Art Nouveau, where a whole school of architects and craftsmen grew up around the great ceramist Emile Gallé.

The Nancy School, like Paris, first came to prominence in the field of decorative arts, thanks to its ceramists and glassmakers. Emile Gallé himself passed from one technique to another in the production of his first pieces of furniture, and his work was continued by Eugène Vallin, who had been trained as a neo-Gothic cabinet-maker, and who was to create some of the finest Art Nouveau furniture made in Nancy, often in collaboration with Majorelle.

The transition from furniture to architecture was not easy. Vallin attempted it, not always with great success, as for example in 22 rue de la Commanderie, built between 1901 and 1902 in collaboration with the Nancy architect Georges Biet. It took the return of Majorelle to his native town, and the ambition he felt on settling there to construct an exemplary building, for this desire to crystallise. Majorelle was helped at the beginning by advice from the young Parisian architect-decorator Henri Sauvage, whom he knew through his wallpapers which he had ordered for his projected villa in Nancy. Sauvage gradually took over as official architect, and created an extraordinary villa which remains the major architectural achievement of the Nancy school.[12]

The Villa Majorelle drew both from the experiences of rationalist architecture and the picturesque, and presented an equivalence of distribution/mass

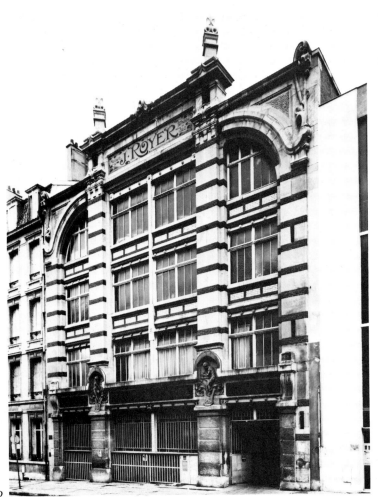

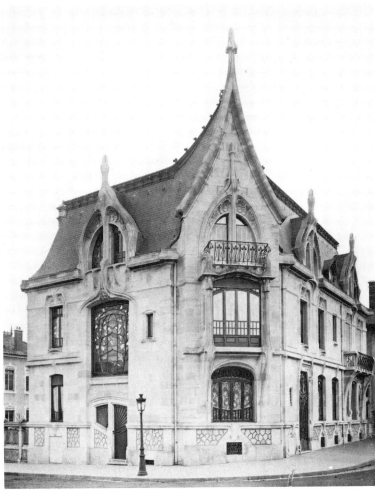

4.30

4.31

which made the organisation of the interior particularly legible. Nothing is gratuitous – every projection of the facade, every articulation of the roof, every opening expresses some interior function. And the decoration exists only as a means of accentuating the main features of the building – the fragile graphic network forms a counterpoint to the large bare surfaces of the wall panels or windows, and brings them to life.

Sauvage is important as one of the great Art Nouveau decorators, despite the fact that almost all his work has now disappeared, as in the case of the Café de Paris in the avenue de l'Opéra, or the Magasins Jansen in rue Royale. With the Loïe Fuller pavilion for the 1900 Exhibition, he showed his ability to work in the grand ornamental style of Art Nouveau, in this case with emblematic tendencies.

Even at Nancy, the only figures who could rival the Sauvage/Majorelle duo were on the one hand Emile André, and on the other Lucien Weissenburger. André settled in Nancy in 1902, which was the year in which he produced both the Parc de Saurupt (and in particular the villa 'Les Glycines' in the style of Majorelle) and the fine apartment building at 69 avenue Foch. The following year, he created his most famous work – the semi-detached houses on the quai Claude-le-Lorrain, which constitute a pleasant variation on the neo-Gothic style, this time of late Gothic inspiration with a few 'balneal' touches. The studio he built for one of his friends in the avenue du Sergent-Blandan shows that he was in touch both with contemporary popular architecture and with the German Jugendstil, especially that of Weimar. Generally speaking, André handled the picturesque detail with a sharp sense of rhythm and scale. If the inspiration is never very profound, it is at least always gracious – and justified.

Weissenburger is much less consistent. A little older, he dabbled in the eclecticism of the 1880s and remained faithful to rationalist aesthetics – the Royer Press, built in 1900, is a stone, iron, brick and glass construction which could even be taken for a Formigé building! Later, he was to be inspired by Art Nouveau – as in his house for the printer Bergeret (a specialist in post cards), built at 24 rue Lionnois between 1903 and 1904. His decorative style, heavily

4.30 WEISSENBURGER *Royer Press* Nancy 1900 (photograph Rose)

4.31-32 WEISSENBURGER *24 rue Lionnois* Nancy 1903-04, exterior view (contemporary photograph) and facade detail (photograph Bastien)

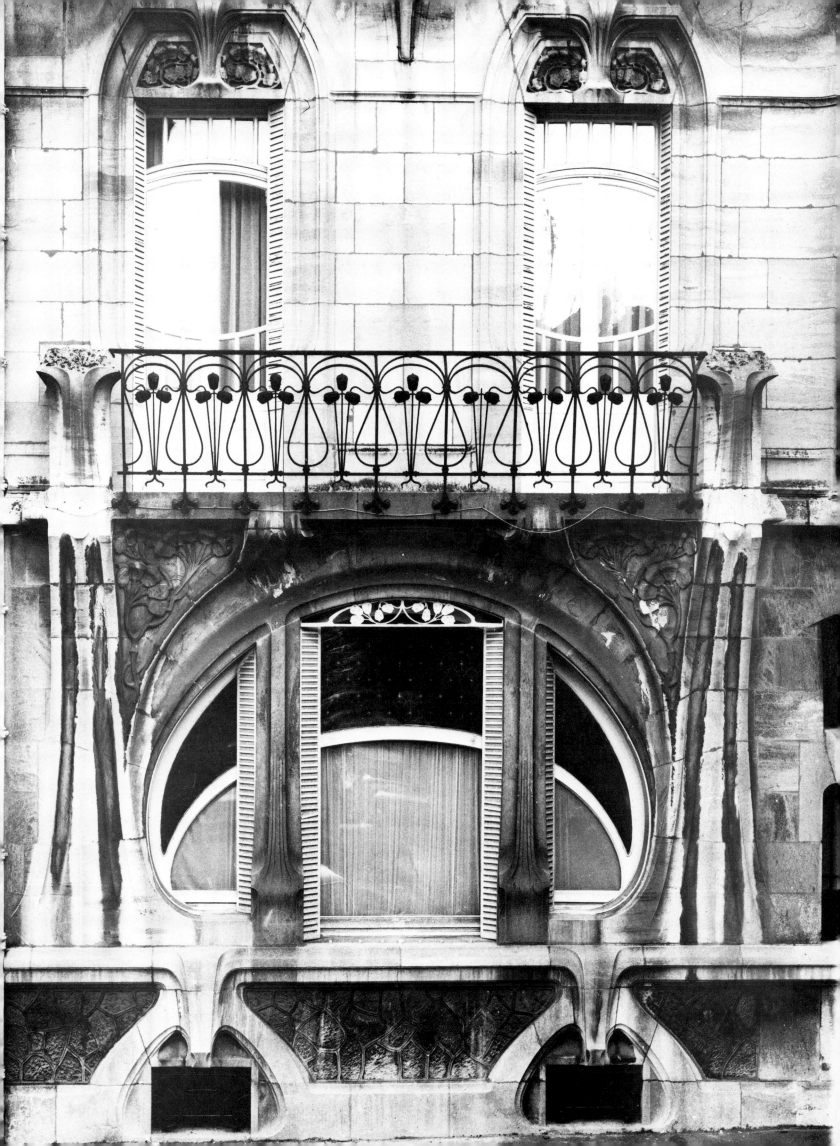

FRANCE

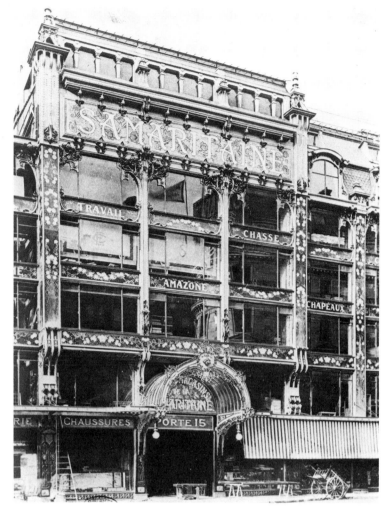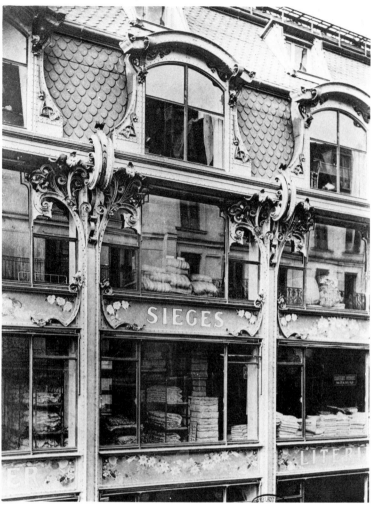

influenced by Eugène Vallin, was a paroxysm of late Gothic treated with much elegance and invention in the ornamental detail. Most important is the moulding, and the floral ornamentation is adapted to it, providing a discreet accompaniment which highlights the major accents.

For his own house in the boulevard Charles V (1904) Weissenburger again confirmed his talents as an ornamentalist. In the same building, however, the dislocated arrangement and brutal articulation of volumes reflects a desire for a formal expressionism which is still closely linked to the traditions of picturesque architecture, and is at odds with the rigid frame of the rectangular box which encloses the construction – a reflection of a Haussmann-like desire for urban order.

The backward, often incoherent character of the work of the Nancy school prevented it from becoming the major home of French Art Nouveau architecture, as it was for the decorative arts. By its very indecision it remained a provincial art – certainly more fully developed than elsewhere, but steeped in the surrounding eclecticism from which it never managed to escape. It is nevertheless notable that the Nancy School was able to exist as a recognised architectural movement – for elsewhere Art Nouveau was the product of either isolated individuals (as in the work of Charles Bourgeois at Roubaix) or is found only in unique works, the accidental echo of a Parisian fashion. One could mention, among many others, the work of Jobbé-Duval or Emmanuel Leray in Rennes, architect of the Leray house, rue de Viarmes (1906), or even the unusual glazed ceramic decoration of the facade of a block of flats at 14 place de la République, Cherbourg, although no other such building exists in the town. No doubt one day a chance sales catalogue brought the contractor or local client in contact with a Parisian manufacturer . . .

This sort of diffusion shows the limitations of a style which was above all decorative and for which the name 'art floral' is more apt than the somewhat excessive 'art nouveau'. Certain contemporaries were well aware of this, and refused to follow the fashion, continuing instead the innovative development begun by the rationalists twenty-five years previously.

The most notable of these was certainly Frantz Jourdain,[13] designer of the

4.33-34 JOURDAIN *Grands Magasins de la Samaritaine* Paris 1905-07 (contemporary photographs)

Opposite left
LAVIROTTE *29 avenue Rapp* Paris 1900-01, details of facade and doorway (photographs Joly)

Opposite above right
LAVIROTTE *34 avenue Wagram* Paris 1904, detail of facade (photograph Joly)

Opposite below right
GUIMARD *Castel Béranger* Paris 1894-98, detail of doorway (photograph Sapieha)

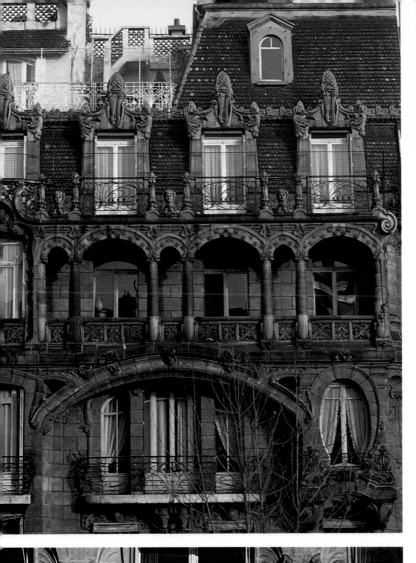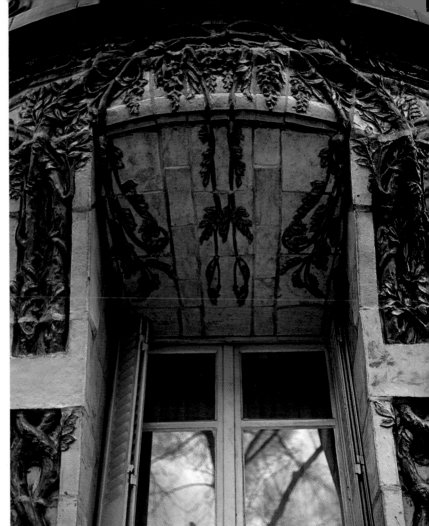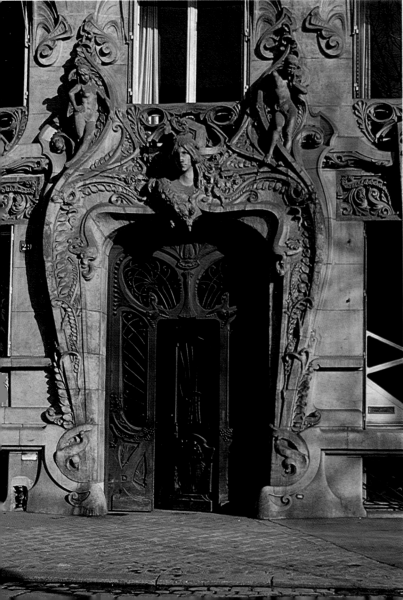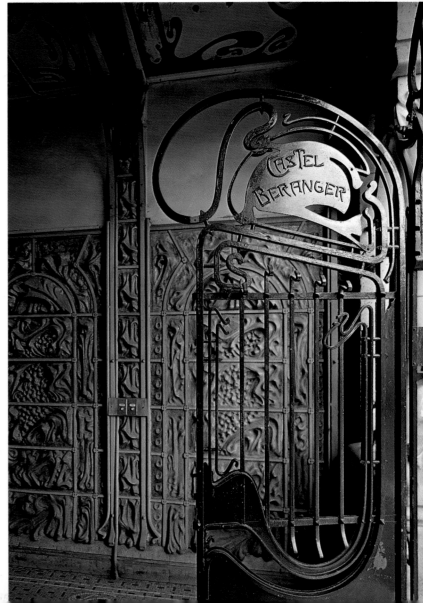

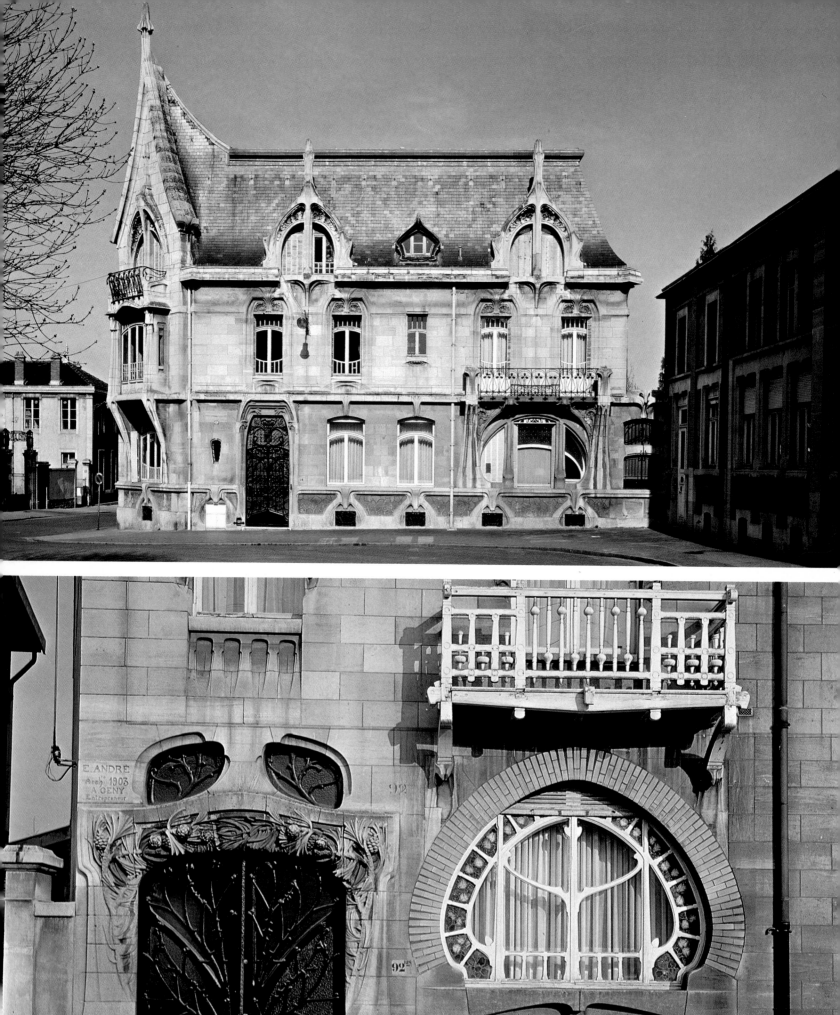

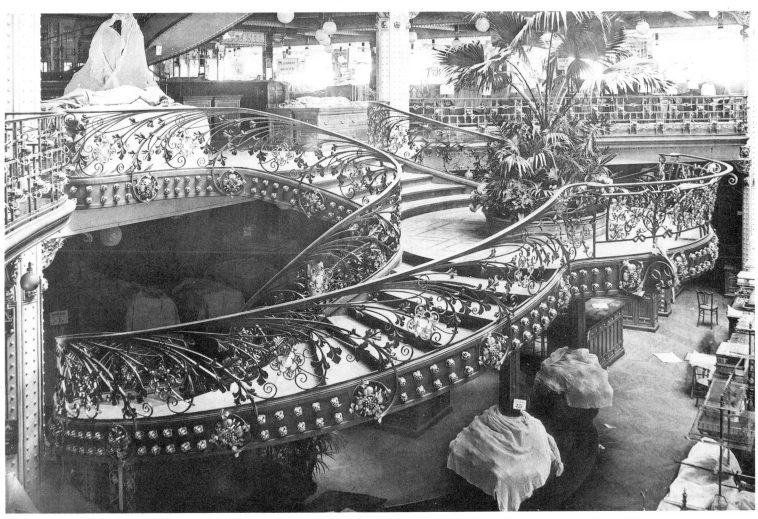

4.35 BINET *Grands Magasins du Printemps* Paris
c.1907, remodelled interior (contemporary
photograph)

Grands Magasins de la Samaritaine in Paris (1905). Although it is tempting
to make comparisons, 'la Samaritaine' in fact owes little to Sullivan's Carson
Pirie Scott department store (1899-1904) and is more indebted to Paul Sédille's
'Printemps', using the same steel construction, decorative mosaics and ornamental structures as well as a similar arrangement of fluid spaces around
the large covered courtyard of the interior. Jourdain, an extremist, was to
complete this model French department store by replacing the opaque floors
with glass tiles decorated with translucent tracery – an exceptional idea which
together with the artificiality of the electric lighting created an elusive atmosphere, the lights seeming to come from nowhere and sink down, from floor to
floor, to the basement of the store. The building was now totally iron and
glass, an architecture of light and space admirably combined. A rich wrought
iron decoration, made up of finely-drawn leaves, penetrates all the angles of the
framework and covers, this time in the form of mosaic friezes, the posts and
panels of the balustrades.

Another great Parisian decorator, René Binet, designer of the admirable
'Porte de la Concorde' for the 1900 Exhibition, was also working along the
same lines as Paul Sédille. The huge steel arch spanning the Cours-la-Reine was
framed on either side by two large riveted triangular pillars, and topped by the
symbolic ship and the allegory of the City of Paris. This composition, which
marked the entrance to the exhibition, was covered with multicoloured
cabochons made of glazed pottery and affixed to the metal. Binet also
participated in the project for the Grand Palais and, although it is not certain,
he was probably the designer of the admirable steel structure which made up
the interior vaulting. In his design for the new 'Printemps' store in 1907, he
adopted Sédille's solution, which he amplified, adding delicate polychromatic
decoration (only the facades have survived after a fire in the interior which also
destroyed Sédille's work). Binet continued his innovative architectural experiments until his death in 1911, and his work, like that of Jourdain, marked the
rejection of a certain form of Art Nouveau and the desire, in the radical fringe
of the architectural profession, to establish a continuity between the prototypes
of rationalism found in the 1880s and the 'modern' character of an emergent

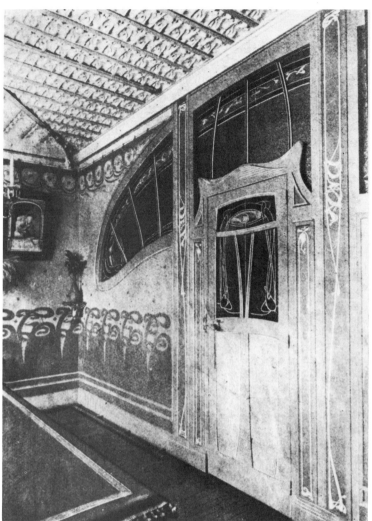

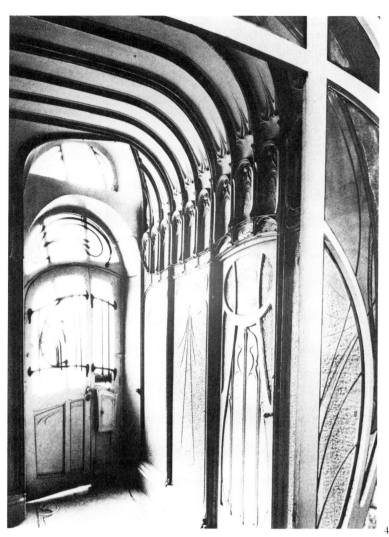

4·36

4·37

architecture, above considerations of fashion and instant success.

The work of the engineer François Hennebique was more limited and architecturally less sure, but nevertheless innovative in the use he made of reinforced concrete, of which he was France's largest contractor. If the apartment building on rue Danton (where he had his office) was undoubtedly a fine demonstration of technology, it was deplorably designed from a stylistic standpoint, displaying an enfeebled academicism. On the other hand, the improbable house which the engineer built for himself at Bourg-la-Reine in 1904 provides a staggering demonstration of the possibilities of overhanging concrete. As a simple demonstration – taken to the point of absurdity – it cannot be faulted.

The use of reinforced concrete, a form of construction which was both skeletal and moulded, presented some difficulties in its adaptation to the formal language of Art Nouveau. While both Binet and Jourdain had been able to master the elegant delicacy of iron, others failed in their attempts at construction in cement. The transposition attempted in 1904 by P. Auscher in his Félix-Potin apartment building, rue de Rennes, was based on the casting potential of the material and was an attempt to transpose the pliable cast iron forms of Guimard's style onto a large scale – a costly, inconvenient and non-repeatable process. For unlike cast iron moulds, which could be easily re-used, a framework moulded in concrete could not be used more than once without incurring great difficulties, each building having specific characteristics of site and plan which profoundly affect its requirements.

The architect Anatole de Baudot, one of Viollet-le-Duc's favourite pupils and one of the major forces behind the respected body of the Architectes des Monuments Historiques, reacted very differently when he explored the possibilities of reinforced concrete[14] as a result of a meeting with the engineer Cottancin.

In de Baudot alone we can see the transition from Second Empire to Art Nouveau. Winner of the competition for the Church of Rambouillet in 1864, he used the principles of overhang in his building, while his partial recourse to

4.36 GUIMARD *Hôtel Roy* Paris 1898, interior (contemporary photograph)

4.37 GUIMARD *Maison Coilliot* Lille 1897-1900, interior (photograph Miotto Muret)

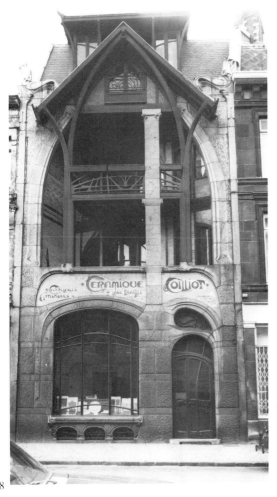

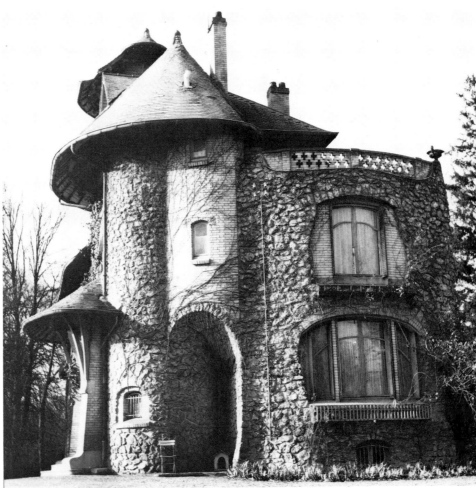

4.38

4.39

4.38 GUIMARD *Maison Coilliot*, façade
(photograph Godoli)

4.39 GUIMARD *Castel d'Orgeval* Paris 1904-05
(photograph Pelzel)

cast iron showed him to be an admirer of Viollet-le-Duc. His early schools (for example the Lycée Lakanal in Sceaux, 1882) were examples of the sort of inflexible construction which was later to influence Vaudremer himself. Such analytical work in brick and cast iron was not enough, however; in 1892 (at the end of a course in the History of Architecture, which he was giving to the future Architectes des Monuments Historiques at the Trocadéro centre), de Baudot met one of his pupils and admirers, Cottancin, who was just beginning his research. From the exchange between the two men the 'Cottancin system' was developed – a system of fine, sinewy concrete structures which de Baudot was to use for the first time in 1893 for a pavilion at Antony.

He then had the idea of applying this system to the whole of a building in the church of St-Jean-de-Montmartre, which was built in 1897, with plans dating from 1894 to 1895. De Baudot's architectural language was derived both from Gothic architecture (in the elevation and his use of the principle of intersection, a characteristic of Gothic rib vaults) and from Byzantine architecture by the use he made of a central square. Structure and decoration are closely linked, and are based on the intersection of the lines of the skeleton, which are filled in by a thin (7 cm.) veil of cement. In fact, the structure was so audacious that it provoked a veritable scandal. A very damning statement, drawn up by three of the best-known rationalist architects, ordered the closure of the building to the public for three years until the facts themselves had testified to its solidity.

An exceptional inventor, de Baudot continued his research into reinforced concrete structures until 1914, and anticipated the work of people like Pier-Luigi Nevi by half a century. Unfortunately, the radically innovative character of his work and of the related ornamental system he evolved (a décor of ashlar cabochons, coated in wet concrete, which transposed Binet's research into the field of cement) made Anatole de Baudot a utopian architect. It is a great pity that none of his projects after 1900 was ever realised, for his was undoubtedly the boldest and most attractive work of the first decade of this century.

Jourdain, Binet, de Baudot – three major figures of an Art Nouveau based on structural innovation and the keen search for a *bonne forme* of ornament, to be attained by a total equivalence of structure and ornament. Floral Art Nouveau, dynamic as it was, seemed very limited in comparison. It developed in the opposite direction – uninterested in structural innovation, it accepted programmes, techniques and customs hallowed by experience. Its revolution took place elsewhere – in the powerful vitality it injected into decoration and in its mad desire for a plastic renovation which made it undertake the difficult transformation of neo-Gothic into a new language, if not into a veritable 'new art'.

Public opinion was very sensitive to the limitations of this purely decorative movement, especially as the flamboyant image given it by someone like Jules Lavirotte was not always appreciated. A reaction built up as a consequence, unusual in that it arose almost simultaneously with the actual production of Art Nouveau, a fact not always appreciated by the critics. Strangely enough, this almost implicit denial came from the most reputed Art Nouveau architects, almost as if their own work embarrassed them and they were trying to escape it by a divergent, less exacting route.

The 'balneal' (literally 'bathing resort', or picturesque) style, so popular between 1890 and 1930, can be considered either as a non-monumental branch of Art Nouveau or as an alternative style in its own right. Both standpoints are equally possible, depending on the date from which the movement is viewed – from 1895 or 1905, before or after the turn of the century which saw both the birth and death of Art Nouveau.

Guimard himself was above all a master of picturesque architecture, as his first works clearly show (Maison Roszé, 1891; Maison Jassedé, 1893). His conversion to Art Nouveau was realised through an essentially picturesque work – the Castel Béranger, with its millstone and brick walls, its complex masses and its marked asymmetry belongs wholly to the anti-monumental language of the picturesque, and the same can also be said of the Maison Coilliot in Lille with its vaguely regionalist characteristics.

Even during his most brilliant period, Guimard remained a convinced exponent of the picturesque – the Castel Henriette in Sèvres (1899-1900) was an improbable display of various types of architecture in the style of a châlet, forming a composite whole which was a humourous variation on suburban architecture. Less ridiculous, but typically *balneal* was Villa 'La Surprise' at Cabourg (1903), the first of a series of buildings in a more sober style (equivalent in the *balneal* branch of Art Nouveau to urban works such as the Villa Agar or the Villa Flore in Paris), of which the beautiful Castel d'Orgeval (1904-05) is the most interesting example. Even in his later works, Guimard still remained faithful to this style, using it for the modest 'Châlet Blanc' in Sceaux (1908), the Villa Hemsy at St-Cloud (1913) and even in 'La Guimardière' in Vaucresson (c. 1930) which was built during a period of total artistic self-denial.

The monumental Guimard of the floral style and the picturesque Guimard of cavernous millstone found their counterparts in Emile André at Nancy, as they did in many others – of the two villas built by André in 1902 for the Parc de Saurupt, one is in ashlar and the other, the Villa 'Les Roches', with its elegant little lodge for the caretaker of the park, is in millstone and is a magnificent example of the picturesque style.

Since these two forms of expression, radically different from a plastic standpoint, could co-exist in the work of two of the greatest French Art Nouveau architects, it is very difficult to see them as opposed movements, and it is important to realise that eclecticism, by introducing considerations of style into the architectural syllabus (and by creating a fundamental distinction between urban and suburban, as Lewis Mumford has pointed out[15]), left Art Nouveau no choice other than to conform. Strangely enough, the radical opposition of various 'manners' is of no chronological significance – the period as a whole was marked by a diversity of plastic languages, expressed superficially by the variety of historical references.

This explanation, however, was no longer to hold true in the work of other architects after 1900 – Henri Sauvage for example, in his progression towards a freedom of form, used the *balneal* only as a basic stepping-stone. At the Atelier Pascal he was influenced by the example of his teacher and by the regionalist atmosphere which the latter seemed to communicate to his pupils, and he used this to free himself from the facile virtuosity of the floral style. The

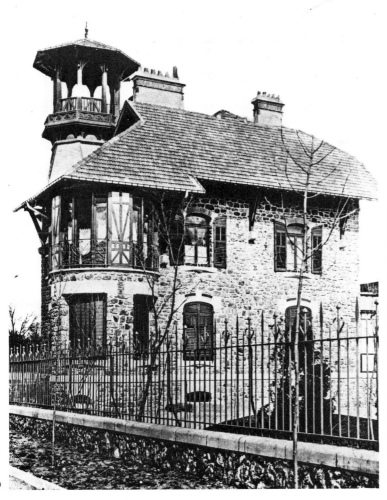

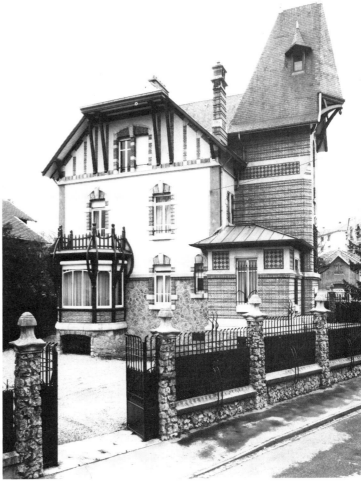

4.40

4.41

4.40 GUTTON & HORNECKER *Villa 'Les Marguerites'* Nancy 1905 (contemporary photograph)

4.41 WEISSENBURGER *Villa Lang* Nancy 1908 (photograph Bastien)

Villa Oceana in Biarritz dates from 1903, and is a severe work, built from quarried granite, without decoration, and with brutalist details – both in the articulation of masses and the treatment of ornament. At the same time, Sauvage tried to renew his decorative language by abandoning the curve in favour of rigorously analysed and articulated elements: historically it was a return to the lessons of rationalism – almost a form of plagiarism for Sauvage which nevertheless helped him to cross the stylistic barrier. The idea of functionality in ornament had again become fashionable. Art Nouveau, as such, was dead – it was 1903.

The regionalist reaction was shared by all of the Atelier Pascal (Provensal, Sézille and the Swiss architect Laverrière), but its influence was far greater, affecting many Art Nouveau artists. While the Villa 'Les Marguerites' by Henri Gutton and Joseph Hornecker (1905) in the Parc de Saurupt in Nancy is pure picturesque in its skilful mixture of châlet style and millstone, the Villa Lang (1905) by Weissenburger is altogether different – here, among the composite diversity of elements, we find an amusing citation of the work of Sauvage in the direct imitation of the covered stairs of the Villa Oceana.

Balneal and regionalism were inextricably mixed. *Balneal*, as a conventional style, became increasingly marked by regionalism – the Villa Oceana at Biarritz, for example, is typically neo-Breton – for reasons which were at first purely picturesque. Later, the preoccupation with regionalism grew more insistent and became an essential feature of all suburban architecture until the 1930s (and even today, this final stage of Art Nouveau is still alive in certain provinces).

Regionalism is the *balneal* equivalent of Art Deco. Supporting a mythical 'return to nature', it presented idealised images of rural architecture. Using the social world of the village as a reference, the architecture it produced was thus in principle 'village-like'. Certain urbanists, basing their views on the theories of Camillo Sitte, believed it possible to reproduce this environment in an urban context, as was the case with Louis Bonnier who, after drawing up the important Parisian bye-law of 1902 which gave the city its post-Haussmann apartment blocks, constructed many typically regionalist buildings using brick and tiles, such as the schools in rue Sextus-Michel and rue Schutzenberger (1912) or the fine swimming pool at Butte-aux-Cailles (1924).

Although it may seem far removed from Art Nouveau, regionalism was nevertheless clearly derived from it, prolonging the use of flexible forms – albeit with more restraint – and becoming a sort of 'sober' Art Nouveau, producing works without any pointless extravagance which were perfectly adapted to the situation and working methods. Regionalism was in fact only a negation of Art Nouveau in so far as it claimed to have gone beyond it and brought it under control.

It is interesting to find an identical reaction in the urban field, also marked by a conscious regionalism. This reaction, as can be seen in Parisian housing of the period, soon showed its hostility to the architecture of Lavirotte (and even Guimard), defining itself as a middle course in Art Nouveau, neither eclectic nor formalist.

The link between this prudent formula and Art Nouveau, with important works by people like Guimard or Lavirotte, has not been so neglected as the unexpected relationship between Art Nouveau and *balneal*. Both of these are simply a convenient means of categorisation, however (urban or 'anti-urban' as the case might be). It is not a question of a different language, simply the same one refined.

The ashlar apartment block built in 1902 by the Perret brothers at 119 avenue Wagram was a confirmation of the new feeling of restraint – a restraint found also in Sauvage's house at 22 rue Laugier (1904) or in the villa he built later (1908) for his client Majorelle in Compiègne (this house, 'Majorelle-bis', reveals a lot about the evolution of Art Nouveau over the preceding ten years).

A whole architectural movement developed in construction, especially in Paris, from 1907 to 1908[17] which tried to make use of the lessons gained from Art Nouveau and of its plastic system in the monumental field while avoiding its excessive iconography, whether explicit (floral art) or implicit (oneirism). Often described as 'French' art[18] because of the use it made of mediaeval and regional sources, this trend blossomed in the fine apartment buildings of Maurice Du Bois d'Auberville at 1-5 avenue Mozart (1907-08), which still showed traces of Japanese influences, in those of Louis Sorel like that at 29 rue de Sèvres (1912), or in the work of a decorator like Théo Petit at 132 rue de Courcelles (1907), who was responsible for some of the finest Parisian Art Nouveau furniture.

This 'sober' (or rather 'softened') Art Nouveau – for its plastic dynamics were developed with much elegance and restraint – was even to influence the great 'stars' of the movement. Hector Guimard was very quickly converted to this way of thinking, which brought his post-1900 works nearer to their late Gothic sources (8 Villa de la Réunion, 1904-07; Hôtel Guimard, Villa Flore, 1909-12). Finally, the 'groupe des six' began to become as renowned in the field of architecture through the work of Charles Plumet as it was in the fields of applied art and furniture through Selmersheim or Charpentier: after the model group of apartment buildings he built at 15-21 boulevard Lannes (1906), Plumet was to remain faithful to himself in the sobriety of his form (39 avenue Victor Hugo, 1912-13; 33 rue du Louvre, 1913).

This school, so typical of late Parisian Art Nouveau, has been judged very harshly by modern critics who regard them as mere imitators, soon to be overtaken by the inventions of modern architecture. In 1903 another reaction appeared, simultaneously with the reaction against decoration by the 'softened' Art Nouveau movement, this time far more radical, for it denied Art Nouveau as such. This reaction also tried to create a totally different language, better adapted to the techniques and ideas of the industrial age.

'Studio' architecture was a complete formal system which developed, in the 'Cité industrielle' of Tony Garnier, from new constraints in the construction of reinforced concrete frames.[19] The innovation was not so much in the forms themselves – these had impressed themselves upon the engineers, for material or financial reasons, and had been in use for at least ten years – but rather in the act of putting into practice a syntax based on the evidence of the structure, on the nudity of the planes, and on their geometrical arrangement in elementary forms . . .

The parallel development of Auguste Perret or Henri Sauvage was more pragmatic. In the case of Sauvage in particular, the evolution of his formal

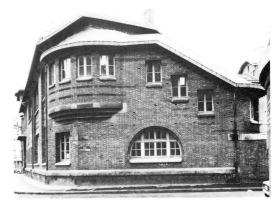

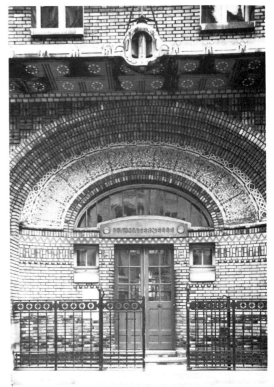

4.42-43 BONNIER *School in rue Sextus-Michel* Paris 1912, facade and entrance detail (photographs Benton)

research had the air of a demonstration. In his Cité l'Argentine, 111 avenue Victor Hugo (1903), he used a steel framework for the last time, reduced to a skeleton by the most rigorous simplification. For the remarkable assembly of workers' houses which he created the same year in rue Trétaigne, he attempted a double transposition: technical (from steel to concrete) and plastic (from a bourgeois apartment building to workers' housing). The systematic character of his development can be seen by the regression which his work was to show over the next few years – the brick apartment building at 20 rue Sévero is much more conventional in form, much less adventurous in technique (and therefore less costly). With the house in rue Vavin (1912-14) and the sociological transposition he made for the Amiraux swimming pool (1923), Sauvage took his system to its furthest limits, at which point it ceased to be purely formal, becoming instead an integral part of a general conception of modern architecture – ranging from the details of construction to urbanism and including all the technical, financial and sociological factors involved in the act of building (which is what Garnier, who remained in a utopian, if sociological field, was unable to do).

The Perret brothers' development, better known than that of Sauvage,[20] might seem more spectacular in that the orthogonality of the forms of the house at 25 bis rue Franklin (which also dated from 1903) was certainly an innovation. To us, it might seem more superficial – the graceful sandstone veneer of Bigot, in a Japanese style, with which Perret covered his facade is a proof of the problems he encountered when it came to creating a new language, for although the geometry is refined, the style is not. The same thing occurred later in the affair of the Théâtre des Champs-Elysées. When in 1912 the Perret brothers succeeded in ousting their Belgian rival Henry van de Velde (undoubtedly the most brilliant European representative of the refined Art Nouveau), it was not to create a revolutionary work, but to fall flatly (under the unhappy influence, in the circumstances, of Antoine Bourdelle) into a sort of neo-classical monumentalism, both conventional and boring. The contrast in the Théâtre des Champs-Elysées between the parts designed by van de Velde (furniture, corridors . . .) and by the Perret brothers (facade, foyer) makes their intervention in this work, which could have been one of the most perfect in the Paris of 1910, seem regrettable.

It is significant, however, that Art Nouveau should be reassessed so soon after the beginning of the century, for Garnier's projects, which he developed from 1901 onwards at the Villa Médicis in Rome, and which were the object of a major scandal at the Ecole des Beaux-Arts, became known in 1904. The houses of Sauvage and Perret were both finished in 1903. At the same time, an 'interior' reaction against Art Nouveau developed – another, more moderate branch of the fundamental opposition to decorative architecture which is called 'modernism'.

In our chronology of French Art Nouveau architecture, the latter finally appears as the last off-shoot of nineteenth-century architectural rationalism in the deeply eclectic context of the period, simultaneous with other types of formal delirium whose sole crime was to have been, at the same date, neo-Louis XVI or neo-Louis XV (but with no less conviction). The modernism which followed after 1903 constituted a drastic revolution in the mode of architectural thinking and belongs to another society, if not to another civilisation.

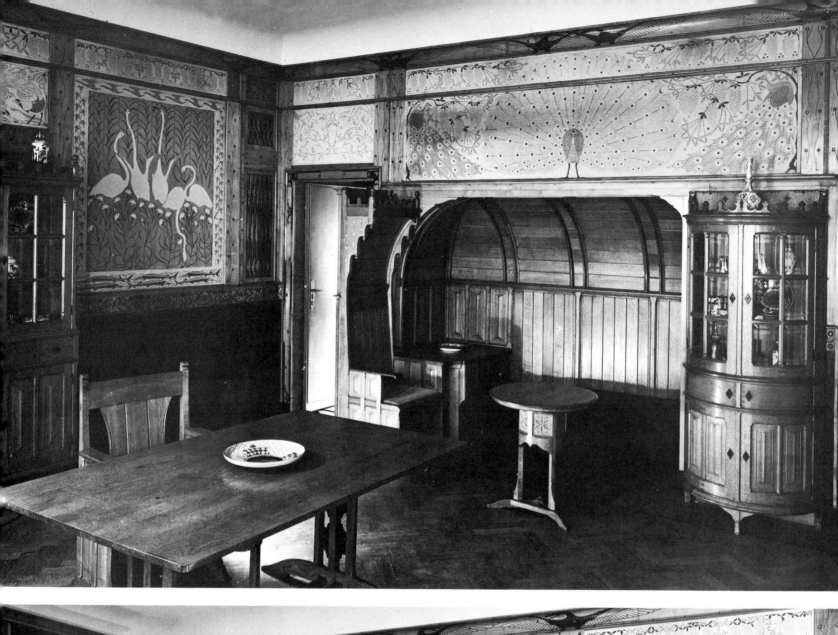

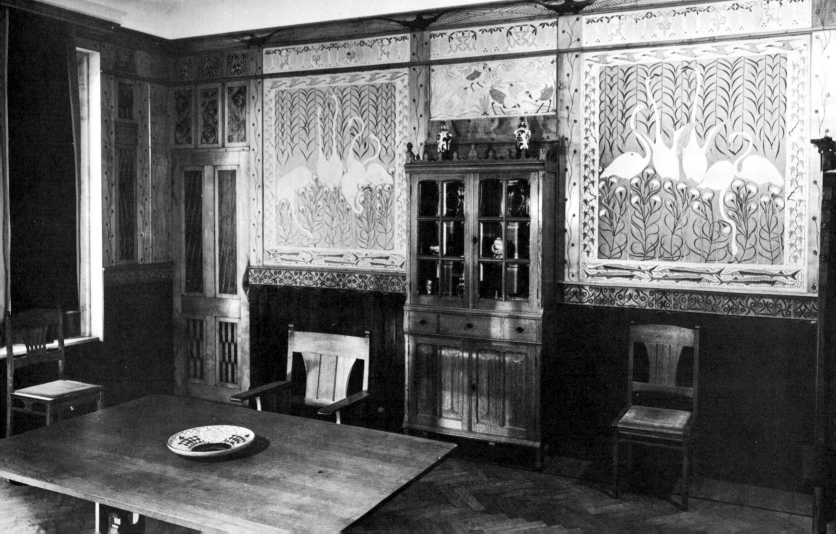

5. HOLLAND
Building towards an ideal: progressive architecture in Holland

Richard Padovan

The poet Heinrich Heine declared that if he heard that the world was about to come to an end he would move to Holland – because there everything happened fifty years later. The country which in the seventeenth century had led the world with its brilliant achievements in art, philosophy and science had by the nineteenth declined to an insignificant provincial backwater. In 1840 the Dutch Association for Fine Arts and Sciences promoted a prize essay 'to ascertain the reasons for the lack of progress of architecture in our country'. The competition produced no answer to the problem.

Yet by the early decades of the twentieth century Holland had become, with Russia, France and Germany, a centre of the most advanced movements in art and architecture. This reversal came about through a process of artistic and cultural renewal accompanied by a general social and political awakening of the Netherlands which began around 1865 and gained momentum from about 1890 onwards. Just as the achievements of the Golden Century coincided with the sudden emergence of the United Provinces as a great political and economic power, so the period 1865-1915 saw both an explosion of creativity in the arts and the rapid development of a backward pastoral nation dominated by a paternalistic oligarchy into one of the most advanced industrial democracies in Europe.

The rebirth of Dutch architecture, which was begun by the Gothic Revivalist P. J. H. Cuypers (1827-1921) and culminated with the flowering of Art Nouveau in the work of H. P. Berlage (1856-1934) and others, was paralleled by the simultaneous appearance of innovative artists in other fields. Josef Israëls, the leader of the Hague School, was a near contemporary of Cuypers; Vincent van Gogh, G. H. Breitner and Jan Toorop were born within a few years of Berlage, as was the great Dutch novelist Louis Couperus.

This remarkable rebirth must have been more than an accident of history. In part it was clearly stimulated by influences from abroad: the processes of industrialisation and democratization in neighbouring countries like England, France and Belgium preceded those in Holland. These countries also led the way in architecture, both through the introduction of new materials like iron and glass into building, and by giving birth to the Arts and Crafts Movement and Art Nouveau. However, the Dutch contribution was unique both for the speed and thoroughness with which the artistic revolution was carried through, and for the degree to which it became integrated into every aspect of life. The reform of architecture spread into every sphere of design activity from public building to working-class housing, and from the revival of handicrafts to art and design education. Dutch Art Nouveau was unusual moreover in its freedom from fin de siècle pathos or sentimentality, and in the fact that instead of exhausting its creative impulse soon after 1900 it continued to develop up to the First World War and was a direct source for the avant-garde movements which followed it. Above all it was unique in being sustained by a philosophical and mystical belief in the spiritual significance of art, a profound idealism which animated its best production.

Intellectual and political life in Holland were dominated, to a greater extent

5.1 DIJSSELHOF *'Dijsselhof Room'* 1890-92, two views in situ at the Gemeentemuseum

than in other Western countries, by spiritual and theological tendencies: by the tradition of religious enquiry and freedom of the individual conscience. As a result, the political parties represented (and still tend to represent) religious groups rather than social classes. Even the socialist movement (led by an ex-Lutheran pastor, Ferdinand Domela Nieuwenhuis) was motivated by an idealistic anarchism, at least until its reorganization as a political party, the SDAP, in 1894. Other reflections of the spiritual and intellectual ferment which permeated Dutch culture in the 1880s and 1890s were the widespread impact of theosophy and of Willem Meng's mystical-aesthetic-anarchist movement 'Wie Denkt Overwint' (He who thinks overcomes); the mediaevalist social-reformism of Catholics like Cuypers; and utopian experiments like the 'Walden' community at Bussum inspired by Thoreau's writings. Most of the leading progressive figures in Dutch art and architecture – the painters Roland Holst, Toorop and Thorn Prikker, the architects De Bazel, Lauweriks, Bauer, Walenkamp and Berlage – were involved in one or other of these movements. Dutch Art Nouveau therefore acquired a social and moral impetus and idealism, and a freedom from aestheticism or modishness, which link it with the modern movement of the period after 1918.

In writing about Art Nouveau architecture in Holland one is faced with a dilemma: the apparent co-existence of two quite distinct and even opposed currents. If one identifies Art Nouveau with the decorative style based on the leitmotif described by Nikolaus Pevsner in *Pioneers of Modern Design* – 'the long, sensitive curve . . . undulating, flowing, and interplaying with others, sprouting from corners and covering asymmetrically all available surfaces . . .' – then Art Nouveau is most easily recognised in a number of Dutch architects whose work was more or less directly inspired by Belgian models: A. P. Otten and J. Verheul in Rotterdam; J. Mutters, W. B. van Liefland, L. A. H. de Wolf, and Hoek and Wouters in The Hague; G. van Arkel and E. Breman in Amsterdam. The alternative current, which included all the front rank architects of the period – H. P. Berlage, K. P. C. de Bazel, Willem Kromhout and J. L. M. Lauweriks – was associated with the circle of P. J. H. Cuypers and the Amsterdam association Architectura et Amicitia. The work of this group was less obviously Art Nouveau in character, being far removed from the curvilinear plasticity of Antoni Gaudí, Victor Horta or Hector Guimard and having more in common with the straight line geometry and plain surfaces of C. F. A. Voysey and Charles Rennie Mackintosh in Britain or Otto Wagner and Josef Hoffmann in Vienna. Is one justified in calling it Art Nouveau at all? And if it does represent the indigenous current of Dutch Art Nouveau what attitude must one take to the rival imported style?

Hitherto most studies of Art Nouveau in Holland – such as L. Gans' *Nieuwe Kunst* (1960), or the special issues of *Forum* (10 and 11, 1958) have concentrated on the more obviously Art Nouveau output of the Belgian-influenced group. However, this approach raises a number of difficulties. It excludes the work of the most important progressive architects of the period, in favour of a kind of architecture which for all its charm is often no more than chic surface modernism overlaying a fundamentally banal conception, and lacks both the intellectual integrity of Berlage or Lauweriks and the revolutionary spatial virtuosity of Horta or van de Velde. Consequently the Dutch contribution to Art Nouveau architecture is reduced to a position of minor importance in relation to that of other Western European countries – a conclusion which is hard to reconcile with the fact that the achievement in other fields of art and design was of major significance. Furthermore, this latter achievement was directly inspired and fostered by the activity of Cuypers and his followers, and relatively unconnected with either Belgian Art Nouveau or its Dutch imitators – with the single exception of the work of Johan Thorn Prikker, who was a participant in the Belgian movement from the start, rather than a follower of it.

Between 1885 and 1895 Cuypers' atelier became the nursery of the group of progressive designers and architects which was to emerge in the 1890s and 1900s – the designers Theodore Nieuwenhuis, C. A. Lion Cachet and G. W. Dijsselhof and the architects J. L. M. Lauweriks, K. P. C. de Bazel and H. J. M. Walenkamp – very much as Peter Behrens' office was to become the training ground for Gropius and Meyer, Mies van der Rohe and the future Le Corbusier twenty years later. Lauweriks, Berlage and Cuypers himself were

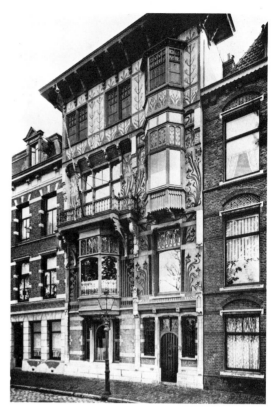

5.2 MUTTERS *Wassenaarseweg 11* The Hague 1898, curvilinear facade

5.3 DE WOLF *Laan van Meerdervoort 215* The Hague c.1898, facade

5.4-5 DE WOLF *Krue confectioner's shop* The Hague 1903, facade and interior

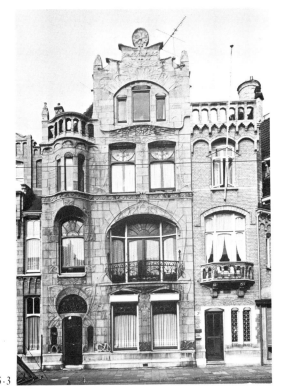

5.3

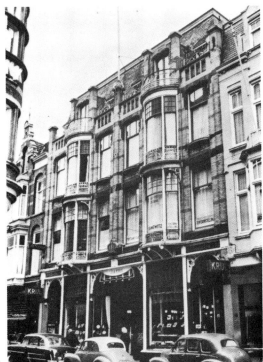

5.4

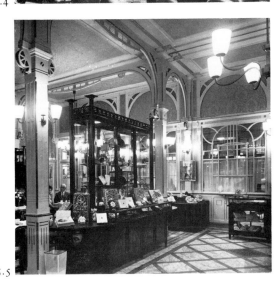

5.5

actively engaged in the education of artists and craftsmen at the Quellinus School and the Rijksmuseum Schools, which Cuypers founded in 1880 and in 1881. De Bazel and Lauweriks set up their 'Atelier for architecture, arts and crafts and decorative arts' in 1895 and founded the periodical *Bouw- en Sierkunst* (Architecture and Decorative Art) in 1898. In 1897 they established the 'Vâhana' course in drawing, art history and aesthetics, and from 1900 to 1904 Lauweriks taught at the School of Arts and Crafts in Haarlem. Finally the firm 't Binnenhuis (The Interior), founded in 1900 by Berlage and Jac. van den Bosch, provided an outlet for the production of designs by architects, artists and designers alike, bringing together most of the members of the progressive design movement, including the architects De Bazel, Kromhout, Lauweriks, Stuyt and Walenkamp, the sculptors Mendes da Costa and Zijl, the furniture designer W. Penaat, the silversmiths J. Eisenloeffel and Frans Zwollo and the potter W. C. Brouwer. The extent of the participation by the architects of the Cuypers/Berlage circle in the Art Nouveau movement in art and design, both as teachers and sponsors and as practitioners, was so great that it seems totally illogical to deny the major relevance of their architectural output to the history of Art Nouveau.

The attitude of the Architectura et Amicitia group to the fashion for Belgian Art Nouveau was unequivocally critical. In 1900 Kromhout published an article in the society's journal *Architectura* entitled 'Five Lost Years?': 'In the last few years 1895-1900 a movement has grown up in the sphere of art which has no time for the patient effort needed to develop an architecture capable of giving expression to our still slumbering ideals, and which by demanding instant progress will inevitably bring about its opposite unless the more serious among us take a firm stand against it. This is the so-called *libre aesthetique* in its various forms – the "Van de Velde School" in Belgium, the "Secession" in South Germany and in Vienna. It has also taken a strong hold in our own country. It is the style of the upholsterers, wallpaperers and furniture-makers, the style of seaweed sinuosities, and now lays exclusive claim to the term "modern". The tragic side to this farce is that so many people take it seriously . . . But still sadder is the ease with which some Dutch architects have mastered this importation, the enthusiasm with which they have thrown themselves into it in order to stand in the front line of the self-styled "moderns". Tomorrow they will turn to something else as soon as the wind of fashion changes direction.'

The following year the 74 year old but still active Cuypers, in an address to Architectura et Amicitia, compared the Art Nouveau to 'a consumptive, who with an insidious flush on his cheeks sets out to enjoy his few years of life with a frenzied intoxication. I see Dutch modernism on the other hand as a sturdy young Hollander who knows what he wants but still approaches his surroundings with awkward hands, awaiting the time when talent and devotion will complete his education . . .'

The rather chauvinistic condemnation of foreign Art Nouveau in these statements now seems short-sighted, but their main message proved extraordinarily prophetic. Two years later the completion of Berlage's Beurs in 1903 marked the coming-of-age of the home-grown modern movement. Belgian influence also reached a peak in the same year with the building of Henry van de Velde's Leuring house in The Hague. However, this was the work of a Belgian, not a Dutch architect, and after 1903, as Kromhout had predicted, the Dutch exponents of Belgian Art Nouveau either fell under Berlagian influence or turned to various forms of eclecticism.

It seems reasonable to conclude that the most significant manifestations of Art Nouveau in Dutch architecture are to be found not in the sometimes charming but fundamentally gratuitous use of themes borrowed from Belgian Art Nouveau, but in the marvellous stirring into life, as if by a magic wand, the sudden joyful outburst of light, colour and spatial invention in the scrupulously honest and rational works of Berlage and his contemporaries. This is Art Nouveau of the same quality as one recognises in the best work of Horta or Guimard, of Hoffmann or Mackintosh.

It is not the aim of this essay to catalogue the vast quantity of minor Art Nouveau architecture to be found in Holland, but to concentrate on the relatively small number of seminal buildings and projects, beginning with the work of Cuypers, the father of Dutch Art Nouveau, and concluding with that

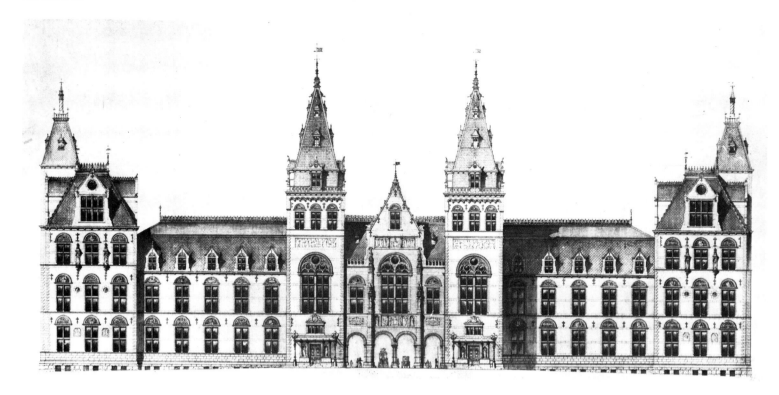

5.6 CUYPERS *Rijksmuseum* Amsterdam 1877-85, front elevation

of J. F. Staal and Michel de Klerk who went on to become leaders of the movement which grew out of it – the Amsterdam School.

Never himself an Art Nouveau architect, P. J. H. Cuypers (1827-1921) by his teaching and example created the intellectual climate in which it could grow. A near contemporary and friend of Viollet-le-Duc, who more than anyone established the basic rationale of Art Nouveau architecture, Cuypers also began his career as a restorer of mediaeval buildings (Viollet visited Roermond in Limburg to advise him on the restoration of the Munsterkerk in 1864). Both architects understood and loved mediaeval architecture above all as *logical construction*. Viollet's aesthetic theory grew out of his profound study of mediaeval buildings in France, which led him to the conclusion that Gothic architecture was based on a system of triangular figures – *générateurs de proportions* – which gave it both its structural stability and its harmony of proportion: 'Architectural proportion is established primarily by the laws of statics, and the laws of statics are derived from geometry.' His theory had a strong influence, through Cuypers, on his pupils and followers – Lauweriks, De Bazel, Berlage and J. H. de Groot.

Although much of Cuypers' output consisted of churches, his two masterpieces – the Rijksmuseum (1877-85) and the Central Station in Amsterdam (1881-89) – were answers to secular and peculiarly modern problems and involved ingenious and complex planning solutions and the frank expression of iron construction. Here again he was in line with Viollet-le-Duc's teaching (Viollet combined iron and masonry in the design for a concert hall illustrated in his *Entretiens* in 1872) and with the example of other French architects like Henri Labrouste and Louis Charles Boileau. The integral use of iron as a monumental element in architecture, begun by Cuypers, was completed by Berlage with the Beurs design of 1898.

An equally important factor in the development of Dutch Art Nouveau was Cuypers' active support for the reform of the applied arts on the model of the work of Ruskin, Morris and their followers in England, both through his teaching at the Quellinus and Rijksmuseum Schools and by the training of designers like Dijsselhof, Nieuwenhuis and Lion Cachet in his own office. The so-called 'Dijsselhof Room' now in the Gemeentemuseum in The Hague was originally designed in 1890-92. More advanced than anything executed by a Dutch architect at so early a date, it is regarded as the first Art Nouveau interior in Holland, though it is closer to the work of Mackmurdo's Century Guild, or to Whistler's Peacock Room. At the same time it is typically Dutch in its use of batik and in the straightforward construction and solidity of Dijsselhof's furniture.

In his own work Cuypers never shook off his mediaevalism, and it is still

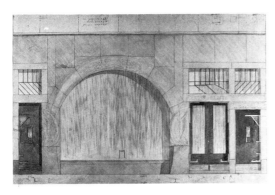

5.7 BAUER *Competition design for an artist's studio-house* 1893

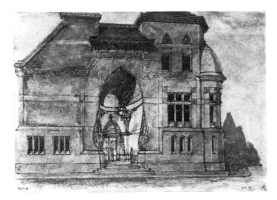

5.8 BAUER & THORN PRIKKER *'Arts and Crafts' shop* The Hague 1898, elevation

5.9 BAUER *Project for a Volksgebouw* 1894, side elevation

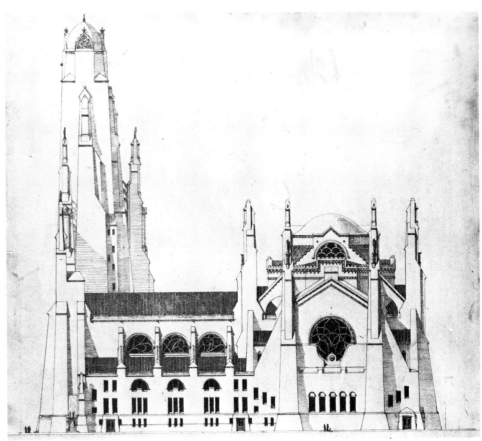

5.9

evident in the early work of his pupils De Bazel and Walenkamp and of other members of the Architectura circle like Willem Kromhout and W. C. Bauer (1862-1904). Bauer studied at the Craft School in The Hague, and later at the Art Academy. He became a member of Architectura et Amicitia in 1888, and during the next five years participated unsuccessfully in a number of competitions with a series of eclectic designs combining Gothic, Baroque and Byzantine elements. However in 1893 he submitted a design for an artist's studio-house which broke free from direct historical references and is the first appearance of Art Nouveau in an architectural project in Holland, within a year of Victor Horta's Tassel house. The following year he anticipated Bruno Taut's Stadtkrone project and Walter Gropius' Bauhaus address of 1919 ('. . . let us conceive and create the new building of the future . . . which will rise one day toward heaven from the hands of a million workers like the crystal symbol of a new faith . . .') with a utopian design for a Volksgebouw (People's Building). This was conceived as the cathedral of a future socialist community in which 'the people, living in a harmonious society, will build themselves places in which they can come together . . . Monuments out of which the light of science and art will shine over the multitude, they will rise high over their surroundings and become the centres from which will come the bond which unites the people . . .' Sadly Bauer was never given the opportunity to realise any large-scale projects; he collaborated with Johan Thorn Prikker on the design of the shop 'Arts and Crafts' in The Hague in 1898 and in the same year joined the agricultural cooperative 'Walden' founded by Frederik van Eeden, where he built a few huts and small villas for its members. Disillusioned by years of neglect and frustration, he committed suicide in 1904.

The long career of H. P. Berlage (1856-1934), continuing that of Cuypers, forms a bridge between the mid-nineteenth century and the mid-twentieth century. The whole patient development of his work and thought was an extension of the teachings of the great rationalist theorists of the 1860s – Gottfried Semper and Viollet-le-Duc. As a delegate at the first CIAM conference in 1928 he witnessed, not without misgivings, the outcome of the revolution which he had done as much as anyone to bring about.

Unlike the other members of the Architectura circle, Berlage studied abroad – at the Polytechnikum in Zurich, which was strongly influenced by Semper who had directed the Bauschule from its foundation in 1855 up to 1871. Semper's teachings about style and the spatial organization of buildings

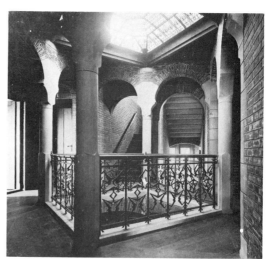

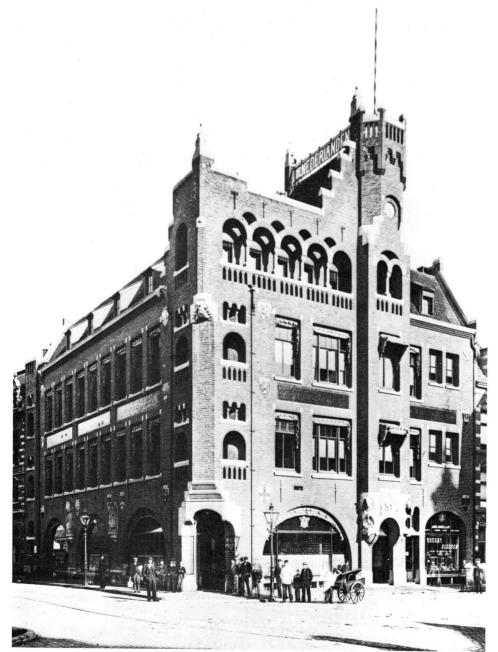

5.11-12 BERLAGE *Villa Henny* The Hague 1898, first floor landing and dining room

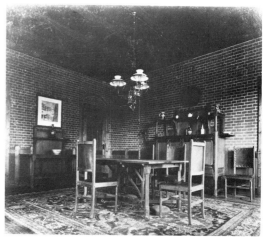

became the basis of Berlage's own architecture and theoretical writings, just as his radical politics (he was a lifelong exile from Germany as a result of his part in the Dresden uprising of 1849) inspired Berlage's socialism.

Returning to Amsterdam in 1881 after his studies in Zurich and a long Italian journey, Berlage formed a partnership with the engineer T. Sanders. The work of the partnership, like the two competition designs for the Beurs (1884/5) and the Focke & Meltzer building on the Spui (1884-86), was conservatively neo-Renaissance in style, giving little indication of what was to follow. Berlage's gradual emergence from eclecticism first appears in his still vaguely Gothic insurance office for De Algemene in Amsterdam (1893). Historicist overtones have almost disappeared in his buildings for another insurance company, De Nederlanden van 1848, in Amsterdam (1894) and The Hague (1895), in which flat planes of naked brickwork are pierced by rectangular or semi-circular openings, key points in the structure being accentuated by flush stonework. However, until regularised by Berlage's later additions, both buildings had picturesque mediaeval outlines broken by pinnacles, turrets and stepped gables.

Carel Henny, the managing director of De Nederlanden (and financial sponsor of both 't Binnenhuis and Thorn Prikker's rival 'Arts and Crafts') was again the client for Berlage's first fully Art Nouveau work. The Villa Henny in The Hague (1898) embodies all the elements of Berlage's mature style – the modular grid, the spatial inventiveness and the rigorously honest expression of

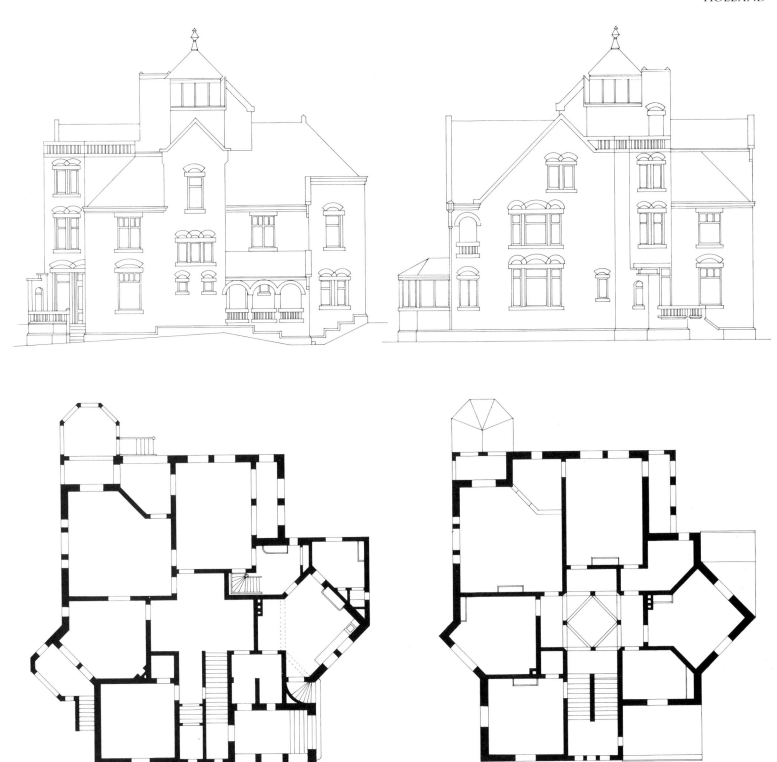

5.13-16 BERLAGE *Villa Henny*, North East and South East elevations and ground and first floor plans (from the original drawings)

materials and construction. The plan is based on a square grid which is used to generate a complex series of rectangular and diagonal spaces whose focus is a central staircase hall in the shape of a Greek cross. The central square of this cross is given a diagonal emphasis by the inscribed square vaulted opening of the first floor landing, through which light pours down from a skylight in the apex of the roof. The use of diagonals and changes of direction (by the time he reaches this extraordinary space the visitor has had to make three right-angled turns since entering the house) gives an air of mystery and an unexpectedly grand scale to this moderately dimensioned building. The complex spatial articulation of the Villa Henny is comparable to the similar diagonal treatment of space in Horta's van Eetvelde house (1895-96). In his *Grundlagen und Entwicklung der Architektur* (1908) Berlage wrote: 'The art of the master-builder lies in this: the creation of space, not the sketching of facades. A spatial envelope is established by means of walls, whereby a space or series of spaces is manifested, according to the complexity of the walling.' The daring use of bare brickwork even in the interiors of the house must have seemed at the time the

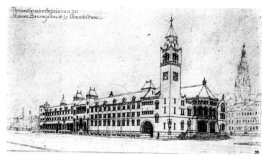

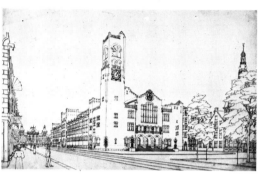

5.19

5.20

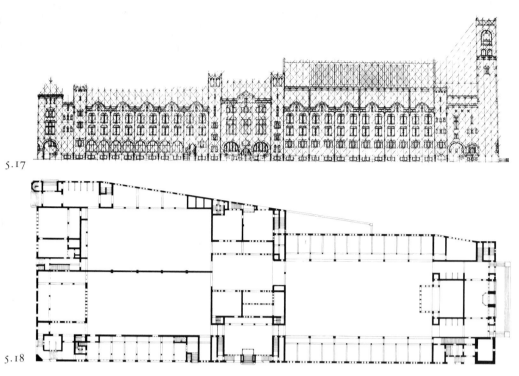

5.17

5.18

5.17-18 BERLAGE *Beurs* Amsterdam 1898-1903,
West elevation showing system of proportioning
based on the Egyptian triangle and ground floor
plan (from the original drawing)

5.19-20 BERLAGE *Beurs*, perspective of the first
design 1896 and third design 1897-98

most extreme aspect of Berlage's radicalism. Carel Henny must have been a
brave man! Here again Berlage stated his principle in writing: 'Before all else
the wall must be shown naked in all its sleek beauty, and anything fixed onto it
must be shunned as an embarrassment.' (*Gedanken über Stil*, 1905) 'The
plasterer will not have much work' he observed laconically about his design for
the Beurs. The furniture designed by Berlage for the Villa was equally radical
in its spartan simplicity and straightforward construction, coming close to
Rietveld's leather armchair of 1908 or even his 'Military' series of 1923. After
1900 't Binnenhuis sold similar furniture, designed by Berlage, Jac. van den
Bosch, Penaat and others.

Almost contemporary with the Villa Henny was the headquarters building
for the Diamond Workers' Union or ANDB (1898-1900). With its strong
asymmetry, the unbroken plane of the facade, flat roof and 'ribbon windows',
this comes closer to the later modern movement than any other of Berlage's
designs before 1914. The heart of the building, as of the Villa Henny, is the
staircase hall with its central well running through three storeys, surrounded
by arcaded galleries on three sides and by the staircase on the fourth, and lit by
the shaft of light which falls from the skylight overhead. The textile-like
pattern of the white and yellow glazed brickwork completes the sparkling
effect of space, light and colour.

The third in the trilogy of buildings which Berlage began in 1898 was his
most famous work, the Amsterdam Beurs (Exchange). The contrast between
the final design and the two competition entries of 1884/5 is astonishing, but it
was arrived at by a typically painstaking process of clarification and purifica-
tion of language, a gradual self-liberation from eclecticism, beginning with the
still fully Romanesque first design of 1896 and culminating in the stark
simplicity of the final statement.

Here again a square grid underlies the discipline of the plan. In fact this is
the base of an imaginary pyramid which creates a three-dimensional diagonal
grid with a base to height ratio of 8:5 – the so-called 'Egyptian triangle'
prescribed by Viollet-le-Duc in his *Entretiens* – which controls all the proportions of the facades and the interior spaces. The use of mathematical
systems of proportion and modular grids was a preoccupation which Berlage
shared with other members of the Cuypers circle, in particular Lauweriks, De
Bazel, Walenkamp and De Groot.

The building occupies the whole area of its irregular site, and the oblique
alignment of the eastern side is exploited to create a sequence of dramatic
spatial effects. The entrance front is more conventional, with an arcaded porch,
gable and campanile reminiscent of an Italian Romanesque church. Yet everything is reduced to a smooth unbroken plane; nothing is allowed to project

Opposite above left
KROMHOUT *American Hotel* Amsterdam 1898-
1903, elevation drawing

Opposite above right
BERLAGE *Diamond Workers' Union (ANDB)*
Amsterdam 1898-1900, section through hallway

Opposite below
KROMHOUT *Competition design for a Peace Palace*
1905, perspective drawing

Page 146 above left
DE KLERK *Competition design for a sports club* 1907,
perspective drawing

Page 146 above right
DE KLERK *Competition design for a Café-Restaurant*
1907, elevation drawing

Page 146 below
LAUWERIKS *Cologne Werkbund Exhibition* 1914,
interior perspective

Page 147
5.21-22 BERLAGE *Beurs*, final design 1898-1903,
perspectives of the exterior and Produce Exchange

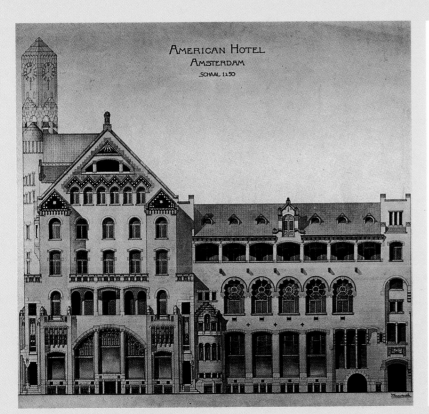

AMERICAN HOTEL
AMSTERDAM
SCHAAL 1:50

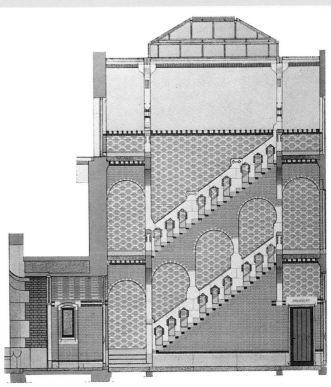

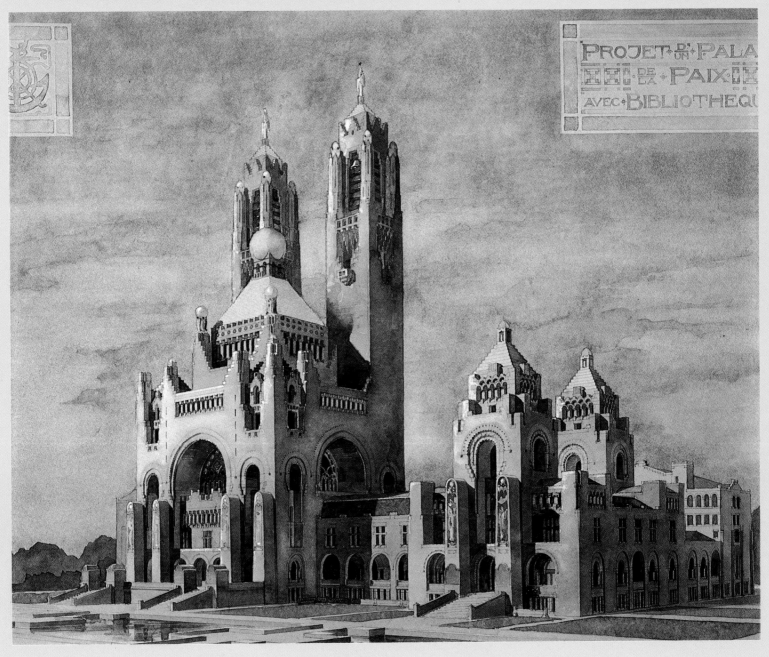

PROJET·D'UN·PALA
····DE·LA·PAIX····
AVEC·BIBLIOTHEQU

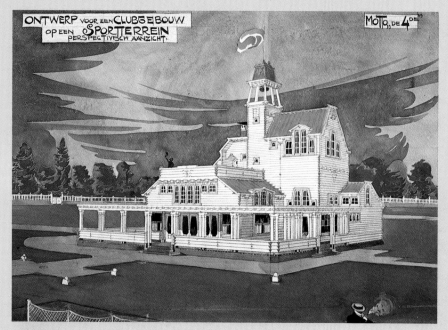

ONTWERP VOOR EEN CLUB EBOUW OP EEN SPORTTERREIN PERSPECTIVISCH AANZICHT. MOTTO, DE 4 DE

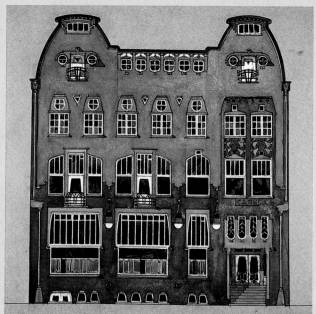

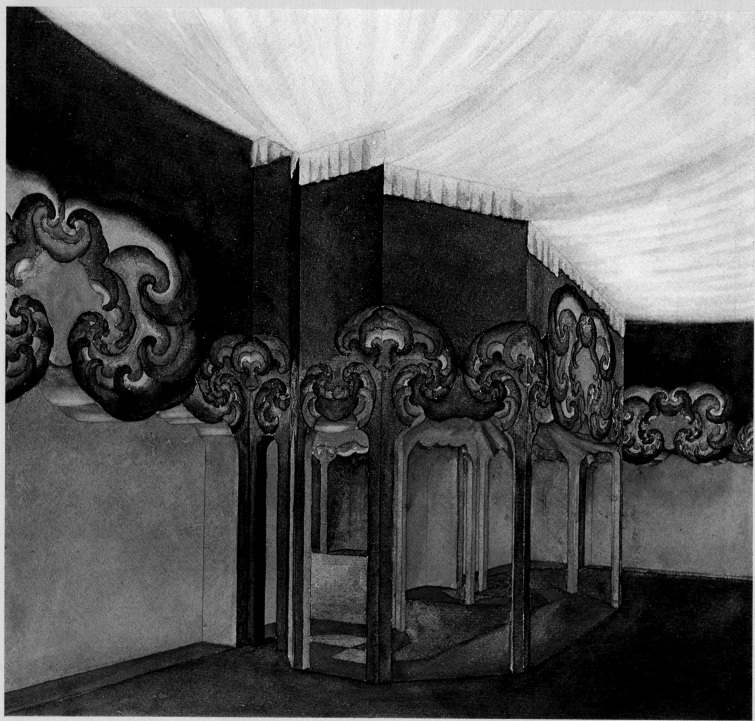

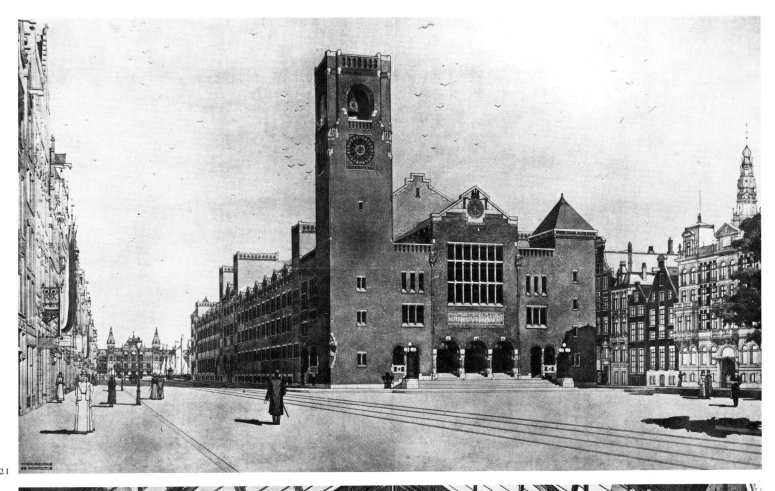

5.21

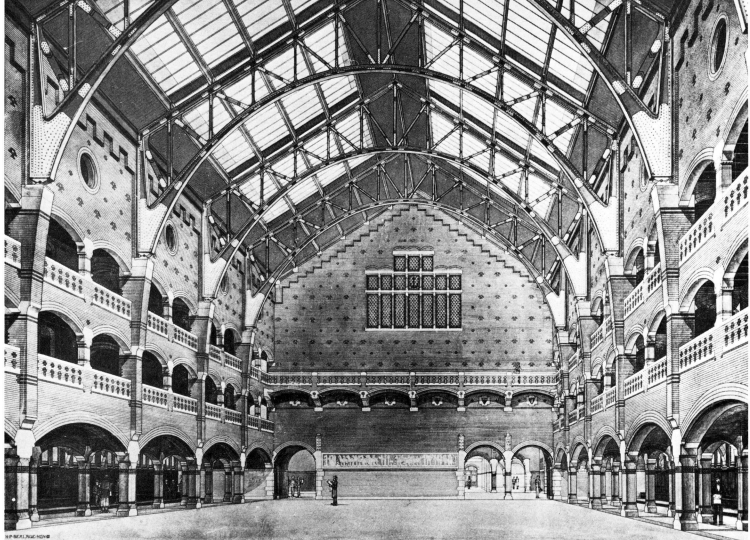

5.22

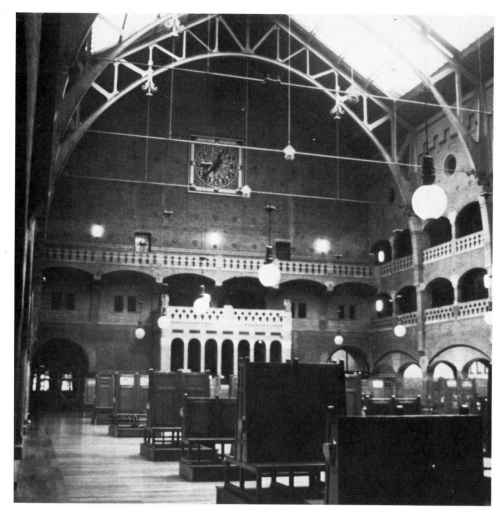

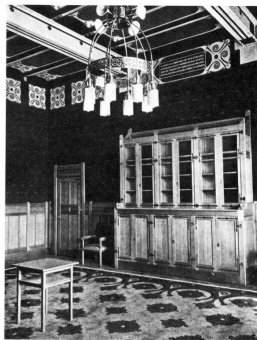

5.24 BERLAGE *Beurs*, committee room

5.23 BERLAGE *Beurs*, Produce Exchange
(photograph La Rue)

beyond this surface, all relief – even the statue by Lambertus Zijl which stands at the angle of the tower – being incised into the thickness of the wall. The other elevations are still more austere, enlivened only by the massing of regularly spaced square towers recalling Walenkamp's public library project of 1895 and his design for an academy of fine art of 1899: it is probable that Walenkamp, who worked for Berlage on the Beurs and drew the perspective renderings of it, may have influenced the design.

Internally the Corn and Stock Exchanges are minor variations on the major theme of the Produce Exchange. This grand space, exactly two squares on plan, is unexpectedly light and colourful compared with the sombre exterior. The brick is yellow, with rust-red motifs picked out at intervals in the large surfaces. The columns are black and white speckled polished granite, while the capitals and other stone members are in blue-grey unpolished granite. The lower part of the walls and the back walls of the galleries are of glazed blue and red brick. The roof trusses are painted yellow with bright blue rivets, and the glass roof is bordered with coloured glass. The two long walls of the hall constitute a fascinating play with space. The projecting buttresses which support and continue the curve of the arched roof trusses intersect the plane of the wall and continue into the space beyond, creating an effect of intersecting spatial volumes which anticipates De Stijl. The subdivision of the wide arches of the lower arcade in 1909 to prevent further settling of the building has weakened the intended effect of spatial layering created by three parallel wall-planes one behind the other. Originally, between the wide arches of the nearest wall appeared a line of columns which were smaller but twice as numerous; through these the outer wall itself was visible. (A similar layering, in the Cistercian Abbey of Le Thoronet, was illustrated by Viollet-le-Duc in his *Dictionnaire*.)

The concept of the total work of art in which architecture would absorb and be completed by the other arts was fundamental to Art Nouveau. In the Beurs the sculpture of Zijl and Mendes da Costa, the paintings and ceramics of Roland Holst and Toorop and the stained glass of A. J. de Kinderen were

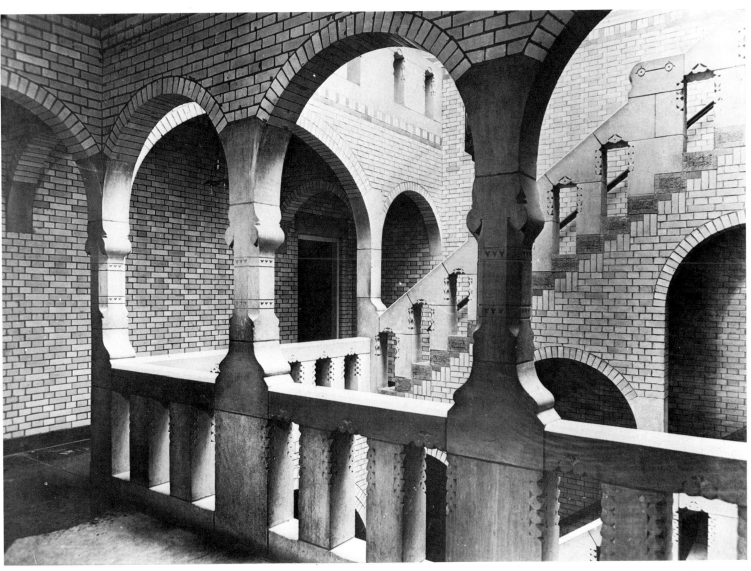

5.25 BERLAGE *Diamond Workers' Union (ANDB)* Amsterdam 1898-1900, central staircase

inseparable from the architecture, as were the furniture and fittings which Berlage himself designed for the building.

The decade which followed the completion of the Beurs produced no dramatic change in Berlage's work. His most important activity was in the areas of working-class housing and town-planning – including master-plans for the expansion of The Hague and Amsterdam (1908 and 1909) with detailed designs for the principal buildings and open spaces. It was not until after his visit to the United States and his encounter with the work of Henry Hobson Richardson, Louis Sullivan and Frank Lloyd Wright that his work took a new leap forward in terms of style. This visit was decisive not only for Berlage but for Dutch architecture as a whole, since through Berlage's articles and the illustrated lectures he gave on his return, Wright's work became widely known in Holland for the first time, and its influence on the future De Stijl movement through Jan Wils who was an assistant of Berlage and J. J. P. Oud who was a close friend was fundamental. Holland House, Bury Street (1914-16) – the London headquarters of the W. H. Müller Company for which Berlage worked exclusively from 1913-19 – shows the impact of Sullivan (especially of the vertical mullioned facades of the Guaranty Building in Buffalo) but it also looks forward to much recent modern architecture. The hunting-lodge St Hubertus (1915-19) for the owners of the Müller firm, Anton and Hélène Kröller-Müller, again takes up on a more generous scale the spatial complexity, diagonal planning and austere interior finishes of the Villa Henny. The De Stijl artist Bart van der Leck collaborated on the design of the interiors. The unexecuted design for the Kröller-Müller Museum (1917), the successor to the equally abortive projects by Peter Behrens and Mies van der Rohe, contained the germ of Berlage's last and one of his finest works, the Gemeentemuseum in The Hague (1919-35), completed a year after his death at the age of 78.

Starting as a rather conservative Renaissance Revivalist, long before the appearance of Art Nouveau, Berlage developed far beyond it, to occupy finally an advanced post which only now is beginning to be recognised fully. His integration of the concepts of space and style was an essential precondition for the creation of modern architecture. By establishing a new *immaterial* basis for style, independent of ornament and construction alike, he liberated architecture from both the eclecticism and the arbitrary formalism from which not even Art Nouveau had been able to escape.

After studying at the Craft School in The Hague, Willem Kromhout (1864-1940) worked as assistant in a number of architects' offices while continuing his studies through evening classes at the Academy of Art, where W. C. Bauer and K. P. C. de Bazel were his fellow-students, eventually setting up his own practice in 1890. He was an active member of Architectura et Amicitia, of which he was President in 1895-96 and 1908-10. Through its mouthpiece *Architectura*, of which he was assistant editor from 1893 to 96 and editor in 1905, he helped to lay the critical foundations of Dutch Art Nouveau. In the first issue (1893) he wrote: 'Once we accept that style, in its totality, must always be the reflection in architecture of the spirit of the age and the life of the people, and that the language of forms must be in harmony with the ethos and character of a civilization, we must conclude that the forms which we can call our own cannot be sought in the work of any foregoing period.' Paradoxically, he retained strong historicist and more specifically Gothic elements in his work throughout the Art Nouveau period. His competition design for the Rotterdam Town Hall (1913) was a fantastic mixture of Gothic, Byzantine and proto-Expressionist elements, a wilder version of Bauer's Volksgebouw twenty years earlier.

In his best known work, the American Hotel on the Leidseplein in Amsterdam (1898-1902), the Gothic spirit is still evident in the verticality of the general composition and particularly in the flamboyant tracery of the West facade. However, underlying Kromhout's spirited plastic invention is a simple, almost warehouse-like building form: a massive rectangular block with a steep gabled roof in the tradition of a mediaeval town hall or an Amsterdam grachthuis (canal house). This basic form is partially disguised by the addition of a number of subordinate elements: the rounded corner-tower, corbelled bow-windows surmounted by gabled dormers, and deep arched loggias at the lower levels. The superb café-restaurant on the ground floor combines the lively comfortable atmosphere of the Café De Kroon on the Rembrandtsplein (G. van Arkel, interior by Jac. van den Bosch, 1898) with something of the structural grandeur of Berlage's Beurs. Kromhout seems to have aimed at achieving an effect of richness and vitality in the American Hotel in reaction to the severity of Berlage. The building's continuing popularity indicates that he succeeded, although at a stylistic level it is somewhat immature compared with Berlage's work of the same date.

The exuberance and fantasy of Kromhout's work contrasts with that of the other members of the Architectura circle, with the possible exception of Lauweriks. This difference is very apparent in Berlage's and Kromhout's entries to the Peace Palace competition of 1905. Berlage's entry is one of his less engaging works, seemingly weighed down by its own excessive solidity and seriousness, while Kromhout's design is as dreamlike as a visionary composition by John Martin or Joseph Gandy. In an open letter published in 1913 Kromhout complained: '. . . Do you know when the misery starts for an architect in our country? When he becomes fantastic. That is unpardonable . . .' Yet the Amsterdam School which grew out of Dutch Art Nouveau was closer in spirit to Kromhout than to any of his contemporaries. The Scheepvaarthuis (1912-16) by J. M. van der Mey with M. de Klerk and P. Kramer seems to have been designed in answer to Kromhout's protest.

After studying at the Academy in The Hague K. P. C. de Bazel (1869-1928) obtained a place in P. J. H. Cuypers' office in 1889. There he made such rapid progress that at barely twenty years of age he was made responsible for the detailed design of the St Vitus church in Hilversum. However, the strain exhausted him and in 1892 a breakdown of his health forced him to stop work. He returned to become Cuypers' chef de bureau at the end of the year, but his health never fully recovered. The monumentality of his work suggests a wish to compensate for his physical frailty.

In Cuypers' office he came in contact with many of the future leaders of Dutch Art Nouveau – Lauweriks, Jan Stuyt, Walenkamp and others. The

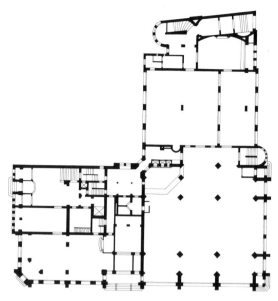

5.26-28 KROMHOUT *American Hotel* Amsterdam 1898-1902, ground floor plan (from the original drawing), exterior and corner detail (contemporary photographs)

5.29 VAN ARKEL & VAN DEN BOSCH *Café De Kroon in the American Hotel* 1898 (contemporary photograph)

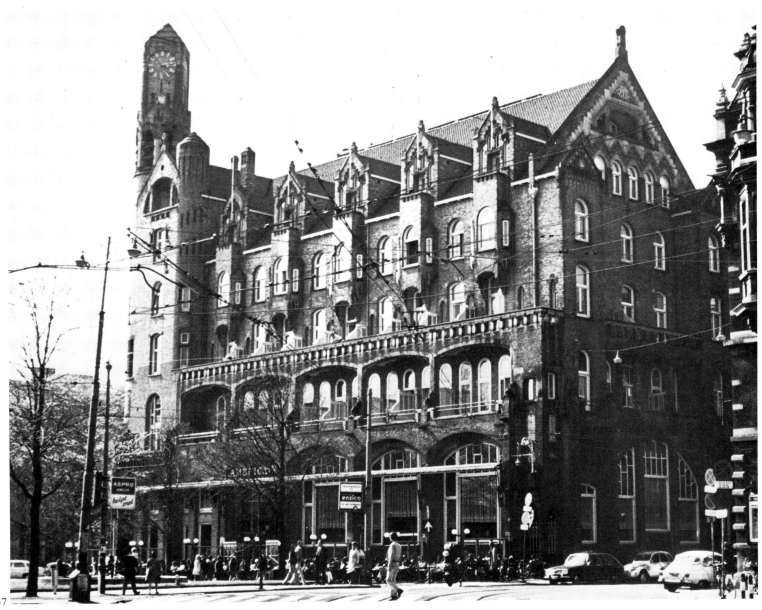

5.27

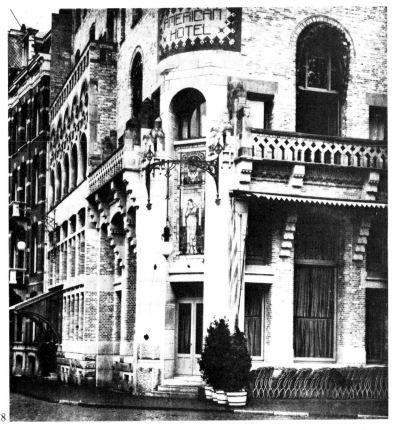

5.28

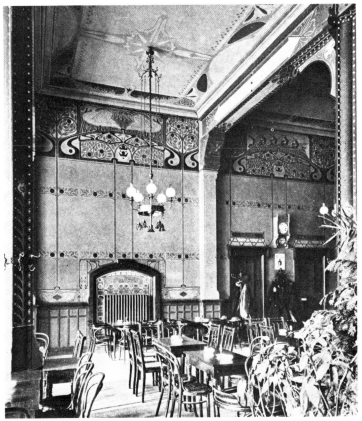

5.29

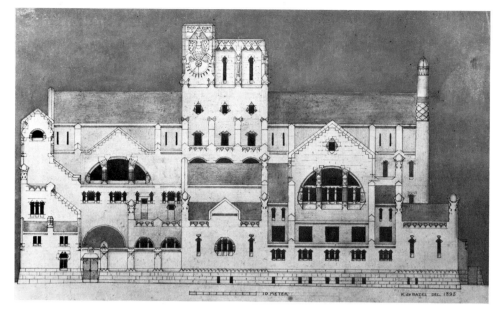

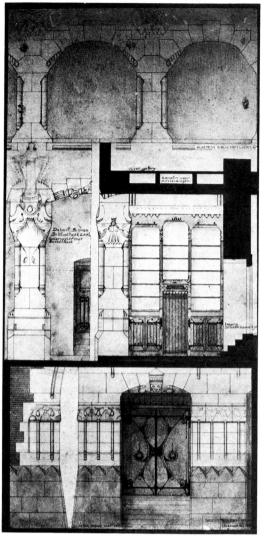

5.30-31 DE BAZEL *Competition project for a public library* 1895, South elevation and interior details

young group shared a common interest in the mathematical basis of design and a receptiveness to the political and intellectual idealism which was shaking the country in the 1890s – from Ferdinand Domela Nieuwenhuis' Social Democratic Union to the anarchism of Kropotkin and Willem Meng and the theosophy of Mme Blavatsky. Lauweriks and De Bazel joined the Theosophist Union in 1894, a move which caused a rift with the Catholic Cuypers and led to their setting up their own 'Atelier for architecture, arts and crafts and decorative art' in 1895. With the exception of a small conversion for Walenkamp's parents no architectural work of the partnership was ever realised, but if the three competition projects which De Bazel designed in this period had been built they would eclipse Berlage's roughly contemporary De Nederlanden buildings, and rival the much later ANDB building and the Beurs in importance. In fact the final version of the Beurs seems much indebted to De Bazel's somewhat Romanesque projects of 1895 for a public baths complex and a public library, as it does to Walenkamp's public library design entered for the same competition. De Bazel's architects' club project (1896-97) is an astonishing work for its time, making brilliant use of contrasts of texture and scale.

Both De Bazel and Lauweriks produced a quantity of graphic work and furniture, and participated in the work of 't Binnenhuis. De Bazel's architectural work after the dissolution of the partnership in 1900 is characterised by a monumental classicism, already visible in the formality of the model dairy-farm 'Oud Bussum' (1903) and the design for a World Capital (1905). His major executed work, the Dutch Trading Company building in Amsterdam (1920-26) has little connection with Art Nouveau and is closer to the monumental expressionism of contemporary German architects like Wilhelm Kreis or Paul Bonatz.

J. L. M. Lauweriks (1864-1932) was born and grew up in the Cuypers household: his father was a Belgian artist whom Cuypers employed in his atelier in Roermond. When Cuypers moved to Amsterdam in 1865 the Lauweriks family went with him and lived under the same roof in a wing of Cuypers' house, sharing the earnest religious and artistic atmosphere of its daily life. The young Lauweriks began teaching at the Quellinus School at the age of sixteen, and remained throughout his life a teacher, writer and theorist as much as a designer. His whole architectural output was produced between the years 1909 and 1915, when he was in his late forties, and none of it was built in Holland. Despite this its importance in the Dutch architecture of the period 1895 to 1915 is surpassed only by that of Berlage.

After leaving Cuypers and setting up the Atelier with De Bazel in 1895 Lauweriks concentrated on furniture and graphic design. Together they ran the 'Vâhana' course from 1897 to 1902, and published the magazine *Bouw- en Sierkunst*. They were also active contributors to *Architectura*, which Lauweriks edited from 1902 to 4. Both taught at the School of Arts and Crafts in Haarlem, De Bazel from 1897 to 1902 and Lauweriks from 1900 to 1904. In that year, on Berlage's recommendation, Lauweriks was offered a teaching appointment at the Kunstgewerbeschule in Dusseldorf by its newly-appointed Director, Peter

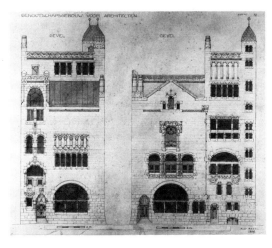

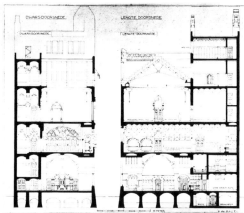

5.32-33 DE BAZEL *Project for an architects' club* 1896-97, elevations and sections

5.34 DE BAZEL *Competition project for a public baths complex* 1895, front elevation

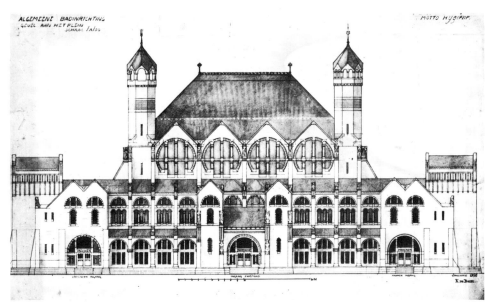

5.34

Behrens, and entered a sphere which was becoming the centre of the progressive design movement in Germany. Hermann Muthesius, who had sponsored Behrens' appointment as Director of the School, was preparing the ground for the creation of the Deutsche Werkbund, founded in 1907. Among Lauweriks' pupils in the five years he taught at Dusseldorf were Gropius' future partner Adolf Meyer, and Christian Bayer whose system-designed church project was published in Lauweriks' magazine *Ring* in 1909.

The foundation of *Ring* in 1908 gave Lauweriks an outlet for his theories about the mathematical generation of architectural form and the metaphysical purpose of art; it was also revolutionary in its typography, using typesetting material in an entirely new way which anticipated the work of Van Doesburg and El Lissitzky. Lauweriks' artistic philosophy was, like Mondrian's, permeated by his theosophical belief. In an article entitled 'The Purpose and Aim of Art' published in the periodical *Theosophia* in 1907 he wrote: 'Art is a performance of the cosmic drama in which by means of images and symbols the cosmic events are played out in eloquent, profoundly convincing actions. The cosmic novel, cosmic theatre, cosmic sculpture, cosmic painting, cosmic building – in short the harmony of the entire cosmos distilled in a single image, just as a tiny photograph can contain a whole panorama.'

Lauweriks' work can be seen as an attempt to rediscover a lost esoteric tradition, to recreate an architecture based on forgotten archetypes. His first opportunity to put his ideas into practice came with the Exhibition of Christian Art at Dusseldorf in 1909. In the same year he was invited to Hagen by the millionaire Karl Ernst Osthaus, who was creating there an artists' colony and school which would rival Grand Duke Ernst Ludwig's Mathildenhöhe at Darmstadt. Van de Velde had designed the interior of the Folkwang Museum in 1900-2, and Osthaus' own house the Hohenhof in 1906-7. With Behrens he produced an overall plan for the development of the Hohenhagen, where Behrens would build his Schröder, Cuno and Grodecke houses. The Dutch artists Thorn Prikker and Frans Zwollo were already active in Hagen: Thorn Prikker designed the stained glass window in the railway station and Zwollo set up the Hagener Silbersmiede studio which was to produce a quantity of silverware to designs by Lauweriks in the years 1910-14.

In 1910 Osthaus commissioned Lauweriks to design a group of houses on the Stirnband in Hohenhagen. These houses were among the last important manifestations of European Art Nouveau. The leitmotif which had first appeared a quarter of a century earlier in Mackmurdo's designs of 1882-83 was now no longer the slender undulating curve but a spiral meander generated by mathematical law, whose energy gives life to every line in the design, from the ridgeline of the roofs down to the smallest details. The content of this architecture is extraordinarily complex. Alongside references to the work of Richardson and Wright, which Lauweriks visited on a journey to the United States in 1909, the houses embody both expressionist fantasy and a rigorous geometric rationalism – elements which look forward to opposed tendencies in the European modernism of the post-war period.

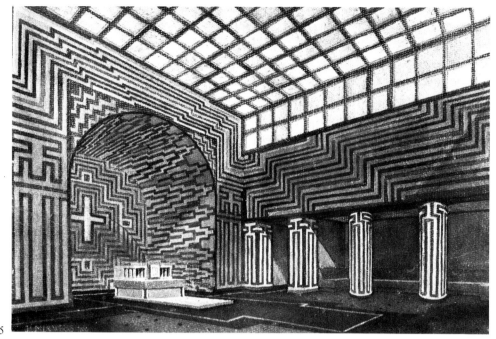

5.35

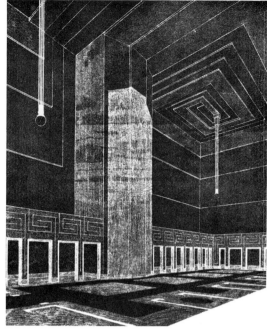

5.36

While Lauweriks was building the first of these houses, for Johan Thorn Prikker, Charles-Edouard Jeanneret must almost certainly have met Lauweriks in Hagen while supervising the construction of Behrens' Cuno house. This encounter was probably a source of Le Corbusier's preoccupation with the tracés régulateurs and ultimately of the Modulor. Lauweriks' influence, through his pupil Adolf Meyer, on the work of Walter Gropius was still more decisive, as can be seen by comparing his furniture designs for the Steger house on the Stirnband with Gropius' office at the Weimar Bauhaus (1923). His impact is likewise evident in the work of J. J. P. Oud and Van Doesburg in the early twenties – especially in Oud's design for the site manager's hut at Oud Mathenesse (1923) and Van Doesburg's project for a monument at Leeuwarden (1918). As N. H. M. Tummers writes in *De Hagener Impuls* (1967): 'The situation in Hagen is extremely significant as a turning point . . . between Jugendstil and the Bauhaus, between Art Nouveau and De Stijl . . . The figure and work of Lauweriks were central to this situation and constitute a further key intersection in the historical development.'

The Stein house at Göttingen (1912) elaborated themes already stated in the Stirnband housing. The following year Lauweriks created perhaps his finest architectural work: a room at the International Exhibition at Ghent. His last designs before leaving Germany, for the 1914 Werkbund Exhibition at Cologne and for a World War Memorial (1915) seem at first to be a return to curvilinear Art Nouveau, but they are in fact based like his other work on a modular system: a spiral generated by the root two series. In 1916 Lauweriks returned to Amsterdam and became the Director of the Quellinus School. He never had the opportunity to build in Holland, and perhaps for this reason has been almost totally ignored until recently. It is still extraordinarily difficult to evaluate his importance. Was he no more than the designer of a few eccentric buildings based on obscure mystical beliefs? Or was he almost alone among Art Nouveau architects in developing the organic essence of Art Nouveau into an intellectual framework which became the basis of later modern architecture? In an article published at the time of Lauweriks' death the Amsterdam School architect C. J. Blauw wrote: 'His system was not merely an attempt to invent artistic form through a meaningless play with line. For him it was the divine thread with which things were embroidered by a higher force. The artist's task was to seize hold of this divine thread and to weave it by creative effort into the work of art, so that it would thrill with the beauty and harmony which stamped it as a thing of a superhuman order.'

J. F. Staal (1879-1940) belonged, with A. J. Kropholler, H. F. Sijmons, J. C. van Epen, J. Crouwel and others to the slightly younger generation of architects who belonged to the school of Berlage and De Bazel. In his extraordinary career he passed from a Berlagian Art Nouveau phase to play a very important part in the Amsterdam School (he was the architect of the Nether-

5.35 LAUWERIKS *Dusseldorf Exhibition of Christian Art* 1909, project for an interior

5.36 LAUWERIKS *Ghent International Exhibition* 1913, project for an interior

5.37 LAUWERIKS *Thorn Prikker house*
Hohenhagen c.1910, perspective

5.38 LAUWERIKS *Stein house* Göttingen 1912,
elevation

5.39 LAUWERIKS *Project for a World War
Memorial* 1915, plan

5.40 LAUWERIKS *Houses on the Stirnband*
Hohenhagen 1910, site plan

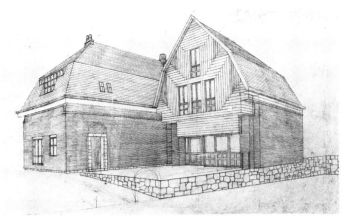

5.37

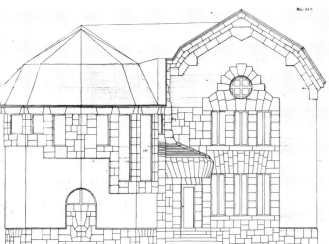

5.38

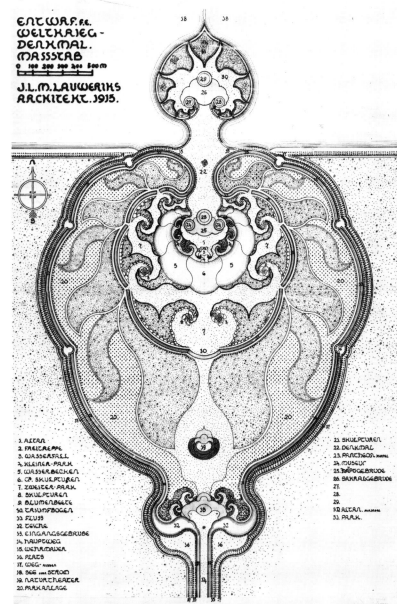

5.39

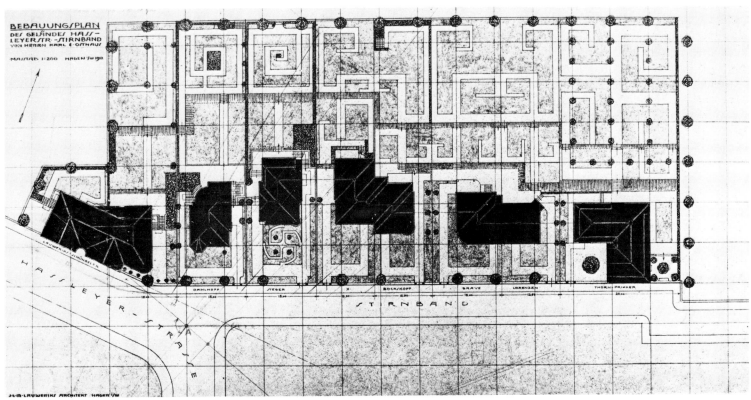

5.40

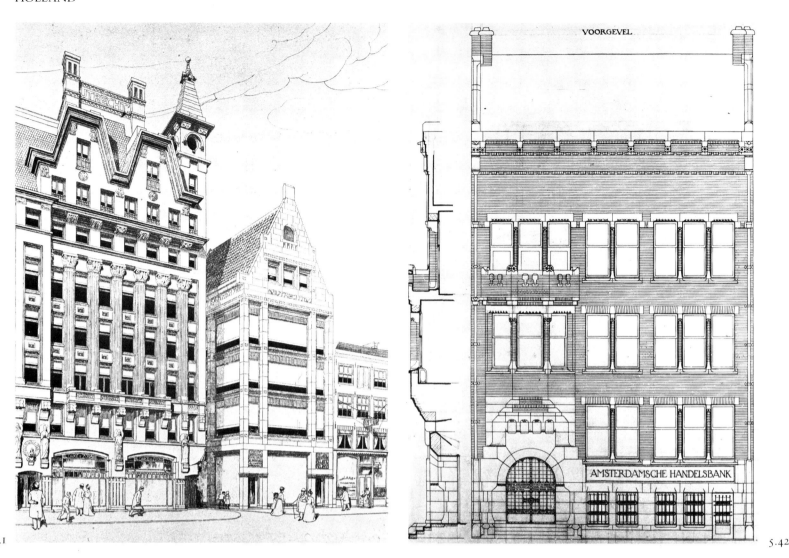

5.41

VOORGEVEL

AMSTERDAMSCHE HANDELSBANK

5.42

lands Pavilion at the Paris Exhibition of 1925) and end in the 1930s as an International Style functionalist. This evolution does not imply a superficial eclecticism; in each phase he made original and significant contributions – he was a leader, not an imitator. His most important Art Nouveau works were the De Utrecht insurance buildings in Amsterdam (1904-6) and Utrecht (1907), the new premises for 't Binnenhuis in the Raadhuisstraat, Amsterdam (1907) – all designed in partnership with A. J. Kropholler – and an office building on the Heerengracht in Amsterdam (1915), of which the interiors, now senselessly destroyed by recent modernisation, were among the richest and most original examples of Dutch Art Nouveau architecture.

Michel de Klerk (1884-1923) was the most brilliant member of the Amsterdam School, and his tragically early death brought to an end its most daring and original phase. His career, like Staal's, forms a link between the Amsterdam School and Art Nouveau. His early work – competition designs for a Café-Restaurant and a club (both 1907) and the first housing blocks on the Spaarndammerplantsoen (1913-14) – show the influence of Olbrich. Like many leading members of the Amsterdam School – J. M. van der Mey, P. L. Kramer, Dick Greiner, J. Boterenbrood and others – De Klerk was trained in the office of P. J. H. Cuypers' nephew Eduard who, beginning as a typical late nineteenth-century eclecticist, produced after about 1900 a number of Art Nouveau buildings, furniture and interiors influenced by van de Velde, Baillie Scott and Olbrich.

In an article in *Architectura*, De Bazel wrote in 1919: 'De Klerk is one of the few who have the gift of animating stone and awakening it into life – one of the few who must become the many so that all stone can be brought to life. This can only be done by injecting oneself into the work, giving one's life-power to it, sacrificing one's own soul and spirit to it; thus vitalised the stone reveals the mystery of the creative force and lives on to invigorate and inspire distant generations.' There could be no better summary of the visionary ideal which inspired the Dutch Art Nouveau movement, and which it transmitted

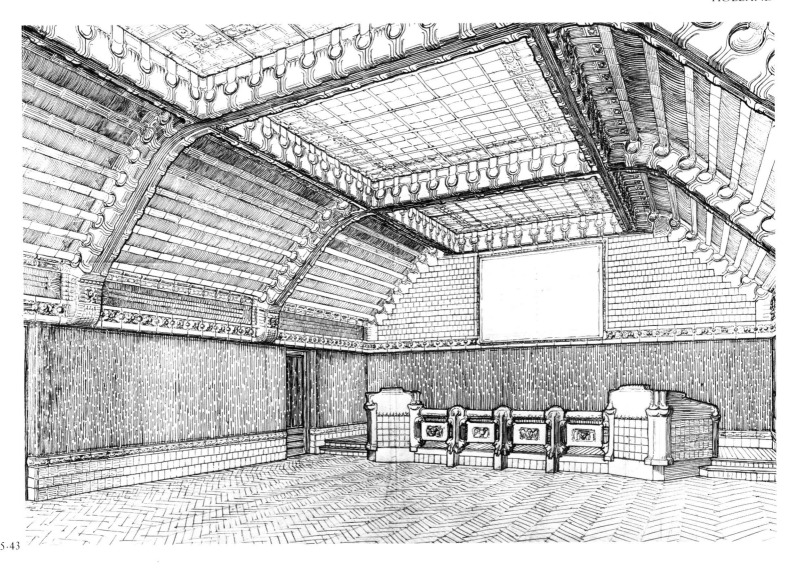

5.43

5.42-43 STAAL *Office building on the Heerengracht* Amsterdam 1915, elevation and conference room

to the movements which grew from it – the Amsterdam School and De Stijl.

★   ★   ★

Art Nouveau architecture was slow to develop in Holland and its output was apparently conservative compared with the revolutionary production of Belgium, France or Austria: Berlage, De Bazel and Kromhout retained strong historicist elements in their work until the post-war period and only Lauweriks was free from any trace of eclecticism. Yet unlike the Art Nouveau of other countries, which flowered brilliantly for a decade but faded and gave way to reaction in the first years of the new century, Dutch Art Nouveau architecture lived on to become a primary source of the heroic movements of the 1920s, and its relation to the work of recent Dutch architects like Aldo van Eyck is no less significant. Perhaps its relevance has never been greater than now, when its central concerns – the twin problems of space and style – are once again fundamental preoccupations in architectural thought.

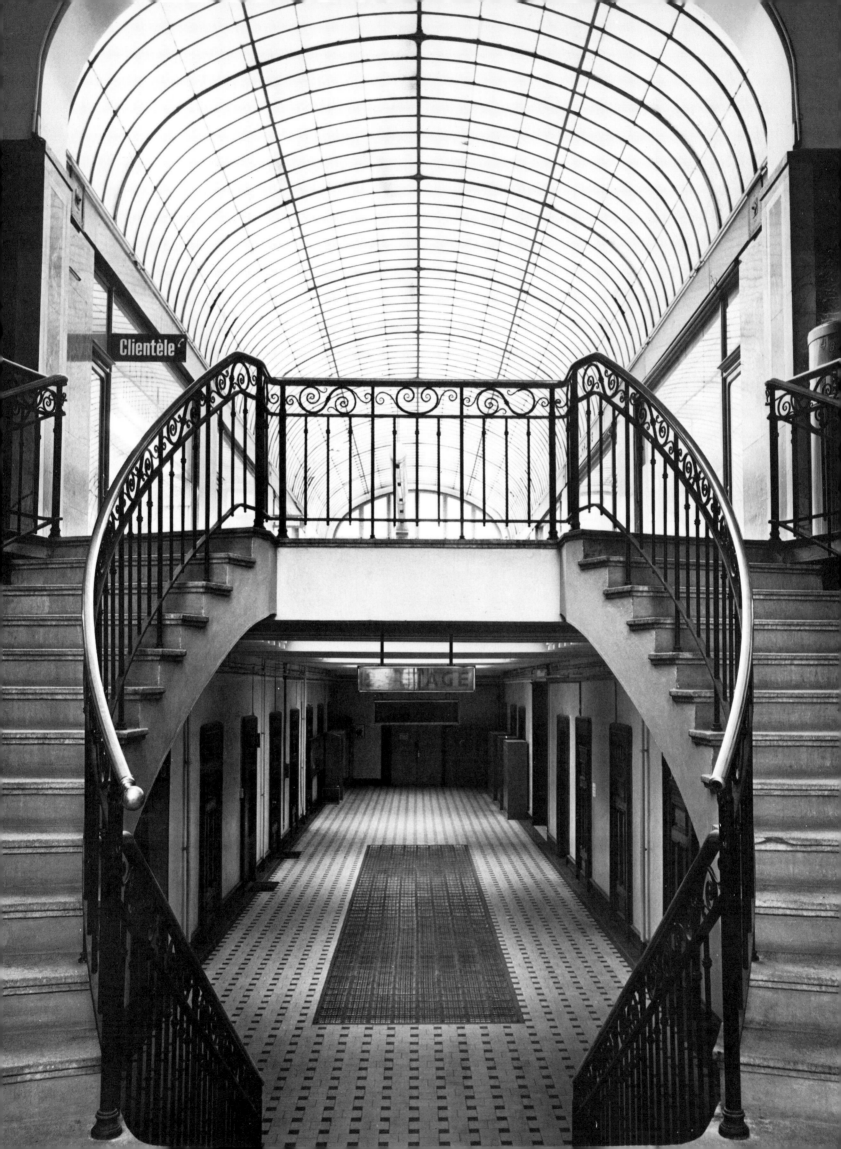

6. SWITZERLAND
The temperate presence of Art Nouveau

Jacques Gubler

During the last decade of the nineteenth century, industry ultimately became the leading sector in Switzerland's economy. While in 1850, 55% of the working population was occupied with agriculture, 35% with industry and 10% with administration, the corresponding figures for the year 1896 ran as follows: 33% (primary sector of agriculture), 44% (secondary sector of industry), 23% (tertiary sector of administration). This shift in the socio-professional distribution of the population corresponded to an increased demand for architecture, particularly in the urban centres. The building industry, whether in the field of housing, commerce, tourism or public works, developed on a broader base and played an important role in the economy of the cities. Since the middle of the 1890s the variety of the products, materials and technical equipment controlled and promoted by the contractors, such as reinforced concrete, synthetic stone, bath tubs, elevators and radiators, strengthened the fragmentation of the operations carried out on the building site and widened the gap between skilled labour and the so-called 'unskilled' workers, most of them imported from Northern Italy. The years 1897-1907 testify to the fight for higher wages, shorter working hours and elementary social security on the part of the masons, bricklayers, labourers, plumbers and carpenters.

This brief historical outline of Switzerland at the turn of the century shows that both the urban and industrial spheres were ready to welcome the advent of Art Nouveau. It seems that both clients and spectators could easily be found by architects, whether in the launching of a crusade for social reconciliation by renovating the arts and crafts, or in experimenting with new formulae of design to answer the demand for singularity and exclusiveness expressed by the nouveaux riches and the new intelligentsia.

Now, on the contrary, critics have discovered how slight the international impact of Art Nouveau in fact was in Switzerland, particularly when compared with the creative neighbouring centres of Germany, France and Northern Italy. It has even been proposed to substitute for the term Jugendstil the more appropriate label of 'Nationale Romantik' (National Romanticism), now generally in use.[1] Indeed, a decisive event in Swiss history during the period 1890-1910 was the codification and crystallisation of nationalism in a whole set of picturesque and colourful clichés associated with recurrent cultural practices. The celebration of the 'Fête nationale' was instituted in 1891. The Landesmuseum (National Museum) was inaugurated at Zurich in 1898, with a sequence of rooms illustrating the history of the Swiss since prehistoric times. Perhaps the most significant manifestation of the 'new tradition' was staged at the National Exhibition of Geneva in 1896, when a complete model village was built to personify the moral and cultural identity of the country. As a vehicle for nationalism, the architectural mise en scène of the Swiss Village was amplified by the poets and the mass-media. Innumerable images circulated such as post cards and films made by the Lumière brothers. The Swiss Village was rebuilt at the Parisian World Exhibition of 1900 where it was hailed as one of the most attractive, exotic and popular exhibits.[2]

In Switzerland itself, the architectural scenery of the Village produced two

6.1 ROSSET & SCHMID *Galeries du Commerce* Lausanne 1908-09, central staircase of the upper passage (photograph Collomb)

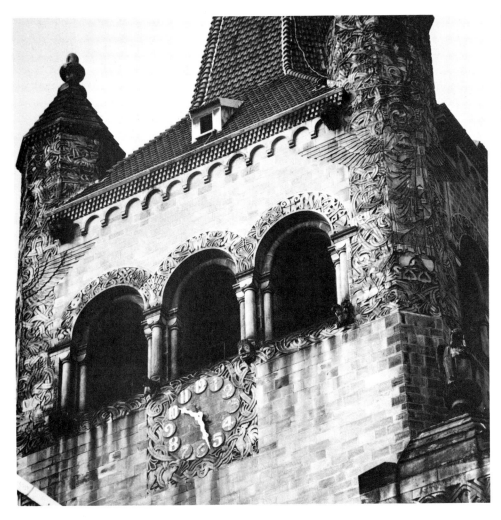

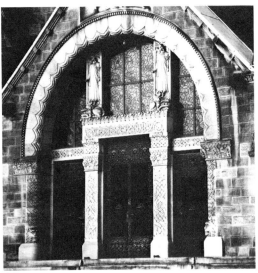

6.2-3 MOSER *St. Paul's Church* Basel 1898-1901, tower and entrance detail (photographs Collomb)

consequences. First it settled a national 'commonplace'. Second it created a whole set of picturesque images used by the architect's client. Art Nouveau could be dismissed as non-Swiss or even dangerous in its 'cosmopolitan' or international, circulatory aspects.[3] In other words, the very ideological motivation which served Art Nouveau in Scotland, Catalonia or Piedmont, i.e. the quest for an autonomous national identity, in fact worked to its detriment in Switzerland.

The Swiss nationalist mistrust of Art Nouveau[4] should not be overstressed. Fairly often the anti-academic tendencies of Art Nouveau have been described as subversive for society, probably because historians needed 'pioneers' to prove the alleged 'revolution' of the Modern Movement. Such an interpretation does not account for the ability of promoters to use fashion as an advertising signpost, nor for the capacity of academies to absorb novelties. The case of Switzerland shows the conjunction of Art Nouveau and Regionalism, i.e. 'local art' or 'local architecture'. In this respect, Eugène Viollet-le-Duc, who died at Lausanne, should be recalled for three reasons: 1) his ambiguous position vis-à-vis the Academy; 2) his ability to produce mixed systems; 3) his arguments in defence of vernacular architecture, 'an architecture subservient to the needs and appropriate to the habits of the people, the climate, the materials'.[5]

The importance of Regionalism at the turn of the century constituted one of the main topics of the Henri Sauvage Exhibition of 1976.[6] The section entitled the 'entourage' contained works typical of the corporate identity of the studio of Jean-Louis Pascal at the Ecole des Beaux-Arts. The entries submitted by Alphonse Laverrière to the juries of the annual Concours d'Emulation,[7] show that Pascal's students had been using Art Nouveau typography and 'dynamographic' mise en page since 1897, often combined with the picturesque rendering of rural, touristic, sportive, alpine or oceanic programmes, such as the upper station of a funicular or the villa on a cliff. Laverrière's diploma project of 1901, showing a mountain inn in Haute-Savoie,[8] might be considered as a personal 'gentle manifesto' for the picturesque synchronisation of Regionalism and Art Nouveau. The ability to use Art Nouveau formulae demonstrated by the younger architects with academic training, born in the 1870s and working in

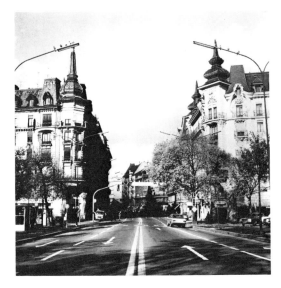

6.4 CAVALLI & GOLAY *Maison des Pans* (left)
and *Maison des Paons* (right) Geneva 1902-03
(photographs Collomb)

6.5 CAVALLI & GOLAY *Maison des Paons*
(photograph Collomb)

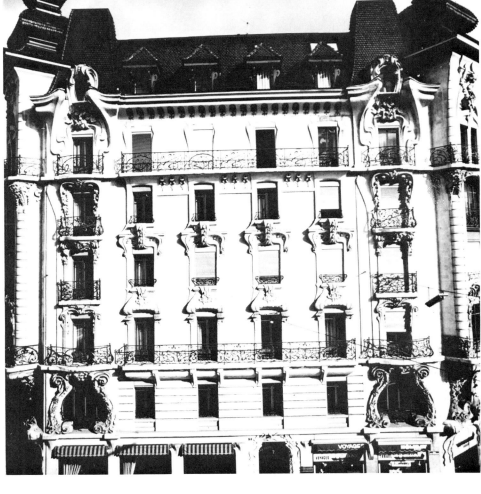

Switzerland during the first decade of the twentieth century, was equalled by the considerable ease shown by older practitioners – some of them born in the 1840s or 1850s – not only in reproducing Jugendstil but also in creating new variations of it, as in the case of Hans Karl Eduard Berlepsch-Valendas' remodelling of the Villa Tobler[9] (1898-1900) in Zurich. Unlike Horta, Mackintosh or Gaudí, the Swiss architects consciously failed to produce new typologies. Art Nouveau entered routine office work, and the years 1903-1905 show a general escalation. Synchronised with Regionalism, seasoned with the picturesque, or subsiding into the mellow tone of neo-Baroque, Art Nouveau became part of the urban landscape in practically all the cities of large and medium size. Adopting Loos' metaphors, Charles-Edouard Jeanneret described the situation a little later in terms of tattooing or make-up: 'Let us be careful that the error lies basically in the *maquillage* and not in the organ.'[10]

When applied to turn of the century Switzerland, the fashionable method of pioneer-hunting proves unsuccessful. This lack of success arises from the method rather than from the architecture itself. Many Art Nouveau works were in fact created in Switzerland and these should be placed within the context of the professional efficiency and relatively high level of culture of the architectural aristocracy, which included architects trained at the Polytechnic in Zurich, such as H. P. Berlage, or at the Ecole de Beaux-Arts in Paris, or even at both schools, such as Karl Moser whose St. Paul's Church in Basel, designed in 1898, was consecrated in 1901. Early Christian interlacing sculpture was reinterpreted for that building in the sense of Art Nouveau 'dynamography'.

It would perhaps be better to follow the typological identity of the buildings than the personalities of their architects. In the field of housing, the apartment house of the upper middle class, with commercial activities on the ground floor, determined the 'street-scape'. The vertical stratification (gabarit) used by Haussmann in Paris, typical of the boulevard Sébastopol and the rue de la Paix, was used in Geneva and sporadically in Lausanne and Fribourg at the turn of the century. The Maison des Paons (House of the Peacocks), 7 avenue Pictet-de-Rochemont in Geneva (1902-03) was built by the firm of two 'non-pedigree' but successful architects, Eugène Cavalli and Ami Golay. The facade of this building

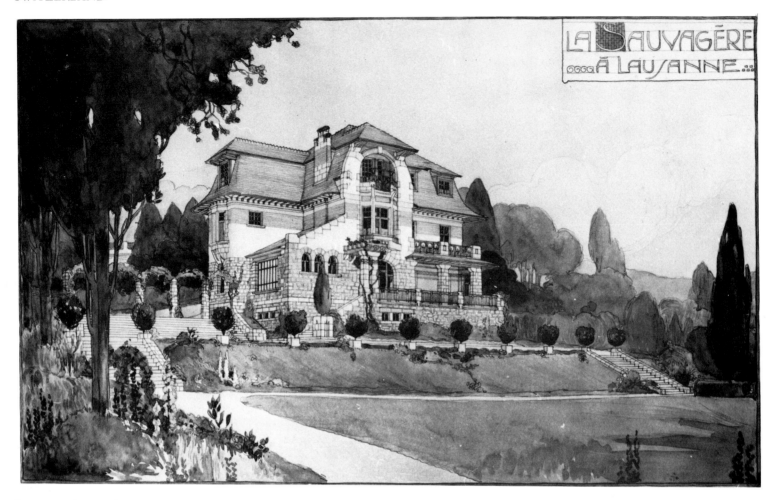

6.6 LAVERRIERE *Villa 'La Sauvagère'* Lausanne 1905-06, perspective drawing

has now been placed under legal protection. But its alter ego, the Maison des Pans, similar in typology and volumetrics and produced at the same time by the same firm, has been ignored because of its neo-Baroque decoration. In fact, a mere pun accounts for the alternative use of an Art Nouveau and a Baroque facade; the word paon (peacock) in French is pronounced the same as the name of the god Pan, whose effigies reign on the second building. Conventional in typology, but utterly 'belle époque' in decoration, the facades of the Maison des Paons and the Maison des Pans are pieces of applied and talented sculpture signed 'Fasanino', probably a craftsman of Italian origin.

Characteristic features of Art Nouveau decoration on apartment houses can be seen at Lausanne, Bienne, Basel, Zurich and elsewhere in Switzerland. As far as the villa is concerned, the English expression 'domestic architecture' was adopted in French at the very beginning of the twentieth century by Gabriel Mouray, one of the editors of the Parisian magazine *Art et Décoration*. For Mouray, the term 'architecture domestique' designated the 'lodging for a family of the enlightened bourgeoisie',[11] thus situating Art Nouveau under the banner of Maecenas. The banks of Lake Geneva[12] provided an ideal situation for such houses, the most prestigious of which is situated at Evian, where the baron Vitta had his Italianesque Villa 'La Sapinière',[13] modernised in 1900-01 by the craftsmen Alexandre Charpentier, Félix Braquemond and Jules Chéret.

The political concept of 'Gesamtkunstwerk', first used by Michael Bakunin in 1850, had been interpreted by Richard Wagner as a synthesis of the arts and was to enable distinguished practitioners to create completely integral architectural mises en scène.

The Villa 'La Sauvagère', avenue Verdeil, Lausanne (1905-06) by Alphonse Laverièrre is typical both of Gesamtkunstwerk and of the type of house commissioned by the enlightened bourgeoisie. On the ground floor are the reception rooms and the kitchen, while the first floor contains the intimate circuit of bathroom, dressing room, bedroom, a large library and a studio.[14] At first sight it would appear that the Villa Mayer-Daguet, avenue du Gambach 19, Fribourg (1905-06) by Frédéric Broillet and Charles-Albert Wulffleff is organised in the same way, although it contains three apartments. The proprietors of both houses in fact belonged to the same social group of university professors and enlightened financiers. The type of the 'villa locative' (tenement villa) which implies that an

Opposite above
LAVERRIERE *Villa 'La Sauvagère'* (photograph Collomb)

Opposite below
BELLI *Crematorium* La Chaux-de-Fonds 1908, interior roof detail (photograph Collomb)

Page 164
JEANNERET & CHAPALLAZ *Villa Fallet* La Chaux-de-Fonds 1905-07, exterior and detail of staircase (photographs Collomb)

Page 165
6.7 CHARPENTIER, BRAQUEMOND & CHERET *Villa 'La Sapinière'* Evian 1900-01, billiard room (photograph Collomb)

6.8 HERTLING *Weissenbach building* Fribourg 1902 (photograph Collomb)

6.9-10 BROILLET & WULFFLEFF *Villa Mayer-Daguet* Fribourg 1905-06, facade and detail (photographs Collomb)

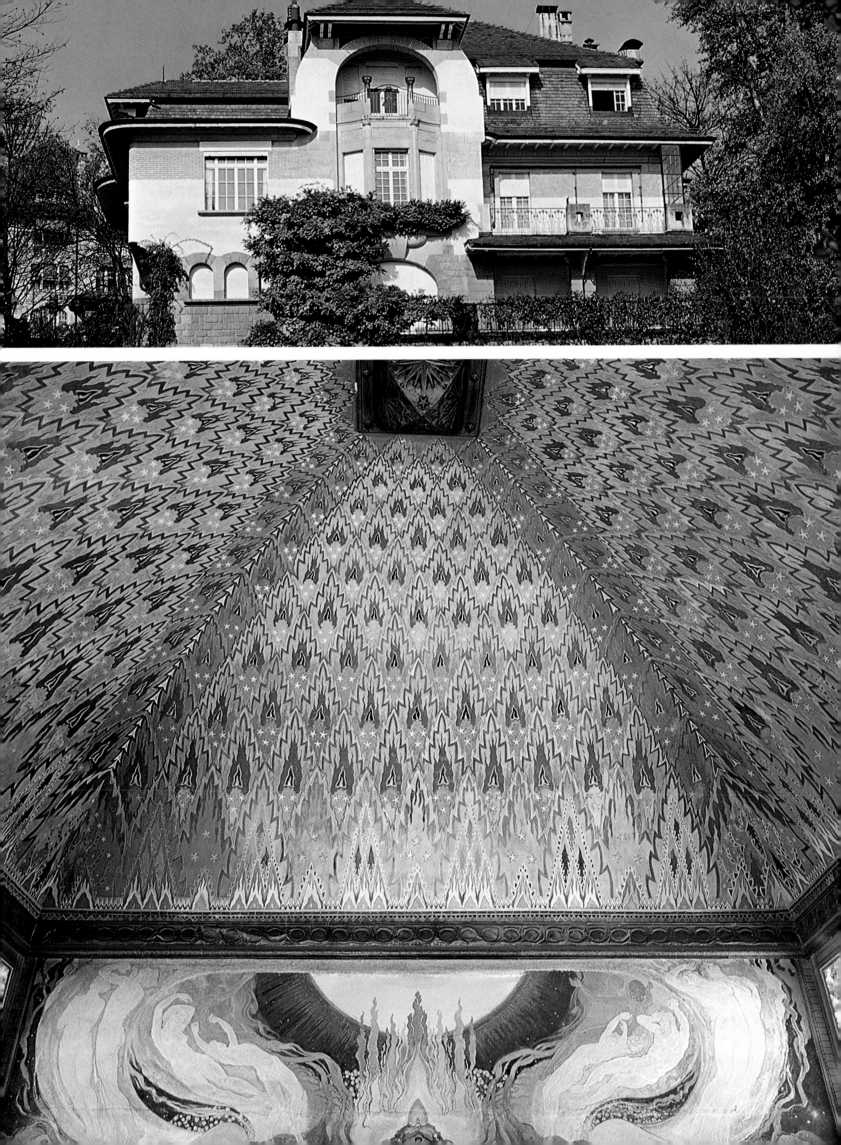

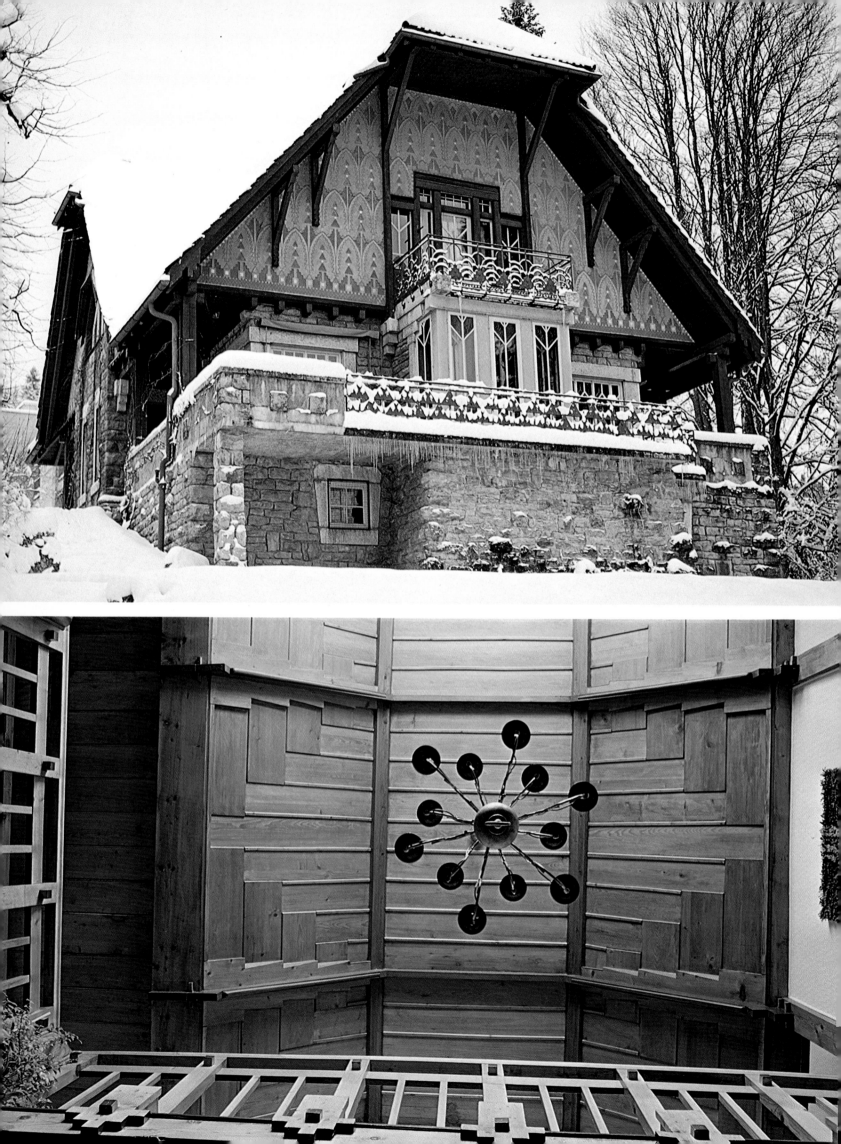

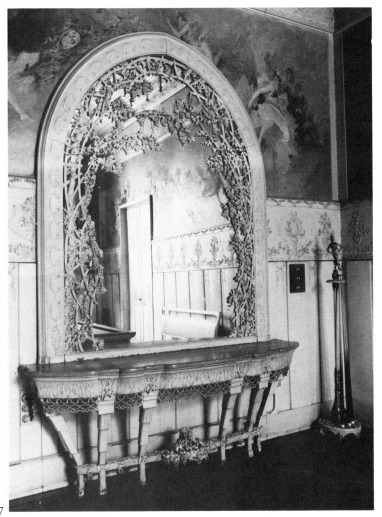

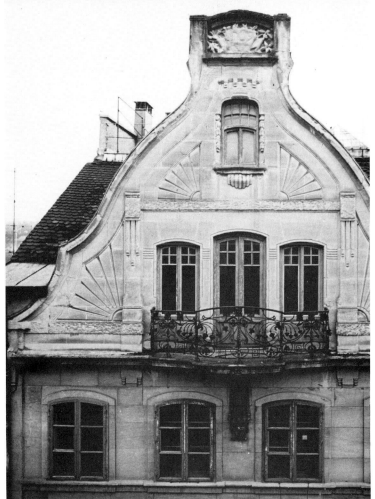

6.7

6.8

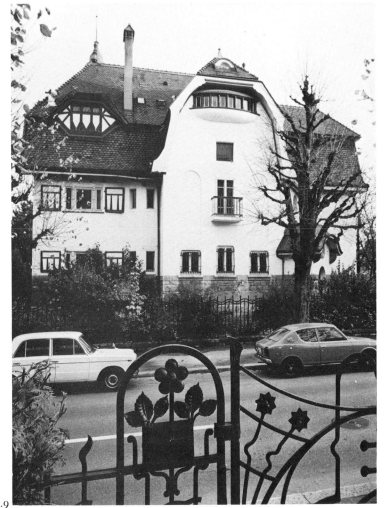

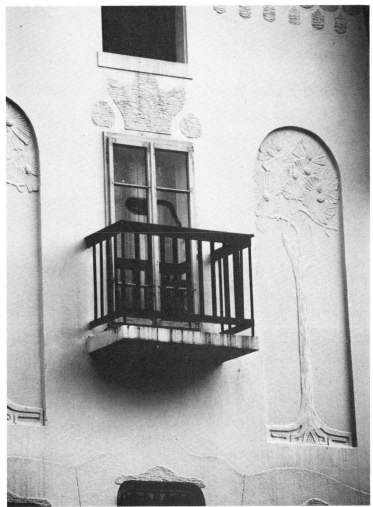

6.9

6.10

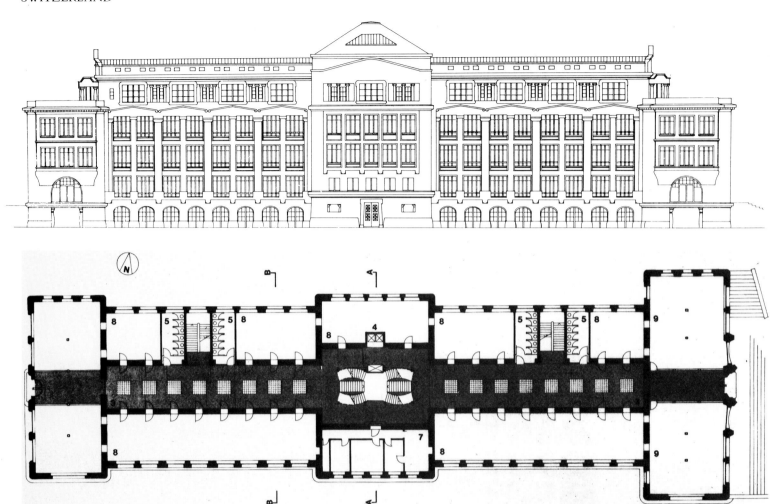

apartment house should look like a private house, was developed on a large scale in Switzerland from the middle of the 1890s, less for the convenience of the tourist than for the local intelligentsia. The Villa Mayer-Daguet at Fribourg is situated on the local 'Matildenhöhe', and its decoration and inner organisation reminds one of the work of Joseph Maria Olbrich. The partnership of Broillet and Wulffleff, active at the peak of the building boom, lasted from the years 1903 to 1911 and produced a considerable catalogue of buildings, on the whole much closer to Regionalism and academicism than to Art Nouveau. Of the two architects, the first was Swiss and had studied at the Polytechnic in Zurich and the Ecole des Beaux-Arts in Paris, whilst the second, born in London, was trained at H. Deglane's Parisian Beaux-Arts atelier.

The advertising potential of Art Nouveau obviously made it suitable for commercial architecture, as demonstrated by the Volkart store at St. Gall (1904) by the architects Ernst Jung and Otto Bridler. The restructuring of mediaeval urban centres to accommodate the increase in commercial activity was witnessed in all Swiss cities at the turn of the century. The Art Nouveau gable of the Weissenbach building, 22 rue de Lausanne, Fribourg (1902) by Léon Hertling functions as a new shop sign. It appears as an additional storey in the feudal cityscape and proves how extensively the Darmstadt magazine *Deutsche Kunst und Dekoration* circulated in Switzerland.

Among several commercial monuments built in the first decade of the twentieth century, the Galeries du Commerce, 2 rue de la Grotte, Lausanne, is particularly interesting for the typological synthesis of an urban thoroughfare in the attic storey of a multi-purpose office building. Like Léon Hertling, the architects of this work, Paul Rosset and Otto Schmid, were educated at the Zurich Polytechnic in the tradition of Gottfried Semper. Academic rationalism accounts for the plan[16] and volumetrics of the Galeries at Lausanne. But the glazed thoroughfare and the central bi-elliptical staircase belong to the world of purified and precious Viennese ornamentation. It should be recalled that Adolf Loos was active at Montreux in 1904-06, when starting the Villa Karma. The marble panelling of the upper thoroughfare at Lausanne appeared in 1908-09.

In the field of public works, the Chauderon bridge (1904-05) at Lausanne is

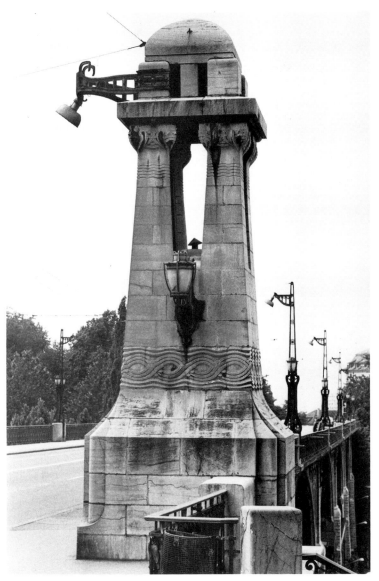
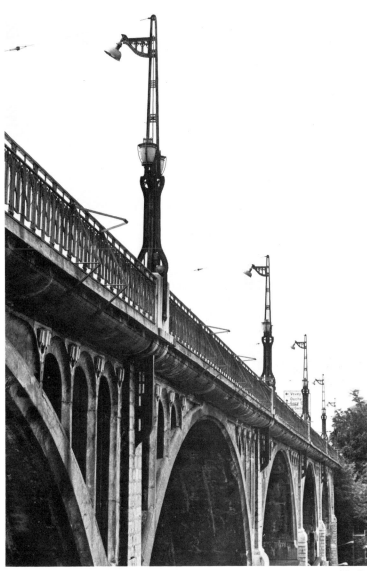

6.13-14 LAVERRIERE *Chauderon Bridge* Lausanne 1904-05 (photographs Mandelmann)

worthy of attention. It resulted from a competition won by a Lausanne engineering firm using the Melan patent for reinforced concrete arches. According to a corporative practice often used in Swiss cities during the period 1896-1912, engineering firms entering public competitions had to collaborate with architectural firms. The Chauderon bridge was designed by Alphonse Laverièrre and his associate Eugène Monod, both from Pascal's atelier at Paris.

The bridge becomes a feature of the urban landscape by means of its four pylons. Pylon, street-lamp, balustrade and the technical system of the Melan arch are treated in the best manner of geometricized nature. 'Dynamographic' is the appropriate expression for it, and Henry van de Velde, who created the word as a personal manifesto, would make a little pilgrimage to the Chauderon bridge when passing through Lausanne.[17]

Returning to the problem of nationalism and Art Nouveau, the case of La Chaux-de-Fonds should be isolated as a possible exception.[18] At the turn of the century, this city was a world centre of the watch industry.[19] Both the local intelligentsia and the workers' unions tried to develop cultural models specific to the Jura. The need for highly efficient work and skilled labour had generated a surprising number of schools for a town of 35,000 inhabitants (in 1900) and produced a strong professional division in the technical fields of watch-making, mechanics, business and the arts and crafts. During the years 1904-05, the School of Art was gradually reorganised by its new director, the young painter Charles L'Eplattenier who was to become Charles-Edouard Jeanneret's first mentor, later receiving the affectionate epithet 'my old master'. Three areas of study were defined. The first, 'general and basic', coped with 'the arts of drawing' or, the 'Grammaire des Arts du Dessin', to quote Charles Blanc, whose two volumes served as text-books in the school library.[20] Drawing courses were given at night to compliment the training of apprentices. The second area was 'professional', the emphasis being mainly on metalwork, and the four-year course aimed at providing a refined artisan training for students already interested in the arts. The third area, whose theoretical and practical importance was to increase until 1912, focused on interior decoration and architecture. The latter students were a small group, often chosen by the director from among the 'best elements' of the 'professional classes', and themselves contributed to the teaching. Like Henry van de Velde and Peter Behrens, L'Eplattenier was primarily a painter. His involvement in the Arts and Crafts movement came comparatively late, at a time when works produced at Nancy and Darmstadt, for example, filled the magazines.[21] L'Eplattenier's campaign for the renovation of the Ecole d'Art gained much local credibility when the school was awarded an honorary degree for exhibiting 108 watches at the Milan International Exhibition of 1906, which celebrated the opening of the Simplon tunnel. At that time the La Chaux-de-Fonds watch industry was subjected to increasing competition, whilst the amount of building work was increasing rapidly in the city, which could offer prospects of immediate development. Built in 1906-07, the Villa Fallet, 1 chemin de Pouillerel, La Chaux-de-Fonds must be seen not only as Charles-Edouard Jeanneret's first house, but also as a manifesto of the new tendencies inside the School of Art. L'Eplattenier found not only the client but also a young architect willing to share his knowledge and provide official supervision, René Chapallaz.

The plan of the house is unmistakably Jeanneret's in its logic. It consists of two floors and a basement. On the first floor, the kitchen with its own 'chemin de ronde' is clearly separated from the large single living area facing South and lengthened by a closed loggia. An open staircase occupies the whole Northern gable and provides the 'spatial surprise' of a hall on two levels. The fireplace as a focusing element is rejected, and central heating is used instead. The second floor consists mainly of large bedrooms. The separation of day and night areas is another strong feature of the house, probably influenced by English domestic architecture via Muthesius. The Villa Fallet is an exercise in the synthesis of Regionalism and Art Nouveau.[22] The crossed gables of the roof give it a picturesque articulation. Yellow ochre limestone, the local stone in the canton of Neuchâtel, serves as the opus rusticum of the basement and Western entrance front. The polychromic facades, executed in collaboration with the painter André Evard, illustrate Art Nouveau. The fruit and the profile of the fir tree are conjugated in a denticulated pattern, a play on the word cone. The fir tree motif is also taken up in the metalwork and woodwork.

The Villa Fallet aimed at identifying specific Jura formulae. The result is almost Wrightian in its expression of 'nature' by means of contrasted materials. And this attempt is carried further in Jeanneret's next two houses, the Villas Jaquemet and Stotzer. Both villas were built in 1908, in association with René Chapallaz. Again, the composed roof and the yellow stone base show the prudent life-style of the mountain intelligentsia. The strong protruding pillars boisterously express the system of construction, i.e. reinforced concrete according to the Hennebique patent. François Hennebique used the expression 'fibrous monolith' to advertise the resistance of his system to fire and earthquake, and his patent had been used in Switzerland since 1894.[24] At the turn of the century it became general practice in the cities of Lausanne, Neuchâtel, Berne and Basel. At La Chaux-de-Fonds itself, the Cantonal Bank (1901) was the first to use Hennebique's system. Factories, apartment buildings, villas, and a hotel had been completed before Chapallaz and Jeanneret were commissioned by Jaquemet and Stotzer. Indeed, the Villa Stotzer is a lived-in monolith, and the application of a monolithic structure to housing was soon to become one of Jeanneret's main preoccupations.[25]

L'Eplattenier's School of Art gave final public proof of its vitality in the construction of the crematorium, designed in 1908 by Robert Belli, the 'architect of the Commune of La Chaux-de-Fonds', and Henri Robert. An axial porch penetrates the central plan of the 'block'. The machinery of the crematorium is situated in the ground floor. The stairs in the open 'triumphal arch' convey the mourners to an upper room, a cubic space 'swallowed' by the pavilion dome. L'Eplattenier and his work-shop used the typically Art Nouveau symbolism of the Four Elements. The intrados of the cupola is related to fire, in close relation to the outer central chimney, the black fumes of which, visible after the ceremony with the help of an ingenious mechanism, are intended to express the sublimation of ashes, i.e. the earth. The geometricization of the fir tree reappears as the main motif in the decoration, hence the conjunction of flames and denticulated

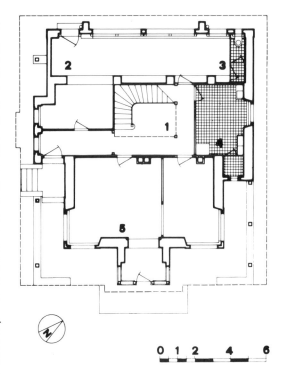

6.15 JEANNERET & CHAPALLAZ *Villa Fallet* La Chaux-de-Fonds 1906-07, ground floor plan (from the original drawing)

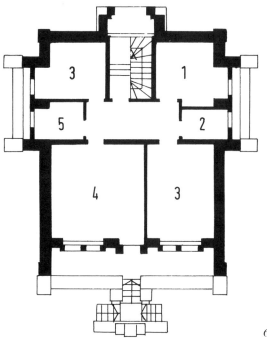

6.16

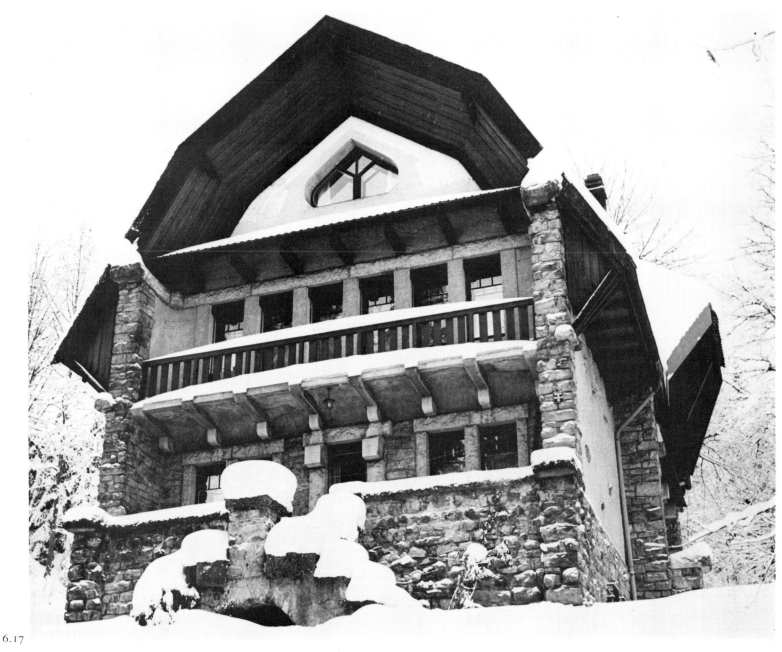

6.17

6.16-17 JEANNERET & CHAPALLAZ *Villa Stotzer* La Chaux-de-Fonds 1908, ground floor plan (from the original drawing) and facade (photograph Collomb)

6.18 BELLI *Crematorium* La Chaux-de-Fonds 1908 (photograph Collomb)

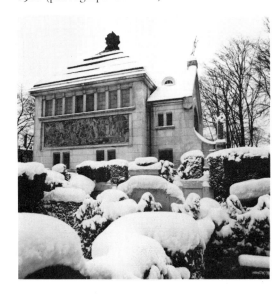

flat cones in the cupola.

Returning to the problem of Art Nouveau and Regionalism in Switzerland, it is interesting to quote Jeanneret. His attitude towards the subject might have been shared by several distinguished practitioners such as Laverrière, Broillet, Hertling, Robert Rittmeyer and Walter Furrer. These architects rejected copyism and the caricature of local monuments, but not the adaptation of their works to the mental and physical landscape of the genius loci. 'I shall proceed by being true to the things I admire, whatever these may be, and by undergoing influences, wherever they come from. A set of dogmatic laws, issuing from the surrounding milieu, has never proclaimed itself. But I would hope that long, sincere work could be my teacher; that, little by little, nature and the life of my surroundings would permeate me; and that my work would betray this influence. The esprit local is not acquired by an act of will but comes from a gradual ascendency, from an intuition.'[26]

Such sentiments, partly tabooed by Le Corbusier, could not be abolished later without also destroying a good many buildings completed in that first decade of the twentieth century.

Alan Colquhoun, Gilles Barbey and Allan Brooks contributed to the discussion of this chapter.

169

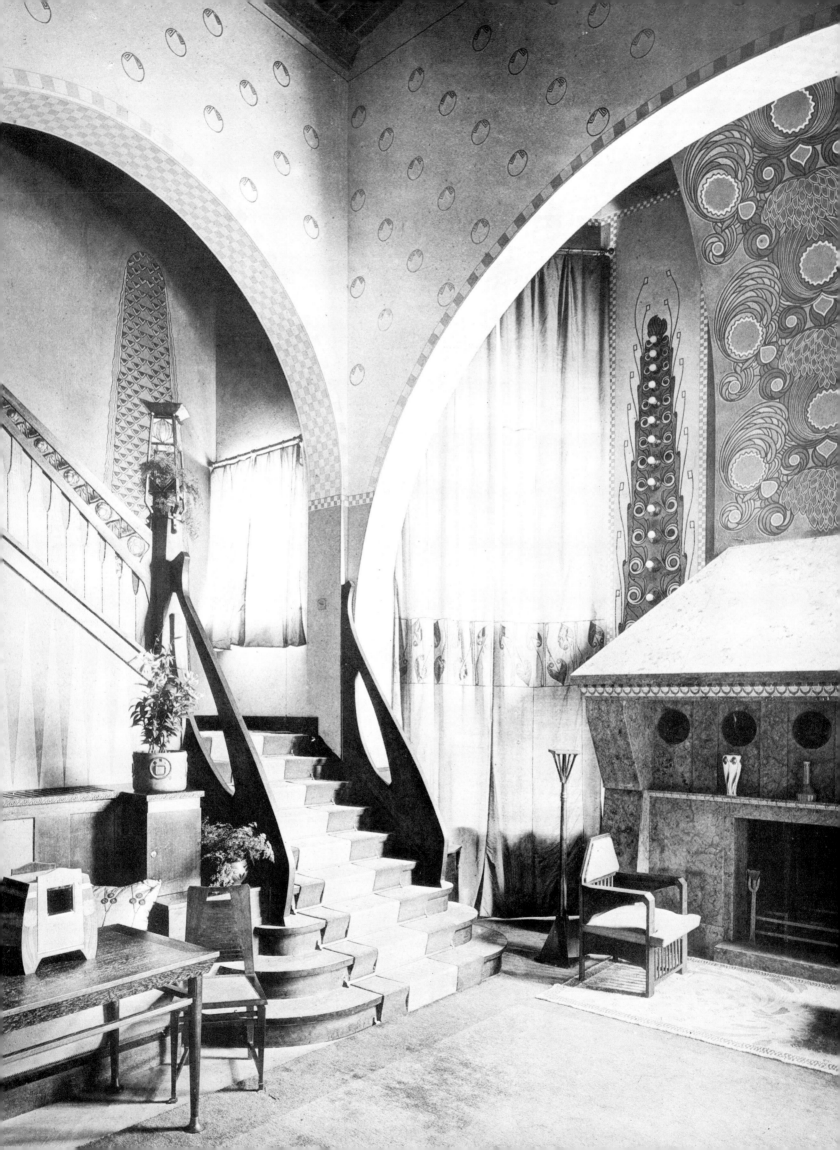

7. GERMANY

Jugendstil: the early morning of the Modern Movement

Ian Latham

'Germany is in the happy situation that it has not yet shown its strength . . . Here it is indeed the early morning that we experience. Perhaps the midday can bestow beautiful things upon us.'[1] The accuracy of Julius Meier-Graefe's optimistic assessment of Germany's artistic potential, made in the final year of the nineteenth century when Art Nouveau was at its zenith, was soon to be proven.

The Jugendstil, as Art Nouveau became known in Germany, was a short yet important phase in the architectural development of the country. Compared with other European countries its appearance came relatively late and its abandonment early, but for the brief period between 1895 and 1904 its influence pervaded and extended the spheres of artistic awareness.

During the latter half of the nineteenth century dramatic changes were taking place in Germany. Rapid industrial development together with imperial expansion brought increased wealth and a striving for national identity. This found architectural expression in neo-Renaissance and neo-Baroque forms, though dissatisfaction with their ornamental exuberance led also to a Romanesque revival which was felt to offer a truer German style. By the 1890s there existed such a confusion of styles that the need for reform became evident; the path was clearing for the introduction of the radical movements that were spreading across Europe.

The three most important influences on German Art Nouveau, as described by Joseph Lux, were the English Arts and Crafts movement of William Morris and John Ruskin, the distinctive work of the Glasgow School, which reached Germany primarily through Vienna, and the individual efforts of the Belgian designer Henry van de Velde.

The call for a return to craftsmanship values and the social reforms suggested by Morris and his followers found a receptive audience in Germany, where the ideas were to be further developed, culminating in the establishment of the Deutscher Werkbund in 1907. The associated revival of interest in domestic architecture was brought to light by Hermann Muthesius who spent seven years at the German Embassy in London before producing a number of well-documented books which included the work of Voysey, Baillie Scott, Townsend and Ashbee.

Improved printing techniques and production methods meant that rapid artistic communication became possible on an unprecedented scale. *The Studio* magazine, founded in 1893, was crucial in the dissemination of English ideas on the Continent. It also precipitated the introduction of many similar journals, particularly in Germany: *Pan* 1895, *Jugend* 1896, *Kunst und Kunsthandwerk, Dekorative Kunst, Deutsche Kunst und Dekoration,* and *Kunst und Dekoration* 1897.

Not until 1896 did the collective efforts of the Glasgow Four achieve recognition in *The Studio,* by which time continental Art Nouveau was generally well advanced. However, in Austria and Germany, where the movement was in its infancy, the work of Mackintosh provided additional impetus and inspiration particularly to the Vienna Secession which was developing from a comparable geometric/symbolist basis. The Austrian architect Joseph Maria Olbrich was personally responsible for introducing the 'Secessionstil' to Germany when, in

7.1 OLBRICH *Grosses Glückert house* Darmstadt 1900, hall (contemporary photograph)

1899, he accepted an invitation from the Grand Duke of Hesse to come to Darmstadt.

The importance of patronage in the architectural development of Germany should not be underestimated. The same benefactor who offered Olbrich the means for his architectural experimentation in Darmstadt had earlier commissioned Baillie Scott and Ashbee. Van de Velde owed much of his success to Julius Meier-Graefe, Karl Ernst Osthaus and the Grand Duke of Saxe-Weimar, and in 1907 the AEG company gave Peter Behrens total responsibility for the design of their products, their factories and even their publicity information.

Henry van de Velde was enthusiastically received in Germany in 1897, calling for a reappraisal of design standards much along the lines of the English Arts and Crafts movement with an emphasis on function and construction. His teaching influenced the direction taken by many of the Jugendstil designers, although van de Velde's own architectural solutions did not always fulfil expectations. Like William Morris he felt unable to reconcile artistic quality with a commitment to machine production.

The diversity of influences on Germany, both external and internal, resulted in almost as many modes of expression as there were individual architects. Many artists developed a Jugendstil vocabulary of form and pattern which they could apply to graphics, sculpture, the applied arts and architecture; indeed it was not uncommon for them to work in all fields at the same time. They were united in their conviction of the need for a thorough reappraisal, to free the arts from the plagiarism that had been accepted without question for so long.

Munich gradually developed as an important centre of Jugendstil during the 1890s, supported after 1896 by the *Jugend* (Youth) magazine, from which the style acquired its apt name, reaching its height in 1897 with the establishment of the Vereinigte Werkstätten. In 1899 on the instigation of Grand Duke Ernst Ludwig, an artists' colony was set up in Darmstadt, with the arrival of Olbrich from Vienna, and among others Peter Behrens from Munich. Darmstadt and Munich therefore represent successive epicentres of the new ideas although their periods of Jugendstil activity had virtually ceased by about 1904.

The earliest indications of an Art Nouveau movement in Germany appeared in Munich around the early 1890s. 1892 saw the foundation of the Munich Secession by Fritz von Uhde and Franz Stuck, and the Dutch symbolist Jan Toorop held an important exhibition in the city in 1893. Many young artists gravitated towards Munich, soon establishing it as the avant-garde centre of German art. The magazines *Jugend, Simplizissimus, Kunst und Kunsthandwerk* and *Dekorative Kunst* began publication in Munich during the next few years, providing vehicles for both local illustrators and foreign artists.

One of the few direct precursors of Jugendstil in Germany was the painter and sculptor Max Klinger (1857-1920), who became president of the Secession in 1897. His graphic work from 1878 onwards reveals most of the salient characteristics of Munich Jugendstil, notably its linearity and asymmetry in composition and pattern, often based on natural sources and substantially influenced by Japanese art.

It was this passion for nature that proved fundamental to the varied work of one of the central and most influential figures of the Munich Group, Hermann Obrist (1863-1927). Son of a Swiss doctor and a Scottish aristocrat, he originally studied medicine and natural sciences before turning to ceramics (Karlsruhe 1888) and sculpture (Paris 1890, Florence 1892). This conversion to the arts was reputedly the result of a daydream Obrist experienced in 1886: 'A whole city appeared in the sky, where the strange architecture excelled all he had seen before; everything was in motion in this town; the streets shifting, revealing squares with fantastic fountains; the houses opened up and revealed inconceivably fine rooms and mysterious devices.'[2] In 1892 Obrist together with Berthe Ruchet founded an embroidery workshop in Florence, and two years later they brought it to Munich and exhibited 39 examples of their work at the Odeonsplatz. These pulsating organic forms caused a sensation. Having set a precedent for the direct use of plant and animal sources, Obrist returned to three dimensions, his subsequent output including an impressive series of early expressionist sculptures.

Dissatisfaction with the established artistic limits in Munich came to a head in 1897, when about thirty young artists joined to form the 'Vereinigte Werkstätten für Kunst und Handwerk'. Members of this so-called Munich Circle included

Opposite above left
OLBRICH *Haus Stöhr* St. Pölten 1899, perspective drawing

Opposite above right
OLBRICH *Haus Olbrich* Darmstadt 1900, perspective drawing

Opposite below left
BEHRENS *Haus Behrens* Darmstadt 1901, detail of doorway (photograph Benton)

Opposite below right
OLBRICH *Grosses Glückert house* Darmstadt 1900, entrance (photograph Latham)

Page 174 above
OLBRICH *Grosses Glückert house* (photograph Godoli)

Page 174 below
OLBRICH *Ernst Ludwig Haus* Darmstadt 1899 (photograph Godoli)

Page 175
OLBRICH *Hochzeitsturm* (Wedding Tower) Darmstadt 1905-08 (photograph Godoli)

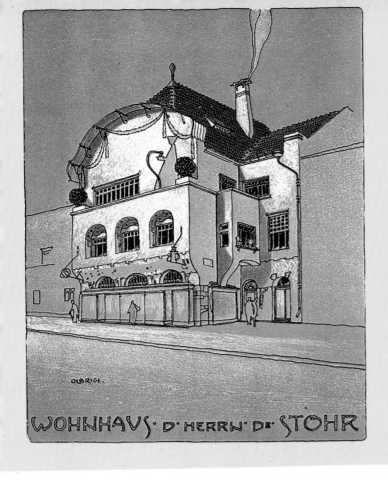

WOHNHAVS D: HERRN D: STOHR

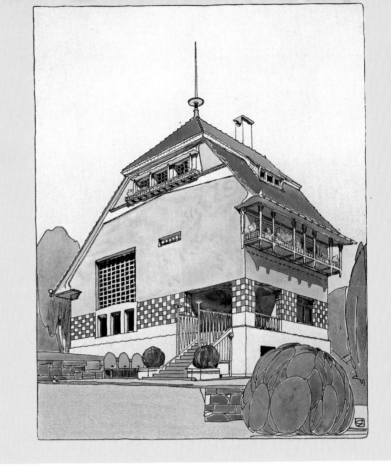

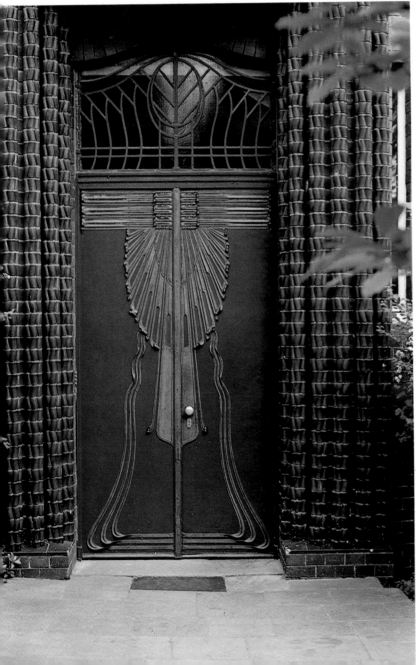

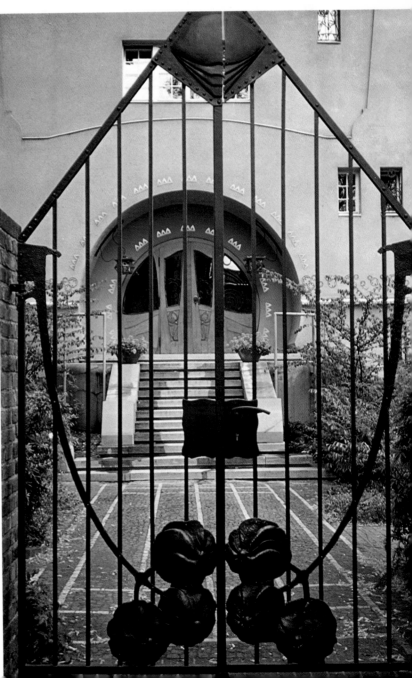

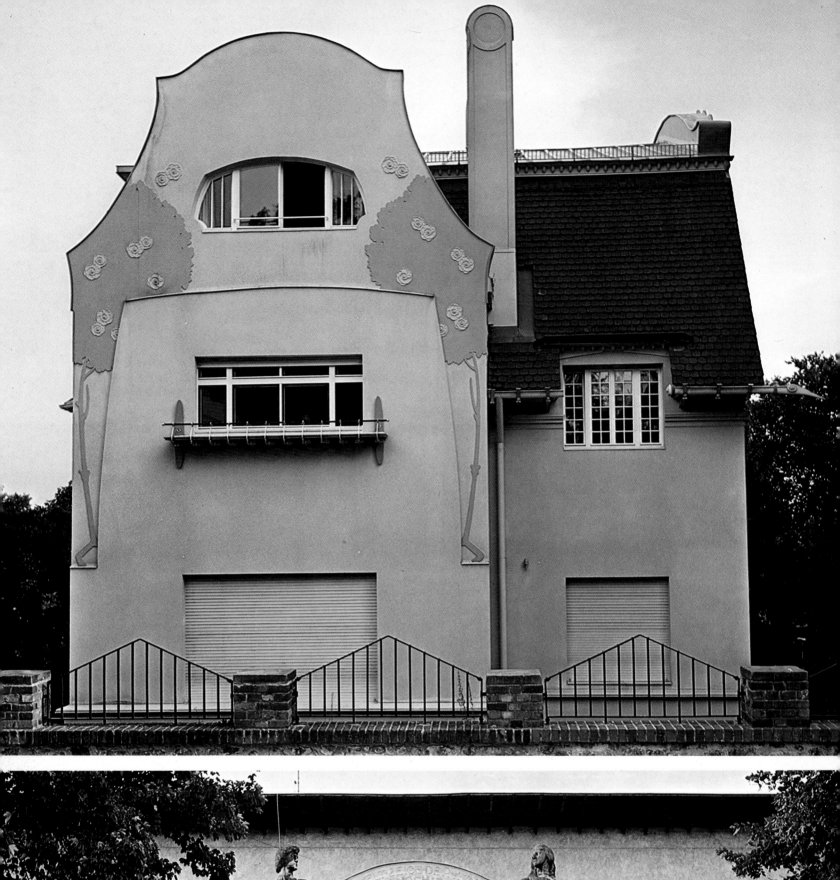

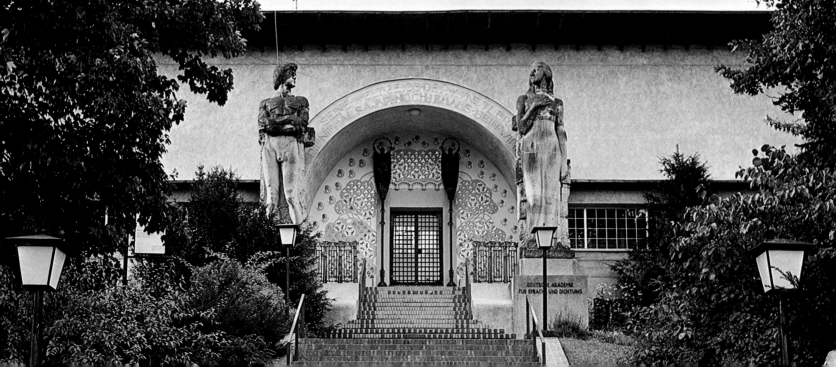

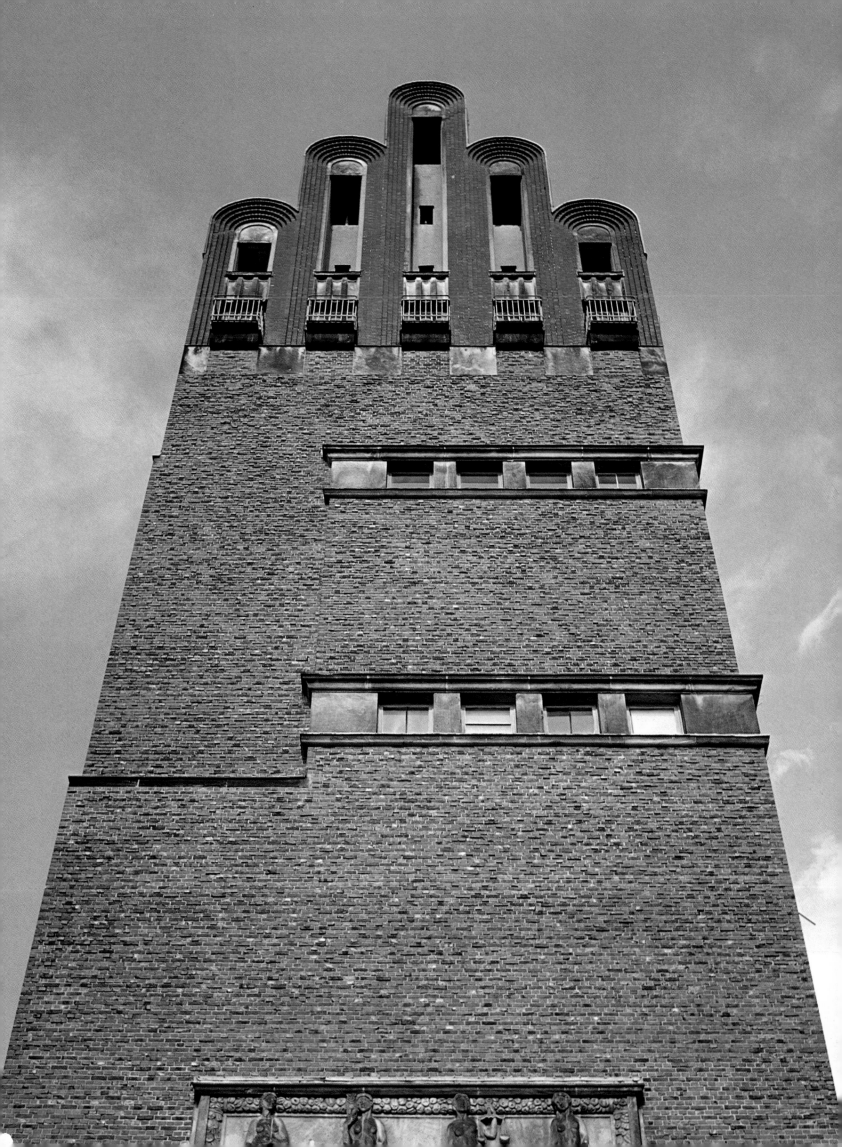

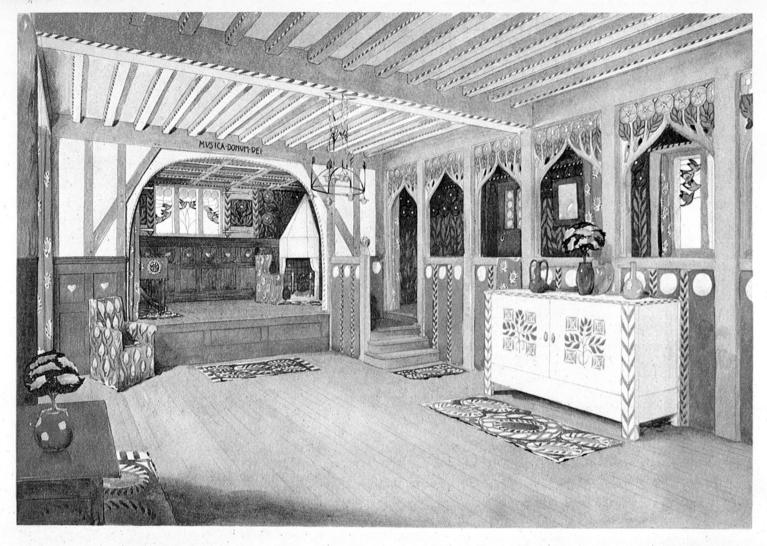

MUSIC ROOM

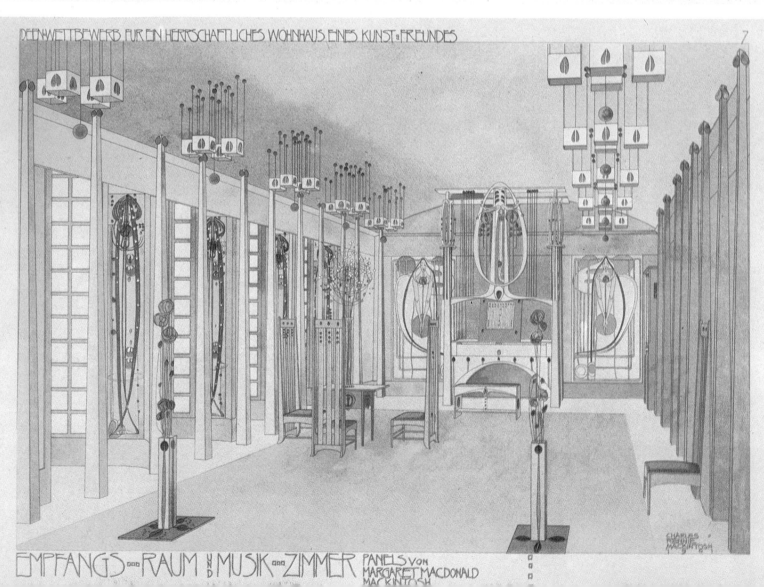

IDEEN-WETTBEWERB FÜR EIN HERRSCHAFTLICHES WOHNHAUS EINES KUNST-FREUNDES

EMPFANGS-RAUM UND MUSIK-ZIMMER   PANELS VON MARGARET MACDONALD MACKINTOSH

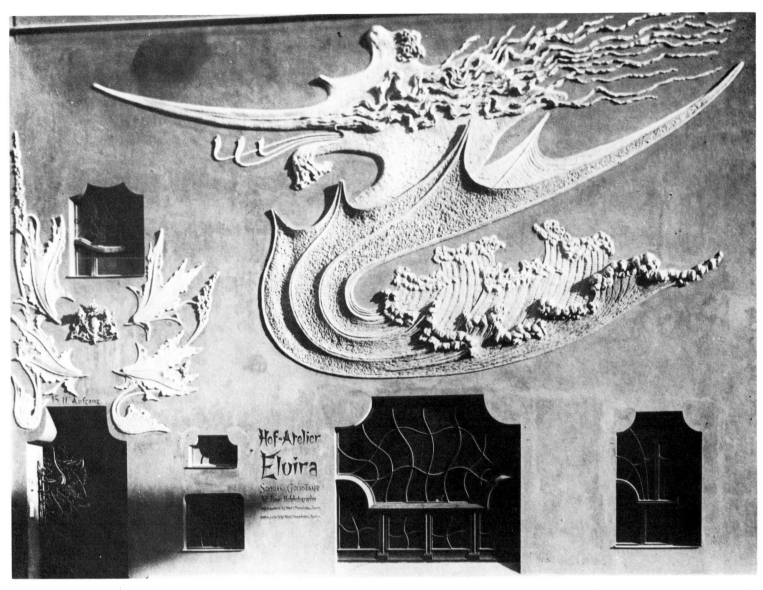

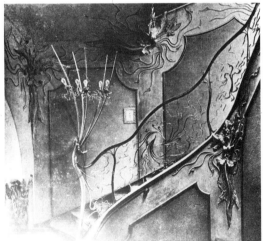

7.2-3 ENDELL *Atelier Elvira* Munich 1897-98, facade and interior (contemporary photographs)

Opposite above
BAILLIE SCOTT *Haus eines Kunstfreundes competition project* 1901 'Dulce Domum', interior perspective of Music Room

Opposite below
MACKINTOSH *Haus eines Kunstfreundes competition project* 1901 'Der Vogel', interior perspective of Music Room

Hermann Obrist, Otto Eckmann, August Endell, Richard Riemerschmid, Bernhard Pankok, Bruno Paul and Peter Behrens.

Otto Eckmann (1865-1902), together with Obrist, was the earliest artist in Munich to develop the characteristic floral Jugendstil when in 1894 he turned his attentions from painting towards the applied arts. Eckmann was born in Hamburg, where in his early years he acquired his passion for the Japanese arts when they were first introduced to Germany by Justus Brinckmann of the Museum of Arts and Crafts. This interest is clear in Eckmann's graphic work for *Pan* and *Jugend,* whereas his furniture has a more abstract basis.

The influence of Hermann Obrist is evident in the work of August Endell (1871-1925) who arrived in Munich to study philosophy and aesthetics. As a self-taught designer he echoed the sentiments of his older friend: 'We have to follow forms with our eyes, exactly and everywhere, every curve, every bend, every broadening, every contraction – in short we must experience every change. If we use our eyes like this, a whole new world of enormous wealth is created for us.' Throughout his life, Endell's artistic output was complemented by a series of important theoretical writings. In his article 'Möglichkeit und Ziele einer neuen Architektur' (Potential and Objectives of a New Architecture, 1897/8), Endell warned against the dangers of an exclusive commitment to function in design: 'The demand for suitability provides only the framework for the building . . . How one completes it depends on other, aesthetic factors. Still no one has dared to frankly show all the constructive features of a building, one always hides certain things. There are structures that are truly aesthetic, and some that aren't; the former excite one, the latter don't.'[3] In a later essay, 'Formenschönheit und dekorative Kunst' (Formal Beauty and Decorative Art), in which Endell illustrated some remarkably advanced window arrangements, an indication was provided of his move towards teaching, made in 1904 with the opening of the 'Schule für Formenkunst'.

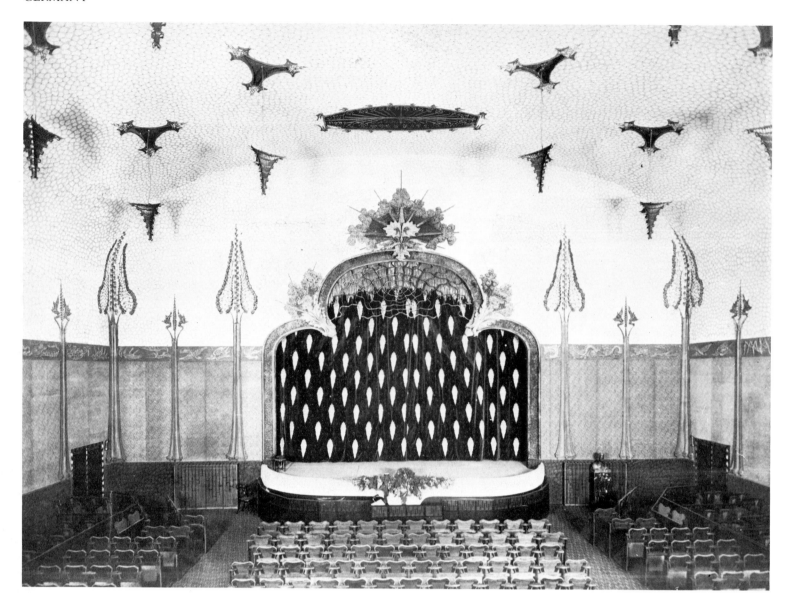

Endell's earliest artistic undertakings consisted of vignettes and textile designs with floral and other biological sources. As a co-founder of the Vereinigte Werkstätten, his contribution towards their first interiors shown at the 7th International Art Exhibition was a decorative relief frieze 'that was strange and thorny, reminiscent of the forms of marine creatures'.[4] A further development of this theme is apparent in Endell's remarkable Atelier Elvira, the Munich photographic studio (1897-8). In a period of such intense architectural experimentation this building must rank as one of the most original and daring.

The Atelier Elvira's facade was dominated by a large brightly coloured decorative relief, of neither floral nor abstract Jugendstil origins, but resembling a fiery serpent-like creature made up from a gamut of organic pattern. This motif stood out boldly from a surface that was otherwise flat and free from articulation. The door and window recesses were cut into the plane without any projecting definition, yet retained compositional relevance with their bowed lintels, curvilinear bars and their functionally based asymmetry. The upper window was not originally part of Endell's design, and he was understandably very disappointed when its addition became necessary during construction. Inside too, Endell unleashed his exuberant organic decoration, particularly on the staircase where the twisting, agitated ironwork of the banisters was set against a background which echoed the window shapes with more relief plasterwork.

The Wolzogen Theatre, or 'Buntes Theater' interior was Endell's next important work. Executed in 1901 for Ernst von Wolzogen it was recognisably Jugendstil, but now the decoration was integrated more with the building rather than overwhelming it. Again Endell employed a whole range of organic motifs. Stylised trees climbed up the walls to the vaulted ceiling, which was covered in an intense mass of cell-like material, and from which hung coral-shaped lamps. A perimeter frieze revealed 'marine creatures, dragons, sea-snakes, sea-horses

7.4-5 ENDELL *Buntes Theater* Berlin 1901, interior views of the auditorium (contemporary photographs)

178

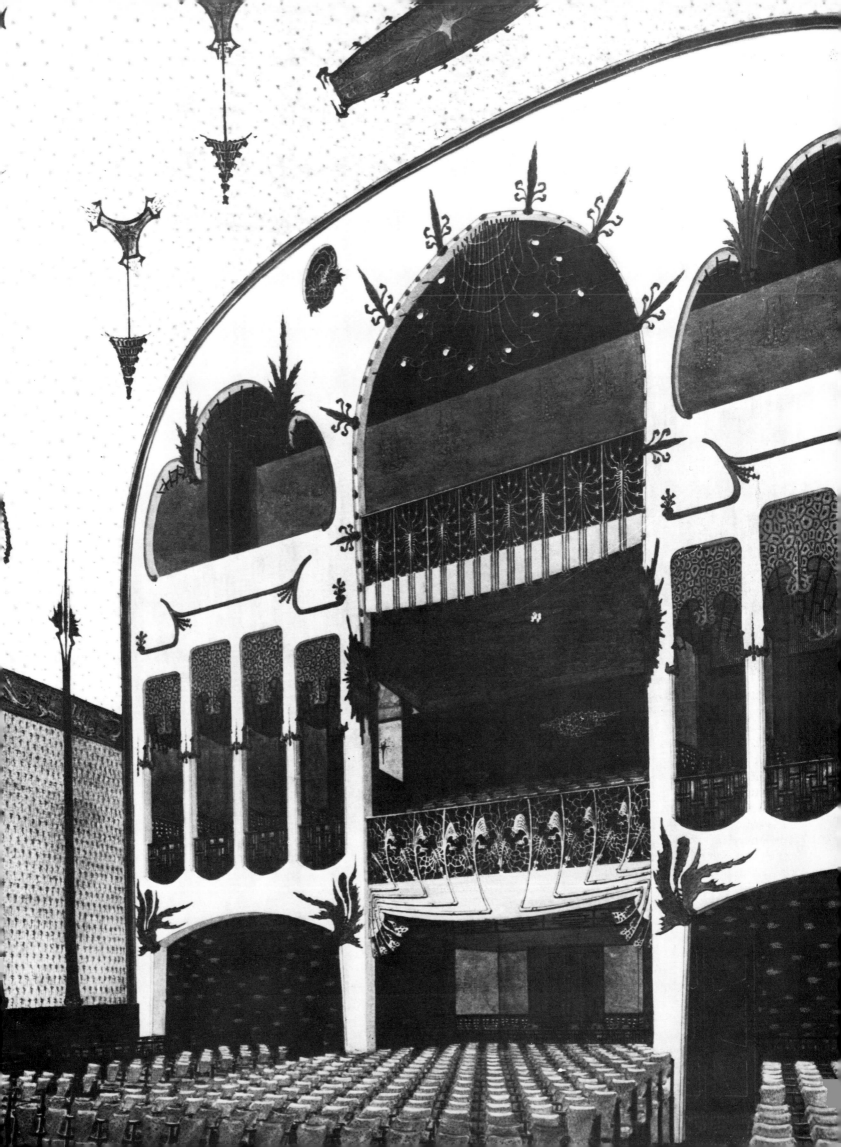

and insects'[5] whilst the railings resembled spiders' webs. The seats were even coloured according to their price, corresponding also to the colour of the particular usherette's costume.

After several years dogged by illness, August Endell concentrated his energies on teaching. His later buildings retained some characteristic Jugendstil elements but these became fused with neo-classical, oriental and Secessionstil influences, unfortunately losing much of the vitality and originality of his early work in the process.

Munich born Richard Riemerschmid (1868-1957), who was later to provide a most important contribution to the development of industrial design, began his career as a painter in 1888 at the Akademie, where he soon became involved in the struggle for a total artistic renaissance. Gabriel Seidl, the Gothic revival architect, had advised Riemerschmid that historical styles were necessary, indeed inevitable, wonderful though it may seem to be rid of them. Unperturbed, Riemerschmid continued the fight. He tells of how, one day, he lay down in a meadow and there before his eyes he saw the direction for the future in the abundant forms of nature. Riemerschmid adopted the organic Jugendstil, not unlike that of Endell, but even in his early work other influences are evident. Riemerschmid was able to integrate the rural and cultural traditions of the Southern German crafts, the 'Volkskunst', with the Jugendstil on a distinctly functional basis, his work earning the praise of both Hermann Obrist and Henry van de Velde.

In 1896 Riemerschmid designed a house for himself at Pasing bei München, just one year after van de Velde had built Bloemenwerf at Uccle. Riemerschmid's house was, for its date, just as startlingly simple as Bloemenwerf; these almost simultaneous actions reveal the coincidental dissatisfactions that existed in Belgium and Germany at the time. With the formation of the Vereinigte Werkstätten in 1897 Riemerschmid concentrated on the applied arts, producing some remarkably advanced designs, particularly for furniture; until recently, the American furniture company of Dunbar was producing a Riemerschmid chair dating from the turn of the century.

The earliest examples of a unitary room concept to come from the Munich group can be attributed to Riemerschmid, whose Music Room was displayed in 1899 in Munich, and a year later his 'Room of an art lover' was shown at the Paris Exhibition. Here he produced an encircling relief frieze with similarly decorated door frames in a refined, almost structural form of Jugendstil.

Riemerschmid's most important architectural contribution to the Jugendstil was his interior scheme for the Munich Schauspielhaus (1901). Here the ornamentation was subtle and carefully controlled, yet sufficiently coherent to generate an overall unity in the hall. No excessive decoration was allowed to distract from the functional requirements; everything was aimed at providing an essential feeling of intimacy.

Recognising that the raising of design standards required an understanding of and a commitment to machine production, Riemerschmid set about tackling the problems. As early as 1899 the Vereinigte Werkstätten designed a range of inexpensive furniture, and Riemerschmid was responsible for their earliest machine-made furniture, shown at the 1905 Dresden Exhibition. In 1898 Karl Schmidt, Riemerschmid's brother-in-law, started the Werkstätte für Handwerkskunst in Dresden, where he employed many of the Jugendstil designers and began the mass-production of furniture. Schmidt later combined many of the German craft workshops as the Deutsche Werkstätten. They settled at Hellerau, near Dresden, where in 1909 Riemerschmid planned Germany's first low cost housing suburb: Hellerau Garden City.

Riemerschmid became actively involved in design education from 1902, teaching at Nuremberg, Munich and Cologne, and in 1907 was instrumental in the establishment of the Deutscher Werkbund.

Bernhard Pankok (1872-1943) initially studied sculpture and painting in Düsseldorf and Berlin and came to Munich in 1892 where his interest in natural forms led him to combine the floral Jugendstil of Obrist and Eckmann with a Germanic formal strength, as in his Alcove Room, exhibited by the Vereinigte Werkstätten in 1900 at Paris. His later work, including a house at Tübingen for Dr Konrad Lange (1901) and his studios for the Stuttgart Association of Art-lovers, reflects Pankok's move towards a functional simplicity, which is also embodied in his machine-made furniture for the Deutscher Werkbund.

Bruno Paul (1874-1968) came to Munich from Dresden in 1894, where he

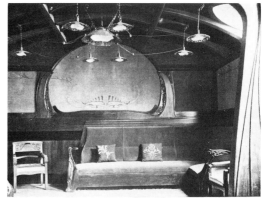

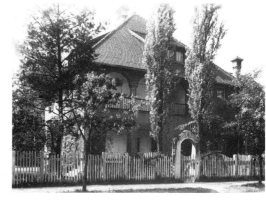

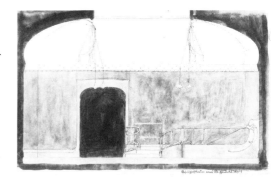

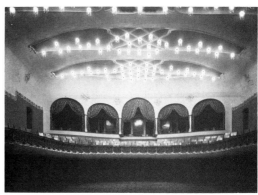

7.6 PANKOK *Paris Exhibition* 1900; Alcove Room for the Vereinigte Werkstätten (contemporary photograph)

7.7 RIEMERSCHMID *Paris Exhibition* 1900, 'Room of an art lover' elevation drawing

7.8 RIEMERSCHMID *Own house* Pasing bei München 1896

7.9 RIEMERSCHMID *Schauspielhaus* Munich 1901, auditorium

7.10-11 PANKOK *Lange house* Tübingen 1901, exterior and detail of the loggia (contemporary photographs)

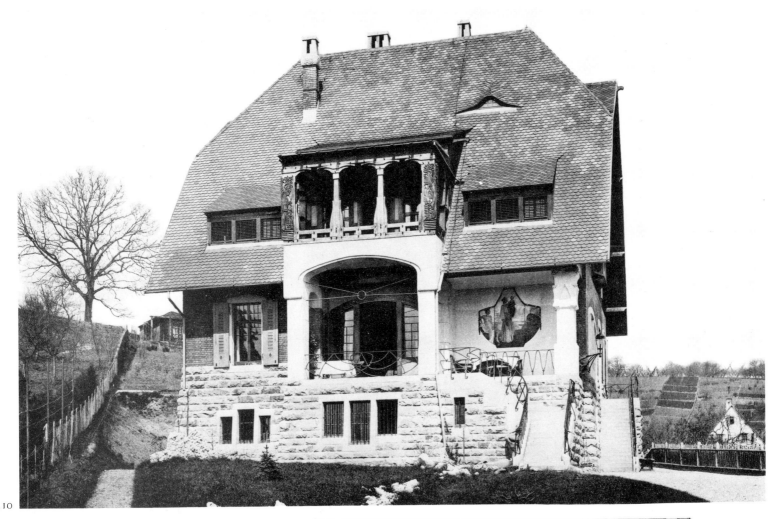

7.10

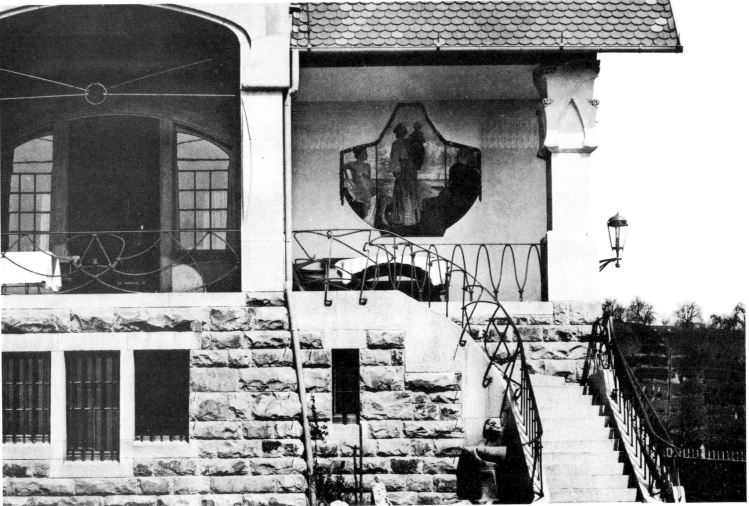

7.11

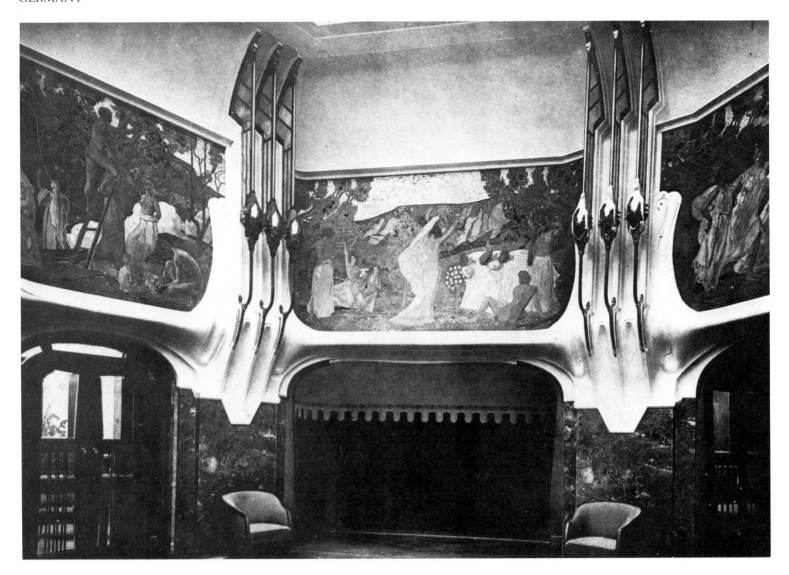

developed a close working relationship with Riemerschmid in the Vereinigte Werkstätten. His versatility as a designer was shown in his early work which included his 'Jagdzimmer' for the 1900 Paris Exhibition and a wide range of graphics and magazine illustrations. Paul's initial training in the building industry provided him with a sound technical basis for his numerous varied projects as a member of the Werkbund.

'Above all, it is this Belgian who has made us Germans aware of Brussels, this man who, for the last ten years, has made Germany the centre of his activity, through whom our arts have found an encouraging direction, and around whom we have fought for recognition; a man whose work has endowed the evolution of German applied arts with an undeniable energy.'[6] This appreciation of Henry van de Velde (1863-1957) appeared in the catalogue for the 1906 Dresden Exhibition at which the Belgian designer was responsible for the Central Hall of Applied Arts.

Van de Velde's first appearance in Germany was in the spring of 1897 when he brought several interiors, including his 'Paris Room' and 'Quiet Room', to the Dresden Exhibition. After an enthusiastic reception he visited Berlin and was introduced to the *Pan* circle. *Pan* was the magazine started in 1895, with the intention of 'transforming the foreign doctrine in accordance with the national spirit', under the control of Julius Meier-Graefe, who had been an early visitor to van de Velde's house in Uccle. The interest he aroused in Berlin resulted in several commissions for the Belgian, who moved his office to the city in 1899.

The German audience proved receptive to van de Velde's abstract, structural form of Art Nouveau, though his arrival was too late to dramatically influence the immediate course of the Jugendstil. In 1900-01 he undertook a lecture tour around Germany, and published several important papers, 'Renaissance im Kunstgewerbe' (Renaissance in Arts and Crafts) and 'Kunstgewerbliche Laienpredigten' (Arts and Crafts Lay Sermons) in which he adopted the English Arts and Crafts principles, calling for a functional clarity and justifying decoration:

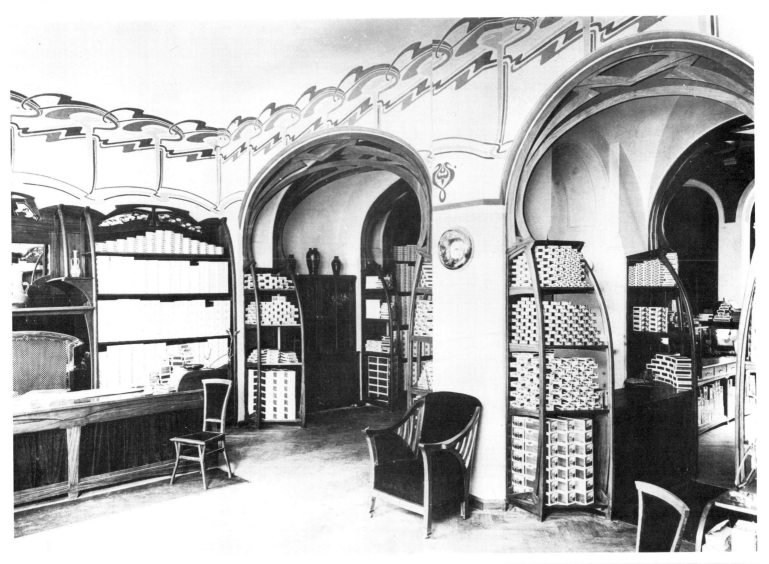

7.13 VAN DE VELDE *Havana Company Cigar Shop* Berlin 1899-1900, interior (contemporary photograph)

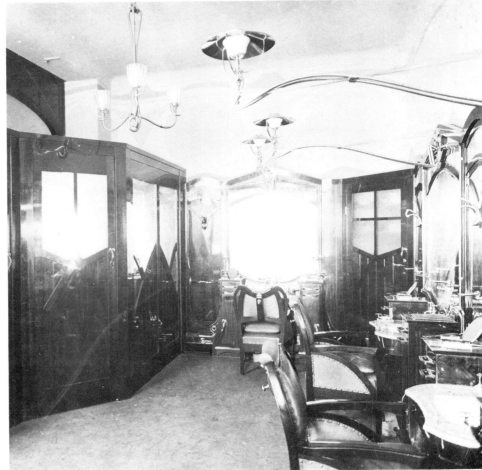

7.14 VAN DE VELDE *Haby Barber's Shop* Berlin 1900-01, interior (contemporary photograph)

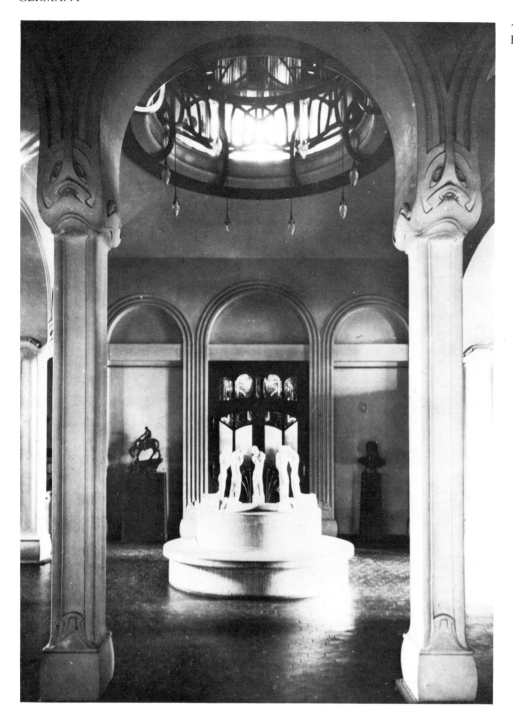

7.15 VAN DE VELDE *Folkwang Museum*
Hagen 1900-02, interior

7.16-19 VAN DE VELDE *Folkwang Museum*,
details of staircase, roof light and decorative
mouldings

'This ornamentation is necessary above all, it arises from the object, stays associated with it, indicating its purpose or construction method, it helps it to adapt still more to its use.'[7]

The first of van de Velde's five Berlin commissions was the interior of the Havana Company Cigar Shop (1899-1900). The distinctive curvilinear motif was employed wherever possible in an attempt to unify the various elements, sometimes at the expense of convenience; no wonder Lenning has described the shop as a 'non-functional tour de force'.[8] The display case supports bowed outwards, springing up apparently to support dividing arches, whilst an abstract frieze encompassed the interiors.

More consistent with van de Velde's theoretical development towards functionalism was his Barber's Shop interior for François Haby (1900-01). Here the decorative extravagance of the Havana Shop was avoided; the functional arrangement of mirrors, chairs, lamps and brackets was conceived with honest clarity. Brass, marble, glass and mahogany were combined with subtlety and maturity to produce an elegant interior exactly suited to its purpose.

An article about van de Velde by Meier-Graefe in *Dekorative Kunst* prompted Karl Ernst Osthaus, a wealthy banker and collector of contemporary art, to visit Uccle in order to meet the Belgian designer. Osthaus' Folkwang Museum at Hagen had been built in 1898 by the Berlin architect Karl Gerard in a neo-

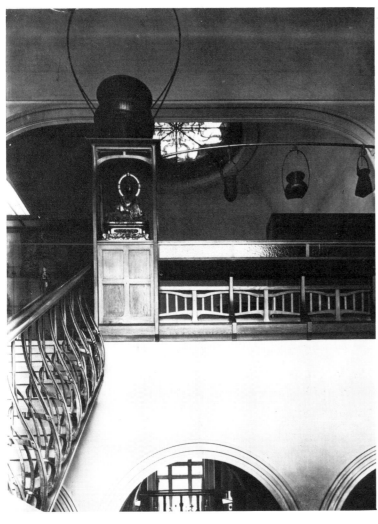

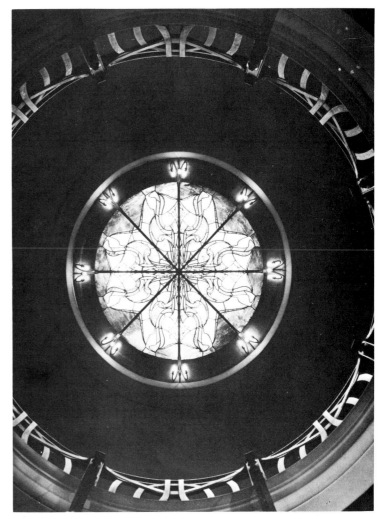

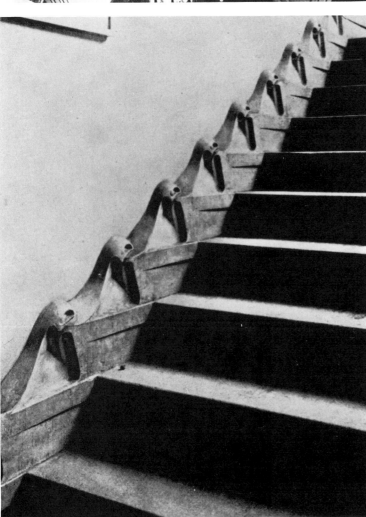

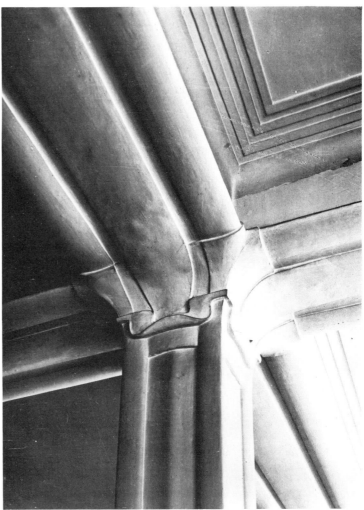

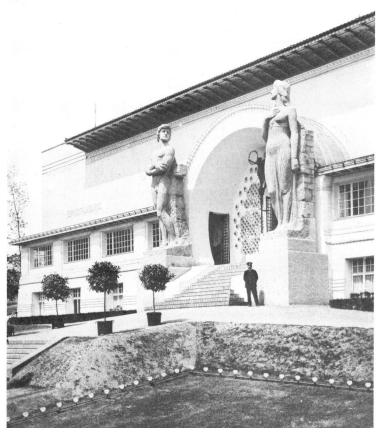

7.20

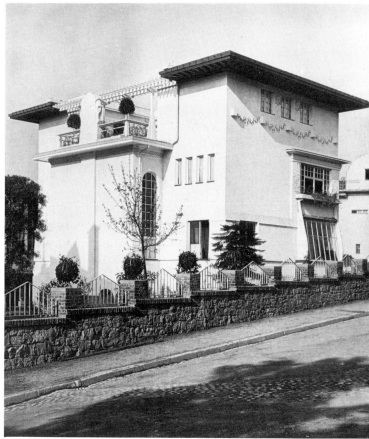

7.21

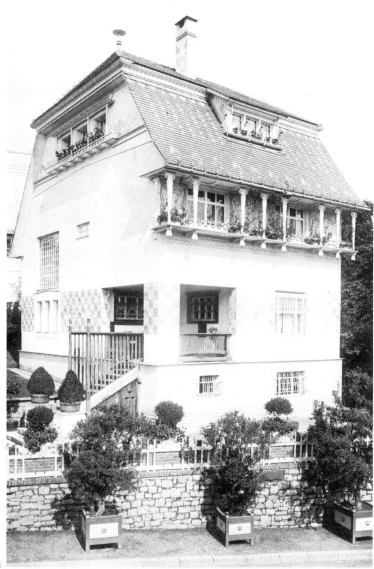

7.22

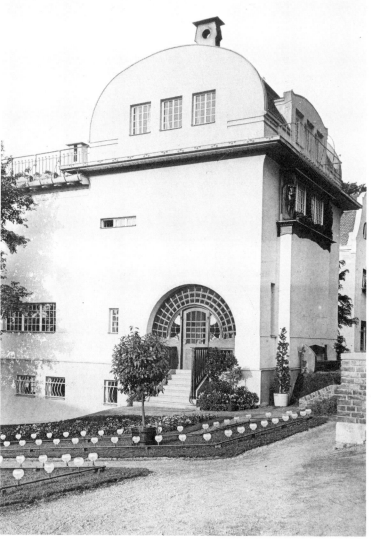

7.23

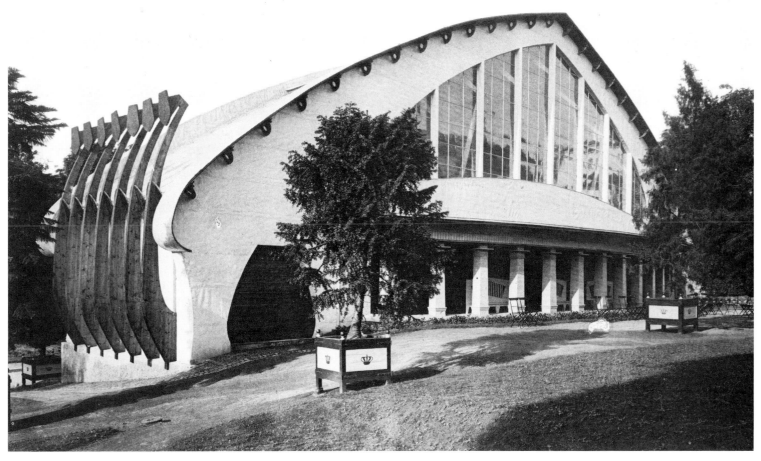

7.24 OLBRICH *Darmstadt Exhibition* 1901,
Gallery of Fine Arts (contemporary photograph)

7.20 OLBRICH *Ernst Ludwig Haus* Darmstadt
1899 (contemporary photograph)

7.21 OLBRICH *Haus Habich* Darmstadt 1900
(contemporary photograph)

7.22 OLBRICH *Haus Olbrich* Darmstadt 1900
(contemporary photograph)

7.23 OLBRICH *Kleines Glückert house*
Darmstadt 1900 (contemporary photograph)

Renaissance style, and van de Velde was invited to design the interiors. This is often regarded as van de Velde's finest work, occurring in 1900-02 between his early decorative period and his later bulky, sculptural architecture. The sophisticated harmony of the interiors was achieved through a balance of unobtrusive display areas and decorated columns, friezes and staircases.

In 1902 Henry van de Velde was invited to Weimar by the Grand Duke of Saxe-Weimar to renovate the Museum, to build a theatre (which remained as a project) and a school of applied arts, and generally to help increase the design standards of local industry. The School of Applied Arts was opened in 1908, and van de Velde's radical teaching methods formed the background to those used when the school later became part of the Bauhaus.

During 1899 Ernst Ludwig, the Grand Duke of Hesse and grandson of Queen Victoria of England, extended invitations to seven young artists to establish an artists' colony on the Mathildenhöhe hill in Darmstadt. Already acquainted with the new movements in art and design through his visits to England and subsequent commissions he had given to Baillie Scott and Ashbee, Ernst Ludwig wished to revitalise the traditional industries of Hesse with the direct help of the colony. The original members were: Rudolf Bosselt (sculptor), Paul Bürck (painter), Patriz Huber (designer and interior architect), Hans Christiansen (painter), Ludwig Habich (sculptor), Peter Behrens (painter), and Joseph Maria Olbrich.

In September of 1899 Olbrich (1867-1908) arrived in Darmstadt from Vienna, only ten months after the completion of his controversial Secession Building. As a co-founder of the radical Secession movement Olbrich had, together with Josef Hoffmann, developed the particular geometric forms of Art Nouveau that became known as the 'Secessionstil'. In Darmstadt he was the only architect and, with one exception, took complete architectural responsibility for the colony during the following eight years. After their initial success at the 1900 Paris Exhibition with the 'Darmstadt Zimmer', the colony members prepared plans for a major exhibition to be held in Darmstadt in 1901 under the title 'Ein Dokument Deutscher Kunst' (A Document of German Art). The intention was to build an 'Acropolis on the Mathildenhöhe' with, as Bosselt described, 'an harmonic pervasive basic feeling, which has its origin in the intellectual qualities, life-feeling and life-direction of the inhabitant'.[9]

The Ernst Ludwig Haus, the work studio of the colony, was to be the centre of its activity. Appropriately Olbrich sited it high on the hillside, with the artists' houses grouped around at a lower level. The long, low facade is dominated by a central arched entrance, a characteristic feature of many of Olbrich's buildings, which is flanked by a pair of statues by Habich. Here the Jugendstil decoration was concentrated, notably in the gilded stucco surrounding the door frame. A band of casement windows contrasts with the blank brow above, helping to emphasise the horizontality; possible precursors for this distinctive building may lie in the vernacular houses of the Mediterranean regions which so impressed Olbrich on his travels. As in the Secession Building, Olbrich's primary concern with the planning of the Ernst Ludwig Haus has been the functional requirements; the Art Nouveau influence was confined to only a few areas of decoration, but provided the basis to the rejection of classical precedents.

Equally original was the Haus Habich, which bears a closer resemblance to the Ernst Ludwig Haus than to the remainder of Olbrich's Mathildenhöhe houses. With its flat roof, projecting over solid unadorned walls, and its functionally positioned recessed windows, the Haus Habich could easily be mistaken for some of the houses built twenty years later in the early days of the 'International Style'.

The Haus Olbrich, Haus Christiansen, Haus Keller and Haus Deiters were more traditional in appearance, drawing from rural Germanic dwellings, yet conceived with subtlety and sophistication. The roof, balcony, windows and decorative tiles of the Haus Olbrich were integrated in a totally functional manner to form an asymmetric unified whole. The interior spatial arrangements derive directly from contemporary English houses with a central living-hall, extending to two storeys in height.

The Grosses and Kleines Glückert houses remain today closer to their original form than the other Mathildenhöhe houses. They provide interesting examples of Olbrich's careful consideration of the site which has resulted in a basis for their built form. The Kleines Glückert is perhaps one of Olbrich's most advanced houses. A cubic block is surmounted on its road frontage by a vaulted roof containing the dining room, the two forms being held by a projecting panel with windows which runs vertically across them.

For the 1901 Exhibition Olbrich designed not only the houses and much of their contents but also the entrance portal, a flower stall, a postcard kiosk, a games room, orchestra pavilion and a gallery: the Gebäude für Flächenkunst, the latter being of particular interest. Consisting of a large timber-framed gabled structure, the bold outline appeared again in Olbrich's 1903 project for Basel railway station.

The marriage of the Grand Duke in 1905 presented Olbrich with an opportunity for which he had waited five years; to erect a tower at the top of the Mathildenhöhe, to complete the 'Acropolis'. The Hochzeitsturm (Wedding Tower) and its associated Exhibition Buildings were eventually inaugurated at the 1908 Exhibition. The red brick tower was crowned by a five-arched element which was faced in glazed tiles and covered in copper, whilst lower horizontal bands of windows served to relieve the verticality. Even today the Wedding Tower provides Darmstadt with one of this century's most distinguished monuments.

Alexander Koch, the influential Darmstadt-based art publisher had helped prepare the ground for the success of the artists' colony. His magazines *Deutsche Kunst und Dekoration* (1897) and *Zeitschrift für Innendekoration* (1890) were founded with the intention of bringing art to the ordinary people, and it was through the latter that Koch sponsored an architectural competition in 1901. Entrants were asked to design a *Haus eines Kunstfreundes* (House for an Art-lover); the two most outstanding submissions were received from Baillie Scott and Charles Rennie Mackintosh. The judges, who included Joseph Maria Olbrich, favoured Mackintosh's entry but, as he had not complied fully with the competition conditions, the top prize was awarded to Baillie Scott. (This was in fact 2nd prize, with no 1st prize given.) Baillie Scott's design was an early form of the four-winged 'Butterfly' or 'Sun-trap' plan with its protected South face and distinctive curved gables. Mackintosh's scheme, on the other hand, was much more radical: 'The exterior of the building . . . exhibits an absolutely original character, unlike anything else known. In it we shall not find a trace of the conventional forms of architecture, to which the artist, so far as his present

7.25 OLBRICH *Ernst Ludwig Haus*, elevation (from the original drawing)

7.26 OLBRICH *Gallery of Fine Arts*, elevation (from the original drawing)

7.27 OLBRICH *Hochzeitsturm* (Wedding Tower) Darmstadt 1905-08, elevation (from the original drawing)

Overleaf
7.28-29 MACKINTOSH *Haus eines Kunstfreundes competition project* 1901 'Der Vogel', perspective view from the South East and North elevation

7.30-31 BAILLIE SCOTT *Haus eines Kunstfreundes competition project* 1901 'Dulce Domum', bird's eye perspective from the North and South and West elevations

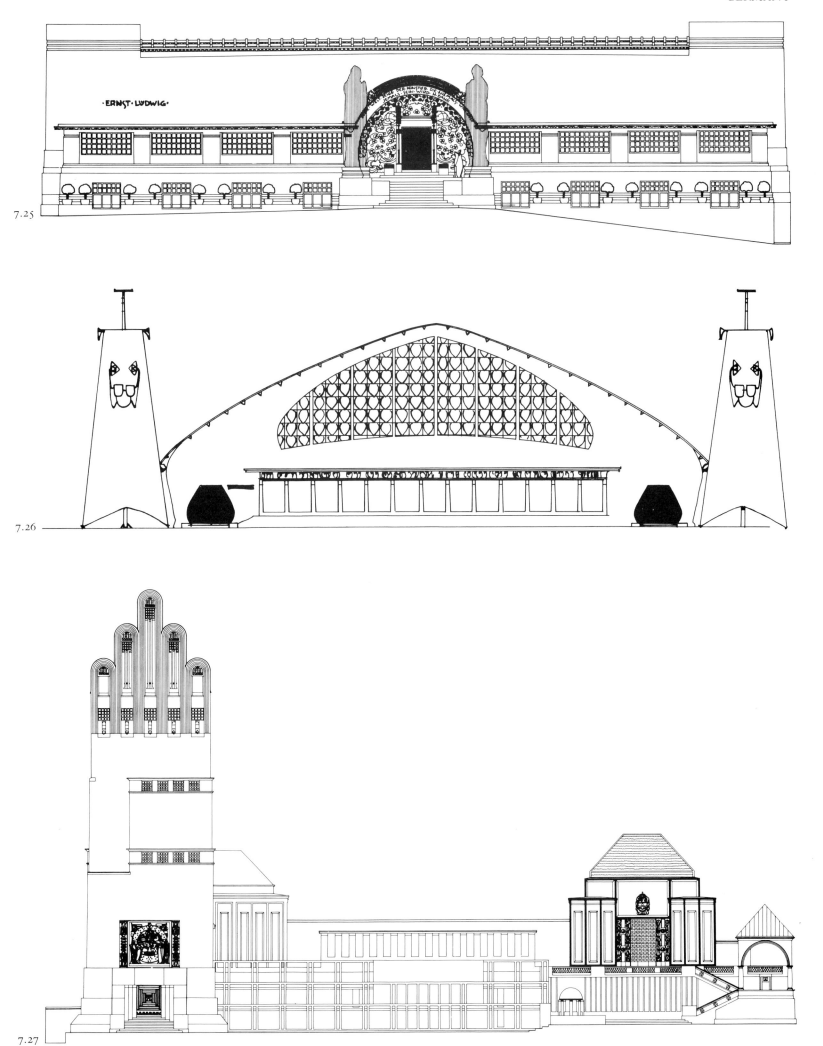

7.25

·ERNST·LUDWIG·

7.26

7.27

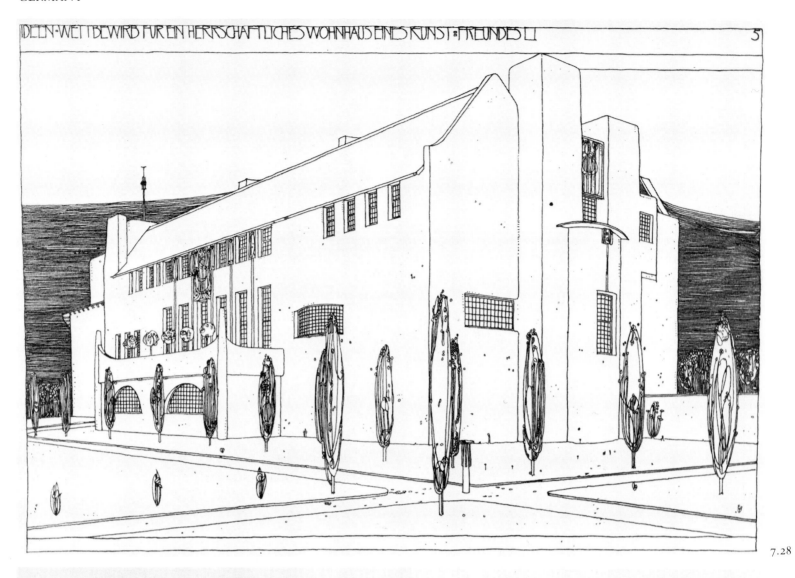

7.28

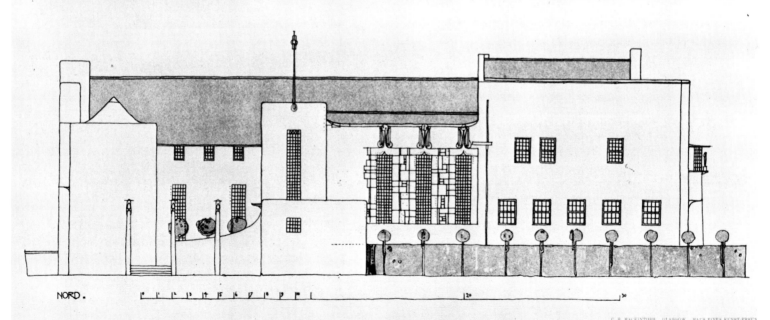

7.29

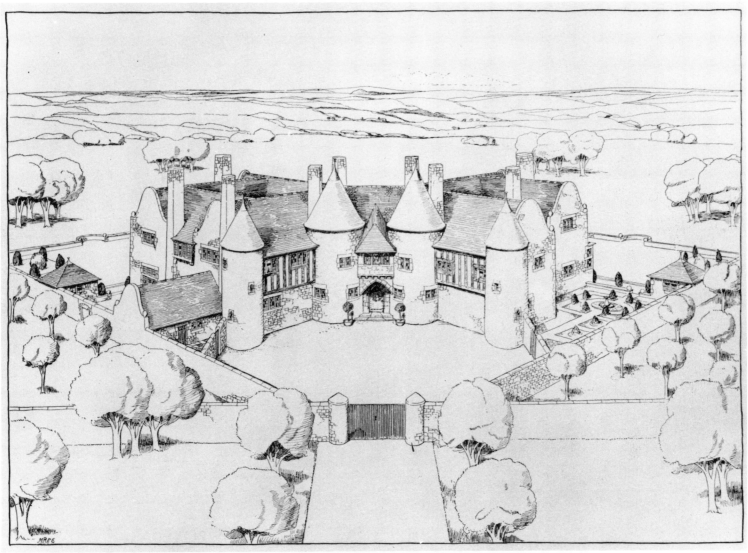

7.30

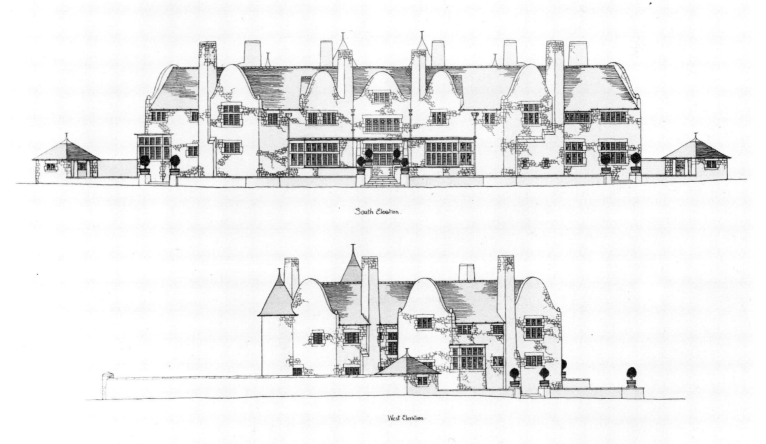

South Elevation.

West Elevation

7.31

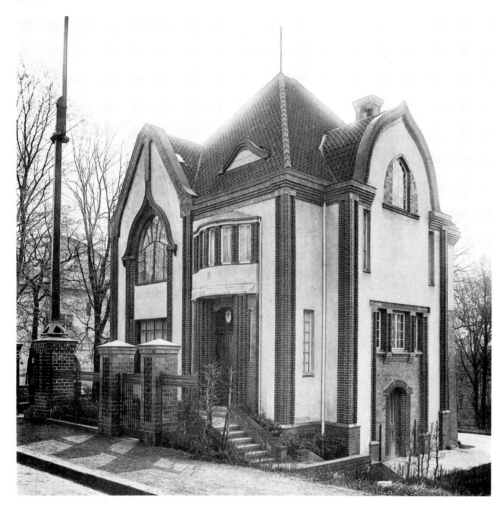

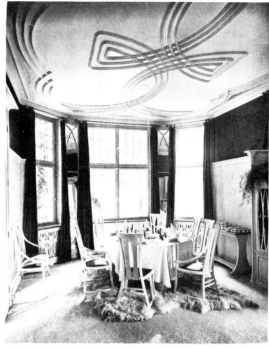

7.32-33 BEHRENS *Haus Behrens* Darmstadt 1901, exterior and interior (contemporary photographs)

intentions were concerned, was quite indifferent.'[10]

An examination of the early career of Peter Behrens (1868-1940) reveals how his movements coincide remarkably with the flourishing of the various artistic centres of Germany during the brief Jugendstil period. Behrens arrived in Munich in 1890 having spent the previous four years studying painting at Karlsruhe and Düsseldorf. He soon made contact with the revolutionary artists and was a founder member in 1892 of the Munich Secession. Behrens travelled to Italy in 1896 and the year after his return, as a co-founder of the Vereinigte Werkstätten and a close friend of Otto Eckmann, he extended his interests to the applied arts. His early work in Munich was varied, though mostly in two dimensions; Behrens developed an abstract, sometimes symbolic form of Jugendstil.

In 1899 Peter Behrens was invited to join the Darmstadt artists' colony, where he would receive the title of 'Professor' and was to be paid a salary second only to that of Olbrich. Here Behrens was also given the opportunity of building his own house for the 1901 Exhibition. The Haus Behrens was the only building on the Mathildenhöhe that Olbrich, Behrens' senior by only one year, did not design himself; it was Behrens' first architectural work and cost considerably more to build than the other colony houses. The Haus Behrens lacks the originality and subtlety of Olbrich's houses but provides an interesting comparison. The influence of Vienna is evident in the clarity of conception and the interplay of plain surface and decoration, both interior and exterior. The work of Mackintosh and van de Velde has not gone unnoticed, especially in the interiors, but Behrens has also incorporated his own theories about symbolism, which give a mystical quality to the building and which characterised many of the activities of the colony. The somewhat clumsy exterior of the Haus Behrens reveals an interest in the Germanic vernacular but there is also an indication of the sober classical spirit that was to become more prominent in Behrens' later buildings.

Behrens left Darmstadt in 1903 to take up the post of Director at the Düsseldorf School of Applied Arts where he developed further his ideas on mystical significance in shape, pattern and colour, under the influence of the Dutch architect J. L. M. Lauweriks.

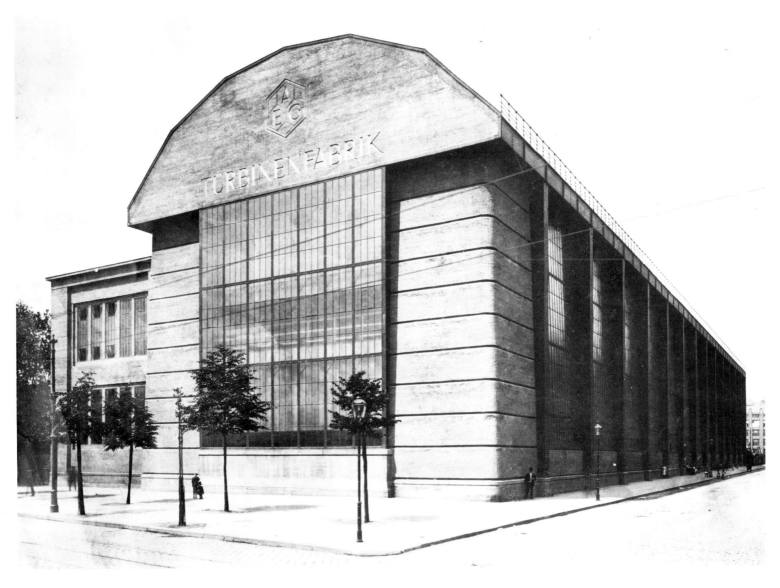

7.34 BEHRENS *AEG Turbine Factory* Berlin
1908-09 (contemporary photograph)

The engagement in 1907 of Peter Behrens as designer to the AEG company (Allgemeine Elektricitäts Gesellschaft) by its president, Emil Rathenau, was an important breakthrough in the development of industrial design. Rathenau had previously employed Adolf Messel and Otto Eckmann in lesser capacities but now Behrens was asked to design not only the AEG products but also their publicity and their factories; to establish and promote quality of design through the AEG corporate image. Behrens' AEG Turbine Factory (1908-9) on the Huttenstrasse in Berlin was one of the most influential buildings of its time, often described as heralding the new age in architecture. Nevertheless, the factory retains the classical solidity, characteristic of Behrens' architecture, that was apparent even in his Darmstadt house. The interpretation of the factory as a glorification of both the machine and the large corporation seems to have been as important to Behrens as his attempt to produce a frank functional building.

During this period of artistic renewal Berlin remained of lesser importance as a centre of Jugendstil than Munich or Darmstadt, primarily because of its deeply rooted classical traditions. Ludwig Hoffman became City architect in 1896 and dominated the architectural scene with his sixteenth- and eighteenth-century revivals. The group associated with the journal *Pan* were the most active Jugendstil supporters in the city, and it was largely through their encouragement that van de Velde came to Berlin. Among significant buildings in the city that bore the influence of Jugendstil were Alfred Messel's Wertheim Store (1896), of which Olbrich had taken note before designing his Düsseldorf Store, and Sehring's Tietz Store (1898), though the prevalent themes in these are clearly Gothic and Baroque respectively.

In the same year that the Wertheim Store was completed, a former architecture student from Berlin Technical College, Hermann Muthesius (1861-1927) was appointed as an attaché to the German Embassy in London to carry out a study of low-cost housing. On his return, he published the three-volume study *Das*

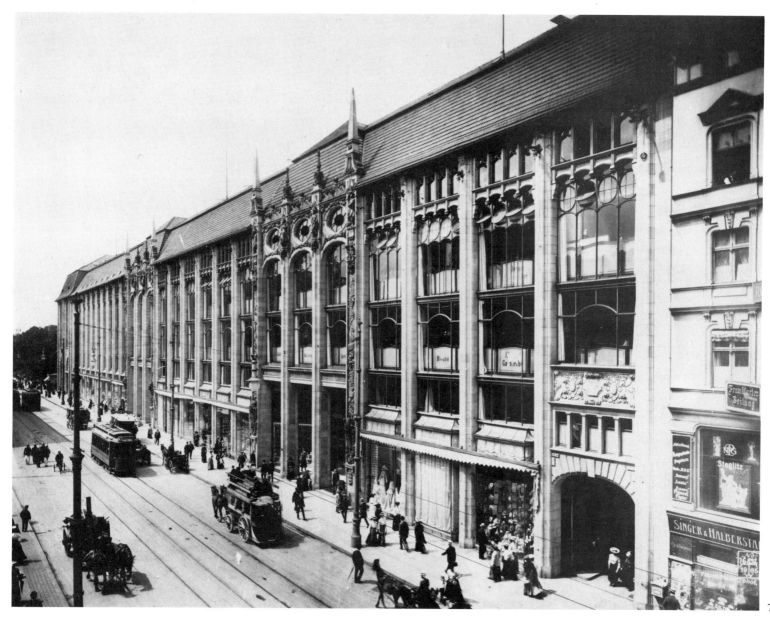

7.35

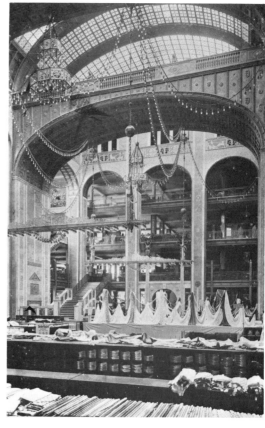

7.36

Englische Haus (1905) which illustrated the work of Baillie Scott, Voysey, Mackintosh and their contemporaries. Muthesius was appointed Inspector to the Prussian Ministry of Trade and Industry in 1904 and was responsible for Behrens' move to the Düsseldorf School of Applied Arts as well as other significant engagements. Muthesius began lecturing, advocating reason and simplicity in design and warning against plagiarism, quoting from English examples: 'The actual decisive quality of the English house is its Sachlichkeit [objectivity]. It is simply a house in which one wants to live . . . it is without pomp or decoration and has that natural decency which – natural as it ought to be – is so rare in our present culture.'[11] By this time the Jugendstil had become debased through cheap repetition and misinterpretation and the leading architects were rejecting superficial ornamentation, and were already moving in the direction that Muthesius advised. He invited artists, designers and industrialists together to form a body united in the search for quality in industrial design, resulting in the establishment of the Deutscher Werkbund on October 6th 1907. Nearly all of the leading Jugendstil designers took part, including Riemerschmid, Behrens, Olbrich, van de Velde, Paul, Pankok as well as Karl Schmidt, Theodor Fischer, Hans Poelzig, Heinrich Tessenow and Josef Hoffmann. The Werkbund aimed at 'selecting the best representatives of art, industry, crafts and trades, of combining all efforts towards high quality in industrial work, and of forming a rallying point for all those who are able and willing to work for high quality'.[12]

Although most of the Jugendstil designers had progessed beyond the superficialities of the style by about 1904, it was not until a decade later that the final battle was fought and the path cleared for the so-called 'Modern Movement'.

The Annual Meeting of the Deutscher Werkbund was held in Cologne in

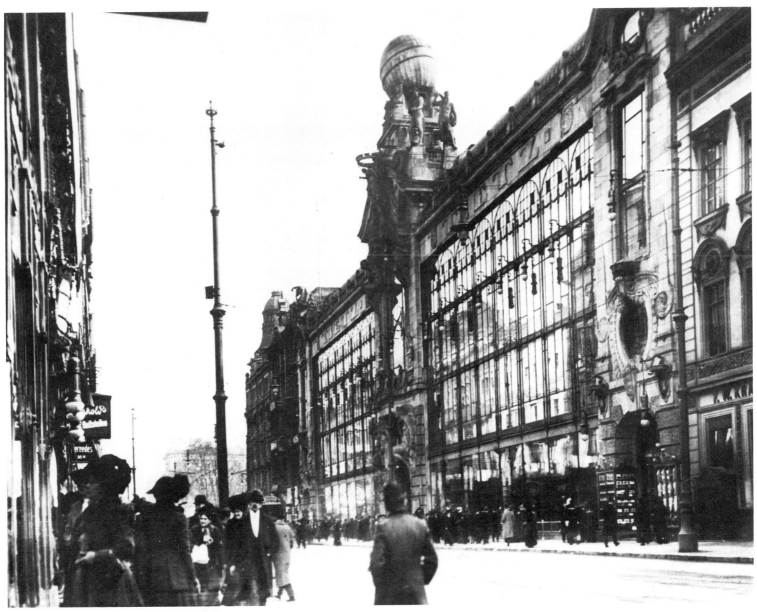

7.37 SEHRING *Tietz Store* Berlin 1898 (contemporary photograph)

7.35-36 MESSEL *Wertheim Store* Berlin 1896, facade and interior (contemporary photographs)

1914, where the celebrated debate between Muthesius and van de Velde took place. Muthesius proclaimed his faith in machine production: 'Architecture and the entire sphere of activity of the Werkbund tend towards standardisation (Typisierung). It is only by standardisation that they can recover that universal importance which they possessed in ages of harmonious civilization. Only by standardisation . . . can a generally accepted and reliable taste be introduced.'[13] Van de Velde argued the case for individualism: 'As long as there are artists in the Werkbund . . . they will protest against any proposed canon and any standardisation. The artist is essentially and intimately a passionate individualist, a spontaneous creator. Never will he, of his own free will, submit to a discipline forcing upon him a norm, a canon.'[14]

The Cologne Werkbund Exhibition of the same year highlighted the contrasting views in architectural thinking at the time. Josef Hoffmann's Austrian Pavilion and Peter Behrens' Main Hall were classical in spirit; Bruno Taut's Glass Pavilion heralded the period of expressionism; van de Velde, in collaboration with Hermann Obrist, designed the Werkbund Theatre, its curvilinear, plastic form representing the final flourish of Art Nouveau; whilst Walter Gropius and Adolf Meyer built the uncompromisingly 'Modern' Model Factory with its Administration Building and Machine Hall.

1914 also saw van de Velde's resignation from the leadership of the Weimar Kunstgewerbeschule and the Hochschule für Bildene Kunst. Three successors were shortlisted: August Endell, Hermann Obrist and Walter Gropius. Gropius was chosen; he combined the two schools soon to form the 'Staatliches Bauhaus Weimar'. Germany's early morning of Jugend was over, the midday was fast approaching.

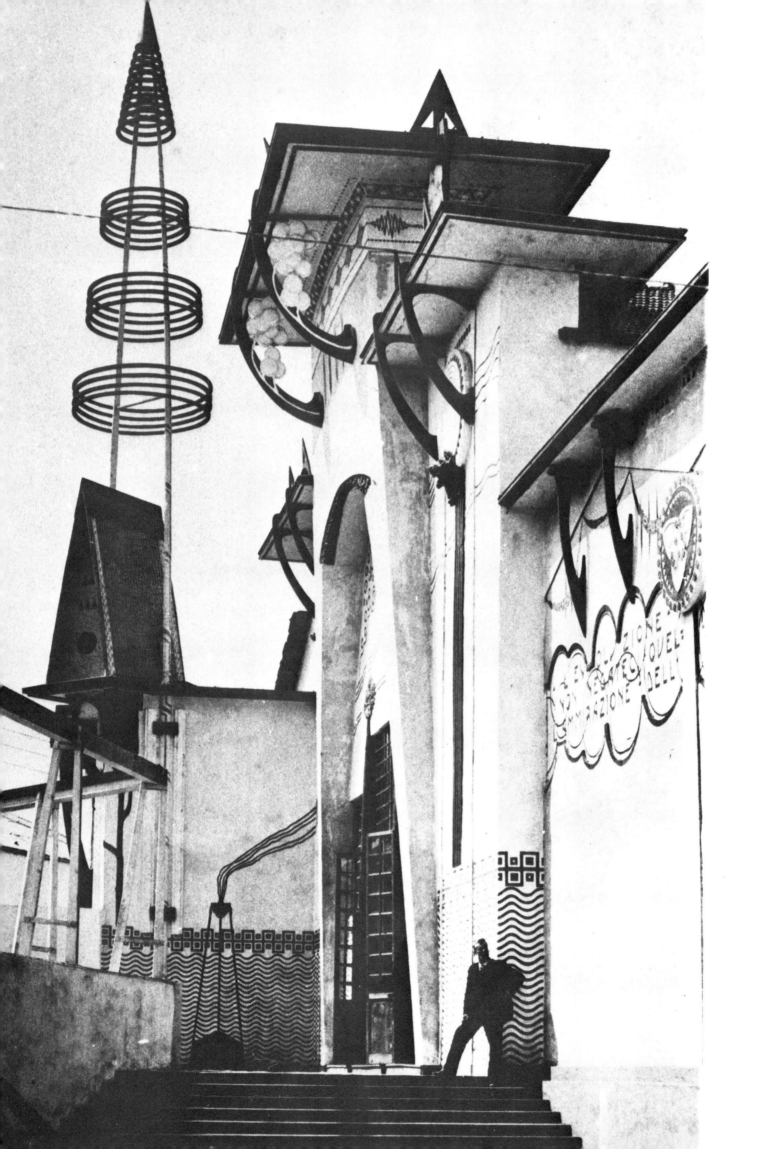

8. ITALY
Liberty architecture in Italy

Ezio Godoli

The expression 'Liberty Architecture'[1] does not denote a single homogeneous Italian stream of Art Nouveau, but is rather a convenient generalisation embracing a number of tendencies united by a common urge to be free of nineteenth-century eclecticism and align themselves with current European developments. These aspirations were held back, however, by the desire to preserve a national architectural character, as well as by the Positivist belief that the new style should evolve gradually from the heritage of the past, rather than constitute a drastic break in historical continuity. Liberty's potential to evolve a unified artistic language was therefore compromised, and it became instead a sophisticated stylistic development from eclecticism. In its pluralism this reflected the multiplicity of regional revivals which arose paradoxically out of the debate about a national style which followed the political unification of the country.

Tracing back the sources of the unification struggle to the attempt at various points in mediaeval and Renaissance history to overcome the political disunity of those times, the romanticism of the Risorgimento gave birth to a parochialism which valued local cultural traditions as expressions of the rivalry between the regions for national leadership. This conception of history underlay the battle for recognition between the various revivals – Venetian Gothic, Tuscan Renaissance, Lombard Romanesque and so on – as the official architecture of the 'New Italy'.

Only the Stile Umbertino – both in its neo-Renaissance manifestations and in the triumphal and philologically indefensible classicism of Guglielmo Calderini's Palace of Justice in Rome (1888-1910) or the Victor Emmanuel Monument (1888-1911) by Giuseppe Sacconi – managed to acquire a position of supremacy, and then only in the field of official architecture supported by State patronage. In its opposition to the academic circles which supported the Stile Umbertino, Liberty inevitably found itself in alliance with those progressive trends within revivalism (especially the mediaeval revivals) which showed most openness to the problem of modernising constructional technique. The anti-academic stance of Liberty did not, however, translate itself into a rigid anti-classicism: on the contrary, classicist tendencies within it are not uncommon.

The dialogue with historicism, implicit in the development of Art Nouveau throughout Europe, constituted the main obstacle to the acceptance of the internationalist aspect of Modernismo in Italy. However, this internationalism corresponded not so much to an aesthetic trend as to a current of thought identified with the so called 'Self-help' trend in Italian literature under the influence of the Scottish writer Samuel Smiles. This had a marked success amongst a wide cross-section of public opinion in the last three decades of the nineteenth century. There was a correlation between the poetic of Arte Nuova and the advocacy of a policy of industrial expansion in the writings of Enrico Fano, Michele Lessona, Carlo Lozzi, Gustavo Strafforello and others. Without minimising the structural causes of the backwardness of the Italian economy these writers insisted on the importance of education as a cultural factor in the development of a new economic structure. Just as the Smilesian economists pointed to the dominance of classical-humanist over technical and scientific

8.1 D'ARONCO *Turin Exhibition* 1902, entrance to the Furniture Gallery (contemporary photograph)

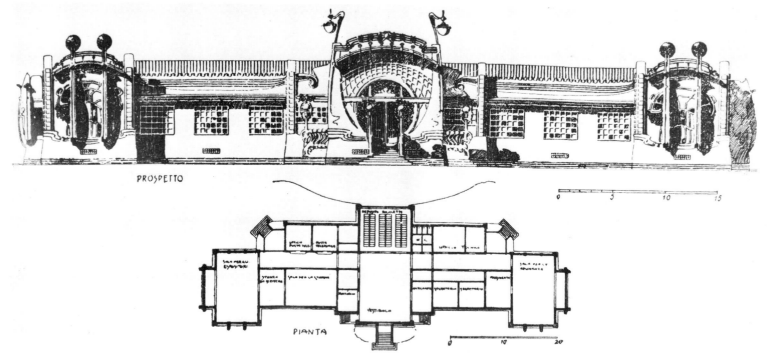

PROSPETTO

PIANTA

education, and to the lack of interest in education as a whole amongst the working classes as principal impediments in the way of industrial growth, so the most aware theorists of the Arte Nuova, in proposing a transformation of the means of production from a handicraft to an industrial dimension, accentuated the primary need to combat the discrimination between 'fine' and 'applied' arts and to modernise the teaching programmes of the schools of art. In the most advanced committed criticism (and especially in the essays of Alfredo Melani whose organic method and conceptual profundity merit a more thorough evaluation in the context of Art Nouveau theory) Modernismo was considered not merely as a renewal of taste, but as the outcome of a revolution in the methods and scope of artistic activity, which in making itself available, with the help of industry, to a wide public would achieve an 'aesthetic socialism' by raising the level of artistic sensibility even of the less well-off classes. 'The Arte Nuova', wrote Melani, 'is not an isolated fact in life, but the product of a movement in society which aims to change every aspect of human activity. Therefore those who are timid in politics . . . and cannot give up any of the forms of the past find it difficult to enter into the ideology and the beauty of the Arte Nuova.'[2]

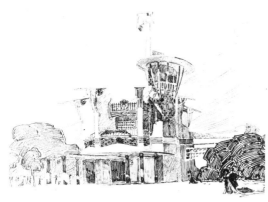

8.2-3 D'ARONCO *Competition projects* 1901, elevation and plan for Administrative Pavilion and Photography Pavilion

It is no accident that the first echoes of this aesthetic programme in the field of decorative art were felt around 1896 – in other words coinciding with the take-off of Italian industrialisation which followed an upward curve until 1907. The development of Liberty can be broken down schematically into three phases: the pioneer period (c. 1896-1902); the period of expressive maturity between the Turin and Milan Exhibitions of 1902 and 1906 during which the phenomenon began to permeate architecture; and the period of regression towards a more emphatically historicist compromise (1907-1914). The parabola can therefore be contained between the beginning of the period of industrial growth and the end of the 'Age of Giolitti' (1901-14)[3] during which this economic development had been effectively supported by government policy.

The relationship between the establishment of the Arte Nuova and the existence of an industrial base is confirmed by the prominent role played by Northern regions like Piedmont and Lombardy in the spread of Modernismo. Here the conditions favourable to the success of Liberty were first created: the formation, in the circle of the critics Melani, Thovez, Morasso and Pica of an intellectual attitude of commitment to the ideological and cultural case for Modernismo, and to the spread of its formal example by means of a number of magazines;[4] and the existence of an identifiable public in a middle class which 'modelled itself on international patterns' and 'countered the abstract literary rhetoric for an "Italian" style with a rationalist conviction that social classes were not confined by national frontiers'.[5] Predominant among the clients of Liberty artists and architects were in fact members of the very middle class which had staked its own future on the success of the industrial development promoted by

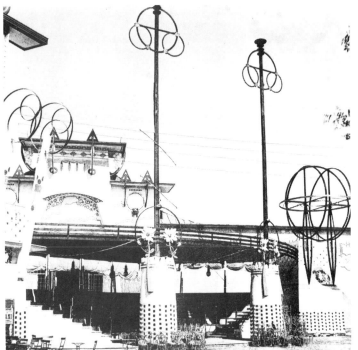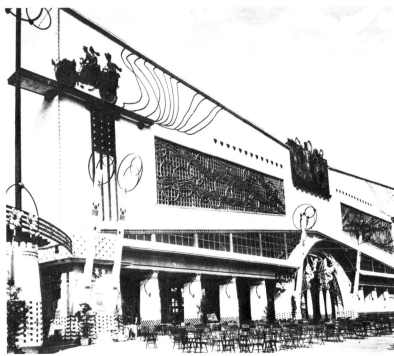

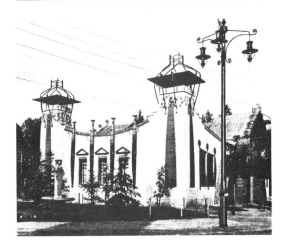

8.4-6 D'ARONCO *Turin Exhibition* 1902, Auditorium, Automobile Pavilion and Offices Pavilion (contemporary photographs)

Giovanni Giolitti's economic policy, and which traditionally shared a wider European culture.[6] On the other hand public patronage was lacking, as well as, with rare exceptions, that of the landed classes which controlled building development through the great property companies. The latter, involved in huge speculative operations in the historic city centres, clung to stylistic formulae of proven commercial profitability and which were unlikely to meet with opposition from municipal planning committees.

Together with the current economic changes, the political climate created by the reformism of the first years of the 'Age of Giolitti' indirectly favoured the spread of the Weltanschauung of Modernismo. Giolitti's rise to power had coincided with a reversal of the reactionary and anti-working-class[7] policies of the Di Rudini and Pelloux governments (1896-98 and 1898-1900), and with a quest for collaboration between employers and employees and between the government and the moderate wing of the socialist party. In the democratic myths of the Arte Nuova, in the vision of an 'aesthetic socialism' the opposite of elitist aestheticism, as well as in the campaign for the cultural and professional betterment of those employed in art manufacture and the appeal to artists to become industrial designers and renounce their attitude of social superiority, there was therefore a reflection of a general political trend.

The same ideological content inspired the International Exhibition of Decorative Art at Turin in 1902, perhaps the most complete review of the world-wide achievement of Art Nouveau. The Organising Committee aimed to demonstrate the validity of the concept neatly expressed in Melani's slogan: 'Design applied to industry has the most direct influence on the nation's prosperity'.[8] Two intentions were clearly evident in the exhibition programme: to launch Italian products on the international market; and to promote closer co-operation between the artistic and industrial avant-gardes by demonstrating to industry the power of the Arte Nuova to win over as consumers the upper layers of the urban proletariat which had benefited from Giolitti's high-incomes policy. These themes were hinted at in the minister Nasi's inaugural speech, in which he welcomed Liberty as 'an art which like science is becoming democratic . . . in order to raise up the masses to the level of its divine inspiration', with 'the dual purpose of spreading the benefits of aesthetic education, and creating new sources of work'.[9] In accordance with these aims a competition was held for 'a room of economic type', whose results were, however, mediocre and merely confirmed conservative critics in their opinion that Modernismo was too highly priced for popular consumption.

Partially successful on the other hand were the attempts to dispel the poor impression given by Italy's participation at the Paris Exhibition of 1900, and to win the support of big industry for the new style.[10] In addition to confirming the reputations of artists like Carlo Bugatti, Giacomo Cometti, Eugenio Quarti,

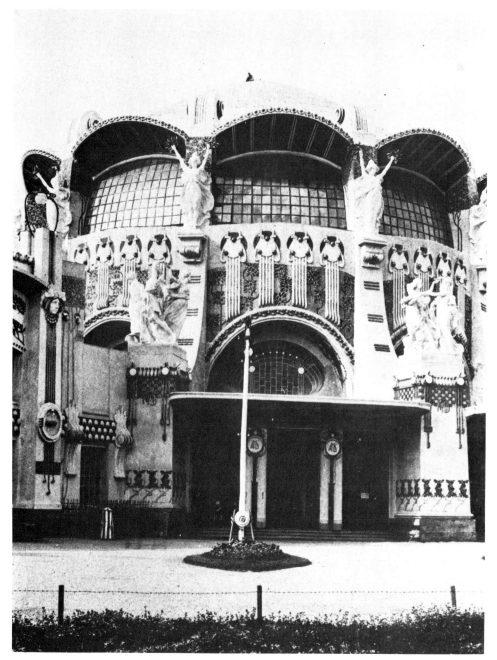

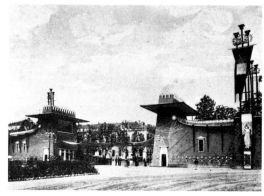

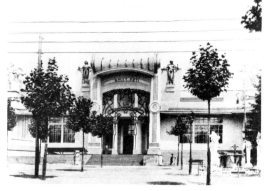

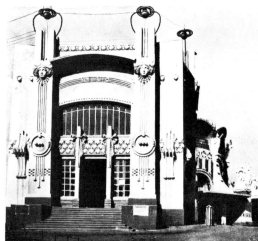

8.7-10 D'ARONCO *Turin Exhibition* 1902, Central Rotunda, Main Entrance, Fine Arts Pavilion and Belgium Gallery (contemporary photographs)

Galileo Chini and the designers for the Valabrega furniture factory in Turin, who had already distinguished themselves at Paris in 1900, the Exhibition brought international fame to Alessandro Mazzucotelli's ferronneries, Ernesto Basile's furniture and the stained glass work produced by the Beltrami workshop in Milan. The up-to-date impression conveyed by Italian decorative art was no sudden readjustment to fashion but the outcome of a long process of development, not without certain elements of originality, which was already apparent in the Turin Exhibition of 1898. This modernising endeavour won little encouragement even from the most progressive foreign critics. They tended to see Liberty as a mere imitation of foreign trends, and were more impressed by the compromising neo-mediaeval and neo-Renaissance traditionalism of, for instance, the Aemilia Ars company of Bologna. They thus supplied ammunition to the supporters of a continuous national tradition who claimed that 'in the attempt to be modern one had just succeeded in being exotic'.[11]

Similar objections were raised against Raimondo D'Aronco's pavilions,[12] dismissed by Pica as 'a servile imitation of Austrian models'. They undeniably incorporated a variety of influences and embodied quotations from Olbrich's buildings at the Exhibition of the Künstlerkolonie in Darmstadt of 1901. These are particularly evident in the form of the main entrance which imitated that of the Matildenhöhe, and in the facade of the pavilion housing the Committee's offices which reproduced on a smaller scale the front elevation of the Haus für Flächenkunst. Underlying this eclectic stance, however, an original leitmotiv in D'Aronco's creative development was discernible: the translation into a basically

Opposite
MICHELAZZI *Villino Giulio Lampredi* Florence c.1910, detail of facade (photograph Godoli)

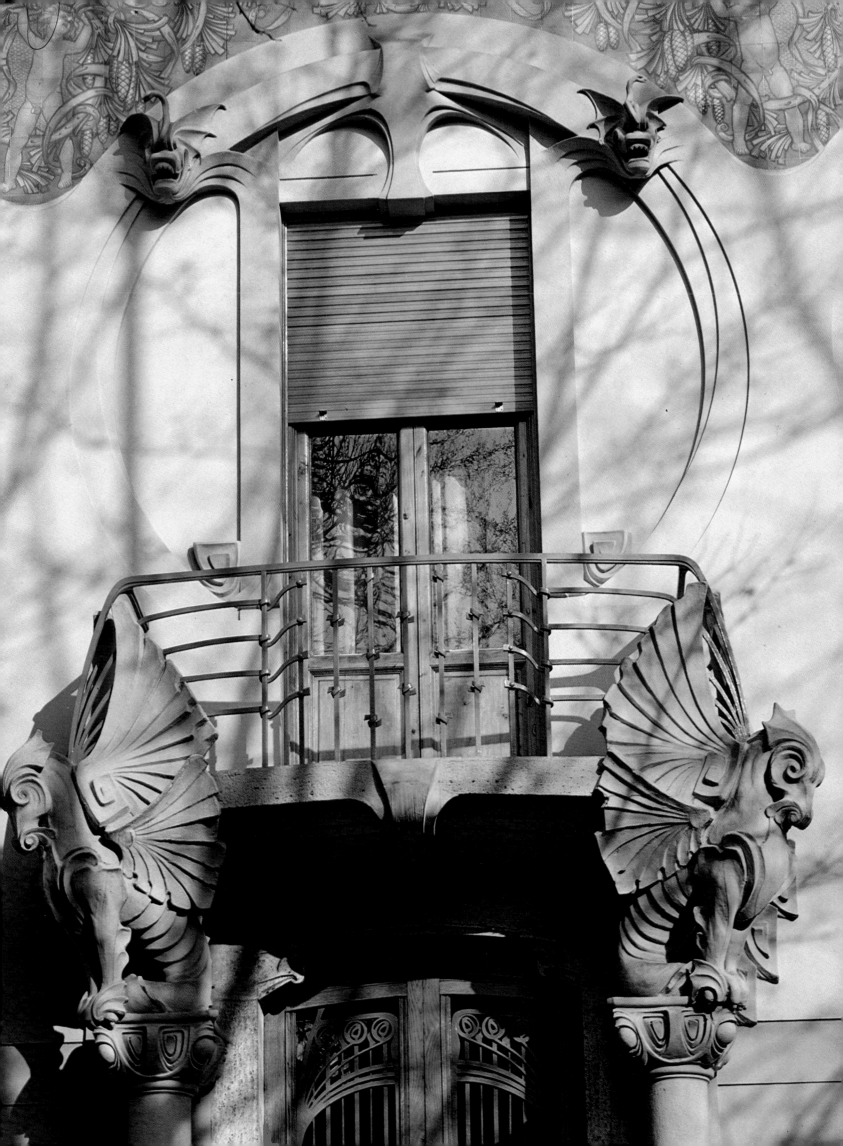

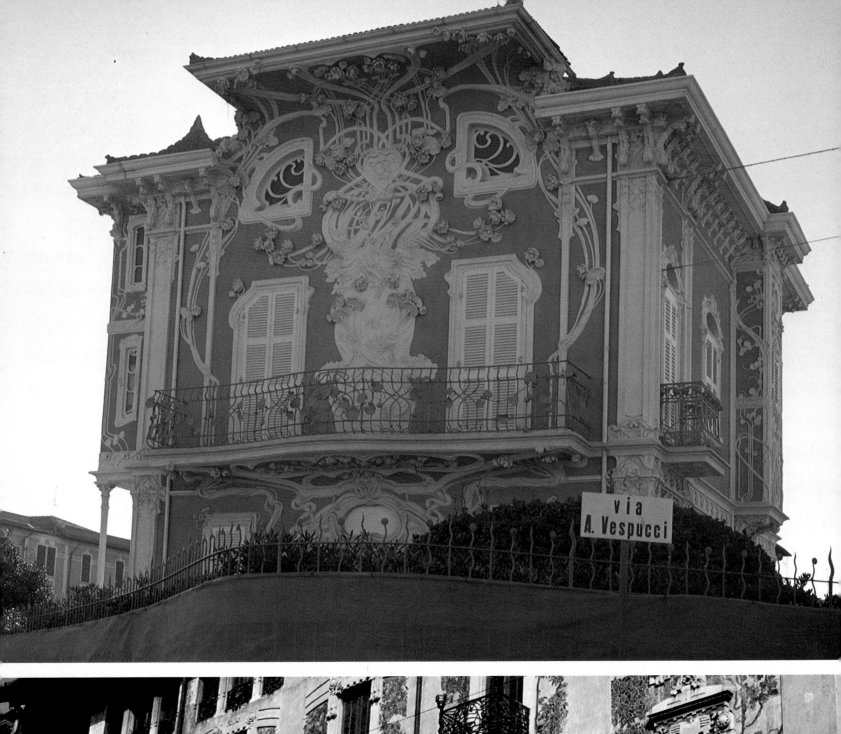

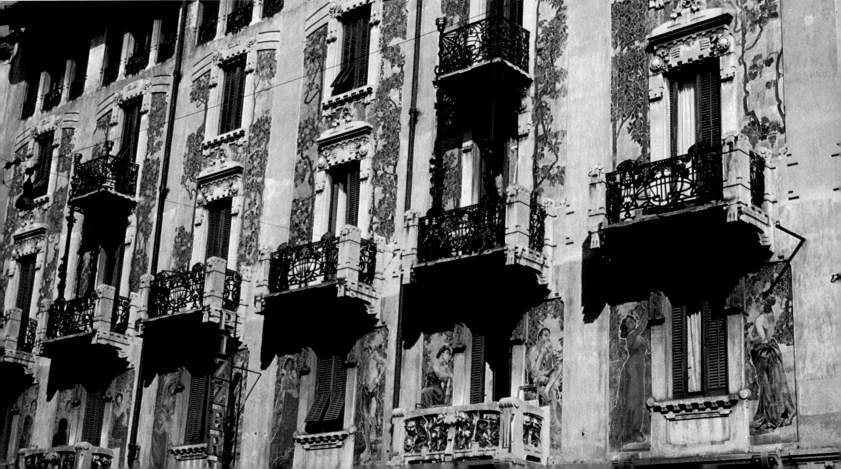

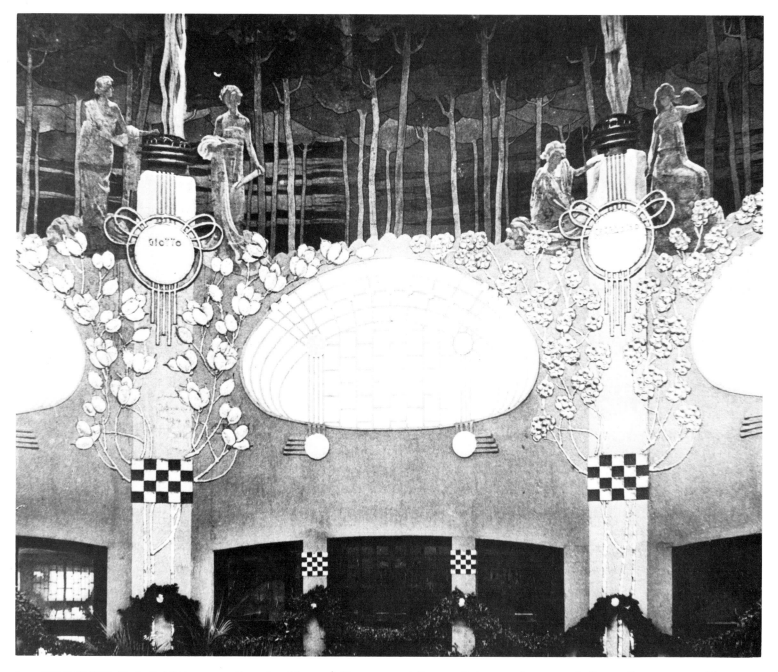

8.11 D'ARONCO *Turin Exhibition* 1902, Central Rotunda interior (contemporary photograph)

Opposite above
BREGA *Villa Ruggeri* Pesaro 1902-07 (photograph Godoli)

Opposite below
BOSSI *Galimberti house* Milan 1905, detail of facade (photograph Touillon)

Central European idiom of themes borrowed from Ottoman architecture. D'Aronco had been appointed Superintendent of Public Works in Turkey in 1896 and he found in Constantinople an environment which not only opened up for him a brilliant career but also encouraged him to free himself from the residue of his academic training. It gave the impetus to a spontaneous experimentalism in his work, in which echoes of the Wagnerschule and of Belgian Art Nouveau (reflected in his use of the narrow-fronted house-type) were combined with influences derived from local architectural tradition.

His competition designs for the Turin Exhibition submitted in 1901 showed D'Aronco at the most eclectic phase in his empirical search for a personal cultural identity. The facades of the main building and the administrative pavilion, and the elaborate decoration, the symmetrical organisation and the figurative dominance of the entrance area, show the influence of Otto Wagner and the Wagnerschule. The auditorium combined Guimard's Metro style with ornamental motifs in the style of Olbrich. The geometric character of the coffee-house was softened by a profusion of decoration. In the 400-seat theatre an interesting spatial duplication was achieved by fusing two rotated volumes roofed with shallow Turkish domes, while the photography pavilion was a variation on the theme of the mosque and minaret.

In the pavilions carried out following new designs[14] the festive/fantastic atmosphere appropriate to the function of the exhibition complex was created not only by formal elaboration but also by the skilful use of light and colour to break down surfaces and volumes into their component elements. In the automobile pavilion a glazed tympanum over the entrance isolated at night the cruciform upper part of the facade, in which 10,000 coloured lights produced changing light-effects as on a cinema screen. The Rotonda, which served as a vestibule to the five principal galleries in which the major part of the exhibition was concentrated, was a modern re-interpretation of the fusion of light and space in Byzantine architecture. 'I took this idea', D'Aronco confessed, 'from S. Sophia where the base of the dull yellow cupola is circumscribed by a band of light and takes on the appearance of a huge sail bellied out by the wind and held down by slender guy-ropes.'[15]

D'Aronco's subsequent work in Turkey tackled a similar set of problems, following Otto Wagner's maxim: to interpret the genius loci without taking refuge in the vernacular. His little mosque at Galata (1903) re-states a traditional building form in terms of a restrained Viennese manner with thin marble facing slabs fixed with metal bolts and gilded bronze cover-strips. This and the proto-rationalist Santoro house at Constantinople (1907) are among D'Aronco's most successful works. In Italy he would never have had the opportunity to equal these achievements. The following buildings in his homeland are worth mentioning: the pavilions for the Udine Exhibition of 1903, which developed themes already introduced at Turin the previous year, and the Favelli house in Turin (1903). The latter, besides the usual Viennese influences is interesting for its volumetric articulation and for its varied fenestration which shows a functionalist concern to subordinate the exterior shell to the needs of the interior spaces. By the time he returned finally to Turkey in 1908 D'Aronco's creativity seems to have burned itself out. His eclecticist town hall at Udine (1908-17), with its funereal monumentality, places a seal on the sudden and untimely termination of his Art Nouveau period.

The Turin Exhibition ushered in the most fertile period of Liberty architecture. Before 1902 it comprised only a handful of works: Alfredo Premoli's prize-winning design for wrought iron railings (submitted in a competition promoted by the magazine *Memorie di un Architetto* and inspired, as was pointed out by one of the competition judges, by Guimard's railings for the Castel Béranger); the same architect's house in Via Donizetti in Turin (1900) now the Hotel Eden; various designs for facades submitted to the Municipal Technical Bureau of Turin – one for a house in Via Verona; and Basile's Villino Florio and Villa Igea at Palermo which combined historicist references with floral decorative themes.

Turin's advanced position in the general panorama of the nation was confirmed by the high quality of its architectural production. It was compromised, however, by a tendency occasionally to interpret Art Nouveau merely as a stylistic alternative to revivalism. A search for plastic effects often takes precedence over the organisation of building form, producing 'facade architecture'. Gottardo Gussoni's apartment block in Via Palmieri (1912) and Vivarelli's in Corso Re Umberto (1911) are not exempt from this weakness. They stand out from the norm of contemporary building by their importation of elements foreign to local tradition like circular or bow-windows, and by the sinuous design of the window surrounds and pilasters contrasted with unbroken wall surfaces in fair-faced brickwork. The same is true of Giuseppe Velati-Bellini's apartment building in Via Cibrario, in which geometric and floral decorative motifs incised into the rendering make up for the lack of any more formal definition of constituent elements. A similar attitude is recognisable in Eugenio Bonelli's designs for the Bonelli and Besozzi houses in Via Papacino (1904). Here a two-dimensional facade unbroken by projecting features and pierced by unframed windows is relieved by elegantly drawn decoration based on architectural and naturalistic motifs in a manner typical of the Wagnerschule and particularly of certain designs by Hans Schlechta and Wunibald Deininger. This is an architecture in which everything is drawn, from the bow-windows to the window-surrounds and from the diagonals of the flying gulls to the birch woods at ground floor level quoted from a Schlechta design of 1900. It is not known whether the architect originally intended to use ceramic cladding, as in the Austrian examples, or a fresco technique. The use of ceramics and other materials like wrought iron made respectable by Art Nouveau was becoming general practice in Italy. However, Liberty architects seem to have been more attracted by their potential for expressive virtuosity than by their technological interest. This attitude is, for example, unmistakable in Antonio Vandone's

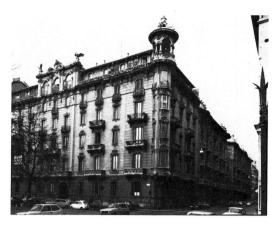

8.12 GUSSONI *Via Palmieri apartment block* Turin 1912 (photograph Godoli)

8.13 VANDONE *Maffei apartment building* Turin 1904 (photograph Godoli)

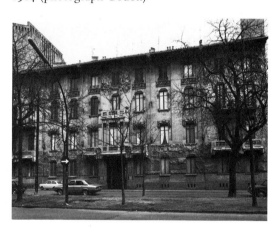

8.14 FENOGLIO *Fenoglio house* Turin 1902 (photograph Godoli)

8.15 FENOGLIO *Villa Scott* Turin 1902 (photograph Godoli)

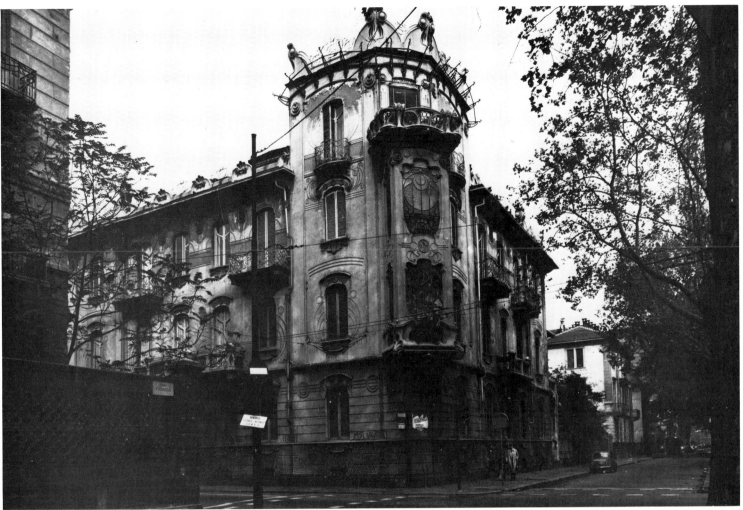

8.14

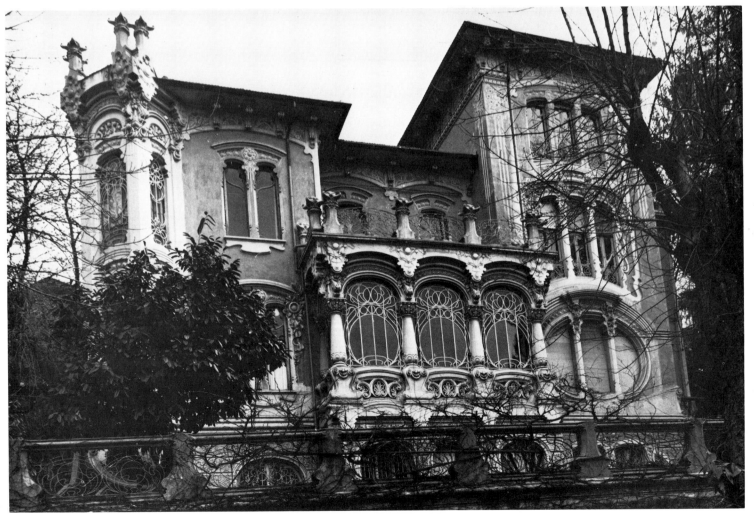

8.15

Maffei apartment building (1904), in which wrought iron superstructures consisting of balconies carried by paired columns (manufactured by the Mazucotelli firm) contrast strangely with the massive stone backdrop decorated at the upper storey with sculptured reliefs by Alloati, a hybrid mixture of neo-Renaissance rhetoric and Liberty taste. Lorenzo Parrocchia's apartment building and department store in Via Nizza (1904) is an almost unique example of the attempt to integrate technical innovation with advanced composition. Exploiting the freedom offered by reinforced concrete construction Parrocchia here rationalised the plan and subordinated the elevations to the needs of the interior spaces.

The most representative figure in the Torinese circle was Pietro Fenoglio, one of the promoters of the 1902 Exhibition whose extremely active professional career is demonstrated by more than a hundred buildings.[16] His apartment block in Corso Francia (1902), regarded as his masterpiece, comes close to Horta and Franco-Belgian Art Nouveau, substituting an abstract treatment of naturalistic motifs for the realism of the Stile Floreale. The building's main interest lies, however, in the concept of its composition, which stresses the diagonal symmetry implicit in the plan and translates it into a play of volumes dominated by the surging plasticity of the corner turret with its stained glass bow-window. The building forms a pivotal fixture at the junction of two streets; it was therefore logical to emphasise the corner feature most exposed to view, treating it as the focal point in the composition. In the contemporaneous Villa Scott (1902), a pleasing and dynamic play of volumes reflecting the intricacy of the plan coincided with Fenoglio's involution towards a greater idiomatic hybridism. The attempt to create an impression of haut-bourgeois opulence led to a mingling of Rococo allusions and Art Nouveau stylistic devices which brings this design close to the work of French architects like Lavirotte and Schoellkopf.

Some of Velati-Bellini's output – for instance the 'Palazzina Lauro' at the 1902 Exhibition and his house in Via Bezzecca (1904) – exemplifies a tendency common in much of the so-called minor Liberty: that is to say the style characteristic of middle class and lower middle class building, seen above all in the small one-family villas which proliferated in the suburbs of many Italian cities. Typically, a simple basic composition was combined with a modest sprinkling of stucco floral decoration concentrated mainly in horizontal bands, and in window-surrounds and crowning features.

Annibale Rigotti's example had by contrast very little influence. Few traces remain of his intense activity both abroad in England, Bulgaria and Siam and in Italy. His Oils and Wines Pavilion and Cinema at the 1902 Exhibition were adjudged at the time as being 'too lacking in ornament'. They typified Rigotti's proto-rationalism and his inclination to a straightforward expression of function without indulging in decorative distractions. This Purism recurs in his Villa Falcioni at Domodossola (c. 1902). The bareness of the elevations is here relieved, not so much by a sparing use of floral ornament (two rose bushes in stucco on either side of the front door and a climbing wistaria on the main facade), as by a skilful use of external features which express the varied functions of the interior spaces: windows of varied size and design, inset balconies and projecting bays.

*　　*　　*

Despite the occurrence of Franco-Belgian accents in Piedmontese Liberty, not surprising in a region bound by political and cultural links to France, the models to which Italian architects were most drawn were German and Austrian. This cultural orientation was clearly not unconnected with Italy's political involvement with Germany and Austria under the terms of the Triple Alliance of 1882. As De Fusco observed, Italy 'shared with Germany similarities in its recent history . . . and its internal politics (for instance between the "Roman Question" and the *Kulturkampf*). These affinities were reinforced by a desire to imitate Germany's rapid and efficient industrial growth.'[17] This imitative tendency is evident in the modernist magazines of the period, which repeatedly held up as patterns for Italian artists to follow the work of the Vereinigte Werkstätten fur Kunst und Handwerk of Munich, of the Künstlerkolonie at Darmstadt and of the Verband deutscher Kunstgewerbe Vereine. As regards Austria, the refined culture of Vienna remained a strong influence in the Northern regions formerly ruled by the Habsburg Empire, tinged with a nostalgia which anti-Austrian nationalism could not dispel. Furthermore the classicist basis of the

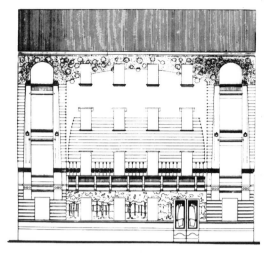

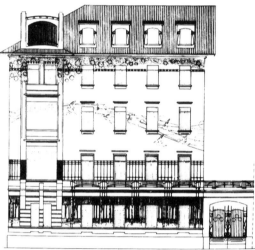

8.16-17 BONELLI *Projects for the Besozzi and Bonelli houses* Turin 1904, elevations

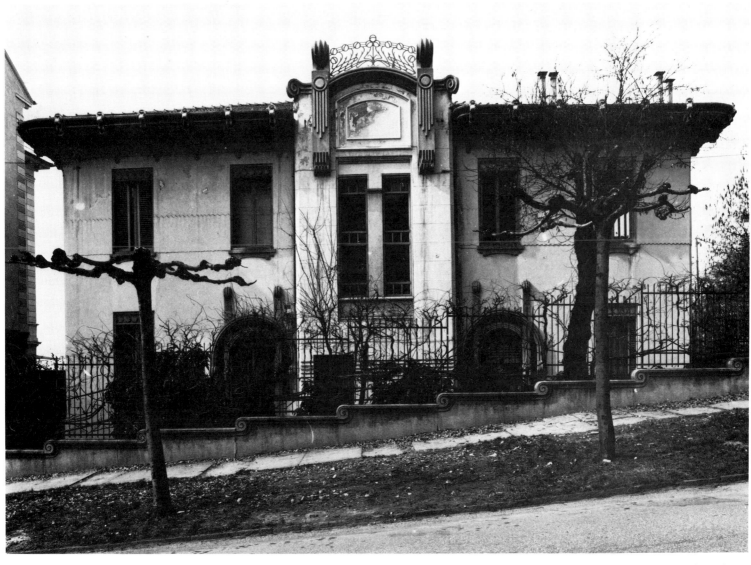

8.18 VELATI-BELLINI *Via Bezzecca house* Turin 1904 (photograph Godoli)

Wagnerschule and its revival of forms and typologies characteristic of Mediterranean architecture made it seem more sympathetic to Italian national tradition than other currents of European Art Nouveau.

Architects trained under Wagner or who, like Mario Sandonà and Max Fabiani, had worked in his office were active in the cities of Venezia Giulia which still belonged to the Habsburg Empire – particularly Trieste. Through this channel the influence of Viennese architecture reached the neighbouring Veneto and Venice itself, a city unusually resistant to the penetration of modern ideas. Guido Costante Sullam and Giuseppe Torres were leading figures in the movement to free local architecture and craftsmanship from the prevailing Byzanto-Gothic revivalism sustained by the dogma of the inviolability of the architectural heritage of the historic city centre, and as regards craft production, by the demands of mass tourism. However, Sullam's and Torres' only Liberty buildings were confined to the fashionable bathing station of the Lido or to Mestre on the Venetian mainland. Sullam visited Darmstadt where he was fascinated by the personality of Olbrich. 'My meeting with Olbrich' he confided to Bruno Zevi 'and the study of his buildings proved to me that it was impossible to create good Liberty architecture in Italy without first modernising the crafts. The art of architecture could only be realised with the help of specialised craftsmen. It was necessary to devote all one's energies to the reform of the schools of art and technical colleges . . . Architecture would follow in due course.'[18]

The unusual qualities of the Villas 'Thea' and 'Mon Plaisir', built by Sullam in 1905 on adjoining sites in Via Lepanto on the Lido, derived from this concern. His attention to detail and the overriding importance he gave to craftsmanship found superb expression in balcony railings and window-sills, in the balustrade of the typically Venetian roof-terrace, the pictorial decoration and the tiled surrounds of the arched windows. The interesting spatial articulation of the Villa 'Mon Plaisir' matched the high quality of its decoration. The interior spaces were skilfully organised around a central stairwell rising through the full height of the

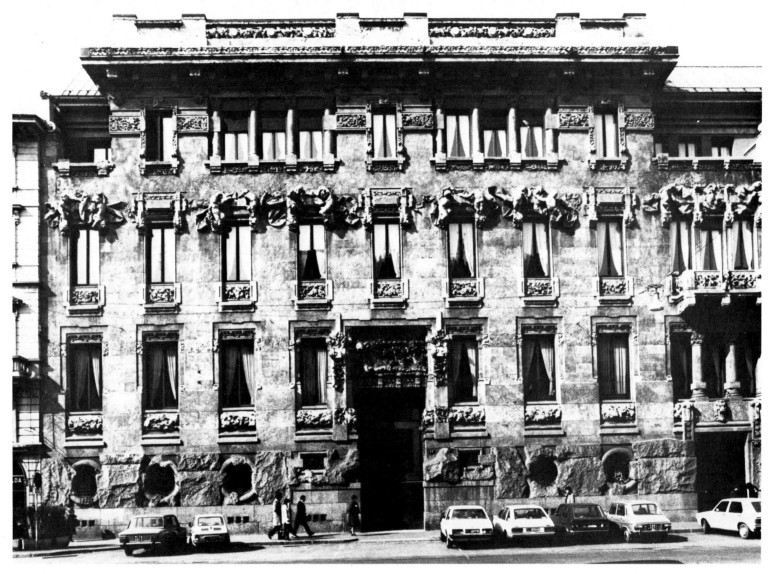

building. This acted, with its landings and galleries, as the circulation hub of the villa.

Slightly later than Sullam, Torres, having likewise started as a mediaeval revivalist, developed compositional and formal themes invented in the orbit of the Wagnerschule. His designs for the 'House of Silence' and the 'House of the Poet' published in 1908 in the magazine *L'Architettura Italiana* with their precise build-up of primary volumes, the predominance of solids over voids and the use of flat roofs or stepped terraces have an affinity with the numerous variations on Capriote and other Mediterranean vernacular themes in the work of Hoppe, Kammerer and Deininger. On the eve of the First World War, however, Torres demonstrated in his interiors for the Villa Tretti at Bevadoro di Padova and in the design for a group of villas on the Lido Promenade his total mastery of the example of Josef Hoffmann. The success of Hoffmann's lucid classicism was by then widely established in Italy. Even in Turin, for example, it became dominant after about 1910 in the work of Pietro Betta, Vittorio Ballatore di Rosana and Giuseppe Hendel.

★　　★　　★

In Milan Liberty architecture took on a more distinctly national and homogeneous character than in the internationalist climates of Piedmont and the Veneto. At the same time it was compromised to a greater degree by the historic heritage. The academic curbs on Italian Liberty are completely summed up in the work of Giuseppe Sommaruga[19] whose personality had an overpowering influence on the development of Milanese architecture. In his best known building, the Palazzo Castiglioni (1903), the idiomatic repertoire of Liberty is substituted for the trabeation, cornices and capitals of the academic hand-books. However, it is congealed within a monumental classicist composition suggestive of Roman Baroque. This Baroque flavour was given not only by the massive basement of

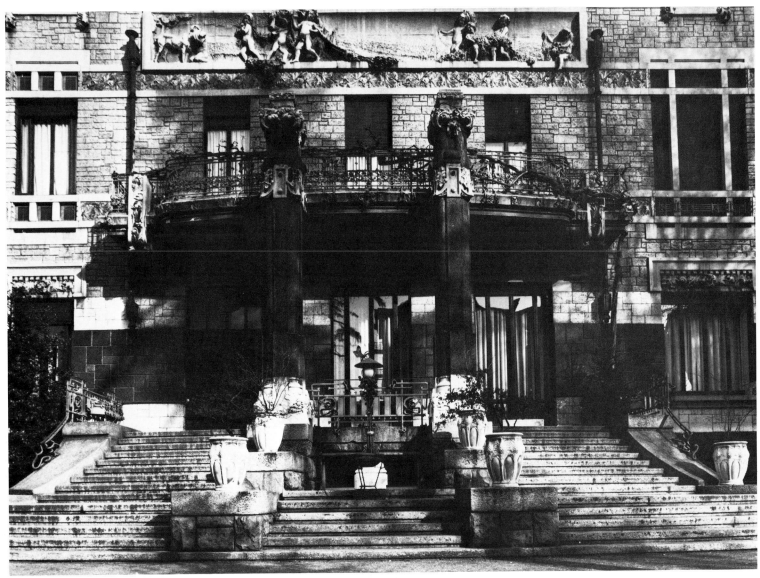

8.20 SOMMARUGA *Villa Romeo* Milan 1908
(photograph Godoli)

rough-hewn stone, but also by Ernesto Bazzaro's sculptured group representing Peace and Industry which stood at the entrance (until hastily removed following a public outcry over the nudity of the two figures) and re-interpreted Bernini's dialectical contrast between inert matter and animated form. The symmetry of the facade and of the plan are combined with great freedom in section. The interior spaces are organised on several different levels around a complex system of vertical circulation. A spacious top-lit staircase hall gave access to a number of entrance lobbies and stairwells serving the individual apartments. The dignified atmosphere of haut-bourgeois luxury implicit in the internal organisation was reinforced by the use of precious materials and by the richness of the decoration.

In some of Sommaruga's other buildings – like the Villa Aletti in Rome (1897) and the Comi and Samoiraghi houses in Milan (1900 and 1906) – monumentality is expressed by an effective play of masses comparatively free from classical stereometry. Here, as again in the Villa Romeo (now the Columbus Clinic) in Milan (1908) the skilful exploitation of different materials – alternating bands of brick, smooth ashlar and rusticated stone – to create effects of colour contrast reappears as a recurrent theme in Sommaruga's vocabulary. Liberty overtones are subdued in his orchestration of the means of expression – confined to marginal features like wrought iron work, occasional bands of relief sculpture, and door and window surrounds. One of Sommaruga's most unusual works was his design for the Hotel Tre Croci at Varese (1908), altered in the course of construction. Its exuberant monumentality, incorporating suggestions of the surrounding mountain landscape, was achieved by a complex accumulation of building masses with turrets and angular pillars, buttressed plinths and connecting bridges halfway between the megalomania of certain drawings by Emil Hoppe and Sant'Elia's preliminary sketches for the 'città futurista'.

Alfredo Campanini's apartment building in Via Bellini (1904–06) was inspired by the example of the Palazzo Castiglioni. It made extensive use of concrete corroded by water and salt to simulate stone, in a riot of sculptured decoration from which emerge two caryatids representing Painting and Sculpture (typical themes in Liberty iconography) on either side of the main entrance. The deceptive use of materials to give a false impression of luxury becomes in Campanini, as in many Milanese architects, a device for disguising the meanness of a speculative building whose real nature is revealed, however, in its banal planning and maximum exploitation of floor areas.

Sommaruga's influence is perceptible not only in private building – in Silvio Gambini's work at Busto Arsizio and in some designs by Giulio Ulisse Arata – but also in a conspicuous quantity of cemetery monuments, characterised by the imitation, stripped of their usual decoration, of the Indian stūpa and shikkara. Funerary architecture was a field in which Liberty architects were particularly active, producing a series of works which included the Crespi Mausoleum (1896-1907) at Crespi d'Adda by Gaetano Moretti, the sketches and designs for the cemetery of Monza (1912) by Antonio Sant'Elia and Italo Paternostro and the drawing entitled *A Vision* (1913) by Silvio Gambini. The forerunners of this series were Sommaruga's ossuary at Palestro (1893) and his competition design for the cemetery of Bergamo (1897). This orientalism, with its esoteric overtones suggestive of Buddhist teachings and the Hindu doctrine of the transmigration of souls, was clearly intended to express the brilliant progressive destiny and the transcendentalism of the bourgeois ethos. It was no accident that the clientele for these mausolea often consisted of families like the Crespi which represented the enlightened paternalism and reformism of the progressive wing of North-Italian capitalist society.

The hydro-electric station at Trezzo d'Adda (1906) embodied a different brand of orientalism – Middle-Eastern rather than Indian. Its architect, Gaetano Moretti, began as a mediaeval revivalist. His first use of Liberty themes was in the three rooms he designed for the Ceruti Company at the Turin Exhibition, which exemplify an amalgam of neo-Renaissance and Floreale which was to have a wide influence on architecture as well as on applied art.

A widespread trend within the continuous upsurge of nostalgic eclecticism in Milanese architecture consisted of a compound of Louis XV reminiscences and Liberty motifs. Among the exponents of this manner were Cattaneo, Menni, Giachi and Manfredini. An advantage of this infusion of historicist elements was that it made the employment of modern materials like iron in facade design more readily acceptable to the general public. The dualist use of a near-Baroque stone cornice in combination with enormous metal-framed windows in Luigi Broggi's Contratti Department Store recalls similar compromise solutions in other commercial buildings of the period like the interesting series of commercial buildings in the rue de Rennes in Paris. This ambiguous and unresolved attitude to the use of new materials, wavering between their exclusive employment in decoration and their subordination to the repertoire of eclecticism, is again evident in Giovan Battista Bossi's Galimberti house in Via Malpighi (1905). This uses ceramic cladding extensively, apparently less to facilitate cleaning of the facades (as in Lavirotte's or Klein's buildings in Paris) than to make possible a purely graphic introduction of Liberty themes. The point of maximum corruption of Liberty by Rococo in Milanese architecture is seen in the 1906 Exhibition held to celebrate the piercing of the Simplon Tunnel. Achille de Lazzari's Goldsmiths' Pavilion was a paradoxically kitsch example of this degeneration. However it also affected the main entrance, the Aquarium by Sebastiano Locati, the Gallery of Work by Bianchi, Magnani and Rondoni and the French Pavilion by Orsino Bongi. Signs of the reversion to a reactionary eclecticism were noticeable also in the decorative arts, which had now exhausted the impulse to innovation given by the Turin Exhibition.

The triumph of an hybrid 'Liberty en rocaille' in the Milan Exhibition was immediately echoed on the Ligurian Riviera where it proliferated in the work of architects like Dario Carbone, Giuseppe Bregante, Gino Coppedè and Gottardo Gussoni (an associate of Pietro Fenoglio). The distinguishing marks of this output were Baroque rhetoric, superfluous decoration and a tendency to pastiche associated with an inclination to Moorish, Egyptian or Assyrio-Babylonian exoticism. Although classified as Liberty it was really a reflection of the taste of the new parvenu aristocracy; it belongs more properly to the history of manners than to that of architecture.

An important place among the revivalist trends within Liberty was occupied

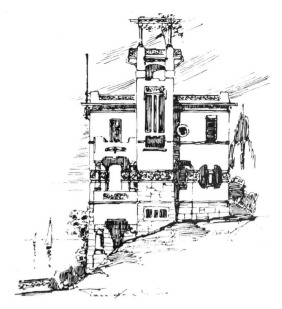

8.21 GAMBINI *Project for a villa on the Adriatic coast* 1906

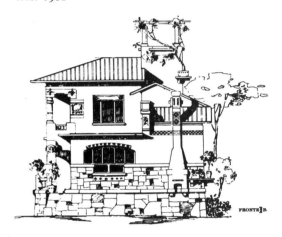

8.22 GAMBINI *Project for a small villa* 1909

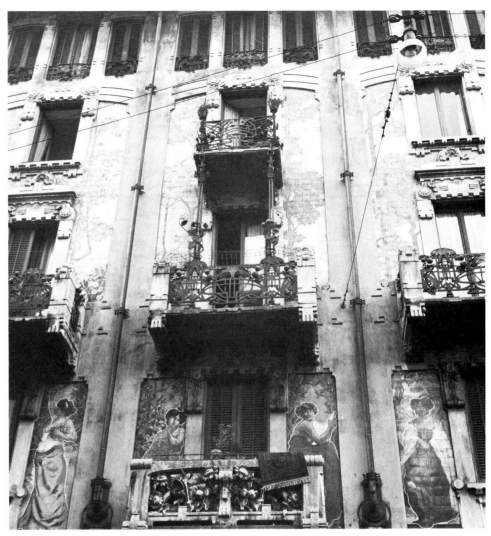

8.23 BOSSI *Galimberti house* Milan 1905
(photograph Bairati)

by the firm Aemilia Ars of Bologna, founded in 1898 by a group of artists and their aristocratic patrons with the aim of improving the artistic quality of the arts and crafts in the Emilia-Romagna region by commissioning craftsmen to make objects designed by its members. The theorist of the group was an architect known for his restorations of mediaeval buildings, Alfonso Rubbiani. The Floreale signified for him far more than a stylistic tendency based, like Pre-Raphaelitism, on the use of naturalistic decoration derived from Gothic and early Renaissance models. It was also the symbol of a socialistic utopia. In its rejection of industrialism and its revival of handicrafts, with its anti-urban ideology and its yearning for a rural society in which 'the gentle future humanity will work the land instead of fashioning a multitude of things demanded by the artificial consumption of the cities'[20] echoed the most backward-looking myths of Ruskin and Morris, blending them with a criticism of luxury of a physiocratic and illuminist stamp. Despite individual artists' varying degrees of freedom from eclecticism the Floreale tendency promoted by Aemilia Ars constituted a unifying influence in the architecture of Emilian and Romagnolo cities like Bologna, Parma and Ferrara. Among its most significant products, on account of their lack of concessions to historicism, must be numbered some of Ciro Contini's buildings in Ferrara. In his plain little villa for the flower-grower Melchiorri a disciplined use of floral decoration introduced a naive symbolic allusion to the owner's occupation.

★ ★ ★

Alongside Turin and Milan the third important centre of Liberty was Palermo. Although the city lacked a corresponding industrial hinterland, here too the success of the new style, and particularly the rising career of Ernesto Basile[21] depended on the support either of the upper middle class families which gravitated around the Florio financial empire, or of a dynamic business tycoon like Vittorio Golia Ducrot, the owner of the furniture factory of the same name. It was in the role of designer for the Ducrot Company that Basile first liberated himself from the residue of his eclecticist training. He won for himself an

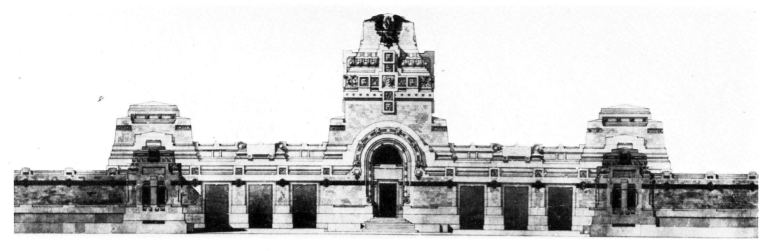

8.24

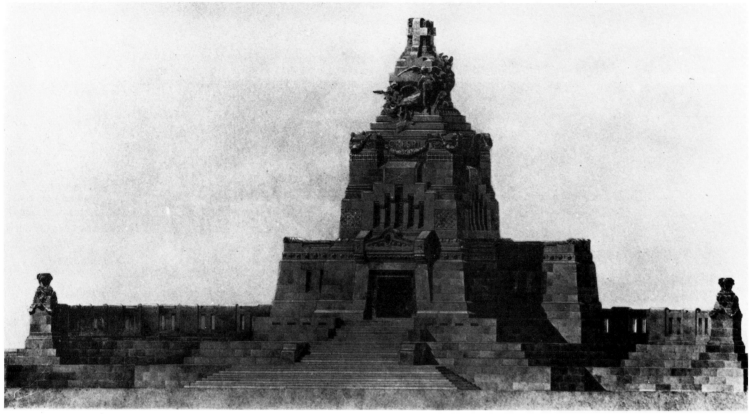

8.25

outstanding position in Liberty circles, confirmed by the prizes he carried off at the Turin Exhibition of 1902, the Exhibition of Fine Arts at Venice in 1903 and the Milan Exhibition of 1906, and exerted by his example a pervasive innovatory influence on the arts and crafts in Sicily and Southern Italy. His uncompromising fidelity to Modernismo in the field of applied art contrasted with a stylistic ambivalence in his architecture which betrayed the continuance in it of typological distinctions of an eclectic nature. A corollary of this concept was the practice of relegating Liberty motifs to the private sphere and adopting a historicist idiom for exteriors. His Villino Florio at Palermo (1899-1903) exemplifies this dualism, as does the Villa Igea of the same date, originally intended as a sanatorium but later converted into a Grand Hotel. The exteriors of these buildings were characterised by a revivalism borrowing predominantly from the Sicilian Quattrocento, and particularly from the works of Matteo Carnelivari, which Basile had carefully studied and measured. Traces of Floreale are discernible only in a few details. In the interiors by contrast it explodes without historicist inhibitions. They were carried out by the Ducrot firm with the help of skilled artists like Ettore de Maria Bergler, who executed the paintings in the dining room at the Villa Igea. Basile's interest in the revival of the applied arts and in the training, in his own workshops, of specialised craftsmen proficient in the repertoire of Floreale contributed to the spread of Liberty in Palermo and throughout Sicily. On the other hand his recurrent use of motifs borrowed from Siculo-Norman, Hispano-Moresque and also Carnelivaresque architecture (which

8.24 SOMMARUGA *Project for the cemetery of Bergamo* 1897

8.25 MORETTI *Crespi Mausoleum* Crespi d'Adda 1896, perspective drawing

8.26 SANT'ELIA & PATERNOSTRO *Project for the cemetery of Monza* 1912

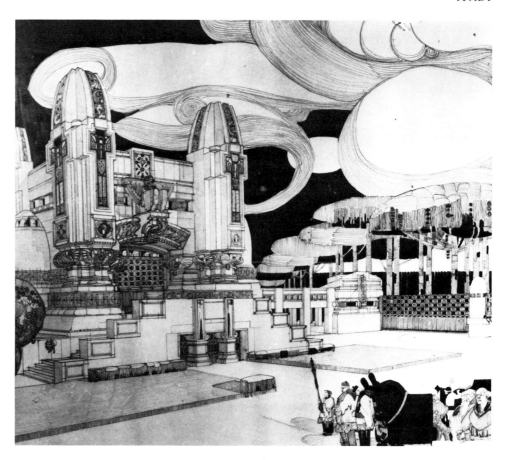

constituted a transitional phase between Catalan Gothic and Renaissance) made him the authoritative representative of the eclectic regional tradition. Rooted in a submerged desire for greater political autonomy from the rest of Italy, this would find many supporters among disciples of Basile like Ernesto Armò, Giovan Battista Santangelo, Saverio Fragapane and Francesco Fichera. Sicilian Modernismo has been compared with that of Catalonia,[22] especially with its more historicist elements, on account of the similarities between the politico-cultural situations of the two regions and because of their sources in similar architectural traditions. However, despite the undeniable affinities between the two cultures, the linguistic gulf between the mediaevalism of Puig i Cadafalch, Domènech i Montaner and their followers and that of Basile and his successors (who did not share the Catalan Modernists' liking for heterodox idiomatic compounds and structural paradox) makes the comparison between the two movements unworkable.

Liberty also had a considerable influence outside Palermo in the cities in the East of Sicily like Catania and Caltagirone, which experienced both rapid industrial growth and strong electoral support for left-wing parties. Thanks to the political initiative of its Mayor, don Luigi Sturzo, the founder of the Catholic People's Party, Caltagirone became through a series of urbanistic and architectural transformations a unique and homogeneous example of the città modernista. The Catholic People's Party, which offered an alternative to the Socialist Party, pursued a policy of reform which concentrated primarily on the solution of the agrarian problem and the expansion of employment in the construction industry also due to public participation. Thanks to Sturzo's support Saverio Fragapane was made responsible for the major public works, except the power station designed by Basile in 1907. Both in the historic centre and in the new suburbs Fragapane's combination of Liberty with Gothic and Baroque allusions gave a uniform imprint to the urban character of the city which embraced commercial and industrial as well as religious and residential architecture.

Outside Sicily Basile's influence was also noticeable in Naples, above all in the field of industrial art. Neapolitan art manufacturers were represented in the Halls of the Mezzogiorno arranged by Basile at the Fifth International Exhibition of Art held at Venice in 1903. The remarkable expansion of Naples in the early 1900s was characterised in the architecture of the new quarters West of the city centre and of the Vomero and Posillipo districts by the external use of Floreale motifs in a vain attempt to disguise a basic conventionality. The best examples of

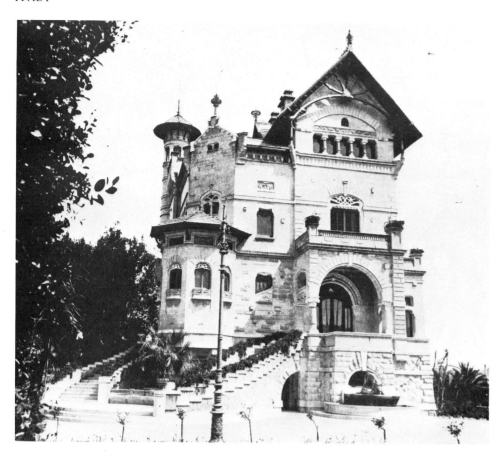

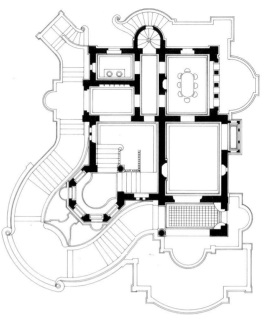

8.27-28 BASILE *Villino Florio* Palermo 1899-1903, exterior (contemporary photograph) and plan (from the original drawing)

Neapolitan Liberty are to be found in interior and shop design rather than residential building. One of the most representative examples is the Knight jewellery shop (1906) by Leonardo Paterna Baldizzi, a former pupil of Ernesto Basile. In his interiors in the Hotel Santa Lucia (1906) Giovanni Battista Comencini employed wooden ribbing to serve a dual function; both to subdivide the walls and ceilings into panels decorated with floral motifs, and to integrate them with the furnishing scheme. These interiors recall those of Henri Sauvage.

★   ★   ★

In Central Italy Liberty architecture found a more receptive climate in holiday resorts like the spas and the seaside towns on the Tyrrhenian and Adriatic coasts than in cities with established academic traditions like Florence and Rome. An outstanding example of seaside Liberty was the villa on the promenade at Pesaro built between 1902 and 1907 for the pharmaceutical manufacturer Oreste Ruggeri by the architect Giuseppe Brega in accordance with the owner's instructions. In this playful architecture the designers lavished their invention on the exterior shell of the building at the expense of the interior. Revivalist echoes – pagoda-shaped roofs, neo-Gothic pinnacled turrets and Corinthian columns – mingle with stucco arabesques, suggesting the interlacing of seaweed, which decorate the facades and the naturalistic lobster-shaped corbels which support the eaves. The internal organisation, in which a small central entrance lobby, hardly more than a staircase landing, gives access to all the rooms, is by contrast rigid and banal. The arbitrariness and affectation of the building is revealed in the lack of correspondence between exterior massing and interior space clearly readable in the sections. The turret and the bow-windows, which from outside appear to be subdivided into two storeys, are found actually to be reachable only at first floor level.

The work of the Florentine architect Giovanni Michelazzi[23] shows a quite different level of stylistic maturity and inventiveness in the organisation of interior space. Michelazzi was an almost isolated figure in the artistic panorama of a city in which the hegemony of a strict neo-Renaissance academicism had remained unscathed by the success at home and abroad of the group of artists associated with Galileo Chini and the Arte della Ceramica workshops which he founded in 1897. Michelazzi collaborated with Chini in the Villino Broggi-Caraceni in Via Scipione Ammirato (1911), commissioning him to carry out the

8.29-30 MICHELAZZI *Villino Broggi-Caraceni* Florence 1911, plan (from the original drawing) and exterior

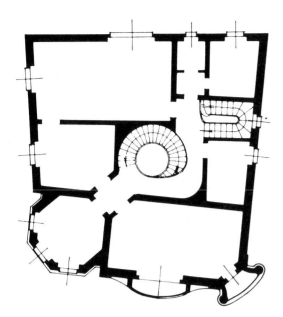

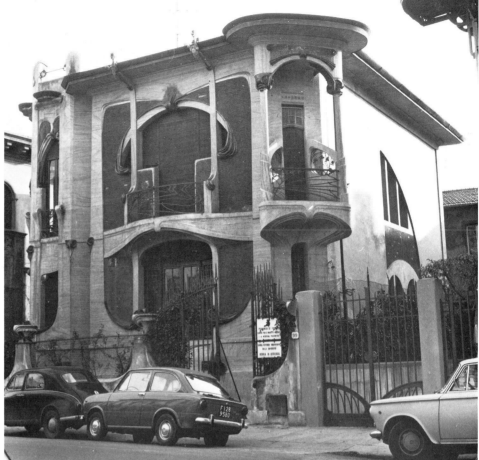

8.31 BREGA *Villa Ruggeri* Pesaro 1902-07

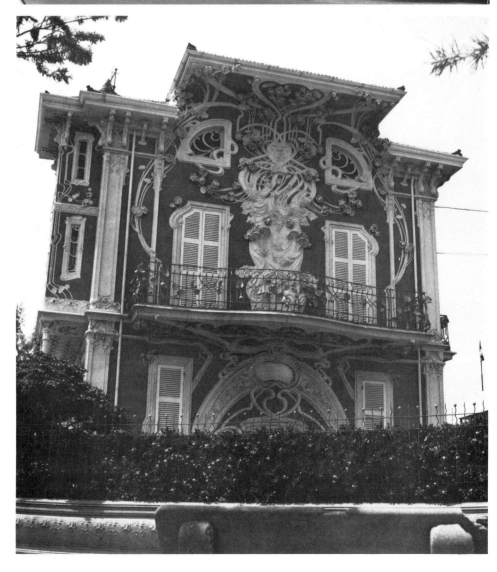

ceramic decorations. Apart from its formal qualities this building was remarkable for its brilliant planning solution. The interior spaces focused around a central eliptical staircase top-lit from a domed skylight, which gave direct access to all the rooms with the minimum waste of space. The house and gallery in Via Borgognissanti, a unique and exceptional intrusion of Liberty into the historic centre of Florence, has also been attributed to Michelazzi. It came close to the manner of Belgian Art Nouveau, both in its use of the narrow-fronted house-type (necessitated by the shape of the deep narrow site) and in the design of the openings, characterised, as in many buildings in Brussels, by the circular window of the top floor studio.

The case of Rome constitutes an irrelevant chapter in the history of Liberty architecture. The city's negative attitude to the Stile Moderno reflected the rooted conservatism of the government machine. The Roman environment exerted a corrupting influence even on men like Sommaruga and Basile, directing their innate historicism towards a neo-Renaissance classicism. From the Palazzo di Rudinì in Via Quintino Sella to the Villino Florio in Via Piemonte and the Parliament Building, the course of Basile's Roman career makes utterly clear his eclecticist willingness to adapt his style to suit the representational purpose of each architectural theme. Among the few Liberty buildings in Rome, there are none which are not conditioned by eclectic compromises and reservations. The same applies to the unusual villa which the sculptor Ettore Ximenes designed for himself in collaboration with Paterna-Baldizzi. This reveals a fundamental dichotomy between the Olbrichian flavour of the studio wing, and the house proper in which Floreale motifs are combined with Siculo-Norman mediaeval influences. However, it also incorporates pleasing formal effects like the curious fireplaces whose elaborate whimsy recalls Gaudí.

Liberty was unable to gain a foothold in Rome even in the field of temporary architecture. On the contrary, the Exhibition of 1911 marked the dramatic defeat of Modernismo in this sphere by a Barocco-imperialist classicism (to which the pavilions at the Turin Exhibition of the same year likewise conformed). This trend matched the upsurge of nationalism which accompanied the Italo-Turkish War over Libya, declared on the 29th of September 1911. The twilight of the 'Age of Giolitti' was characterised by the resurgence of colonialist policies, the sharpening of anti-Austrian irredentism and a general swing to nationalism which contaminated even the world of culture. These were accompanied by a hardening of attitudes towards the Left on the part of the governing class. The fortunes of Liberty, tainted with suspicions of both internationalism and socialism, were likewise in full decline, despite occasional tremors of activity which continued up to the eve of the First World War.

Alongside the anti-Liberty polemics mounted in academic circles one must also consider that of the Futurists. 'I combat and despise' declared Sant'Elia in the *Manifesto of Futurist Architecture,* 'all the pseudo-architecture of the avant-garde, Austrian, Hungarian, German and American.' It is still open to dispute whether this statement, which set out indirectly to vilify the whole output of Liberty, was an interjection demanded by Marinetti who as the leader of the Futurists was in the van of the anti-Austrian irredentist movement. It appears in fact to contradict the entire previous output of Sant'Elia, for whom the Wagnerschule folios in his library were like a new Vitruvius. Sant'Elia's designs of the period 1910-14 comprise the most complete summary of the figurative and compositional themes of Austro-German Art Nouveau to be found in the whole panorama of Italian Liberty. Graphic and decorative devices inspired by Franz von Stuck and Gustav Klimt (who had been the star of the Venice Biennale of 1910) appear in these projects combined with a monumentalism which exploits the entire repertoire of the Wagnerschule and of the drawings of Schönthal, Hoppe and Bastl, transmuting their archetypal forms – the pyramidal structures and 'cosmic cupolas', the massive buttresses and inclined processional stairways. The Liberty tradition repudiated in the *Manifesto* was destined to outlive the scene-painting of the 'città futurista', whose stepped buildings had been anticipated within the architectonic culture of Art Nouveau in the pioneering projects of Sauvage.

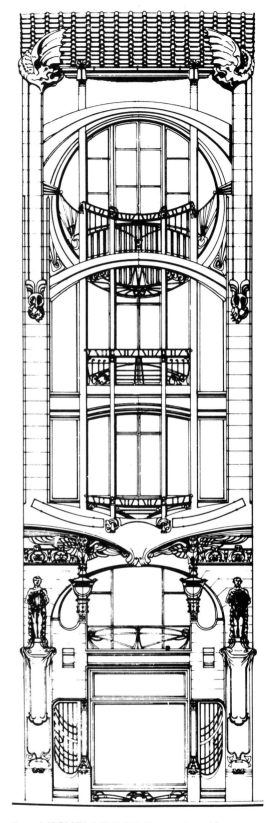

8.32 MICHELAZZI *Via Borgognissanti house* Florence 1896-1915, elevation

8.33 SANT'ELIA *Project for the new headquarters of the Società dei Commessi* Como n.d., perspective

8.34-35 SANT'ELIA *Città Nuova* c.1913-15

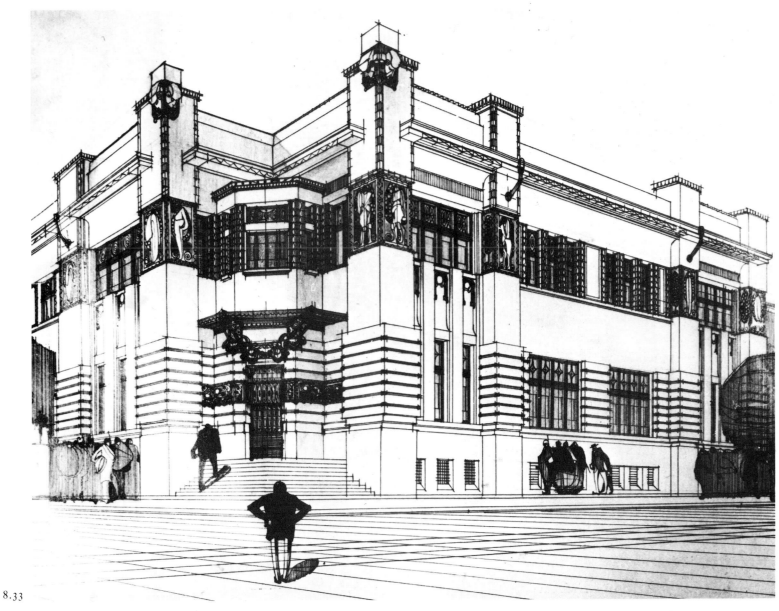

8.33

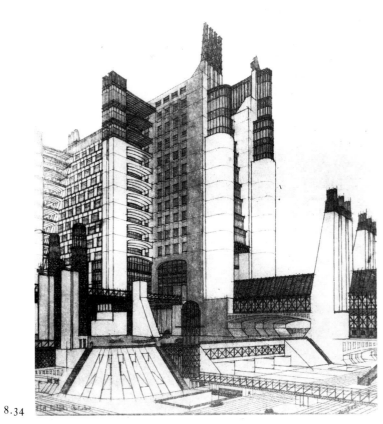

8.34

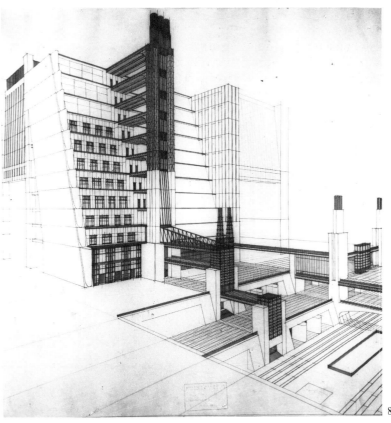

8.35

9. CZECHOSLOVAKIA
The Secession in Eastern Europe
Anna Masaryková

The casual visitor to the Paris 1900 Exhibition would have discovered, next to the deceptively classical Austrian pavilion,[1] the oriental style pavilion of the Balkan States of Bosnia and Herzegovina with interior decorations by Alfons Mucha. Although the countries which were to constitute the future Republic of Czechoslovakia – Bohemia, Moravia, part of Silesia and Slovakia – were at the time still part of the Austro-Hungarian Empire, it is not altogether incorrect to talk of a Czechoslovakian Art Nouveau, for the Czech and Slovak people have always had a strong sense of national identity which found expression as much in architecture as in other cultural achievements.

The development of Secession architecture in Czechoslovakia was influenced by neo-Baroque, local examples of high and late Gothic and by the perfect, classical neo-Renaissance style as exemplified in the work of Josef Zítek and Josef Schulz, to which Antonín Wiehl, Zítek's pupil, gave a rustic character. Zítek and Schulz were both professors at the Prague Polytechnic,[2] and in 1883 Schulz completed the Prague National Theatre, begun by Zítek in 1864. Its opening, and the accomplishment of the Art House in Prague (1885) by Zítek, represented not only a major step towards a state of national self-realisation and independence[3] but also a very real and successful cooperation between practitioners in all fields of architecture and the applied arts, so typical of Art Nouveau in general.

In 1885 the School of Arts and Crafts was founded in Prague under the direction of František Schmoranz. Bedřich Ohmann from Lvov was appointed Professor of Decorative Architecture, Celda Klouček Professor of Decorative Sculpture and Josef Václav Myslbek Professor of Plastic Arts. It was the pupils of Zítek and Schulz at the Prague Polytechnic, especially Schmoranz, Fanta, Koula and Polívka, who made the first break with the neo-Renaissance style of their tutors and also with their own initial historical eclecticism and historicism. These architects, together with Ohmann, his best pupils Dryák and Bendelmayer, his successor Jan Kotěra and a great number of Czech architects such as Hilbert, Balšánek, Klenka z Wlastimilu, Pfeiffer, Stibral, Hybschmann, Bílek and K. Zasche, a German architect prominent in Prague and Jurkovič from Slovakia, were to establish after 1900 the Secession in Czechoslovakia. They were all fortunate in that the beginning of their careers coincided with a greatly augmented building programme, for the changes brought about by industrialisation had rendered many existing buildings inadequate. The resultant problems of urbanisation in the larger cities and an increased expenditure on building by both local government and individual clients stimulated the demand for administrative buildings, schools, banks, offices, water and electricity plants, markets, restaurants, hospitals and villas.[4]

The first opportunity for the older generation to show its work was at the Jubilee Exhibition held in Prague in 1891. Though still tainted by various types of historicism – the pavilions of retrospective and modern art, for example, were mostly in a neo-Renaissance style – certain works such as Křižik's electric fountains, as well as tramways and telephones, represented the technological innovations which had contributed to the renovation of Prague. Also noteworthy were the Industrial Palace by Bedřich Münzberger, an iron construction

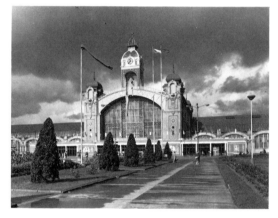

9.1 MÜNZBERGER *Prague Jubilee Exhibition* 1891, Industrial Palace (photograph Hyhlík)

Opposite above
FANTA *Central Railway Station* Prague 1899-1914, detail of facade (photograph Adamík)

Opposite below
KOTERA *District House* Prostějov 1905-07 (photograph Adamík)

Page 220 above
POLIVKA *Topič Building* Prague 1904, detail of facade (photograph Hnízdo)

Page 220 below
KOULA *Svatopluk Cech bridge* Prague 1906-08 (photograph Hnízdo)

Page 221
9.2 KOTERA *District House* Prostějov, detail of facade (photograph Adamík)

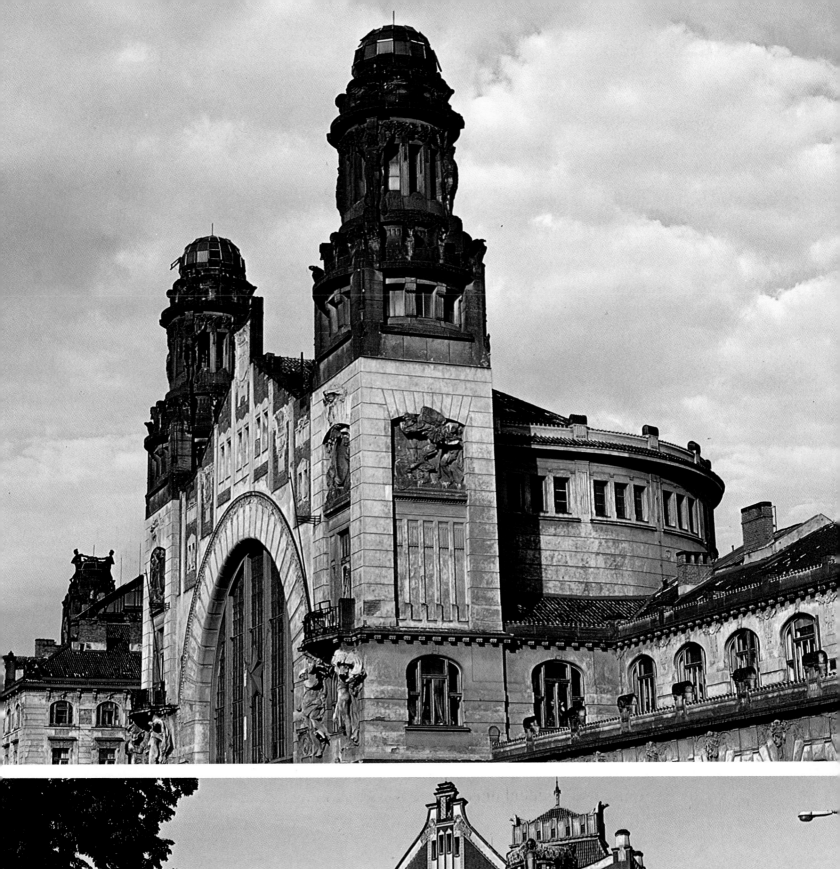

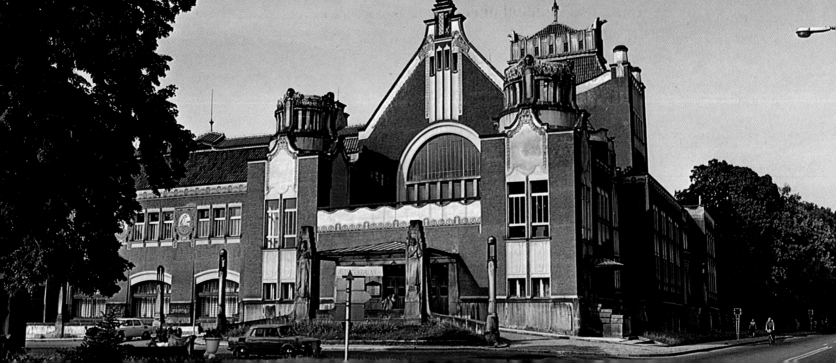

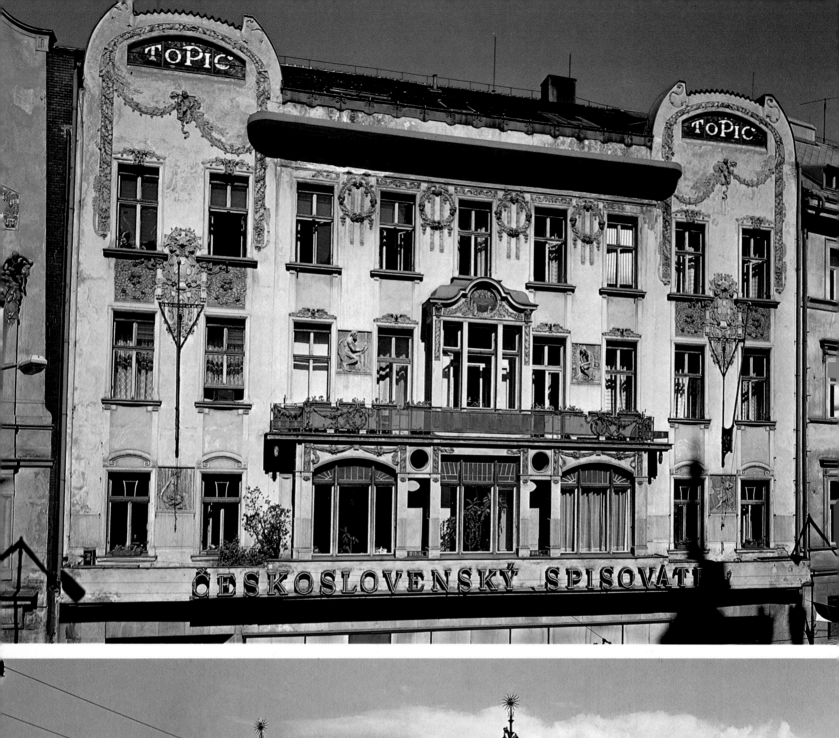

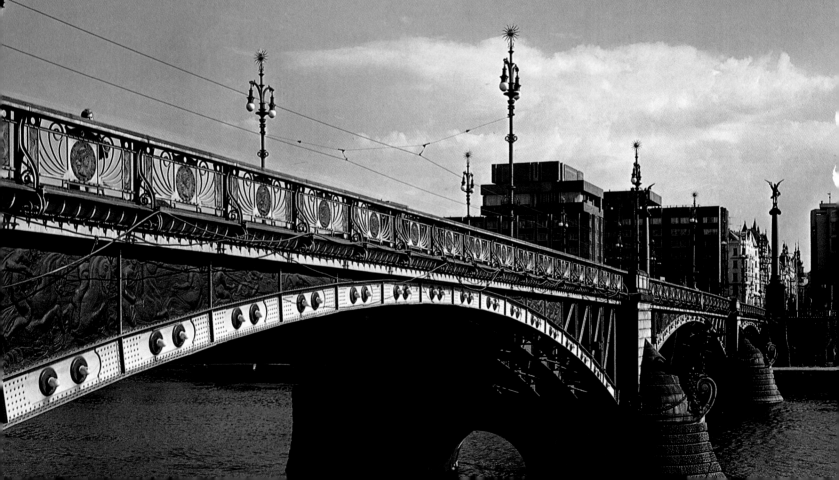

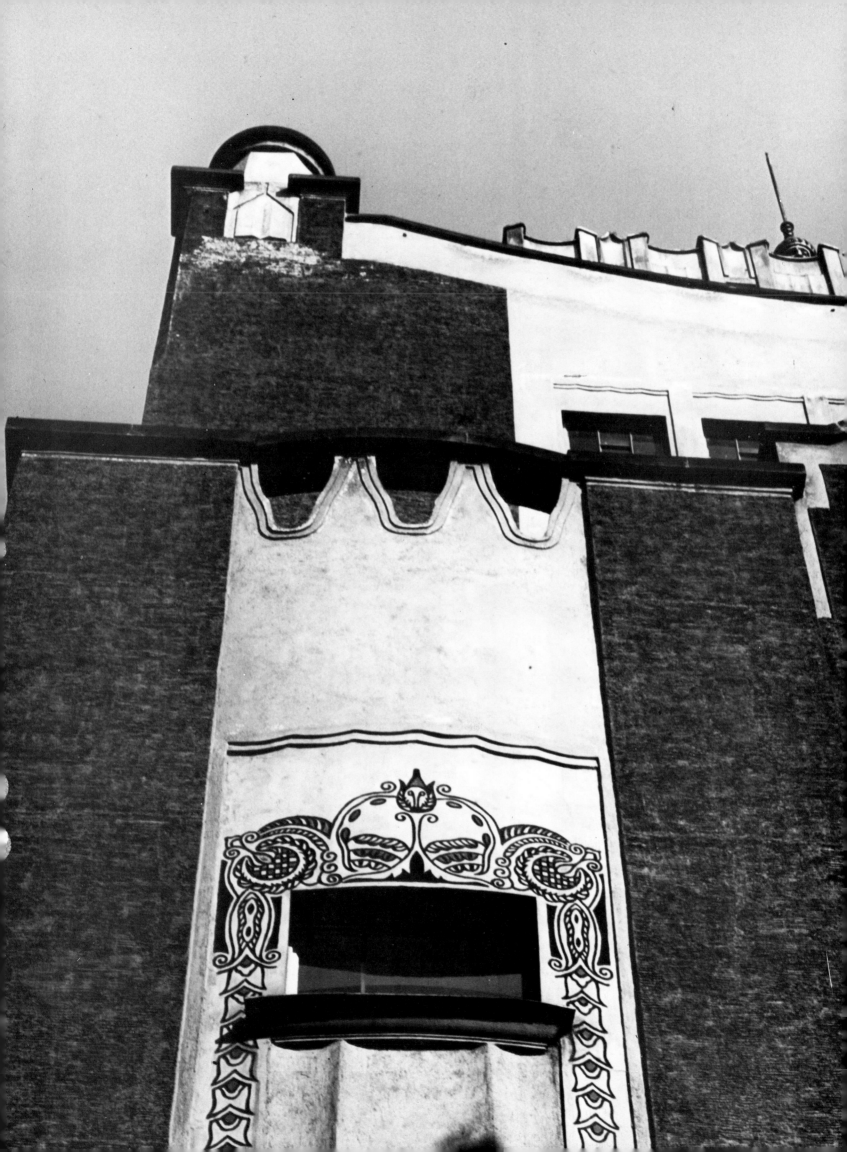

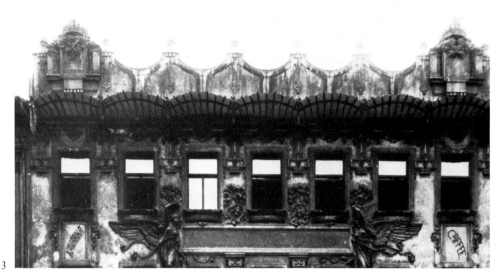

9.3

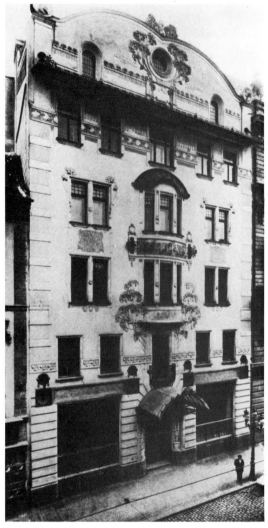

9.4

borrowing much from Czech Baroque, and the main entrance gate by Antonín Wiehl. In 1895 an Ethnographical Exhibition was held, and part of a Slovac village designed by Jurkovič was widely acclaimed. This was followed by an Exhibition of Architecture and Technology held on the same site in 1898.

At the Paris 1900 Exhibition, the work of Czech artists and architects was much praised, especially the interiors of Josef Fanta, which were awarded the Gold Medal, and the interior frescoes of the Bosnia-Herzegovina pavilion by Alfons Mucha. Mucha's project designs for a Humanity Pavilion are also significant and contain the lattice interlacings and eclectic Byzantine haloes which characterised his graphic work.

Among Zítek's pupils, Antonín Wiehl designed a number of buildings in a Czech neo-Renaissance style, including the Old Town water supply station and the Prague Credit Bank, Na Příkopě Street (1891) in collaboration with Osvald Polívka and the sculptor Celda Klouček. Polívka also came to Art Nouveau via the neo-Renaissance – a development which began with the Zemská Bank (1896) in Prague and reached its climax in the exceptionally modern Novák Department Store, Vodičkova Street, Prague (1900), the Insurance Company Offices (1903) and the Topič Building, National Street, Prague (1904). Here the dominant street facades were softened by relief sculptures and sgraffito decoration. In the Insurance Offices there is a remarkable, very expressive attic with monumental iron work and plastics by L. Saloun, while the sgraffito decoration and balcony railings are both very typical of all Czechoslovakian Secessionist facades. The same type of heavy upper decoration in an expressionist Secession style by the same sculptor Saloun is also to be seen in an Insurance Office by J. Stibral, built in Prague in 1902. Polívka also collaborated with Balšánek in designing the Municipal Buildings in Prague (1906–11).

Other of Zítek's pupils to design works in an Art Nouveau style were Fanta and Jan Koula. Koula influenced his contemporaries as much by his teaching and writing as by the example of his works, although he did design several large urban projects, notably the Svatopluk Cech bridge in Prague (1906–08). Fanta's greatest work was the Central Railway Station, begun in 1899 and built in two stages between 1901 and 1909, although the iron construction of the hall and platform was not completed until 1914. His other notable Art Nouveau building was for the choral society Hlahol, Gottwald Embankment, Prague (1905) with plastic decoration by Josef Pekárek, a student of Klouček and Myslbek, a large ceramic picture by K. Klusáček and remarkable rich iron work.

In Bohemia, Moravia and Slovakia there are some vigorous Art Nouveau buildings by S. Ďušan Jurkovič. Jurkovič combined a knowledge of the work of the English domestic revival and other European developments with his lifelong interest in the folk architecture of the Valašsko and Cičmany regions to produce works such as the 'Peklo' (Hell) restaurant near Náchod in Bohemia, the powerful urbanistic design of the Spa buildings in Luhačovice in Moravia or the simple, modern National House in Skalice in Slovakia. He was also responsible for the interiors of the Vesna Girls School, Brno, designed by Antonín Pfeiffer. Jurkovič's work was linked with Prague from the very beginning, although other Art Nouveau architects in Slovakia were drawn more to Hungary, due to the geographical and political reality of the period.

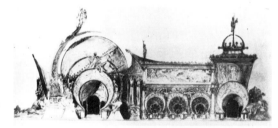

9.5

9.3 OHMANN *Café Corso* Prague 1897-98, detail of facade (contemporary photograph)

9.4 BENDELMAYER, DRYAK & OHMANN *Central Hotel* Prague 1900 (contemporary photograph)

9.5 MUCHA *Project for a Humanity Pavilion* 1900

9.6 BENDELMAYER *Hotel Europa* Prague 1905-07 (photograph Hnízdo)

9.7 KLOUCEK, POLIVKA & WIEHL *Prague Credit Bank* Prague 1891 (contemporary photograph)

9.8 POLIVKA *Insurance Company Offices* Prague 1903 (photograph Hnízdo)

9.9 FANTA *Hlahol building* Prague 1905 (photograph Hnízdo)

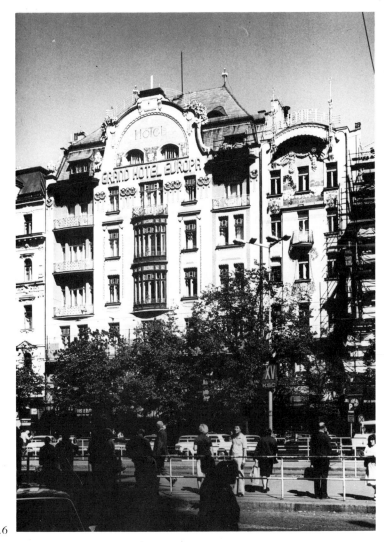

9.6

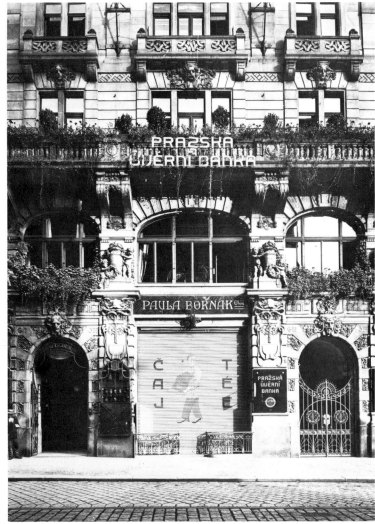

9.7

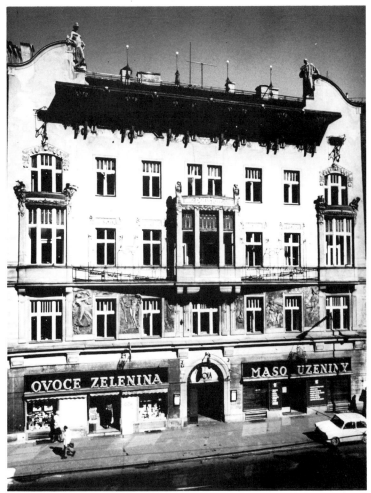

9.8

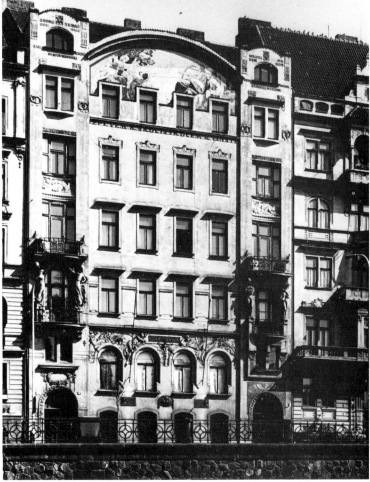

9.9

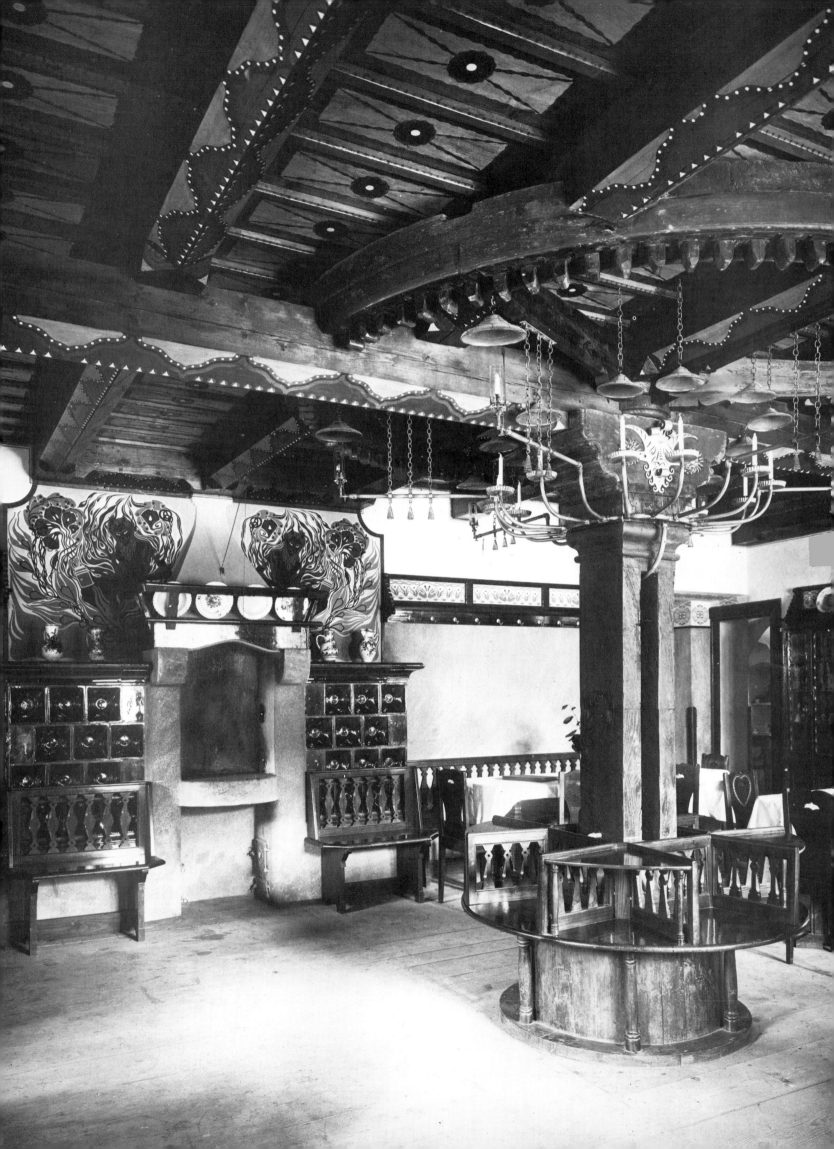

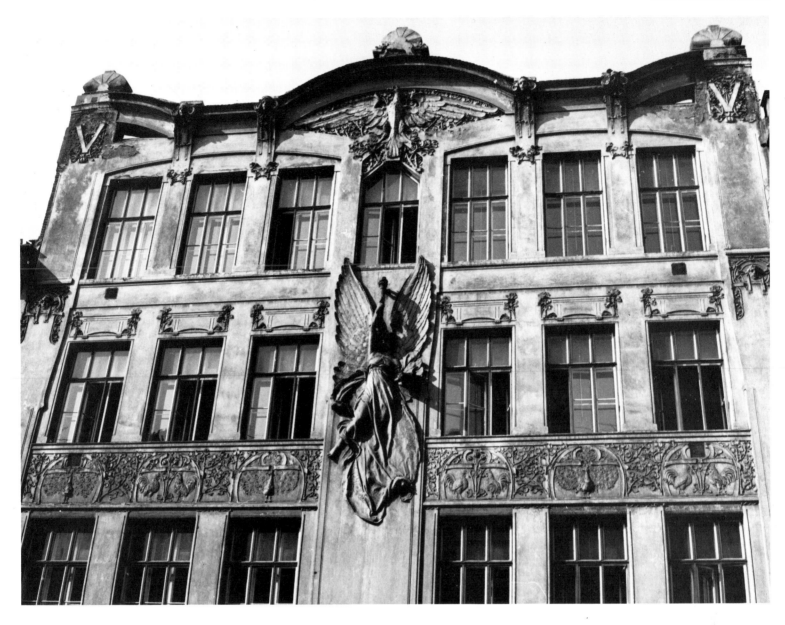

9.11 JURKOVIC & PFEIFFER *Vesna Girls School*
Brno c.1900, detail of facade

9.10 JURKOVIC *'Peklo' restaurant* Náchod c.1900,
interior (contemporary photograph)

In Prague the first truly Art Nouveau building – although still influenced by Wiehl's Czech neo-Renaissance – was the Café Corso, Na Příkopě Street (1897-98) by Bedřich Ohmann. An exponent of late Baroque and high Gothic, Ohmann passed from historicism to Art Nouveau, and his last building in Prague, the Central Hotel, Hybernská Street (1900), designed in conjunction with his erstwhile student Bedřich Bendelmayer and Alois Dryák, was also in a Secession style. Bendelmayer's own finest achievement of the first part of his career, before moving towards modernism, was the Hotel Europa, Wenceslas Square, Prague (1905-07).

If Ohmann finally renounced historicism with the first Secession building in Prague, Kotěra on the other hand began his career with the Secession style, becoming a major exponent of modern architecture and a beloved teacher of many modern architects. His artistic career began auspiciously well. After studying in Bohemia he became a prominent student at the Vienna Academy under Otto Wagner, along with Jože Plečnik from Jugoslavia and other exponents of the Secession such as Joseph Maria Olbrich, Leopold Bauer and A. Hoffmann, all of whom were born in Czech territory.

In 1899 at the age of twenty-seven Kotěra succeeded Bedřich Ohmann as Professor of Decorative Architecture at the School of Arts and Crafts in Prague, and like Wagner, he was an exceptional teacher. Wagner was highly sympathetic to the new ideas of his pupils, believing in the necessity to find a style of architecture orientated towards modern life,[6] and the motto of the Secession group from 1897 'Der Zeit ihre Kunst, der Kunst ihre Freiheit' (To the time its art, to art its freedom) reflects the atmosphere of artistic tolerance and innovation found in Vienna at the time. Kotěra arrived in 1894, and in 1896 he was awarded the State Prize for Architecture. The following year his project for an imaginary

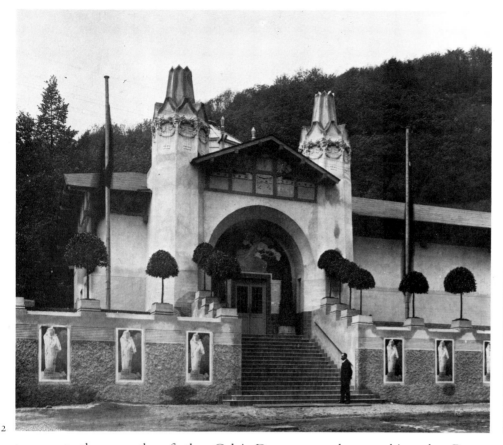

9.12

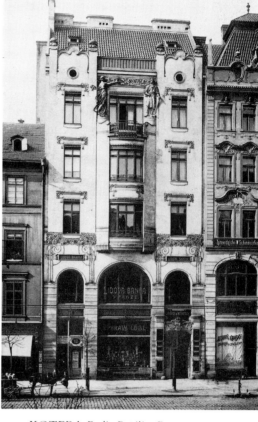

9.13

town at the mouth of the Calais-Dover tunnel won him the Rome Prize – a travelling scholarship to Italy. Both the project and the prize reflect the Secession's preoccupation with technical innovations and its interest in the progressive architecture of the rest of Europe. Kotěra's design could only have been conceived during a period which witnessed the birth of iron construction, the subway and the skyscraper, and his drawing of a seaside town was a perfect expression of the age. The project, with its urban plan and idea for a communications network, was proof of his premonitory vision, and already contained the features which were to characterise his future work – a feeling for beauty and harmony combined with a confident use of modern technology and deployment of space.

Returning from Italy to Prague in 1898 as an assistant of Ohmann, Kotěra had exhibited drawings, watercolours and projects from his year in Italy at the Topič Gallery. Throughout his career he was to be interested in a wide range of activities, from the design and construction of buildings to interior design and decoration incorporating all branches of the arts, always in collaboration with the best craftsmen, painters and sculptors. As well as forming part of Kotěra's duties at the School of Arts and Crafts and later at the Academy, this diversity of interests was also one of the fundamental qualities of Secession architects in general. Kotěra expounded his aims in 1907 in his preface to the book *Práce mé a mých žáků* (My work and that of my students) and in his article 'About modern Art', published in the magazine *Volné Směry* (Free Trends), the mouthpiece of the avant-garde group Mánes, founded in 1887 by students of the School of Arts and Crafts and the Academy.[5]

Like Wagner, Kotěra was opposed to historical eclecticism, believing that the clear and simple expression of materials in building would automatically lead to the creation of a new style. His first house, the Peterka house, Wenceslas Square, Prague, designed in 1899 and completed in 1900, bears on its facade Secession style motifs and a gentle floral stucco with sculptures by Sucharda. In 1902 Kotěra designed a pavilion for the Rodin Exhibition – one of a number of exhibition installations in collaboration with the Mánes group. Rodin himself, who visited Prague for the occasion, is reported to have described Kotěra's light pavilion with dark violet pansies as 'inoubliable'. For the St. Louis World Exhibition of 1904, Kotěra designed the interior of the Czech School of Arts and Crafts pavilion, and in 1907-08 he produced a design for a pavilion for the Jubilee Exhibition of the Czech Chamber of Commerce and Trade – his first collaboration with the young sculptor Jan Stursa.

9.12 KOTERA *Rodin Pavilion* Prague 1902

9.13 KOTERA *Peterka house* Prague 1899-1900, facade (contemporary photograph)

9.14 KOTERA *Project for an imaginary town at the mouth of the Calais-Dover tunnel* 1897

9.15-16 KOTERA *Jubilee Exhibition of the Chamber of Commerce and Trade* 1907-08, pavilion exterior and interior (contemporary photographs)

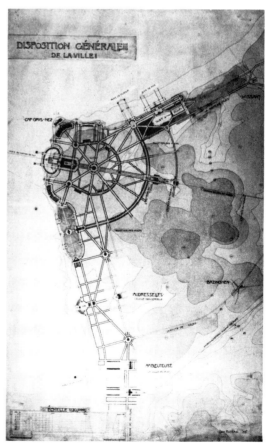

9.14

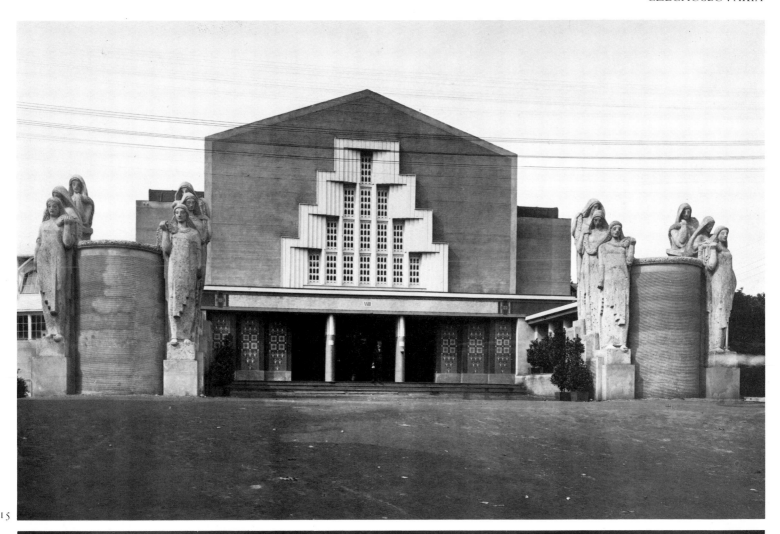

9.15

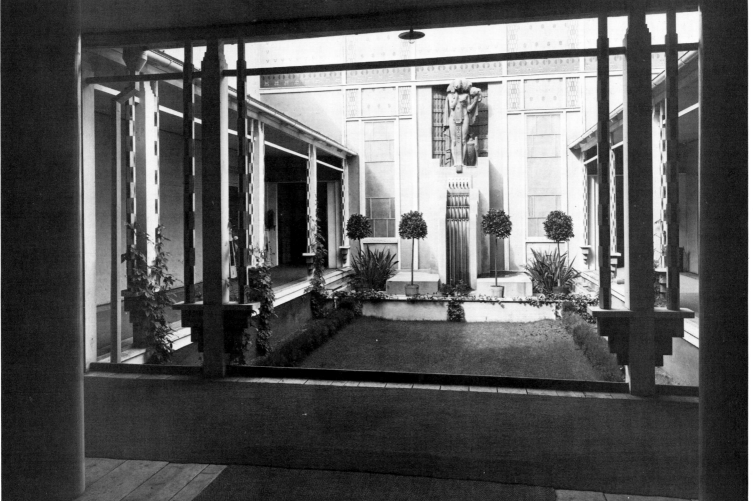

9.16

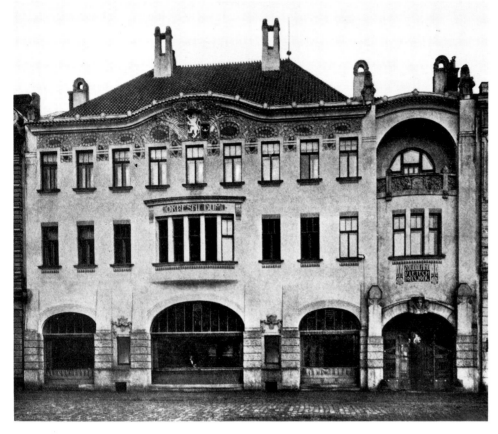

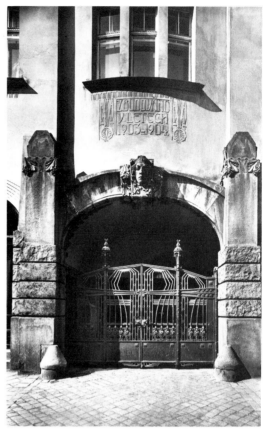

The climax of the Secession phase of Kotěra's career, however, came with the District Houses in Prostějov, Moravia, and in Hradec Králové, Bohemia, where he also designed a museum (1906-12). The Hradec District House (1903-04) is adorned with the Czech national emblem and has relief sculpture and the typical decorative ironwork on the main entrance. The interiors of the restaurant and common rooms are enriched by the decorative canvas of the painter Jan Preisler and by decorative stained glass designed by Kotěra himself. The building of the Prostějov District House (1905-07), besides the large staircase and common rooms, also includes a theatre, all with decorative and sculptural work by Sucharda.

In 1910 Kotěra was the right person to be appointed as an expert of the Czech lands regulations committee, and a year later he became a professor at the Prague Academy, and was succeeded by Plečnik at the School of Arts and Crafts. His later works include the Austro-Hungarian Bank in Vienna, projects for a hotel in Abazzia (both 1911) and a Royal Palace in Sofia (1912). His urbanistic work was as remarkable as his teaching, and he designed workers' settlements in Louny (1909-13), Záběhlice (1914) and after the war, the new reurbanisation of Prague. But he produced no more work in a Secession style.

By 1908 the age of pure Art Nouveau had come to an end, and although Secession decoration continued to appear on a few buildings, Czechoslovakia, like the rest of Europe, turned towards the progressive ideas of the Modern Movement.

9.17-18 KOTERA *District House* Hradec 1903-04, exterior view and detail of facade (contemporary photographs)

9.19-21 KOTERA *District House* Prostějov 1905-07, plan (from the original drawing), exterior and interior (contemporary photographs)

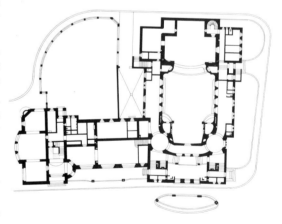

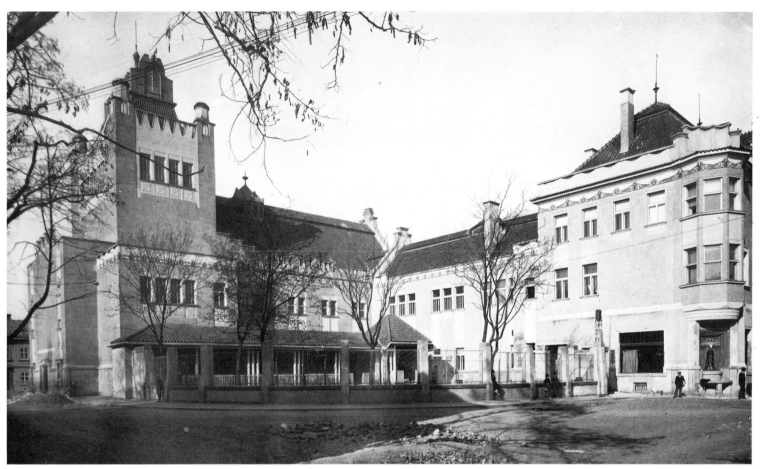

9.20

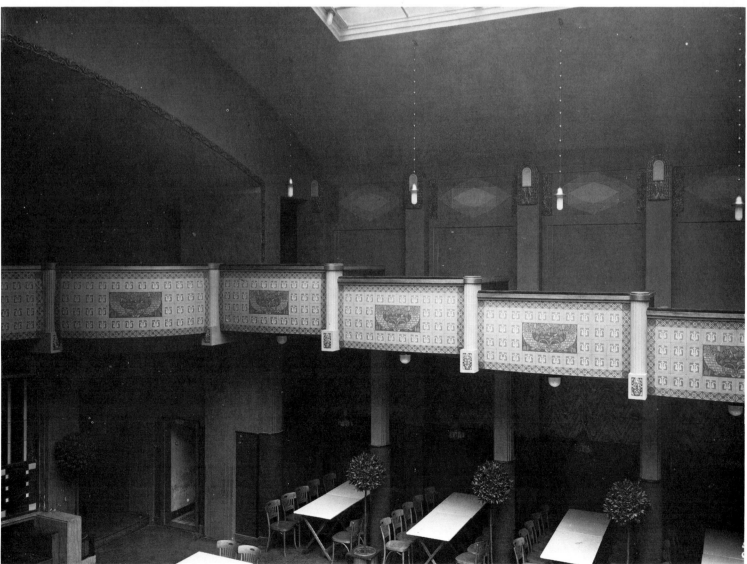

9.21

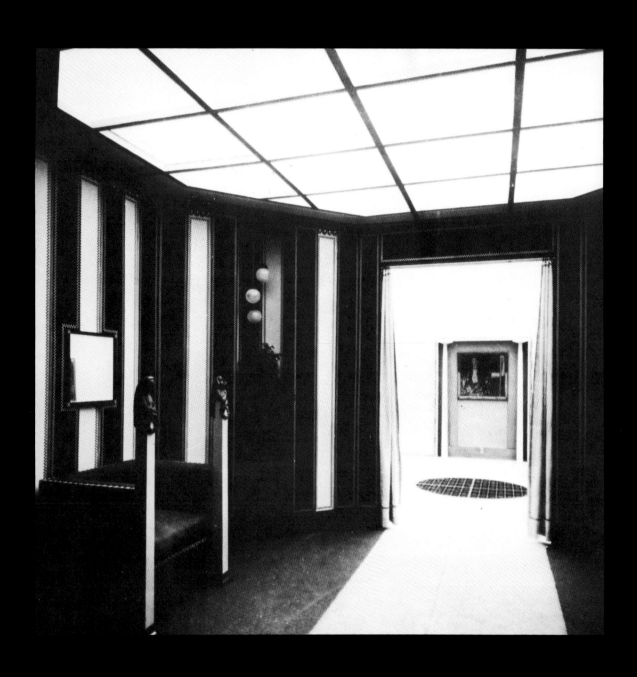

10. AUSTRIA

To the limits of a language: Wagner, Olbrich, Hoffmann

Ezio Godoli

'Wir führen, wir gehen siegreich voran, wir haben die Hegemonie, bei uns sind die richtigen Leute und die richtige Kunst.' (We lead, we move triumphantly forward, we hold the leadership, the right people are with us and the right art.)[1]

With this exultant affirmation regarding Viennese architecture, Otto Wagner in 1903 clearly expressed his own satisfaction on observing that the message of his *Moderne Architektur* (published in 1895) and his professorship of almost ten years standing in the Spezialschule für Architektur at the Akademie der bildenden Künste had not been unfruitful. To unusual teaching skills, and a flexible approach to the young who were challengingly heterodox in a world in which – as Stefan Zweig recalls in *Die Welt von Gestern* – 'Whoever had the misfortune of being too young in appearance had to fight everywhere against widespread mistrust', Wagner united the fine intuition of a talent-scout to guide him in the choice of colleagues for his studio, such as Joseph Maria Olbrich – who worked there from 1895 to 1898 – and Max Fabiani. In this way some of the leading figures in Austrian architecture and the architecture of countries within the Habsburg domains developed within his circle in the first half of the twentieth century: Olbrich and Josef Hoffmann, founders of the Secession to which even Wagner had belonged in 1899, Josef Plečnik, Otto Schönthal, Leopold Bauer and Jan Kotěra, as well as architects like Karl Ehn, Rudolf Perco, Franz and Hubert Gessner and Max Fellerer, actively engaged between the two World Wars in the 'Rote Wien' popular building scheme. In the Vienna where 'to be a fin de siècle Viennese artist or intellectual . . . one had to face the problem of the nature and limits of language, expression and communication',[2] Wagner had learned from his own school and studio, receiving contributions from young pupils and colleagues without departing from an autonomous line of research, and thus creating a laboratory where linguistic experiences were ripening through an osmotic relationship which was to shape the architecture of the Habsburg empire.

The Wagnerschule, as the centre of gravitation and subsequent divergence of the architectural avant-garde of central Europe, acted as a sounding-box for their peculiar problems, from the dialectics of the Secession – between the Dionysian vitalism of Olbrich and the formal Apollonian order of Hoffmann – to a rationalism which, derived from the technological experimentation of the engineers of the 1880s, was to lead him to unpublished linguistic results. Wagner's teaching, his cultural promotion work – in which he used his own personal prestige to support the activities of the Secession, among other things – and his theoretical and architectural work, were fundamental elements in the revival of Austrian architecture. The experiments of Olbrich and Hoffmann at this time also played a far from secondary role and Wagner himself was unable to ignore their influence, for trends inspired by them were emerging even within the Wagnerschule. The absence of sectarianism and the non-dogmatic character of Wagner's teaching encouraged in his pupils a free and open-minded receptiveness towards a variety of cultural influences. From this came the composite character of the Wagnerschule which, besides its avant-garde beginnings and its

10.1 HOFFMANN *18th Secession Exhibition* Vienna 1903, vestibule for the Klimt exhibition (contemporary photograph)

search for a 'Zeitstil' – a style, that is, expressing the needs of modern man, a metropolitan 'Weltanschauung' (world view), and new building technologies – also led to a last attempt to preserve tradition, seen by Wagner as a genius loci, but misunderstood by some of his pupils as a 'Heimatstil' (vernacular style). Because of the great variety of cultural combinations it contained, the Wagnerschule formed the trunk of a genealogical tree which branched out into a number of other schools (Kotěraschule, Plečnikschule, Bauerschule, Hoffmannschule, etc.) and reflected the complexities and contradictions of the Habsburg architectural panorama, registering the forward thrusts of this architecture as a regressive resistance. From Wagner's circle came Olbrich and Hoffmann,[3] who were founders together with the painters Koloman Moser, Max Kurzweil, Leo Kainradl, Karl Moll and Theodor Gottlieb Kempf, of the Siebenerclub (Club of the Seven), a group of artists who joined together in the Secession, responding to the call of Gustav Klimt. But among Wagner's pupils were also sympathisers and members – like Oskar Laske – of the Hagenbund, a society founded in 1900 with the aim of counterbalancing the 'internationalism' of the Secession with a 'national' art revival, which in architecture found a point of reference in the new appreciation of the 'Biedermeier' and the 'Heimatstil' of Robert Oerley.[4]

Although some architects of the Wagnerschule were part of the Secession, the two movements remain clearly distinguished entities, not only because of their divergent range of interests (the first was a specifically architectural phenomenon, while the second extended its field of activity and its influence into all the figurative arts), but also on account of the different degree of homogeneity shown in their linguistic researches. The extreme multiplicity of directions followed by the Wagnerschule contrasted with the closely knit cultural dialectic of the Secession between the two poles established by the work of Olbrich and Hoffmann. In the eight years of Secession activity from 1897 to the breakaway of the Klimtgruppe[5] in 1905 and their establishment of a new movement – the Kunstschau – two periods may be clearly distinguished in architecture and the decorative arts, dominated by the personalities of Olbrich and Hoffmann respectively. Olbrich made his influence felt at least until 1900, whilst the output of Hoffmann was to characterise the opening phase of the Secession. In the dining-room shown at the 8th exhibition of the Secession in 1900, in which Charles Rennie Mackintosh also took part, Hoffmann already appears free of the Olbrichian influence and orientated towards a language which, purged of any trace of naturalism and tending to rationalise itself in geometric designs, was to characterise his later output and that of the Wiener Werkstätte. This change of direction in Hoffmann marks the end of the Olbrichian phase, more rightly termed Jugendstil within the Secessionist movement, although its repercussions continued to be felt in Viennese architecture for a few years to come.

*   *   *

The expression 'der Schrei des Lebens' (the Cry of Life) applied by contemporaries to Olbrich's work, effectively sums up the meaning of 'an architecture of Erlebnis [experience], of life embodied in forms',[6] of automatic writing, of 'Empfindungen' (mental states) as well as the ideology of work seen as an expression of liberty, as 'a long bout of jovial parties'.[7] Because of these descriptions about his work – which perhaps constitute the only authentic expression in Austria of an aesthetic ideology of Art Nouveau – the poetry of Olbrich becomes, for contemporary critics, the emblem of an anti-positivist reaction, of an 'Idealismus' contrasted with the 'Materialismus' of nineteenth-century culture.[8] But it was on account of these very elements that it met with resistance in the nineteenth-century fin de siècle milieu of Vienna, and found excellent conditions to express itself during its self-imposed 'exile' in the Künstlerkolonie of Darmstadt or through those professional occasions organised by an 'elite' circle of discerning clients, like the art critic Hermann Bahr. Only by withdrawing into the private sphere could Olbrich's fervour for an artistic mission, which he saw as a search for hitherto unknown forms and a reification of an oneiric world, express his own rejection of an institutional language of architecture, and his anti-historicist vocation. On the metropolitan scene, however, architecture, if it wishes to 'communicate', cannot express itself purely subjectively; it cannot avoid some dialogue with history even if this is in a metaphorical rather than a mimetic form. Here it must perforce come to some compromise

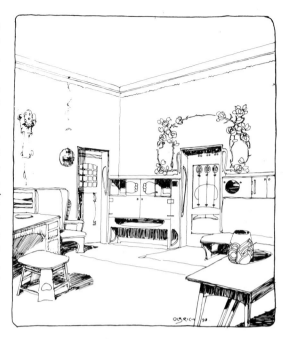

10.2 OLBRICH *Villa Friedmann* Hinterbrühl 1898, ladies' room (from the original drawing)

10.3-4 OLBRICH *Villa Bahr* Wien-Ober-St. Veit 1899-1900, elevations (from the original drawings)

10.5 OLBRICH *Villa Stifft* Vienna 1899, dining room window elevation (from the original drawing)

10.6-7 OLBRICH *Berl house* Vienna 1899, music-room and bedroom wall elevations (from the original drawings)

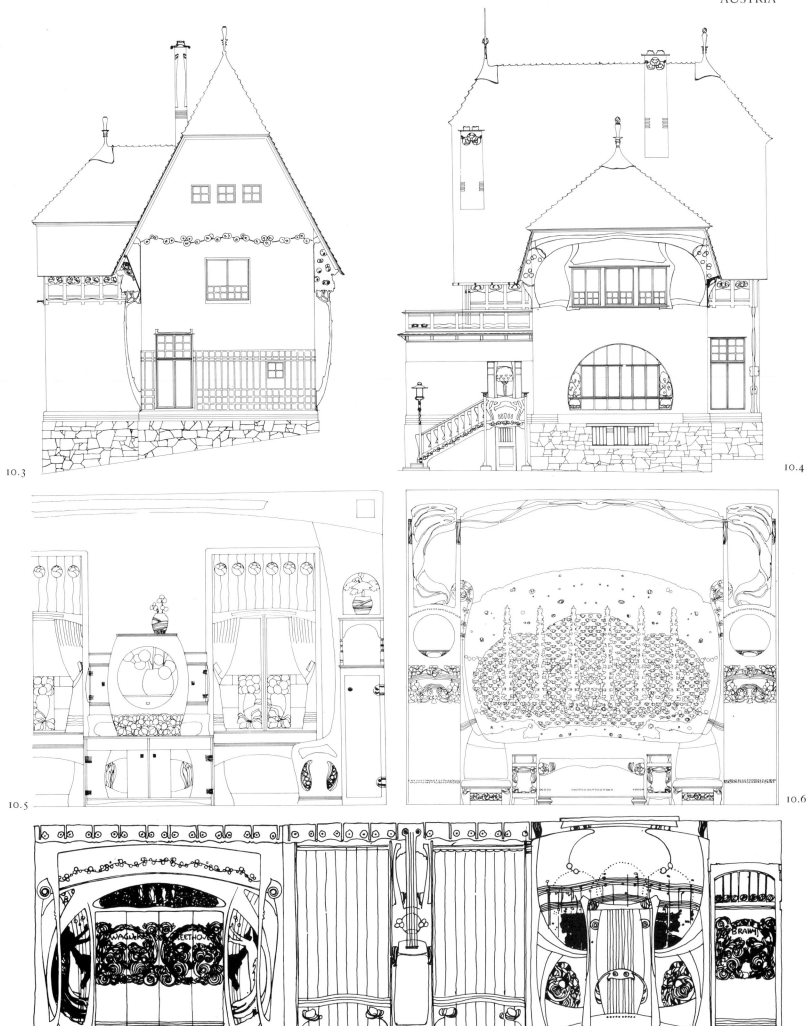

10.3

10.4

10.5

10.6

10.7

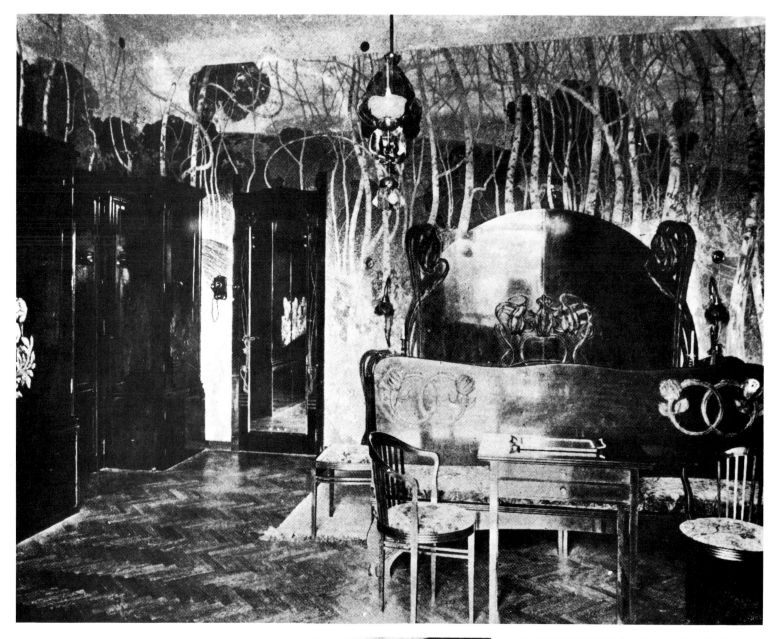

10.8 OLBRICH *Villa Friedmann* Hinterbrühl 1898, bedroom (contemporary photograph)

10.9 OLBRICH *Spitzer house* Vienna 1899, music-room (contemporary photograph)

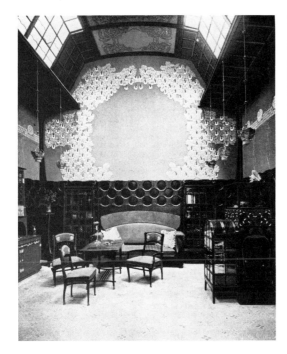

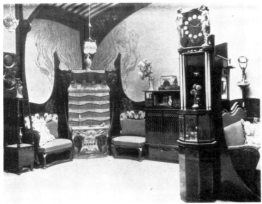

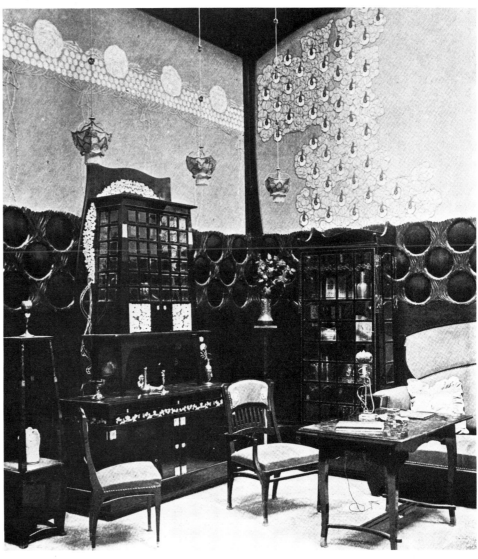

10.10-12 OLBRICH *Paris Exhibition* 1900, interiors (contemporary photographs)

with the conventions of language in order to explicitly define its own symbolic values.

This dual tension towards a free cryptography of inner emotions and towards the recovery of means of communicating through symbolic forms is inherent in the early output of Olbrich, and shows itself on the one hand in the bipolarity of the interiors of the Stifft (1899), Von Diriztaj (1899), Berl (1899) and Spitzer (1899) houses, and in the Villa Friedmann at Hinterbrühl (1898), the Stöhr house at St. Polten (1899) and the Bahr house at Wien-Ober-St. Veit (1899-1900), and on the other hand in the Secession House. The only piece of urban architecture among the Austrian works of Olbrich, the main exhibition building of the Secession already expresses in the choice of a cruciform plan its own idea of the 'temple of art', and that 'sacral quality' which the same writer, in a short piece which appeared in the magazine *Der Architekt,* declares he is pursuing as a given characteristic of that building.[9] But beyond this explicit affirmation, the idea of the 'Haus der Secession' as a metaphor of the temple is even more unmistakably expressed in an illustration to Olbrich's text,[10] where the foreground of the building – photographed from the rear – stands out distinctly against the Karlsplatz in the background from which the Trajan columns rise, and from the dome of the Baroque Karlskirche, designed in 1715 by Johann Bernard Fischer Von Erlach and completed about 1736 by his son Josef Emanuel. The allusion to the symbol is revealed: the 'temple of art' like a distorted reflection of the church of S. Carlo Borromeo that stands almost opposite it in the same square.[11] As Jolanda Nigro Covre has rightly pointed out:[12] 'The masterful dome [of the Karlskirche] that rises on a lofty tambour is contrasted by a soap-bubble wedged between four pilasters in the shape of a truncated pyramid, a precious dome made of nothing, a fragile thread guilded with laurel leaves, light and transparent . . . The jutting, classical portico of the Karlskirche is contrasted by a plain, concave entrance in half-light; the Baroque corner-towers are balanced by two flat, denuded wings; the towering Trajan columns are balanced by the shorn

10.13-14 OLBRICH *Secession House* Vienna 1897-98, final elevation before construction (from the original drawing) and view from Friedrichstrasse (photograph Simoner)

Opposite
OLBRICH *Secession House*, detail of facade (photograph Pezzato)

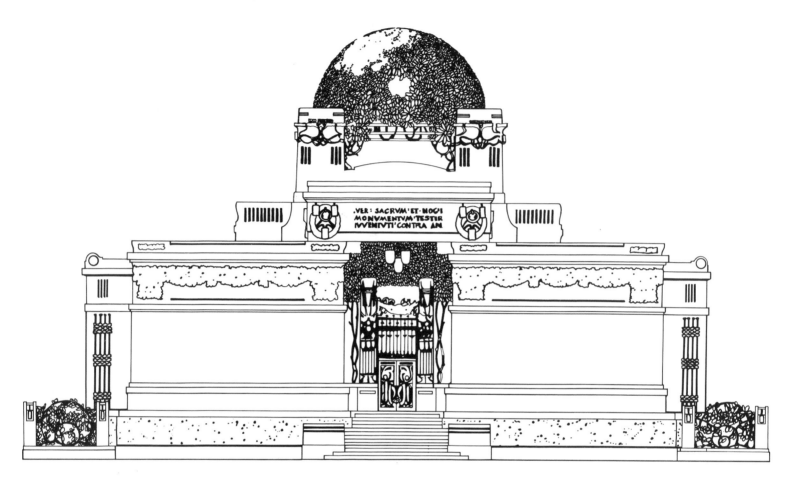

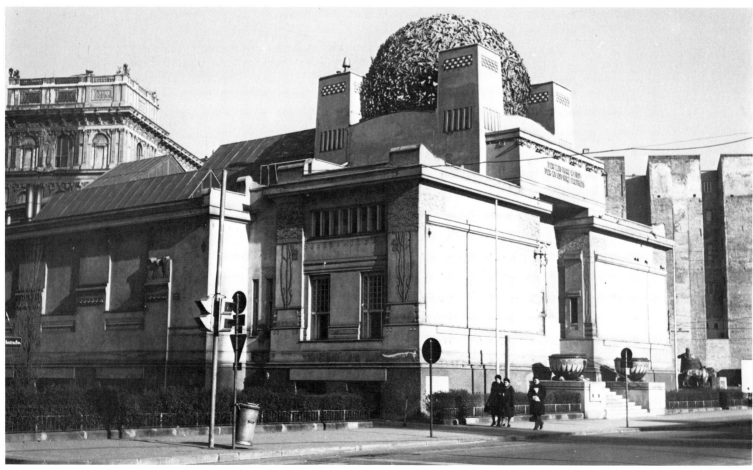

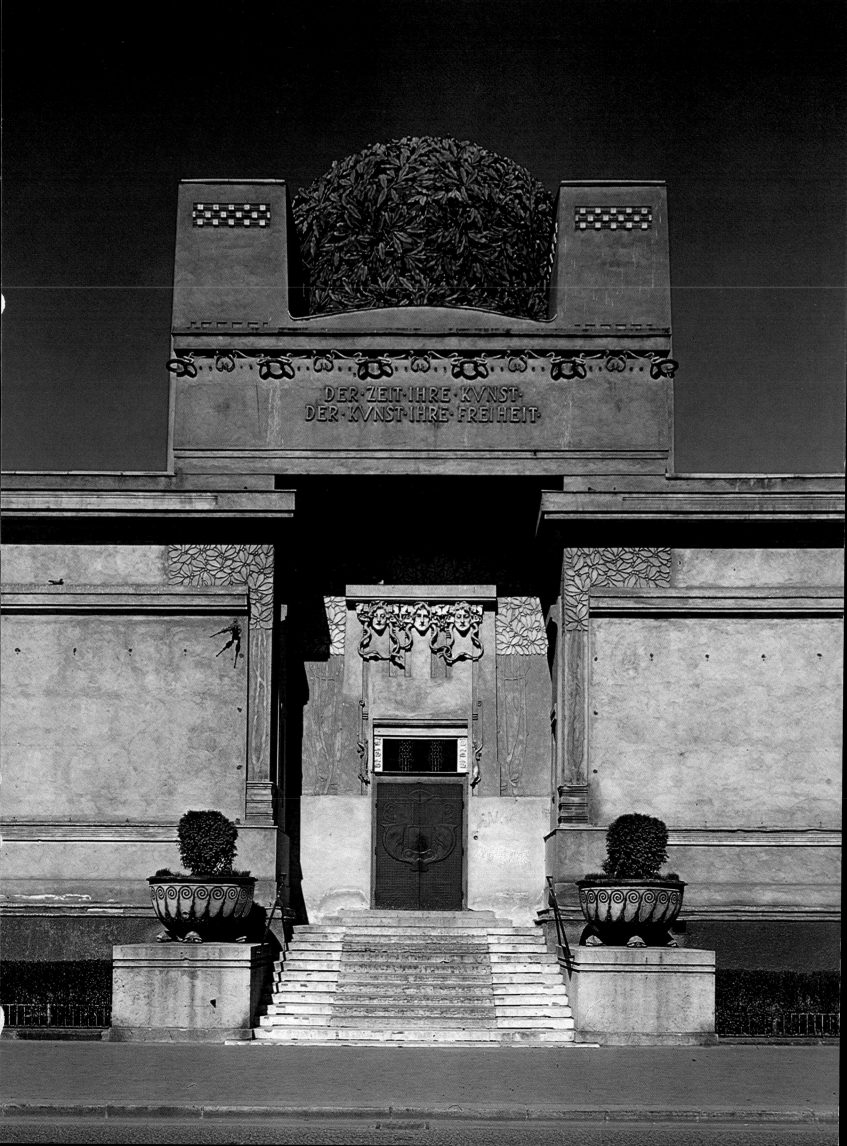

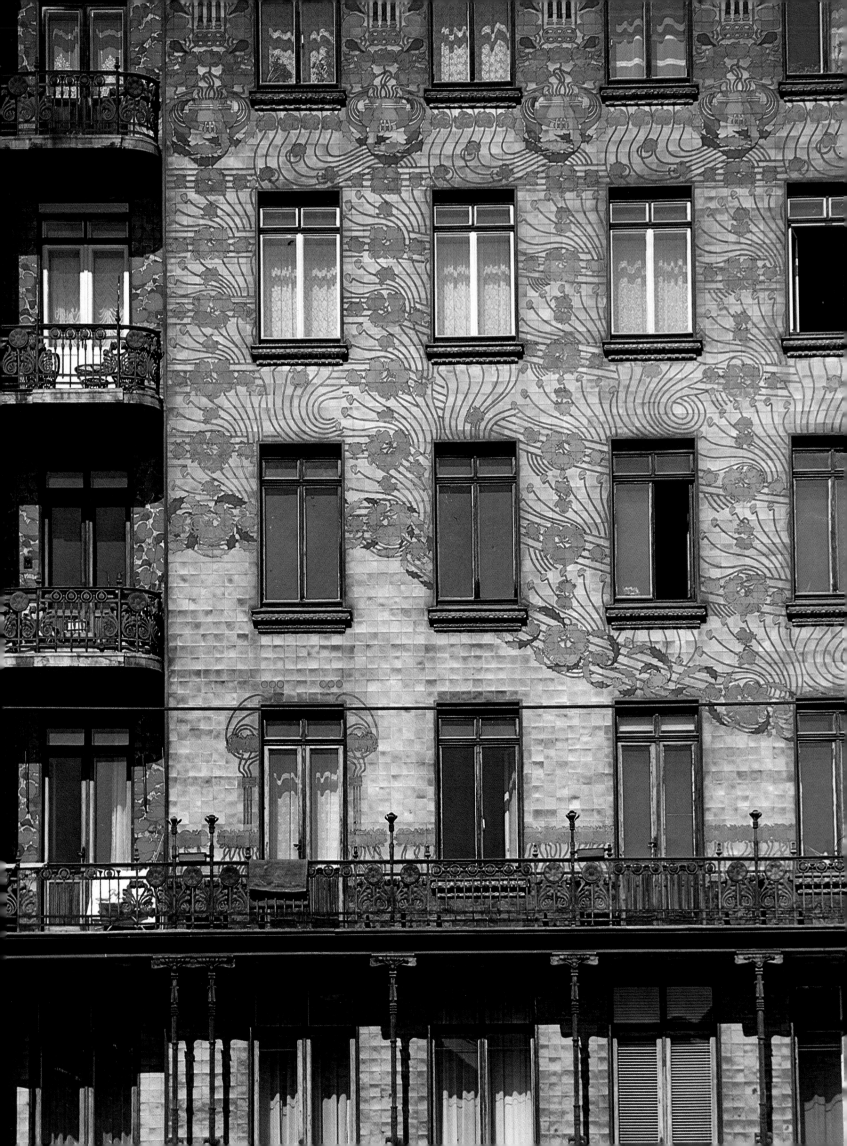

Opposite
WAGNER *Majolikahaus* Vienna 1898, detail of
facade (photograph Pezzato)

10.15–16 WAGNER *Karlsplatz station* Vienna
1899–1900, elevation (from the original drawing)
and exterior (contemporary photograph)

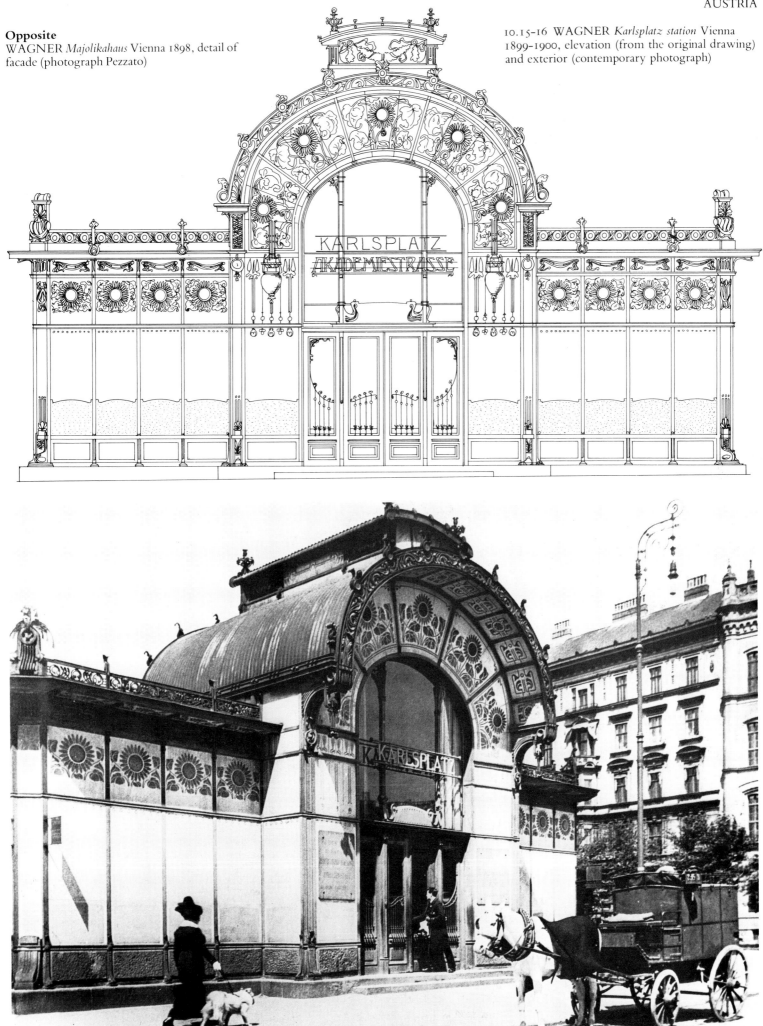

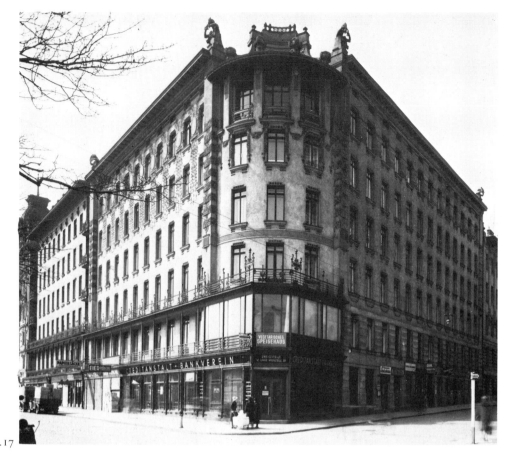

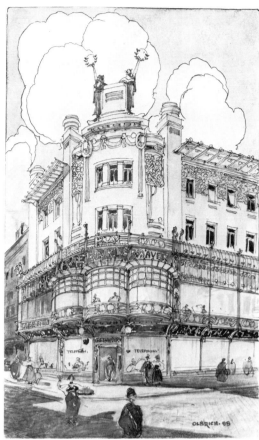

10.17 WAGNER *38 and 40 Linke Wienzeile* Vienna 1898-99

10.18 OLBRICH *Project for the Café Niedermeyer* Troppau 1898

pillars – almost like sepulchral stones; the rhetorical plasticity of a religiosity allied to power is balanced by the naked stereometry and the restrained, two dimensional bas-reliefs . . .' This interpretation also finds confirmation in the successive stages of the project – from the first studies of 1897 to the working drawings of 1898 – which show a progressive decanting of classical-Baroque elements more directly linked with the church of Fischer Von Erlach the Elder. The metaphor 'temple of art', used to mean a place where the 'profane' are initiated into the mysteries of 'beauty', not only makes use of the reference to the Karlskirche but also uses symbolism drawn from the hermetic-esoteric tradition: the dome with its transparent interlacing laurel branches is no more than a transformation of the 'hermetic tree', which in its many images – 'tree of good and of evil, sacred Indian tree, tree of Jesse, tree of Christ' – will reappear frequently in the iconography of the Wagnerschule,[13] as is shown for example in Otto Schönthal's design for a cemetery church (1901). The presence of mystical-esoteric ideologies within the Wagnerschule is also shown by other documents, such as the remarkable projects by Alois Bastl for a Palace of Occult Sciences (1902).

★   ★   ★

Notwithstanding the resistance of the Viennese milieu to Olbrich's poetry, the imprint he left on contemporary architecture was far from insignificant. In the years around 1900 a deluge of admirers started to use Olbrichian designs, especially in the ephemeral architecture of shops and exhibitions; a genuine fashion was created, with involutions towards kitsch of which the magazine *Der Architekt* has left us some accounts. Not even Wagner was immune from the influence of the young colleague who worked in his studio during the planning of the Stadtbahn and the dwelling-houses at 38 and 40 Linke Wienzeile. The building at the corner of the Linke Wienzeile where it meets the Köstlergasse (1898-99) is a redesigned version of Olbrich's project for the Café Niedermeyer in Troppau (1898). The cylindrical mass that acts like a hinge between the bulk of the two buildings on the Linke Wienzeile and the Köstlergasse, the articulation of surfaces by means of pilasters extending beyond the line of the roof, the symmetrical grouping of decorative relief-work in stucco on the top-most storeys (designed by Koloman Moser), and the iron superstructure – with shop windows, verandas and balconies – juxtaposed on the facade up to a height of

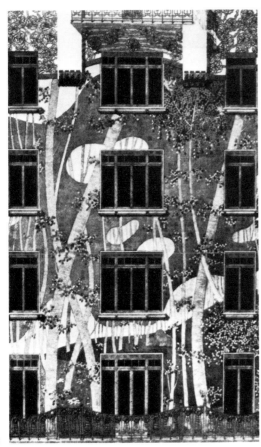

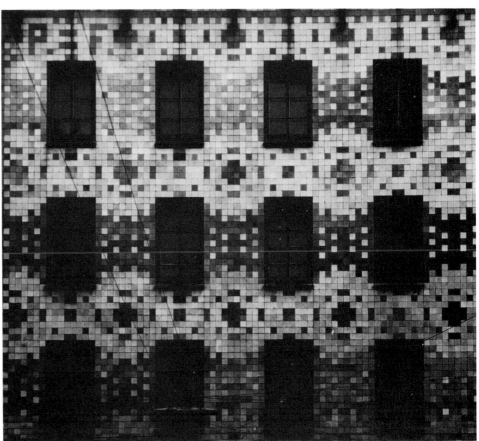

10.19

10.20

10.19 SCHLECTA *Project for a facade* 1900

10.20 FABIANI *Portois & Fix apartment building*
Vienna 1899-1900 (photograph Pezzato)

two storeys from ground level, are all features that Wagner borrowed from the
Café Niedermeyer; from which, however, he omitted the asymmetry of the
plan, replacing it with an austere diagonal symmetry. The use of characteristics
taken from the Olbrichian repertoire and grafted onto a composite syntax, which
singles out in a formal, classic order the linguistic idiom most suited to nineteenth-century engineering structures, is also to be found in some stations of the
Stadtbahn, and in particular in the two most famous ones of the Karlsplatz, and
in his design for a modern art gallery (1900). The dual spirit of Wagner's work in
the years between 1890 and 1900, torn between Jugendstil influences and the
urgency of 'Sachlichkeit' (objectivity), finds model expression in the Majolikahaus (1898) at 40 Linke Wienzeile, a prototype of a series of buildings and designs
that Adolf Loos would have defined as 'tattooed architecture'. Between the
'Sachlichkeit' of the building organism based on standards of economy, functionalism and simplicity, and the Art Nouveau mask of its facade there is only
contradiction, not a dialectical synthesis. Beyond this cleavage, beyond the
breaking-down of the Secessionist-Olbrichian repertoire to a mere tattoo, there
emerges already that conviction in the incompatibility of the architecture of
'Erlebnis' (experience) and 'Rationalisierung' (rationalism) which was to make
the language of Wagner develop towards the purist results of his last works. The
Majolikahaus model met with considerable success within the Wagnerschule as
certain designs for facades done in 1900 by Wunibald Deininger and Hans
Schlechta show.[13] The recovery of the naturalistic element as 'pure painting', as
representation independent of any architectural 'ratio', is clearly defined in
Schlechta's drawing where a dense growth of birch trees – taken from mural
paintings in the bedroom of the Villa Friedmann by Olbrich – is superimposed
like a film onto the symmetric and proto-rationalist plan of the facade. The
language of Jugendstil thus absolves the wholly external function of introducing
a note of artistry into architecture, which conforms to the precept of Wagner's
Moderne Architektur: 'to be aware of man's innate chromatic instinct by making
use of the sister arts', whilst keeping to the use of 'the simplest shapes possible;
smooth surfaces, Majolika, stone, mosaic . . .'[15]

One applied example of these maxims, which has remained a model of its
kind, can be seen in the Portois & Fix apartment block, 51-53 Ungargasse,
Vienna (1899-1900) by Max Fabiani. Here the naturalistic shapes of the
Majolikahaus and the designs of Deininger and Schlechta are replaced by an
abstract chromatic quality achieved through a mosaic facing done with tiles of

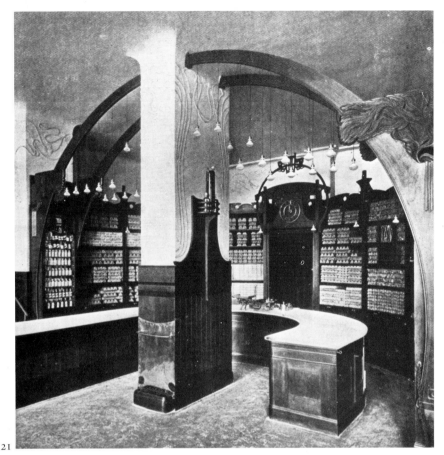

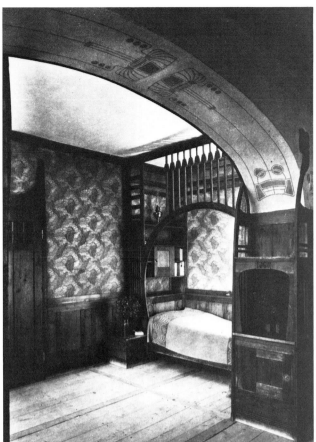

10.21

10.22

pyrogranite powder baked until vitrified. Apart from this variation, the Portois & Fix apartment block does not depart from the standard type of commercial building developed by the Wagnerschule, from which it takes the symmetric composite plan, the absolute two dimensional quality and the interplay between convexities and concavities on the facades, divided in two on the glazed surfaces of the shops (occupying the ground-floor and mezzanine) and the extreme simplicity of architectonic features in those above which are faced in ceramic material taken from the office floors.

The influence of Olbrich on the Wagnerschule was not confined to the use of some of his figurative themes, but also showed itself in a conspicuous stream of designs – especially for country houses – by Oskar Felgel, Otto Schönthal, Leopold Bauer, Max Joli, Karl Benirschke and others, that re-present the symbiosis of Jugendstil and 'Heimatstil' of the Villa Friedmann and the Stöhr and Bahr houses.

Even more obvious parallels with Olbrich's work are shown in the early output of Hoffmann, from the interior designs for the Haus auf der Bergerhöhe (1899) to the décor for the stand of the School of Handicraft at the Paris Exhibition of 1900, and the 'Apollo' candle shop (1899-1900) in Vienna. The use of wooden structures in curvilinear progression to connect walls, ceilings and furniture in a homogeneous and continuous whole, the subdivision of spaces into a series of niches, the chromatic hedonism, a preference for the interlacing of curved, circular and elliptic lines, and rosette floral decoration, are the features that link these interiors with Olbrich's work.

*   *   *

Towards 1900, however, Hoffmann was beginning to free himself from Olbrichian mannerisms. This change in direction was due in some measure to the influence of the work of Mackintosh, invited in 1900 to take part in the exhibition of the Viennese Secession following his success the year before at the Munich Secession Exhibition. The interest shown in the work of Mackintosh must be seen in the context of a more widespread expression of anglophile sentiment then spreading throughout the artistic cultural circles of Germany and Austria. Even before the publication in Germany of the writings of Hermann Muthesius, in Vienna A. Von Scala, curator of the Österreichisches Museum für angewandte Kunst (Austrian Museum of Applied Arts) from 1897, had

10.21 HOFFMANN *Apollo candle shop* Vienna 1899-1900, interior (contemporary photograph)

10.22 HOFFMANN *Haus auf der Bergerhöhe* Vienna 1899, bedroom (contemporary photograph)

10.23 HOFFMANN *Paris Exhibition* 1900, interior of the Vienna School of Handicraft (contemporary photograph)

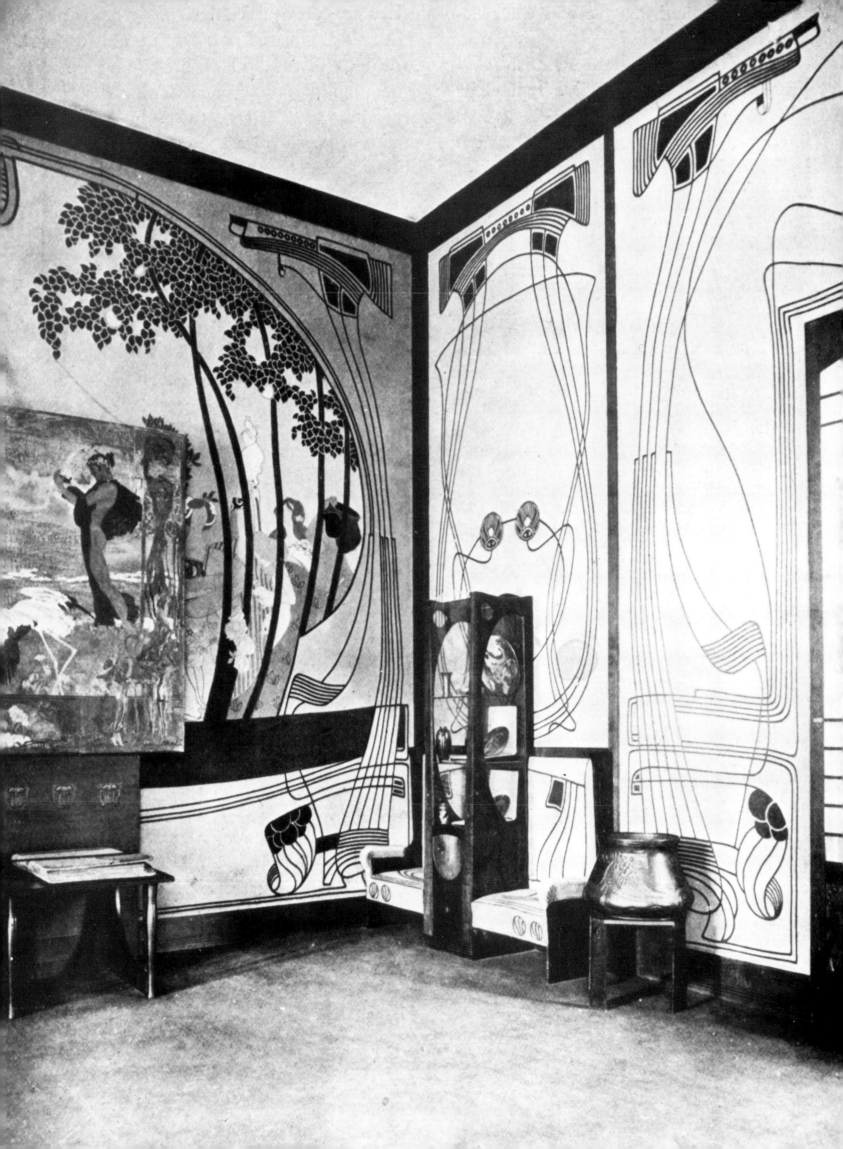

repeatedly published articles on English architecture and the decorative arts[16] in the magazine *Kunst und Kunsthandwerk* (Art and Craft) founded by him in 1898, thus helping to make known in Austria the achievements of Charles R. Ashbee, M. H. Baillie Scott, Richard Norman Shaw and Charles F. A. Voysey. Not only avant-garde groups responded to the influence of English architecture, but also the members of conservative associations like the Hagenbund, which was to foresee in the revival of English domestic architecture a possible means of reconciling the needs of modern comfort and the 'Heimatstil'. On this score it is symptomatic that passages from Voysey, Baillie Scott and Ashbee frequently appear in the works of Robert Oerley, as his one-family house (c.1905) in the Lannerstrasse, Vienna, unmistakably shows; a work which seems to come directly from the studio for Britten of 1891 and from some of Voysey's contemporaneous designs for cottages.

In the case of Mackintosh there is much evidence of his success in the Viennese milieu, from repeated invitations to take part in the Secession exhibitions to the commercial success of his furniture and interior decoration.[17] In 1902 Fritz Wärndorfer, the future Maecenas of the Wiener Werkstätte, commissioned from him a music-room for his own residence (now destroyed), and Hoffmann used his furniture for the interiors of the Henneberg and Moser houses on the Hohe Warte in Vienna. The contact with Mackintosh's work was undoubtedly one of the factors in renovating Hoffmann's style, at least as far as interior design was concerned. It would, however, be inaccurate to try to see any deterministic rapport between the anti-Olbrichian reaction of Hoffmann – which immediately found followers in architects of differing cultural extraction such as Leopold Bauer, Rudolf Tropsch, August Vaugoin, Ernst Lichtblau, Teo Deininger, Otto Prutscher and Marcel Kammerer – and the 'discovery' of Mackintosh. The favourable reception given to the Scottish architect in Austria and Germany might appear incomprehensible if one were to ignore the link between his design research and the movement towards a rappel à l'ordre then emerging in German speaking countries. As Maria Grazia Messina has rightly pointed out,[18] 'The presence of the Glasgow group in Vienna exerted a mainly psychological role, confirming the severely geometric guide-line followed by Hoffmann within the Secessionist movement, in contrast to the excesses and superficialities of a decorative Jugendstil which by now had become fashionable.'

On the German scene the tendency towards a formal abstract-geometric order was already present with the change in fashion represented by the 8th Secession Exhibition of 1900. In an article which appeared in the magazine *Dekorative Kunst* in 1898, August Endell had attempted to spread Theodor Lipps' system of aesthetics – a source from which even Wilhelm Worringer drew in his famous book *Abstraktion und Einfühlung* (Abstraction and Empathy) – by translating it into operative terms. Endell advanced a theory of form, illustrated with graphic diagrams of facades, based on the use of a network of vertical and horizontal lines which, subject to their varying combinations, would have exerted different emotive effects on the observer. Although still classified, like the poetic ideas of Jugendstil, within a theory of 'Einfühlung', Endell took as the cardinal point of his thesis the 'scientific' analysis of means of communication, so claiming the possibility of rationally controlling them. Already implicit in this last premise is the overcoming of the need to surrender to the powers of the unconscious found in Jugendstil 'naturalism' and 'symbolism', in favour of a 'Gestaltung' which, by adopting as its own postulates the aesthetic categories formulated by the Viennese school of art history, made geometric abstraction into its own basic morphological law and freed the expression of 'necessity' and the response to precise rules of form from the emotive free-will of the poetic ideals of 'Erlebnis'. Hoffmann's approach to Mackintosh was governed by a similar intellectual attitude, in carefully selecting those elements from the Scottish architect's work compatible with an anti-naturalistic urge of 'Abstraktion': the dual black and white colour scheme of the interiors, the visually pervasive quality of the furniture reduced to slender, transparent structures, their lacquering expressing itself as a negation of the nature of the material, straight lines instead of curved ones endowed with greater emotive force. The interiors of Hoffmann in point of fact redeploy the elements of Mackintosh's language, purged of all symbolist residue, in morphologic structures which pursue not only the geometric forms of abstract representation but also – according to Alois Riegl and Worringer – the peculiar vacuum-like quality of the third dimension,

10.24-26 HOFFMANN *Henneberg house* Vienna 1901, interiors (contemporary photographs) and exterior (photograph Godoli)

10.27 HOFFMANN *Spitzer house* Vienna 1902-03 (contemporary photograph)

10.28 HOFFMANN *Spitzer and Moser houses* Vienna 1902-03 (contemporary photograph)

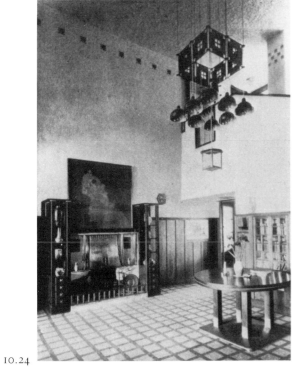

10.24

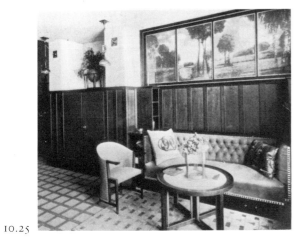

10.25

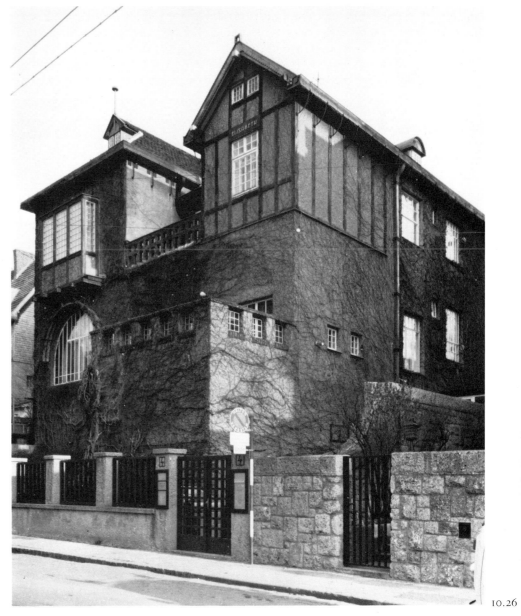

10.26

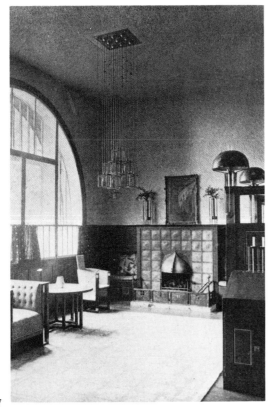

10.27

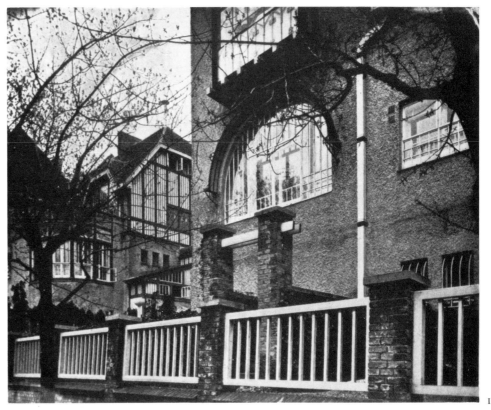

10.28

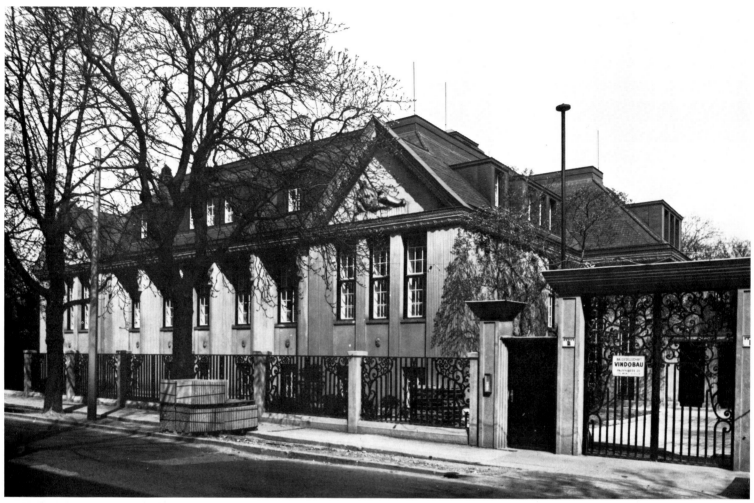

10.29

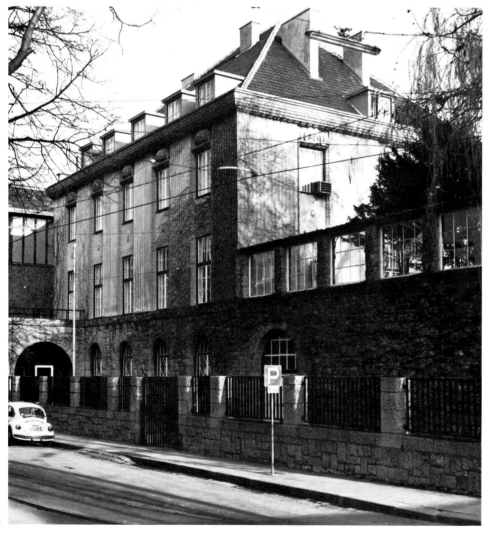

10.30

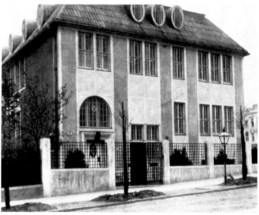

10.31

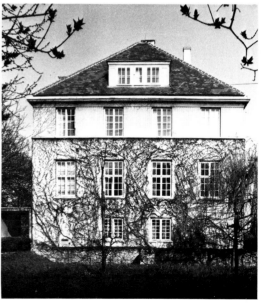

10.32

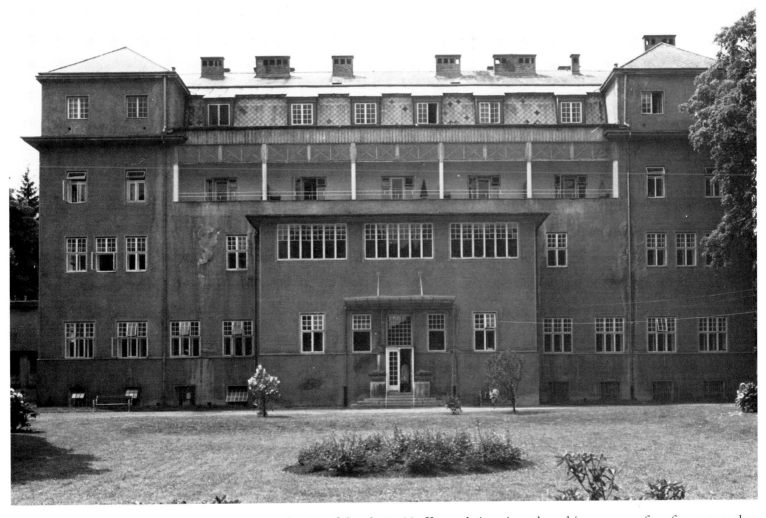

10.33 HOFFMANN *Purkersdorf Sanatorium* Vienna 1903-05 (photograph Benton)

that is of depth. In Hoffmann's interiors the white veneer of surfaces, together with the diffuse light, perform the function of annulling the three dimensional volumes, reducing them to two dimensional planes. An analogous function is performed by the transparency of the fittings – whether they be items of furniture or lattice-shaped partitions with orthogonal lines – that hollow out the three dimensional substance in the perception of their forms as projections onto the white screen of the walls, through a visual effect sharpened by reducing the chromatic element to a simple contrast of black against white. The articulated spaces of Olbrich's architecture and concatenation of forms like living organisms are replaced by immobile spaces, visible at once in their composite laws which already contain within themselves that aspiration towards a meta-historical classicism which was to develop in Hoffmann's architecture immediately preceding the First World War. If, in this journey towards 'Abstraktion', Hoffmann on the one hand uses means of expression borrowed from Mackintosh, on the other he anticipates the final results of the Scottish architect's design research: certain interiors of tea-rooms in Ingram Street, Glasgow (c.1911), in particular the Cloister Room, and the bedroom of Bassett-Lowke's house in Northampton (1916) bear a close resemblance to earlier interiors designed by the Wiener Werkstätte after drawings by Hoffmann.

10.29 HOFFMANN *Villa Skywa* Vienna 1913 (photograph Godoli)

10.30 HOFFMANN *Villa Ast* Vienna 1909-10 (photograph Godoli)

10.31 HOFFMANN *Villa Beer-Hoffmann* Vienna 1906 (contemporary photograph)

10.32 HOFFMANN *Villa Bernatzik* Vienna 1911-14 (photograph Godoli)

★   ★   ★

Besides the reappraisal of Mackintosh's language through the filter of the aesthetic theories of Viennese artistic historiography, further cultural elements acted on Hoffmann as a stimulus to free him from his earlier Olbrichian style: the latent classicism of Wagner's teaching, the interest in the typologies and structural shapes of the Bauernhaüser, which transferred the whole question of the revival of English domestic architecture within the context of the Austro-German traditions of building, and finally the influence of the spontaneous architecture of the Mediterranean, in particular that of Capri, which he knew directly, as certain sketches done by him during a study visit to Italy in 1896 show. The imperative 'il faut méditerraniser l'architecture' – a paraphrase of the call to 'méditerraniser la musique', uttered by Nietzsche in his campaign against Richard Wagner – had become the symbol, after the stylistic orgy of the historicist eclecticism, of the need for a return to an elementary language of clear-cut volumetric units and smooth white walls, which found followers among the pupils of the Wagnerschule. Models of Capri architecture became the direct linguistic medium through which the proto-rationalism of Wagner's pupils – such as Hoppe, Kammerer, Schönthal, Deininger, Felgel and Fenzl – expressed itself in designs during the years 1900-04.

The architecture of Hoffmann developed, through the interaction of these diverse cultural factors, from the modified 'Heimatstil' of his first four villas on the Hohe Warte (Moll, Moser, Henneberg, Spitzer, 1901-04) – and above all in the villa for Koloman Moser (1901), a version in a modern key of the local Landhaüser with a typical wooden structure shown on the facade – to the purism of the Purkersdorf Sanatorium (1903-05). Hoffmann, whilst keeping to the composite canons of Wagner's *Moderne Architektur* in the rigorous symmetry of the planimetric and volumetric plan, reaches in the Sanatorium pure economy of language, without precedent in the Viennese milieu and which anticipates the 'nihilism' of Loos.

The author of *Ornament and Crime* was probably referring to this work when, after attacking Hoffmann's early Olbrichian output (in particular the 'Apollo' shop), he admitted: 'Hoffmann, after the Café Museum,[19] has given up fretwork and as far as the structure is concerned, has come close to what I am doing myself. But even today he still believes he can decorate his furniture with curious engravings, applied ornament and inlay.'[20] In spite of the distinction maintained by Loos, there is no dichotomy on a level of language to be found between the architecture and furniture of Hoffmann. The definition of his buildings put forward by the critic Max Eisler as 'furniture conceived on an architectural scale', beyond its literal meaning, captures the close relationship which exists between the two fields of activity in Hoffmann. Even in the Purkersdorf Sanatorium there emerges that same tendency towards 'Abstraktion' implied in the accepted significance of reducing all plastic values to surface qualities which distinguishes the furniture and the interior architecture of Hoffmann: articulation of volume is transformed into a two dimensional expression of thin linear strips – in black and white squares – that mark out the edges; these strips frame the apertures in place of traditional jutting cornices. The tendency to mediate the perception of volumes by the use of the more direct and incisive image of lines framing their surface areas is also the distinctive feature of the Palais Stoclet in Brussels, which represents the summit of Hoffmann's work. The originality of the language of this work did not fail to have a notable influence also on the Viennese circle, as can be seen in some of the projects and work of Adolf O. Holub and Emanuel J. Margold, an architect who, following Olbrich's example, was to leave Austria and, after 1910 move to the Darmstadt Künstlerkolonie. Within a 'Kunstvollen' that had inwardly injected the theories of 'pure visuality' is also contained the idea of the reduction of the classical language to the two dimensional and a-tectonic; a feature of Hoffmann's architecture during the years around 1910, from the Villas Beer-Hoffmann (1906), Ast (1909-10), Skywa (now Primavesi, 1913) and Bernatzik (1911-14) in Vienna, to the Austrian pavilion for the German Werkbund Exhibition in Cologne (1914). Here the classicist's lexicon, uprooted from the syntactic norms of its own code and deprived of any static function, becomes the ingredient of the degrading and ultra-refined divagations of form that herald Art Deco taste.

It was mainly in this, his last classicist deviation, that Hoffmann's architecture exerted an influence on contemporary works which was not confined to the circle of the master's pupils; a circle which also included names of interest such as E. J. Margold, H. Ofner, A. O. Holub, O. Prutscher and C. Witzmann.

*　　*　　*

Although a leaning towards Hoffmann's style in Austrian architecture[21] has been

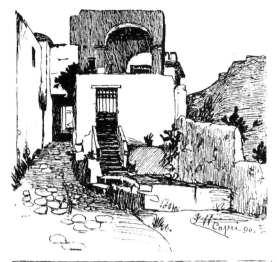

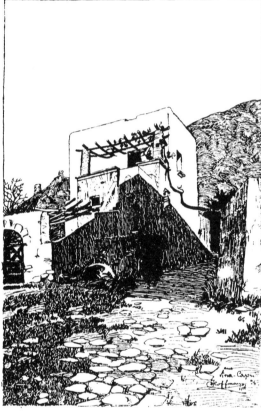

10.34-35 HOFFMANN *Capri sketches* 1896

10.36-37 MARGOLD *Projects for a great staircase and a war memorial* 1908-09

10.38 HOPPE *Project for a country house* 1902

10.39 DEININGER *Project for a villa* 1903-04

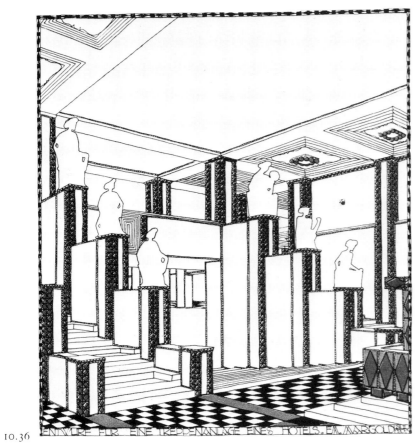

10.36

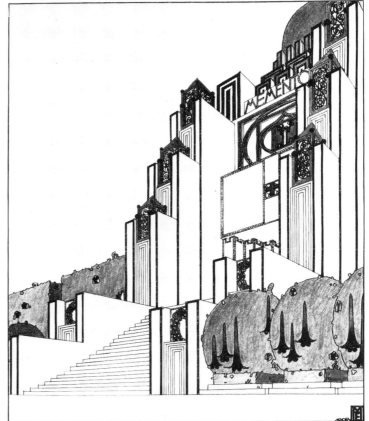

10.37

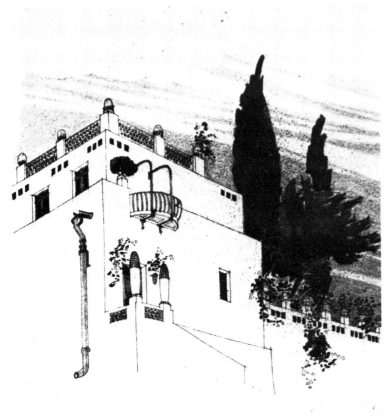

10.38

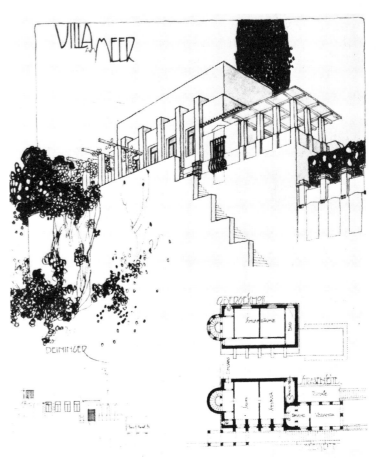

10.39

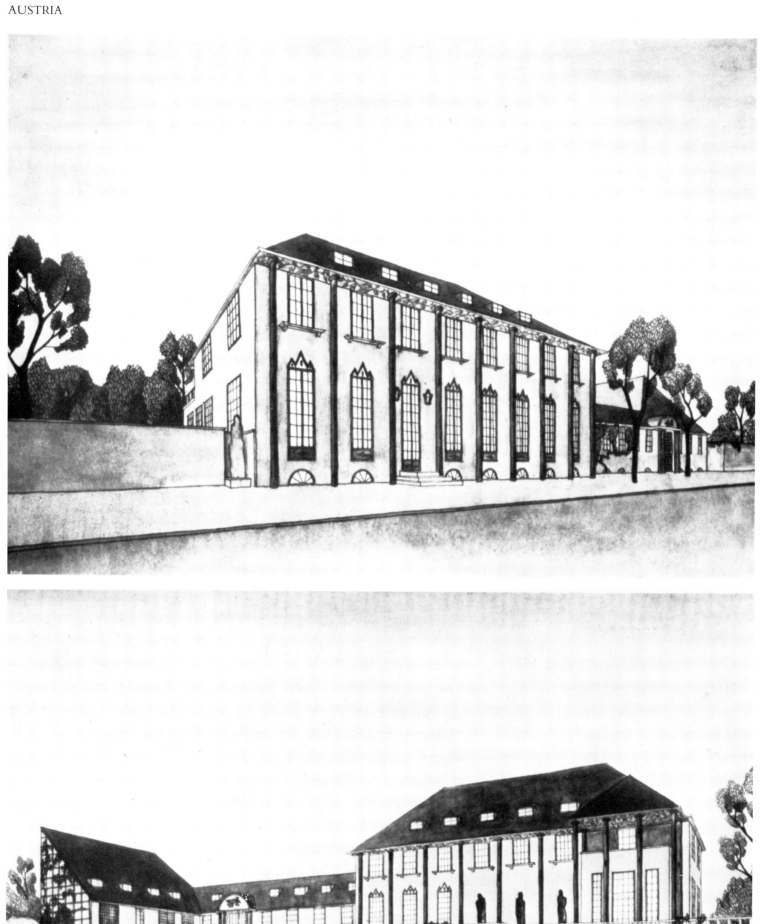

clearly traced – recognisable also in some work of Wagner's pupils, as for example the Wiesler Hotel in Graz by Kammerer, the interior of which seems to be inspired after that of the Purkersdorf Sanatorium – it was mainly within the context of the decorative arts and of interiors that Hoffmann's approach found the greatest number of followers. In this context above all he continued his own work up to the First World War, firstly as a teacher at the Kunstgewerbeschule, (a post he had been appointed to in 1899 together with Koloman Moser by the director F. Von Myrbach who was a member of the Secession movement), then as the leading figure in the Wiener Werkstätte. Founded in 1903 through the initiative of a group comprising – apart from Hoffmann and Moser – C. O. Czeschka and D. Peche, with the financial help of Wärndorfer, the Wiener Werkstätte concentrated its own programme on a nostalgic attempt to restate the aims of Austrian craft and on a rear-guard resistance to the industrial system of production, thus placing itself in opposition to the aims of associations like the German Werkbund. In the *Arbeitsprogramm der Wiener Werkstätte* compiled in 1905 by Hoffmann and Moser, could be read the following: 'The incalculable damage inflicted on the crafts by, on the one hand, the mass-production of inferior articles, and on the other hand by the thoughtless imitation of styles of the past has now spread throughout the entire world like a raging torrent . . . Hands have been replaced by machines, the craftsman has been replaced by the businessman. To swim against the current today seems pure folly. Yet we have established our own workshop. This must become a rallying point in our country amidst the hum of craft-work, and it must be a welcoming call for those who invoke the name of Ruskin and Morris . . . We cannot and we do not wish to compete with cheap production; this above all is made at the worker's expense, whilst we consider that our first duty is to give him happiness in his work and a life worthy of a man.' And again in 1923, justifying the bitter prophecy of Karl Kraus that 'Berlin will get accustomed to tradition before Vienna gets accustomed to the machine',[22] Hoffmann declared: 'It is true that in the past ten years work has been largely ruined by the introduction of machinery. But here [in Vienna] there still prevails a noble contempt for the mass-produced, industrial article; the ideal of the true craft as work created and executed by a single person, continues to exist.'[23]

Even in times of the greatest expansion of its business, the Wiener Werkstätte, which in 1905 employed around one hundred craftsmen and was turning out, apart from individual items, complete interiors for the buildings designed by Hoffmann, remained faithful to those ideals and used the machine only when absolutely necessary to meet persistent orders from clients. If on the one hand the programme of the Wiener Werkstätte differed from that of the Deutscher Werkbund on account of its fundamental remoteness from the whole question of the integration of art and industry, on the other hand it also dissented profoundly from the call of Loos to restore the values of a 'true craft', a call which, once Olbrichian aestheticism had been eliminated, selected both these groups as the main targets for its own controversial writings. The significance of Loos' polemical writings has been effectively described by Karl Kraus when he wrote: 'Adolf Loos and myself, he literally, I verbally, have done no more than show that there is a difference between an urn and a chamber-pot, and that culture "plays" on this difference. But the rest, those who defend positive values, are divided into two kinds: those who mistake the urn for a chamber-pot and those who mistake the chamber-pot for an urn.'[24]

The main theme of Loos' writings from *Die Überflüssigen* (Deutscher Werkbund) to *Ornament und Verbrechen,* is an awareness of the impossibility – accepted as an historic destiny – of a synthesis between the ideals of 'Kultur' and the rationale of production, the impossibility of recovering the values of a pre-industrial culture within the capitalist 'Rationalisierung'. As opposed to 'ornament', seen as a superimposing on the article of 'values of quality' that go beyond strictly functional limits, is the whole process of capitalist-industrial development: 'The evolution of civilisation [Kultur] is synonymous with the elimination of ornament from the utensil . . . Ornament usually increases the cost of the article. It happens that an ornamental article, made in a material costing the same and which needs . . . three times as much work on it, is offered at a price half that of a plain article . . . Ornament is wasted work-effort and as such is a waste of health. It has always been thus. But today this means waste of material, and the two things put together signify waste of capital.'[25] Further-

10.40-41 HOFFMANN *Project for a country house* 1918

more it is the same industrial 'Zivilisation' which carries within itself, in the shape of its own products, the seeds of a new 'Kultur': '. . . Do we need artists of applied art? No. All industries which succeeded . . . in keeping far from their own work shops this superfluous phenomenon have attained their highest level. Only the products of these industries represent the style of our time. They represent the style of our time so well that we – and this is the only valid criterion – do not even notice we have a style.'[26] Where the Deutscher Werkbund and the Wiener Werkstätte advocated integration, Loos speculated a separation: not 'industrial art', not 'artistic handicraft', but art and industry, art and craft. Just as he had counter-balanced the Deutscher Werkbund with the new self-contained forms, the anti-style of industry, so he counter-balanced the Wiener Werkstätte with 'pure craft': 'All products that . . . failed to correspond with their age were the work of craftsmen done under the supervision of artists and architects . . . : if you wish for a craft agreeing with the spirit of the age, if you want utensils agreeing with the spirit of the age, then poison all architects.'[27] To whoever mistakes 'urn' for 'chamber-pot', 'art' for 'utensil', Loos replied: 'Mistaking art for the utensil is the greatest humiliation that art can be subjected to.'[28] It is not therefore an argument against art, but against 'applied art', which foresees the only possibility of survival for art in isolating itself from the sphere of manufacture and from any utilitarian purpose.

★   ★   ★

The principal themes stirring the Austrian controversy on architecture and the applied arts were all echoed in the writings of Wagner, from *Moderne Architektur* (1895) to *Die Grossstadt* (1911). Wagner's idea of architecture attempts a re-synthesis, through the concept of 'Nutz-Stil' (useful style), of terms that for Loos were necessarily and irrevocably separated. 'Useful style' for Wagner means restoring to the utensil, to the work of architecture, that artistic value which for Loos could exist only as an absolute 'otherness' in the face of a 'utilitarian' world; it means the moment of dialectical synthesis between 'Idealismus' and 'Realismus' inherent in the practice of architecture: 'One is of the opinion', he writes, 'that realism and idealism are irreconcilable terms. The mistake lies in the false belief that utility can totally alienate all that is spiritual, and in the logical conclusion that humanity could live without art; whilst it can be accepted that utility and realism precede, condition and make ready that which art and spirit must accomplish.'[29] The new style as an expression of this synthesis was for Wagner – who in this respect allies himself to Gottfried Semper – the result of an evolutionary process: 'Each new style is born little by little out of the preceding one by means of new constructive methods and new materials; new tasks for man and new visions required a transformation and a new expression of existing forms . . . Each form [of the past] was recovered and developed by different peoples according . . . to their way of seeing and thinking, until it corresponded with the aesthetic ideal of the age.'[30] In this formulation, besides the readiness to recover the historicist inheritance as a storehouse of forms to be transformed, adapting them to the needs of modern life and new techniques of construction and new materials, some indication appears of a problem which goes beyond Semperian evolutionistic determinism. Wagner, whilst linking the genesis of the 'new style' to the material factors that conditioned it, transcends his own Semperian premises, laying emphasis on the moment the formal process frees itself from its material conditionings, with expressions like 'way of seeing' and 'aesthetic ideal of the period' that re-echo Riegl's concept of 'Kunstvollen'. 'In this way', as Adriana Giusti Baculo observes, 'Wagner shifts the relationship between materials, technique, aim and form, arranged by Semper within the vast compass of nature, outside the latter within the area of culture, that is within the historical-critical and specifically aesthetic edifice of reality. The technique-form relationship is thus included in the idea of architecture as intentioned form, as the expression of an aesthetic ideal.'[31]

Wagner in his *Moderne Architektur,* in stating precisely his own aesthetic theory, almost in the style of a manual, translating it into exact formal canons (symmetry, centering of the focal point of vision, equilibrium of bodily mass, stereometry of volume, etc.), frequently uses concepts borrowed from the theories of the 'Sichtbarkeit', from the writings of Von Marées, Fiedler, Von Hildebrand, Wölfflin and Riegl. This reference to the contributions of con-

10.42 WAGNER *Austrian Postal Savings Bank* Vienna 1904-06, great staircase (photograph Godoli)

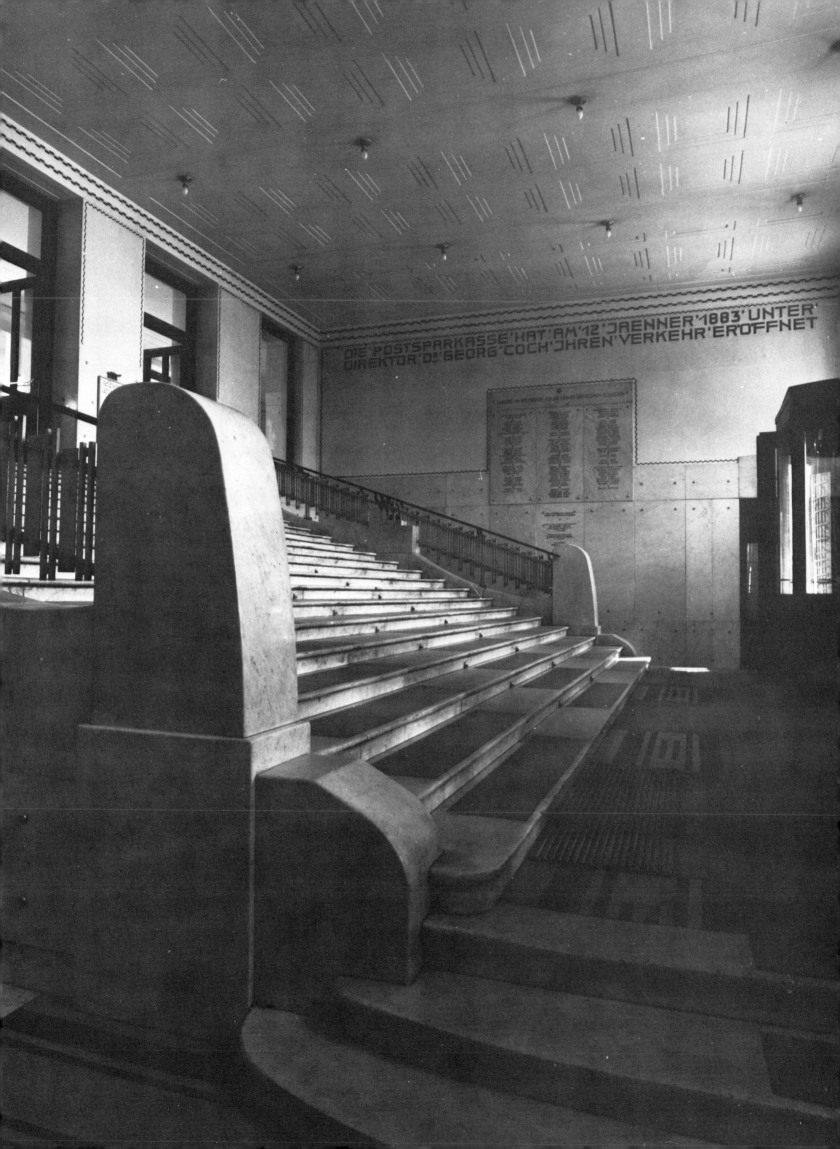

DIE·POSTSPARKASSE·HAT·AM·12·JAENNER·1883·UNTER·
DIREKTOR·D⁵·GEORG·COCH·IHREN·VERKEHR·EROEFFNET

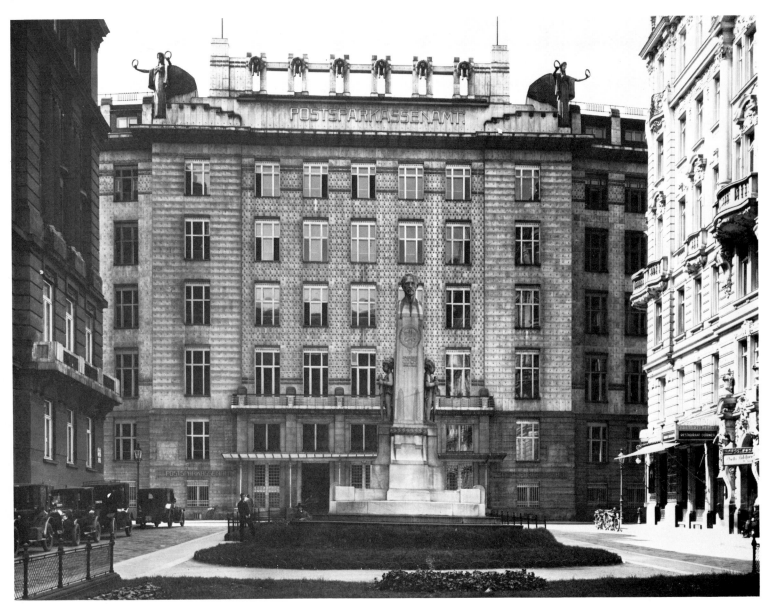

10.43 WAGNER *Austrian Postal Savings Bank* Vienna 1904-06, view from Georg Coch-Platz

temporary aesthetics is not just learned quotations, but on the operative level becomes the cultural filter through which Wagner effects a recovery of the classical-Baroque tradition, and as such provides the most relevant key to interpret the 'historicism' of the architect in works like the Österreichisches Postsparkasse (Austrian Postal Savings Bank) (1904-06), the Church of Steinhof (1905-07), the dermatology ward in the Wilhelminen Hospital (1910-13), or in the projects for the War Ministry (1907-08), the Kaiser Franz Joseph Stadtmuseum on the Karlsplatz (1909-12) and the University Library (1910-12). Wagner's classicism is not so much the result of a search for symbolic representationalism, for the will to express universalistic contents, as the outcome of a rationale restricted to the specific problems of form. The classical code is not used by him as a morphology of style, but as an abstract formal schema capable of 'objectivising' the form: in the classical vocabulary certain composite constants interest him, certain fundamental 'methods of vision', the hierarchy of the parts in terms of visual enjoyment. His break-down of the classical vocabulary to a-tectonic representation is consistent with this position, coloured by the aesthetics of 'Sichtbarkeit', but also with a proto-rationalism summarised by Wagner in the motto 'artis sola domina necessitas' (necessity sole mistress of art), and with the need, affirmed by him in a programmatic way, to relate style to the requirements of materials and modern construction techniques. In *Moderne Architektur* Wagner wrote: 'Modern architecture proceeds impressionistically in the use of figurative and ornamental decoration, using only those shapes out of which a bold visual effect can emerge. From which the new style takes its resoluteness, the integration of tectonic form with figurative, in general the most sparing use of figurative and ornamental decoration possible, the refusal to give sculptural elements the appearance of being constructional ones, the purity of ornamental forms and various further results.'[32]

Opposite above
WAGNER *First Villa Wagner* Vienna 1885-86, interior of studio (photograph Godoli)

Opposite below
HOFFMANN *Villa Skywa* Vienna 1913, view from the garden (photograph Godoli)

Page 256
WAGNER *Church of Steinhof* Vienna 1905-07, interior (photograph Pezzato)

Page 257
10.44-46 WAGNER *Austrian Postal Savings Bank*, counter section, pillar and hot air blower (photographs Godoli)

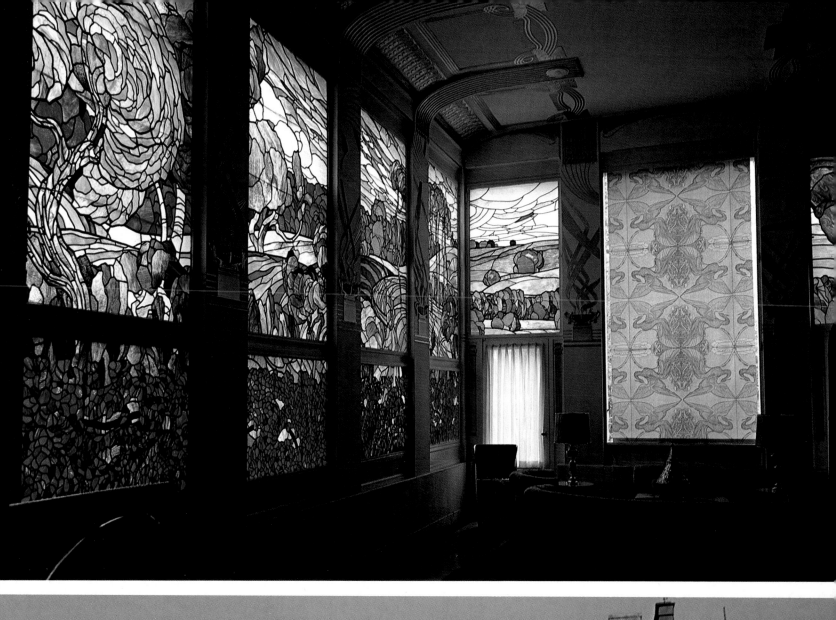

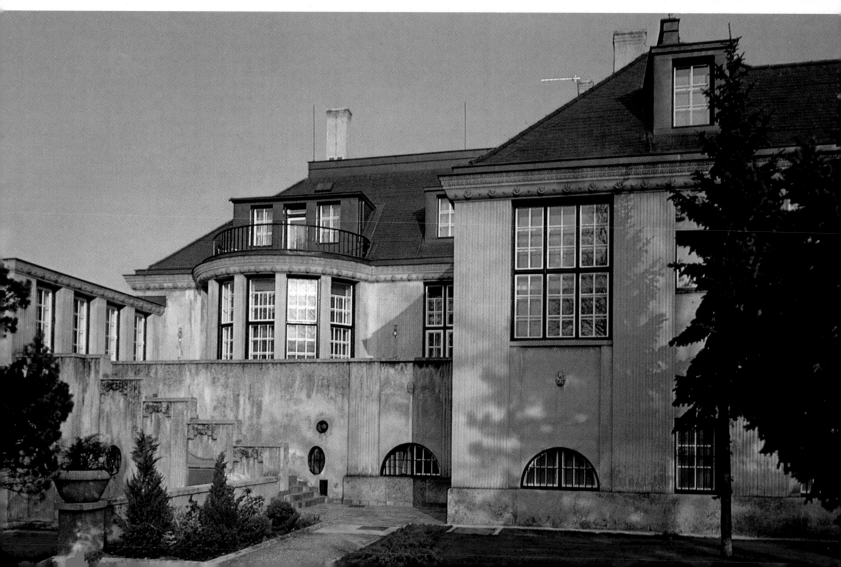

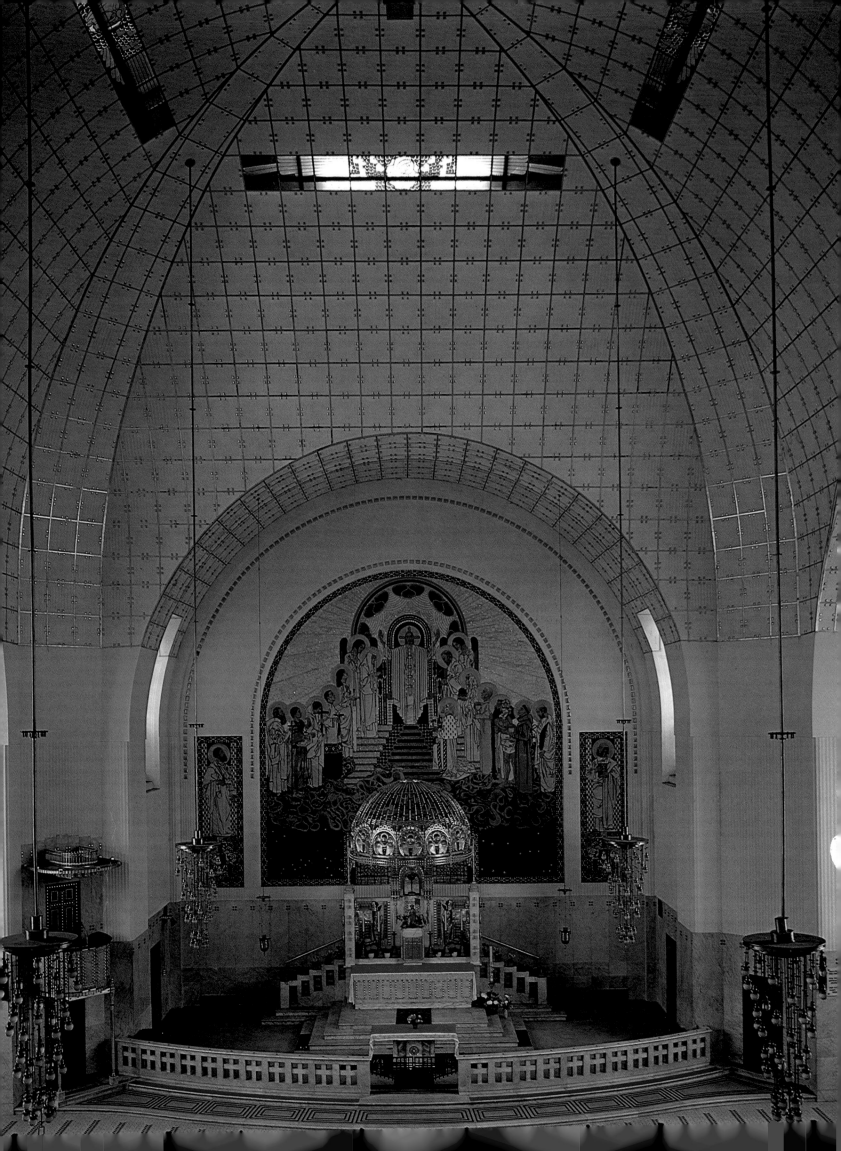

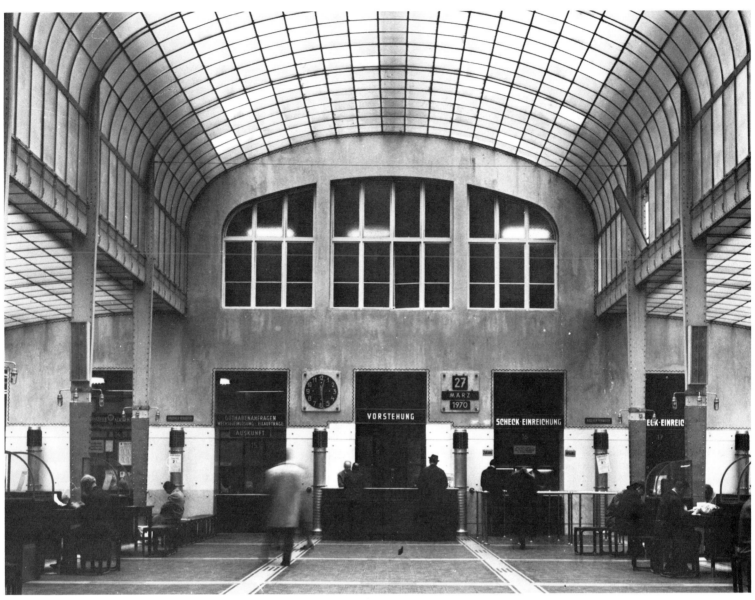

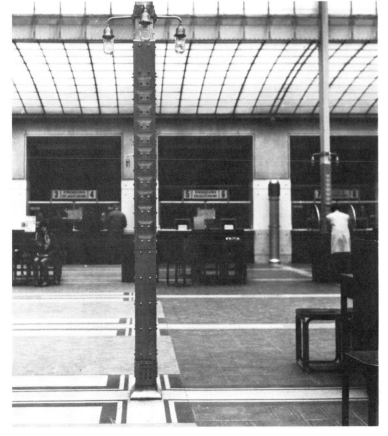

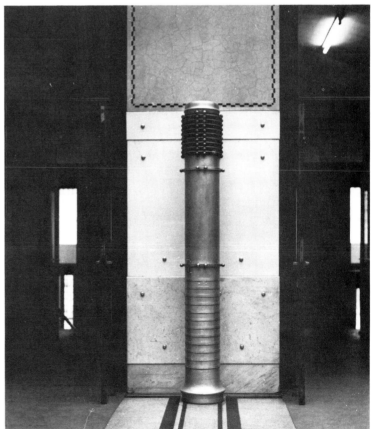

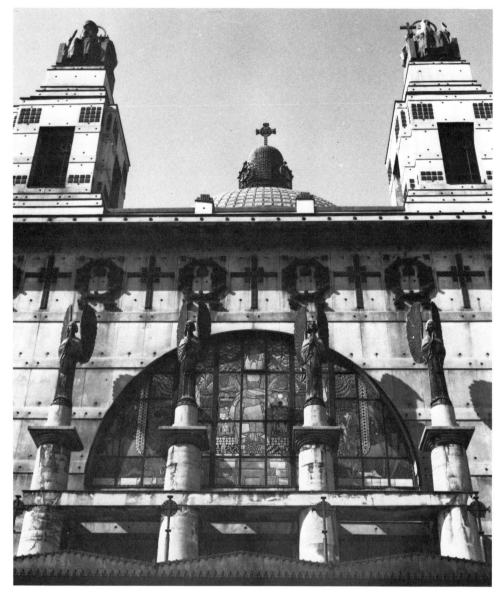

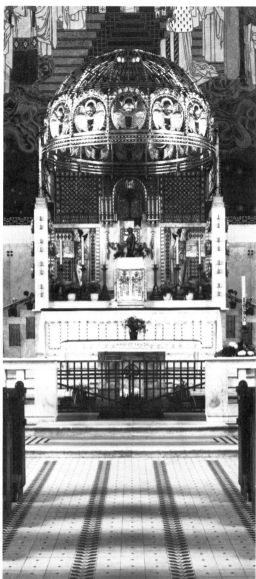

10.47-48 WAGNER *Church of Steinhof* Vienna 1905-07, facade detail and altar (photographs Godoli)

An allusive language, pursuing the integration of buildings with their urban environment not in a mimetic but in an analogical form, replaces the nineteenth-century philological classicism – rendered obsolete by new building methods – of the Ringstrasse, disparagingly called 'Potemkin City'[33] by Adolf Loos. In the facades of the Österreichisches Postsparkasse – facing the Georg Coch-Platz adjacent to the Ringstrasse – or in that of the Wilhelminen Hospital ward, the traditional plastic relief made up of classical style elements is replaced by a two dimensional image with a few essential features: the jutting pilasters are replaced by smooth surfaces over which thin strips of blue ceramic tiles trace the tripartite division of the ideal pilasters into capital, shaft and base, lending rhythm to the facades. This evoking of the classical style makes use of expressive devices which are particularly refined in the Postsparkasse, where even the varying numbers of metal discs holding the thin slabs of marble facing in place on the walls contributes towards defining the visual urgency of the centre section of the facade, projecting slightly as regards the side-wings, and at the same time stresses the classical texture. If on the outside the constructional data is manipulated to carry a special meaning, inside – in particular in the public hall of the Postsparkasse – it expresses itself without any stylistic mediation: all searching for the representational is annulled in the immediate expression of the functional data, the constructional structure (in iron with glass tamponning) and the mechanical installations (e.g. air radiators) transformed into articles of furnishing.

The dialectic between urgency of form and technological 'ratio' inherent in the Postsparkasse seems to resolve itself in other works of Wagner, either in the second factor outweighing the first or in a radical renunciation of style. These two approaches are exemplified in the Schützenhaus (1904-06), annexed to the Kaiserbad watergate on the Donaukanal, and in the two dwelling-houses in 40

10.49 WAGNER *Church of Steinhof*, longitudinal section

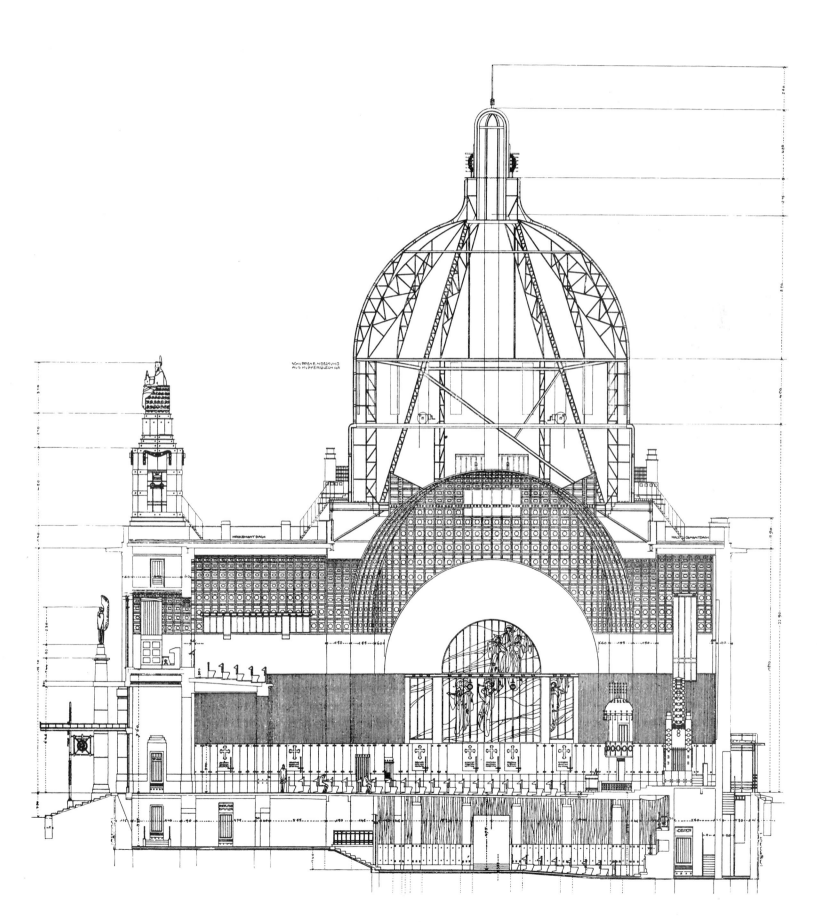

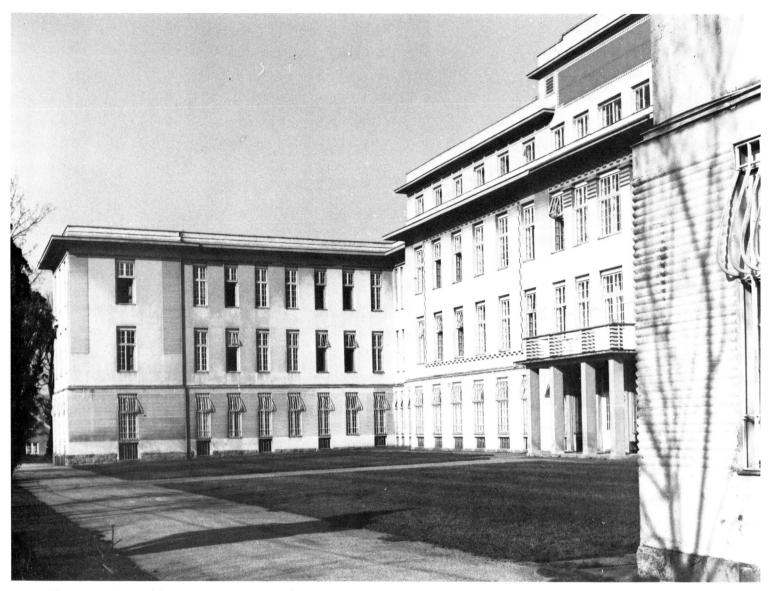

10.50 WAGNER *Wilhelminen Hospital dermatology ward* Vienna 1910-13 (photograph Godoli)

Neustiftgasse and 4 Döblergasse (1909-11). In the first, where a small structure in which a crane used to lift the moving parts of the watergate is kept, the technical factors dictate the shape of the building; whilst in the second the search for 'rationality' expresses itself by the absence of any decorative protuberances. Here two parallelepipeds, sealed on top by the overhanging cornice, reveal the bareness of their own surfaces, perforated by windows proportioned according to a modular lattice of squares and rectangles, rendered visible on the facade by the border lines between the marble slabs.

Compared with this extreme, this puritan demand for simplicity and economy, the second villa of Wagner's in Hüttelbergstrasse (1912) indulges in a careful graphic lay-out and in decorative episodes entrusted to the talent of Koloman Moser. Basically, however, its problem is the same as that of the earlier houses in Neustiftgasse and Döblergasse: for even here, to quote Dagobert Frey, the dominant theme is the 'rediscovery of the beauty of fundamental geometric forms'.[34] Particularly relevant to this work, and helpful in understanding the reasons for its success, are the following reflections of Frey relating to Wagner: 'All his buildings are a cube or a prism with a slab covering; in the simplicity of their relationships lies their monumental beauty, their classical perfection. All ornamental elements are accessories. The fundamental aesthetic need of today is clarity of stereometric form, defining it by means of large surfaces, and compactness and simplicity of volume . . . The value that this architecture holds for us lies in this, this is its fruitful matrix. The geometric interpenetration and optical clarity of the visual square have become the aesthetic experience of our time . . .'[35] If, on the one hand, these observations of a contemporary adequately sum up the didactic strength of Wagner's architecture, on the other hand by accurately taking the search for form back to the classicist matrix, to the 'optical clarity of the visual square', to an appetite for the closed and completed form, the historical limitation is implicitly admitted. As Giusti Baculo appropri-

10.51 WAGNER *First Villa Wagner* Vienna 1885-86 (photograph Godoli)

10.52 WAGNER *Second Villa Wagner* Vienna 1912-13 (photograph Godoli)

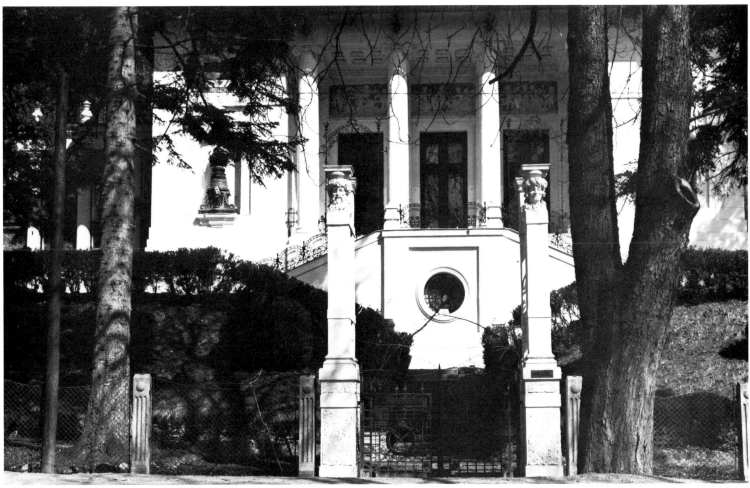

10.51

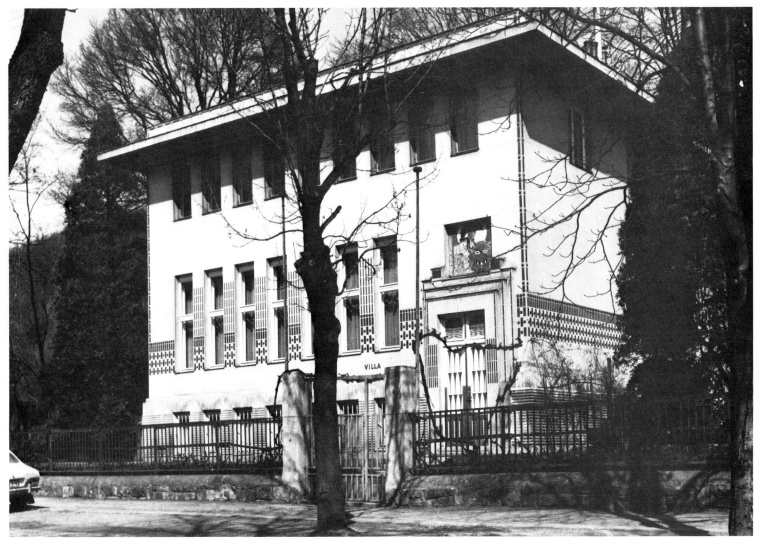

10.52

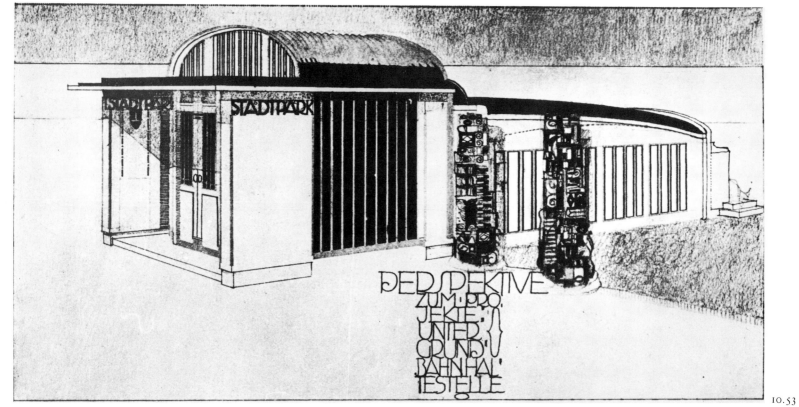

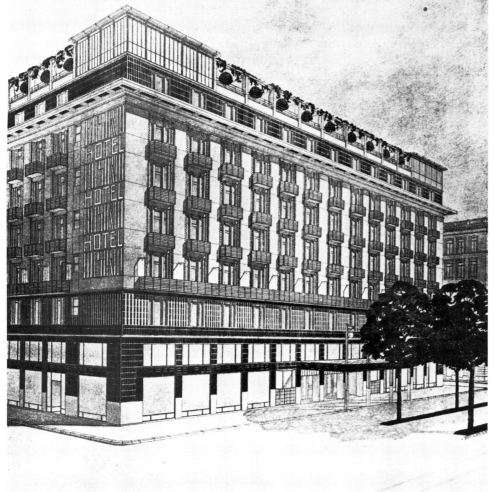

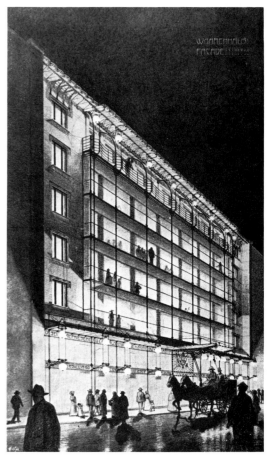

10.53 REINHARDT *Project for an underground railway pavilion* c. 1912

10.54 KLEINOSCHEG *Project for the Hotel Austria* 1912

10.55 BENKO *Project for a department store* 1902

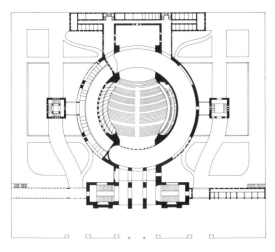

10.56 BAUER *Project for a theatre* 1899 (from the original drawing)

ately observes: 'Wagner's work does not . . . go beyond the boundary line between the composition of simplified, purified and rationalised forms, and the neo-plastic break-down, for example, whilst preparing a language . . . that seems to anticipate the crossing of that line . . . If on the one hand the geometric and stereometric transcript of architecture proposed by Wagner at this stage brings it nearer to proto-rationalism, to abstract art, etc., on the other hand it draws it further away from the cubist break-down, from neo-plastic asymmetry, from the spatial dynamism of modern architecture, since geometry for Wagner still means a perfect composition of the parts in an harmonious and completed whole.'[36] This was the frontier before which Wagner's design research came to a halt: crossing it would be accomplished by some of his best pupils, if only with unrealised projects.

*   *   *

Beyond the fluctuations in taste brought on by external influences already mentioned, over a period of almost twenty years during which Wagner's school was active – a school which had about 190 pupils – one can trace various threads in projects which develop themes and problems pointing directly back to the theoretical and architectural works of Wagner. There are designs of Oskar Felgel and Karl Maria Kerndle for example, which go beyond Wagner's break-down of forms to elementary volumes, and attempt a break-down of the volumetric box into its constituent elements, foreshadowing the experiences of the post-war avant-gardists. Others express the Wagnerian aspiration towards 'Nutz-Stil' in the immediate identifying of the form with functional and technological data, with linguistic results expressing architectonic images devoid of data, which could have been developed in the twenties and thirties. Among these are an interesting group of designs for large stores and 'Grand' hotels: Istvan Benkó's or Karl Dorfmeister's department stores of 1902 for example, where the transparent glass film of the facade reveals the floor structure (comprising the ceiling of one room and the floor of the next) and – in Dorfmeister's project – the pillars which extend beyond the roof allude to the unfinished significance of the building, to its unlimited vertical extensibility. Numerous projects from 1898 onwards faced the problem of finding a new architectural language to suit reinforced concrete buildings. This interest in new technologies produces futuristic solutions at times, which would involve a radical upheaval of traditional architectural typologies. This was the case for example with the project for a theatre by Leopold Bauer in 1899, where the circular shaped stage revolves around the space reserved for the audience. Even if all these ideas remained on the drawing board, and only a few of Wagner's pupils (Kotěra, Plečnik, Schönthal, Hoppe, Kammerer, and the Gessner brothers) were able to carry on their normal professional activity before the First World War, the output of the Wagnerschule was much discussed and exercised a strong influence, even beyond the confines of the Habsburg empire, mainly as a result of certain publications (the supplements to the magazine *Der Architekt* and issues devoted specifically to the work of the school) which made known its contribution. But it was, above all, after the First World War, with the dispersion of architects of different nationalities who had been trained at the school of the author of *Moderne Architektur,* that the Wagnerschule finally unfolded the wealth of its own cultural merits. With the disappearance of the central and unifying figure of Wagner, the composite character of the school dissolved into a plurality of tendencies which shaped, in the post-war years, the architecture of countries once under the Habsburg monarchy. But even in this scattering process, in the progress of Wagner's best pupils towards solutions far removed from the teachings of the master, it is often possible to recognise traces – which frequently reappear – of experiences discovered within the Wagnerschule.

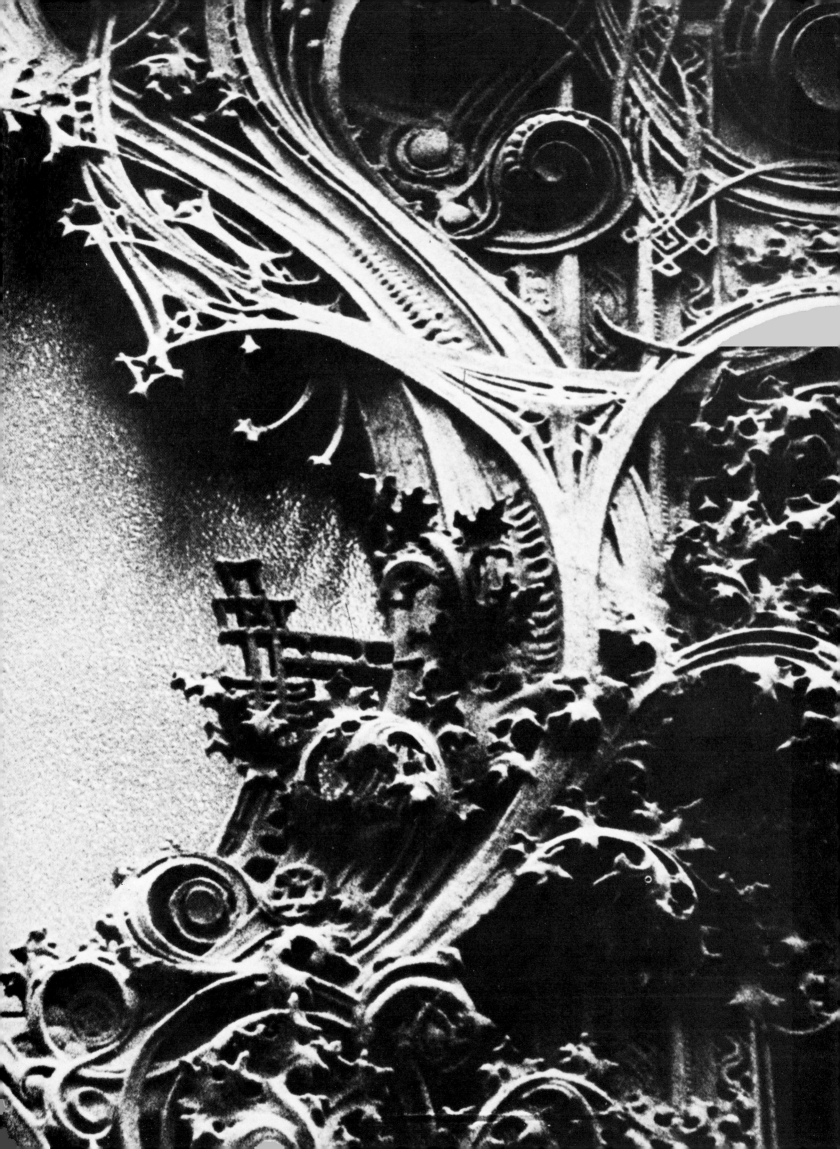

11. USA
Louis Sullivan, Greene and Greene, and Frank Lloyd Wright

William Chaitkin, Randell L. Makinson & Thomas A. Heinz

Louis Sullivan
William Chaitkin

To begin with a paradox: on the one hand, American Art Nouveau has often been regarded as if somewhat incidental to European styles, no more so than in architecture. On the other hand, when the decorative work of Louis Henri Sullivan and his Chicago School contemporaries *is* subsumed within the terms of Art Nouveau, it tends to be 'detached' and considered independently from the 'architecture', which is *not* treated as Art Nouveau. Since the importance to the Modern Movement of those tall, steel-framed, commercial buildings resides in their proto-functionalist design, the very presence of ornament contradicts their non-eclectic rationalism, mitigates against their modernism. Fortunately these historiographic problems did not inhibit the Chicago School architects themselves. In a literal sense they did engender a 'New Art' in both ornament and expression of modern functions. Certainly the creative span of, say, Sullivan – 1879 to 1924 – not only encompassed European Art Nouveau chronologically but began earlier and extended later a consistent exploration of decorative themes corresponding to those of Paris, Brussels, Glasgow and Barcelona. A dichotomy remains, however, in the buildings of Chicago.

Pevsner, for example, can describe Sullivan's Guaranty Building (1894-95), as if a house divided against itself: 'In technique and in its strong vertical emphasis it points forward to the twentieth century, but its elaborate and complex ornament places it still in the age of Art Nouveau'.[1] Yet despite Sullivan's own insistence that ornament must be integral with or *of* the structure instead of *applied,* curiously the drastic operation of stripping it off – for separate stylistic identification – can be performed with some success to the actual buildings. Without its ornament the Guaranty – or Wainwright, Schiller, and Bayard Building – is organised like a classical column into distinct base, fluted shaft, and strong terminating capital (by a heavy cornice). Facades are usually bilaterally symmetrical; massing is solid, even monumental, pierced by voids of simple geometric shape like semicircular arches, rarely soft or compound curves; proportions are firmly controlled in static repose without exaggerated tensions. There is nothing particularly 'Art Nouveau' about such a Sullivan building unadorned. The only attenuation is that vertical emphasis, which Sullivan said made it 'every inch a proud and soaring thing, rising in sheer exaltation from bottom to top'.[2] But every inch of it is also, unto the thirteenth storey, covered with an exquisite skein of ornament, incised or in low relief, much of its detail lost from the ground.

At the time, commercial buildings were expected to be decorated. Even John W. Root's Monadnock Block of 1890-91, admired as severe and monolithic, was *intended* to be decorated (as it is internally) but the client interposed his own taste for austerity[3] . . . and that was a rare exception in Chicago School practice. Apart from its artistic prestige-value, ornament served valid architectural needs in both construction and visual function.

The Chicago School received its initial impetus, drew its continuing livelihood from, and found new forms for the energetic building boom following the great Chicago Fire of 1871. To prevent a recurrence of that conflagration, building codes and methods were revised, especially with regard to the new skyscraper construction which was itself generated by the opportunity for economic expansion.[4] Vulnerable steel members had to be insulated within a thickness of non-structural fireproofing. The ideal material for this was terra-cotta: of cheap, plentiful, heat-resistant clay, capable of mass manufacture in unit moulds, lightweight so as to minimize its own additional dead load on the structure.

Since this constituted the enclosing fabric of a building invariably designed for profit, if ornamentation had not been economically feasible it would not have been incorporated so effusively. But the decorative terra-cotta panels and hollow tiles – necessary for fireproofing anyway – were as easily mass-produced as bricks, and the embossed or openwork cast iron of lushly decorated elevator grilles, stairway railings, window surrounds and the like were as much industrial products as the structural posts and beams. When S. T. Madsen wrote 'Art Nouveau offered no solution to the problem of how to relate the machine to aesthetic norms . . . only Bauhaus could offer a solution',[5] he was not thinking of the skyscrapers of the Chicago School, which does differ in that respect from European Art Nouveau.

That they are rooted in the new technical realities, therefore, didn't obviate ornament, nor need there be any conflict between art and technology. In the Auditorium (1886-90) interior, complex mechanical systems are integrated into the famous concentric 'Golden Arches'. Sullivan's partner and collaborator Dankmar Adler[6] used flattened curvatures here, not as a stylistic motif, but to prevent the focussing of sound waves while reflecting them into the audience, reducing spatial volume and hence reverberation time. They contain ventilation ducts with outlets built into Sullivan's decorations, and multitudinous rows of electric lightbulbs whose clear glass sheds a mellow, golden glow upon the overall gilding. Yet they simply hang non-structurally from huge spanning trusses above, as acoustical and visual modulators.

On the vast facades of offices, ornament helped mediate between disparate scales, relieving expansive surfaces with texture, pattern, and colour. The Wainwright Building's elevations reveal the extreme skill with which Sullivan deployed his ornamental media to unify the hierarchy – ascending by size – of spandrels, piers, and whole facade, all in rich, earthy, red-brown hues, whether terra-cotta spandrels, brick piers, or granite and sandstone base. Intricate curves, almost intimately tactile, act as foils to the rectilinear mass; two dimensions play against three; the repeated panel commands interest in itself. The way ornament – commensurate with construction – works architecturally, is also what Sullivan meant by his misappropriated dictum 'form follows function'.

Late nineteenth-century Europe and America did share similar new building types, such as commercial offices and department stores, without historical precedent. That past styles could not be adapted, without risible results, accounts for much of the freshness of Art Nouveau. In Chicago, experimentation was further facilitated by rejection of a 'reactionary' European tradition; character-istically, demise of the Chicago School was blamed (by Sullivan at the time[7] and historians ever since) on the 'foreign' neo-classicism imported to the Columbian Exposition of 1893. There, only the Transportation Building by Adler and Sullivan retained architectural integrity, yet it is revealing that it impressed not only Chicago visitors but a Commissioner of the Union Centrale des Arts Décoratifs, which awarded it Gold, Silver, and Bronze medals. As commended, 'It has the special merit of recalling no European building'.[8] When Sullivan was invited to exhibit at the Músee des Arts Décoratifs in Paris, he sent photographs, a model of the Transportation Building's 'Golden Door', and casts of ornament. These aroused such interest that duplicates were made for dissemination all over the continent, thus evincing the possibility that some influence could have flowed *from* Sullivan *to* European Art Nouveau.

Indeed, Sullivan could not have seen much of the latter before his own style matured. Still his ornament seems to have been spontaneously in sympathy with, or parallel to, the new art in Europe; in particular his polychromatic sense was just as liberal and striking. The temporary Transportation Building, dismantled after the Exposition without benefit of colour photography, is lost to

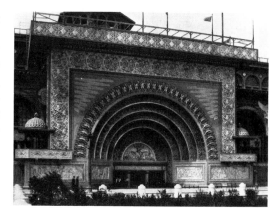

11.2 ADLER & SULLIVAN *World's Columbian Exposition* Chicago 1893, entrance to Transportation Building (contemporary photograph)

11.3 ADLER & SULLIVAN *Wainwright Building* St. Louis 1890-91 (contemporary photograph)

11.4-5 SULLIVAN *Auditorium Building* Chicago 1886-90, exterior and auditorium (contemporary photographs)

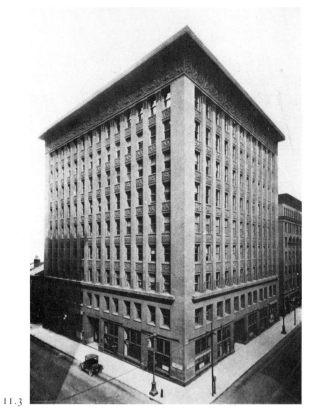

11.3

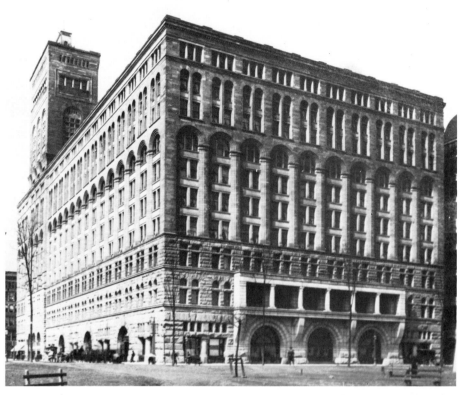

11.4

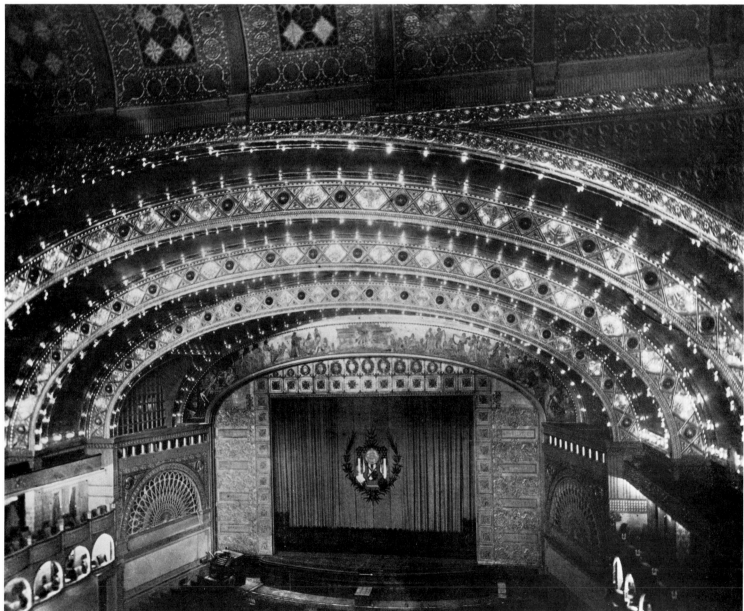

11.5

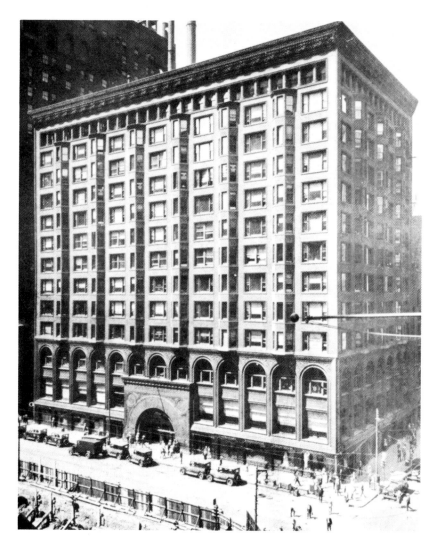

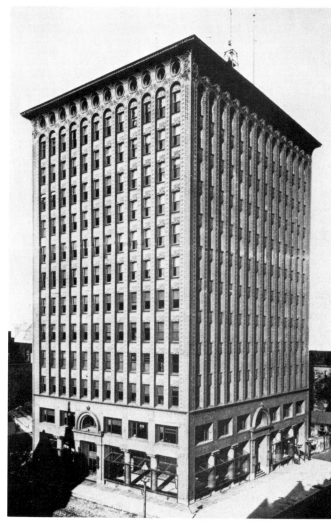

11.6 SULLIVAN *Chicago Stock Exchange* Chicago 1893-94 (contemporary photograph)

11.7 SULLIVAN *Guaranty Building* Buffalo 1894-95 (contemporary photograph)

us in that respect. Its lively palette was much admired. Unlike its neo-classical neighbours at the White City, it made no attempt to imitate marble or other stonework, and was anything but *white*.[9] Rather, its Golden Door 'was covered with gold leaf, set off by arabesques in orange, red, and yellow stucco';[10] on the rest of the vast facade ultramarine blue and green vibrated against the warmer hues. Apparently the flat surfaces – of what was effectively a decorated shed without 'architectural' mouldings or the like – were graphically coloured like the stencilled friezes of the Auditorium interiors. Sullivan's proficiency as a colourist culminated in the late banks, aglow with sybaritic splendour like exotic prairie-jewels in mosaic, stained glass, terra-cotta, glazed tiles, bricks burnt to special shades, gilt cast iron, bronze and copper patinas and, internally, chosen woods. It can be rather heady, unrestrained as Midwestern autumn.

As for the *content* of Sullivan's ornament, credence has been given by some commentators[11] to 'Celtic' strains in it, or in him: either by the observed internal evidence of those entwined spirals, dense interlacings, and folded ribbons, or circumstantially by his having had an Irish father, as if such tendencies were genetically transmitted through dominant male genes (his Swiss mother being French-German).[12] A literary and artistic Celtic Revival did thrive in the British Isles and Scandinavia around the 1890s,[13] but by the same token its nationalistic implications would have been literally alien in melting-pot America. Liberty's neo-Celtic jewellery dates from no earlier than 1899, nor could Sullivan have seen much of Mackintosh's work before then, or again, other Art Nouveau.

What European Art Nouveau had in common with the Chicago School was not an abstract language of stylisation but ideas to conjure with; a sort of 'intellectual nature-worship' informs both. The prevalent allusion in Sullivan's ornament is to biomorphic nature and, while he expressed that content visibly, it stands for something more. Charles Darwin's scientific rationale for natural forms had early and lasting repercussions for the young Louis Sullivan to whom, as he recounts in his *Autobiography of an Idea,* 'The Theory of Evolution seemed stupendous'.[14] Yet, although his friend and kindred architectural spirit John Root tried to define a biological basis for beauty,[15] Sullivan's ornament reads as

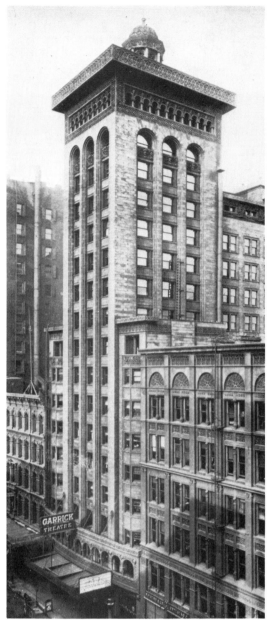

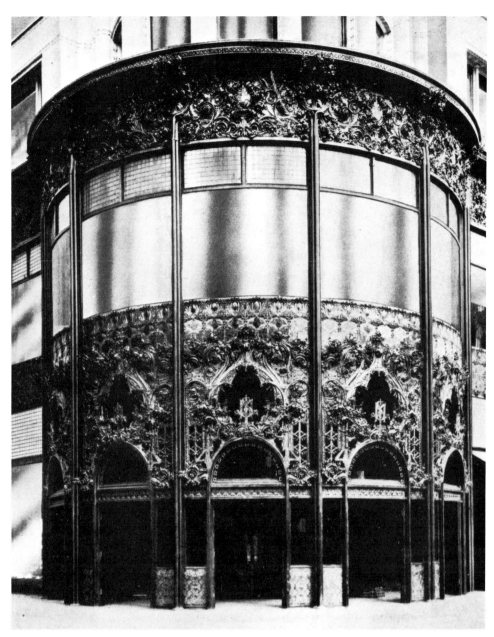

11.8 SULLIVAN *Schiller Building* Chicago 1891-92 (contemporary photograph)

11.9 SULLIVAN *Carson, Pirie, Scott Store* Chicago 1899-1904, detail of cast iron corner entrance (from a Winslow Brothers advertisement)

visual poetry rather than the expository prose of rationalism, and Sullivan's written poetry is largely about Romanticised nature – or Nature – as well. As he averred, 'I should not wish to see a rose reduced to the syllogism'.

It was Root who brought these attitudes, by no means mutually exclusive, together by ennunciating: 'To other and older types of architecture these problems [office buildings etc.] are related as the poetry of Darwin's evolution is to other poetry.'[16] Root dilated this Darwinian analogy to argue that past architectural forms, however 'admirable and inspiring', had been made *extinct* by new functions of modern life, from which in turn *evolved* its own mutant species of architecture. In 1860 the German Gottfried Semper had written an evolutionary interpretation of architecture, which Root translated and introduced to his fellow Chicago School designers in 1889.[17] Adler, Sullivan, Root, and others were meeting regularly around 1890 – the halcyon time of the Monadnock and Wainwright – to discuss this application of Darwin to architecture. Sullivan delivered a paper to them articulating his organic principle 'form follows function',[18] and Adler subsequently added a proviso even more in accord with Semper:[19] 'Returning to Mr Sullivan's aphorism, we find that he bases it upon studies and observations of nature . . . although the common function of all organic creation is to maintain and propagate the species, yet an ever changing environment has produced an infinite number of species . . . Therefore, if "form follows function" it does not follow in a straight line, nor in accordance with a simple mathematical formula, but along the lines of curves whose elements are always changing and never alike . . .' Function *and environment,* he concluded, determine form. In the case of Chicago that environment presumably consisted of technological, economic, and other circumstances.

Still, there was not essential disagreement here, and 'lines of curves whose elements are always changing' could well describe a passage in Sullivan's ornament itself. This he took very seriously too (it might be said to lack one quality of much European Art Nouveau: whimsy), conceiving it as a meta-phorical schematic of the building's life – *like* an organism – and of design process rather than stylistic predetermination. Despite any resultant ambiguities, it is precisely because his ornament *is not* integral with architectonic mass that its invested meaning is reinforced; it is *about* the architecture if not quite of it, since a proper metaphor must not merge with its own referent. 'All art is at once surface and symbol,' said Oscar Wilde, himself often construed as a spokesman for Art Nouveau aesthetics, and who had lectured in America on 'Art Decoration' in 1882.

As organic symbolism, Sullivan's biologically-charged ornament conjoins function with feeling through its intuitive poetics of the 'organic' in the broadest sense of 'system, organised structure'. The word also connotes *products* of natural growth and form, from which Sullivan derived his working vocabulary. Prof. Morrison's detective work in Sullivan's library led him to conclude: 'Gray's *Botany* influenced him more than any single book. He had a dog-eared copy, showing extensive use in studying the morphology of plants . . . His sketch book was full of drawings from this source: complex organic developments from single germinal ideas.'[20] So far from a modernist's *reductive* abstraction, Sullivan – remembering his Darwin – worked from the simple to the higher visual organisation of botanical motifs, often overlaying or compounding them with still others.

Celtic influence in Sullivan's exfoliations may be doubtful, but perhaps he, drawing those convolutions, became as hypnotically absorbed in the metamor-phic exercise as any Hiberno-Saxon monk illuminating a manuscript, truth revealed; perhaps Sullivan's ornament 'illuminates' his buildings. His micro-cosmic diagrams of life can be rigid, angular, and crystalline – as on the Guaranty – or rhythmic, lyrical, and flowering as on the Bayard; most often he comingles the geometric and fluid, both *organic*. It is not all, to every taste, beautiful (as all is not in the natural world). 'While man once invented a process called composition,' Sullivan said, 'Nature has forever brought forth organisms.'[21] But it is convincingly syncretic in a way seldom essayed by European practitioners of Art Nouveau: *either* the univalent curves of Paris and Brussels *or* the univalent linearity of Glasgow and Vienna. However, while *they* progressively pared down or abandoned ornament after about 1906, in consonance with the Modern Movement's aesthetic of exclusion, Sullivan's involvement with ornament actually *intensified* into the twentieth century. Having become an historical anomaly in any but its own terms, it speaks for itself in its own sensuous, eloquent language.

In his later work, as Sullivan's buildings got smaller,[22] his ornament grew bigger. Always concerned with framing elements, his generative motifs begin splaying over their compositional borders in delirious efflorescences. The piers of his Gage Building, 1898-99, had been 'pinned there by vast ornamental brooches',[23] but still related structure to skin. In his later series of Midwestern banks, which had no steel skeletons, an equivocal tension is effected between them – or between surface and symbol.

Perhaps the most astonishing single piece of Sullivan's (or anybody's) dis-proportionate ornament is the medallioned 'rose-window' of the Merchants' National Bank, Grinnell, Iowa, 1914. Like giant jewellery writ rather too large, it may not comport well with 'human scale', may seem a geometric game overwrought with foliate complexities too insistent for mere adornment, but the *conception* is elegantly simple, organising the otherwise blank elevation and giving great presence to the entry. In contrast, the stylised dragon on Endell's Atelier Elvira, Munich (1897-98), is rendered at nearly such size, and is easily as detachable, yet floats uncertainly and arbitrarily across the facade, without Sullivan's assured placement. In detail or relation to the whole his treatment is unique in architectural history.

His last executed building, the Krause Music Store of 1922, back in Chicago, sprouts as literal a plant-form as any he ever gave life to, its vital stem bursting into luxuriance. It was not yet his last work. In Sullivan's terminal year, having completed his *Autobiography of an Idea* 1922-23, he prepared nineteen accompanying plates of pencil designs to be called 'A System of Ornament

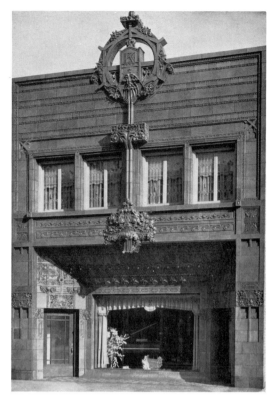

11.10 SULLIVAN *Krause Music Store* Chicago 1922, facade

11.11-14 SULLIVAN *Schiller Building* Chicago 1891-93, *Bayard Building* New York 1897-98 (photographs Nickel), *Wainwright Building* St. Louis 1890-91 and *Getty Tomb* Chicago 1890 (photographs Barford), decorative details

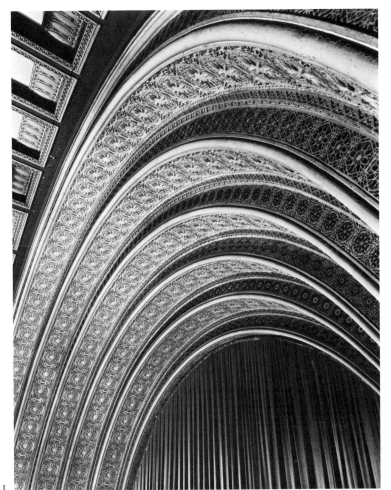

11.11

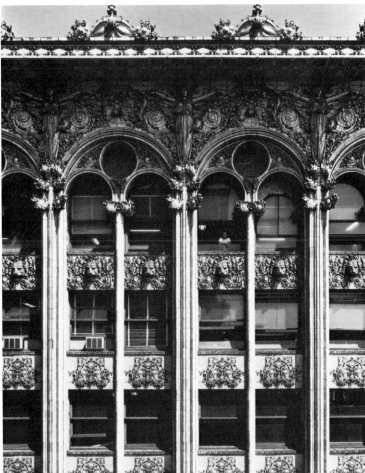

11.12

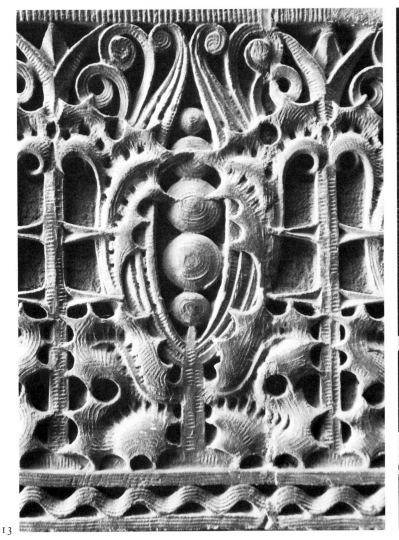

11.13

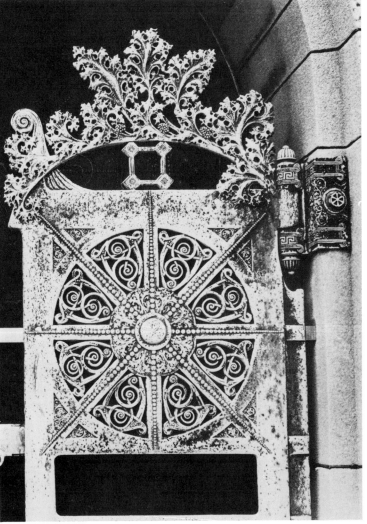

11.14

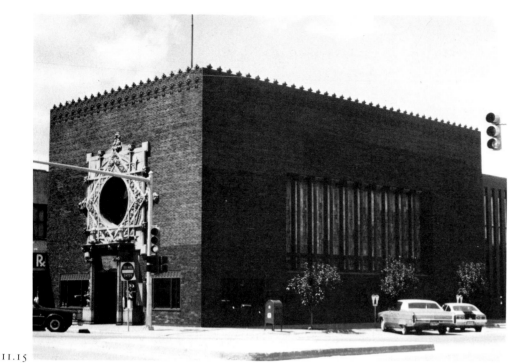

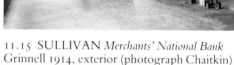

According with a Philosophy of Man's Powers'. An advance printed copy was presented to him,[24] poignantly more-or-less on his deathbed, in the sordid Chicago hotel room to which his straitened fortunes had reduced him. The drawings may posit Louis Henri Sullivan's final testament but, like Picasso, Sullivan's art was always the *summa* of what he had found, not what he was experimentally looking for, the organic *idea* which, he hoped, his life had conclusively autobiographied.

If it is to be wondered how he could create ornament *autonomous* of the specific architectural occasions or physical context out of which he had maintained it must grow, perhaps his ornament was not a metaphor so much for any given building's design as for his ideal Organic Architecture itself. That this could, in its heyday, be an architecture 'nouveau' and entire, was appreciated at the time – regardless of whether modernist historians might retrospectively relegate its ornament (and Art Nouveau generally) to the swansong of an older kind of architecture rather than the beginning of a new. To conclude with a contemporary appraisal, the following is extracted from a review of Sullivan's Carson, Pirie, Scott Store, brand new in 1904:

'For, let it be well understood, Mr. Sullivan is really our only Modernist. He is, moreover, strictly of our soil . . . the first American architect. To say that he has invented a style would, of course, be to say too much, but he has certainly evolved and elaborated a highly artistic form of superficial decorative expression in logical connection with the American steel skeleton building . . . Here, is L'Art Nouveau indigenous to the United States, nurtured upon American problems . . .'[25]

11.15 SULLIVAN *Merchants' National Bank* Grinnell 1914, exterior (photograph Chaitkin)

11.16 SULLIVAN *National Farmers' Bank* Owatonna 1907-08, interior (photograph Barford)

Opposite above
SULLIVAN *Chicago Stock Exchange* Chicago 1893-94, column and capital of the original structure of the Trading Room, incorporated in 1977 in the new wing of the Art Institute of Chicago (photograph Barford)

Opposite below
SULLIVAN *Carson, Pirie, Scott Store* Chicago 1899-1904, detail of facade (photograph Barford)

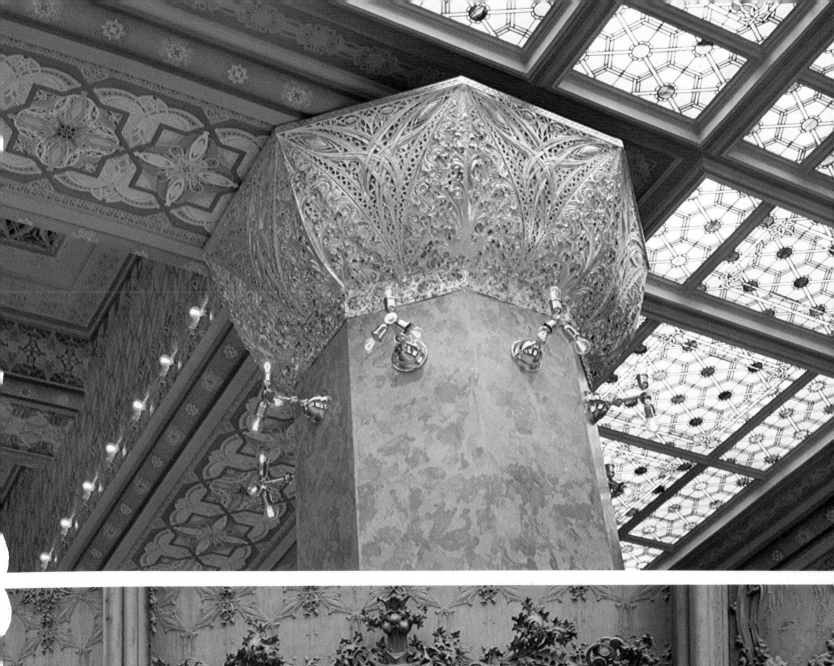

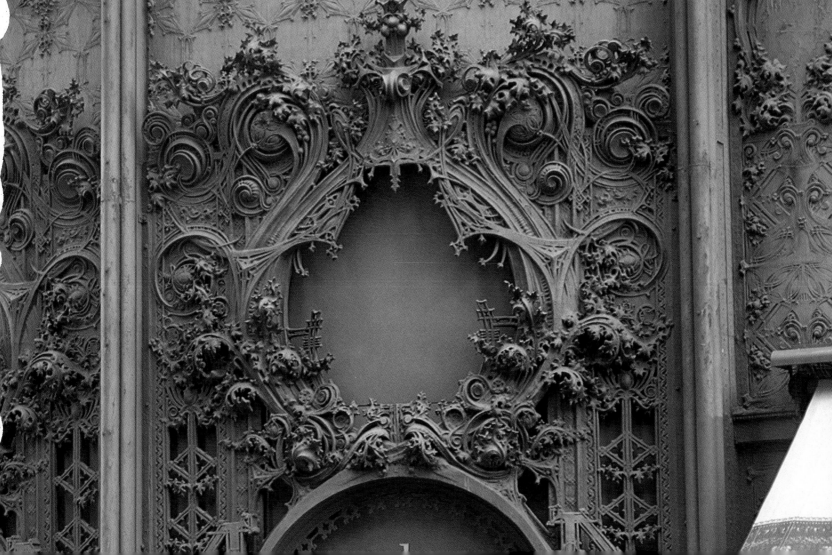

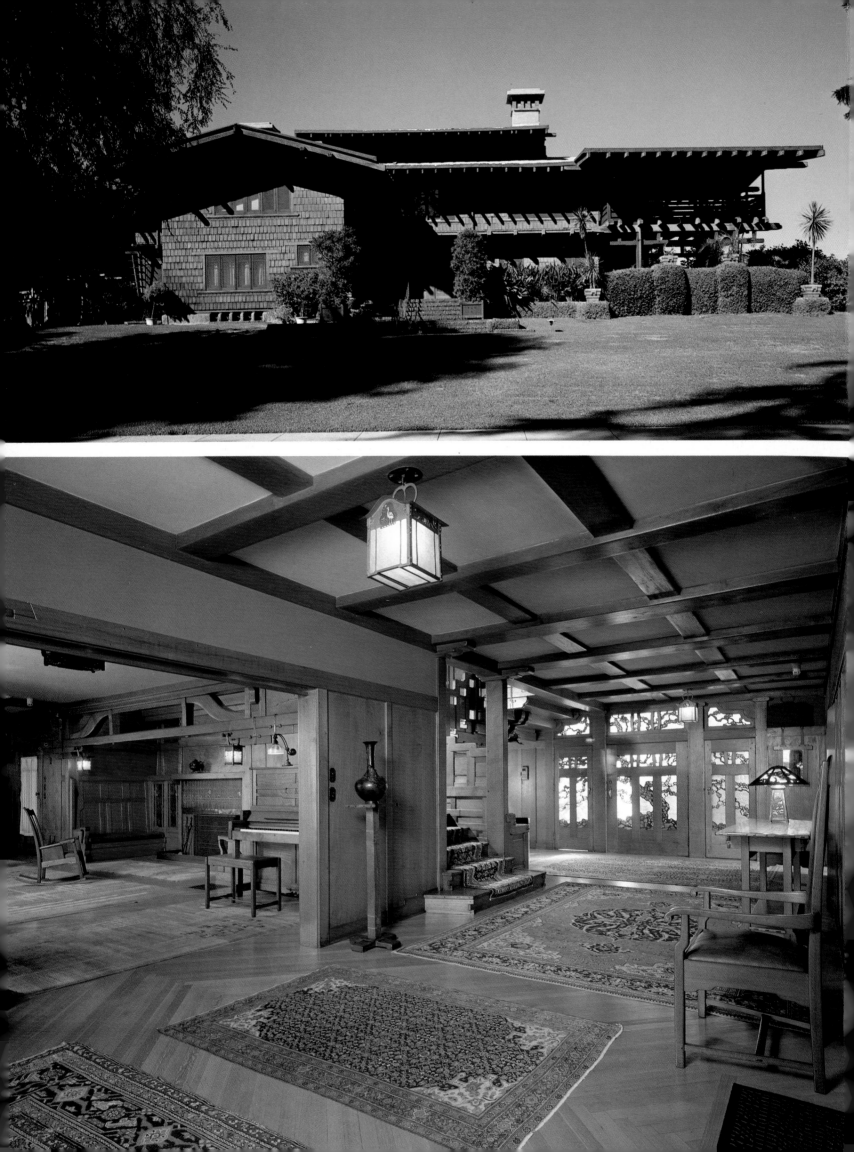

Greene and Greene
Randell L. Makinson

Fields of California poppies and groves of ripening oranges in the San Gabriel Valley are seldom associated with Art Nouveau architecture. Yet here along the bluffs of the great Arroyo evolved a new architecture possessing such richness in spirit and craftsmanship that it changed the quality of living and the character of neighbourhoods. At first glance, the California bungalow designs of architects Greene and Greene may seem independent of the Art Nouveau movement. In place of the identifiable twists and curves, the graceful wending of sinuous line and fluid forms of the 'new art', the works of Greene and Greene are carefully orchestrated symphonies in wood, free of applied decoration, and a straightforward statement of the linear properties of a timbered structural system. However, such discipline allowed for an equally straightforward expression of non-linear forms when the Greenes found that the properties of differing materials encouraged the variation so often identified with the Art Nouveau.

The brothers Charles and Henry Greene wove together the rural integrity of the American countryside with the freedoms and philosophies emanating from William Morris's Arts and Crafts movement. They also integrated their classical training in architecture under the Beaux-Arts system with the regional characteristics of Southern California to produce a new vocabulary which was to influence a generation of fellow architects, builders and home owners.

The Greenes' embrace of the fundamental principles of the 'new art' was not surprising, despite their distance from European centres of the Art Nouveau movement. California was at the outset relatively free from borrowed tradition. That which existed in the form of the Franciscan Missions and courtyard dwellings embracing outdoor living was quiet, unpretentious and appropriate to the environment. The cultural atmosphere encouraged freedom of artistic expression. The rolling countryside, open spaces and pace of daily life attracted the creative mind. Along the Arroyo of Pasadena there developed groups of artists and craftsmen with interests not dissimilar from William Morris's followers and the earlier craft guilds of England. When the Southern California building boom developed newcomers flocked into the state, bringing with them differing cultural traditions. Building styles were transplanted and intermixed; and the prevailing democracy allowed for the logical and creative development of new architectural expression, as well as for an explosion of inappropriate designs springing from foreign styles. Charles Greene in his writings depicted the chaotic residential character as 'nameless but may be described as the union of a Franciscan Mission and a Mississippi steamboat'.

For Charles and Henry Greene the fundamental principles which became the basis of their interpretation of the 'new art' and the evolution of their independent style were set early in their lives. Their childhood and training led naturally to their master works though not without the careful filtering of the multiple cross-currents which influenced the last decade of the nineteenth century. Their youth spent on the family farm in Virginia impressed them greatly. There was in nature no unnecessary or applied decoration. The structure of a tree or a leaf exhibited the true character of its function, and that logic was to become the basic element of the Greenes' individual beliefs. The farm life proved also to be an excellent background for their enrolment in the first and newly established Manual Training High School in the United States. Located in St. Louis, its formation had been the vision of its director, Calvin Milton Woodward, who was an enthusiastic follower of John Ruskin and William Morris. The concepts in the manual used in the three year training programme clearly followed the principles of Morris and instilled the young architects-to-be with a sensible approach to the fundamentals of design. When the Greenes then entered the formal architectural curriculum at Massachusetts Institute of Technology they were immediately confronted with a totally different set of architectural determinants. Designs were now derived from history, although society had undergone great changes and was far different from the cultures, civilisations and regional variances which had produced the classic architectural styles of bygone civilisations. This was perplexing to the Greenes.

Between 1891 and 1893 Charles and Henry apprenticed in key architectural offices in Boston. Correspondence shows that the brothers were aware of the emerging energy and new architectural expressions in and around Chicago and, at one point, planned to seek employment there. These plans were interrupted, however, by their decision to visit their parents who had moved to Pasadena. On the way to California they made special notes on their visit to the 1893 World's Columbian Exposition in Chicago. In almost every direction they were confronted with the trappings of history, all carefully rewoven to represent the epitomy of the latest taste. The Japanese pavilion especially impressed them by its straightforward structural integrity, grace and simplicity. To them it possessed the qualities of Woodward's teachings at the Manual Training School. Consequently, the following year, they made a special effort to visit the Japanese exhibits of the San Francisco Exhibition. The Greenes were deeply moved and, though they would never visit Japan, they developed such an appreciation of the principles behind Oriental designs that they would blend them with their own. When filtered through the culture of Southern California, their work hinted of the Orient yet possessed a truly refreshing regional spirit.

Pasadena and the adjacent valleys immediately fascinated both Charles and Henry, and they sensed that its cultural patterns were much more oriented to Morris's principles than to their Beaux-Arts training. These dramatic philosophical differences, coupled with the uncontrolled importing of tastes into Southern California, delayed the flowering of the Greenes' developing talents. It was almost a decade before they divorced the differences of their classical training and embraced its lessons in scale, proportion, optics and movement into the mainstream of their own emerging beliefs. Some years later, near the peak of their careers, Charles clearly defined the brothers' thoughts on this point in an article in 1907: 'How in the name of reason . . . can we copy things two thousand years old? Is the Paris opera house built onto the front of a railway station or a Greek temple plastered over the entrance to an office building good art? One is apt to seize the fact for the principle today and ignore the very lesson time should teach. The old things are good, they are noble in their place; then let our perverted fingers leave them there.'

Before and after the turn of the century the various publications of the day, particularly the *International Studio,* interested Greene and Greene. Clippings and entries in their scrapbooks between 1891 and 1905 indicate a keen interest in all that was emerging in other parts of the world, particularly where the Arts and Crafts movement was most prolific. Not until publications of the 'new art' began to feature the work of those who looked beyond pure freedom to the order and discipline found in geometry did the Greenes respond.

At the turn of the century their own work was free of nearly all applied decoration and affectations of historicism. Its character exhibited their interest in volumetric form and mass composition. However, a rapid change occurred in the work of the firm following Charles Greene's visit to England in 1901, publication of the first issues of Gustav Stickley's magazine *The Craftsman,* the articles and designs of Harvey Ellis, and the later series by Will Bradley appearing in the *Ladies Home Journal.* Little is known of Charles' contacts in Europe but qualities of the English Tudor country house appeared briefly in his work following his return. Stickley's Mission oak furniture advertised in *The Craftsman* was promptly selected for furnishings. The Ellis articles tend to be the strongest tie between the Greenes and the geometric concepts of Josef Hoffmann, Charles Rennie Mackintosh and their followers. However, Charles and Henry were apparently interested in the philosophy of the architect's involvement with the totality of interior designs and furnishings in Bradley's articles rather than in the elaborateness of his Art Nouveau decorative surface designs.

Greene and Greene were not at all responsive to the two dimensional graphic quality of the Art Nouveau as practised by many of their contemporaries. In their own work, Art Nouveau was a three dimensional expression of the integrity of concept and structure, freedom from tradition, and appropriate form drawn from the nature of materials, tools and craftsmen. They were paramount among the American Art Nouveau movement, and their work represented a synthesis of international tradition freed by a pioneer regionalism and boldly woven together with an almost impish systematic seriousness. Their independent feelings for design can be identified by a careful study of the planning, organisation, interiors, detailing and decorative elements which comprise their total designs. Charles' rampant imagination was given order by Henry's sense of system and discipline, and their combined efforts produced an extraordinary

11.17-18 GREENE & GREENE *David B. Gamble house* Pasadena 1908, detail of stained glass entrance doors and living room (photographs Rand)

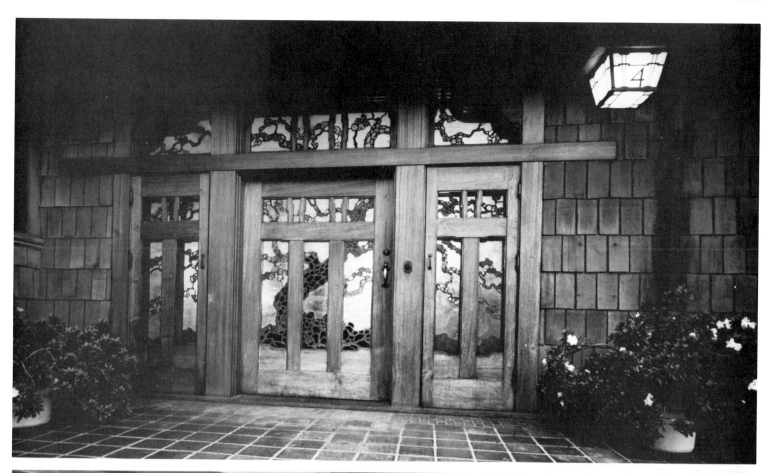

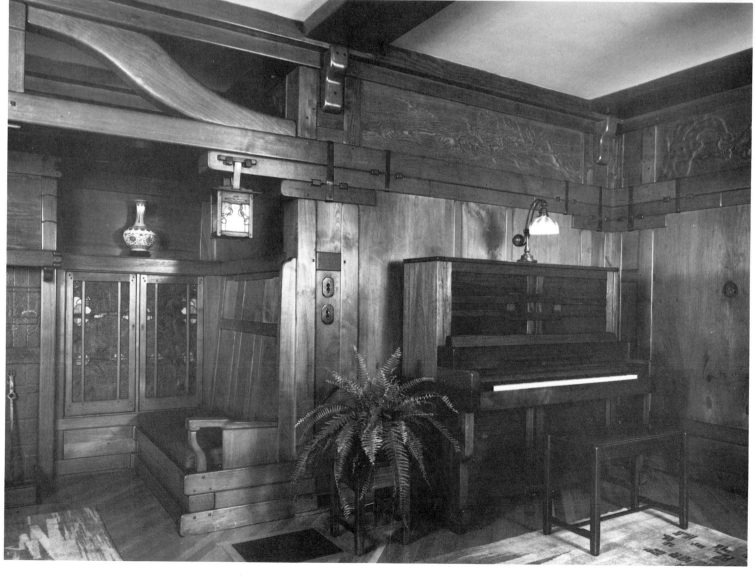

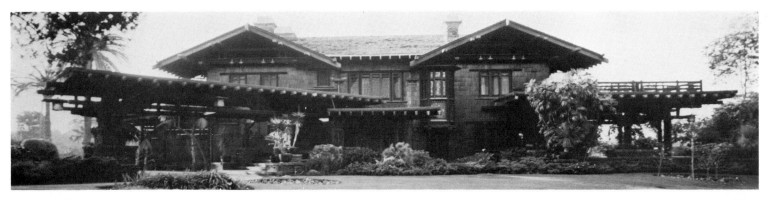

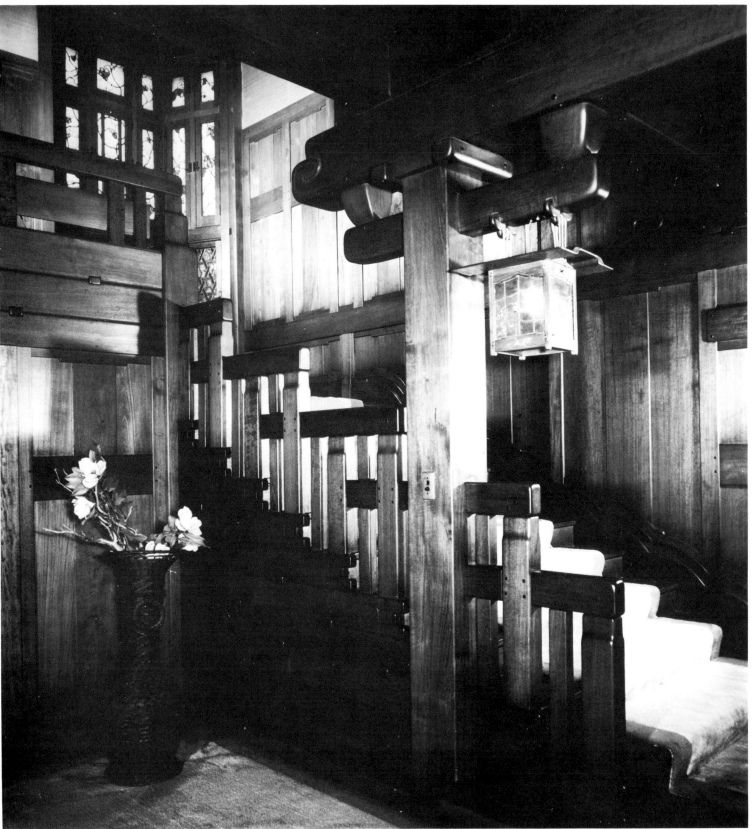

directness and practicality, touched by the magic of a truly creative spirit.

In less than a decade Greene and Greene evolved their highly individual architectural vocabulary, distinguished by an appropriate use of materials, joinery and superb craftsmanship. By 1902, their simple, direct, wood-structured bungalows embraced the landscape, as well as furnishings, which later included carpets, stained leaded glass, lighting fixtures, hardware, silver pieces, and graphic patterns for stitchery on fabrics – all of which contributed to a total architectural expression drawn from the nature of the site, the quality of life and the character of the individual client. Within five years Greene and Greene had fully mastered their concepts, had attracted both craftsmen and clients who encouraged the creation of some of the most sensitive and beautifully crafted spaces of the Art Nouveau movement.

The Greenes were, and indeed still remain, in the forefront of American creative architects. They brought to craftsmanship what Frank Lloyd Wright brought to space. In the Greenes' work there is a concern for the whole as well as for each and every part. There was a hierarchy of relationships between scale and space and materials which allowed for human sensitivities and at the same time dealt with bold dimension. There was no limitation to the various media from which they were to draw different and varying expression. They wove together the simple elements of wood, metal, glass, brick, boulders, tile and plant materials, each with differing characteristics calling for differing forms. So sensitively was each element composed into the highly articulated overall design that each was a necessary element contributing to the enrichment of one harmonious unified whole. In their bungalow designs, whether small or large, the elements were common but the language was new. As Charles described it: 'Let us begin all over again. We have got to have bricks and stone and wood and plaster; common, homely, cheap materials, every one of them. Leave them as they are – stone for stone, brick for brick, wood for wood, plaster for plaster . . . The noblest work of art is to make these common things beautiful for man.' The brothers had found the vocabulary which clearly allowed for the direct applications of their firm but varied beliefs. Their confidence catapulted their imaginations so quickly that new construction was dated by the designs on the drawing boards. The new work frequently brought former clients back for alterations and additions to earlier houses to bring them into line with their newer creations.

While the Greenes' architectural language is consistent and clear and each design has decidedly individual qualities, in earlier designs the plans are clustered and tight. Before long a casual flow developed, and outdoor space considerations were incorporated into the initial planning processes. The English plan, as the Greenes put it, was not appropriate. They recognised in the American people a distaste for secluded interior spaces. They frankly admitted that the early California ancestral building pattern of client Arturo Bandini (1903) introduced them to the Mission or courtyard plan which utilised the out-of-doors as an integral part of planning. This principle quickly became a keystone in the Greenes' new thinking and was interpreted in not only central court plans but also frequently in 'U' and 'L' formed plans as well as rambling angular compositions with wings reaching out to varying areas and vistas of the site.

Classic illustrations were the plans for the Freeman Ford (1907) and Charles M. Pratt houses (1909). In the plan for the Ford house, the formal geometry of the interior court gives way on the interiors to a variation in the shape and size of rooms. This then was naturally expressed on the periphery of the plan where the outer forms dance in and out depending on the demand of each interior space, whether it be view, use, or need to capture passing breezes. Its random exterior wall line thus exhibits a disciplined and ordered freedom – a true example of the original precepts of Art Nouveau. The angular flowing form of the plan for the Pratt house reflects the refined evolution of the Greenes' response to a differing site. Its vast acreage and location along the rocky barrancas in the foothills of the Ojai Valley offered an opportunity to respond to the daily breezes and vistas without the constraints of privacy or the rigidity of property lines.

When necessity called for more concentrated plan forms as for the David B. Gamble house (1908), the Greenes maintained their concerns for indoor-outdoor planning by providing broad tiled terraces and verandas which served also as a functional transition between the structure and site. In so doing, retaining walls of masonry, boulders or the burned rejected 'klinkers' from the brickyards

11.19-20 GREENE & GREENE *Robert R. Blacker house* Pasadena 1907, front elevation and entrance hall staircase (photographs Rand)

provided an easy transition between the rigid wood structural system of the house and the earthy and undulating configurations of the landscape. It was in the use of masonry or boulders that Greene and Greene delightfully played with free form in a manner reminiscent of the works of Antoni Gaudí. Nevertheless, these seemingly meandering forms were graceful and compatible with the disciplined structural system of the house.

Wood was the Greenes' primary structural material and the foundation of their design repertoire. It was plentiful, readily available in the local ports and because of their Manual Training School experience, the Greenes were able to exploit its properties and opportunities to the fullest.

In a wooden structure Greene and Greene believed in the integrity and expression of the linear stick. Artificial configurations and cutting of wood into beautiful but unnatural forms was, in their minds, not an appropriate use of the material. In this they differed from the great body of practitioners of Art Nouveau who in varying degrees of creativity forced the fluid forms which generally depict the era and distinguish it readily from other stylistic forms. They were not, however, unaware of the visual and sometimes functional necessity to soften the character of timbers by rolling the edges or giving sculptural change of dimension by shaping of the projecting ends. In so doing they accomplished the essential transition between the massive, heavy timbered structure and the detail which produced designs that were bold and at the same time sensitive to human scale.

Broad overhanging eaves were supported by heavy cantilevered timbers which projected beyond the structure giving variation and change to the exteriors – their shadows constantly changing under the clear California sun. The bold timber structures were softened by the rhythm of repetitive projecting expressed rafter tails. To further break down the scale hierarchy, the Greenes frequently utilised the shingle for siding, a carryover of the shingle style of the East, from Henry Greene's Boston apprenticeship with Shepley, Rutan and Coolidge – successors to the firm of H. H. Richardson. Wood became equally articulated in the interior designs where exquisite joinery, square pegging and natural oil-rubbed surfaces contributed to the richness of the integrated design. Detail revealed their strong respect for the Japanese, for the Swiss, for the dwellings of the Black Forests, and yet they are none of these. There is, however, woven together the images of those who throughout the ages have built lovingly with wood. Roof lines were kept low, pitches shallow with always a concern for the horizontal line. Structures were eased into the site – softened by subtle earth toned stains and easy transitions from interior to exterior, house to garden. Exterior spaces were equally important to the living patterns of Southern California and their development received great attention from the brothers.

Leaded and stained glass was an equally important and integral part of the Greenes' building vocabulary. Utilising it in windows, doors and lighting fixtures, both in and out, they took full advantage of its opportunities to provide desired colour, to set mood according to the time of day or night, to allow light to enrich space without the sacrifice of privacy and to enrich and complement the material texture of the interior. Because of the latitude and malleability of the leading process, both Charles and Henry exercised their imaginations fully with free form and linear compositions. Here and in the inlay work of their furniture designs, the Greenes' work relates most obviously to their Art Nouveau contemporaries.

The earliest designs for the furniture followed the work of Gustav Stickley. Swiftly, however, the lines of their designs were softened, gently sculpted yet retaining the integrity consistent in all Greene and Greene work. As Henry Greene stated it: '. . . we try to find what is truly necessary and then try to make it beautiful.' The natural grain of the woods was important and enhanced by oil finishes hand rubbed until the craftsman's hands were almost raw. Decorative elements emerged naturally from the manner of construction, the joinery, hardware and, in time, the careful incorporation of inlay work which subtly enriched the scale and character of the furnishings. The rapid evolution of the Greenes' architecture and furnishings coincided with their association with master-wood-craftsmen Peter and John Hall; with glass artisan Emile Lange, formerly with the studios of Louis Tiffany; and with a group of loyal and dedicated craftsmen.

Of the Greenes' work Ralph Adams Cram observed in 1913: 'Where it comes

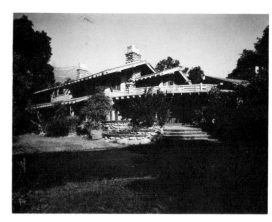

11.21-22 GREENE & GREENE *Charles M. Pratt house* Ojai 1909, exterior (photograph Rand) and plan

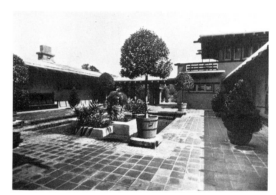

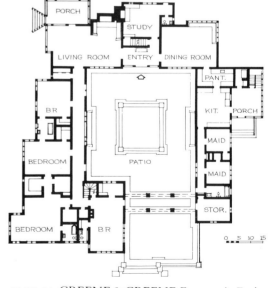

11.23-24 GREENE & GREENE *Freeman A. Ford house* Pasadena 1907, central courtyard and plan

11.25 GREENE & GREENE *David B. Gamble house*, plan

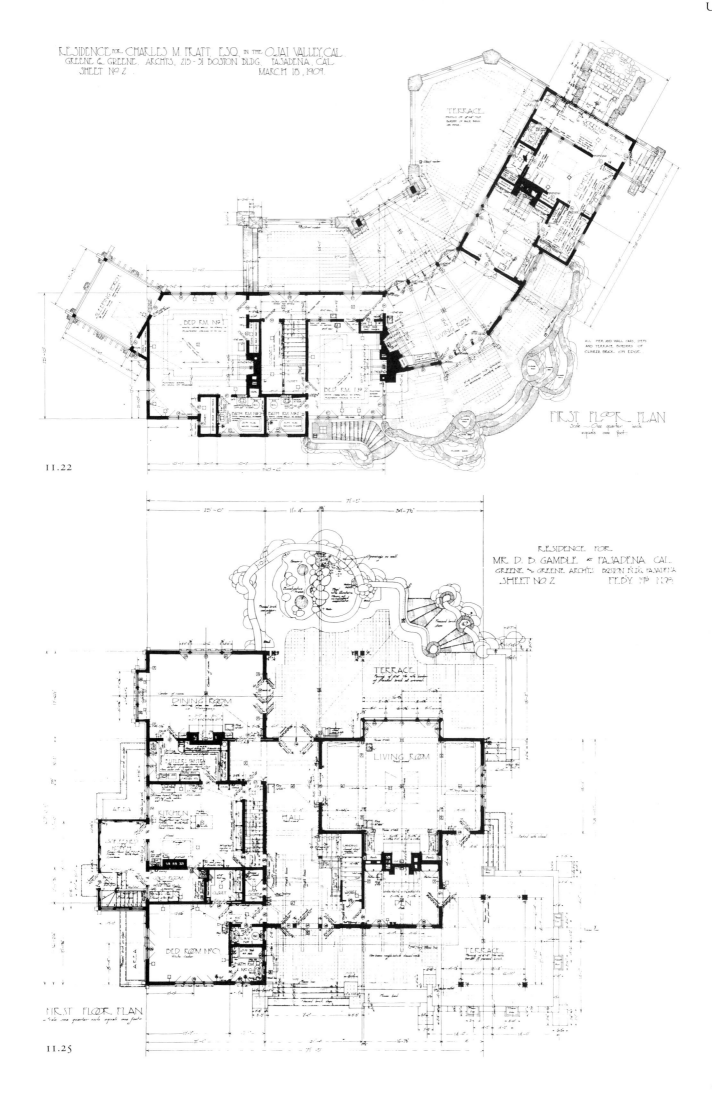

RESIDENCE FOR CHARLES M. PRATT, ESQ, IN THE OJAI VALLEY, CAL.
GREENE & GREENE, ARCHTS, 215-51 BOSTON BLDG, PASADENA, CAL.
SHEET No 2   MARCH 15, 1909.

FIRST FLOOR PLAN
Scale One quarter inch
equals one foot.

ALL PIER AND WALL CAPS, STEPS
AND TERRACE BORDERS OF
CLINKER BRICK ON EDGE.

11.22

RESIDENCE FOR
MR. D. B. GAMBLE AT PASADENA CAL.
GREENE & GREENE ARCHTS BOSTON BLDG PASADENA
SHEET No 2   FEBY 9th 1909

TERRACE

DINING ROOM

LIVING ROOM

HALL

KITCHEN

DEN

TERRACE

BED ROOM No 1

FIRST FLOOR PLAN
Scale one quarter inch equals one foot.

11.25

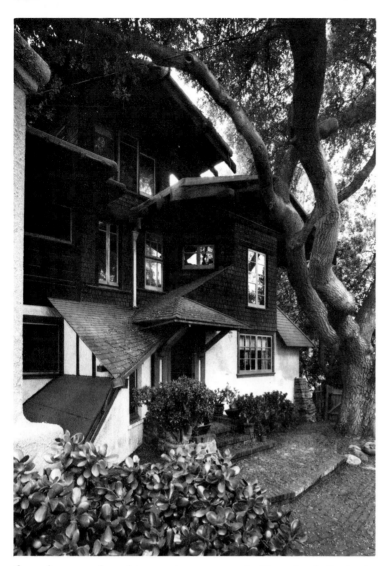

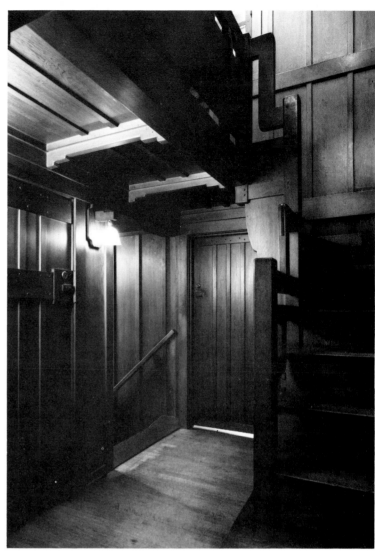

11.26-27 GREENE & GREENE *Charles S. Greene house* Pasadena 1902-06, side elevation and second floor hallway (photographs Rand)

from heaven alone knows, but we are glad it arrived, for it gives a new zest to life, a new object for admiration. . . Structurally it is a blessing; only too often the exigencies of our assumed precedents lead us into the wide and easy road of structural duplicity, but in this sort of thing there is only an honesty that is sometimes brazen. It is a wooden style built woodenly . . . [and has] the elusive element of charm that comes only from the personality of the creator, and charm in a degree hardly matched in other modern work.'

Charles Robert Ashbee had included in his memoirs comments from his meeting with Charles Greene in 1909 in which he stated in part: '. . . the arts and crafts that all the others were screaming and hustling about, are here actually being produced by a young architect, this quiet, dreamy nervous, tenacious, little man, fighting . . . until recently against tremendous odds.'

For Charles and Henry Greene the Art Nouveau would never have been embraced as an applied art. To them it was a way of thinking – a realistic approach to a design process, ever changing, ever refining – and in this way it achieved the distinction of a true 'new art' totally three dimensional in concept, evolved from the confidence of an inner soul and expressed as one single harmonious entity.

Frank Lloyd Wright
Thomas A. Heinz

Frank Lloyd Wright is rarely thought of in connection with Art Nouveau. Wright is known to be angular and geometric and Art Nouveau is recognised by its soft sinuous reversing curves. However, the underlying principles of these two are identical. Art Nouveau sought a return to the craft guilds with products that had unusual effects, were colourful, consistent, harmonious and functional, and were appropriate for modern life. This new art was to trample established order, making way for revolutionary manifestations. These were all to be executed by a universal artist, one who was accomplished in many fields and media.[1] These statements are true of the best Art Nouveau art and artists, and of Frank Lloyd Wright and his work.

Wright's background made him receptive to the principles of Art Nouveau. At the age of nine, he was instructed in the Froebel Kindergarten system which taught children to see the world in geometric abstractions.[2] With this training, he then began to abstract from nature in order to represent the essence of nature. The Froebel 'gifts' had a very strong effect on Wright's aesthetic once he began to design on his own. Similarly, the proponents of Art Nouveau saw the world in abstractions which were curvilinear rather than geometric.

Chicago and Frank Lloyd Wright were greatly influenced by the principles that William Morris was espousing in England: honesty in the use of materials and a return to handicraftsmanship. Wright agreed with the first of these principles and disagreed with the second; Wright was a modernist and he knew that society would never return to the ways of an earlier time. In contrast to Morris, Wright saw new possibilities with the use of the machine. In his lecture to the Chicago Arts and Crafts Society at Hull House in 1901, 'The Art and Craft of the Machine', he expressed many of these views. Wright called for a return to honesty in the use of materials.[3] An object produced according to this principle could be adapted to the lifestyle envisioned by Art Nouveau artists and at the same time could simplify the daily routines of the people using these designs, thus improving life. It was surely Morris's example which Wright emulated, not Sullivan's, when he began to design many different items using various materials. For many commissions, he designed the landscaping, the house itself, the lighting fixtures, rugs, furniture, and art glass. Therefore, his architecture and all elements of it were in perfect harmony with each other in scale, colour and texture.

As Norris Kelly Smith has elucidated so well, Wright was designing with an attitude quite different from most of his contemporaries. Wright's organic architecture had its roots in the Hebrew culture and his architecture had a life and vitality. In contrast and conflict, most contemporary buildings were influenced by Greek classicism in that they were complete and static; they could be taken in and understood immediately (in one look) and did not have to be experienced to be comprehended.[4] Wright's buildings are adapted to the prevailing conditions in the most logical ways, like nature. Another influence on Wright's designs was the Japanese. Perhaps in reaction to the Victorians of the Midwest and certain designers in Belgium and France, he was trying to simplify his structures by rethinking the uses of the occupants and then reflecting that change in the building. In the Japanese prints that he collected he saw a simplification of line and a return to the absolute minimum of line that would still produce the image of the artist to the observer.

The most profound influence, one that is often overlooked, is that of the client. During this period (1895-1910), Wright seemed to have plenty of them. This fact is very important in his development. Wright always seemed to have a very good grasp of three dimensions, but without seeing and experiencing what his ideas produced this thought process would be strictly an academic function. By building as much as he did while so young, and building for the most part in his own town of Oak Park, he was able to see every stage of construction and have a very good rapport with the contractors. If there appeared to be something wrong with his paper perception of the structure, then he could alter the building design before construction got too far. He never let something go if he was convinced that it could be done better and simpler.

Chicago is a city which has had a great impact on its inhabitants almost since its incorporation in 1837. This city has always had a reputation for getting things

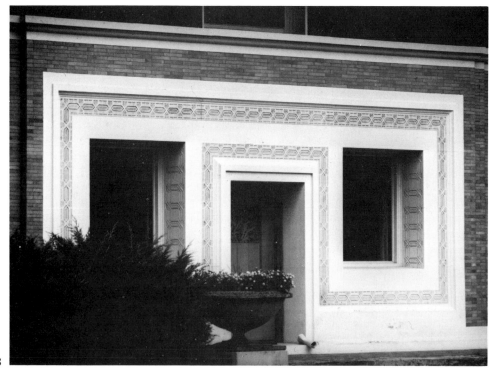

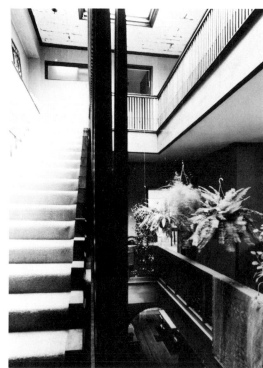

11.28

11.29

11.28 WRIGHT *Winslow house* River Forest 1892, entrance detail (photograph Heinz)

11.29 WRIGHT *Charnley house* Chicago 1892, staircase and roof skylight (photograph Heinz)

done. It is a city that takes things seriously. Wright had first-hand knowledge of how well this can work when he drew designs for one of the buildings for the 1893 World's Columbian Exposition in Sullivan's office – the Transportation Building. He was acquainted with Daniel Burnham, the organiser of the Fair. He saw how things were conceived and executed, and he experienced a growth of a city that was unprecedented in the history of the world. Chicago's population grew from half a million in 1880 to over a million in 1890, to 1.7 million in 1900 and to 2.2 million in 1910, almost five times the number of people in one area in less than thirty years.[5] With that many people expanding and building, there were almost unlimited possibilities for architects in Chicago. Wright often said that in terms of the population he needed only a handful in order to keep him busy. Indeed he was right; in his entire life he designed for less than one thousand people.

Now knowing that the Charnley house was totally designed by Wright in his off hours while in the employ of Adler and Sullivan, gives us an exciting indication of how he applied Sullivan's principles. First there is a great deal of simplification in the plan and volumes of the building; the surfaces have become planes that appear as if they are made by machines with machine-cut holes for windows. On the interior, the spaces flow in three directions, a first for a Sullivan (Wright) residence. The space flows past, over and through the machine-cut balusters. The spaces are defined by light as well as by walls and partitions all the way up to the skylight at the roof.

The Winslow house of the next year, 1892, in River Forest next to his own Oak Park, is very similar in feeling to the Charnley house in volume and wall surface, but recalls some of what he learned from the Lieber Meister before the break with the firm. The dark frieze under the great roof is a reworking of Sullivan's ornament, and the detail of the front door is an expansion of this theme. The geometric design around the windows, however, is wholly his own. It is interesting to note that here Wright reverts to hand-carved, not machine-made elements. It appears that he is not quite comfortable with his new forms, or it could be that the client, who had worked much of Sullivan's ornament in iron (Winslow Brothers Ornamental Iron Works) preferred hand-carved ornament and insisted upon it.

In 1896 Isadore Heller commissioned Wright to design a dwelling for him on a tight city lot on South Woodlawn, not far North of the Robie house site. This was Wright's first complete design of a building and its interior appointments and furnishings. On the exterior, as Donald Hallmark has pointed out, the lyrical frieze may have been derived from Viollet-le-Duc and combined with a touch of the Beaux-Arts.[6] It is a splendid piece; for the first time Wright combines a figure and a geometric background. The figure is not abstracted as it is in most of his

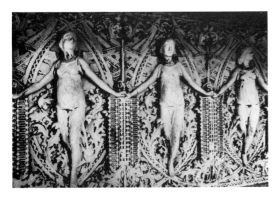

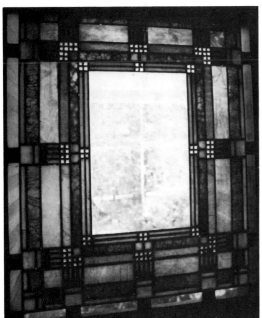

11.30-31 WRIGHT *Heller house* South Woodlawn 1896, detail of exterior frieze and staircase windows (photographs Heinz)

11.32 WRIGHT *Husser house* Chicago 1899, plans, elevations and sections (from *Architectural Review* June 1900)

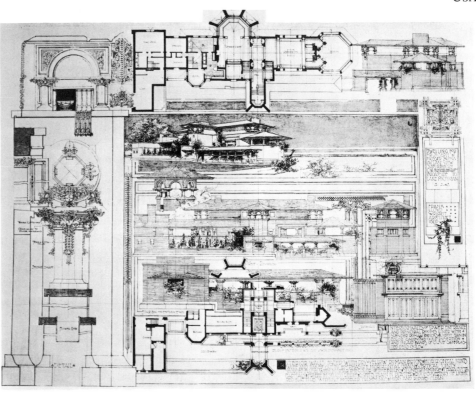

11.32

work. The stairway windows are the first that are not derivative but which come from his Froebel Kindergarten training. These are the only existing ones that were constructed using the American Luxfer Prism Company's electroglazing process (actually patented by Winslow for the company; Wright was their architectural consultant). It is similar to Tiffany's foil method but instead of soldering, the glass is dipped into an electrolyte, and a very thin shoulder builds up and thus becomes very strong and waterproof. These designs are of the border type: squares and rectangles around a central panel of clear glass. The other type which Wright used was an overall pattern, as in the Winslow and Thomas houses.

The graphic presentation of the Heller house, together with three plates, appeared in an article on Wright's work in the June 1900 issue of *Architectural Review*, (Boston), pp. 62-72, written by his friend Robert C. Spencer. The Heller house plate is a delightfully complex piece of graphics. Another plate in the article is of the Joseph W. Husser house (1899) that was built along the lake in Chicago. It is similar in style to the Heller house but shows evidence of his advances in thinking about how a dwelling is to be planned. With the main living rooms on the second level, it catches the breezes, affords a spectacular view of the lake, and gives a great deal of privacy to the occupants. The ornamental piers illustrated in the *Architectural Review* article show a continued effusion of the Sullivanesque ornament and indicate how well Wright could design this type of decorative detail. Unfortunately with the loss of the house we also lost the first art glass mosaic in Wright's work, executed by Orlando Giannini in a wisteria motif in greens, violets and crackled gold (a process which the firm of Giannini and Hilgart patented).

Judge Foster of the far South side in Chicago must have been aware of the architect's interest in the Japanese, for in his house is the most pervasive use of this influence. In Wright's own house and studio we also observe the use of Japanese-inspired details. The abstracted floral design of the cut wood screen over the dining room table of 1895 in Wright's house was backed with rice paper to diffuse the light from the lightbulbs hidden above, perhaps constituting the first use of concealed incandescent light. Similar screens were used as a skylight in the playroom addition with additional lightbulbs behind them for night use. The light source for both day and night was through these screens. Another cut wood screen was in the front door of the 1895 Chauncey Williams house, a neighbour of Winslow. Previous to this 1895 work, at least two of the second floor bedrooms in Wright's house were decorated with Sullivanesque stencils on the upper section of the walls. In one room, to the South, the stencil was rendered in silver metallic, and in the North it was paint. Giannini also painted three murals of American Indians. In the North or master bedroom they were of a man

285

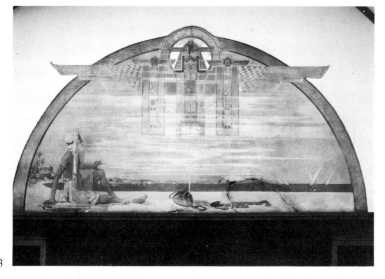
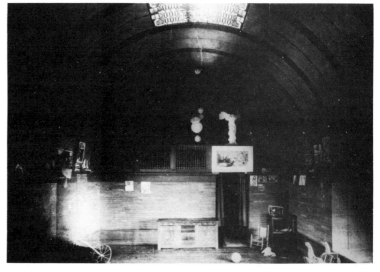
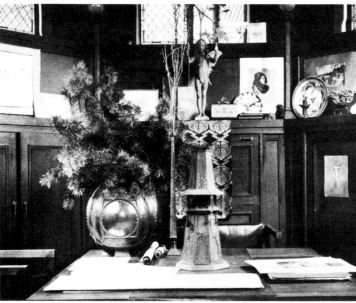
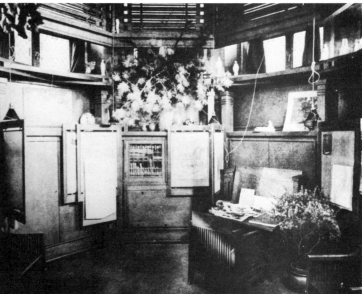

and a woman. The mural in the playroom depicts an allegorical theme from the *Arabian Nights* – the Fisherman and the Genie. The rendition of this is, like the Heller house frieze, a combination of abstracted geometry and naturalistic forms. This mural is more than decoration: it provides an illusion of the extension of space past the confines of the wall of the room. On the other end Wright actually extended the space above the wall and into the attic, making an otherwise modest space feel monumental.

Initially one of the most interesting rooms of the 1898 addition of Wright's studio to his house was the library. It is especially interesting to compare the photograph of the 1898 room with a photograph taken after the 1906 remodelling; both photographs were arranged and taken by Wright and both in their own way show his development. In each he chose to include an early piece of copperwork, a copper urn, which presents the continuing problem in geometry of the circle and the square and combines the two as he would do later with tables and chairs. The Wright-designed lamp in the earlier photograph is very much from the Arts and Crafts background of Morris and the American offshoots, Craftsman and Roycrofters. The building itself changes. The 1898 version is very similar in feeling to the interior of the Heller house with its post and globe fineals; in 1906 the fineals became more linear and square. Both photographs are taken on axis but the arrangements are asymmetrical. This is an example of the conflict in Wright's work between the Greek formality and the dynamic asymmetry of the Hebrew. Leonardo da Vinci described the resolution of this conflict graphically with his circle/square with the man in the centre. Man is the element that can bridge the gap between the two forms. Moving dynamically he forms a circle and statically, a square.

In 1895 Wright executed three significant floral designs in terra-cotta: the Roloson Row house apartments, Francisco Terrace and Francis apartments.

11.33-34 WRIGHT *Own house* Oak Park 1895, playroom mural (photograph Heinz) and attic extension (contemporary photograph)

11.35-56 WRIGHT *Own house*, library as it was in 1898 and 1906 (contemporary photographs)

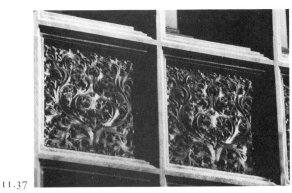

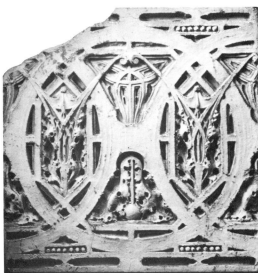

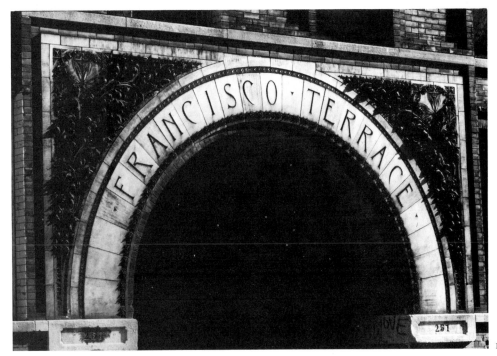

11.37 WRIGHT *Roloson Row house apartments* Chicago 1895, detail of terra-cotta spandrel panel (photograph Heinz)

11.38 WRIGHT *Francis apartments* Chicago 1895, decorative panel (photograph Heinz)

11.39 WRIGHT *Francisco Terrace* Chicago 1895, terra-cotta entrance frieze (photograph Heinz)

Two of these were for his continuing client Edward C. Waller, a neighbour in River Forest to Winslow. Again, this may have been an imposed client request which was handled in three different ways. The Roloson terra-cotta was a spandral panel and was used to soften a very severe and hard facade. In Francisco Terrace it was for the accent of the entrance and in the Francis apartments it was intended to lighten the volume of the building and bring the scale of the building down to that of the pedestrian. What is missing in each of these is the geometric backgrounds that he used on the Winslow and Heller houses; in the Francisco Terrace the background is native American oak leaves (not Greek acanthus leaves). These later designs have strength but not the lightness of the contemporary Europeans. An independent American design has come forth.

In 1901, the *Ladies Home Journal* published a design by Wright that heralded his new style.[7] This was before the Kankakee works and the Thomas house. This design was the basis for the Ward Willits house, Highland Park, Illinois. The preliminary design was taken directly from the *Ladies Home Journal* design and elaborated to what we see in the Willits house, with much attention from both the client and the architect. The paper design and the subsequent Willits building were both influenced by the principles and visual qualities of the Japanese residential style. Both Wright and Willits were very interested in the Japanese; in fact, they went together to Japan after the house was completed.

The dining room of the Willits house was very important to the development of Wright's dining rooms for the next decade. It may be the prototype for all his dining rooms from this time to the Robie house. The furniture itself was the second set that we are aware of in this new style of Wright's; the first being the Husser house set of 1899,[8] and this second set of 1901. This style was consistent, harmonious and functional, just as Art Nouveau said that it should be.

The glass in the Willits house that was executed by Giannini and Hilgart was interesting because it used ceiling lights that were constructed mostly of the conventional came between glass method. Some of the centre glass pieces, however, were just cut and then assembled without the cames, making only a hairline in a herringbone pattern. It is interesting to note that most of the innovation in Wright's glass took place when Giannini and Hilgart were doing the execution, which leads one to think that the members of the firm might have piqued the designer's imagination, and provided him with the technological information necessary to make his pieces more interesting.

The Dana house of Springfield, Illinois came at a very good time for us. In it we see the amount of time Wright's office spent on fanciful detailing that was actually executed in this grand scheme for two ladies, mother and daughter. Wright's inventiveness was only rarely put to use as it was here. Almost every window opening has a different design. They are all related by colour, and most of them by motif, but on many occasions they relate only to the specific room for which they were designed. At the entrance, one is overwhelmed by the three

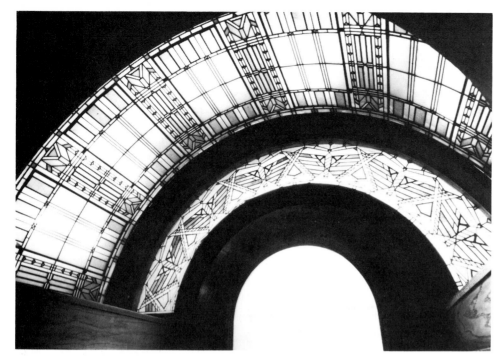

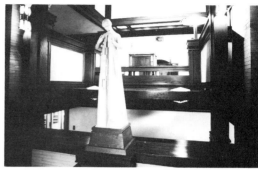

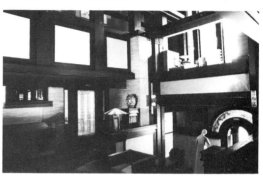

11.40-42 WRIGHT *Dana house* Springfield 1903, stained glass arch over entrance, and two views of the interior (photographs Heinz)

arches of art glass; two of the same scene of abstracted butterflies, and another connecting the two in a vaulted arch. Then one encounters the terra-cotta sculpture, 'The Flower in the Crannied Wall', executed by Richard Bock and the Northwestern Terra Cotta Works. In this statue, there is a very exquisite and harmonious blend of natural and geometric female forms, comprising a very geometric construction. Wright also designed a terra-cotta fountain in the entry hall. His first freestanding art glass lamps are also here. He must have been pleased with these designs because some of them show up in his later buildings such as the Robie house, built nine years later.

Another innovation in art glass in this building was in the ballroom. In one end of the barrel-vaulted room is installed a plate glass semi-circular window. Hung on a wooden frame on the interior side of this window is a very fine and delicate art glass design. This method was not repeated again, however.

Three years later, in 1904, in the D. D. Martin house of Buffalo, New York, Wright got another chance to design everything, but not on so grand a scale. As in the Dana house, the glass here is designed with a very strong graphic sense, and a good colour sense, but the lines and line weights of the zinc cames are stronger than the colours of the green iridescent glass used. Wright was the first to utilise the thick and thin cames for graphic effects not just for strength. The strength is in the lines. (Wright was also almost the only one to use this idea). The four-sided fireplace mosaic that once existed here is gone. It too was executed by Orlando Giannini of Giannini and Hilgart. This was a wisteria motif of green purple, dead gold, and a patterned effect on green glass of crackled gold. It was the focal point of the whole first floor and gave some visual warmth to the severe lines of the dwelling. Another curvilinear element was the barrel chair design for the living room. Wright, who worked in geometrics, here contrasted his square chairs with a round one.

Darwin D. Martin was the President of the Larkin Company, and in 1904 Wright designed the administrative headquarters for it. This building is one of the most important in modern architecture. The number of technical innovations used here is staggering. The visual strength of the design is outstanding as are the planning concepts. The design of the Larkin Building as an administrative building is superior to most contemporary office buildings for several reasons. It was an office building with large windows, but these were not for viewing, thus wasting the time of the worker. They were for light so that he could be a more efficient worker. The windows were high above the heads of the employees and also provided more wall space for filing cabinets. The large well in the centre was also to provide light. The staircase was to the side, almost a separate building, and easy to close off in case of fire. It was articulated on the exterior. In the large corner piers were air shafts that delivered conditioned air to the floors. This was not the same as the air-conditioning by refrigeration that we know today, but the air was humidified in the winter and de-humidified in the summer. The air was

11.43-44 WRIGHT *Larkin Building* Buffalo 1904, exterior and steel furniture (contemporary photographs)

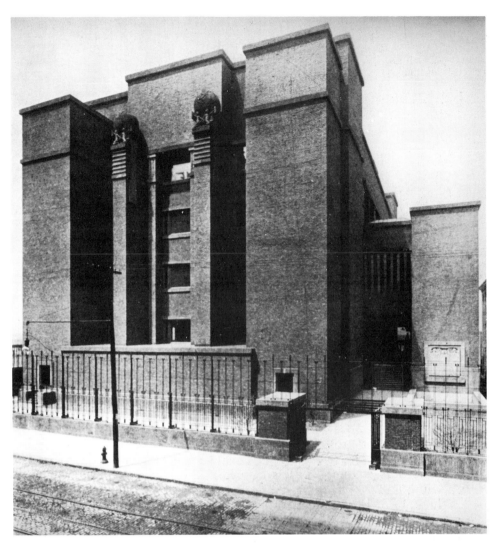

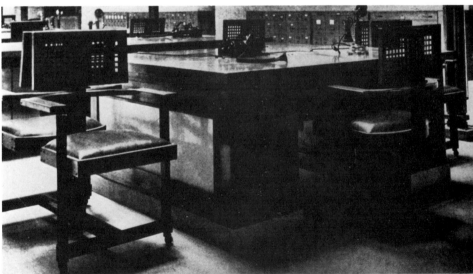

filtered all year. The reason for this closed system was that the building was in a heavy industrial railroad area.

The office furniture that was designed for the Larkin Building was the first ever to be made of steel. The desks, chairs, and filing cabinets were all steel. The chairs at the desks were attached to the desk leg with a pivot to facilitate floor cleaning. In the bathrooms, the first wall-hung toilets were installed – again for ease of cleaning. (This toilet design was discovered by Donald Kalec in an advertisement by the manufacturer in a contemporary publication.) It was an amazing structure incorporating, as it did, all of these advanced ideas at once.

Unity Temple of Oak Park, Illinois was designed with some of these same advanced systems, such as the conditioned air, and tall windows to avoid distractions. It was very different in some ways too. The construction was of poured-in-place reinforced concrete, which up to this time was strictly an

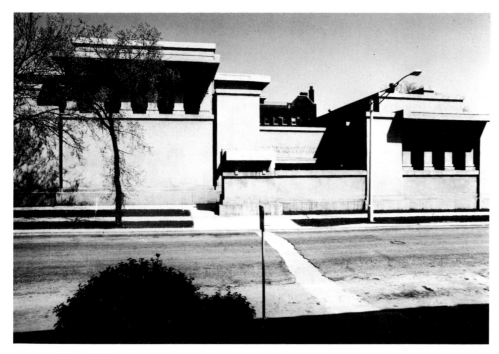

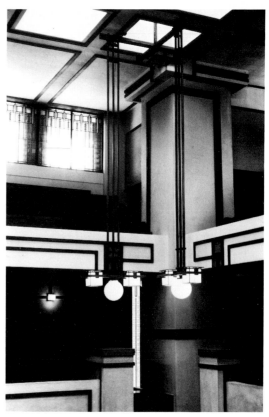

11.45-46 WRIGHT *Unity Temple* Oak Park 1905, exterior and interior detail (photographs Heinz)

Opposite above
WRIGHT *Winslow house* River Forest 1892 (photograph Heinz)

Opposite below
WRIGHT *D. D. Martin house* Buffalo 1904 (photograph Heinz)

Page 292 above
WRIGHT *Dana house* Springfield 1900, interior (photograph Heinz)

Page 292 below
WRIGHT *Unity Temple* Oak Park 1905, interior (photograph Heinz)

industrial building material. Concrete was inexpensive and because of its mass it was able to delay the environmental effects of the outside for some hours, especially helpful on Sunday summer mornings. Most important are the visual effects that Wright achieved here. Previous to this, Wright's spaces flowed in and around posts and partitions. Here he takes space around the corners with his wood trim, which also acts as a construction joint. In effect he is making the three dimensional column two dimensional with this trim, making it quite plastic and joining the space on one side with that of the other.

Early in his career Wright became fascinated with materials and their technological possibilities. An example was his work as the architectural consultant to the American Luxfer Prism Company of Chicago. Edward Waller, William Winslow and others headed the company that had its headquarters next to Wright's in Waller's Rookery Building in 1898. (Wright was able to build his Oak Park studio building with the fee he received from these services.) Wright took out many of the design patents for the patterns that were to be on the face of these four-inch glass squares. These patterns have a very Art Nouveau feeling. Some appear to be architectural details drawn in elevation. Some are very simplistic, perhaps suggesting that there was a quota of designs to be filled as part of the position; others are quite innovative for two dimensions.

Another important Art Nouveau design executed by Wright during this time is his design for the exhibition of his work at the Art Institute of Chicago in 1902. The exhibition itself included many of the pieces that have already been discussed but their arrangement here is interesting. His use of space and display techniques had not been seen up to this date. The exhibition makes it very clear that he was a master in all media and at all scales.

Wright also designed rugs and fabrics for furniture and draperies for his buildings, such as the Robie and Coonley houses. He even, like Horta, designed clothing for his wife and some of his clients' wives.

Wright was not afraid to attempt any type of design. He studied the materials to be used for the particular purpose, the technology of its production and then its execution in order that each design was perfectly suited to its purpose. He thus achieved a harmonious, colourful design which heralded the new and modern life that he was helping to bring about. Only now are we beginning to understand and use the principles that he developed. The conservation of line and integration of ornament that he learned from Froebel and Sullivan are there for us also, but we will perhaps see them more clearly if we look at them through the eyes of Wright, and closely analyse his understanding and interpretation.

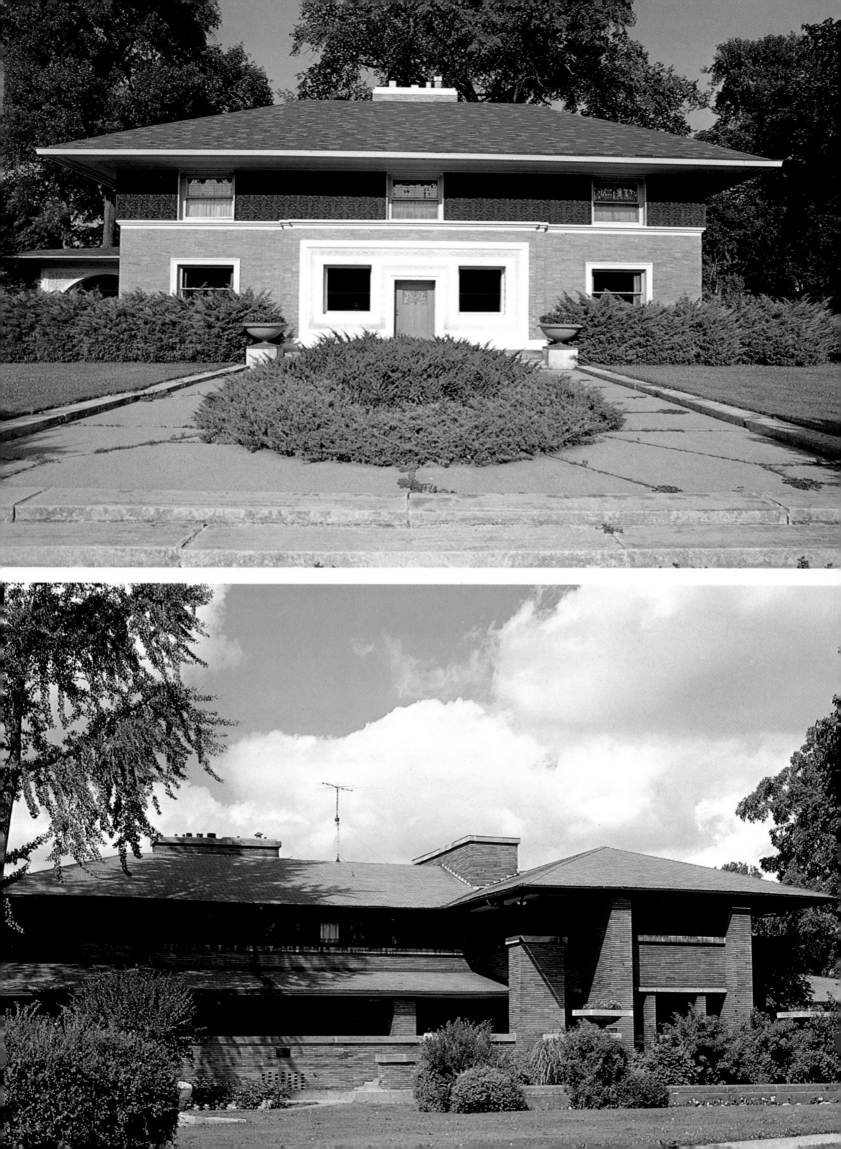

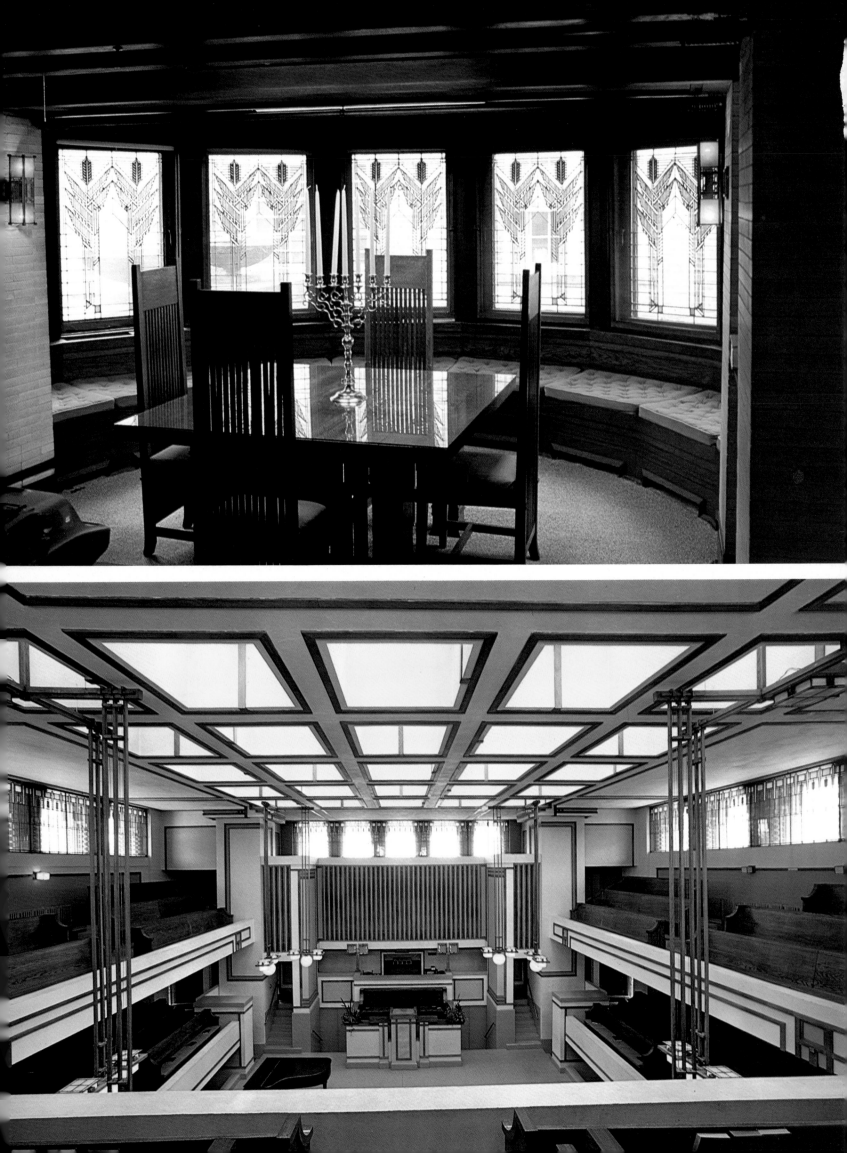

BIOGRAPHIES

Compiled by Brian Hanson and Vicky Wilson

ADLER, Dankmar (1844-1900)

Adler was born near Eisenach, Germany, and moved to Detroit, USA, with his family in 1859. In 1861 his father was offered a post as Rabbi in Chicago, where Adler received his architectural training under John Schaeffer and E. Willard Smith, and worked as a draughtsman for Augustus Bauer and O. S. Kinney. In 1871 he went into partnership with Edward Burling, and in 1881 formed the firm Adler & Sullivan with Louis Sullivan. His independent works after the dissolution of the firm in 1895 include buildings for the Morgan Park Military Academy, and the Isaiah Temple Synagogue, Chicago (1897-98). *See also Sullivan.*

ANDRE, Emile (1871-1933)

André's architectural career began with the Anciens Magasins Vaxelaire et Pignot, rue Raugraff, Nancy, built in collaboration with his father Charles, also an architect, and Eugène Vallin. His subsequent buildings in Nancy include work on the Parc de Saurupt, in collaboration with Henri Gutton, for which he designed the wrought iron entrance gates, porter's lodge and two villas, 'Les Roches' and 'Les Glycines'; 69 and 71 avenue Foch (1902-04); 92 and 92 bis quai Claude-le-Lorrain, and 30 rue du Sergent-Blandan (1903). At the 1904 Ecole de Nancy exhibition, initiated by his father, André was represented by photographs of these buildings. His later work includes a bank (1910) with interiors by Charbonnier, and 'Les Pins', rue Albin-Haller, Nancy (1912).

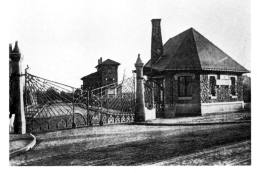

1 ANDRE *Parc de Saurupt* Nancy 1902, porter's lodge and gateway (contemporary photograph)

ASHBEE, Charles Robert (1863-1942)

Ashbee was born in London and studied history at King's College, Cambridge. In 1886 he was articled to the architect G. F. Bodley. He afterwards taught at Toynbee Hall in East London and, in 1888, founded the Guild and School of Handicraft which was dissolved in 1908 but survived in a reduced form until 1914. In 1898 he founded the Essex House Press, for which he designed a typeface. His London buildings include numbers 37 (1894, for himself), 72-73 (1897), 38-39 (1899-1901), 75 (1902) and 71 Cheyne Walk

(1912-13), and in 1905 he also converted a Norman chapel at Broad Campden into a house for himself. His interest in history led him in 1894 to found the London Survey Commission, and in 1900 he was editor of the first Parish volume of the *Survey of London*. From 1904 to 1914 Ashbee ran a school of Arts and Crafts. His work was publicised abroad in such periodicals as *Kunst und Kunsthandwerk*, and Ashbee himself travelled widely. During the First World War he was in Egypt and then from 1919 to 1923 was Civic Adviser to the Palestine Commission in Jerusalem. His other works include a chapel and additions, Wambourne Wodehouse, near Wolverhampton (1895-97); Little Coppice, Iver Heath, Bucks (c.1905); Stanstead House and Five Bells, Iver Heath, Bucks (c.1905); The Shoehorn, Orpington, Kent (c.1905); industrial cottages, Ellesmere Port, Cheshire (1906); Byways, Yarnton, Oxon (1907) and Villa San Giorgio, Taormina, Sicily (1907).

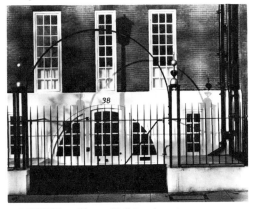

2 ASHBEE *38 Cheyne Walk* London 1899-1901, entrance detail (photograph Goulancourt)

AUSCHER, Paul (1866-n.d.)

Born in Marseilles, Auscher was admitted to the Ecole des Beaux-Arts in 1883, under Julian Guadet. He built the Banque Heine, hotels and a bazaar in Rheims and Galéries in Bordeaux. His best known building is the Félix Potin department store, rue de Rennes, Paris (1904).

BAILLIE SCOTT, Mackay Hugh (1865-1945)

Baillie Scott was born near Ramsgate in 1865 and studied at the Agricultural College in Cirencester. He soon decided on a career in architecture and was articled to C. E. Davis, the City Architect of Bath, for three years from 1886. After this he went to the Isle of Man, working for F. Saunderson. From 1893, Baillie Scott practised alone, first in the Isle of Man and from 1901 in England. While based in the Isle of Man he built the Red House, Douglas (1892-93), the Village Hall at Onchan (1897-98) and White Lodge, St Mary's Convent, Wantage, Berks (1899). His work was

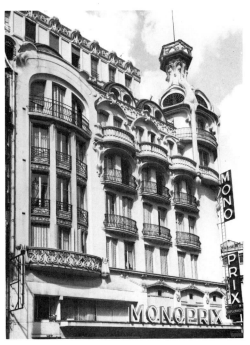

3 AUSCHER *Félix Potin department store* Paris 1904 (contemporary photograph)

widely published in America and Europe and he gained commissions for a house in Zurich (1903); for designs for Princess Marie of Romania, and for a house, 'The Close', in New Jersey (with F. E. Tappan). His winning design for the *Haus eines Kunstfreundes* competition was published by Koch in 1901. In 1905 Baillie Scott was successful in the Letchworth Cheap Cottages Competition, and consequently built Elmwood cottages on Norton Way. Between 1908 and

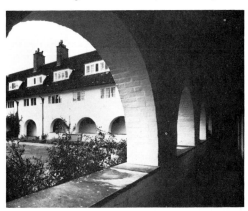

4 BAILLIE SCOTT *Hampstead Garden Suburb* London 1908-09, Waterlow Court (photograph Goulancourt)

1909 he designed houses for Hampstead Garden Suburb and he later designed Cloisters for Regent's Park. He wrote a number of articles for *The Studio*, which were compiled in his book *Houses and Gardens* (1906). Like Voysey he built very little after 1910 because of a shortage of clients.

BALSANEK, Antonín (1865-1921)

Born in Prague, Balšánek studied architecture at the Prague Polytechnic and drawing at the School of Arts and Crafts. He also studied privately in Italy and Germany. His work includes designs for a theatre in Pilsen (1899-1902); the Municipal Museum and buildings, Prague (1906-11); a theatre, Pardubice (1907) and a savings-bank, Prague (1913). He was also Professor of Architecture at the Prague Polytechnic.

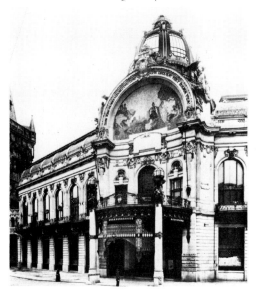

5 BALSANEK & POLIVKA *Municipal Building* Prague 1906-11 (contemporary photograph)

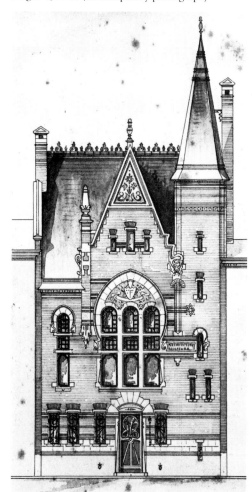

6 BASCOURT *House at corner of Dolfijnstraat and Tweelingenstraat* Antwerp c.1897, elevation

BASCOURT, Joseph (1863-1927)

Bascourt completed his architectural studies at the Antwerp Academy as a night student, working as a clerk and foreman for a brick mason to support himself. In 1889 he won notice when his design for a press club took first prize in a competition sponsored by the Société Royale des Architectes. Soon afterwards, his marriage to a daughter of the architect Vereecken introduced him into the wealthy circles of Antwerp, from whom he gained many commissions. Between 1894 and 1906 he built more than twenty-five dwellings for the Société Anonyme de la Construction du Quartier d'Est d'Anvers, the majority of which still exist. Bascourt remained faithful until his death to the eclectic style he had developed, later adapting and simplifying it to suit the needs of a clientele less fortunate than the wealthy merchants of Zurenborg.

BASILE, Ernesto (1857-1932)

Basile's introduction to architecture was through his father, an architect and designer of the Teatro Massimo, Palermo, with whom he worked during his early years. He then went on to study at the University of Palermo where his father held the Chair of Architecture – a post which was later to pass to his son. Basile also taught architecture at the Scuola di Applicazione, Palermo, was Professor of Architecture at the Scuola di Applicazione, Rome throughout the 1880s and became Director of the Reale Accademia di Belle Arti in 1897. His independent works from the late 1890s include the Villa Paterno, Palermo (1898); Villino Florio (1899-1903); Villa Igea, Palermo (1899); Monumento al Redentore, Caltanissetta (1900); pavilion for the Exhibition of Fine Arts, Palermo (1900); Palazzo Utveggio, Palermo (1901-03); Library in the Palazzo Francavilla, Palermo (1903) and the Villino Ida, Palermo (1903). He provided buildings for the Agriculture Exhibition at Palermo in 1902, and won prizes for his furniture at the 1902 Turin Exhibition and for the Mezzogiorno Halls at the fifth International Exhibition of Art in Venice (1903). His works in Rome include the Palazzo Antonio di Rudini, the Villa Carlo di Rudini, the Villino Flori and an interior in the Palazzo di Montecitorio, and he also built the theatre and Villa Lombardo, Canicatti, and designed the Palazzo Municipale in Licata.

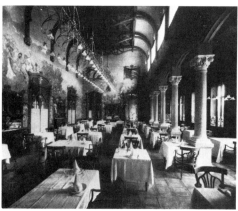

7 BASILE *Villa Igea* Palermo 1899-1903, dining room (contemporary photograph)

BAUER, Leopold (1872-n.d.)

Born in Silesia, Bauer was first destined for a career in music. In 1890, however, he went to Vienna to study architecture under Hasenauer and Wagner, during which time he met Olbrich and Hoffmann. He won a number of prizes during his student days, and visited Italy, Germany and Paris on a travelling scholarship. In 1899 he published his architectural travel sketches with a text. On his return to Vienna in the same year, he projected a theatre design and entered the competition for the Vienna Jubiläumskirche. In 1900, with Mackintosh and Baillie Scott, he entered the competition for a *Haus eines Kunstfreundes*, and his design was published by Koch. He went on to design country seats in Klostermühle, Bohemia and the Villa von Kralik at Leistungen. He was also involved in restorations – the Klin, Knetzitz and Steinitz castles in

Mähren – and produced a number of unexecuted schemes. Later in his career he concentrated more on decorative art and furnishing.

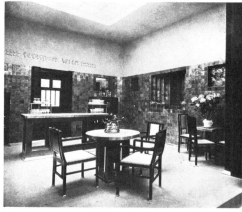

8 BAUER L. *Düsseldorf Exhibition* 1902, tea-room (contemporary photograph)

BAUER, Wilhelm Cornelis (1862-1904)

Bauer's father ran an interior decoration business in The Hague together with his eldest son under the name of 'G. H. Bauer & Zoon'. W. C. Bauer was a student first at the Craft School, and later at the Art Academy (1881-87). In 1887 he travelled in Belgium, France, Germany, Italy and Austria. In 1888 he moved to Amsterdam and joined the office of G. B. and A. Salm. In the same year he also became a member of the group Architectura et Amicitia. Between 1888 and 1893 he unsuccessfully entered eclectic designs using Gothic, Baroque and Byzantine styles in competitions for a monumental bank, a concert hall, an exhibition gallery, a theatre and a church facade, among others. He also designed a studio-house (1893) and a Volksgebouw (1894). He never realised the vision of these projects, building only on a small scale for the Walden cooperative, and, in 1898, with Johan Thorn Prikker, he designed the shop 'Arts and Crafts' in The Hague. He committed suicide in 1904.

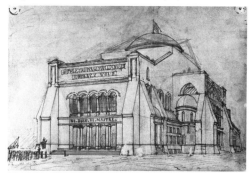

9 BAUER W. C. *Competition design for a Volksgebouw* 1894

BEHRENS, Peter (1868-1940)

Born in Hamburg into a fairly wealthy family, Behrens had an early education at the Technical School of Hamburg. In 1886 he started to attend painting classes in Karlsruhe, and in 1889 in Düsseldorf. In 1890 he visited Holland before settling in Munich. He was a member of the Munich Secession, and exhibited with them in Berlin and Vienna. He visited Italy with Harleben in 1896, and on his return the following year to Munich became one of the founders of the 'Vereinigte Werkstätten für Kunst und Handwerk', or the Munich Circle. He produced some graphic work for the publication *Pan*, and exhibited in Zurich. In 1899 he was invited by Ernst Ludwig von Hessen to Darmstadt to be Professor at the Künstlerkolonie on the Mathildenhöhe. He built his own house there at the time of the colony's exhibition in 1901, providing for it mosaic, ceramic and painted decorations. In 1902 he provided the German entrance hall for the Turin Exhibition. Throughout his life he was a respected teacher, in and out of the studio. He directed the master course at Nuremburg (1901-02), was Director of the Düsseldorf Kunstgewerbeschule (1903-07) and later taught at the Düsseldorf Academy, the Vienna Academy and the Berlin Academy. In 1910 Gropius, Mies van der Rohe and Le Corbusier were in Behrens' Berlin office. His work includes additions to the Haus Wetter an der Ruhr (1904); the Obernauer house, Saarbrücken (1905); projects for a warehouse and a crematorium, Hagen, Westfalia (1906); the Cuno house, Hagen (1908) and the Schröder house, Hagen (1909). In 1907 Emil Rathenau invited Behrens to become artistic adviser to the AEG, in which capacity he designed lighting, electrical equipment, advertising, typefaces, shop fronts and a Turbine Factory (1908-09).

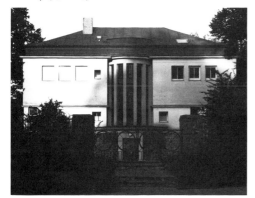

10 BEHRENS *Cuno house* Hagen 1908 (photograph Godoli)

BENDELMAYER, Bedřich (1871-1932)

Bendelmayer was a student of Ohmann, and collaborated with him on the design of the Central Hotel. He created his most notable works in the period before the First World War, for example the Hotel Europa, Wenceslas Square, Prague (1905-07) and the houses at 1-3 U prašné bráný. His later work includes the Hvězda house, Wenceslas Square, and a number of houses in the centre of Prague built during the early 1920s.

BERENGUER I MESTRES, Francesc (1866-1914)

Born in Reus, Berenguer was educated at his father Francesc's school. He left for Barcelona in 1881 to attend the Schools of Art and Architecture but due to the responsibilities of marriage he had to leave in 1887 and find work. In the mornings he worked for Augusto Font and in the afternoons for Gaudí, with whom he collaborated on enlargements of the Palau Güell, the Finca Güell buildings, the Colonia Güell, the crypt of the Colonia Güell chapel and the Park Güell. From 1902 until his death he worked under Migel Pascal in the Architect's Department of the borough of Gracia. He was the president of the Centra Moral de Gracia, for which he provided buildings in 1909 as well as a parish house for St Juan de Gracia (1900), and the restoration of the church of St Juan (1909). Independently, he also designed the altarpiece for San José de Calasanz, Montserrat; the Mercat de la Llibertad, Barcelona (1893); a house in the Park Güell occupied by Gaudí, now the Gaudí Museum (1904); the Torre Berenguer in the via Puxtet, Barcelona (1906); a chapel in Els Hostalets (1909) and the Sanctuary of San José de la Montana, Barcelona (1910-14).

BERLAGE, Hendrik Petrus (1856-1934)

Berlage was born in Amsterdam and studied at the Polytechnikum, Zurich between 1875 and 1878. He visited Italy, Austria and Germany during 1880-81, returning to Amsterdam and later forming a partnership with Thomas Sanders, which lasted until 1889. They designed warehouses, the Amsterdam Panopticum and submitted two competition designs for the Beurs in 1884 and 1885. After setting up independently Berlage produced three designs for insurance offices in the early 1890s – for De Alegemene, Amsterdam (1893), and for De Nederlanden in Amsterdam and The Hague in 1894 and 1895 – the Villa Henny, The Hague (1898), a house for the

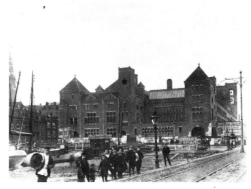

11 BERLAGE *Beurs* Amsterdam 1898-1903 (contemporary photograph)

Diamond Workers' Union, Amsterdam (1899-1900) and his masterpiece, the Amsterdam Exchange. His *Gedanken über Stil* (Thoughts on style) were published in Leipzig in 1905, and in 1908 and 1909 he produced master plans for the enlargement of The Hague and Amsterdam. Soon after this he visited America, being particularly struck by the work of H. H. Richardson, Louis Sullivan and Frank Lloyd Wright, whose work he introduced into Holland through his subsequent lectures and articles. In 1919 work began on his Gemeentemuseum in The Hague. The work was finished in 1935, one year after his death.

BERLEPSCH-VALENDAS, Hans Karl Eduard (1849-1921)

Born at St. Gall, Berlepsch-Valendas studied architecture at Zurich Polytechnic. In 1873 he was draughtsman/designer for four Ortwein contractors going under the name of 'Deutsche Renaissance'. He then spent two years in Frankfurt, moving in 1875 to the Munich Academy where he learnt history painting under Diez. In 1879 he travelled to the Balkans with the battle painter Kotzebue. He became in time a member of the Munich Secession, and due to visits to England, where he met William Morris and Walter Crane, he became interested in architecture and decorative art. His first opportunity to exhibit came in 1897 at the Annual Exhibition in Munich. The following year he exhibited two rooms, and the success of these brought him a commission for a villa – the Villa Tobler, Zurich. In 1898 he published his *Dekorative Anregungen*. In 1900 he built his own house at Maria-Eich near Planegg.

BINET, René (1866-1911)

René Binet was both an architect and a gifted watercolourist. He was a student of Laloux, studying at the Ecole des Beaux-Arts from 1892. He designed the 'Porte de la Concorde' for the Paris 1900 Exhibition and is thought to have contributed to the structural skeleton of the Grand Palais. His other works include the Maison Comédiens, the Pont-aux-Dames and the new 'Printemps' store. In 1902 he exhibited watercolours of Paris, Versailles, Tunis, Spain, Venice, Naples, Palermo, Assisi and Nuremburg at the Salon Durand-Ruel. In his later years he was the architect of Postes, Télégraphes et Téléphones.

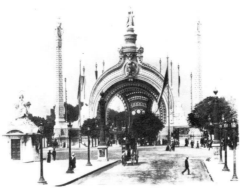

12 BINET *Paris Exhibition* 1900, 'Porte de la Concorde' (contemporary photograph)

BLEROT, Ernest (1870-1957)

Born in Brussels, Blérot studied at Saint-Louis College and Saint-Luc Academy. His work includes terraces along the rue Vanderschrick, rue Ernest Solvay and rue Saint-Boniface; his own house, 1 rue Vilain XIV (1901-08); houses on the rue du Monastère (1897), rue de Belle-Vue, boulevard Maurice Lemonnier and place L. Morichar (1899 and 1900); apartments, rue de la Vallée (1901) and a house in rue Blanche (1904). The First World War severed a large part of his market, and afterwards he devoted himself to the reconstruction of the Château d'Elzenwalle near Ypres, which belonged to his wife's family, for his own use.

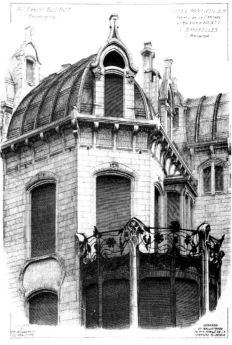

13 BLEROT 1 *rue Vilain XIV* Brussels 1901-08, drawing of the veranda and balustrade

BRIDLER, Otto (1864-1938)

Born in Altnau, Bridler attended the Kantonsschule at Frauenfeld. After one year of practical work in Basel he attended, from 1882 to 1886, the Stuttgart Polytechnic, followed by the Berlin and Munich Polytechnics. He travelled for study purposes in England, Holland, France and Germany. From 1889 he worked in association with Ernst Jung in Winterthur, designing villas and schools in Winterthur, Schaffhausen and the surrounding area, as well as the station in Winterthur, the Wald Sanatorium, factories in East Switzerland and the Volkart store, St. Gall (1904).

BROILLET, Frédéric (1861-1927)

Born at Givisiez near Fribourg and educated at local primary schools, then at St Michel's College, Fribourg (1873-78), Broillet attended the Zurich Polytechnic from 1878 to 1883, where he gained some architectural training. In 1884 he went to the Ecole Nationale et Spéciale des Beaux-Arts, Paris, where he joined the atelier of the architect Gaspard André. Following this he worked as a draughtsman and clerk of works for Ernst in Zurich (1886-89), for Bringolf in Lucerne and for Dürler in St. Gall. From 1890 to 1891 he travelled in Northern Italy, Vienna and Budapest, returning to Ernst as architect. From 1893 to 1896 he was in A. Hodler's office in Berne. He set up on his own in Fribourg in 1896, and designed small hotels, schools at Givisiez, prisons, orphanages, clinics, houses in town and country, a printers' works, a restaurant, and stations in Gruyère. He also built a large number of churches and chapels, including restorations at Cugy, Neirivue, Chevilles, Altetswill, Böesigen, Belfaux, Lechelles, Villarimboud and Malie Seychelles. His restorations of historic monuments include the church and cloister of Hauterive near Fribourg; Romont parish church; the Château de Vaulruz, Surpierre; the ramparts of Romont and Estavayer and the parish churches of Estavayer and Meyriez. From 1903 to 1911 Broillet worked in association with Charles

Wulffleff and together they won a number of competitions. Broillet was also President of the Société fribourgeoise des ingénieurs et architectes.

CAUCHIE, Paul (1875-1952)
Born at Hainaut, Cauchie studied at the Brussels Academy of Fine Arts. Primarily a designer of wall decoration, he created a sgraffito frieze 'les phases de la construction' (1900) for an apartment building in the rue Malibran, Brussels, and frescoes for buildings in the rue de Tyrol. In 1905 he took on the full role of architect by designing his own house in the rue des Francs, Etterbeck. His decorative work includes two café interiors near Brussels; the Maison Blanche, Saint-Gilles, and the 'Palais de l'alimentation', Ixelles.

CHAMBON, Alban (1847-1928)
A youthful familiarity with the Loire valley châteaux inspired Chambon's vocation as an architect. He first studied sculpture and then attended the Ecole des Beaux-Arts in Paris. In 1868 he moved to Belgium. After working for several years there as a designer, he was commissioned to build the Eden Théâtre in Brussels (1880), the Park-Schouwburg in Amsterdam (1893) and the Théâtre de la Bourse in Brussels (1885). From 1885 to 1888 he built no fewer than five theatres in London. In 1894 he directed the construction and decoration of the Métropole Hotel in Brussels, from 1894 to 1900 he built the first villas at the new beach of Westende – an enterprise of the senator and financier Otlet – and from 1898 to 1906 he transformed, enlarged and decorated the Kursaal in Ostende. Leopold II gave him his full support and honoured him with several commissions. Besides his architectural designs Chambon also created a number of urban planning projects, most notably the Mont des Arts at the request of Leopold II. The First World War, and the profound social and political changes that followed, effectively ended his career.

CHAPALLAZ, René (1881-1976)
Chapallaz studied at the Zurich Polytechnic and later collaborated with L'Eplattenier at La Chaux-de-Fonds. He supervised Charles-Edouard Jeanneret's early houses at La Chaux-de-Fonds, beginning with the Villa Fallet (1906). He took on the entire supervision of the Villa Jacquemet in 1908, Jeanneret being in Vienna at the time. In 1923-25 he designed and built, in collaboration with L'Eplattenier, the Musée des Beaux-Arts, La Chaux-de-Fonds.

COMENCINI, Giovanni Battista (c.1850-n.d.)
Born in Udine, Comencini studied in Padua and then began work in Rome. He settled in Naples in 1884, where he undertook engineering work in the Piazza del Castello. He did much important work in Naples, including interiors for the Hotel Santa Lucia (1906) and the Hôtel de Londres, and the Miccio Kiosk, Piazza San Ferdinando (1907).

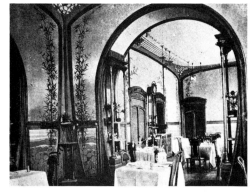

14 COMENCINI *Hotel Santa Lucia* Naples 1906, dining room (contemporary photograph)

CUYPERS, Petrus Josephus Hubertus (1827-1921)
Born in Roermond, Cuypers attended the Antwerp Academy, graduating in 1848 and working briefly for Viollet-le-Duc before setting up his own practice in Roermond in 1850. Soon afterwards he began work on the restorations of the Munsterkerk in Amsterdam, supplying many neo-Gothic church furnishings over

the following decade through his workshop 'Cuypers & Stoltenberg Co.', opened in Roermond in 1852. He built some private houses, but his early career is best measured by his churches – St Lambertus Kerk, Vegel (1854-62); St Catharina Kerk, Eindhoven (1859); St Willibrordus Kerk, Amsterdam (1864-66); St Barbara Kerk, Breda (1866) and Kerk van het Heilige Hart, Amsterdam (1873-80). He also led the restoration work on St Martin's Cathedral in Mainz between 1872 and 1875. In 1865 he transferred his practice to Amsterdam, and collaborated on later churches with the architects Eberson and Vogel. In 1876 they were successful in the competition for the Amsterdam Rijksmuseum, which was completed in 1885. In 1879 Cuypers founded a school for applied arts, the Quellinus School. His other major secular commission in Amsterdam was the Central Railway Station (in collaboration with A. L. van Gendt) of 1881-89. Cuypers was still consistently building churches into the 1880s and 1890s – in Bussum, Amsterdam (St Mary Magdalen, 1887), Delft, Nijmegen, Groningen, Hilversum (St Vitus, 1890-92), Dongen and Leeuwarden (St Boniface, 1881-89). In 1890 he began the Castle de Haer at Haarzuylen near Utrecht. His best domestic work of this period is the 'Oud Leyerhoven' on the corner of Vandelstraat and Tesselschadestraat in Amsterdam (1890).

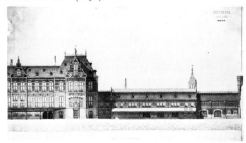

15 CUYPERS *Central Railway Station* Amsterdam 1881-89, side elevation

CZESCHKA, Carl Otto (1878-1960)
Born in Vienna, Czeschka studied under Griepenkerl at the Vienna Academy, where he subsequently taught for six years. In 1908 he took up a post as Professor at the Kunstgewerbeschule in Hamburg. He was a member of the Klimtgruppe, and in 1907 joined the Wiener Werkstätte, for whom he designed jewellery, woodcuts, silverware, enamel work and fabrics. He also designed sets and costumes for a production of Hebbels' Nibelungen, and was well-known as a graphic artist and illustrator.

D'ARONCO, Raimondo (1857-1932)
D'Aronco was born in Gemona near Udine, spent some years in Austria apprenticed to a stonemason at Graz, then studied at the Accademia di Belle Arti in Venice under Giacomo Franco from 1871, obtaining his diploma of architecture. In 1882 he projected a design for the Tenaglia gate in Milan, and in 1887 provided decorations for the National Exhibition at Venice. For the competition for a monument to Victor Emmanuel II in Rome in 1884 he entered a project which was awarded a gold medal and was exhibited at Turin in 1902. In 1892 the Sultan Abdu'l-hamid summoned him to Constantinople to take part in a project for an Ottoman exhibition. He was appointed the Sultan's chief architect four years later, designing the Imperial Palace Archives at Yildiz (1896); buildings for the guards corps at Quai di Galata (1896); the Torre del Suli at Beyoğlu (1896) and the Bazar di Charité in Constantinople (1897). For the 1902 Turin Exhibition, which he directed from Turkey, D'Aronco provided a main entrance, administrative offices, auditorium, coffee house, photographic pavilion, automobile pavilion and a Rotunda. He also provided pavilions at Udine the following year. The cultural cross references continued in a Viennese-inspired mosque at Galata (1903) and in the buildings he designed in Turkey during the remaining five years of his stay, including the Santoro house in Constantinople. Returning to Italy in 1908, and beginning work on Udine Town Hall in 1909, D'Aronco passed his remaining days with less flair. He died in San Remo.

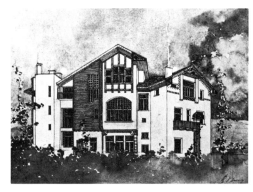

16 D'ARONCO *Casa D'Aronco* Turin 1903, perspective drawing

DE BAUDOT, Anatole (1834-1915)
A pupil of Labrouste and Viollet-le-Duc, de Baudot's work shows the rationalist influence of the latter blended with an equal feeling for the Gothic. He was opposed to the system of education fostered by Guadet at the Ecole des Beaux-Arts, and remained in his teaching a faithful disciple of Viollet-le-Duc. He taught History of Architecture at the Musée des Monuments Historiques for twenty-five years, and was one time Vice-President of the Comité des Monuments Historiques. His work includes the Rambouillet church (1869); St Jean de Montmartre, place des Abbesses, Paris (1894-1903) and the Lycée Lakanal, Sceaux.

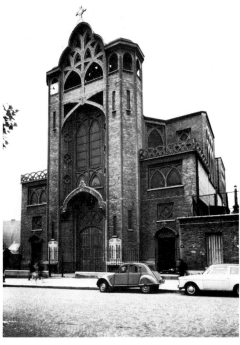

17 DE BAUDOT *St Jean de Montmartre* Paris 1894-1903

DE BAZEL, Karel Petrus Cornelius (1869-1928)
Born at Den Helder, De Bazel moved with his family to The Hague in 1873, where he studied as an apprentice joiner. In the evenings he attended the Academy of Fine Arts where Vogel, Faber and Mialaret were teaching. In 1888 he became draughtsman to J. F. van Nieukerken and one year later assistant to P. J. H. Cuypers. Very soon he was directing construction on Cuypers' St Vitus church, Hilversum, which exertion cost him his health in 1892. Throughout this time he entered competitions and built some houses and villas. He rejoined Cuypers after a break for recuperation in 1892, and in the following year visited England with J. L. M. Lauweriks, whom he had met in Cuypers' office. He remained with Cuypers until 1895, attending evening classes at the Rijksacademie. The break came when he and Lauweriks joined the Theosophist Union and contributed woodcuts to the related

publication *Licht und Waarheid* which offended the Catholic Cuypers. Together De Bazel and Lauweriks formed their own 'Atelier for architecture, arts and crafts and decorative arts' and though their built work is negligible, their two competition designs of 1895 for a public baths and a general library, and the scheme of 1896-97 for an architects' association building were highly influential. They also produced graphic work, interior designs, furniture designs and a design for a set of postage stamps. From 1897 until 1902 they held classes at the old American Hotel in the evenings under the auspices of Vâhana during which time De Bazel also taught at the School of Arts and Crafts in Haarlem. Later in his career, after leaving Lauweriks, De Bazel's work tends towards monumentality – the 'Oud Bussum' dairy farm (1903); the plan for a World Capital at The Hague (1905); the De Maerle house (1906); the competition design for Rotterdam Town Hall (1913); offices at Arnheim (1912-13). His last major work was for the Nederlandsche Handel Maatschappij offices in Amsterdam (1919-26).

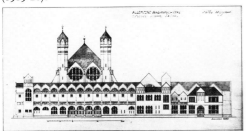

18 DE BAZEL *Competition project for a public baths complex* 1895, side elevation

DEININGER, Wunibald (1879-n.d.)

The son of Julius Deininger, the head of the Board of Works in Vienna, Wunibald was educated at the special school of Professor Luntz for one year before attending Otto Wagner's classes at the Academy of Fine Arts from 1899 to 1902, when he was awarded the Rome Prize. From 1900 he worked in collaboration with his father Julius, entering a series of competitions after 1901, and winning a number of prizes in them. His work includes country houses and villas (1900-04); a house for J. E. Steiner in Fulnek and a villa for the chemist Ptaczek. At the Vienna Annual Exhibition of 1910 he exhibited a stand for the Allgemeines Gewerbe group.

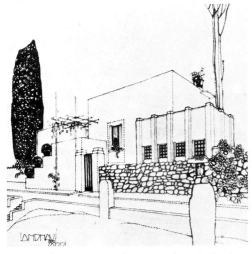

19 DEININGER *Project for a country house in Capri* 1903

DE KLERK, Michel (1884-1923)

Architect, artist and draughtsman, De Klerk was born in Amsterdam and was leader of the Amsterdam School of architects. He is best known for his low cost housing around Amsterdam in a style based on vernacular Dutch building, in traditional materials, with expressionistic tendencies. As an eleven year old, a drawing by him of one of his teachers led to an interest being taken in him by the architect Eduard Cuypers, nephew of P. J. H. Cuypers. De Klerk was in Cuypers' office from the age of fourteen until 1910,

with only one interruption. He also attended evening classes at the Industrieschool under B. W. Wiefink. During 1910 and 1911 he travelled in Scandinavia. His early works include unexecuted projects for a railway station (1906), a sports club (1907), four workers' houses (1908) and a seaside hotel (1909). In Amsterdam West De Klerk built in 1915, 1918 and 1921 the Eigen Haard housing, Zaanstraat, and in Amsterdam Zuid he built terraced houses on Henriette Ronnerplatz.

DOMENECH I MONTANER, Lluis (1850-1923)

Domènech was born in Barcelona, and joined the political group La Jove Catalunya at the age of nineteen. In 1873 he qualified as an architect from the University of Madrid, and soon became known through his competition schemes with Vilaseca for a monument to Clave and a building for the Instituciones Provinciales de la Instrucción Publica. In 1875 he began to teach at the Barcelona School of Architecture. Domènech was made President of the Lliga de Catalunya in 1887, of the Unio Catalunya in 1892, of Jocs Floral in 1895, and of the Ateneo Barcelones for three sessions from 1898 to 1906. In 1904 he temporarily gave up his active political life, leaving the Lliga. In 1900 he became Director of the Barcelona School of Architecture. Domènech designed a Café-Restaurant and an International Hotel for the Barcelona Universal Exhibition of 1888, when he also restored and converted the Town Hall for the use of the Royal Family, and designed the lay-out of the via Transversal. Following this he built the Palau Montaner (1893) and the Casa Thomas (1895-99), both on the calle Mallorca; the Palau de la Musica Catalana (1905-08); Casa Lléo Morera (1905); Casa Fuster (1908-11) and the Hospital de San Pablo, Avenida (1902-12), all in Barcelona. In Reus he built the Pere Mata Institute (1897-1919); Casa Rull (1900); Casa Navàs (1901) and Casa Gasull. He also built the Gran Hotel, Palma (1902-12), and some works for the Marqués de Comillas at Comillas. He was involved in the restoration of the Castle of Santa Florentina at Canet de Mar, and the Casa Solà at Olot. In 1905 he published his *Estudis politics*. He died in Barcelona and is buried at Canet de Mar.

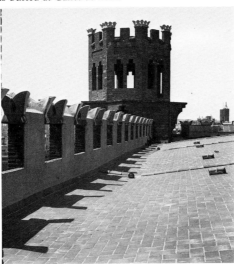

20 DOMENECH *Café-Restaurant* Barcelona 1888, detail of roof

DRYAK, Alois (1872-1932)

A pupil and later a collaborator of Ohmann, Dryák was Professor of Decorative Architecture at the Prague School of Decorative Arts. He completed Ohmann's Central Hotel after the latter's death, and in 1912 built a gymnastic stadium in Prague.

DU BOIS D'AUBERVILLE, Maurice-Paul (1863-n.d.)

Born in Paris, Du Bois d'Auberville entered the Ecole des Beaux-Arts in 1886 as a pupil of Pascal, and later worked as an architect at Paris and Versailles. His work includes hotels, villas and apartment blocks, sometimes in collaboration with Bossis.

DUTERT, Charles-Louis-Ferdinand (1845-1906)

Dutert was born in Douai, and came to Paris to enroll at the Ecole des Beaux-Arts, where he was later to make a brilliant impression as a teacher. He was an equally brilliant student, obtaining the Grand Prix de Rome in 1869. Collaborating with the engineers Contamin, Pierron and Charton, he designed the 'Galerie des Machines' for the Paris Exhibition (1889) for which he received a Lauréat. He also worked on the Musée d'Histoire Naturelle, rue Buffon during the 1890s, producing a notable design for the Gallery of Paleontology.

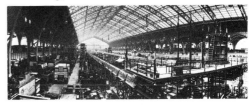

21 DUTERT *Paris Exhibition* 1889, 'Galerie des Machines' (contemporary photograph)

ECKMANN, Otto (1865-1902)

Eckmann was born in Hamburg and studied at the Kunstgewerbeschule there and at Nuremburg, and later at the Academy in Munich, the city where much of his short-lived artistic activity was to be centred. At first purely a painter, in 1894 he began to study the techniques of Japanese colour printing, sold off all his old paintings and concentrated on Japanese influenced applied arts. His first works in the new style were prints of swans on water backgrounds of different shades. He was a contributor to the Munich *Jugend* and provided illustrations for *Pan* between 1895 and 1897. In 1897, the year in which he became involved with the foundation of the Munich Circle, he taught decorative art at the Berlin Kunstgewerbeschule. He also designed some furniture.

EIFFEL, Gustave (1832-1923)

Eiffel was born in Dijon, and was originally marked for a career in chemistry although he went on to study at the Ecole des Arts et Manufactures, and then became an engineer. In the years after leaving the Ecole and before setting up on his own in 1866-67 he worked with various engineers, including Nougier and Koechlin. During the 1870s he specialised in railway bridges, employing the lattice construction by

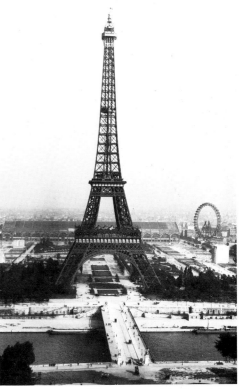

22 EIFFEL *Tour Eiffel* Paris 1889, originally built for the Paris Universal Exhibition of the same year

which he was to revolutionise steel construction in the Ponte Mario Pio at Porto, Portugal (1877-78) and the Ponte Truyère at Garabit (1880-84), among others. Eiffel also designed the metal framework which holds up the figure of Liberty by Bartholdi (1885), and four years later his 300 metre 'tour de force' appeared at the Paris Universal Exhibition. His last years, from 1910 onwards, were spent studying the action of wind on high structures.

ELMSLIE, George Grant (1871-1952)

Born in Aberdeenshire in 1871, Elmslie came to Chicago in 1885, joining the firm of Adler & Sullivan around 1889. For a time he shared an office with Frank Lloyd Wright. When Sullivan left Adler in 1895 Elmslie became his assistant and a lot of Sullivan's domestic work of the post-Adler years must be attributed to him. His own work includes a project for a dwelling for Ellis Wainwright, St Louis (c.1898); a project for a house for Mrs N. F. McCormick, Lake Forest, Illinois (c.1898-1900) and his first executed commission, a residence for his brother-in-law, W. G. H. Miller, Pitts, Pennsylvania (1907, designed 1904). Sullivan's Babson and Bradley houses of these years were executed by Elmslie, and they became prototypes for some of his later work with William Gray Purcell, from 1909. Also prototypical for Purcell & Elmslie were the small-town banks built with Sullivan – the Merchants' Bank of Hector, Minnesota (1907) and the National Farmers' Bank, Owatonna, Minnesota. Elmslie practised alone from 1920, and had a fruitful career in domestic and other work.

ENDELL, August (1871-1925)

Endell was born in Berlin, where his father was Oberbaudirektor at the Ministerium für öffentliche Arbeit. In 1891 he graduated from the Askanische Gymnasium in Berlin and went first to Tübingen and then to the University of Munich, where he studied aesthetics and philosophy. In 1897 he was one of the co-founders of the Vereinigte Werkstätten, contributing a relief frieze to their first exhibition. His work includes the Atelier Elvira, Munich (1897); Buntes Theater, Berlin (1901); Sanatorium, Föhr (1898); Festsäle, Rosenthalestrasse, Berlin (1905-06); houses in Berlin on the Steinplatz (1906-07), Kastanienallee (1907), Eichenallee (1908) and Akazienallee (1909); Trabrennbahn (grandstand), Mariendorf (1910-11); country house, Potsdam (1910-11), and the Puma Stiefel shoe shop, Berlin (1910-11). Due to illness, Endell's later years were increasingly devoted to teaching. In 1904 he opened the Schule für Formenkunst in Berlin and in 1914 was short-listed for the post of Director of the future Bauhaus. In 1918 he became Director of the Akademie für Kunst und Kunstgewerbe, Breslau.

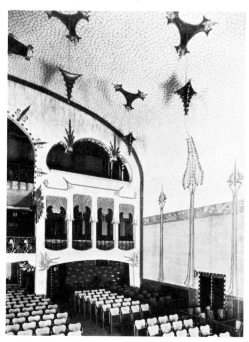

23 ENDELL *Buntes Theater* Berlin 1901, auditorium (contemporary photograph)

FABIANI, Max (1865-1947)

Born in Kobdil, Fabiani studied at the Technische Hochschule in Vienna from 1882 to 1889, receiving a diploma in engineering and, in 1892, a doctorate. From 1890 to 1892 he was also employed as assistant at Graz Technische Hochschule and was working on university buildings. He then travelled through Greece, Italy, Germany, France, Belgium and England before returning to Otto Wagner's studio in Vienna, where he assisted on the building of the Stadtbahn. He was with Wagner for two years, during which time he produced a plan for the rebuilding of the city of Ljubljana, Yugoslavia, destroyed by an earthquake in 1895. In 1900 he produced the first master plan for the city, and in 1901 built an infirmary there. Over the years he was to add other buildings to Ljubljana – the Hribar house, Wienerstrasse (1903); Krispar house, Gerichtsplatz (1903); Pfarrhaus, St Jakob (1906) and the Palais Bamberg (1907). After leaving Wagner, Fabiani became König's assistant at the Vienna Technische Hochschule (1896-98), and he later built in Vienna three tax offices, Wieden Starhemberggasse and Favorizenplatz (1898, 1899 and 1900); 4 Favorizenplatz; a monumental entrance project for Vienna general cemetery (1898); the Portois & Fix apartments, Ungargasse (1899-1900); Artaria & Co., Wienkohlmarkt (1901); Anna Riess house (1900); Haus der Libertas, Piaristengasse (1903) and Iglhaus, Wien Wildpretmarkt (1908). In 1910 he became Professor of Ornament and Interior Design at the Vienna Hochschule.

FANTA, Josef (1856-1954)

Born in Sudoměřice, near Tábor, Fanta studied at the Prague Polytechnic and then in Italy. After his studies he started to work at the design studio of the National Theatre in Prague, designing the decoration of the auditorium and the lounges. In 1881 he became assistant to Profesor Schulz at the Prague Polytechnic and in 1909 became himself a professor. Buildings he designed include the Central Railway Station in Prague, a house for the choral group Hlahol on the Gottwald embankment, an observatory at Ondrejov, numerous houses in Prague and the surrounding area, and a monument commemorating the battle of Slavkov (1907).

FELGEL, Oskar (1876-n.d.)

Born in Vienna and a pupil at the Academy of Fine Arts from 1893 to 1900, Felgel built a large number of country houses in the South Tyrol, a synagogue in Trieste, and produced a scheme for a Stipendistheim in Rome (1901). With E. Felgel he founded a home for artists in Hietzing bei Wien.

FELLERER, Max (1889-1957)

Born in Linz, Fellerer studied at the Technical University in Vienna and then at the Vienna School of Arts and Crafts. From 1919 to 1926 he had a post in Hoffmann's office, and from 1926 to 1932 he worked with Holzmeister. He designed numerous buildings for the Vienna City Council, including the reconstruction of the Houses of Parliament (1955-56), as well as houses on Geyschlägergasse 2-12 (1928-29), Woinovichgasse 6-8 (1930), Moissigasse 21 (1930) and Karl Renner-Ring 3 (1955-56). He also built the open-air baths at Gänsehäufel (1948-49) and did some work in Linz. A teacher for most of his life, Fellerer's posts include Professor at the Academy of Fine Arts, Vienna (1932-34), Director of the Kunstgewerbeschule (1934-38) and President of the Academy of Applied Arts (1946-55).

FENOGLIO, Pietro (1867-1927)

Fenoglio was born in Turin, and produced over 100 buildings there, including industrial buildings; the Besozzi house, Corso Siccardi (1905); Villa Raby, Viale de Francia (1905); Casa Fenoglio (1902-03) and Villa Scott (1902). He was also one of the promoters of the 1902 Turin Exhibition. At the outbreak of the First World War he gave up architecture for banking.

GARNIER, Jean Louis Charles (1825-1898)

Born in the rue Mouffetard in Paris, Garnier attended the Ecole des Beaux-Arts under H. Lebas, gaining the Grand Prix de Rome in 1848. After this he went to the Mediterranean for a few years, returning in 1853. In

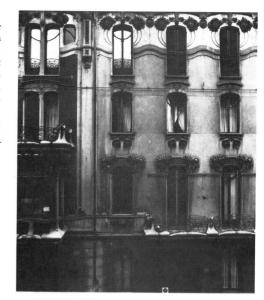

24 FENOGLIO *Rossi Galateri house* Turin 1903, facade detail (photograph Godoli)

1860 he obtained the commission for his most important work, the Paris Opéra, which was to take fifteen years to complete, and to cost fifty million francs. His works after this include a casino at Monte Carlo (1878-81); his own house at Bordighera (1872) and the Cercle de la Librairie, boulevard Saint-Michel (1878). In 1889 at the Paris Exhibition he exhibited an 'Histoire de l'Habitation Humaine'. Garnier was made Grand Officier of the Légion d'Honneur in 1895, three years before his death.

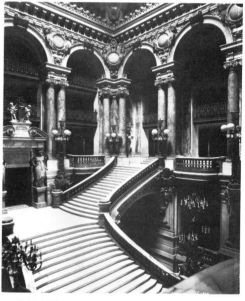

25 GARNIER *Paris Opéra* Paris 1860-75, grand staircase

GAUDI I CORNET, Antoni (1852-1926)

Gaudí was born in Reus, where he was educated in the school run by Francesc Berenguer, the father of one of his later collaborators. After this he went to the Convent of San Francisco, Tarragona to study for his Bachillerato, which he gained in 1869. He then went to Barcelona for pre-University training at the Convent of the Carmelites. In 1873 he entered the new School of Architecture in Barcelona, where he remained, doing extra-curricular work as a draughtsman to help finance his course, until 1878, when he set up practice in the calle del Call, Barcelona. His early work includes fencing and monumental gates for the Parque de la Ciudadela (1875-77) in collaboration with Fontseré; pews and other furnishings for the Pantheon chapel of the Marqués de Comillas, Santander (1878); a machine shed for Obrera Mat020nense and a showcase for the glove manufacturer Comella, exhibited in Paris in 1878 with Gaudí's housing project for

Mataró. In 1879 Gaudí was the winner of a competition for street lamps in Barcelona, now in the Plazas Real and del Palacio. Between 1879 and 1883 he received several commissions from local religious associations, designing altar decorations, lighting and furniture. His secular works, mainly houses in and around Barcelona, include Casa Vicens (1883-85); 'El Capricho', Comillas, Santander (1883-85); Los Botines, Léon (1891); Bishop's Palace, Astorga (1887-93); Casa Calvet (1898); Park Güell (1900-14); Palau Güell (1885-90); Bellesguard (1900-02); remodelling of the Casa Batlló (1904-06) and the Casa Milá (1906-10). In 1883 Martorell recommended that Gaudí succeed Villar as architect of the Sagrada Familia, Barcelona, and after 1910 Gaudí renounced secular commissions to concentrate on this and on the Colonia Güell chapel, the crypt of which was built between 1908 and 1914.

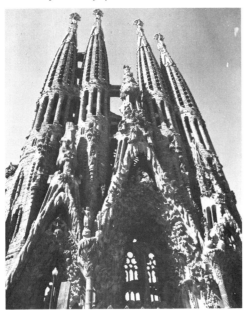

26 GAUDI *Sagrada Familia* Barcelona 1883- , facade detail

GESSNER, Franz (b. 1879) and Hubert (1871-1943)
Brothers, born in Wallachisch-Klobouk, they were both at one time in Wagner's studio in Vienna, Hubert in the 1890s and Frantz in 1907. Together they produced work influenced by their common master – workers' housing, Vienna (1903); Hotel Schlesischer Hof, Troppau (1905); Hotel Heinrichishof, Neutit-schein (1906) and the 'Vorwarts' building, Vienna (1910), among others.

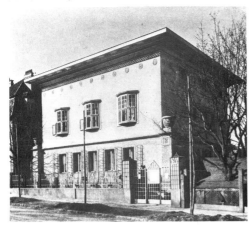

27 GESSNER F. & H. *Haus Gessner* Vienna 1907 (contemporary photograph)

GODWIN, Edward William (1833-1886)
Born in Bristol, the son of a decorator, Godwin was first articled to the Bristol City Surveyor William Armstrong. He left Armstrong in 1854 to set up his own practice, and later went into partnership with Henry Crisp. The firm built town halls at North-ampton (1860-64) and Congleton (1864-67), Dromore Castle, Limerick (1866-73) and Glenbergh Towers, Kerry (1867-70) as well as schools, houses and ware-houses in and around Bristol. After the death of his wife in 1865, Godwin moved to London where he came into contact with Gothic revivalists and estab-lished a friendship with Whistler, for whom he built a house on Tite Street (1877-78). Little of his work there remains. In his last years he designed theatrical costumes and sets, Japanese inspired furniture made by Watt, assisted Burges in his Law Courts design, and R. W. Edis in his designs for a Berlin House of Parliament. He also built the Fine Arts Society premises on Bond Street and a studio for Princess Louise at Kensington Palace.

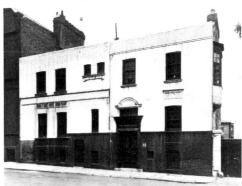

28 GODWIN *Whistler's house* London 1877-78

GREENE, Charles Sumner (1868-1957) and Henry Mather (1870-1954)
Born in Cincinnati to a physician, the Greenes spent their early childhood in Virginia, moving later to St Louis where their father enrolled them in his friend Professor Calvin Woodward's experimental Manual Training High School. They then attended the Massachusetts Institute of Technology, graduating in 1891 after an academic training. After some years in Boston they settled with their parents in Pasadena. Their house designs, comprising the major part of their output, are in a version of the stick style, relying on finely wrought craftsmanship – all of which was supervised on site by the designers. They include the Cuthbertson house (1902); the Bandini house (1903); the Gamble house (1908); the Blacker house (1907) and the Thorsen house (1909). The First World War affected their market and the Spanish Colonial vogue emanating from the San Diego Exhibition also affected their popularity. In 1914 Charles retired to Carmel, Henry continuing to practise alone until the 1930s.

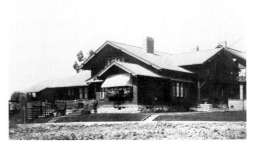

29 GREENE & GREENE *Henry M. Greene house* Pasadena 1904 (contemporary photograph)

GUIMARD, Hector-Germain (1867-1942)
Born in Paris, Guimard was a student of Genuys at the Ecole des Beaux-Arts, and later of de Baudot. In 1895 he was awarded a travelling scholarship which enabled him to visit England and Belgium. From 1894 to 1898 he was himself teaching at the Ecole des Arts Décoratifs. He was designing from the late 1880s – a Café-Restaurant on the quai d'Auteuil (1888); the electricity pavilion at the 1889 Paris Exhibition; a number of villas and private houses between 1891 and 1895, and the Ecole du Sacré Coeur, avenue de la Frillière, Paris (1895). His first work in a recognisably Art Nouveau manner was the Castel Béranger, rue Lafontaine, Paris (1895-97) and this was followed by the Maison Coilliot, Lille (1897); the Humbert de Romans concert hall (1898-1900); the Maison Canivet and the Villa 'La Bluette' at Hermanville (1898-1901); the Castel Henriette, Sèvres (1899-1903); the 'Châlet Blanc', Sceaux (1908); Hôtel Guimard (1909) and a synagogue, rue Pavée (1913). He is best remembered for his work on the Paris Metro, for which he provided the plant-like entrance canopies in cast iron in 1900. In the 1920s he built some speculative apart-ments, and his last important commission was for the 'Mairie du Village Français' exhibited at the Paris Exhibition of 1925. In 1930, due to the actions of his old friend Frantz Jourdain, he was given a position on the Comité de l'Architecture d'Aujourd'hui. He went to New York in 1938 and died there four years later.

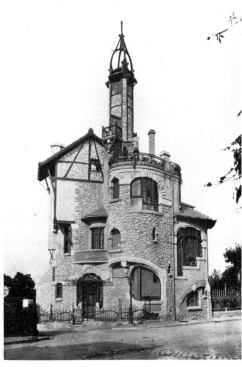

30 GUIMARD *Castel Henriette* Sèvres 1899-1903 (contemporary photograph)

HAMESSE, Paul (1877-1956)
Hamesse was born in Brussels and was at one time a pupil of Paul Hankar. His work includes a studio for the painter Potvin, rue Charles-Quint (1898); a project for a house at Schaerbeck (1899); two apartment buildings with shops, place Fontainas and rue du Lombard (1905); 17 place Antoine Delporte (1907); 17 rue Meyerbeer (1908) and a house and studio on the Champs Elysées (1909). Hamesse often worked in partnership with his brothers Georges and Léon, both painters.

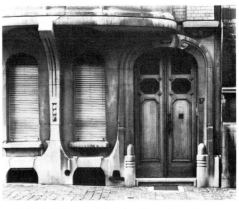

31 HAMESSE *17 rue Meyerbeer* Brussels 1908, entrance detail (photograph Wieser)

HANKAR, Paul (1861–1901)

Born at Frameries, Hankar studied and worked with Henri Beyaert from 1879 until the latter's death in 1894. Together they worked on the restoration and decoration of the church at Everberg, Brabant. His independent works include the house for the painter Ciamberlani, rue Defacq, Ixelles (1897); the Zegers-Regnard building, avenue Louise, Brussels (1894); the Peeters Pharmacy, rue Lebeau; the Niguet Shirt Shop, rue Royale (1899); the Senec-Sturbelle Chocolate Shop, rue Neuve; Magasins Clasens, rue de l'Ecuyer (1896); P. Henrion Jewellers' shopfront, rue Mathieu, Namur (1896); a house for M. Zegers, avenue Louise (1897); Maison Kleyer, Brussels (1898); Grand Hôtel, Brussels (1896); residence and studio for the painter Bartholomé, Etterbeck (1898) and for the painter Janssens, rue Defacq, Ixelles (1898); house, rue Antoine Bréart, Saint-Gilles (1898); Compagnie Générale de Céramiques d'Architecture, quai à la Houille (1899); country cottage and studio for the sculptor Philippe Wolfers, La Hulpe (1900). Hankar left an unfinished scheme for a 'Cité des Artistes' when he died in Brussels. For a time he also worked in partnership with Adolphe Crespin.

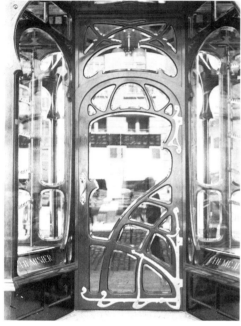

32 HANKAR *Niguet Shirt Shop* Brussels 1899, entrance detail (contemporary photograph)

HENNEBIQUE, François (1842–1921)

Hennebique was a pioneer in the use of reinforced concrete and patented a system of employing the

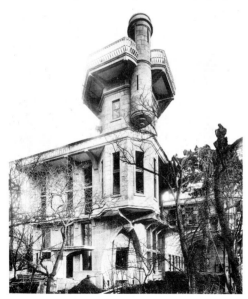

33 HENNEBIQUE *Own house* Bourg-la-Reine 1904 (contemporary photograph)

material in 1892. He set up his own firm in 1867 and gained experience of all types of construction. His first use of reinforced concrete was in 1880, and the first building under the perfected system was the Charles VI Spinning Mills at Tourcoing (1893). In the 1890s Hennebique built a 100ft span bridge at Viggen in Switzerland, the first reinforced concrete bridge (1894), and a curved staircase using the same material in the Petit Palais, Paris (1898). He collaborated with a number of architects in the early years of this century – with E. Arnaud on apartments in rue Danton (1900), with Charles Klein on apartments in rue Claude Chalin (1902), with Perret on 25 bis rue Franklin (1903–04) and with P. Auscher on his Félix Potin store in the rue de Rennes (1904).

HERTLING, Léon (1867–1948)

Born in Fribourg, Hertling studied from 1879 to 1884 at St Michel's college there, in the technical section. From 1884 to 1885 he studied at the Winterthur Technical School and then at the Zurich Polytechnic until 1879 when he got a job in Zurich. He set up his own office in Fribourg in 1890. There he designed banks and stores, including the Weissenbach building of 1902, rue de Lausanne. In Gambach he built a girls' school (in collaboration with Camoletti) and an Ecole Reformée (in collaboration with Hemann) as well as houses and villas in the new quarters of Gambach and Pérolles. With Bracher and Widmer he produced schemes for a Bibliothèque Cantonale and a university. From 1903 to 1907 a member of the Fribourg town council, Hertling was also Director of the Department of Public Works.

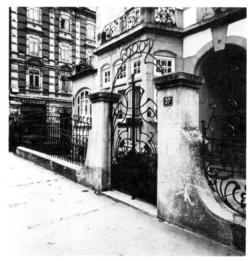

34 HERTLING *Villa Sallin* Fribourg 1904–05 (photograph Collomb)

HOFFMANN, Josef (1870–1956)

Born in Pirnitz, Moravia, Hoffmann moved to Vienna in 1892 to study at the Academy under Hasenauer and Wagner. In 1895 he was awarded the Prix de Rome, and spent the following year in Italy, joining the studio of Otto Wagner on his return to Vienna. In 1895 he joined the Siebenerclub, and in 1897 was co-founder of the Vienna Secession, designing a room for the 1898 Secession Exhibition, the Max Klinger room for the exhibition of 1902 and the Klimt exhibition in 1903. His other early works include a house on the Bergerhöhe (1899), the 'Apollo' candle shop (1899–1900) and a stand for the Kunstgewerbeschule at the Paris Exhibition of 1900. During this period Hoffmann also worked in the studio of Franz Krásny. Between 1902 and 1904 he produced his first designs for villas – for Henneberg, Moser, Moll and Spitzer on the Hohe Warte, Vienna. In 1903 he founded the Wiener Werkstätte with Koloman Moser. His mature works include the Palais Stoclet, Brussels (1905), the Purkersdorf Sanatorium (1903–05) and villas such as Beer-Hoffmann (1906), Ast (1909–10), Skywa (1913–15) and Bernatzik (1911–14). In 1912 Hoffmann founded the Austrian Werkbund, and his subsequent work includes Haus Knips (1923–24); houses for the Vienna City Council on Stromstrasse (in collaboration with Peter Behrens, 1924), Prager Strasse (1925), Laxenburger Strasse (1931) and Silber-

gasse (1949–53); the Haus Ast, Velden (1923) and a monument to Otto Wagner (1930). He also collaborated in the exhibitions Kunstschau Wien (1909), Paris 1911 and 1925, for which he provided the Austrian Pavilion, and the Cologne Werkbund Exhibition of 1914. Hoffmann taught for most of his life, and was a Professor at the Kunstgewerbeschule, Vienna from 1898 to 1941.

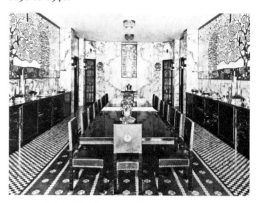

35 HOFFMANN *Palais Stoclet* Brussels 1905, dining room (contemporary photograph)

HOLDEN, Charles Henry (1875–1960)

Born in Bolton and educated locally and in St Helens, Holden was introduced through his brother-in-law into the architectural office of E. W. Leeson in Manchester. At the same time he took classes at Manchester School of Art and Technical College, winning prizes for his studies in brickwork and for the student competitions he entered. After a brief period with Jonathan Simpson in Bolton he came in 1897 to London as assistant and pupil of C. R. Ashbee. In 1899 he joined Percy Adams, a well-known hospital designer, and worked on the Newcastle Infirmary competition scheme, the Belgrave Hospital, Kennington (1903) and the Midhurst Sanatorium. In 1907 he became a partner. Other buildings include the Law Society extension (1902), the Bristol Library (1905–06) and the British Medical Association Building, Strand and Agar Street (1906). In 1915 Holden was a founder member of the Design and Industries Association, and in March of that year he met Frank Pick, for whom he was to design a series of underground stations in London in the 1920s and 30s. In 1928 he built the London Transport Headquarters at 55 Broadway, employing Jacob Epstein and a number of other sculptors including Henry Moore. His last executed work was for the University of London.

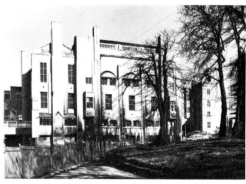

36 HOLDEN *Central Reference Library* Bristol 1905–06 (photograph Benton)

HOLUB, Adolf Otto (1882–n.d.)

Born in Vienna, Holub studied at the Staatsgewerbeschule under Brenek and at the Kunstgewerbeschule. In 1900 he organised a course in modern art for Josef Hoffmann, and he continued to teach until 1906. Holub worked for various firms in Vienna and also did designs for the Wiener Werkstätte. In 1909 he produced a town plan for Amstetten. He participated in several exhibitions and was responsible for the organisation of the Jubilee Exhibition in Steyr (1908), the Breakfast Room at the Kuntschau Wien 1908, an altarpiece and belltower for the Vienna Exhibition of Church Architecture (1912) and interiors for the

Kriegsausstellung Wien 1917. From 1913 he taught at the Kunstgewerbeschule at Essen an der Ruhr. Although Holub built some country houses, he was primarily interested in interior decoration and all areas of Arts and Crafts, designing carpets, fabrics, jewellery and metalwork. He also did some church decoration.

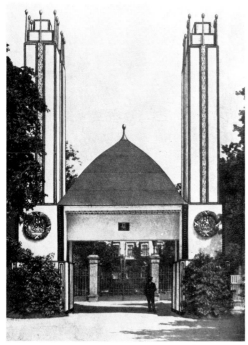

37 HOLUB *Country Crafts Exhibition* 1908, entrance pavilion (contemporary photograph)

HOPPE, Emil (1876-1957)
In the Wagnerschule from 1898 to 1901, Hoppe later collaborated with Wagner and a fellow pupil Schönthal. His work includes dwellings and commercial structures in Vienna; the Ludwig family tomb; villas and country houses, and a synagogue in Trieste. *See also Kammerer and Schönthal.*

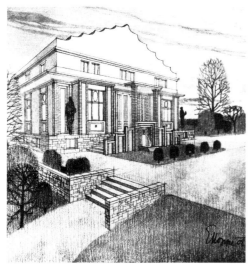

38 HOPPE *Project for a villa* 1908

HORTA, Victor (1861-1947)
Horta was born in Ghent, and after studying music for one year at the Ghent Conservatoire, he enrolled at the Ghent Académie des Beaux-Arts where for three years he studied drawing and architecture. In 1878 he was in Paris working with the architect/decorator Jean Dubuysson. In 1880 he went to the Brussels Académie des Beaux-Arts. After graduation Horta joined the office of Alphonse Balat, the reputed neo-classical architect, and his first independent works were three houses in rue des Douze Chambres, Ghent. In 1887 he entered a competition for the Museum of Natural History in Brussels, and won the Grand Prix de Concours at the Brussels Academy's Triennale. In

1890 he built the Maison Mattyn, Saint-Gilles, in 1892-93 the Tassel house, rue Paul-Emile Janson, and in 1894 the Hôtel Solvay, avenue Louise. In 1896 Horta began to work on the Maison du Peuple in Brussels – the headquarters of the Belgian Socialist Party. Other works include the Maison Autrique, Schaerbek (1893); Maison Winssinger, rue Hôtel des Monnaies (1895); the Jardin d'enfants, Brussels; the Hôtel Deprez-van de Velde, rue Boduognat; the Hôtel van Eetvelde, avenue Palmerston (1897-1900); the atelier Victor Horta, rue Américaine, Brussels (1898); the Hôtel Aubecq, avenue Louise (1900) and the Hôtel Dubois, avenue Brugmann, Saint-Gilles (1901). In 1901 he built the store 'A l'Innovation' in Brussels using an exposed skeleton of iron. This led to other stores – the Grand Bazar in Frankfurt (1903) and the Grand Bazar Anspach, rue l'Evêque, Brussels (1903-05). In 1903 he designed the last of his great Art Nouveau houses, the Hôtel Max Hallet, avenue Louise. Horta taught at the Free University of Brussels from 1897. In 1912 he became Professor at the Académie des Beaux-Arts in Brussels. In 1915 he travelled to London, and from 1916 to 1918 he was in the USA. On his return he designed the Palais des Beaux-Arts, Brussels (1922-28). Horta continued to teach, becoming head of the Académie des Beaux-Arts in 1927. In 1932 he was made a baronet.

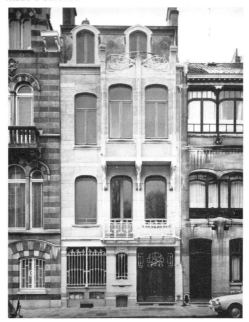

39 HORTA *Maison Horta* (now Musée Horta) Brussels 1898 (photograph Wieser)

JANAK, Pavel (1882-1959)
Janák was a student of Otto Wagner from 1906 to 1908. His work includes a crematorium, Pardubicích; the Hlávka Bridge, Prague (1909-11); a lock and weir, Předměřice (1914) and a building for the Riunione Adriatica di Sicurtà, Municipal Square, Prague. He also designed furniture in cubist forms. His articles 'Prism and Pyramid' of 1911, and 'Revival of the Facade' of 1913 were to form the basis of later nationalistic cubism.

JASPAR, Paul (1859-1945)

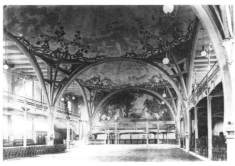

40 JASPAR '*Salle Royale de la Renommée*' Liège 1905, interior (contemporary photograph)

Born at Liège, Jaspar studied at the Academy there and in Brussels. After leaving the Academy he joined H. Beyaert, with whom he stayed for five years. His studies took him to Italy and Northern France. In 1895 he collaborated with Paul Hankar in the unexecuted design for a new theatre in Liège, using a steel skeleton. His first important independent work was on the Hospital at Glain, this being followed by a number of apartments, houses and villas in Liège and Brussels and the astounding steel and reinforced concrete 'Salle Royale de la Renommée', Liège. After the First World War Jaspar worked on a number of restorations, some at Dinan and Herbeumont. He also worked on the restorations of the Municipal Buildings at Bisé, and designed a number of monuments.

JEANNERET, Charles-Edouard (1887-1965)
Jeanneret was born at La Chaux-de-Fonds. His father and grandfather were engravers, his mother a musician. In 1900 he entered the School of Applied Arts at La Chaux-de-Fonds to study engraving and chasing under the painter L'Eplattenier, and in 1904 he began L'Eplattenier's 'Cours supérieur de décoration'. His first architectural commission was for the Villa Fallet, chemin de Pouillerel, La Chaux-de-Fonds (1905-07). In 1907 he journeyed to Northern Italy and Tuscany, finishing in Budapest and Vienna, where he worked for a few months with Josef Hoffmann. Leaving Vienna in 1908 he travelled via Nuremburg, Munich and Nancy to Paris. He worked with Auguste Perret for a time, returning to his home town in the spring of 1909. He helped to initiate the Ateliers d'art réunis, and went on their behalf to Germany in 1910 to form links with the Werkbund, working for five months in Behrens' office with Gropius and Mies van der Rohe. His two works of 1908, the Villa Stotzer and the Villa Jacquemet, chemin de Pouillerel, La Chaux-de-Fonds, were supervised by René Chapallaz, Jeanneret being in Vienna. Jeanneret's other work includes the Jeanneret house (for his father), chemin de Pouillerel (1912); the Favre-Jacot house, Le Locle (1912); the Cinéma Scala, rue de la Serre, La Chaux-de-Fonds (1916) and the Schwob house, rue de Doubs, La Chaux-de-Fonds (1916). In 1917 Jeanneret settled in Paris, and three years later took on the pseudonym of Le Corbusier. The aforementioned buildings were excluded from the extensive volumes of his *Oeuvre Complète* and were only rediscovered in 1963, two years before his death.

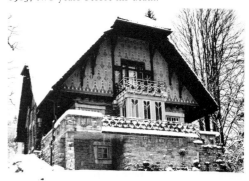

41 JEANNERET & CHAPALLAZ *Villa Fallet* La Chaux-de-Fonds 1905-07 (photograph Collomb)

JOLI, Max Hans (1879-n.d.)
Born in Vienna, Joli studied from 1900 to 1903 at the Academy under Otto Wagner. He then moved to Teschen, where he undertook various architectural commissions, including the Realgymnasium (1909), a court of honour for Franz Joseph I and villas and tombs for private clients.

JOURDAIN, Frantz (1847-1935)
Novelist, dramatist, journalist and protagonist of Art Nouveau, Jourdain was born in Antwerp and entered the Ecole des Beaux-Arts, in the atelier of Daumet, in 1865 where he remained until 1870. In his writings in *La Patrie, Le Figaro, Le Petit Parisien, Le Courrier Français, La Revue Bleue* and *La vie moderne* he attacked traditionalists and defended the new young artists. His best known work of architecture is the store 'la Samaritaine', rue de Rivoli, Paris, which was com-

missioned by Ernest Cognacq in 1883, built in 1905, and extended by Jourdain and Henri Sauvage in 1929. Before this he had built a factory at Pantin (1888), and a reinforced concrete hôtel for the ironmonger Schenck in the rue Vergniand (1894). He also designed the tombs of Alphonse Daudet and Emile Zola, built houses in the rue Galilée, a villa in Bouffémont, and a printers' in the rue Cadet. He was a member of the jury at the Paris Exhibition of 1900, when he also designed pavilions and street decorations, and was involved in the foundation of a number of artistic bodies including the Société du Nouveau Paris in 1903 and the Salon d'Automne in 1905. He took part in restorations at the Châteaux of Vertheuil, la Roche-Guiyon, and Chateauneuf-sur-Sarthe. In 1893 he published *L'Atelier Chantorel*. In 1930 he helped out the then forgotten Guimard by securing him a position on the Comité de l'Architecture d'Aujourd'hui.

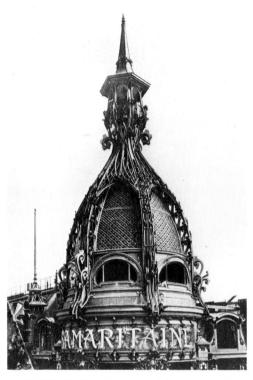

42 JOURDAIN *Grands Magasins de la Samaritaine* Paris 1905-07, detail of roof (contemporary photograph)

JUJOL I GIBERT, Josep Maria (1879-1949)

Jujol was born in the parish of Sant Joan Despí, Tarragona. The family moved to Barcelona in 1888 after their son had had an early education at his father's own school. In Barcelona he attended the school of Señor Gavalda, obtaining his Bachillerato in 1896, and then the School of Architecture. His first designs for furniture date from 1898. He trained with Gallinà from 1901 to the latter's death in 1903, collaborating with him on the ornamentation of the calle Fernando for the Fiesta de la Merced in 1902, and with Font i Gumà in 1903, before joining Gaudí. In 1904 he began, with Gaudí and Rubió, works concerned with the restoration of the cathedral at Palma de Mallorca. He also provided metalwork and ceramics for Gaudí's Casa Batlló (1904-06) and Casa Milá (1906-10), and contributed a great deal to the Park Güell (1900-14), notably the famous ceramic mosaic on the serpentine bench. His independent works include the Torre Sansalvador, Barcelona (1909); the facade and interior of Tienda Manach, Barcelona (1911); the Torre de la Creu, Sant Joan Despí (1913-16); the Casa Bofarull, Tarragona (1914); the Casa Negre, Sant Joan Despí (1914-30) and the Casa Planells (1923-24). His ecclesiastical work includes the church at Vistabella, Tarragona (1918), and the Santuario de Montferri, Tarragona (1926-29).

JUNG, Ernst (1841-1912)

Jung was born in Basel and studied under Schinkel at the Berlin Bauakademie and then at the Kunstakademie. He travelled subsequently to Italy, and

returned to Switzerland to open an office at Winterthur. His works include the rebuilding of Winterthur station; a school and bank buildings in Winterthur; a church in Trüllikon and the Volkart store, St. Gall, with Otto Bridler. He was for a long time President of the Winterthur Kunstverein and from 1899 to 1905 was President of the Swiss Kunstverein.

JURKOVIC, Dušan Samo (1868-1947)

Born in Tutá Lúka, Slovakia Jurkovič was educated in Vienna from 1884, and spent much of his life studying the regional architecture of the Valašsko and Cičmany. His work includes the spa buildings at Luhačovice, Moravia (1902-14); the 'Peklo' restaurant near Náchod; the Resek house, Nové Město nad Metují and the Farmers' Cultural Centre, Skalice (1905). He also designed the reconstruction of numerous Czech and Slovac castles, including adaptations of the interiors of the Renaissance château at Nové Město nad Metují and the castle at Zbraslav, and designed monuments to the victims of the Second World War.

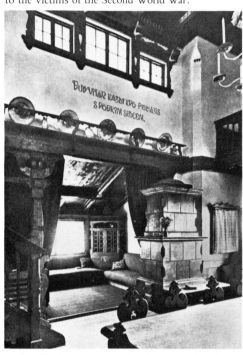

43 JURKOVIC *Restaurant* Rezek 1900-01, interior (contemporary photograph)

KAMMERER, Marcel (1878-1958)

Born in Vienna, Kammerer studied painting under Franz Rumpler and architecture under Camillo Sitte and Otto Wagner from 1898 to 1901. Until 1901 he worked with Otto Schönthal in Wagner's office, setting up his own practice with Schönthal and Emil Hoppe in 1911. Their joint works include Dorotheergasse 5-7 (1912); Ramperstorffergasse 2 (1912); Plenergasse 24; the Central Bank of the Deutsche Sparkasse (1913-15); the Electoral Palace of Abbazia; alterations and facade of the Grand Hotel Wiesler, Graz and stations for the Niederösterreichischen Landesbahnen. In 1908 the work of Kammerer was shown at the

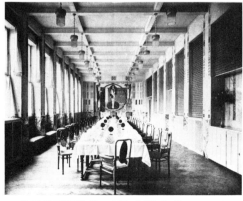

44 KAMMERER *Grand Hotel Wiesler* Graz c.1908, dining room (contemporary photograph)

exhibition Kunstschau 1908, and he also collaborated with Hoppe and Schönthal on the Ver Sacrum room for the 2nd Secession Exhibition. After the First World War, Kammerer turned exclusively to painting, his most important exhibition being at the Salon Artin in 1923.

KOTĚRA, Jan (1871-1923)

Kotěra was born in Brno. In 1887 he entered the Craft School at Pilsen, leaving in 1890 to do four years of building practice, and then going to Vienna to the studio of Otto Wagner. In 1896 he won the State Prize for architecture, and in the following year the Rome Prize which enabled him to travel to Italy in 1898, after which he went to Prague as successor to Ohmann at the School of Arts and Crafts there. Kotěra was an exceptional teacher, and he founded a school in Czechoslovakia similar to the Wagnerschule in Austria. His first house, in Wenceslas Square, was built between 1899 and 1900, and for a period in 1900 he also worked in Fanta's studio on the project for the Central Railway Station. In 1902 he built a pavilion for the August Rodin exhibition held by the avant-garde group Mánes, of which he was a member. His first major work was the District House at Hradec (1903-04), with decorations by Jan Preissler. In 1904 he built a villa and studio for the family of Stanislav Sucharda, his sculptor friend, at Prague-Bubeneč, and provided an interior for the Czech School of Arts and Crafts' Pavilion at the St Louis Exhibition. With Sucharda he built the District House at Prostějov between 1904 and 1905, and he collaborated with another sculptor, Jan Stursa, in a pavilion for the Czech Chamber of Commerce and Trade at the Jubilee Exhibition of 1907-08. Other works include a bank (1911) and a museum (1906-12) in Hradec; a hotel project for Abazia (1911); projects for a Royal Palace in Sofia (1912); for workers' settlements in Louny (1909-13) and Zábčhlice, Prague (1914). He built a number of memorials during the war and afterwards worked on urban projects. Until his death

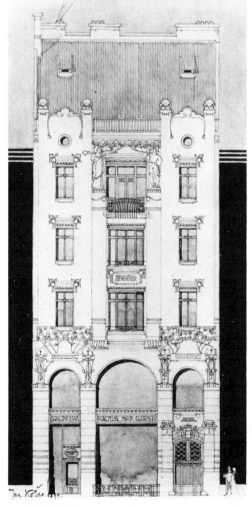

45 KOTERA *Peterka house* Prague 1899-1900, facade elevation

he worked on a project for Prague University. He taught architecture from 1911 at the Prague Academy, and from 1910 served on the Czech Land Regulation Committee. He was made a member of the Czech Academy of Arts and Sciences in 1920, and was behind the formation of the Czech Werkbund svazceského.

KOULA, Jan (1855-1919)

Koula was born in Český Brod and studied at the Prague Polytechnic and under Professor Hansen in Vienna. In 1897 he was appointed Professor of Architecture and Ornamental Drawing at the Prague Polytechnic. He was concerned with large urban projects such as the design of the Czech bridge in Prague and the competition design for the Letná hill. He also designed reconstructions of historical monuments, such as the Town Hall in Pilsen and the Minuta house in Prague. An expert in Czech architectural history and folk architecture, he collaborated in the Ethnographical exhibition in Prague in 1895. He was also a prolific writer.

KROMHOUT, Willem (1864-1940)

Born in Rotterdam, Kromhout spent two years at the Kunstnijverheidschool in The Hague followed by three years in the studio of Weestra, during which time he took evening classes at the Academy. After graduating as an architect he lived for a short time in Amsterdam before taking up a post with J. J. Winden in Antwerp in 1885, and attending evening classes at the Antwerp Academy. In 1887 he travelled to France, Italy and South Germany, and in 1890 he set up independently as an architect, teaching in the evenings at the Kunstnijverheidschool. His early works include dwellings and offices in the Reguliersbreestraat, Amsterdam (1887); St Nicolaskerk, Amsterdam, with A. S. B. Leijs (1888), and the 'Oud Holland' tourist village, built in Amsterdam in 1895. He succeeded Berlage at the Quellinus School in Amsterdam in 1897, remaining until 1910 when he took over the architecture section of the Academy of Art, Rotterdam. He also disseminated his theories through the publication *Architectura*, for which he was assistant editor from 1893 to 1896, and editor in 1905. His later works include coronation decorations for Queen Wilhelmina on the streets and canals (1898); the facade of the De Fakkel printing works, Amsterdam (1900); the American Hotel, Amsterdam (1898-1901); project for a Palace of Justice, The Hague (1900); Kampen Hospital (1910-12); competition design for Rotterdam Town Hall (1913); Villa Bussum (1913) and numerous exhibition pavilions.

LASKE, Oskar (1874-1951)

Born in Czernowitz, Laske studied at the Technical University in Vienna and under Wagner at the Academy of Creative Arts. He was a member of the

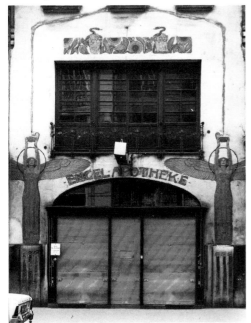

46 LASKE *Engel Pharmacy* Vienna 1902, facade detail (photograph Godoli)

Hagenbund from 1907, and from 1929 to 1939 and 1945 to 1950 a member of the Vienna Secession. A self-taught painter, Laske produced oil paintings, watercolours, etchings, lithographs and book illustrations. His architectural works include the Engel Pharmacy, Bognergasse 9 (1902) and the Flora Hof, Wiedner Hauptstrasse 88 (1901).

LAUWERIKS, Johannes Ludovicus Matheus (1864-1932)

Born in Roermond in 1864 to a father who was chef d'atelier to P. J. H. Cuypers, Lauweriks moved with his family and Cuypers to Amsterdam when the studio was relocated in 1865. He began teaching at Cuypers' Quellinus School in 1880 and studied drawing at the Rijksnormaalschool from 1883 to 1887, obtaining a state diploma for freehand drawing in 1885, and one for architectural drawing in 1887. He taught drawing for a short period at the Industrial School in Amsterdam. From 1887 to 1895 he worked in Cuypers' office during the day and attended evening classes at the Rijksacademie. He left Cuypers' office with De Bazel in 1895, after the two of them had joined the Theosophist Union, and formed the 'atelier for architecture, arts and crafts and the decorative arts'. Together they produced competition schemes, graphic designs and furniture, but little building. Primarily a teacher, Lauweriks taught from 1900 to 1904 at the School of Arts and Crafts in Haarlem, and in 1904 was invited by Peter Behrens to teach at a similar school in Düsseldorf. His ideas also found expression in the avant-garde publication *Ring*, which he founded in 1905. The realised output of Lauweriks' architectural thought is compressed between the years 1909 and 1915, after a brief trip to America. All of the buildings are outside Holland – interior designs for an Exhibition of Christian Art at Düsseldorf (1909); work on the artists' colony at Hagen for Karl Ernst Osthaus; houses for Thorn Prikker, Milly Steger, Lauweriks, Schüngeler and Harmann; a house for Professor W. Stein at Göttingen (1912-13); a room for the International Exhibition, Ghent of 1913; houses on the Stirnband (1910-14); renovation of the Osthaus bank, Hagen (1914) and a pavilion for the Deutsche Werkbund Exhibition, Cologne (1914). Returning to Amsterdam in 1916 he became Director of the Quellinus School and taught in the architectural section of the Instituut Voor Kunstnijverheid. From 1919 to 1925 he co-edited the publication *Wendingen*.

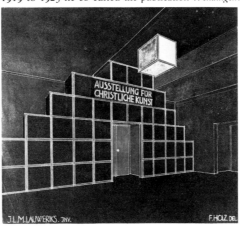

47 LAUWERIKS *Exhibition of Christian Art* Düsseldorf 1909, interior perspective

LAVERRIERE, Alphonse (1872-1954)

Laverrière was born in Carouge in 1872 and his early studies were in Genfer. In 1893 he entered the atelier Pascal at the Paris Academy. He returned to Switzerland to practise, setting up an office in 1902 with another of Pascal's students, Eugène Monod. His work includes a project for a mountain inn in Haute-Savoie (1901); the Chauderon bridge, Lausanne (1904); 'La Sauvagère', avenue Verdeil, Lausanne (1905-06); villas on the Genfer See; Lausanne Central Station (with Monod, J. Taillens and Charles Dubois) and the Reformation Memorial, Genfer. In 1911 Laverrière and Monod won a prize for their advanced scheme for a stadium in Stockholm.

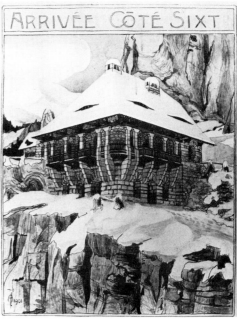

48 LAVERRIERE *Project for a mountain inn in the Haute-Savoie* 1901

LAVIROTTE, Jules Aimé (1864-1924)

Born in Lyon, Lavirotte was a student of Louvier there. In 1892 he became a student of P. Blondel in Paris for two years. His work includes apartment buildings in square Rapp (1899), avenue Rapp (1901-02), rue de Grenelle (1897), rue Sédillot (1899), rue d'Abbeville (1900) and avenue Wagram (1904). He also built the Château of St-Cyr-au-Mont-d'Or near Lyon (1913); a château, villa and restoration of the church in Chaouat, Tunisia (1904) and low-rent accommodation on the rue Lefèbvre, Paris (1906) and at Juvisy (1913).

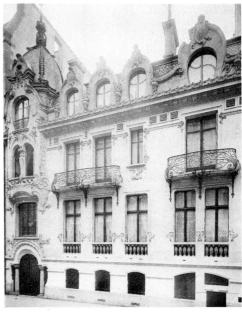

49 LAVIROTTE *12 rue Sédillot* Paris 1899 (contemporary photograph)

L'EPLATTENIER, Charles (1874-1946)

L'Eplattenier was born in Neuenberg and grew up in Geneveys-sur-Coffrane. He trained as an artist, coming under the influence of the architect and watercolourist Paul Bouvier. Going to his father's sister in Budapest in 1891 he spent a year at the Decorative Art School there and from 1893 to 1896 he studied at the Ecole des Arts Décoratifs in Paris. After also studying painting, sculpture and architecture at the Ecole des Beaux-Arts he returned to Geneveys-sur-Coffrane in the spring of 1896. A year was then spent visiting London, Belgium, Holland and Munich. In 1898 he began to teach at the Ecole d'Art at La Chaux-de-

Fonds, and in 1903 he was made Director. He worked in furniture, ceramics, metalwork and small scale decoration, as well as doing large scale work with his pupils – the decoration of a hall in the new Post Office and the new Crematorium at La Chaux-de-Fonds. He also designed monuments. He resigned from the Ecole d'Art after the First World War. In 1923-25 he designed and built, in collaboration with René Chapallaz, the Musée des Beaux-Arts, La Chaux-de-Fonds.

LETHABY, William Richard (1857-1931)

Born at Barnstaple in Devon, Lethaby was educated at the local School of Art, then articled to Alexander Lauder of Barnstaple and Richard Waite of Derby. In 1879 he gained the R.I.B.A. Soane Medallion for architectural study abroad and in 1881 the Pugin Studentship. He studied at the R.A. Schools and travelled in Northern France drawing Gothic cathedrals. He was in Norman Shaw's office until 1889, eventually as chief draughtsman, and in 1891 set up his own practice. He built little, being chiefly known as an author, teacher and critic. What he did build, however, is of great interest – a house at Avon Tyrrel, Hampshire (1890); house at Melsetter, Orkney (1898); a stone church at Brockhampton (1900-02) and the Eagle Insurance Building, Birmingham (1899). He assisted Shaw in the design of New Scotland Yard, and assisted in an Arts and Crafts competition scheme for Liverpool Anglican Cathedral. As a teacher, Lethaby was promoter and first principal of the L.C.C. Central School of Arts and Crafts in 1894. From 1900 he was the first Professor of Design at the Royal College of Art. His publications cover a wide historical range – *Architecture, Mysticism and Myth* (1892); *Form and Civilisation* (1922); 'Philip Webb and his work', in *The Builder*, 1925. From 1906 to 1928 he was Surveyor of Westminster Abbey, and through his cleaning and restoration work on the Abbey came to be considered an expert on the care of old buildings. Lethaby was Master of the Art Workers' Guild in 1911.

LOOS, Adolf (1870-1933)

Loos was born in Brno, Moravia, the son of a sculptor and stonemason, and his initial training was as a mason. He studied from 1890 to 1893 at the Technischen Hochschule Dresden, and after this time spent three years in America, visiting Chicago, Philadelphia and New York. On his return to Vienna in 1896 he became an assistant to Carl Mayreder. In 1897 he began to write for the Free Press of Vienna and the best known of his writings, *Ornament und Verbrechen*, appeared in 1908. Loos' architectural designs are numerous, although little was realised. In 1898 he began the remodelling of the Café Museum in Vienna, and ten years later provided interiors for the American Bar in the Kärntnerdurchgang. Early executed works include a villa for Dr Beer, Genfersee (1904); the Karma house, Montreux (1904-06); the Steiner house, Vienna (1910-11) and the Goldman Building on the Michaelerplatz (1910). In 1912 Loos formed an independent school of architects, but this closed with the war. His later houses and projects link him firmly with the developing aesthetic of the Modern Move-

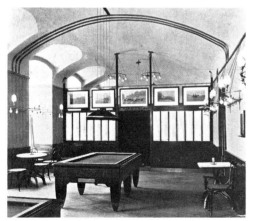

50 LOOS *Billiard Room* Vienna c.1899 (contemporary photograph)

ment, and in 1923 he became involved with a group of avant-garde artists – Kraus, Altenberg, Schönberg and Kokoschka. From these years dates his unusual competition entry for the Chicago Tribune Tower. In 1926, due to his revived celebrity in France, he taught at the Sorbonne, returning in 1928 to Vienna where he built more houses, and probably his finest work, the Müller house of 1920, in Prague.

MACKINTOSH, Charles Rennie (1868-1928)

Mackintosh was born in Dennistown, Glasgow, where he attended Alan Glen's School. At the age of seventeen he attended the Glasgow School of Art, then under Francis Newbery, where he was to study for seven years. Meanwhile he became apprenticed to the architect John Hutchison, and in 1889 joined the firm of Honeyman and Keppie as a draughtsman. In 1890 he visited France and Italy on the Alexander Thomson Travelling Scholarship. In 1891 he was back in Glasgow, and with Margaret Macdonald, his future wife, her sister Frances, and Herbert MacNair produced work as 'The Four', exhibiting posters at Bing's L'Art Nouveau in Paris in 1895. His buildings include the Glasgow Herald Building, executed with Keppie in 1893; the Martyr's Public School in Barony Street (1895); Queen's Cross Church, Woodside (1898-99); Windyhill, Kilmalcolm (1899-1901); Hill House, Helensborough (1902-04); Scotland Street School (1904-06); the Glasgow School of Art (1897-1909) and four tea-rooms for Mrs Cranston. In 1899 he was successful at the Munich Secession Exhibition, and this led him to be invited to exhibit at the 8th Exhibition of the Vienna Secession the following year. While in Vienna Fritz Wärndorfer of the Wiener Werkstätte commissioned him to design a *Haus eines Kunstfreundes*. His project came second to Baillie Scott's in the ensuing competition and was published with Scott's and Leopold Bauer's by Alex Koch in 1902. In 1902 Mackintosh became a partner in the firm of Honeyman and Keppie, and in the same year he provided the Scottish pavilion at the Turin Exhibition, through which he obtained openings to exhibit in Venice, Munich, Dresden, Budapest and Moscow. Sadly his personal problems led him to drop sharply out of sight after 1910. He resigned his partnership in 1913 and moved to London, and but for the Cloister Room in the Ingram Street tea-rooms in Glasgow, the remodelling of Bassett-Lowke's house in Northampton, and the studio house for Harold Squire in Glebe Place, Chelsea, he did no more architectural work, concentrating on textile designs, flower studies and landscape painting. He spent his latter days as a watercolourist at Port Vendres in the South of France, where he moved in 1919.

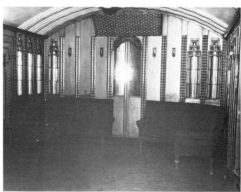

51 MACKINTOSH *Ingram Street tea-rooms* Glasgow, Cloister Room 1911

MACKMURDO, Arthur Heygate (1851-1942)

Architect, craftsman, and later economist, Mackmurdo was introduced to architecture through Ruskin's 1873 Oxford lectures, and in 1874 – and later in 1878 and 1880 – accompanied Ruskin to Italy. He later received a more strictly architectural training under T. Chatfield Clarke and James Brooks, and in 1875 started his own practice. In 1882, with Herbert Horn, Selwyn Image and Bernard Creswick, Mackmurdo formed the Century Guild, producing designs

for interiors, wallpapers, furniture, carpets and metalwork. In 1884 the Guild published the first issue of *Hobby Horse*, with Mackmurdo as first editor. His architectural work includes Brooklyn, Private Road, Enfield (1886-87); exhibition stand for the Century Guild at the Liverpool International Exhibition (1886); house, Redington Road, Hampstead (1890); house, Hans Road, Knightsbridge (1891); 25 Cadogan Gardens, Chelsea (1893-94); Old Swanne, Sloane Street, Knightsbridge (1899); cold storage warehouse, Charterhouse Street, Smithfield (1900) and Little Ruffins, Wickham Bishops, Essex (c.1900). Around 1900 Mackmurdo gave up architecture to devote himself to economics – although he did build a house for himself, Great Ruffins, Wickham Bishops, Essex, in 1904.

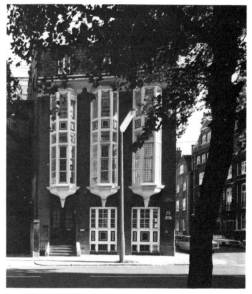

52 MACKMURDO *25 Cadogan Gardens* London 1893-94 (photograph Goulancourt)

MACLAREN, James M. (1843-1890)

Born in Stirling in Scotland, MacLaren began his architectural career with James Salmon the elder, and later worked in Glasgow for Cambell Douglas and J. J. Stevenson, and in London for Edward Godwin and Richard Coade. He started his own office in 1886, and his work includes The Park, Ledbury (1886); Stirling High School (1887-88); the Town Hall, Aberfeldy, Perthshire (1889-90); 10 and 12 Palace Court, London (1889-90) and Heatherwood, Crawley Down, Sussex (1890-91). He also built in Las Palmas, and between 1889 and 1890 a number of cottages in Perthshire. In the year of his death he was successful in the competition for the London Eiffel Tower, to be built at Wembley.

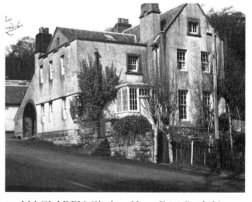

53 MACLAREN *Glenlyon House Estate* Perthshire c.1889, tenant farmer's house

MAJORELLE, Louis (1859-1926)

Majorelle was born in Toul and exhibited in the painting section of the Salon at the age of sixteen. He spent two years in Paris at the Ecole des Beaux-Arts, and in 1879 took over his father's family cabinet-making and ceramic business in Nancy, concentrating on furniture design. He was represented at Bing's establishment L'Art Nouveau in 1895, and at the Paris Exhibition of 1900 he exhibited a dining room and bedroom in a style he dubbed 'Nénuphar', based on the waterlily. He also exhibited in 1902 in Turin. Also an expert metal-worker, he provided fittings for his own villa at Nancy and made decorative railings, such as those on the stairs of the Galerie Lafayette, Paris.

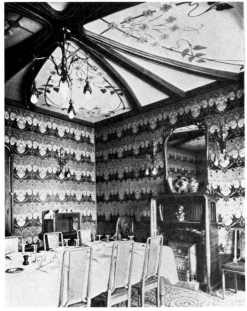

54 MAJORELLE *Café de Paris* Paris 1899, salon (contemporary photograph)

MARTORELL I MONTELLS, Juan (1833-1906)

Martorell was born, worked, and died in Barcelona. His work there, mainly ecclesiastical, includes the Jesuit church; the Sagrado Corazón de Maria; Las Adolatrices; Las Salesas and Montesión. He also built the Sagrado Corazón at Sarriá, churches at Castellar del Vallero and Port-Bou and the dome of the Mercenary Church in Barcelona. Secular work includes buildings for the Crédito Mercantil, Barcelona, and houses in the colony of the first Marqués de Comillas at Comillas. He designed funerary chapels for Comillas in San Ignacio, Comillas, and for the Countess Olmo at San Sebastian. It was Martorell, in 1884, who recommended that Gaudí succeed Villar as architect on the Sagrada Familia.

MELANI, Alfredo (1859-1928)

Melani was born in Pistoia, and settled in Milan in 1881 after an education at the Accademia di Firenze, where he studied the applied arts and the history of architecture. In 1883 he became a Professor at the Scuola Superiore d'Arte Applicata a l'Industria, where Giuseppe Sommaruga was among his pupils. His architectural work includes a project for the restoration of the Palazzo Municipale, Pistoia (1881); the Merli Maggi chapel in Milan cemetery and Villa Rosa, Carlanzone. His publications include *L'architettura, il secolo XIX nella vita e nella cultura dei Pololi* and works on Palladio (1928).

MICHELAZZI, Giovanni

Michelazzi studied at Trieste, and in Vienna under Wagner. His works, mainly in Florence, include villas in Viale del Poggio Imperiale (1902-03) and in Viale Michelangiolo (1904); Villino Lampredi, Via Giano della Bella (1908-12); Villino Broggi-Caraceni with ceramics by Galileo Chini, Via Scipione Ammirato (1911); Villino Ravazzini (1912) and Villino Toccafondi, Via XX Settembre (1913). Also attributed to Michelazzi is the house and gallery in Via Borgognissanti.

MORETTI, Gaetano (1860-1938)

Born in Milan, Moretti attended the Accademia di Brera, and took his laureat at Milan Polytechnic. He became a student of C. Boito, and also collaborated with Luca Beltrami. His works, mainly in Piedmont and Lombardy, include a chapel for Chiavari cemetery (1892); a scheme for Crespi d'Adda cemetery (executed in 1907); cemeteries in Annone and Milan;

the Casati monument, Milan (1900); three rooms for the Ceruti Company at the 1902 Turin Exhibition; a hydro-electric station at Trezzo d'Adda (1906); a competition project for the Palazzo del Parlamento, Rome (1899), won by E. Basile; winning competition design for a monument to Argentinian independence, Buenos Aires (1909); Palazzo del Parlamento, Montevideo; museum, Lima; restorations at Gallarate (S. Pietro), Vigevano (S. Francesco), S. Sepolcro, Milan and St Mark's Campanile, Venice (1912).

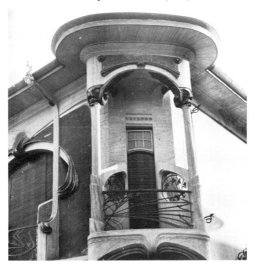

55 MICHELAZZI *Villino Broggi-Caraceni* Florence 1911, corner detail

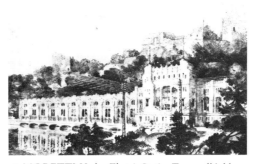

56 MORETTI *Hydro-Electric Station* Trezzo d'Adda 1906, perspective drawing

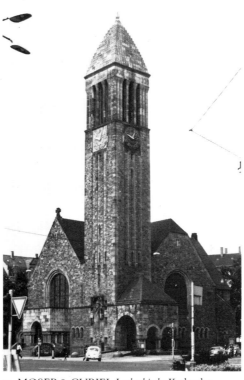

57 MOSER & CURJEL *Lutherkirche* Karlsruhe 1905-06 (photograph Godoli)

MOSER, Karl (1860-1936)

Moser studied at the Zurich Technical High School, where he was also a professor from 1915, and at the Ecole des Beaux-Arts in Paris. From 1888 until 1915 he worked with Curjel in Karlsruhe, and the partnership designed a bank (1898-1901) and the Lutherkirche (1905-06), both in Karlsruhe, the Palace of Art, Zurich (1910), the Badischer station, Basel (1912) and Zurich University (1914). Moser's independent works include the churches of St. Paul (1898-1901) and St. Anthony (1926-27), both in Basel. In 1928 he became the first president of CIAM.

MOSER, Koloman (1868-1918)

Born in Vienna, Moser studied from 1886 to 1892 at the Academy of Creative Arts with Rumpler and Griepenkerl and from 1892 to 1895 with Matsch at the Vienna School of Arts and Crafts, where he was also a Professor from 1900 until 1918. He was a founder member of the Vienna Secession in 1897, leaving in 1905 as part of the Klimtgruppe. He was also founder member of the Wiener Werkstätte and the Siebenerclub. A painter, graphic designer and craftsman, Moser collaborated with Hoffmann, Wagner and Olbrich in the designs of their buildings.

MUTHESIUS, Hermann (1861-1927)

Born in Gross-Neuhausen, Muthesius studied at Berlin Technical College, then became a student of Ende and later worked in Wallot's office. From 1887 to 1891 he worked in Japan for Ende and Bockmann and on his return to Berlin he joined the Ministry of Works. From 1896 to 1903 he was attached to the German Embassy in London, and he published books on English architecture – *Englische Baukunst der Gegenwart* (1900-02) and *Die neuere kirchliche Baukunst in England* (1902). His most important and influential work, published on his return to Germany, was *Das englische Haus* (1905). His own architectural works include country houses; some developments at Duisburg, Dresden-Hellerau, and Berlin-Wittenau; a building for the mechanical silkweavers, Michels & Co., Nowares and buildings for a woollen manufacturer, Grünberg, Silesia. He was connected with the foundation of the Deutscher Werkbund, and designed the Fabenschau Halle for the 1914 Cologne Exhibition.

MYSLBEK, Josef Václav (1848-1922)

Born in Prague, where he lived and worked for most of his life, Myslbek was a sculptor and studied under T. Seldon (1864-66), V. Levy (1867-70) and M. Trenkwald (1868-71). From 1872 to 1873 he was in Germany, spending a short time with E. J. Hähnel of Dresden. In 1875 he became Professor at the Prague School of Decorative Art, moving in 1876 to the Academy. In 1885, following the foundation of the School of Arts and Crafts, he was appointed Professor of Plastic Arts – a post he held until 1919.

NEWTON, Ernest (1856-1922)

Born at Hoxton, Newton was educated at Uppingham under Edward Thring. In 1873 he entered Shaw's office, where he met Prior, Macartney and Lethaby, with whom he was later to found the Art Workers' Guild. In 1879, he set up his own office, designing a series of small suburban houses and several larger works, including Red Court, Haslemere (1894); Martins' Bank, Bromley (1898); Steep Hill, Jersey (1899); Ardenrun Place, Blindley Heath (1906); Luckley, Wokingham (1907) and Ludwick Corner, Herts (1907). From 1899 to 1910 Newton provided a number of cottages and small buildings for Overbury in Worcestershire, and from 1902 to 1905 a dozen type houses for the Bickley Park Estate.

NOVOTNY, Otakar (1880-n.d.)

Born in Benešov, Novotný was a student of Jan Kotěra, and worked for most of his life in Prague. His best known work is the Stenc house in Prague (1909-11) which foreshadows to some extent his later cubist works, such as his boarding house for single workers, Cernožice (1924) and his Bilkova Street flats in Prague. His other works include private houses and gymnasia at Holice (1911) and Rakovnik (1912); a stand for the Federation of Czech Arts and Crafts at the 1914 Cologne Werkbund Exhibition; teachers' cooperative houses, Prague (1919) and the Steinsky house, Hradec Králo é (1926). From 1920 Novotný was Chairman of the avant-garde group Mánes, and in 1929 became Professor of Architecture at the Prague School of Arts and Crafts.

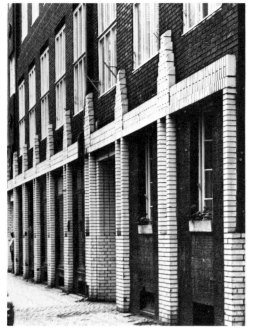

58 NOVOTNY *Commercial building* Prague 1908-09, facade detail (photograph Godoli)

OBRIST, Hermann (1863-1927)

Obrist was born at Kilchenberg, near Zurich, son of a doctor. At first he studied medicine and the natural sciences, but in 1886, purportedly as the result of a visionary daydream, he renounced science to study ceramics at Karlsruhe and sculpture in Paris and Florence. In 1892 he founded an embroidery workshop in that city with Berthe Ruchet, and together they exhibited in Munich in 1894. Obrist went on to develop his sculpture. In 1897 he was one of the thirty artists who made up the 'Vereinigte Werkstätten für Kunst und Handwerk'. In 1907 in Jena his *Neue Möglichkeiten in der bilden de Kunst* was published, and he was shortlisted with Gropius in 1914 for the Directorship of the Bauhaus.

OERLEY, Robert (1876-1945)

Oerley was born in Vienna, and was a student at the Kunstgewerbeschule there. He led an opposite movement to that of the Secession – a move towards the nationalism of a 'Heimatstil'. His work includes a one-family house, Lannerstrasse (c.1905); the Strauss-Lanner Memorial, Rathauspark, with the sculptor Fr Seifert (1907); the Luithlen Sanatorium (1908) and the Carl Zeiss optical works (1917), all in Vienna.

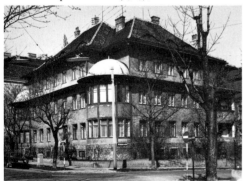

59 OERLEY *98 Weimarer Strasse* Vienna 1904-05 (photograph Godoli)

OHMANN, Bedřich (1858-1927)

Ohmann was born in Lvov and studied in Vienna at the Technische Hochschule under Ferstel and König, and at the Vienna Academy under Professor Schmidt. From 1888 to 1898 he taught at the School of Arts and Crafts in Prague. His work includes the Café Corso, Na Příkopě Street and the Storch house, Old Town Square, and he also collaborated on the design of the Central Hotel (1899-1902). He took part in a number

of church restorations and decorations in Zlonic, Pristec and elsewhere.

OLBRICH, Joseph Maria (1867-1908)

Born in Troppau, Olbrich studied in Vienna under Hasenauer, visited Italy and Tunisia, and returned to Vienna in 1894, working until 1898 in the studio of Otto Wagner. In 1897 he was a founder member with Josef Hoffmann and a number of other artists of the Vienna Secession. In 1898 he constructed the Villa Friedmann, Hinterbrühl, and the Secession House in Vienna, which acted as an exhibition centre for the group. In 1899 Ernst Ludwig von Hessen invited Olbrich and six other young artists to found an artists' colony in Darmstadt. Over the next eight years this Künstlerkolonie was erected, chiefly to Olbrich's designs, on the Mathildenhöhe in Darmstadt. The colony exhibited a 'Darmstadt Zimmer' in Paris in 1900, and as this met with some success they held a major exhibition on the Mathildenhöhe the following year. For this Olbrich built the Ernst Ludwig Haus (the colony studio), houses for a number of artists, an entrance portal and ancillary structures, including the Gebäude für Flächenkunst. The colony was later enlarged following the marriage of Ernst Ludwig in 1905, and Olbrich's Hochzeitsturm (Wedding Tower) and Palace of Freikunst were finished by 1908. Olbrich also built a number of other houses in the locality – a two-family house on the Mathildenhöhe (1902); the Romheld house (1902); the Ganss house (1902) and the Wilhelm Opel house (1903). His final works were the Feinhals house, Marienburg, and the Tietz department store in Düsseldorf. Before the latter was completed he died of leukaemia, leaving behind some forty built works and 28,000 drawings.

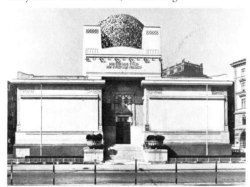

60 OLBRICH *Secession House* Vienna 1897-98

PANKOK, Bernhard (1872-1943)

Pankok was born in Münster im Westfalia, studied sculpture and painting at the Düsseldorf Academy and in Berlin, and in 1892 settled in Munich for a decade.

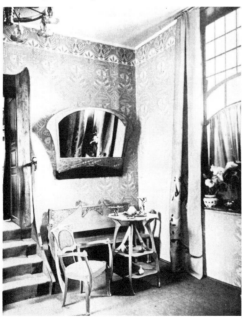

61 PANKOK *Munich Secession Exhibition* 1899, interior (contemporary photograph)

During this period he founded, together with Obrist, Eckmann, Endell, Riemerschmid, Paul and Behrens, the 'Vereinigte Werkstätten für Kunst und Handwerk' – the Munich Circle. Two of his works were exhibited by this group at international exhibitions – an Alcove Room in Paris (1900) and a Music Room in St Louis (1904). In 1900-01 he built a house for Konrad Lange at Tübingen, and did some work at Dessau Town Hall (1900-02). In 1902 he transferred to Stüttgart, going on to design studios for the Stüttgart Association of Art Lovers. He also produced designs for the Deutscher Werkbund for machine-made furniture. In 1913 he became Director of the State Kunstgewerbeschule.

PAUL, Bruno (1874-1968)

Born at Seifhennersdorf, Paul was attached to the Kunstgewerbeschule in Dresden from an early age. He also gained some training in the building industry before entering the Munich Academy in 1894. Three years later he became a leading figure in the Munich Circle, developing a particularly close working relationship with another member of the group, Richard Riemerschmid. Ten years later he joined the Deutscher Werkbund and contributed numerous projects on its behalf. Apart from his architecture, Paul was a gifted illustrator, producing caricatures for the publication *Simplizissimus* and illustrations for *Jugend*. In 1900 he exhibited a 'Jagdzimmer' at the Paris Exhibition. He was a respected teacher and a reformer of art education, organising many representative German exhibitions. His architectural work includes offices in Berlin; the Schloss Heinerberg in Taunus; the Rose-Livingstone-Stiftung house, Frankfurt-am-Main; drawing rooms on the Lloyd steamers Prinz Friedrich Wilhelm and George Washington; and the Asiatische Museum in Berlin-Dahlem.

PAXTON, Sir Joseph (1801-1865)

Son of a Bedfordshire farmer, Paxton was trained as a gardener and in 1826 became head gardener and subsequently landscape designer and business agent for the Duke of Devonshire at Chatsworth. In 1831 he invented the 'ridge and furrow' roof for glass houses, a technique which he first used in the Great Conservatory and Lily House at Chatsworth, and perfected in his most famous work, the Crystal Palace of 1851. His other works include the design of the grounds at Sydenham; several public parks, including one at Birkenhead, Cheshire (1843); a new

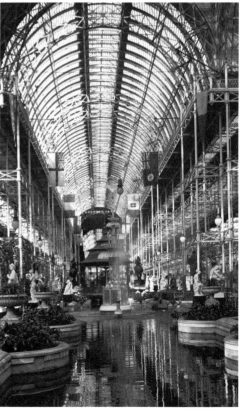

62 PAXTON *Crystal Palace* London 1851, originally built for the Great Exhibition of the same year

village, Edensor, at Chatsworth and fountains at Chatsworth and Sydenham. He was also involved in several architectural commissions in collaboration with G. H. Stokes, including mansions for the Rothschild family, and designed a number of unexecuted glass and iron projects.

PECHE, Dagobert (1887-1923)

Born in St Michael, Salzburg, Peche studied at the Vienna Technical University and then under Ohmann at the Vienna Academy. In 1910 he travelled to England, and in 1912 won a prize from the Academy of a two month stay in Paris. On his return, he joined the publisher Alexander Koch in Darmstadt, and while in Darmstadt he also converted the Daberkowsche Haus, 29 Neubaugasse. In 1913 he moved to Vienna and worked for the firm 'Wiener Keramik'. In November 1913 he designed a Reception Room for the Secession Exhibition, and in 1914 Josef Hoffmann entrusted him with the direction of the Austrian section of the International Exhibition in Rome. In 1915 Peche joined the Wiener Werkstätte, and from 1917 until 1919 he was head of their branch in Zurich, designing embroidery, silverware and jewellery. On his return to Vienna he participated in the exhibitions Kunstschau 1920 and Kunstschau 1921. In 1922 he went to Cologne to supervise the production of a series of his carpet designs by the firm Flammersheim & Steinmann. His work in jewellery, fabric and carpet design, ceramics, ivory, and metal was shown at a memorial exhibition in Vienna in 1923.

PERRET, Auguste (1874-1954)

Perret was born in Brussels, son of a French builder fleeing from the Paris Commune. Auguste and his brothers continued their father's business, Auguste and George leaving the Ecole des Beaux-Arts in order to do this in 1901. The first building Auguste designed himself was at the age of sixteen – a house at Berneval-sur-Mer near Dieppe. His later works in Paris include 25 bis rue Franklin (1903); the Magasins Esders; the Casablanca Docks buildings; 119 avenue Wagram; the Garage Marboeuf, rue Ponthieu (1905) and the Théatre des Champs-Elysées (1911-13).

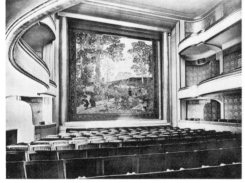

63 PERRET A. & G. *Théâtre des Champs-Elysées* Paris 1911-13, auditorium (contemporary photograph)

PFEIFFER, Antonín (1879-1938)

Pfeiffer first worked in Paris, Brussels and elsewhere. On returning to Prague he teamed up with Jan Kotěra and together they did much work in central Prague. His first work was the Vesná Girls' School, Brno, with interiors by Jurkovič. In 1912 he provided a cubist canopy for a Baroque statue in Prague.

PLECNIK, Jože (1872-1957)

Plečnik was born in Ljubljana, Yugoslavia. Before entering the studio of Otto Wagner in 1894 he worked in Vienna as a freelance artist. After leaving Wagner's studio he practised as an architect in Vienna until 1911, when he succeeded Kotěra as Professor of Architecture at the Prague School of Arts and Crafts. His Viennese work includes the Zachlerhaus store (1903-05); the Carlo Borromeo fountain, with J. Engelhart (1908) and the Holy Ghost Church (1910-11). During his period in Prague he continued to produce designs for churches, houses, book illustrations, furniture and church furnishings, and in 1918 he took part in the restorations of Prague Castle. In 1920 he returned to his home of Ljubljana, where he became Professor of the Technical Faculty.

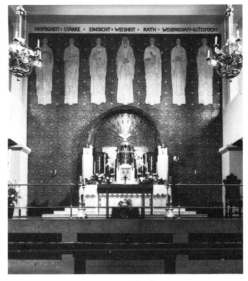

64 PLECNIK *Holy Ghost Church* Vienna 1910-11, interior with altar by Holub (photograph Godoli)

PLUMET, Charles (1861-1928)

Born at Cirey-sur-Vezouze, Plumet studied under Bruneau and de Baudot, and collaborated with Tony Selmersheim from 1898. His early work includes a house on rue Legendre, Paris (1891); houses on rue Truffaut, rue de Lévis and rue Léon Cosnard (1893) and an apartment block, 67 avenue Malakoff (1895). In 1895 he joined the Société Nationale des Beaux-Arts, and was a regular exhibitor at their Salons, showing furniture and ceramic work. In 1897 he was one of the founders of the Société des Cinq. With Selmersheim he designed the interior of the tailor's shop 'Roddy', boulevard des Italiens (c.1898); the Restaurant Auvray, place Boïeldieu (c.1898); Kohler's Chocolate Shop, boulevard de la Madeleine (c.1899); entrance to the Grand Hotel du Havre, rue d'Amsterdam (c.1900) and the Magasin Cadolle (c.1898). Plumet was Architect in Chief of the Paris Exhibitions of 1900 and 1925, and in 1900 won a gold medal for public decoration, and a bronze for architecture. He also exhibited a ceramic kiosk and a dining room, and at Turin, two years later, a buffet for a dining room. In 1903 he was one of the founders of the Salon d'Automne, becoming secretary (1903-05) of the architecture section, and Vice-President (1906-07). In 1904 he was made Légion d'Honneur. His own buildings in Paris include houses on the avenue Victor Hugo (1900 and 1906), boulevard de Lannes (1906), rue Octave Feuillet (1907) and rue Marbeau (c.1907). In 1906 he designed a monument to Stendhal and in 1910 he built a villa at Neuilly-sur-Seine for the musician Gustave Kéfer.

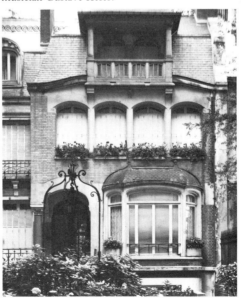

65 PLUMET *50 avenue Victor Hugo* Paris c.1900 (photograph Godoli)

POLIVKA, Osvald (1859-1931)

Born in Enns, near Linz, Polívka was a student at the Prague Polytechnic. He worked for a time with the Prague architect Achille Wolf and in 1899 became an assistant of Professor Zítek at the Prague Polytechnic. His works include the Zemská bank, Prague (1896); the Novák Department Store, Vodičkova Street (1900); a building for the Praha Insurance Company, National Street (1903); a design for the new Town Hall and a savings bank, Hradec Králové.

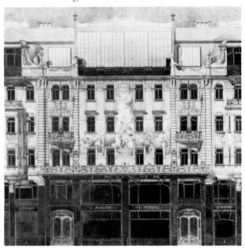

66 POLIVKA *Novák Department Store* Prague 1900

POMPE, Antoine (1873-1965)

Pompe was born in Brussels to a jeweller and was sent to Germany to study the craft of jewellery. In 1886 he entered the Académie Royale des Beaux-Arts in Brussels, going to Munich to study for three years at the Kunstgewerbeschule in 1890. After leaving there Pompe worked for three years for the Demolder works, then in 1898 joined the atelier of Van Parijs, and the following year entered the office of Delpy in Brussels. From 1900 to 1903 he worked in the 'Ateliers d'ameublement et de décoration' of Georges Hobe and from 1904 to 1908 he worked with the architect Lener. In 1900 he drew up the working drawings for Horta's projected Congo pavilion for the Paris Exhibition and in 1901 he drew with Horta the perspective of his house in the rue Americaine. With Lener he designed the Palace Hotel (1904) and cottage and furniture designs. In 1910 Pompe constructed his best known building in Brussels, the orthopedic clinic for Dr Van Neck, rue Wafelaerts. From 1910 he worked with F. Bodson, producing designs for a viaduct (1910), a crematorium (1912), houses, and factories.

PRIOR, Edward Schroeder (1852-1932)

Born to a barrister, Prior was educated at Harrow and Cambridge. From 1872 until the late 1880s he worked with Norman Shaw, though his independent work dates from around 1883. He was one of the founders of the Art Workers' Guild in 1884 and was also Professor of Fine Art at Cambridge between 1912 and 1932. His early work includes the Red House, Harrow (1883); houses at West Bay, near Bridport, Dorset (1885); Holy Trinity Church, Bothenhampton (1887-89); Harrow Laundry Superintendant's House, Alma Road, Harrow (1887-89) and The Barn, Foxhole Hill Road, Exmouth, Devon (1896-97).

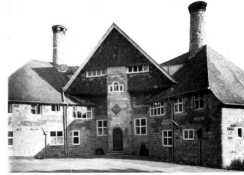

67 PRIOR *The Barn* Exmouth 1896-97

PRUTSCHER, Otto (1880–n.d.)

Born in Vienna, Prutscher studied under Franz Matsch and Josef Hoffmann. From 1909 he taught at the Kunstgewerbeschule, and in 1918 was appointed Inspector of Further Education in Vienna. His architectural works include the Th. Flemmich Haus, Jägerndorf; Villas M. Rothberger and R. Bienenfeld, Baden; a house for Dr O. Wertheim, Mariazell; a country house for W. Kapsch, Mitterbach bei Mariazell; municipal housing in Stöbergasse, Längenfeldgasse, Harkurtstrasse and Güpferlinggasse, Vienna; the Heinrichshof Café, Opernring 3, Vienna; a main entrance for G. Zykan, Kohlmarkt, Vienna; a warm water baths for the Wiener Dianabad and a department store for the Österreichischer Werkbund, Kärntnerring, Vienna. Prutscher also designed silverware for the Wiener Werkstätte and jewellery, ceramics, furniture, glassware, wallpapers and lighting for many Viennese firms.

PUIG I CADAFALCH, Josep (1867–1956)

Puig was born in Mataró, and studied physics and maths in Barcelona before going on to the School of Architecture there, and then in Madrid. He travelled widely in France, England, Austria and Germany. He wrote numerous articles on Catalan art, and a *General History of Art* in collaboration with Domènech. An independent architect from 1891, his works in Barcelona, mainly houses, include Casa Martí (Els Quatre Gats), via Montesión (1896); Casa Amattler, paseo de Gracia (1900); Casa Macaya, paseo del General Mola (1901); Casa Muntadas, avenida del Doctor Andreu (1903) and Hôtel Terminus, via Aragon (1903). He was a member of the Lliga de Catalunya and President of the first united regional government of Catalonia – the Mancomunitat.

RICHARDSON, Henry Hobson (1838–1886)

Richardson was born in St James' Parish, New Orleans. In 1855 he entered Harvard College, and during his time there decided to take up architecture. Graduating in 1859, he went to Paris and entered the atelier of Louis J. André at the Ecole des Beaux-Arts. When the Civil War broke out in America his funds stopped, and on leaving the Ecole he decided to make his own way in Paris, collaborating with Théo Labrouste as draughtsman, and superintending railway station construction for Hittorf. When he returned to America he went to New York and opened a small office with Emlyn Little in 1867, leaving after a few months to form a partnership with Charles D. Gambrill which lasted eleven years. Richardson's great contribution to American architectural practice lay in his use of the Romanesque style – a mixture of French and Spanish motifs. Works in this style include a building on the corner of Commonwealth Avenue and Clarendon Street, New York (1871); the Boston Trinity (1872–77); the New York State Capitol, Albany, with Leopold Eidlitz and F. L. Olmsted, and a warehouse for Marshall Field (1885–87).

RIEMERSCHMID, Richard (1868–1957)

Born in Munich, Riemerschmid studied painting at the Academy there from 1888 to 1890. With Obrist, Eckmann and others he formed the 'Vereinigte Werkstätten für Kunst und Handwerk' in Munich in 1897, and after this concentrated almost exclusively on the applied arts. The previous year he had built his own house at Pasing bei München, and in 1900 he exhibited a 'Room of an Art Lover' in Paris. His advanced furniture designs, including early designs for machine-produced items (1905), found an outlet from 1898 in the Dresden workshop of his brother-in-law Karl Schmidt. Riemerschmid also produced interiors for the Munich Schauspielhaus (1901) and drew up plans for the Garden Cities in Hellerau (1909) and later Nürnberg. He was instrumental in the foundation of the Deutscher Werkbund in 1907, and through his teaching at Nürnberg, Munich and Cologne, his Directorship of the Munich Kunstgewerbeschule from 1913 to 1924, and his establishment of a Werkschule in Cologne in 1926, he provided a basis for modern industrial design.

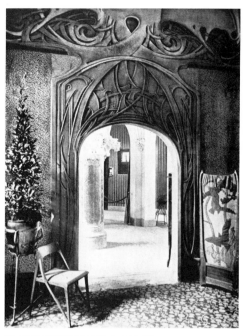

68 RIEMERSCHMID *Paris Exhibition* 1900, 'Room of an Art Lover' (contemporary photograph)

RIGOTTI, Annibale (1870–n.d.)

Born in Turin, Rigotti obtained his diploma in architecture in 1891. From 1893 to 1896 he worked in Constantinople with D'Aronco, returning to Italy in 1899 to teach at the Accademia di Belle Arti in Parma. He later taught at the Academies of Florence, Turin and Venice. From 1907 he worked in the court of the King of Siam. He produced a number of competition designs only a few of which were executed. His works include a project for a cemetery, Treviso (1893); municipal theatre, Sistov, Bulgaria (1896); communal school, Sommariva (1897); the Palazzo Municipale, Cagliari (1898), with Caselli, and the Villa Falcioni, Domodossola (1902). With D'Aronco he did work for the 1901 Esposizione Internationale delle Arte Figurativo, Turin, and at the 1902 Exhibition he produced an Oils and Wines pavilion and Cinema.

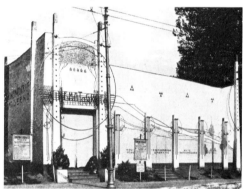

69 RIGOTTI *Turin Exhibition* 1902, project for a Cinema (contemporary photograph)

ROOSENBOOM, Albert (1871–1943)

Roosenboom was born of a family of painters of Dutch extraction living in Brussels. After taking courses at the Académie Royale des Beaux-Arts in Brussels, he became a draughtsman in Victor Horta's office in 1896, and later worked for Jules Barbier. In 1900 he became Professor at the Ecole des Arts Décoratifs, Ixelles, and in the same year designed a house at 83 rue Faider and a villa on the avenue des Cyclistes, both in Brussels. After 1914 he became involved with restorations at Brussels, Ypres, Louvain and Bruly and on the châteaux of Boisselles, Soiron, Bormenville and Elverdinghe, among others.

ROOT, John Wellborn (1850–1892)

Born in Lumpkin near Atlanta, Georgia, Root moved with his father to Liverpool, England, when he was fourteen. He acquired a general education which included architectural drawing. In 1868 he entered

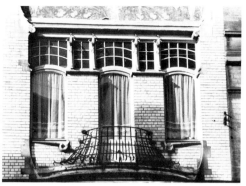

70 ROOSENBOOM *83 rue Faider* Brussels 1900, window detail (photograph Wieser)

Oxford College but left prematurely to return to America where he took an engineering course at City College, New York. He worked for James Renwick, James Snook of Brooklyn and with Peter Wright before setting up practice with Daniel H. Burnham in Chicago in 1873. With Burnham he built a number of business structures in Chicago between 1873 and his death in 1892, the best known being the sixteen-storey Monadnock Building (1880–91), and the Reliance Building (1890–94). Their most distinguished commission was for the Chicago Academy of Fine Arts, Van Buren Street, and they also built a number of private houses, and were consultants for the World's Columbian Exhibition of 1893. In 1889 Root translated Semper's *Development of Architectural Style*.

RUBBIANI, Alfonso (1848–1913)

Born in Bologna, Rubbiani initiated a programme of organic restoration of Bolognese monuments, including S. Paolo, Sta Maria degli Angeli, the Chiesa dello Spirito Santo, the Collegio di Spagna, the Loggia della Mercanzia and the Palaces of Re Enzo, Notari, del Podesta and Bevilacqua. He also restored castles in San Martino, and the Ponte Poledrano. He decorated the new apsidal chapel of S. Francesco, and was a consultant to the association Aemelia Ars.

SAINTENOY, Paul (1862–1952)

Saintenoy's life and career were concentrated in Brussels, although he travelled widely. He was the son of an architect and acquired an academic and traditional education. His work includes a house on avenue Louise, with ironwork by Bogaerts and Merxem (1898); house, rue du Taciturne, with ironwork by P. Desmedt; the Delacre Pharmacy and the Old England Department Store, rue Montagne de la Cour, in collaboration with Becker and Wykowski. He also built the Palais de la Ville de Bruxelles for the exhibition of 1897, and worked on the restoration of the Hôtel Ravenstein.

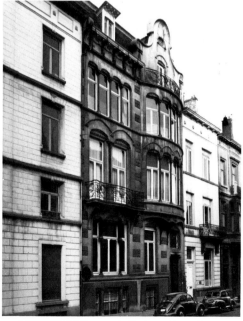

71 SAINTENOY *34 rue du Taciturne* Brussels 1900

SANT'ELIA, Antonio (1888-1916)

Sant'Elia was born in Como in 1888, and studied in Milan and at the Scuola di Belle Arti in Bologna. His designs for monuments include a new cemetery at Monza (1912), in collaboration with Italo Paternostro, and the tomb of the Caprotti family, Como (1914). In 1911 he published a project for a 'Villino Moderno' in *Le case popolari e la città giardino* and in 1912 – the year he settled in Milan – he worked with the sculptor Gerolamo Fontano on the design of a villa. He collaborated on other projects at this time with his artist friends but little is known of these in detail. In 1914 in Milan at the first exhibition of the Nuove Tendenze group he showed his project for a 'città futurista', and it was the catalogue notes for this exhibition, originally written by Sant'Elia, which were modified by Marinetti and republished soon afterwards as the *Manifesto of Futurist Architecture*. Sant'Elia was killed in action at Monfalcone.

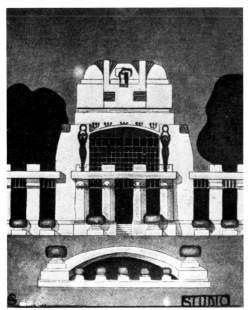

72 SANT'ELIA *Project for an architect's studio* n.d.

SAUVAGE, Frédéric-Henri (1873-1932)

Sauvage was born in Rouen and was a pupil of Pascal at the Ecole des Beaux-Arts. From the beginning of his working life he produced designs for wallpapers, posters and graphics as well as for architecture. From 1900 he worked in collaboration with Charles Sarazin. In 1899 he provided furniture and decoration for the

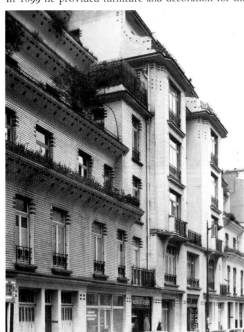

73 SAUVAGE *Maisons Ouvrières* Paris 1912-14 (photograph Godoli)

Café de Paris on the avenue de l'Opéra and between 1898 and 1900 he collaborated with Charpentier, Jourdain and Majorelle on the Villa Majorelle, Nancy. Around 1900 he provided interiors for the Magasins Jansen in the rue Royale, Paris, and for the Paris Exhibition of that year he built another lost work, the Loïe Fuller Pavilion. He built a number of apartment blocks in Paris, in particular 'habitations hygiéniques' for the Société des Logements Hygiéniques à Bon Marché and two villas at Biarritz in 1903 and 1907. In 1903 he and Sarazin published their *Eléments de l'architecture*. Sauvage's later work includes 'maisons ouvrières' or 'gradins' on the rue Vavin, the Cinéma Gambetta (1920) and pavilions and a transformer terminal for the 1925 Paris Exhibition. In 1926 he collaborated with Frantz Jourdain on the extension to 'la Samaritaine', and in 1931 he built the Grands Magasins Decré in Nantes.

SCHMID, Otto (1873-n.d.)

Born at Hilzingen of German-Swiss parentage, Schmid was educated at the Technische Hochschule in Zurich. He settled in Schloss Chillon, Veytaux, in 1897, and began restoration work on the castle. Among his other restorations are the Cathedral of St Ursus, Solothurn. He also built a school in Veytaux, and in Lausanne villas, the church of St Jean and, with P. Rosset, the Galeries du Commerce in rue de la Grotte. He designed other villas, in Vevey and Montreux, where he also provided a bathing beach.

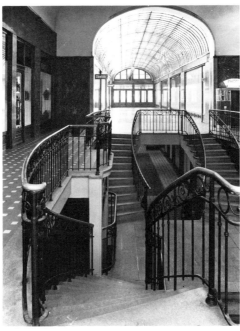

74 SCHMID & ROSSET *Galeries du Commerce* Lausanne 1908-09 (photograph Collomb)

SCHMORANZ, František (1845-1892)

Born at Slatinan, the son of an architect, Schmoranz studied at Prague Polytechnic. After one year in Cairo he returned to Prague and became Director and organiser of the newly constituted Prague School of Arts and Crafts. His own architectural works include the Khedive pavilion at the Vienna World's Exhibition (1873) in collaboration with J. Machytha; a thermal baths at Trenčianské Teplice; state school buildings in Prague (1884), again with Machytha, and a Bishop's residence in Zara.

SCHOELLKOPF, François-Xavier (1870-1911)

Schoellkopf was born in Moscow to French parents, and gained his architectural education in Paris. After studying classics at Sainte-Barbe College he entered the Ecole des Beaux-Arts as a pupil of Guadet and Raulin, graduating in 1895. His Parisian work includes a private house, avenue d'Iena (c.1898); Hôtel Guilbert, boulevard Berthier (1900); apartments, avenue de la République (c.1900); an apartment block, boulevard de Courcelles (1902) and 29 boulevard de Courcelles with the sculptor Rouvière. He also designed maisonettes for Montbéliard (1906) which were exhibited at the Salon de la Société des Artistes Français.

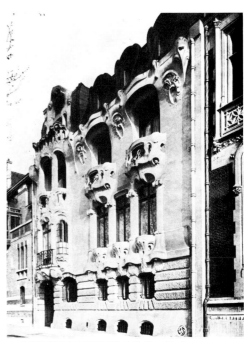

75 SCHOELLKOPF *Hôtel Guilbert* Paris 1900 (contemporary photograph)

SCHÖNTHAL, Otto (1878-1961)

A member of the Wagnerschule from 1898 to 1901, Schönthal went on to assist Wagner on the buildings of the Stadtbahn, the Postsparkasse and the Steinhof church. His houses include a scheme for a Künstler-villa (1900); house on the Linzerstrasse (1901); project for a Sommer Wohnhaus for Dr Bauer; projects for villas and country houses (1902 and 1903) and the Villa Vojczik, Wien-Hütteldorf (1902). Schönthal also designed a church for the Zentralfriedhof (1901); a cemetery church (1901); the Mozart fountain in Vienna, with sculpture by K. Wollek (1904) and other buildings in Vienna. From 1909 he collaborated with Emil Hoppe, and until 1915 with Marcel Kammerer. He was Viennese Baurat and from 1923 to 1925 was President of the Wiener Künstlergenossensch. *See also Kammerer*.

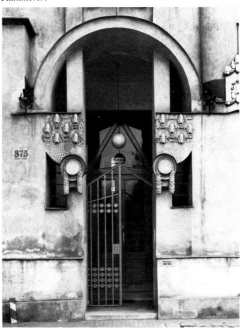

76 SCHÖNTHAL *Villa Vojczik* Vienna 1901, entrance detail (photograph Godoli)

SCHULZ, Josef (1840-1917)

Schulz was born in Prague and was a student of van der Nüll and Siccardsburg at the Vienna Academy. From 1869 to 1871 he was in Italy, and in 1878 he was nominated Professor at the reorganised Czech Polytechnic in Prague. A pupil and assistant of Zítek, he completed the latter's National Theatre, and worked on the Rudolfinum with him (1884). He was also the designer of the National Museum (1885-90) and the Museum of Arts and Industry (1899) in Prague.

SELLERS, James Henry (1861-1954)

Born in Oldham, Sellers began his career as office boy to a local architect, Thomas Boyter. After training himself as a draughtsman, he became an itinerant assistant, working in Liverpool, London, Birmingham and York. In 1893 he was made assistant county architect for Cumberland under George Dale Oliver, and was responsible for several banks and various school buildings. In 1900, Sellers left Carlisle and returned to Oldham, where he went into partnership with David Jones. His work of this period includes a design for two villas in Abbey Hills Road (1901) and extensions to the nearby Manor House (1901) and to a house owned by Dronsfield Brothers in Alexandra Park (1903). In 1904 he formed a partnership with Edgar Wood, with whom he collaborated on many houses in the Manchester area. Sellers' most significant independent work of this period was the office building for Dronsfield Brothers, Oldham (1908), although the Durnford Street and Elm Street schools in Middleton (1908-10) can also be largely attributed to him. In 1922 Wood retired to Italy, and Sellers continued to practise alone until about 1950.

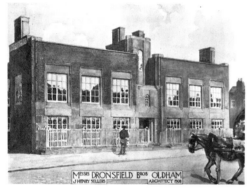

77 SELLERS *Dronsfield Brothers office building* Oldham 1908, perspective drawing

SERRURIER-BOVY, Gustave (1858-1910)

Son of an architect, Gustave Serrurier attended the Liège Academy of Fine Arts, obtaining his diploma in 1882. In 1884 he married Marie Bovy and they opened a porcelain and crystal shop in the rue de l'Université, Liège, under the name of Serrurier-Bovy. In 1887 the shop began to sell Japanese inspired objets d'art and crafts. The following year Serrurier-Bovy visited Liberty's in London, gaining from them the exclusive representation for the province of Liège. By 1890 he was designing furniture to be made by artisans on the premises, and by 1899 he had branches in La Haye and Nice. After exhibiting at Paris in 1900 he was provided with capital to industrialise his production, but finding machine-made products unsaleable he had no hesitation in ceasing to use them. The firm continued until 1924. Serrurier-Bovy's architectural works include an unexecuted project for a University Hospital at Liège; the Pavillon Bleu at the Paris 1900 Exhibition, in collaboration with R. Dulong, and his own house, 'l'Aube', avenue de Cointe, Liège.

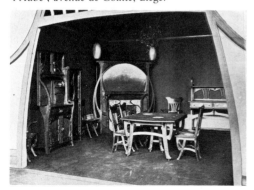

78 SERRURIER-BOVY *Salon de 1899,* dining room (contemporary photograph)

SHAW, Richard Norman (1831-1912)

Shaw was born in Edinburgh and moved to London in 1846. After a brief period with an unknown architect he was articled in 1849 to William Burn, who introduced him to William Eden Nesfield, with whom he shared an office from 1863 to 1876. He attended the R.A. Schools, and as R.A. travelling student he spent from 1854 to 1856 in France, Italy and Germany. The sketches made on this trip were published as *Architectural Sketches from the Continent.* After a brief session with Anthony Salvin, Shaw succeeded Webb as chief assistant in Street's office and was there from 1859 until 1862, when he set up on his own. Shaw's country houses include Glen Andred, Sussex (1866-68); Leyswood, Sussex (1867-69); Cragside, Northumberland (1870); Grim's Dyke, Harrow (1870-72); Merrist Wood, Surrey (1876-77); Adcote, Shropshire (1876-79); Chesters, Northumberland (1891-93) and Bryanston, Dorset. In London he built Lowther Lodge, South Kensington (1873-75); 196 Queen's Gate (1874-76); buildings for Bedford Park (1879-80); Old Swan House, Chelsea (1876); New Scotland Yard (1887-90); New Zealand Chambers (1971-73); Alliance Insurance, St James's (1881-83); The Gaiety Theatre, Aldwych (1901-03); the Picadilly Hotel (1905-08) and his last building, Portland House in the City (1908). He also built sixteen churches, all in a Gothic style, the only one departing from this programme being St Michael's, Bedford Park (1879-80).

SMITH, A. Dunbar (1866-1933) and BREWER, Cecil Claude (1871-1918)

Brewer's architectural training began when he was articled to J. G. Gibbins of Brighton, and he later went on to the R.A. Schools. He obtained an R.I.B.A. Pugin Studentship in 1896. In 1895 he provided the winning scheme for the competition for the Passmore Edwards Settlement in Bloomsbury in collaboration with Smith, and set up a partnership which lasted until the end of Brewer's life. After the Settlement, their works include additions to the Royal Hospital, Kew Foot Road, Richmond (1896); the East Anglian Sanatorium at Nayland (c.1898); Little Barley End House and stables, Aldbury, Herts (1900), and a number of other houses. Their largest commission was for the Cardiff National Museum of Wales (1908-10), before which Brewer made a study of European museums. They also built Heal's store on Tottenham Court Road (1914-16), and with Ambrose Heal and others Brewer was instrumental in setting up the Design and Industries Association, of which he was the first Honorary Secretary.

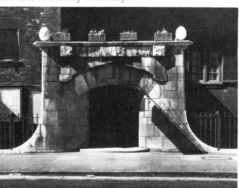

79 SMITH & BREWER *Passmore Edwards Settlement* London 1895-97, entrance detail

SOMMARUGA, Giuseppe (1867-1917)

Sommaruga was born in Milan, and studied at Milan Polytechnic and the Brera Academy. His early works include two competition designs for a Palace of Parliament in Rome, in collaboration with Broggi (1889), and in Buenos Aires (1896), and a project for the Monument to the Fallen at the Battle of Palermo (c.1895). His mature work began with the Villino Aletti, Rome (1897), continuing with the Aletti Tomb, Varese (1898); the Palazzina Comi, Milan (1900); the Palazzo Castiglioni, Milan (1901-03), with statues by Ernesto Bazzaro; a funerary monument for the Cosnati (1905); the Palazzina Salmoiraghi (1905-06); the Philodramatic Theatre at Trieste (1906); the

Mausoleo Faccanoni, Sarnico (1908) and the two Villas Faccanoni at Credaro (1907), and Sarnico (1907). In 1907 he began the Villa Romeo, later the Columbus Clinic. In 1908 in Milan he built the Villa Galimberti, and in Varese he began the monumental Hotel Tre Croci on the Campo dei Fiori. In 1915 he built a monumental cemetery in Milan and laid out a residential area at Lanzo d'Intelvi. In 1904 he was awarded a gold medal for his Italian Pavilion at the St Louis World's Exhibition. In his lifetime he was Consigliere of Brera Academy, Consigliere Superiore di Belle Arti, and was a member of the commission for the facade of Milan Cathedral.

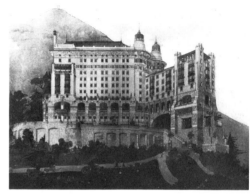

80 SOMMARUGA *Hotel Tre Croci* Varese 1908-11, perspective drawing

STAAL, Jan Frederik (1879-1940)

Staal was born in Amsterdam and after working in various offices there he travelled to New York. His early work, often in collaboration with A. J. Kropholler, includes the De Utrecht Insurance Offices, Damrak, Amsterdam (1905); the Kettner store, Heligenweg (1906) and 't Binnenhuis store and apartments, Raadhuisstraat (1907); the Willemspark houses (1911); country houses in Bergen (1916-18) and the Capi store, Kalverstraat, Amsterdam (1916). From 1920 to 1931 Staal was co-editor of *Wendingen.*

STEVENSON, John James (1831-1908)

Born in Glasgow and intended for the ministry, Stevenson attended a Theological course at Edinburgh. His love of architecture was crystallised by a visit to Italy, and in 1856 he joined the office of David Bryce in Edinburgh. For further training in 1858 he went to Gilbert Scott in London, and after a tour in France with a fellow pupil of Scott he set up his own practice with Cambell Douglas in Glasgow in 1860. In 1870 he went into partnership with E. R. Robson, newly appointed architect to the London School Board. His own house, the Red House, Bayswater Road (1871) became a meeting place for literary and artistic men of the time. Apart from domestic and school work, Stevenson built several churches, took part in the restoration of Oxford and Cambridge colleges, and was one of the first architects to design ship interiors, for the Orient Company. He was one of the founder members of the Society for the Protection of Ancient Buildings, and continued a thriving practice until about 1900.

STRAUVEN, Gustave (1878-1919)

Strauven was born in Schaerbeek, and for two years worked in the office of Victor Horta. His independent works in Brussels include two houses for Mme Spaak, rue Saint Quentin (1899); a house on the rue Van Campenhout (1901) and the Maison Van Dyck, boulevard Clovis (1901). In 1902 he built apartments in the avenue Paul de Jaer, Saint-Gilles, and a house on rue Souveraine, and in 1903 houses for M. Beyens on rue de l'Abdication and for the painter of Saint-Cyr in square Ambiorix.

SUCHARDA, Stanislav (1866-1916)

Sucharda, a sculptor and medallist, was born in Nová Paka and went to Prague in 1886 to study at the School of Arts and Crafts under J. V. Myslbek. He graduated in 1892 and taught there until 1915, when he left to teach at the Prague Academy. He was a great friend of Jan Kotěra and collaborated with him on houses in Wenceslas Square, Hradec Králové and Prostějov, and on the monument to the historian

Frant Palacký. Sucharda's sculpture also graced the Landesbank, the Assicurazioni Generali Building and the Wilson Station in Prague.

SULLIVAN, Louis Henri (1856-1924)

Born in Boston to an Irish father and a French/German mother, Sullivan studied at the Massachusetts Institute of Technology under William C. Ware. He worked as a draughtsman for Furness & Hewitt and in the Chicago office of Major Jenney and in 1874 went to the Ecole des Beaux-Arts in Paris, returning to Chicago in 1875. He was introduced to Adler in 1879 through a friend he had met in Jenney's office, and in 1881 the firm of Adler & Sullivan was established. Early commissions for business premises included the Borden Building, corner of Randolph and Dearborn (1880); the Ryerson Building, Randolph Street (1884) and the Knisel Building, West Monroe (1885). The firm's largest commission to date came in 1886 with the Auditorium Building, a collection of offices, hotel and theatre, and at the time the largest structure in Chicago. The firm also designed libraries, clubs, a synagogue, and exhibition buildings, including the Transportation Building for the Chicago World Columbian Exhibition in 1893 which was awarded the gold, silver and bronze medals by the Union Centrale des Arts Décoratifs. Residential commissions at one time numbered one half of the work of the firm, although Frank Lloyd Wright, who worked in the office between 1887 and 1893, had a large part to do with these. Adler & Sullivan's last major commission was for the Guaranty Building, Buffalo (1894), which, with the Wainwright Building of 1890-98 is the best known of their later work. When the partnership ended in 1895 Sullivan took with him G. G. Elmslie, an assistant, and together they designed the Carson Pirie Scott Store (1899-1904). Sullivan continued to work with Elmslie until 1909, their most successful areas being in housing and small banks. After Elmslie left, he went into something of a decline, realising only twenty buildings in the last thirty years of his life. He died in 1924 with the proofs of his book *A System of Architectural Ornament* just off the presses.

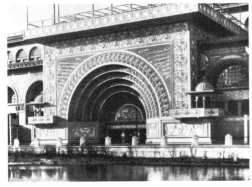

81 SULLIVAN *Chicago World Columbian Exhibition* 1893, Transportation Building (contemporary photograph)

THORN PRIKKER, Johan (1868-1932)

A painter and decorative artist, Thorn Prikker studied at the Academy in The Hague, and in 1893 exhibited with Les Vingts. He was friendly with Verhaeren and van de Velde and contributed ornamental designs to *Van Nu en Straks*. From 1904 he was resident in Germany, teaching at Krefeld, and after 1910 at the Hagen Volkwangschule, Essen, and later in Munich, Düsseldorf and Cologne. In 1898 he designed a simple wooden chair which greatly influenced later functional designs.

TOWNSEND, Charles Harrison (1851-1928)

Townsend was born in Birkenhead, and was articled to a minor Liverpool architect, Walter Scott. Around 1880 he came to London, forming a partnership in 1884 with T. L. Banks, whom he had joined in 1883. He stayed with Banks until 1888 when he became a Fellow of the R.I.B.A., joined the Art Workers' Guild, and began his own Arts and Crafts practice. He designed textiles, wallpapers and joinery as well as buildings, and wrote a great deal for periodicals, often working in collaboration with other artists and craftsmen he met through the Guild. In 1891 he rebuilt the West end of Vulliamy's All Saints, Ennismore Gardens, South Kensington and between 1892 and 1907 built the Bishopsgate Institute; a church (St Martins); a Congregational chapel; a village hall; a number of houses in Blackheath; the Horniman Museum, London Road, Forest Hill (1896-1901) and the Whitechapel Art Gallery (1899-1901). In 1906 he wrote an introduction to an edition of Joseph Nash's *Mansions of England in the Olden Time*, and in 1910 participated in the restoration of Compton Wyngate's House, Warwicks. Between 1902 and 1904 he collaborated with a number of craftsmen in the construction and decoration of the church of St Mary the Virgin near Great Warley, with its adjoining Garden of Rest. Other works include Linden Haus, Düsseldorf (1896-1901); Dickhurst, near Haslemere, Surrey (1900); the Union Free Church, Woodford Green, Essex (1904); the Arbuthnot Institute Hall, Shamley Green, Surrey (1906); a house in The Glade, Letchworth, Herts (1906) and schools at Penn and Holmer Green, Bucks (1909-10).

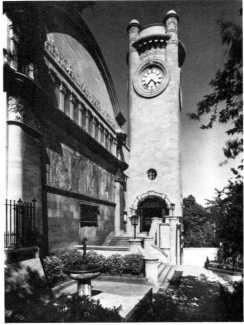

82 TOWNSEND *Horniman Museum* London 1896-1901, facade detail

VALLIN, Eugène (1856-1922)

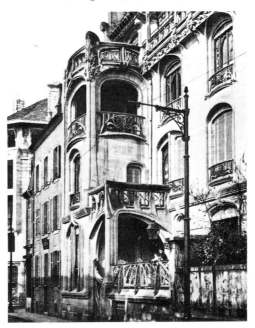

83 VALLIN & BIET *22 rue de la Commanderie* Nancy 1901-02 (contemporary photograph)

Vallin served his apprenticeship at Nancy with his uncle, a maker of ecclesiastical furnishings. Although primarily a cabinet-maker and designer of interior settings, Vallin also practised architecture in Nancy – the Société Générale building, rue St Dizier (1901); the Magasins Vaxelaire, 13 rue Raugaff (1901); apartments on the rue Stanislas (1906); the aquarium of the garden of the Musée de l'Ecole de Nancy, avenue Sergent-Blandan (1906) and the entrance gallery of the Exhibition of Decorative Arts, Nancy (1909).

VAN DE VELDE, Henry-Clément (1863-1957)

Born in Antwerp, van de Velde studied painting at the Académie des Beaux-Arts from 1881 to 1882, and then went to Paris where he was a pupil of Carolas Duran from 1884 to 1885. In 1886 and 1887 he participated in the foundation of the groups Als ik Kan and L'Art Indépendant, and in 1888 was admitted to Les Vingt, through which he met Paul Gauguin and William Morris. His first architectural commission was for the Sethe house in Dieweg, Uccle (1894), and in the following year he designed and built his own house, Bloemenwerf. From about 1890 he provided lay-outs for the publication *Van Nu en Straks*, and he also provided decorations and furniture for Bing's L'Art Nouveau and Meier-Graef's La Maison Moderne. In 1897 van de Velde exhibited textiles, wallpapers and furniture at the Dresden Art Exhibition, and in 1899 he left for Berlin, where he was involved in the decoration of François Haby's Barber's Shop (1900-01) and the Havana Company Cigar Shop (1899-1900). He also received commissions from Karl Ernst Osthaus – notably the Folkwang Museum interiors (c.1900-02) and the Osthaus dwelling on the Hohenhof (1908). In 1902 he moved to Weimar as artistic consul to the Grand Duke. He was also Director of the Kunstgewerbeschule until 1914, and provided buildings for it in 1906. His other works include a house for himself, Ehringsdorf, Weimar (1906); houses in Chemnitz, Schoveningen, Hagen, Lauterbeck, Hanover and Weimar, and the theatre for the Werkbund's 1914 Cologne Exhibition. He left Germany in 1917 for Switzerland, returning to Belgium later in life.

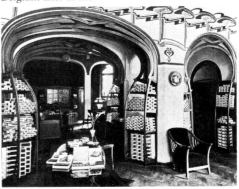

84 VAN DE VELDE *Havana Company Cigar Shop* Berlin 1899-1900, interior (contemporary photograph)

VIOLLET-LE-DUC, Eugène-Emmanuel (1814-1879)

Born in Paris, Viollet-le-Duc's early architectural training began around 1830 with the architects Huvé and Leclère, and he spent the 1830s travelling and sketching in Italy and France. In 1840 he was entrusted by the Commission des Monuments Historiques with the restoration of the Abbey Church of Vézelay, and in the same year became director of the restorations of the Sainte-Chapelle, Paris. He also worked on the cathedrals of Amiens and Laon and, from 1845 onwards, together with Lassus, on the restoration of Notre Dame de Paris. Between 1863 and 1870 he restored the Château at Pierrefonds to serve as a summer residence for Napoleon III. In 1863 Viollet-le-Duc obtained the Chair of History of Art at the Ecole des Beaux-Arts, but protests from the students caused him to step down. His highly influential *Entretiens sur l'architecture* were published between 1863 and 1872, and he continued to write throughout the 1870s. His other major published work is the *Dictionnaire raisonné de l'architecture française* which was published between

1854 and 1868. The one major church to his own design is St Denis-de-l'Estrée, at St Denis.

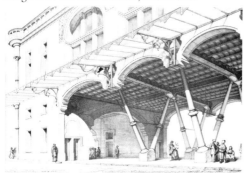

85 VIOLLET-LE-DUC *Design for a covered market* c.1872, perspective drawing (from *Entretiens sur l'architecture* vol. 2, XII, fig. 21)

VOYSEY, Charles Francis Annesley (1857-1941)

Born at Hessle near Hull, Voysey was educated mainly at home. In 1874 he began to work for the architect John Pollard Seddon and between 1879 and the establishment of his own practice in 1883 he worked for Saxon Snell and George Devey. Between 1882 and 1884 he was involved with construction of the South Devon Sanatorium and the adjacent Royal Hospital, Teignmouth. His first domestic commission came through the publication of one of his cottage designs in *The Architect*, which led M. H. Lakin to commission a house for himself at Bishops Itchington, Warwickshire in 1888. At this time he also designed a house and studio for Bedford Park and was involved with the design of stained glass, fabrics, wallpaper, furniture and decorative accessories. His houses were numerous, and were very well publicised in England through *The Studio* and on the continent through Muthesius' *Das englische Haus*. The best known of these are the Studio House, South Parade, Bedford Park (1891); 14 and 16 Hans Road, Knightsbridge (1891-92); Annesley Lodge, Kidderpore Avenue, Hampstead (1896); Broadleys and Moor Crag, near Windemere (1899); Spade House, Sandgate, for H. G. Wells (1899) and The Orchard, Chorley Wood, Herts, for himself (1900-01). He also designed a house in Egypt. In 1902-03 he designed a wallpaper factory in Barley Mow Passage, Chiswick, for Messrs Sanderson – his only industrial commission. The war virtually extinguished his practice, but he was rediscovered by a new generation in the 1930s, and was awarded the R.I.B.A. Gold Medal in 1940.

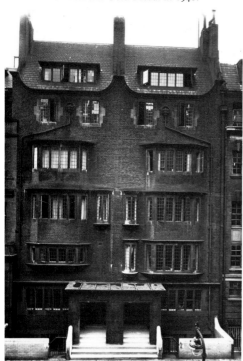

86 VOYSEY *14 and 16 Hans Road* London 1891-92

WAGNER, Otto Koloman (1841-1918)

From an early age Wagner was educated by private tutors and French governesses. In 1850 he attended the Akademisches Gymnasium in Vienna, where he spent two years before proceeding to a Benedictine boarding school at Kremsmünster. In 1857 he returned to Vienna for two years to study civil engineering at the Vienna Polytechnic, and between 1860 and 1861 he was at the Royal Academy of Architecture in Berlin. He finally qualified as an architect from the Vienna Academy of Fine Arts, where he had studied from 1861 to 1863. After qualifying he worked briefly for the Ringstrasse architect Ludwig van Förster. In his first thirty years of architectural practice Wagner produced a large number of buildings and projects including a synagogue in Budapest (1871); contributions to Otto Thienemann's Grabenhof (1873-74); a number of apartment blocks – Stadiongasse 6/8 (1882), Lobkovitzplatz I (1884), Universitätstrasse 12 (1886) and the Villa Hahn, Baden (1885-86). Between 1889 and 1891 he built three houses in Rennweg, and in 1882 won in a competition a commission for a Länderbank. In 1880 he produced his first project for a museum complex, the 'Artibus'. In 1893 Wagner was appointed adviser to the Viennese Transport Commission, and the Commission for the Regulation of the Danube Canal. In the same year he drew up a plan for regulating traffic in the city and he was to be given opportunities for a large number of engineering schemes in the following years. More important, in 1894 Karl von Hasenauer, Professor of Architecture at the Academy of Fine Arts, died, and Wagner was promoted to Oberbaurat and took his place. Thus began the Wagnerschule, a brilliant training ground for the new European artistic life for over a decade, and in his inaugural lecture, later published as *Moderne Architektur*, Wagner set out his principles. He joined the Vienna Secession soon after it was formed by his most brilliant pupils in 1898 and through them was introduced to van de Velde and Mackintosh. His work for the Stadtbahn – thirty-six stations built on four separate lines – was completed in 1900. His other works in Vienna include the Majolikahaus on the corner of the Linke Wienzeile and Köstlergasse (1898-99); the 'Die Zeit' Post Office of 1902, and the Österreichisches Postsparkasse of 1903-07. His two apartment blocks, Neustiftgasse 40 and Döblergasse 4 (1909-11), contained his own flat and studio, Hoffmann's studio and part of the Wiener Werkstätte. His status in the architectural profession grew steadily and in 1914 he was a member of organisations in eight countries.

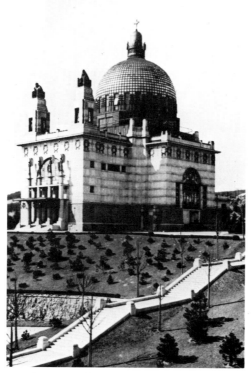

87 WAGNER *Church of Steinhof* Vienna 1905-07

WALENKAMP, H. J. M. (1872-1933)

Born in Amsterdam in 1872, Walenkamp joined Cuypers' office in the 1880s as a draughtsman. From 1899 to 1903 he was draughtsman for H. P. Berlage on the Amsterdam Stock Exchange, for which he provided some remarkable perspectives. His projects of the 1890s include the public library and public baths projects of 1895, and the Academy of Fine Arts project of 1899. He was involved in the work of t'Binnenhuis, and along with De Bazel, Lauweriks and others, was one of the founders of Architectura et Amicitia.

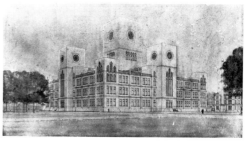

88 WALENKAMP *Project for a Peace Palace* 1905, exterior perspective

WALTON, George (1867-1933)

Born in Glasgow, Walton left school in 1881 and became a junior clerk at the British Linen Bank in Glasgow, attending classes in art in the evenings. In 1888 he set up an interior decoration business in Wellington Street, Glasgow, which in later years was to be extended into a workshop, with other showrooms in the city and elsewhere. In 1896 his decorative hoardings were placed around a frontage in Buchanan Street, the site of Mrs Cranston's tea-rooms, on which he collaborated with Charles Rennie Mackintosh. Between 1897 and 1898 Walton furnished houses at Leadcameroch and York, the latter leading to the establishment of another workshop there. In 1897 he met George Davison, head of Kodak European sales – a connection which led him to design Kodak shops in London, Glasgow, Brussels, Milan, Vienna and elsewhere. Between 1901 and the outbreak of the war he designed and furnished a number of houses, the best known of these being The Leys at Barnet Lane near Elstree, which was illustrated in Muthesius' *Das englische Haus*, and The White House near Shiplake in Oxfordshire. In Wales he realised two schemes – 'Wern Fawr', and the St David's Hotel, both in Harlech. During the war he was surveyor for the Central Liquor Traffic Control Board, and after the war he had a few small commissions including some extensions to his earlier house, The Leys, some stained glass in Boreham Wood Church for the same client, and four suburban houses in Sterne Street, Shepherd's Bush (1923). His final works were textile designs for the Edinburgh Weavers – few of which were executed due to a preference for Art Deco after Paris 1925 – and some building, including a memorial chapel for the wife of the patron of The White House, at Cap d'Antibes.

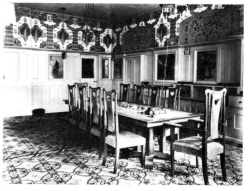

89 WALTON *Kodak offices* London, board room at Clerkenwell Road branch 1902

WEBB, Philip Speakman (1831-1915)

Born in Oxford, Webb's early interests were wildlife and plants. He was educated at Aynho Grammar School, and later articled to the architect John Billing of Reading, and then to an architect in Wolverhampton. In 1852 he returned to Oxford and for four years worked in the office of G. E. Street, where he met William Morris. By 1858 he was designing furniture with Morris and Burne-Jones. Webb set up his own practice in 1856, and in 1859 he designed the Red House at Bexley Heath for Morris and his wife. He also designed church and domestic decorations and furniture, textiles, tiles, grilles and other metalwork for the firm of Morris Marshall Faulkner and Co. In the course of his career he built about fifty or sixty fine houses and one church, at Brampton, Cumberland (1875). He always insisted on the personal supervision of his houses, which include Jolwynds, Surrey (1873); Clouds, Wiltshire (1881-86) and his last complete house, Standen near East Grinstead (1891-94). Webb also made many additions to older country houses, and built in London a terrace of shops at Worship Street, Shoreditch; 2 Palace Green (1868) and 35 Glebe Place (1873). In 1877 he founded with Morris the Society for the Protection of Ancient Buildings. Webb effectively retired from practice in 1900 to design cottages for Mrs Morris at Kelmscott.

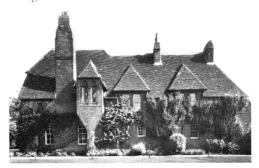

90 WEBB *Red House* Bexley Heath 1859

WEISSENBURGER, Lucien (1860-1929)

Weissenburger began to practise in Nancy in the 1880s. In 1900 he built the Royer Press, rue de la Saltpétrière with sculptures by Bussière and in 1901-02 supervised the construction of the Villa Majorelle. Other works in Nancy include 24 rue Lionnois (1903-04); 10 rue d'Auxonne (c.1908); 1 and 14 boulevard Charles V; 52 cours Léopold (1905); 60 and 62 quai Claude-le-Lorrain (1902); Anciens Magasins Réunis, place Thiers, in collaboration with Victor Prouvé (1907); a villa in the Parc de Saurupt (c.1908) and the collaboration in 1910 with Alexandre Mienville on the Hôtel-Brasserie Excelsior, with decorations by Majorelle.

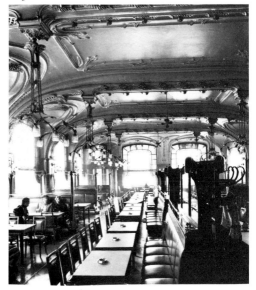

91 WEISSENBURGER *Hôtel-Brasserie Excelsior* Nancy 1910 (photograph Rose)

WILSON, Henry (1864-1934)

Born in Liverpool, Wilson attended a course in design at the Kidderminster School of Art, and later worked consecutively in the architectural offices of E. J.

Shrewsbury, John Oldrid Scott and John Belcher. In 1888 he joined John Dando Sedding in his Oxford Street studio, and on Sedding's death in 1891 took over the practice, completing a number of Sedding's unfinished schemes including Holy Trinity, Sloane Street (1888-1900). He also added portions to completed Sedding schemes, such as towers for St Clement's Church, Boscombe (1893) and Holy Redeemer Church, Finsbury (1895-97) and a chancel for St Mary's Church, Lynton, Somerset (1905). His earliest important personal commission was for a public library in Ladbroke Grove (1890), and he also built the churches of St Peter's, Mount Park Road, Ealing (1892), and St Mark's, Brithdir, Merioneth (1896-97) which he also decorated. Around 1900 he provided furnishings for St Bartholomew's Church, Brighton. From 1915 to 1922 he was President of the Arts and Crafts Exhibition Society, for whom he created a number of architectural exhibition settings and in 1917 he was made Master of the Art Workers' Guild. Also in 1917 he produced a plan for the creation of a Cotswold village for two hundred handworkers, a vision he had had for many years. In 1922 he went to France and passed his remaining years at Menton. The project which occupied a large part of his later years was his design for the Elphinstone Tomb for King's College, Aberdeen.

WITZMANN, CARL (1883-1952)

Born in Vienna, Witzmann studied at the Kunstgewerbeschule from 1900 to 1904 under Josef Hoffmann and Hermann Herdtle. He then worked with Hoffmann in the Wiener Werkstätte. He taught at the Kunstgewerbeschule from 1908 to 1914 and from 1918 to 1949. His works include houses at Elsslergasse 11 (1912), Eitebergergasse 18 (1912), Elsslergasse 8 (1912-13), Beckgasse 32 (1913), Hietzinger Hauptstrasse 20 (1920) and Lainzerstrasse 33 (1922). He was chief architect at the Jubilee Exhibition of 1908 and also built a theatre and several cafés, most of which have since been destroyed.

WOOD, Edgar (1860-1935)

Born in Middleton near Manchester, Wood was educated at the local Grammar School and was then articled to James Murgatroyd in Manchester. On qualifying he set up his own practice, first in Oldham, then Manchester. His independent works include the Manchester and Salford Bank, Middleton (1892); Silver Street Chapel, Rochdale (1893) and a Methodist Church, school and cottages, Middleton (1899-1902). From 1901 he built fourteen houses on Richardson's estate in Hale, Cheshire, and he also built a clock tower at Lindley, Huddersfield (1900-02) and the First Church of Christ Scientist, Victoria Park, Manchester (1903-08). He met his future partner J. Henry Sellers in Oldham in 1903, and they went into partnership in 1904. Between 1914 and 1916 Wood, one time President of the Manchester Society of Architects and the Northern Art Workers' Guild, built his own house at Hale Road, Hale, Cheshire. Two years later he retired to Porto Maurizio in Italy where he built another house, largely decorated by himself. He spent the rest of his life there painting. *See also Sellers.*

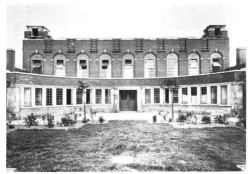

92 WOOD & SELLERS *Elm Street School* Middleton 1908-10

WRIGHT, Frank Lloyd (1867-1959)

Wright was born in Richland Centre, Wisconsin. He studied engineering at the University of Wisconsin, leaving in 1886 for the office of J. L. Silsbee in

Chicago. From 1887 to 1893 he worked as a draughtsman for Adler & Sullivan, and a great deal of the domestic work done by the firm can be attributed to him. In 1893 he opened his own office in Chicago with Cecil Carwin, who left in 1897. Wright first visited Japan in 1906, and in 1915 he established an office in Tokyo. In 1909 he went to Europe, visiting Germany and Italy. His influence on European design was established through an exhibition in Berlin, and the teaching of Berlage and Kotěra. In a career which spanned the periods of Art Nouveau and the Modern Movement, Wright produced over three hundred houses, as well as more important works such as the Imperial Hotel, Tokyo, Florida Southern College, Lakeland and the Soloman R. Guggenheim Museum and Beth Sholom Synagogue, New York.

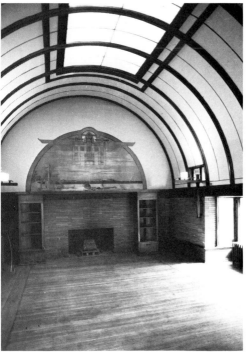

93 WRIGHT *Own house* Oak Park 1895, playroom (photograph Heinz)

WULFFLEFF, Charles-Albert (1874-n.d.)

An architect and painter in watercolours, Wulffleff was born in London, studied under H. Deglane at the Ecole des Beaux-Arts, then worked from 1903 to 1911 in Fribourg in collaboration with Frédéric Broillet on buildings such as the Villa Mayer-Daguet, avenue de Gambach (1905-06). After 1911 Wulffleff became architect to the Colonial Ministry in Paris. He designed a cathedral; a medical school and banqueting room in the Government Buildings at Dakar, French West Africa; buildings for Crédit Agricole and plans for the Colonial Hospital 'Fort de France' in Martinique. With J. H. Verrey he designed a training college at Fribourg. He also designed five churches including the protestant church at Auteuil, and was cofounder of the Institut Colonial Français.

ZITEK, Josef (1832-1909)

Zítek was born in Prague. From 1848 he studied at the Polytechnic there, and from 1851 to 1854 at the Vienna Academy. He worked in Vienna for a while after graduation in the studio of J. Kranners, which he left in 1855 to go on a study tour to Venice. Returning again to Vienna he spent a year in the studios of van der Nüll and Siccardsburg. Between 1859 and 1862 Zítek made two further journeys to Italy – to Rome, Naples and Pompeii – where he met the artist Friedrich Preller, who was to recommend his work to the Grand Duke of Saxe-Weimar. In 1862 he was again back in the studios of van der Nüll and Siccardsburg. Zítek's works include the design for the National Theatre in Prague; the Weimar Museum for Grand Duke Carl Alex and the Mill Fountain Colonnade at Carlsbad (1873-80). Zítek became Professor at the Prague Polytechnic, and from 1899 he was assisted in his work by Polívka.

MAP OF EUROPE

at the turn of the century

KEY TO THE PRINCIPAL CENTRES AND THEIR ARCHITECTS

Glasgow
Mackintosh, Walton

London
Baillie Scott, Townsend, Voysey

Barcelona
Domènech, Gaudí

Brussels
Hankar, Horta, Saintenoy

Nancy
André, Sauvage, Weissenburger

Paris
Guimard, Jourdain, Lavirotte

Amsterdam
Berlage, Cuypers, Kromhout

The Hague
Berlage

La Chaux-de-Fonds
Chapallaz, Jeanneret

Lausanne
Laverrière

Berlin
Behrens, Endell, van de Velde

Darmstadt
Behrens, Olbrich

Munich
Endell, Riemerschmid

Milan
Bossi, Sommaruga

Turin
D'Aronco, Fenoglio, Velati-Bellini

Prague
Fanta, Kotěra, Polívka

Vienna
Hoffmann, Olbrich, Wagner

Chicago
Sullivan, Wright

Pasadena
Greene and Greene

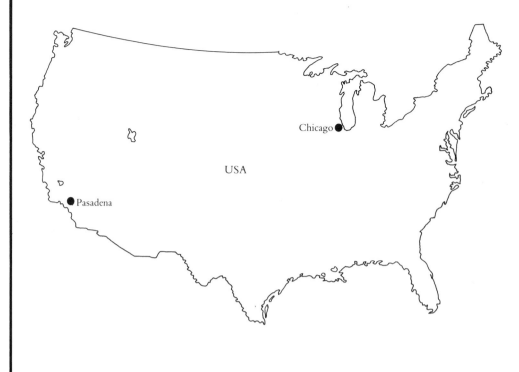

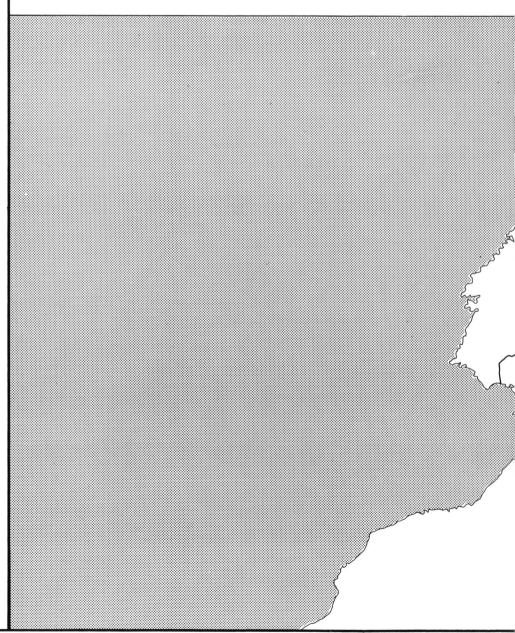

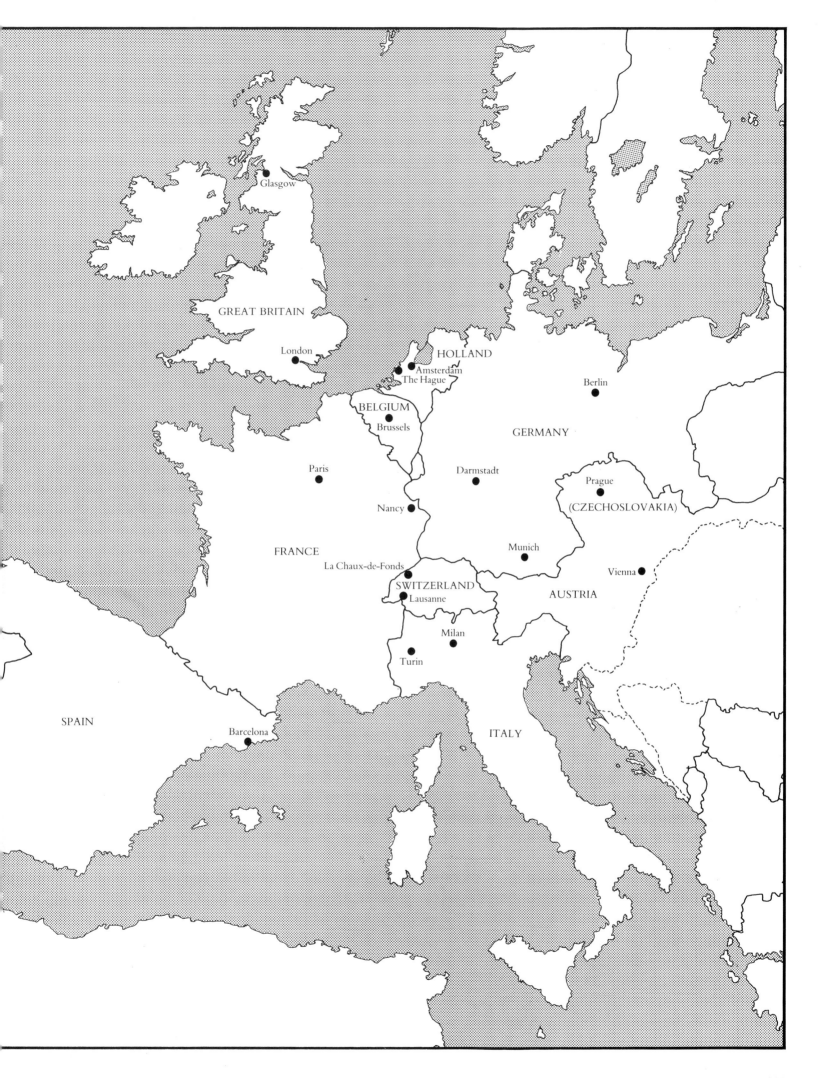

Glasgow

GREAT BRITAIN

London

HOLLAND
Amsterdam
The Hague

Berlin

BELGIUM
Brussels

GERMANY

Paris

Darmstadt

Prague

(CZECHOSLOVAKIA)

Nancy

FRANCE

Munich

La Chaux-de-Fonds

Vienna

SWITZERLAND
Lausanne

AUSTRIA

Milan

Turin

SPAIN

Barcelona

ITALY

BIBLIOGRAPHY

GENERAL

Books

Amaya, M., *Art Nouveau*, London, 1966.
Aslin, E., *The Aesthetic Movement: Prelude to Art Nouveau*, London, 1969.
Battersby, M., *Art Nouveau*, Feltham, 1969.
Bayard, J. E., *El Estilo Moderno*, Paris, 1919.
Behrendt, W. C., *Modern Building. Its Nature, Problems and Forms*, New York, 1937.
Bini, V., Trabuchelli, *L'Art Nouveau*, Milan, 1957.
Bossaglia, R., *Le Mobilier Art Nouveau*, Paris, 1972.
Bott, G., *Kunsthandwerk um 1900: Jugendstil, Art Nouveau, Modern Style, Nieuwe Kunst*, Darmstadt, 1973.
Cassou, J., Langui, E., Pevsner, N., *The Sources of Modern Art*, London, 1962.
Casteels, M., *The New Style. Architecture and Decorative Design*, London, 1931.
Cremona, I., *Il Tempo dell'Art Nouveau*, Florence, 1964.
Denis, M., *Théories 1890-1920*, Paris, 1920.
De Wouters de Bouchout, *L'Art Nouveau et l'Enseignement*, Malnes, 1903.
Emery, M., *Un Siècle d'architecture moderne: 1850-1950*, Paris, 1971.
Evers, H., *Het Orientalisme in de Westersche Architektur*, Rotterdam, 1894.
Geffroy, G., *Les industries artistiques françaises et étrangères à l'exposition universelle de 1900*, Paris, 1900.
Giedion, S., *Bauen in Frankreich. Bauen in Eisen. Bauen in Eisenbeton*, Berlin, 1928.
Giedion, S., *Space, Time and Architecture. The Growth of a New Tradition*, Cambridge, U.S.A., 1941.
Gloag, J., *A History of Cast Iron in Architecture*, London, 1948.
Guerrand, R.-H., *Art Nouveau en Europe*, Paris, 1965.
Hazan, F., *Dictionnaire de l'architecture moderne*, Paris, 1964.
Henri, M., Magne, L., *Le Décor du métal*, Paris, 1922.
Hitchcock, H.-R., *Architecture: Nineteenth and Twentieth Centuries*, Harmondsworth, 1958.
Jackson, H., *The Eighteen Nineties*, London, 1913.
Kaufmann, E., *Von Ledoux bis Le Corbusier*, Vienna, 1933.
Lenning, H. F., *The Art Nouveau*, The Hague, 1951.
Madsen, S. T., *Sources of Art Nouveau*, New York, 1956.
Meyer, P., *Moderne Architektur und Tradition*, Zurich, 1928.
Murdoch, W. G. B., *The Renaissance of the Nineties*, London, 1911.
Muthesius, H., *Architektonische Zeitbetrachtungen*, Berlin, 1900.
Oudin, B., *Dictionnaire des Architectes*, Paris, 1970.
Pevsner, N., *Pioneers of the Modern Movement from William Morris to Walter Gropius*, London, 1936.
Pevsner, N., *Pioneers of Modern Design*, London, 1960.
Pevsner, N., *The Sources of Modern Architecture and Design*, London, 1968.

Pevsner, N., *Ruskin and Viollet-le-Duc: Englishness and Frenchness in the Appreciation of Gothic Architecture*, London, 1969.
Pevsner, N. (ed.), *The Anti-Rationalists*, London, 1973.
Platz, G. A., *Die Baukunst der neuesten Zeit*, Berlin, 1927.
Platz, G. A., *Wohnräume der Gegenwart*, Berlin, 1933.
Rheims, M., *L'Art 1900 ou le style Jules Verne*, Paris, 1965.
Rheims, M., *The Age of Art Nouveau*, London, 1966.
Rheims, M., *The Flowering of Art Nouveau*, New York, 1966.
Rowland, K., *A History of the Modern Movement: Art, Architecture and Design*, New York, 1973.
Scheffler, K., *Moderne Baukunst*, Berlin, 1907.
Scheffler, K., *Die Architektur der Grossstadt*, Berlin, 1913.
Schmutzler, R., *Art Nouveau-Jugendstil*, Stuttgart, 1962.
Sitte, C., *Der Stadtbau nach seinen Künstlerischen Grundsätzen*, Vienna, 1889.
Van de Velde, H., *Der neue Stil*, Weimar, 1906.
Van de Velde, H., *Les Formules de la beauté architectonique moderne*, Brussels, 1923.
Van de Velde, H., *Le Nouveau: Son Apport à l'Architecture et aux Arts Industriels*, Brussels, 1929.
Van de Velde, H., *Les Formules d'une Esthétique Nouvelle*, Brussels, 1932.
Van de Velde, H., *Les Fondements du Style Moderne*, Brussels, 1933.
Venturi, R., *Complexity and Contradiction in Architecture*, New York, 1966.
Viollet-le-Duc, E. E., *Dictionnaire raisonné de l'architecture française du XIe au XVIe siècle*, Paris, 1854-68.
Viollet-le-Duc, E. E., *Entretiens sur l'architecture*, Paris, 1863, 1872.
Wallis, N., *Fin de Siècle*, London, 1947.
Wright, F. L., *On Architecture. Selected Writings, 1894-1940*, New York, 1941.
Zevi, B., *Storia dell'architettura moderna*, Turin, 1950.

Periodicals

Brunhammer, Y., Ricour, M., 'Le Style 1900', *Jardin des Arts*, August, 1958.
Brunhammer, Y., '1900 un Style', *La Maison française*, November, 1964.
Brunhammer, Y., 'Un Oublié de l'Art Nouveau', *Plaisir de France*, no. 421, 1974.
Digaetano, Y. C., 'Art Nouveau', *The Museum*, 23, 1971.
Grady, J., 'A Bibliography of the Art Nouveau', *Journal of the Society of Architectural Historians*, Crawfordsville, Ind., vol. XIV, 1955.
Kielland, T. B., L'Art Nouveau 1895-1925', *Fransk Møbelkunst*, Oslo, 1928.
Lancaster, C., 'Oriental Contribution to Art Nouveau', *The Art Bulletin*, New York, vol. XXXV, no. 3, 1953.
Lange, K., 'L'Art Nouveau – What it is and What is

Thought of it – A Symposium', *Magazine of Art*, New York, March-June, 1904.
Lenning, H. F., 'The Movement in Europe – van de Velde, Horta and Guimard', *World Review*, London, January, 1953.
Roosenboom, A., 'Par Horreur du Modern-Style', *Le Home*, 3-4, 1910.
Waldberg, P., 'Modern Style', *L'Oeil*, Paris, 1960.

Catalogues

Brunhammer, Y., Culot, M., Delevoy, R.-L., *Pionniers du XXe Siècle: Guimard, Horta, van de Velde*, Musée des Arts Décoratifs, Paris, 1971.
Cassou, J., et al., *Les Sources du XXe siècle*, Musée National d'Art Moderne, Paris, 1960-61.
Zurich, Kunstgewerbemuseum, *Um 1900. Art Nouveau und Jugendstil*, 1952.

Miscellaneous

Rehme, W., *Die Architektur der Neuen Freien Schule*, Leipzig, 1901-02, folio of illustrations.
Rehme, W., *Ausgeführte Moderne Bautischler Arbeiten*, Leipzig, 1902, folio of illustrations.
La Maison Moderne, Brussels, 1902-06.

GREAT BRITAIN

Books

Adams, M. B., *Modern Cottage Architecture*, London, 1904.
Baillie Scott, M. H., *Houses and Gardens*, London, 1906.
Baillie Scott, M. H., Unwin, R., et al., *Town Planning and Modern Architecture in the Hampstead Garden Suburb*, London, 1909.
Baillie Scott, M. H., et al., *Garden Suburbs, Town Planning and Modern Architecture*, London, 1910.
Banham, R., *Theory and Design in the First Machine Age*, London, 1960.
Billcliffe, R., *Architectural Sketches and Flower Drawings by Charles Rennie Mackintosh*, London, 1977.
Billcliffe, R., *Mackintosh Watercolours*, London, 1978.
Blomfield, R., *Richard Norman Shaw*, London, 1940.
Brandon-Jones, J., *C. F. A. Voysey: a Memoir*, New York, 1977.
Cason, H., *An Introduction to Victorian Architecture*, London, 1948.
Clark, K., *The Gothic Revival*, London, 1928.
Cobden-Sanderson, T. J., *The Arts and Crafts Movement*, London, 1905.
Cooper, J. (ed.) and Bernard, B., *Mackintosh Architecture*, London, 1978.
Creese, W., *The Search for Environment: The Garden City Before and After*, New Haven, 1966.
Dutton, R., *The English Interior, 1500-1900*, London, 1948.
Farmer, A. J., *Le Mouvement esthétique et décadent en Angleterre 1873-1900*, Paris, 1931.

Frey, D., *Englisches Wesen in der Bildenenkunst*, Stuttgart-Berlin, 1942.

Gebhard, D., *Charles F. A. Voysey*, Los Angeles, 1975.

Henderson, P., *William Morris – His Life, Work and Friends*, New York, 1967.

Heseltine, J., *C. F. A. Voysey*, London, 1979.

Hitchcock, H.-R., *Modern Architecture, Romanticism and Reintegration*, New York, 1929.

Holme, C., *Modern British Domestic Architecture and Decoration*, London, 1901.

Howarth, T., *Charles Rennie Mackintosh and the Modern Movement*, London, 1977.

Kornwolf, J. D., *M. H. Baillie Scott and the Arts and Crafts Tradition*, Baltimore, 1972.

Lethaby, W. R., *Philip Webb and his Work*, London, 1925.

Macleod, R., *Style and Society: Architectural Ideology in Britain, 1836-1914*, London, 1971.

Muthesius, H., *Die Englische Baukunst der Gegenwart*, Leipzig, 1900.

Muthesius, H., *Die neuere kirchliche Baukunst in England*, Berlin, 1901.

Muthesius, H., *M. H. Baillie Scott. Haus eines Kunstfreundes. Meister der Innen-Kunst I*, London, 1902.

Muthesius, H., *Charles Rennie Mackintosh. Glasgowhaus eines Kunstfreundes. Meister der Innen-Kunst II*, London, 1902.

Muthesius, H., *Das englische Haus*, vols I-III, Berlin, 1904-08.

Naylor, G., *The Arts and Crafts Movement*, London, 1971.

Pevsner, N., *Charles Rennie Mackintosh*, Milan, 1950.

Pevsner, N., *Studies in Architecture and Design*, vol. 2, London, 1968.

Raffles Davison, T., *Modern Homes*, London, 1909.

Randolph, W., *A Century of English Architecture*, London, 1939.

Richardson, A. E., *Monumental Classic Architecture in Great Britain and Ireland during the 18th and 19th Centuries*, London, 1914.

Ruskin, J., *The Works of John Ruskin*, vols I-XXXIX, London, 1903-12.

Service, A., *Edwardian Architecture and its Origins*, London, 1975.

Service, A., *The Architects of London*, London, 1979.

Shaw, R. N., *Sketches for Cottages*, London, 1878.

Shaw, R. N., *Architecture. A Profession or an Art*, London, 1892.

Shaw Sparrow, W., *The Modern Home*, London, 1906.

Turnor, R., *Nineteenth Century Architecture in Britain*, London, 1950.

Voysey, C. F. A., *Individuality*, London, 1911.

Voysey, C. F. A., *Reason as a Basis of Art*, London, n.d.

Walker, D., Gomme, A., *Architecture of Glasgow*, London, 1968.

Young, A. M., *Charles Rennie Mackintosh (1868-1928): Architecture, Design and Painting*, Glasgow, 1968.

Periodicals

Antichini, F., 'Incontri con Charles Rennie Mackintosh', *L'Architettura*, Rome, vol. VI, 1959.

Baillie Scott, M. H., 'An Ideal Suburban House', *The Studio*, January, 1895.

Baillie Scott, M. H., 'An Artist's House', *The Studio*, vol. IX, 1896-97.

Baillie Scott, M. H., 'A Small Country House', *The Studio*, vol. XII, 1898.

Baillie Scott, M. H., 'Decoration and Furniture for the New Palace, Darmstadt', *The Studio*, March, 1899.

Baillie Scott, M. H., 'Yellowsands – A Seaside House', *The Studio*, April, 1903.

Baillie Scott, M. H., 'The Ideal House', *The British Architect*, December, 1909.

Banham, R., 'The Voysey Inheritance', *The Architectural Review*, London, vol. CXII, 1952.

Beazley, E., Lambert, S., 'The Astonishing City, Glasgow', *Architect's Journal*, vol. 139, May 6th, 1964.

Betjeman, J., 'Charles Francis Annesley Voysey. The Architect of Individualism', *The Architectural Review*, London, vol. LXX, 1931.

Betjeman, J., 'C. F. A. Voysey', *Architect's Journal*, XCIII, 1941.

Blomfield, R., 'W. R. Lethaby. An Impression and a Tribute', *The Journal of the Royal Institute of British Architects*, London, vol. XXXIX, 1931-32.

Bodenhausen, E. von, 'Englische Kunst im Haus', *Pan*, 11, Berlin, 1896.

Brandon-Jones, J., 'An Architect's Letters to his Client', *Architect and Building News*, CXCV, 1949.

Brandon-Jones, J., 'C. F. A. Voysey', *Architectural Association Journal*, vol. LXXII, 1957.

Carter, E., 'Arthur Mackmurdo', *Journal of the Royal Institute of British Architects*, London, vol. IL, April, 1942.

Chapman-Huston, D., 'Charles Rennie Mackintosh, His Life and Work', *Artwork*, vol. 7, no. 21, Spring, 1930.

Coleman, O., 'Baillie-Scott's Yellowsands', *The House Beautiful*, February, 1904.

Daryll, A. B., 'The Architecture of Charles Francis Annesley Voysey', *Magazine of Fine Arts*, II, 1906.

Fred, W., 'Der Architekt M. H. Baillie-Scott', *Kunst und Kunsthandwerk*, 4, 1901.

Hitchcock, H.-R., 'Early Cast Iron Facades', *The Architectural Review*, London, vol. CIX, 1951.

Howarth, T., 'Mackintosh and the Scottish Tradition', *Magazine of Art*, vol. 41, November, 1948.

Macartney, M. E., 'Recent English Domestic Architecture', *The Architectural Review*, London, 1908.

Macartney, M. E., 'Recent English Domestic Architecture', *The Architectural Review*, London, 1911.

MacDonald, S. W., 'New Church Work at Great Warley', *Art Journal*, London, 1905.

Macleod, R., 'Charles Rennie Mackintosh', *Country Life*, 1968.

Malton, J., 'Art Nouveau in Essex', *The Architectural Review*, London, vol. CXXVI, 1959.

Muthesius, H., 'M. H. Baillie-Scott', *Dekorative Kunst*, 5, 1900.

Pevsner, N., 'George Walton. His Life and Work', *The Journal of the Royal Institute of British Architects*, London, vol. XLVI, 1939.

Pevsner, N., 'Charles Francis Annesley Voysey', *Elsevier's Maandschrift*, Brussels, 1940.

Pevsner, N., 'Richard Norman Shaw', *The Architectural Review*, London, vol. LXXXIX, 1941.

Pevsner, N., 'Arthur H. Mackmurdo', *The Architectural Review*, London, vol. CXI, 1952.

Pevsner, N., 'William Morris, C. R. Ashbee und das zwanzigste Jahrhundert', *Deutsche Vierteljahrsschrift für Literaturwissenschaft und Geistesgeschichte*, Halle, vol. XIV, no. 4.

Raffles Davison, T., 'The recent advances in architecture – country houses', *Magazine of Art*, 1903.

Rendell, B., 'Charles Ashbee als Architekt und Baumeister', *Kunst und Kunsthandwerk*, IV, 1901.

Renzio, T. del, 'Charles Rennie Mackintosh', *World Review*, London, January, 1953.

Rooke, N., 'The Drawings of W. R. Lethaby', *The Journal of the Royal Institute of British Architects*, London, vol. XXXIX, 1931-32.

Rooke, N., 'The Work of Lethaby, Webb and Morris', *The Journal of the Royal Institute of British Architects*, London, vol. LVII, 1950.

Rykwert, J., 'Charles Rennie Mackintosh, 1868-1928', *Domus*, no. 462, 1968.

Shand, P. M., 'Scenario for a Human Drama: The Glasgow Interlude', *The Architectural Review*, vol. 77, January, 1935.

Shaw, R. N., 'Mr Norman Shaw's Architecture', *The Builder*, London, vol. XCVIII, 1910.

Schmid, H., 'Moderne englische Baukunst', *Kunst und Kunsthandwerk*, IV, 1901.

Schmutzler, R., 'The English Origins of Art Nouveau', *The Architectural Review*, February, 1955.

Stamp, G., 'London 1900', *Architectural Design*, London, vol. 48, no. 5-6, 1978.

Townsend, C. H., 'Originality in Architecture', *The Builder*, London, vol. LXXXII, 1902.

Townsend, H., 'Notes on Country and Suburban Houses Designed by C. F. A. Voysey', *The Studio*, XVI, 1899.

Vallance, A., 'A. H. Mackmurdo', *The Studio*, vol. XVI, 1899.

Voysey, C. F. A., 'Ideas in Things', *The Arts connected with Building*, London, 1909.

Voysey, C. F. A., 'Patriotism in Architecture', *Architectural Association Journal*, XXVIII, 1912.

Weaver, L., 'Small country houses of today', *Country Life*, 1910.

White, G., 'Some Glasgow Designers and their Work', *The Studio*, London, vol. XI, 1897.

Wilson, A., 'A. H. Mackmurdo and the Century Guild', *Apollo*, November, 1961.

Anon., 'An Interview with Mr C. F. A. Voysey', *The Studio*, London, vol. I, 1893.

Anon., 'Houses for People with Hobbies: "The Orchard", Chorley Wood', *Country Life*, VI, 1899.

Anon., 'Houses for People with Hobbies: "Walnut Tree Farm", Castlemorton', *Country Life*, VI, 1899.

Anon., 'The Orchard, a house', *Ideal House*, January, 1907.

Catalogues

Brandon-Jones, J., et al., *C. F. A. Voysey: architect and designer 1857-1941*, London, 1978.

Symonds, J., *Catalogue of Drawings by C. F. A. Voysey in the Drawings Collection of the Royal Institute of British Architects*, Farnborough, 1976.

Partnership in Style: Edgar Wood and J. Henry Sellers, Manchester City Art Gallery exhibition catalogue, 1975.

Miscellaneous

Doak, A. M. (ed.), *Architectural Jottings by Charles Rennie Mackintosh*, selected by Andrew McLaren Young, Glasgow Institute of Architects, 1968.

The Royal Institute of British Architects, *One Hundred Years of British Architecture 1851-1951*, London, 1951.

SPAIN

Books

Bassegoda, J., Garrut Roma, J. M., *Guia de Gaudí*, Barcelona, 1969.

Bergós, J., *Antoni Gaudí, l'hombre i l'obra*, Barcelona, 1954.

Bohigas, O., *Resena y Catalogo de la Arquitectura Modernista*, Barcelona, 1973.

Bohigas, O., *Architettura Modernista*, Turin, 1969.

Borràs, M. L., *Domènech i Montaner*, Barcelona, 1971.

Calzada, A., *Historia de la Arquitectura Espanola*, Barcelona, 1933.

Casanelles, E., *Antonio Gaudí: A Reappraisal*, London, 1967.

Cirici Pellicer, A., *El arte modernista Catalán*, Barcelona, 1951.

Cirici Pellicer, A., *L'Arquitectura Catalana*, Palma de Mallorca, 1955.

Cirici Pellicer, A., *1900 a Barcelona*, Barcelona, 1967.

Cirici Pellicer, A., Maspons, O., *Arquitectura Gotica Catalana*, Barcelona, 1968.

Cirlot, J. E., *El Estilo de siglo XX*, Barcelona, 1952.

Cirlot, J. E., *Gaudí*, Barcelona, 1966.

Collins, G. R., *Antonio Gaudí*, New York, 1960.

Cros, J. E. H., Mora, G., Pouplana, X., *Arquitectura de Barcelona*, Barcelona, n.d.

Giedion-Welcker, C., *Park Güell*, Barcelona, 1966.

Hitchcock, H.-R., *Gaudí*, New York, 1957.

Jardi, E., *Puig i Cadafalch*, Barcelona, 1975.

Jujol, J. M., *La Arquitectura de J. Ma. Jujol*, Barcelona, 1974.

Martinell, C., *Gaudinismo*, Barcelona, 1954.

Martinell, C., *Gaudí*, edited by G. Collins, Cambridge, Mass., 1975.

Mooring, S., *Gaudí*, London, 1979.

Perucho, J., Pomes, L., *Gaudí, una arquitectura de anticipación*, Barcelona, 1967.

Puig Boada, I., *El templo de la Sagrada Familia*, Barcelona, 1952.

Ràfols, J., Folguera, F., *Gaudí*, Barcelona, 1929.

Ràfols, J., *Modernismo y Modernistas*, Barcelona, 1949.

Rubio, I. S. M., *Joan Rubio i Bellver y la fortuna del Gaudinismo*, Barcelona, 1975.

Sweeney, J. J., Sert, J. L., *Antoni Gaudí*, London, 1960.

Periodicals

Bidou, H., 'Les Salons de 1910', *Gazette des Beaux-Arts*, July, 1910.

Bohigas, O., 'Lluis Domènech i Montaner 1850-1923', *The Architectural Review*, CXLII, December, 1967, pp. 426-436.

BIBLIOGRAPHY

Borràs, M. L., 'Two apartment houses by Gaudí', *Global Architecture*, no. 17, 1978.

Brunati, M., et al., 'Eredità dell ottocento: spazio e sintesi plastica nel genio de Barcelona', *L'Architettura,* May, 1958.

Burckhardt, E., 'The unfinished cathedral and Antonio Gaudí', *Art News*, January, 1958.

Dali, S., 'De la beauté terrifiante et comestible de l'architecture modern style', *Minotaure*, no. 3-4, 1933.

Hitchcock, H.-R., 'The work of Antoni Gaudí y Cornet', *Architectural Association Journal*, no. 74, November, 1958.

Jimeno, O., 'Antonio Gaudí y la originalidad arquitectonica', *El Arquiteto Peruano*, July-August, 1953.

Jurgen, J., 'Antonio Gaudí', *Architecture d'Aujourd'hui*, vol. 33, June-July, 1962.

Kerrigan, A., 'Gaudianism in Catalonia', *Arts*, vol. 33, December, 1957.

Leblond, M.-A., 'Gaudí et l'architecture mediterrannée', *L'Art et les Artistes*, no. 11, 1910.

Loyer, F., 'La Chapelle Güell', *L'Oeil*, June, 1971.

Mackay, D., 'Berenguer', *The Architectural Review*, December, 1964.

Marquina, E., 'La Sagrada Familia', *L'Art et les Artistes*, no. 6, 1908.

Pevsner, N., 'The Strange Architecture of Gaudí', *The Listener*, August 7th, 1952.

Sellés, S., 'Park Güell', *Associación de Arquitectos de Cataluña*, 1903.

Sert, J. L., 'Introduzione a Gaudí', *Casabella*, no. 202, August-September, 1954.

Sert, J. L., 'Gaudí, visionnaire et précurseur', *L'Oeil*, February, 1955.

Smith, G. E. K., 'Report from Spain and Portugal', *Architectural Forum*, May, 1950.

Sugrañes, D., 'Disposició estàtica del Templo de la Sagrada Familia', *Associación de Arquitectos de Cataluña*, 1923.

Sugrañes, D., 'La estabilidad en la construcción del Templo de la Sagrada Familia', *Ibérica*, March, 1917.

Waugh, E., 'Gaudi', *The Architectural Review,* June, 1930.

Whiffen, M., 'Catalan Surreal', *The Architectural Review*, November, 1950.

Zevi, B., 'Un genio catalano: Antonio Gaudí', *Metron*, September-October, 1950.

'Gaudí en Paris: Salon de la Société Nationale des Beaux-Arts', *Associación de Arquitectos de Calaluña*, 1911.

'Antonio Gaudí', *Architecture and Urbanism*, no. 86, 1977.

Cuadernos de Arquitectura, 1954-.

Catalogues

Brunhammer, Y., Cid, T. C., 'Gaudí', *Pionniers du XXe Siècle 2*, Musée des Arts Décoratifs, Paris, June 19th-September 27th, 1971.

Collins, G. R., *The Drawings of Antonio Gaudí*, The Drawing Center, New York, March 26th-May 24th, 1977.

Hitchcock, H.-R., *Gaudí*, New York 1957-58, catalogue of the exhibition at the Museum of Modern Art, New York.

Miscellaneous

Gaudí, Colegio Oficial de Arquitectos de Cataluña y Baleares, Barcelona, 1960.

Alvarez, A., 'Gaudí Speaks', *Jubilee*, vol. 9, 1962.

Bergos, J. M., 'Las conversaciones de Gaudí', *Hogar y Arquitectura*, no. 112, 1974.

Martinell, C., *Conversaciones con Gaudí*, Barcelona, 1969.

O'Neal, W. B. (ed.), *Papers X: Antonio Gaudí and the Catalan Movement (1830-1930)*: comprehensive bibliography.

BELGIUM

Books

Boelens, V., *L'Architecture pratique*, Brussels, 1902.

Borsi, F., Portoghesi, P., *Victor Horta*, Rome, 1969.

Borsi, F., Weiser, H., *Bruxelles, Capitale de l'Art Nouveau*, Brussels, 1971.

Borsi, F., *Bruxelles 1900,* Brussels, 1974.

Casteels, M., *Henry van de Velde*, Brussels, 1932.

Conrardy, C., Thibaut, R., *Paul Hankar*, Brussels, 1923.

Culot, M., Terlinden, F., *Antoine Pompe et l'Effort Moderne en Belgique*, Musée d'Ixelles, Brussels, 1969.

Culot, M., Delevoy, R.-L., *Antoine Pompe, ou l'Architecture du Sentiment*, Brussels, 1973.

Delevoy, R.-L., *Victor Horta*, Brussels, 1958.

De Maeyer, C., *Paul Hankar*, Brussels, 1963.

Fauconnier, M., *La Structure sociale d'une grande ville*, Brussels, 1929.

Hammacher, A. M., *Le Monde de Henry van de Velde*, Antwerp, 1967.

Horta, V., *Considération sur l'art moderne*, Brussels, 1926.

Horta, V., *L'Enseignement architectural et l'Architecture Moderne*, Brussels, 1926.

Hüter, K. H., *Henry van de Velde*, East Berlin, 1967.

Jaquemyns, J., *Histoire contemporaine du Grand Bruxelles*, Brussels, 1936.

Laurent, M., *L'Architecture et la Sculpture en Belgique*, Brussels, 1928.

Maus, O., *L'Art et la Vie en Belgique, 1830-1905*, Brussels, 1929.

Osthaus, K. E., *Van de Velde: Leben und Schaffen des Künstlers*, Hagen, 1902.

Poirier, P., *Notice sur le Baron Victor Horta*, Brussels, 1968.

Rességuier, C., *Die Schriften Henry van de Veldes*, New York, 1955.

Schmitz, M., *L'architecture moderne en Belgique*, Brussels, 1936.

Spaeth, K., *Die Umgestaltung von Alt-Brüssel*, Leipzig, 1914.

Van de Velde, H., *Amo*, Leipzig, 1909.

Van de Velde, H., *Geschichte meines Lebens,* Munich, 1962.

Van de Voort, J., *Gedenkboek Henry van de Velde*, Gand, 1933.

Van Kuyck, H., *Modern Belgian Architecture*, New York, 1948.

Verniers, L., *Les Transformations du Bruxelles et l'urbanisation de sa banlieue depuis 1795*, Léau, 1934.

Verniers, L., *Esquisse provisoire de l'histoire de la plus-value à Bruxelles depuis un siècle*, Brussels, 1938.

Periodicals

Binney, M., 'The mystery of the style Jules Verne – Victor Horta and the origin of Art Nouveau', *The Country Life Annual*, 1970.

Bodson, F., 'A propos d'Hankar', *La Cité*, no. 6, 1922.

Conrardy, C., 'Victor Horta', *Le Thyrse*, 1919, pp. 1-3.

Conrardy, C., 'L'Oeuvre de Victor Horta', *Architecture*, 1948.

Courtens, A., 'Hommage à Victor Horta', *Le Document*, 1946-47.

Crespin, A., 'La Vie et l'art de Hankar', *La Ligne Artistique*, February, 1901.

De Fusco, R., 'La Maison du Peuple', *Architettura, segno e linguaggio*, Bari, 1973.

Delhaye, J., 'Hommage à mon maître: l'architecte Baron Victor Horta', *Appartement d'aujourd'hui*, Liège, 1946.

Delhaye, J., 'Victor Horta et la Maison du Peuple', *Cahiers Henry van de Velde*, nos. 9-10, 1969.

Dezzi Bardeschi, M., 'A. Pompe e il movimento moderno in Belgio', *Necropoli*, nos. 6-7, 1970.

Duesberg, A. C., 'Le Baron Victor Horta', *Architecture*, January, 1948.

Duesberg, A. C., 'Le Souvenir de Victor Horta', *Rythme*, 1950.

Flouquet, P.-L., 'Paul Hankar', *La Maison*, June, 1950.

Flouquet, P.-L., 'Victor Horta et la "Belle Epoque"', *La Maison*, October, 1957.

Flouquet, P.-L., 'L'Architecte Victor Horta', *Le Phare*, September, 1957.

Ford, G. B., 'The Emancipation of Architecture in Belgium', *The American Architect and Building News*, June, 1907.

Girardi, V., 'Letture di Victor Horta', *L'Architettura*, Rome, vol. III, September 1957-April 1958.

Hamesse, P., 'La brocante, l'archéologie, l'art architectural', *La Vie Intellectuelle*, 1908.

Jacques, G. M., 'Deux façades de Horta', *Art Décoratif*, Paris, 1900.

Kaufmann, E., 'Victor Horta', *Interiors*, February, 1957.

Lacambre, G., 'Le Musée Victor Horta', *Présence de Bruxelles*, December, 1962.

Lacambre, P., 'Horta dans ses propres murs', *Présence de Bruxelles*, April, 1969.

Lannoy, P., 'Le Palais de la Société des Nations', *Art et Décoration*, February, 1926.

Le Grande, L., 'The Home Hankar', *La Ligne Artistique*, October, 1901.

Loyer, F., 'L'Espace d'Horta', *L'Oeil*, no. 194, February, 1971.

Madsen, S. T., 'Horta. Works and Style of Victor Horta before 1900', *The Architectural Review*, London, vol. CXVIII, 1955.

Martiny, V. G., 'L'Architecture en Belgique depuis 1900 jusqu'à nos jours', *L'Industrie de la construction*, 1966.

Maus, O., 'Paul Hankar et Adolphe Crespin', *Art et Décoration*, 1897.

Maus, O., 'Paul Hankar', *Art Moderne*, no. 29, July, 1900.

Meier-Graefe, J., 'Henry van de Velde', *L'Art Décoratif*, 1, 1898.

Osborn, M., 'Henry van de Velde', *Innen Dekoration*, II, 1900.

Pierron, S., 'Le Palais des fêtes à Bruxelles. Les plans de Victor Horta', *Le Home*, January, 1921.

Pierron, S., 'Victor Horta', *Savoir et Beauté*, July, 1924.

Pierron, S., 'Le Palais de la S.N.D.', *Le Soir*, December 26th, 1924.

Sedeyn, E., 'Victor Horta', *Art Décoratif*, October, 1901.

Thiebaut-Sisson, 'Un Novateur: Victor Horta', *Art Décoratif en Belgique*, January, 1897.

Van de Velde, H., 'Notes d'Art', *La Wallonie*, nos. 2-3, Brussels, 1890.

Vehenne, H., 'La Protection de l'oeuvre de V. Horta', *Le Soir*, January 28th, 1961.

Vinson, J. S., 'L'Héritage d'Horta', *Connaissance des Arts*, October, 1969.

Catalogues

Henry van de Velde 1863-1957. Persönlichkeit und Werk, catalogue of Kunstgewerbe Museum, Zürich, 1958.

Miscellaneous

Fierens-Gevaert, P., 'Ecole belge', *Nouveaux essais sur l'art contemporain*, Paris, 1903.

Puttemans, P., 'L'Héritage de Victor Horta', *Bulletin de la classe des Beaux-Arts*, Académie Royale de Belgique, 1968.

Strauven, F., 'La Signification de Victor Horta pour l'architecture contemporaine', in *Victor Horta*, Musée Horta, 1973.

FRANCE

Books

Bigot, A., *Grès de Bigot*, Paris, 1902.

Boileau, L.-A., *La Cathédrale Synthétique*, 1886.

Bonnier, L., *Rapport sur la Révision des ordonnancements de la voie publique*, Paris, 1909.

Burnand, R., *Paris 1900*, Paris, 1951.

Champier, V., *Les Industries d'Art à l'Exposition Universelle de 1889*, Paris, 1903.

Cheronnet, L., *Paris vers 1900*, Paris, 1932.

Culpepper, R., *Bibliographie d'Hector Guimard*, Paris, 1971.

Doniol, A., *Histoire du XVIe arrondissement de Paris*, Paris, 1902.

Escholier, R., *Le Nouveau Paris. La Vie artistique de la cité moderne*, Paris, 1912.

Garnier, C., *La Nouvelle Opéra*, Paris, 1881.

Geffroy, G., *Les Industries artistiques françaises et étrangères à l'Exposition universelle de 1900*, Paris, 1901.

Graham, F. L., *Hector Guimard*, New York, 1970.

Gromort, G., *Histoire abrégée de l'architecture en France au 19e siècle*, Paris, 1924.

Guerrand, R.-H., *Mémoires du Métro*, Paris, 1961.

Guimard, H., *Le Castel Béranger*, Paris, 1898.

Haussmann, G.-E., *Mémoires*, Paris, 1890-93.

Hautecoeur, L., *Histoire de l'architecture classique en France*, vol. 7, *La Fin de l'architecture classique, 1848-1900*, Paris, 1957.

Hénard, E., *Etudes sur les transformations de Paris*, Paris, 1903-09.

Hillainet, J., *Dictionnaire historique des rues de Paris*, Paris, 1963.

Lahore, J., *Les Habitations à bon marché et un art nouveau pour le peuple*, Paris, 1902.

Lambert, T., *Nouvelles Constructions*, Paris, 1900.

Magne, H. M., *L'Architecture: l'art français depuis 20 ans*, Paris, 1922.

Mourey, G., *H. Sauvage. Les Albums d'art*, Paris, n.d.

Naylor, G. and Brunhammer, Y., *Hector Guimard*, London, 1978.

Poëte, M., *Une vie de cité, Paris de sa naissance à nos jours*, Paris, 1924-31.

Rey, R., *Frantz Jourdain*, Paris, 1923.

Roman, J., *Paris fin de siècle*, Paris, 1958.

Soulier, G. and P. N., *Etudes sur le Castel Béranger, oeuvre de Hector Guimard*, Paris, 1899.

Van de Velde, H., *Der neue Stil in Frankreich*, Berlin, 1925.

Weisberg, G. P. et al., *Japonisme: Japanese Influence on French Art, 1854-1910*, Cleveland, 1975.

Periodicals

Bans, G., 'Les Gares du Métropolitain de Paris', *L'Art Décoratif*, no. 25, October, 1900.

Bedel, J., 'Emile Gallé, cet inconnu', *Guide des Antiquités*, no. 40, 1968.

Bénédite, L., 'Les Salons de 1898', *Gazette des Beaux-Arts*, June, 1898.

Blondel, A., Plantin, Y., 'Guimard, architecte de meubles', *L'Estampille*, 10, 1970.

Blondel, A., Plantin, Y., 'Le Monde plastique de Guimard', *Plaisir de France*, XXXVIII, no. 387, 1971.

Blondel, A., Plantin, Y., 'Hector Guimard, la Salle Humbert de Romans', *L'Architecture d'aujourd'hui*, XLIII, no. 155, 1971.

Blondel, A., Plantin, Y., 'Expressionnisme Naturaliste de Guimard au Castel Béranger', *L'Oeil*, no. 194, 1971.

Boileau, L.-C., 'Les Maisons de M. Guimard, rue La Fontaine', *L'Architecture*, IX, December, 1896.

Boileau, L.-C., 'Causerie: L'Exposition des Oeuvres de M. Guimard dans les Salons du "Figaro"', *L'Architecture*, April 15th, 1899.

Boileau, L.-C., 'Castel Béranger, immeuble de rapport à Auteil, 16 rue La Fontaine', *L'Architecture*, XII, 1899.

Boileau, L.-C., 'Critique de l'un des édicules composés pour les stations souterraines', *L'Architecture*, XIII, November, 1900.

Boudon, F., 'Recherche sur la pensée et l'oeuvre d'Anatole de Baudot', *Architecture, mouvement, continuité*, no. 28, 1973.

Brincourt, M., 'Causerie: Hôtel et maison de rapport avenue et rue de Messine', *L'Architecture*, XXIV.

Champier, V., 'Le Castel Béranger et M. Hector Guimard', *Revue des Arts Décoratifs*, XIX, 1899.

Charpentier, F.-T., 'L'Ecole de Nancy et le renouveau de l'art décoratif en France', *Médecine de France*, July, 1964.

Cordier, G., 'A propos des Expositions Universelles, essai d'intégralisme', *Architecture, mouvement, continuité*, no. 17, 1970.

Culpepper, R., 'Les Premières Oeuvres d'Hector Guimard', *L'Architecture d'Aujourd'hui*, no. 154, 1971.

Dali, S., 'The Cylindrical Monarchy of Guimard', *Arts Magazine*, March, 1970.

Derveaux, A., 'Villa à Compiègne', *La Construction Moderne*, series 3, III, 1907-08.

Forthuny, P., 'Un maître d'oeuvre: Charles Plumet', *Revue des Arts Décoratifs*, XIX, 1899.

Frantz, H., 'The Art Movement, Castel Béranger, the new art in architectural decoration', *The Magazine of Art*, vol. XXV, 1901.

Gallé, E., 'Le Pavillon de l'Union Centrale des Arts Décoratifs à l'Exposition Universelle', *Revue des Arts Décoratifs*, 20, 1900.

Gardelle, C., 'Charles Plumet, architecte', *L'Art Décoratif*, 1, 1899.

Guimard, H., 'La Renaissance de l'art dans l'architec-ture moderne', *Le Moniteur des Arts*, series 2, XIII, 1899.

Guimard, H., 'An Architect's Opinion of "L'Art Nouveau"', *The Architectural Record*, New York, vol. XII, 1902.

Grady, J., 'Hector Guimard, an overlooked Master of Art Nouveau', *Apollo*, April, 1969.

Haber, F., 'H. Guimard: surviving works', *Architectural Design*, XLI, 1971.

Jourdain, F., 'La Villa Majorelle à Nancy', *L'Art Décoratif*, IV, 1902.

Léon, P., 'La Querelle des classiques et des gothiques', *La Revue de Paris*, Paris, vol. XX, July, 1913.

Leroy, M., 'L'Ecole de Nancy au Pavillon de Marsan', *L'Art Décoratif*, 5, 1903.

Lesbruère, M., 'Maisons 1900 de Paris', *Bizarre*, no. 123, 1963.

Marx, R., 'René Lalique', *Art et Décoration*, 6, 1899.

Mazade, F., 'An "Art Nouveau" Edifice in Paris . . . Hector Guimard, Architect', *The Architectural Record*, New York-London, vol. III, 1904-05.

Méry, M., 'Le Castel Béranger', *Le Moniteur des Arts*, XLIV, 1899.

Miotto-Muret, L., Palluchini-Pelzet, V., 'Une Maison de Guimard', *Revue de l'Art*, March, 1969.

Osborn, M., 'La Maison Moderne in Paris', *Deutsche Kunst und Dekoration*, 7, 1901.

Poupée, H., 'Actualité de Guimard', *La Construction Moderne*, no. 4, 1970.

Puaux, R., 'La Maison Moderne in Paris', *Deutsche Kunst und Dekoration*, 12, 1903.

Sergent, R., 'Une maison de rapport', *Art et Décoration*, vol. 10, 1901.

Sergent, R., 'Maison Avenue Rapp à Paris', *La Construction Moderne*, series 2, VI.

Soulier, G., 'Henri Sauvage', *Art et Décoration*, vol. V, 1899.

Soulier, G., 'La Plante et ses applications ornementales', *Revue des Arts Décoratifs*, 20, 1900.

Uhry, E., 'Constructions récentes de M. Lavirotte', *L'Art Décoratif*, VII, 1905.

Vauxcelles, L., 'Frantz Jourdain', *L'Amour de l'Art*, III, 1922.

Zahar, M., 'L'architecture vivante: Henri Sauvage', *L'Art Vivant*, IV, 1928.

Catalogues

Alexandre, A., 'L'Oeuvre d'Eugène Grasset', *Catalogue de la Deuxième Exposition du Salon des Cent reservée à un ensemble d'oeuvres d'Eugène Grasset*, Paris.

Blondel, A., Plantin, Y., *Hector Guimard, Fontes Artistiques*, Paris, 1971.

Brunhammer, Y., Bussmann, K., Kock, R., *Hector Guimard, 1867-1942*, Münster: Landesmuseum, 1975.

Brunhammer, Y., et al., *Art Nouveau Belgium, France*, Institute for the Arts, Rice University, 1976.

Charpentier, F.-T., *Le Musée de l'Ecole de Nancy*, Lyon.

Guerinet, E., *L'Exposition de l'Ecole de Nancy*, Paris, 1900.

Lanier, G., *Hector Guimard*, New York, 1970.

Miscellaneous

Berryer, A.-M., 'A propos d'un vase de Chaplet décoré par Gauguin', *Bulletin des Musées Royaux d'Art et d'Histoire*, Brussels, nos. 1-2, April, 1944.

Guimard, H., *Fontes Artistiques pour Constructions, Fumisterie, Articles de Jardin et Sépultures, Style Guimard*, Fonderies de Saint-Dizier, 1907.

L'Architecture au XXe Siècle, vols I-IV: folio of illustrations.

HOLLAND

Books

Berlage, H. P., *Gedanken über den Stil in der Baukunst*, Leipzig, 1905.

Berlage, H. P., *Grundlagen und Entwicklung der Architektur*, Berlin, 1908.

Cuypers, J. Th. J., *Het werk van dr P. J. H. Cuypers 1827-1917*, Amsterdam, 1917.

De Bazel, K. P. C., *De Houtsneden van K. P. C. de Bazel*, Amsterdam, 1925.

Eisler, M., *De Bouwmeester H. P. Berlage*, Vienna, 1919.

Gans, L., *Nieuwe kunst. De Nederlandse Bijdrage tot de Art Nouveau*, Utrecht, 1960.

Gratama, J., *Dr H. P. Berlage Bouwmeester*, Rotterdam, 1925.

Hoff, A., *Johan Thorn Prikker*, Recklinghausen, 1958.

Van de Voort, J., *Gedenboek Henry van de Velde*, Ghent, 1933.

Periodicals

Berlage, H. P., 'Over Architectuur', *Tweemaandlijk Tijdschrift*, Amsterdam, vol. II, 1896.

SWITZERLAND

Books

Baer, C. H., *Einfache Schweizerische Wohnhäuser, aus dem Wettbewerb der Schweiz. Vereinigung für Hermatschutz*, Bümpliz, 1908.

Barting, O., *Vom neuen Kirchenbau*, Berlin, 1919.

Baudin, H., *Villas et Maisons de campagne en Suisse*, Geneva, 1909.

Birkner, O., *Bauen und Wohnen in der Schweiz, 1850-1920*, Zurich, 1975.

Du Bois, P., *Les Mythologues de la belle époque*, La Chaux-de-Fonds, 1975.

Germann, G., *Der protestantische Kirchenbau in der Schweiz von der Reformation bis zur Romantik*, Zurich, 1963.

Godet, P., *Die Schweiz im 19. Jahrhundert*, Lausanne, 1900.

Gubler, J., *Nationalisme et internationalisme dans l'architecture moderne de la Suisse*, Lausanne, 1975.

Hartog, R., *Stadterweiterungen im 19. Jahrhundert*, Stuttgart, 1962.

Periodicals

Baer, C. H., 'Modernes Bauschaffen', *SBZ*, 43, 1904.

Barbey, G., Gubler, J., Paschaud, G., 'Riviera lémanique', *Werk-archithèse*, vol. LXIV, no. 6, June, 1977, pp. 3-40.

Elskes, E., 'Les ponts en fer et l'esthétique', *BTSR*, 28, 1902.

Lambert, A., 'L'Architecture contemporaine dans la Suisse romande', *SBZ*, 40, 1902.

Linder, R., 'Beton- Eisenkonstruktion System Hennebique, ausgeführt am Geschäfthaus Ecke Freie Strasse und Barfüssergasse', *Ingenieur- und Architektenvereins*, 1897.

Malfroy, S., 'Un modèle de passage piétonnier: Les Galeries du Commerce à Lausanne (1909)', *Habitation*, Lausanne, 1977, vol. L, no. 5.

Melley, C., '"Modern Style" et traditions locales', *BTSR*, vol. XXX, Lausanne, 1904.

Rebsamen, H., 'Zürich Total 1890-1919', *Tages-Anzeiger Magazin*, Zürich, no. 36.

Rohn, A., 'Steinerne und eiserne Brücken', *SBZ*, 56, 1910.

Wichert, F., 'Stilbildung, Stadteinheit und moderne Hausform', *SBZ*, 53, 1909.

'Neu Zürich', *SBZ*, 15, 1890.

'Aus der Baugeschichte der Stadt Luzern', *SBZ*, 22, 1893.

'Die Erweiterung der Stadt Lausanne', *SBZ*, 44, 1904.

'Zwei moderne Quartierpläne in Zürich', *SBZ*, 55, 1910.

Catalogues

Birkner, O., *Der Weg ins 20. Jahrhundert*, catalogue of exhibition at the Gerwerbemuseum, Winterthur, 1969.

GERMANY

Books

Ahlers-Hestermann, F., *Stilwende: Aufbruch der Jugend um 1900*, Berlin, 1941, 1956.

Behrens, P., *Ein Dokument Deutscher Kunst: die Ausstellung der Künstler-Kolonie in Darmstadt, 1901*, Munich, 1901.

Bernstein, P., *Am Ende des Jahrhunderts*, Berlin, 1898.

Cremers, P. J., *Peter Behrens. Sein Werk von 1909 bis*

zur Gegenwart, Germany, 1928.

Culot, M., Sharp, D., *Henri van de Velde: Theater Designs 1904-14*, London, 1974.

Eckmann, O., *Neue Formen. Dekorative Entwürfe für die Praxis*, Berlin, 1897.

Ehmig, P., *Das Deutsche Haus*, vols I, III, Berlin, 1916.

Endell, A., *Die Schönheit der Grossen Stadt*, Stuttgart, 1908.

Hirth, G., *Das Deutsche Zimmer*, Munich, Leipzig, 1899.

Hoeber, F., *Peter Behrens*, Munich, 1913.

Hüter, K.-H., *Henry van de Velde*, Berlin, 1967.

Joseph, D., *Geschichte der modernen Baukunst*, vols I-IV, Leipzig, 1912.

Joseph, D., *Geschichte der Baukunst des 19. Jahrhunderts*, vols I-II, Leipzig, 1910.

Koch, A., *Darmstadt, eine Stätte moderner Kunstbestrebungen*, Darmstadt, 1905.

Latham, I., *Olbrich*, London, 1979.

Obrist, H., *Neue Möglichkeiten in der bildenen Kunst (1896-1900)*, Jena, 1903.

Olbrich, J. M., *Architektur von Prof. Joseph M. Olbrich*, vols I-III, Berlin, 1903.

Olbrich, J. M., *Joseph Olbrichs Zeichnungen für Baukunst und Kunstgewerke*, Berlin, 1912.

Olbrich, J. M., *Ideen von Olbrich*, Vienna, 1900.

Olbrich, J. M., *Neue Gärten*, Berlin, 1905.

Osborn, M., *Neue Arbeiten von Otto Eckmann*, Berlin, 1897.

Popp, J., *Bruno Paul*, Munich.

Roh, F., *Geschichte der Deutschen Kunst von 1900 bis zur Gegenwart*, Munich, 1958.

Rosner, K., *Das deutsche Zimmer im neunzehnten Jahrhundert*, Munich, 1898.

Schmalenbach, F., *Jugendstil: ein Betrag zu Theorie und Geschichte der Fläschenkunst*, Würzburg, 1935.

Schumacher, F., *Strömmungen in deutscher Baukunst seit 1800*, Leipzig, 1936.

Seling, H., *Jugendstil – Der Weg ins 20. Jahrhundert*, Heidelberg/Munich, 1959.

Sterner, G., *Jugendstil: Kunstformen zwischen Individualismus und Massengesellschaft*, Cologne, 1975.

Veronesi, G., *Joseph Maria Olbrich*, Milan, 1948.

Periodicals

Anderson, S., 'Peter Behrens', *Architectural Design*, February, 1969.

Bode, W., 'Hermann Obrist', *Pan*, Berlin, 1896.

Endell, A., 'Möglichkeiten und Ziele einer neuen Architektur', *Deutsche Kunst und Dekoration*, Darmstadt, vol. I, 1897-98.

Joyant, M., 'Jugendstil I, II', *Forum*, vol. XIII, 1958-59.

Judson Clark, R., 'J. M. Olbrich', *Architectural Design*, December, 1967.

Meyer, P., 'Umfang und Verdienste des Jugendstils', *Werk*, vol. XXIV, 1937.

Michalski, E., 'Die entwicklungsgeschichtliche Bedeutung des Jugendstils', *Repertorium für Kunstwissenschaft*, vol. XLVI, 1925.

Obrist, H., 'Die Zukunft unserer Architektur', *Dekorative Kunst*, Munich, vol. VII, 1901.

Obrist, H., 'Luxuskunst oder Volkskunst', *Dekorative Kunst*, Munich, vol. IX, 1901-02.

Schaefer, I., 'August Endell', *Werk*, no. 6, 1971.

Serrurier-Bovy, G., 'A Darmstadt', *L'Art Moderne*, 10, 1902.

Architectural Design, February, 1972.

The Architectural Review, 1934, pp. 39, 83, 131.

The Architectural Review, 1935, pp. 23, 61.

Bauen und Wohnen, 111, 1948.

Casabella, nos. 237, 240, 1960.

Die Form, 1932, pp. 297-324.

Catalogues

Bott, G., *Jugendstil*, catalogue of the Hessisches Landesmuseum Darmstadt, Darmstadt, 1965.

Ein Dokument Deutscher Kunst – Darmstadt 1901-1976, exhibition catalogue, 5 vols, Darmstadt, 1976.

ITALY

Books

Accasto, G., Fraticelli, V., Nicolini, R., *L'Architettura*

di Roma Capitale 1870-1970, Rome, 1971.

Arata, G. U., *Costruzioni e progetti*, Milan, 1942.

Bairati, E., Bossaglia, R., Rosci, M., *L'Italia Liberty*, Milan, 1973.

Barilli, R., *Il Liberty*, Milan, 1966.

Basile, E., *Studi e schizzi*, Turin, 1911.

Beltrami, L., *Gaetano Moretti – Costruzioni concorsi schizzi*, Milan, 1912.

Bossaglia, R., *Il Liberty in Italia*, Milan, 1968.

Bossaglia, R., Hammacher, A., *Alessandro Mazzucotelli, l'artista italiano del ferro battuto Liberty*, Milan, 1971.

Bossaglia, R., *Liberty a Milano*, Milan, 1972.

Bossaglia, R., *Il Liberty-Storia e fortuna del Liberty italiano*, Florence, 1974.

Bossaglia, R., Cresti, C., Savi, V. (ed.), *Situazione degli studi sul Liberty*, Florence, 1977.

Brosio, V., *Lo stile Liberty in Italia*, Milan, 1967.

Capelli, G., *Gli architetti del primo Novecento a Parma*, Parma, 1975.

Caramel, L., Longatti, A., *Antonio Sant'Elia*, Como, 1962.

Caronia Roberti, S., *Ernesto Basile e cinquant'anni di architettura in Sicilia*, Palermo, 1935.

De Fusco, R., *Il Floreale a Napoli*, Naples, 1959.

Fratini, F. R. (ed.), *Torino 1902. Polemiche in Italia sull'arte nouva*, Turin, 1970.

Gabetti, R., Portoghesi, P., Ziino, V., *La cultura architettonica in Italia dall'unità politica alla prima guerra mondiale*, Rome, 1959.

Leva Pistoi, M., *Torino: mezzo secolo d'architettura*, Turin, 1969.

Marescotti, X., *Milano e l'Esposizione Internazionale del Sempione 1906*, Milan, 1906.

Meeks, C., *Italian Architecture 1750-1914*, New Haven, London, 1966.

Melani, A., *L'Architettura di Giulio Ulisse Arata, vol. I: Ville*, Milan, n.d. (1913).

Monneret de Villard, U., *L'Architettura di Giuseppe Sommaruga*, Milan, n.d. (1908).

Nicoletti, M., *Raimondo D'Aronco*, Milan, 1955.

Pica, V., *L'arte decorativa all'Esposizione di Torino del 1902*, Bergamo, 1903.

Pirrone, G., *Palermo Liberty*, Caltanisetta-Rome, 1971.

Pirrone, G., *Studi e schizzi di Ernesto Basile*, Palermo, 1976.

Pozzetto, M., *Max Fabiani architetto*, Gorizia, 1966.

Reggiori, M., *Milano Liberty*, Milan, 1970.

Rogers, E., *Raimondo D'Aronco*, Milan, 1955.

Sandoz, G., Roger, Berr, *Turin 1911, Rapport Général*, Paris, 1911.

Walcher, M., *L'architettura a Trieste dalla fine del Settecento agli inizi del Novecento*, Trieste, 1967.

Periodicals

Angelini, L., 'Artisti contemporanei: Giuseppe Sommaruga', *Emporium*, XLVI, 1917, no. 276, pp. 282-298.

Bossaglia, R., 'L'iter Liberty dell'architettura torinese', *Comentari*, XVII, 1966, nos. 1-3, pp. 182-184.

Bossaglia, R., 'Testimonianze critiche dell'età Liberty in Italia', *Arte in Europa*, Milan, 1966.

Brizzi, G., Guenzi, C., 'Liberty occulto e G. B. Bossi', *Casabella*, XXXIII, 1969, no. 338, pp. 22-33.

Calzavara, M., 'L'architetto Gaetano Moretti', *Casabella*, 1958, no. 218, pp. 69-82.

Catto, C., Mariani Travi, L., 'Immagini di Sommaruga', *L'Architettura – Cronache e storia*, XIII, 1967-68, nos. 143-147, pp. 340-344, 410-414, 480-484, 550-554, 620-624.

Cremona, I., 'Discorso sullo stile Liberty', *Sole Arte*, 1952, no. 3, Florence.

Cresti, C., 'Liberty a Firenze', *Antichità viva*, IX, 1970, no. 5, pp. 23-38.

Cresti, C., 'Un episodio del Liberty italiano: villa Ruggeri a Pesaro', *Bollettino degli Ingegneri*, XVIII, 1970, no. 11, pp. 3-10.

Gebhard, D., 'Raimondo D'Aronco – L'Art Nouveau in Turchia', *L'Architettura – Cronache e storia*, XII, 1966-67, nos. 134-137, pp. 550-554, 620-624, 690-694, 760-764.

Labo, M., 'Tempo e gusto del Liberty', *Emporium*, CXVI, 1952.

Meeks, C., 'The Real Liberty of Italy – The "Stile floreale"', *Art Bulletin*, XLIII, 1961, no. 2, pp.

113-130.

Pica, V., 'Revisione del Liberty', *Emporium*, XCIV, 1941, no. 560, Bergamo.

Riva, D., 'Un'architettura Liberty a Milano: la casa dell'architetto A. Campanini in via Bellini 11', *Arte Lombarda*, XVII, 1972, no. 36, pp. 114-118.

Scheichenbauer, M., 'D'Aronco in Turchia', *Casabella*, XXXV, 1971, no. 356, pp. 30-35.

Tentori, F., 'Le origini Liberty di Antonio Sant'Elia', *L'Architettura – Cronache e storia*, I, 1955, no. 2, pp. 206-216.

Tentori, F., 'Contributo alla storiografia di Giuseppe Sommaruga', *Casabella*, 1957, no. 217, pp. 70-87.

Vermeuil, M. P., 'L'Exposition d'Art décoratif moderne à Turin', *Art et Décoration*, 8, 1902.

Catalogues

Bairati, E., Pacciarotti, G. (ed.), *Silvio Gambini. Opere: 1903-1915*, exhibition catalogue, Busto Arsizio, 1976.

Bossaglia, R., *Architettura Liberty a Milano*, exhibition catalogue, Milan, 1972.

Portoghesi, P., 'Art Nouveau in Italy', *The New Domestic Landscape*, catalogue of the Museum of Modern Art, New York, 1972.

Il Liberty a Bologna e nell'Emilia-Romagna, exhibition catalogue, Bologna, 1977.

Mostra del Liberty italiano, exhibition catalogue, Milan, 1972.

Mostra del Liberty a Palermo – Bilancio di studi sul Liberty, exhibition catalogue, Palermo, 1974.

Miscellaneous

Angelucci, G., 'Contributi metodologici e critici per il catalogo dell'architettura Liberty nelle Marche', *Situazione degli studi sul Liberty*, Florence, 1977.

Avarello, P., Conforti, C., 'Stilemi e tematiche liberty nell' architettura borghese a Roma', *Situazione degli studi sul Liberty*, Florence, 1977.

Cittadini, B., De Luca, P., *Album-ricordo della grande Esposizione Internazionale di Milano 1906*, Milan, n.d. (1906).

Romanelli, G., 'L'architetto Torres e il Liberty', *Situazione degli studi sul Liberty*, Florence, 1977.

Zevi, B., 'Guido Costante Sullam', *Annuario dell'Istituto Universitatio di Architettura di Venezia*, 1950-51.

L'Architettura alla prima Esposizione Internazionale d'arte decorativa moderna di Torino, Turin, 1902.

CZECHOSLOVAKIA

Books

Dostál, O., Pechar, J., Procházka, V., *Modern Architecture in Czechoslovakia*, Prague, 1967.

Kotěra, J., *Meine und meiner Schüler Arbeiten*, Vienna, 1902.

Novotný, O., *Jan Kotěra a jeho doba*, Prague, 1958.

Poche, E., *Architektura a užité umění, Ceská secese – umění 1900*, Brno, 1966.

Teige, K., *Moderní architektura v Ceskoslovensku*, Prague, 1930.

Periodicals

Matějček, A., 'Jan Kotěra', *Der Architekt*, vol. XXI, 1917.

Miscellaneous

Symposium sur la protection des monuments d'architecture et d'art du XIXe et du XXe siècle 'Prague 1860-1960', Prague, 1971.

AUSTRIA

Books

Bahr, H., *Secession*, Vienna, 1900.

Bauer, L., *Verschiedene Skizzen, Entwürfe und Studien*, Vienna, 1899.

Eisler, M., *Österreichische Werkkultur*, Vienna, 1916.

Fagiolo, M. (ed.), *Hoffmann. I mobili semplici di Vienna*, Rome, n.d.

Feldegg, F. von, *Friedrich Ohmanns Entwürfe und ausgeführte Bauten*, 2 vols, Vienna, 1906-1914.

Feldegg, F. von, *Leopold Bauer, der Kunstler und sein Werk*, Vienna, 1918.

Feuchtmüller-Mrazek, W., *Kunst in Osterreich 1860-*

1918, Vienna, 1964.

Geretsegger, H., Peintner, M., *Otto Wagner 1841-1918. Unbegrenzte Grossstadt, Beginn der modernen Architektur*, Salzburg, 1964. (English translation, New York-London, 1970.)

Gessner, H., *Bauten und Entwürfe*, Vienna-Leipzig, 1932.

Giusti Baculo, A., *Otto Wagner dall'architettura di stile allo stile utile*, Naples, 1970.

Glück, F., *Adolf Loos*, Paris, 1931.

Graf, O. A., *Die vergessene Wagnerschule*, Vienna, 1969.

Hevesi, L., *Acht Jahre Sezession (März 1897-Juni 1905): Kritik, Polemik, Chronik*, Vienna, 1906.

Hevesi, L., *Altkunst-Neukunst: Wien 1894 bis 1908*, Vienna, 1909.

Hoffmann, J., *Josef Hoffmann*, with an introduction by Armand Weiser, Genf, 1930.

Holme, C., *The Art Revival in Austria*, London, 1906.

Hoppe, E., Schöntal, O., *Projekte und ausgeführte Bauten*, Vienna, 1931.

Kerndle, K. M. (ed.), *Wagnerschule. Arbeiten aus den Jahren 1902-1903 und 1903-1904*, Leipzig, 1905.

Kleiner, L., *Josef Hoffmann*, Berlin, 1927.

Kulke, H., *Adolf Loos*, 1931.

Lanyi, R., *Adolf Loos*, Vienna, 1931.

Larroument, G., *L'Architecture au XXe Siècle*, vols. I-II, Paris.

Lichtblau, E. (ed.), *Wagnerschule. Arbeiten aus den Jahren 1905-1906 und 1906-1907*, Leipzig, 1910.

Loos, A., *Ins Leere gesprochen (1897-1900)*, Berlin, 1925.

Loos, A., *Trotzdem (1900-1930)*, Innsbruck, 1931.

Lux, J. A., *Otto Wagner*, Munich, n.d. (1914).

Lux, J. A., *Josef Maria Olbrich*, Berlin, 1919.

Marilaun, K., *Adolf Loos*, Vienna, 1923.

Markalaus, B., *Adolf Loos. Das Werk des Architekten*, Vienna, 1931.

Münz, L., *Adolf Loos*, Milan, 1956.

Olbrich, J. M., *Architektur von Professor Joseph Maria Olbrich*, 6 vols, Berlin, 1901-1914.

Ostwald, H., *Otto Wagner: ein Beitrag zum Verständnis seines baukünstlerischen Schaffens*, Baden, 1948.

Pagliara, N., *Appunti su Otto Wagner*, Naples, 1968.

Pirchan, E., *Otto Wagner, der grosse Baukünstler*, Vienna, 1956.

Pozzetto, M., *Max Fabiani, architetto*, Görz, 1966.

Pozzetto, M., *Jože Plečnik e la scuola di Otto Wagner*, Turin, 1968.

Rochowanski, L. W., *Josef Hoffmann: eine Studie geschrieben zur seinem 80. Geburtstag*, Vienna, 1950.

Schöntal, O. (ed.), *Das Ehrenjahr Otto Wagners an der K. K. Akademie der bildenden Künste in Wien*, Vienna, n.d. (1912).

Schreyl, K. H., *Joseph Maria Olbrich. Die Ziechnungen der Kunstbibliothek Berlin, Kritischer Katalog*, Berlin, 1972.

Sperlich, H.-G., *Versuch über Joseph Maria Olbrich*, Darmstadt, 1965.

Tietze, H., *Otto Wagner*, Vienna, 1922.

Uhl, O., *Moderne Architektur in Wien von Otto Wagner bis Heute*, Vienna, 1966.

Veronesi, G., *Josef Hoffmann*, Milan, 1956.

Veronesi, G., *J. M. Olbrich*, Milan, 1956.

Wagner, O., *Moderne Architektur*, Vienna, 1895.

Wagner, O., *Einige Skizzen, Projekte und ausgeführte Bauwerke*, 4 vols, Vienna, 1897-1922.

Wagner, O., *Aus der Wagner Schule*, Vienna, 1900.

Wagner, O., *Wagnerschule 1901*, Vienna, 1902.

Wagner, O., *Die Baukunst unserer Zeit*, Vienna, 1914.

Waissenberger, R., *Die Wiener Secession*, Vienna, 1971.

Weiser, A., *Josef Hoffmann*, Geneva, 1930.

Zuckerkandel, B., *Zeitkunst, Wien 1901-1907*, Vienna, 1908.

Periodicals

Fendler, F., 'Um Wiener-Sezession', *Berliner Architektur-Welt*, Berlin, 1901.

Girardi, V., 'Joseph Hoffmann maestro dimenticato', *L'Architettura*, Rome, vol. II, 1956.

Girardi, V., 'Commento a Otto Wagner', *L'Architettura*, Rome, vol. IV, 1958.

Hevesi, L., 'The Art Revival in Austria', *The Studio*, London, vol. IV, 1894.

Levetus, A. S., 'A Brussels Mansion designed by Professor Joseph Hoffmann of Wien', *The Studio*, London, vol. LXI, 1914.

Wagner, O., 'Die Kunst der Gegenwart', *Ver Sacrum*, vol. III, 1900.

Zuckerkandel, B., 'Josef Hoffmann', *Dekorative Kunst*, Munich, vol. VII, 1903.

Catalogues

Mrazek, W., *Die Wiener Werkstätte, modernes Kunsthandwerk von 1903-1932*, exhibition catalogue, Vienna, 1967.

Die Wiener Werkstätte, catalogue of the Österreichisches Museum für Angewandte Kunst, Vienna, 1967.

Joseph M. Olbrich 1867-1908. Das Werk des Architekten, exhibition catalogue of Hessischen Landesmuseum in Darmstadt, Darmstadt, 1967.

L'architettura a Vienna intorno al 1900, exhibition catalogue of Galleria Nazionale d'arte moderna di Roma, Rome, 1971.

Vienna Secession, catalogue of the Royal Academy of Arts, London, 1971.

Wien um 1900: Austellung veranstaltet vom Kulturamt der Stadt Wien, Vienna, 1964.

Miscellaneous

Sekler, E. F., 'The Stoclet House by Josef Hoffmann', in *Essays in the history of architecture presented to Rudolf Wittkower*, London, 1967.

Aus der Wagner-Schule, MDCCCXCVII, supplement of *Der Architekt*, Vienna, 1897.

Aus der Wagner-Schule, MDCCCXCVIII, supplement of *Der Architekt*, Vienna, 1898.

Aus der Wagner-Schule, MDCCCIC, supplement of *Der Architekt*, Vienna, 1899.

Aus der Wagner-Schule, MCM, supplement of *Der Architekt*, Vienna, 1900.

Die Wiener Werkstätte 1903-1928, Vienna, 1929.

Josef Hoffmann zum sechzigsten Geburtstag. 15. Dezember 1930, Vienna, 1930.

Wien am Anfang des 20. Jahrhunderts. Ein Führer in technischer und künstlerischer Richtung hrsg. vom Österreichischen Ingenieur- und Architektenverein, 2 vols, Vienna, 1905-1906.

Wien am Anfang des 20. Jahrhunderts, Vienna, 1906.

Wiener Neubauten im Style der Sezession, Vienna, 1902.

Wiener Neubauten im Stil der Sezession, vols I-VI, Vienna, 1908-10.

Wiener Werkstätte, Modernes Kunstgewerbe und sein Weg, Vienna, 1929.

Wagner-Schule 01, supplement of *Der Architekt*, Vienna, 1902.

Wagnerschule 1902, Vienna-Leipzig, 1903.

USA

Books

Andrews, W., *Architecture, Ambition and Americans: A Social History of American Architecture*, New York, 1947.

Burchard, J., Bush-Brown, A., *The Architecture of America – A Social and Cultural History*, New York, 1961.

Cheney, S., *The New World Architecture*, New York, 1930.

Clark, R. J., *The Arts and Crafts Movement in America 1876-1916*, Princeton, 1972.

Connely, W., *Louis Sullivan as He Lived. The Shaping of American Architecture*, New York, 1960.

Current, W. R. and K., *Greene and Greene: Architects in the Residential Style*, Fort Worth, 1974.

Dredge, J., *A Record of the Transportation Exhibits of the World's Columbian Exposition of 1893*, New York, 1894.

Gilbert, P., Bryson, C. L., *Chicago and its Makers*, Chicago, 1929.

Hitchcock, H.-R., *The Architecture of H. H. Richardson*, New York, 1936.

Jordy, W. H., *American Buildings and their Architects. Vol. 3, Progressive and Academic Ideals at the Turn of the Twentieth Century*, Doubleday, 1972.

Morrison, H., *Louis Sullivan, Prophet of Modern Architecture*, New York, 1935.

Mumford, L., *Roots of Contemporary American Architecture*, New York, 1952.

Mumford, L., *The Brown Decades*, New York, 1955.

Schuyler, M., *Studies in American Architecture*, New York, 1927.

Sullivan, L., *Inspiration*, Chicago, 1886.

Sullivan, L., *The Autobiography of an Idea*, New York, 1924.

Sullivan, L., *A System of Architectural Ornament According with a Philosophy of Man's Powers*, New York, 1924.

Sullivan, L., *Kindergarten Chats and Other Writings*, New York, 1947.

Szarkowski, J., *The Ideas of Louis Sullivan*, Minneapolis, 1956.

Vogel, F. R., *Das Amerikanische Haus*, Berlin, 1910.

Wright, F. L., *An Autobiography*, New York, 1932.

Wright, F. L., *Genius and Mobocracy*, New York, 1949.

Periodicals

Anonymous, 'Structures Designed by Louis H. Sullivan', *Interstate Architect and Builder*, vol. 2, December 22nd, 1900.

Anonymous, 'A Departure from Classic Tradition: Two Unusual Houses by Louis Sullivan and Frank Lloyd Wright', *Architectural Record*, vol. 30, October, 1911.

Anonymous, 'Louis Sullivan, the First American Architect', *Current Literature*, vol. 52, June, 1912.

Bangs, J. M., 'Greene and Greene', *Architectural Forum*, October, 1948.

Barker, A.-W., 'Louis H. Sullivan, Thinker and Architect', *Architectural Annual*, 1901.

Bouilhet, A., 'L'Exposition de Chicago', *Revue des Arts Décoratifs*, vol. 14, 1893-94.

Bragdon, C., 'Letters from Louis Sullivan', *Architecture*, vol. 64, 1931.

Caffin, C. H., 'Louis H. Sullivan, Artist among Architects, American among Americans', *The Criterion*, vol. 20, 1899.

Dean, G. R., 'A New Movement in American Architecture', *Brush and Pencil*, vol. 5, March, 1900.

Desmond, H. W., 'Another View – What Mr Louis Sullivan Stands For', *Architectural Record*, vol. 16, July, 1904.

Greene, C. S., 'Architecture is a Fine Art', *The Architect*, April, 1917.

Grey, E., 'Indigenous and Inventive Architecture for America', *Inland Architect & News Record*, vol. 35, June, 1900.

Hamlin, A. D. F., 'L'Art Nouveau', *The Craftsman*, vol. 3.

Hope, H. R., 'Louis Sullivan's Architectural Ornament', *Magazine of Art*, March, 1947.

Makinson, R. L., 'Greene and Greene: The Gamble House', *The Prairie School Review*, Fourth Quarter, 1968.

McLean, R. C., 'Architects and Architecture in the United States', *Inland Architect & News Record*, vol. 28, January, 1897.

McLean, R. C., 'Louis Henry Sullivan, Sept. 3rd 1856 – April 14th, 1924; An Appreciation', *Western Architect*, vol. 33, May, 1924.

Robertson, H., 'The Work of Louis H. Sullivan', *Architect's Journal*, vol. 59, June 18th, 1924.

Schopfer, J., 'American Architecture from a Foreign Point of View: New York City', *Architectural Review*, March, 1900.

Schuyler, M., 'A Critique of the Works of Adler & Sullivan', *Architectural Record*, December, 1895.

Stickley, G., 'The Value of Permanent Architecture as a Truthful Expression of National Character', *The Craftsman*, April, 1909.

Sturgis, R., 'Good Things in Modern Architecture', *Architectural Record*, July-September, 1898.

Wright, F. L., 'Louis Sullivan, Beloved Master', *Western Architect*, vol. 33, June, 1924.

Wright, F. L., 'Louis H. Sullivan – His Work', *Architectural Record*, vol. 56, July, 1924.

Miscellaneous

World's Columbian Exposition: Memorial Volume, Dedicatory and Opening Ceremonies, Stone Kastler and Painter, Chicago, 1893.

NOTES

INTRODUCTION

1 *L'architecture aux U.S.A., preuve de la force d'expansion du génie français, heureuse association de qualités admirablement complémentaires,* Paris, Payot, 2 volumes, 162 and 174 pp. (Architecture in the United States, a proof of the potential for expansion of French genius, and a happy association of admirably complementary qualities).

BELGIUM

1 Sander Pierron and Henri Nizet, 'Architecture domestique en Belgique', *Le Monde Moderne,* vol.X, pp.757-8, Paris 1899.
2 Comparison of the building regulations of several towns and communes, G. Maukels, architect, professor at the Académie Royale des Beaux-Arts in Brussels.
3 Thus although the furnishing and decoration of the Exposition Coloniale in Tervuren in 1897 was given to Horta, Hankar, van de Velde, Hobé, and other Art Nouveau architects, it was less because Leopold II appreciated this style than to show, through the curves and volutes of the 'Modern Style', that wood from the Belgian Congo was capable of meeting the demands of the most delicate cabinet-making.
4 See, for instance, Jules Destrée, 'Socialisme et Art', in *Révolution Verbale et Révolution Pratique,* a lecture delivered to the Etudiants Collectivistes of Paris on June 13th, 1902. This and other speeches by Destrée were published under the title *Sémailles,* Henri Lamertin, 1913, pp.2-18.
5 Louis Bertrand, a leading figure in Belgian socialism, deputy mayor of the commune of Schaerbeek, awarded the building of all the new communal schools to the architect Henry Jacobs (1864-1935), a pupil of Horta.
6 Emile Vandervelde, *Essais Socialistes,* Paris, 1906.
7 Regarding his reading of Dostoyevsky, Destrée tells how he found pleasure in perusing that author's 'indictments against reason'. Travelling in Italy in 1886 he notes in his diary: 'The decadence of individuals is pitiful; the decadence of societies is as marvellous as a sunset'. Quoted in Richard Dupierreux, *Jules Destrée,* Brussels, Lahor, 1938, p.46.
8 Destrée published a work entitled *Imagerie Japonaise* in 1888, several years before the Goncourt brothers' studies on Japanese art, which had a compelling influence on the taste of the period.
9 The architect Alphonse Balat (1819-95) built the greenhouses of the royal château at Laeken from 1874 to 1886. Victor Horta entered his studio as a probationer in 1884.
10 'At last we move under full sail into the metallurgical order, which will present differences sharper than those that distinguish the Tuscan from the Gothic order . . . All the architectonic masterpieces of the *Thousand and One Nights,* hitherto relegated to albums and memory-books, are realisable in iron and cast iron. Even the haunting biblical nightmares of the painter Martin, the mysterious brahmanic compositions of the erudite Condère, and the elegant arabesques of Midolle

the engineer can be rendered in cast iron lace, bright with stained glass.' From a review of the 1847 Exposition published in the Brussels *Journal de l'Architecture,* no.4, April 1848, p.3.
11 'Don't expect us to define his architecture . . . it's simply twentieth-century. It's a pagoda if you like, a mosque if you prefer, an Alhambra if that suits you better. It's an Alcazar, the delight of Moorish kings and of lots of others who are neither kings nor Moors. It's a composite Eden, motley, teeming, kaleidoscopic, multicoloured, appended to the architectural movement of a time that has no architecture because it has all the architectures, the movement of an electric, ever-changing age that injects criticism even into its art. Stunning fantasy of a composite, cosmopolitan art, artificial, brilliant improvisation that responds to the fever and paroxysm of the moment. It is surely the setting that goes best with modern ballets, exhibitions of *tableaux vivants,* the perilous leaps of gymnasts, the somersaults of acrobats, the lies of Bengal lights, the trumperies of gas, the impostures of electric light. A theatre spangled, starry, rouged, light-headed, fanciful, adorable, and absurd, that looks as if it had been made of dancers' skirts, athletes' jerseys, and the tinseled tights of lion-tamers.' 'La première au Théâtre de la Bourse', *L'Etoile Belge,* Dec.31, 1885.
12 This vogue led to the building of the elegant Galeries Saint-Hubert in Brussels in 1846, following plans drawn in 1837 by the architect Jean-Pierre Cluysenaar (1811-80).
13 The iron church in the royal demesne at Laeken was built in 1892-93 on Alphonse Balat's plans.
14 De Wouters de Bouchout, *L'Art Nouveau et l'Enseignement,* Malines, 1903, p.9.
15 Victor Horta, *Mémoires.* Conserved at the Musée Horta, 25 rue Américaine, 1050 Brussels.
16 'Die Linie' appeared in *Die Zukunft,* Berlin, Sept.6, 1902.
17 'In Nature's creations we can discover all the secrets which the new architectural line will reveal to us in the near future . . . Nature proceeds by continuity, connecting and linking together the different organs that make up a body or a tree; she draws one out of the other without violence or shock . . . This line will be expressive in the manner of the line that determines the shape of trees as well as that of the bodies of humans and animals.' Van de Velde, *Les Formules de la beauté architectonique moderne,* Weimar, 1916, p.81.
18 *Ibid.*

FRANCE

1 *The Architecture of the Ecole des Beaux-Arts,* published by David van Zanten for an exhibition at the Museum of Modern Art, New York, 1976. For a more general picture of eclecticism, see Luciano Patetta's *L'architettura dell' Eclettismo, fonti, teorie, modelli, 1750-1900,* Milan, 1975. For France, the best reference book is still Louis Hautecoeur's *Histoire de l'Architecture classique en France,* vol. VII 'La fin de l'architecture classique, 1848-1900', Paris, 1957.

2 Eugène-Emmanuel Viollet-le-Duc, *Entretiens sur l'architecture,* 2 volumes and atlas, Paris, 1863 and 1872, Republished by Pierre Mardaga, Brussels, 1977.
3 The thesis of Hubert Damish in *Viollet-le-Duc, l'architecture raisonnée,* Paris, 1964.
4 On architecture in iron, the recent work by Giulio Roisecco *L'architettura del ferro La Francia 1715-1914,* Rome, 1973, is better than Siegfried Giedon's *Espace, temps, architecture,* Brussels, 1968; originally published in Cambridge, U.S.A., 1941, which is already outdated. Also useful are the short treaty by Marc Emery, *Un siècle d'architecture moderne 1850-1950,* Paris, 1971, and the interesting catalogue by Paul Chemetov, Marie-Christine Gangneux, Bernard Paurd and Edith Girard *Architectures Paris 1848-1914,* Paris, 1976.
5 Pierre Francastel, *Art et Technique,* Paris, 1956; Stephen Tschudi-Madsen, *Sources of Art Nouveau,* Oslo, New York, 1956; Nikolaus Pevsner, *The Sources of Modern Art,* London, 1962; Robert Schmutzler, *Art Nouveau,* New York, 1964; Maurice Rheims, *L'Art 1900 ou le Style Jules Verne,* Paris, 1965; Peter Collins, *Changing Ideals in Modern Architecture,* London, 1965.
6 The role played by Bing in Impressionism and Post-Impressionism was evaluated long ago by John Rewald (*Histoire de l'impressionnisme,* Paris, 1955).
7 c.f. Jean d'Albis, *Ernest Chaplet,* Paris, 1976.
8 As the long-awaited publication by Alain Blondel and Yves Plantin on Guimard has not yet appeared, the catalogue drawn up by Yvonne Brunhammer, Klaus Bussmann and Roswitha Kock for the exhibition at the Landesmuseum, Münster in 1975 is very useful. Also Franco Borsi and Ezio Godoli's *Paris 1900* (Brussels, 1976) – the best existing synthesis in this field.
9 Drawn up by Yvonne Brunhammer et al; *Art Nouveau Belgium/France,* a catalogue of the exhibition at the Rice Museum, Houston in 1976.
10 There is no work solely devoted to Jules Lavirotte. For want of anything better, see Borsi/ Godoli *Paris 1900* (op. cit.) – although the information they give on Lavirotte is very sketchy.
11 The scarcity of works on French Art Nouveau architecture is flagrantly obvious. There was nothing on Nancy until the purely illustrative catalogue of the recent exhibition organised by the Inventaire Général (Jean-Claude Groussard, Francis Roussel, *Nancy Architecture 1900,* Nancy, 1976).
12 For Henri Sauvage, see the catalogue of the exhibition organised by the Archives of Modern Architecture, Brussels (Paris, S.A.D.G., 1976).
13 There is also a lack of documentation for Franz Jourdain (although his son Francis was the subject of an exhibition in the Parisian suburbs in 1977). There is a good summary of his work in Borsi/Godoli, op. cit.
14 The only available study of Anatole de Baudot is the admirable work by Françoise Vitale-Boudon, 'Recherche sur la pensée et l'oeuvre d'Anatole de Baudot', a special edition of the magazine *Architecture, Mouvement, Continuité* (no. 28, March 1973, Paris, S.A.D.G.).
15 Lewis Mumford, *La cité à travers l'histoire,* Paris,

1964 – *The City in History*, 1961.
16 Camillo Sitte, *Der Stadtbau nach seinen künstlerischen Grundsätzen*, Vienna, 1889. The work was well known and very influential in France, despite the fact that a translation was not published until some time later (*L'Art de bâtir les villes*, Paris, 1918).
17 The catalogue of the exhibition 'Art Nouveau Belgium/France' (Houston, 1976, op. cit.) gives as exhaustive a picture as possible.
18 Raymond Escholier's *Le nouveau Paris: la vie artistique de la Cité moderne*, Paris, circa 1913.
19 Christophe Pawlowski, *Tony Garnier et les débuts de l'urbanisme functionnel en France*, Paris, 1967.
20 Thanks to Paul Jamot's biography *Auguste et Gaston Perret et l'architecture de béton armé*, Paris, 1927, complemented by Bernard Champigneulle's *Auguste Perret*, Paris, 1959.

SWITZERLAND
1 Othmar Birkner coined that label in 1967. 'One understands better the Swiss evolution [in architecture] during the first decade of the twentieth century if the general situation is called National Romanticism [Nationale Romantik] and not Art Nouveau'. See Othmar Birkner, *Der Weg im 20. Jahrhundert*, catalogue of the exhibition at the Gewerbemuseum, Winterthur, 1969, p.26.
2 *Almanach Hachette de l'année 1900*, petite encyclopédie populaire, 'édition complète', Paris 1900, p.335.
3 Such is the argument of a professor of architecture at the Lausanne School of Engineering; see Charles Melley, ' "Modern Style" et traditions locales', in *Bulletin technique de la Suisse romande*, vol.XXX, Lausanne, 1904, pp.72-75.
4 See Othmar Birkner, *Bauen und Wohnen in der Schweiz, 1850-1920*, Zurich, 1975, p.203; and Jacques Gubler, *Nationalisme et internationalisme dans l'architecture moderne de la Suisse*, Lausanne, 1975, pp.32-35.
5 Eugène Emmanuel Viollet-le-Duc, *Lettres d'Allemagne*, Paris, 1856, p.12.
6 Organised by Maurice Culot and Lise Grenier, the exhibition was backed by a catalogue in which François Loyer's contribution discusses the problem of Regionalism. See *Henri Sauvage, 1873-1932*, Archives d'architecture moderne, Brussels, 1976, p.36.
7 *Ibid.*, pp.237-238.
8 Reproduced in *Academy Architecture*, vol.XXII, London, 1902, pp.52-53.
9 See Hanspeter Rebsamen, 'Zürich Total 1890-1919', in *Tages-Anzeiger Magazin*, Zürich, no.36, 19th November 1977, pp.16-34.
10 Charles-Edouard Jeanneret, 'Le renouveau dans l'architecture', in *L'Oeuvre*, vol.I, 1914, p.35.
11 Gabriel Mourey, letter of the 12th May 1903 to Alphonse Laverrière: 'loger une famille de bourgeoisie éclairée'.
12 See Gilles Barbey, Jacques Gubler, Geneviève Paschoud, 'Riviera lémanique', in *Werk-archithèse*, vol.LXIV, no.6, June 1977, pp.3-40.
13 Roger Marx, 'Une villa moderne: la salle de billard', series *Essais de Rénovation Ornementale* published by the Gazette des Beaux-Arts, Paris, 1902.
14 See Othmar Birkner, *Bauen und Wohnen*, loc. cit., p.72.
15 *Ibid.*, pp.153-162.
16 See *Werk-archithèse*, vol.LXIV, no.2, February 1977, pp.45-46; and Sylvain Malfroy, 'Un modèle de passage piétonnier: Les Galeries du Commerce de Lausanne (1909)' in *Habitation*, Lausanne, 1977, vol.L, no.5, pp.9-16.
17 Oral testimony to the author by an eye witness, the architect Henri-Robert von der Mühll (born 1898).
18 See Stanislaus von Moos, *Le Corbusier*, Frauenfeld, Stuttgart, 1968, pp.11-25.
19 See Pierre du Bois, *Les Mythologies de la belle époque*, La Chaux-de-Fonds, 1975.
20 Charles Blanc, *Grammaire des Arts du Dessin*, Paris, 1867.
21 See Paul Turner, 'The Beginnings of Le Corbusier's Education, 1902-1907', in *Art Bulletin*, vol.LIII, 1971, no.2, pp.214-224.
22 See Charles Jencks, *Le Corbusier and the Tragic View of Architecture*, London, 1973, pp.17-27.
23 *Ibid.*, p.23.
24 Othmar Birkner, *Bauen und Wohen*, loc. cit., p.23-24.

25 See Joyce Lowman, 'Corb as structural rationalist', in *The Architectural Review*, vol.160, October 1976, pp.229-233.
26 Thus the future Le Corbusier in 1914, see Charles-Edouard Jeanneret, 'Le renouveau dans l'architecture', loc. cit., p.37: 'L'esprit local ne s'acquiert pas par un acte de volonté; ce doit être une emprise lente, une intuition.'

GERMANY
1 Julius Meier-Graefe, 'Epigonen', *Dekorative Kunst* IV, July 1899.
2 Carola Giedion-Welcker, *Plastik des XX Jahrhunderts*, Stuttgart, 1955.
3 August Endell, 'Möglichkeiten und Ziele einer neuen Architektur', *Deutsche Kunst und Dekoration* vol.I, 1897-8, p.141.
4 Friedrich Ahlers-Hestermann, *Stilwende*, Berlin, 1941.
5 Robert Schmutzler, *Art Nouveau-Jugendstil*, Stuttgart, 1962.
6 1906 Dresden Exhibition Catalogue.
7 Henry van de Velde, *Kunstgewerbliche Laienpredigten*, Leipzig, 1902.
8 Henry F. Lenning, *The Art Nouveau*, The Hague, 1951.
9 *Dekorative Kunst*, 1902, p.443.
10 Hermann Muthesius, 'Haus eines Kunstfreundes', 1901 Competition Folio.
11 Hermann Muthesius, *Das Englische Haus* III, pp.238-9.
12 *Die Form* VII 1932, pp.297-324.
13 *Die Form* VII 1932, pp.297-324.
14 *Die Form* VII 1932, pp.297-324.

ITALY
1 The name of the famous London shop, used originally in an ironical and disparaging sense in the early 1900s to describe Italian Art Nouveau, has gradually ousted the alternative expressions Stile Moderno, Arte Nuova, Modernismo and Stile Floreale. The latter term is still used to indicate that current within Liberty which, basing itself on Pre-Raphaelite precedent, argued for a return to a neo-Renaissance classicism characterised by exuberant floral decoration.
2 Melani, A.,'Di fronda in fronda. Arte nuova e filosofia vecchia', in *Arte e storia*, XXI, 1902, no.11, p.71.
3 It is usual to regard the 'Age of Giolitti' as dating from Giovanni Giolitti's becoming Minister of the Interior in the Zanardelli cabinet.
4 *Emporium* (Bergamo) founded in 1895 and directed by Vittorio Pica was the first to emphasise the need for innovation in the decorative arts, following attentively achievements abroad and particularly in England. Its example was followed by *Arte decorativa moderna* and *Il giovane artista moderno*, both published in Turin from 1902 onwards. These were joined by *L'architettura italiana* (Turin), *Per l'arte* (Turin) and *L'ambiente moderno* (Milan) in 1905, 1909 and 1910 respectively. In the early 1900s the executed work of modernist architects began to enjoy a favourable reception in older magazines like *Memorie di un architetto* (Turin) and *Edilizia moderna* (Milan), founded respectively in 1887 and 1892.
5 Bossaglia, R., 'L'architettura', in *Mostra del Liberty italiano*, exhibition catalogue, Milan, 1972, p.33.
6 Investment of foreign capital contributed in considerable measure to the take-off of Italian industrialisation, and 'these investments' observed De Fusco 'were made precisely by those countries in which Art Nouveau was most firmly established. These economic connections explain, if only in part, the spread of the new stylistic tendency in Italy . . . The Lombard or Piedmontese capitalist adopted in the premises of his company and in his private residence that style which he saw used as an expression of "Progress" in the European environments with which he habitually dealt.'
7 This anti-working-class policy was brutally expressed in May 1898 in the bloody repression of workers' demonstrations in Milan by General Bava Beccaris.
8 Melani, A., 'Di fronda in fronda. Lo studio del disegno', in *Arte e storia*, XXI, 1902, no.11, p.71.
9 'L'Esposizione di Torino. Il discorso del Ministro Nasi', in *L'arte decorativa moderna*, I, 1902, no.4, p.110.

10 Among the firms on an industrial scale which produced Liberty objects were the Società Ceramica Richard-Ginori, the Carlo Zen furniture factory of Milan, the Società Ceramica Italiana Laveno and the Golia-Ducrot Company of Palermo.
11 Angeli, D., 'Per la gloria artistica di Torino', in *Nuova Antologia*, 1902, no.743, p.444.
12 Raimondo D'Aronco (b. Gemona near Udine 1857, d. San Remo 1932) after completing a three-year apprenticeship as stone-mason at Graz in 1871 entered the Academy of Fine Art at Venice, where he obtained the diploma of architect. Following an outstanding success (gold medal) in the international competition for the monument to Victor Emanuel II in Rome in 1884, he acquired a certain fame as an exhibition architect with a series of buildings and projects characterised by a restrained neo-classicism: the building for the Exhibition of Fine Arts at Venice (1887), carried out in collaboration with Trevisanato, and the unrealised projects for the First Architectural Exhibition at Turin (1890) and the Ottoman Exhibition at Constantinople (1890). His success in the competition for the 1902 Exhibition was belated compensation for the outcome of the one for the 1890 Turin Exhibition: on that occasion the Jury, although awarding the First Prize to D'Aronco, in fact decided to carry out the design submitted by Camillo Riccio.
13 See for example Wagner's design of 1900 for a Moderne Galerie and the projects by Plečnik for a Kursalon für Ostende (1899) and by Melichar for a Weltausstellungsgebäude (1899).
14 Since D'Aronco was occupied in Turkey with the reconstruction of the city of Pera which had been destroyed in an earthquake he was unable to supervise the construction of the pavilions. Their execution was therefore assigned to a technical office directed by the engineer Enrico Bonelli, who did not always carry out D'Aronco's postal instructions faithfully.
15 Quoted from *Mostra del Liberty italiano*, op. cit., p.93.
16 Pietro Fenoglio (b. Turin 1867, d. Corio 1927) constructed several industrial buildings in Turin – the Ansaldi Foundry in Via Cuneo (1889), the factory for the Società Termotecnica in Corso Tortona, the Fiorio Factory in Via San Donato – all of which follow the local Romanesque-Gothic tradition. After a brief Art Nouveau interval Fenoglio's work returned – as early as 1905 – to eclecticism. During the First World War he abandoned architectural practice for a position in a bank.
17 De Fusco, R., op. cit., p.17.
18 Quoted from Zevi, B., 'Guido Costante Sullam 1873-1949', in *Annuario dell'Istituto Universitario di Architettura di Venezia*, 1957, pp.83-84.
19 Giuseppe Sommaruga (b. Milan 1867, d. Milan 1917), a pupil of Camillo Boito and Alfredo Melani, qualified at the Brera Academy and at the Milan Polytechnic. Principal works: Villino Aletti, Via Malpighi 14, Rome (1897); Pavilion at the St. Louis Fair (1904); Teatro Filodrammatico Building, Trieste (1906); Villa Galimberti, Stresa (1906); Faccanoni Mausoleum, Sarnico (1908); Villa Carosio, Baveno (1908); Villa Galimberti, Milan (1908); Poletti Residential Complex, Lanzo d'Intelvi (1915).
20 Quoted from Bossaglia, R., 'Significato di una ricerca sull'architettura Liberty in Emilia-Romagna', in *Il Liberty a Bologna e nell'Emilia-Romagna*, catalogue of the exhibition, Bologna 1977.
21 Ernesto Basile (b. Palermo 1857, d. Palermo 1932) was the son of the well-known architect Giovan Battista Basile, the designer of among other things the Teatro Massimo at Palermo, from whom he inherited the Chair of Architecture at the University of Palermo. Leaving aside his early works, designed together with his father, his extensive output included the following buildings notable for their modernist character: the pavilions for the Exhibition of Fine Arts (1900) and the Agricultural Exhibition (1902) at Palermo; the Palazzo Utveggio (1901-03) and the library in the Palazzo Francavilla (1903) at Palermo; the Villino Ida, Via Siracusa 15, Palermo (1903).
22 c.f. Pirrone, G., 'Le stile 1900 alle frontiere europee: la Spagna e la Sicilia, in AA.VV., *Situazione degli studi sul Liberty*, Florence, 1977.
23 Many of Michelazzi's buildings have been demolished in recent years. Notable among his more

important surviving works are the Villino Lampredi, Via Giano della Bella 13, Florence (1908-12); the Villa in Viale del Poggio Imperiale (1902-03) and the Villino at Via Giano della Bella 9.

CZECHOSLOVAKIA

1 The Austrian pavilion was a tactful mixture of a classical exterior and Art Nouveau interiors by Max Fabiani, among others.

2 The reorganised Prague Polytechnic was founded in 1714 and was the oldest school of its kind in Europe.

3 The golden stucco inscription on the National Theatre 'Národ sobě' (The Nation to itself) was an expression of the lawful claims of the country, and a symbol of the strong feelings of national identity.

4 During this period, inspired by a growing spirit of national and cultural identification, local governments financed the construction of Municipal Houses with auditoriums and concert halls in almost every major centre, including three in Prague itself. The Secession style was also used for theatres – for example the Vinohrady Theatre in Prague or the Mladá Bolaslav in Kralik – for gymnasiums ('Sokol') and for stadiums – for example the stadium in Prague of 1912 by Dryák. Prominent architects were called in to design parks and spa buildings and several markets and schools were also built in a Secession style, for example the market at Smíchov by Alois Censký. In the private sector, several publishers commissioned buildings from Secession architects (Vilímek buildings by Pfeiffer; Topič Building by Polívka; Leichter and Urbánek buildings by Kotěra). In Prague itself, the new sanitation laws of 1893 necessitated the demolition or renovation of several buildings, and between 1893 and 1896 competitions for a new sanitation plan to cover the old town were held.

5 The magazine Volné Směry was founded in 1897 (in the same year as Jugend) to mark the tenth anniversary of the Mánes group. Kotěra worked as co-editor for a time.

6 Wagner's ideas on a new architecture were expounded in his inaugural speech on his appointment at the Academy, published as Moderne Architektur in 1895.

AUSTRIA

1 Quoted in Deutsch-German, A., 'Oberbaurath Wagner', in Wiener Porträts, Vienna, 1903, p.30.

2 Janik, A., Toumlin, S., Wittgenstein's Vienna, London, 1973, p.117.

3 Josef Hoffmann, although he had been a pupil – like Olbrich – of Karl Hasenauer, took his degree in the academic year of 1894-95 with Wagner.

4 Together with the painters Ludwig Ferdinand Graf, Rudolf Hejda and Rudolf Konopa, the architect Robert Oerley was one of the four founders of the Hagenbund, whose programme was shared by the Künstlerbund Hagen, another association also founded in 1900. To this belonged the architect Josef Urban, an ex-pupil of Hasenauer.

5 Gustav Klimt, Josef Hoffmann, Otto Wagner, Koloman Moser, Wilhelm Bernatzig, Georg Klimt, Max Kurzweil, Wilhelm List, Karl Moll, Emil Orlik and Alfred Roller all broke away from the Secession which had already become an academy of itself.

6 c.f. Tafuri, M., 'Ordine e disordine', Casabella XLI, 1977, no.421, pp.36-40.

7 Letter from Olbrich to Wagner quoted in Veronesi, G., Joseph M. Olbrich, Milan, 1948, p.42.

8 This interpretation is found for example in Feldegg, F. von, 'J. M. Olbrich', Der Architekt V, 1899, p.37.

9 See Olbrich, J. M., 'Das Haus der Secession', Der Architekt V, 1899, p.5.

10 See Der Architekt V, 1899, p.49.

11 The Karlskirche and the Haus der Secession are not exactly opposite one another but their longitudinal axes are parallel.

12 Nigro Covre, J., 'Vienna 1898-1910 tra rinnovamento ed eredità culturale', La città/Immagini documenti, no.3, 1976, p.160.

13 See Fagiolo, M., 'La cattedrale di cristallo, l'architettura dell'Espressionismo e la "tradizione" esoterica', in Argan, G. C. (edited by), Il Revival, Milan, 1974, p.243.

14 See Graf, O. A., Die vergessene Wagnerschule, Vienna, 1969, ill.46-48.

15 Wagner, O., Moderne Architektur, Vienna, 1895; Italian translation: Turin, 1976, pp.148-149.

16 Among articles on English architecture and the decorative arts which appeared in Kunst und Kunsthandwerk between 1898 and 1901 we would recommend: Newton, E., 'Die Architektur und das englische Home', Kunst und Kunsthandwerk I, 1898, pp.164-176; Hevesi, L., 'Ausstellung preisgekrönter englischer Schülerarbeiten im österreichischen Museum', Kunst und Kunsthandwerk II, 1899, pp.58-77; Fred, W., 'C. R. Ashbee. Ein Reformer englischen Kunstgewerbes', Kunst und Kunsthandwerk, III, 1900, pp.167-176; Fred, W., 'Der Architekt M. H. Baillie-Scott', Kunst und Kunsthandwerk IV, 1901, pp.53-73; Dreger, M., 'Zur Walter Crane – Ausstellung im österreichischen Museum', Kunst und Kunsthandwerk IV, 1901, pp.93-108; Schmid, M., 'Moderne englische Baukunst', Kunst und Kunsthandwerk IV, 1901, pp.329-359; Rendell, B., 'Charles Ashbee als Architekt und Baumeister', Kunst und Kunsthandwerk IV, 1901, pp.461-467; Fred, W., 'Die internationale Kunst- und Industrie Ausstellung in Glasgow', Kunst und Kunsthandwerk IV, 1901, pp.501-518.

17 On the influence of Mackintosh in Austria see Sekler, E. F., 'Mackintosh and Vienna', in Richards, J. M., Pevsner, N. (edited by), The Anti-Rationalists, Wisbech, Cambs., 1973, pp.136-142.

18 Messina, M. G., ' "Einfache Möbel". I "mobili semplici" di Hoffmann', in Fagiolo, M. (edited by), Hoffmann: i 'mobili semplici'. Vienna 1900-10, exhibition catalogue, Rome, 1977.

19 The Café Museum, designed by Loos in 1899, was renamed by his contemporaries 'Café Nihilismus'.

20 Loos, A., Trotzdem, Innsbruck, 1931, p.77.

21 Echoes of Hoffmann's style are also evident in the early works of Le Corbusier – the Maison Jeanneret père at La Chaux-de-Fonds (1912), the Villa Favre-Jacot at Le Locle (1912) and the Villa Schwob at La Chaux-de-Fonds (1916-17) – who had tried to become a member of Hoffmann's studio during a long stay in Vienna in 1908.

22 Kraus, K., 'Pro Domo et Mundo', Beim Wort genommen, edited by H. Fischer, Munich, 1955. (Italian translation: Milan, 1972, p.235).

23 Quoted in Veronesi, G., Josef Hoffmann, Milan, 1956, p.10.

24 Kraus, K., 'Nachts', Beim Wort genommen, op. cit., p.341.

25 Loos, A., 'Ornament und Verbrechen', Trotzdem, op. cit., pp.80, 86.

26 Loos, A., 'Die Überflüssigen', Trotzdem, op. cit., p.71.

27 Loos, A., 'Hands Off', Trotzdem, op. cit., pp.146-147.

28 Loos, A., 'Kulturentartung', Trotzdem, op. cit., p.78.

29 Wagner, O., Die Baukunst unserer Zeit, Vienna, 1914 (4th edition of Moderne Architektur), p.59.

30 Ibid., p.31.

31 Giusti Baculo, A., Otto Wagner dall'architettura di stile allo stile utile, Naples, 1970, p.116.

32 Wagner, O., Die Baukunst unserer Zeit, op. cit., pp.48-49.

33 Loos used this expression to refer to the villages made of cloth, wood and cardboard built in the Ukraine under the ministry of Potemkin in order to transform the desert into a pleasant landscape for the eyes of the Tsarina Catherine.

34 Frey, D., 'Otto Wagner, historische Betrachtungen und Gegenwartsgedanken', Der Architekt XXII, 1919, pp.1-9.

35 Ibid.

36 Giusti Baculo, A., op. cit., pp.209-210.

USA

Louis Sullivan

1 Nikolaus Pevsner, The Sources of Modern Architecture and Design, London, 1968, p.35.

2 Louis Sullivan, 'The Tall Office Building Artistically Considered', Lippincott's, March 1896, pp.403-409.

3 'Monadnock Block' brochure, published by the Commission on Chicago Historical and Architectural Landmarks, 1976. It has elsewhere been assumed that the client's decision was due to budgetary restrictions, but in 1884 he wrote to his partner that he 'would

request an avoidance of ornamentation . . . rely upon the effect of solidity and strength'.

4 According to Condit, The Rise of the Skyscraper, Chicago, 1952, the Fire destroyed $192,000,000 worth of property; then, in the next two decades, buildings costing a total of $316,200,000 were erected. Although flammable 'balloon-frame' wooden buildings greatly fed the flames, no commercial structure in cast iron was adequately protected to survive either.

5 S. Tschudi Madsen, Art Nouveau, New York, 1967, p.234. This criticism is common to concluding chapters on the 'failure' of Art Nouveau to provide the link between the Arts and Crafts Movement and the Bauhaus in the progress of modernism.

6 Separate accounts by Adler and Sullivan of this building complement – and compliment – each other. Adler praised Sullivan's artful ornament in 'The Chicago Auditorium', Architectural Record, April-June 1892. Sullivan praised Adler's technical ingenuity in 'Development of Construction', The Economist, Chicago, vol. 55, 1916.

7 Calling the Columbian Exposition's house style a 'lewd exhibit of drooling imbecility', among other imprecations, Sullivan prophesied that the damage wrought there to American architecture would last fifty years. Cf. Sullivan, The Autobiography of an Idea, New York, 1956 edition, p.322.

8 Quoted in Hugh Morrison, Louis Sullivan, Westport, Connecticut, 1971 edition, p.189.

9 Comparison might also be made to white-stuccoed International Style, with its restricted palette of de Stijl primary and neutral colours; academic purity meets puritanical modern classicism.

10 Wayne Andrews, Architecture, Ambition, and Americans, London, 1947, p.222.

11 Morrison, op. cit., p.35. Albert Bush-Brown, Louis Sullivan, New York, 1960, p.26. H. R. Hitchcock, Architecture Nineteenth and Twentieth Centuries, Harmondsworth, 1958, p.243.

12 Sullivan always introduced himself 'Louis Henri' in the French pronunciation but, since he spoke that language in his student days in Paris, 1874, neither this French connection, nor any Irish one, necessarily came as a filial due. On the other hand, Chicago in the late nineteenth century was a cosmopolitan magnet. Dankmar Adler was a German-Jewish immigrant, so were most of the firm's clients, and through their transplanted culture Sullivan became acquainted with Schiller, Nietzsche, and Wagner – about whose music he became quite passionate. John Root came from the American South, was educated in England, read German, and also gravitated to Chicago.

13 See Madsen, pp. 38-40, 69-70, for a summary of this movement. It contributed to Art Nouveau in the affected areas, but Madsen himself makes no claims on Sullivan's heredity for it.

14 Op. cit., p.254.

15 In his unpublished 'Utilitarian Theory of Beauty', cited by Condit, p.76, and 'Art of Pure Color', Inland Architect and Builder, I, no. 6, July 1883.

16 'A Great Architectural Problem', Inland Architect and News Record, XV, no. 5, June 1890.

17 Gottfried Semper, 'Development of Architectural Style', translated by J. W. Root, Inland Architect and News Record, XIV, no. 7, 1889.

18 This exact phraseology – much abused and mis-interpreted – dates from 1895. Sullivan's own exegeses include, in Kindergarten Chats, '. . . outward appearances resemble inner purposes. For instances: the form, oak-tree . . . expresses the purpose or function, oak; the form, pine-tree . . . indicates the function, pine . . .' and so on ad infinitum. In the Autobiography: '. . . it was not simply a matter of form expressing function, but the vital idea was this: that the function created or organized its form'.

19 In 'The Influence of Steel Construction and Plate Glass upon Style', read to the American Institute of Architects Convention, 1896.

20 Morrison, p.225.

21 Chaper on 'Emotional Architecture as Compared with Intellectual', Kindergarten Chats, New York, 1947, p.201.

22 The Adler-Sullivan partnership was dissolved in 1895, due as much to the Depression beginning in 1893 as to the change in architectural taste betokened by the Columbian Exposition of the same year. Between 1881

and 1895 the firm had produced schemes for more than a hundred commissions, but it was Adler – the more 'practical' partner – who had all the client contacts. Although Sullivan 'inherited' the Carson Store job after the breakup, that was to be his last sizeable building. In his thirty years of independent practice, he built only twenty buildings, none on anything like a skyscraper scale.
23 Vincent Scully, *American Architecture and Urbanism*, London, 1969, p.110.
24 By Max Dunning of the A.I.A., which published them, 1924. Morrison quotes him, p.227: 'Mr Sullivan considered, I believe, that these two efforts constituted his life's greatest accomplishment . . . his last days were among the most pleasant he had experienced for many years, as he felt that his life's work had been so splendidly consumated'.
25 H. W. Desmond, 'Another View – What Mr Louis Sullivan Stands for', *Architectural Record*, vol. 16, July 1904.

Frank Lloyd Wright
1 Rheims, Maurice, *The Flowering of Art Nouveau*, New York, 1966 pp.7-11. This is a discussion of the purposes and goals of the Art Nouveau artists.
2 Manson, Grant C., 'Wright in the Nursery: The influence of Froebel education on the work of Frank Lloyd Wright', *The Architectural Review*, London, 1953, CXIII, pp.349-359. This article was the impetus for Manson, with prodding from Wright who read the article and wrote to Manson, to publish his dissertation that was completed in 1939 and is now known as *The First Golden Age Book*.
3 Wright, Frank Lloyd, *The Architectural Club of Chicago*, catalogue of the 14th Annual Exhibition of the Chicago Architectural Club, Chicago, 1901. This volume published the complete talk by Wright and did away with most of the usual visual material that was normally included.
4 Smith, Norris Kelly, *Frank Lloyd Wright, A Study in Architectural Content*, New Jersey, 1966, pp.51-53. This book is about the only one that begins to analyse the work of Wright. Smith's discussion of the basis of Hebrew and Greek thought and life reflected in their buildings and in Wright's architecture is very thought provoking and should be read before and again after one is familiar with his buildings.
5 Condit, Carl W., *Chicago 1910-1920: Building, Planning and Urban Technology*, Chicago, 1973, p.301. A listing of the population for Chicago in ten year increments.
6 Hallmark, Donald P., 'Richard W. Bock, Sculpture Part II: The Mature Collaborations' *Prairie School Review*, vol.VIII, no. 2, second quarter 1971, p.9. Hallmark identifies some of the possible influences in Bock's and thus Wright's work that are a result of Bock's European travels. By examples Bock's role as collaborator is more clearly shown.
7 Wright, Frank Lloyd, 'A Home in a Prairie Town', *Ladies Home Journal*, XVIII, February 1901, p.17 and Wright, Frank Lloyd, 'A Small House with Lots of Room in It', *Ladies Home Journal*, XVIII, July 1901, p.15. These two articles were part of a series on architecture that could be afforded by most people of modest income. They brought few commissions but tell what Wright's design thoughts were at the time.
8 Strauss, Irma, 'The Husser House dining room set', *The Frank Lloyd Wright Newsletter*, II, no. 1, first quarter 1979, pp.5-9. New evidence of Wright's decorative arts are still being discovered and documented. This fine article by Ms Strauss tells the history of the pieces and their significance in Wright's work.

PHOTOGRAPHIC ACKNOWLEDGEMENTS

The photographers referred to in the captions are as follows:
Ivan Adamík, T. & R. Annan, Eleonora Bairati, Richard Ball, George Barford, Tim Benton, Franco Borsi, Guy Collomb, Ezio Godoli, André Goulancourt, Thomas A. Heinz, Vladimír Hnízdo, Vladimír Hyhlík, Pierre Joly, A. F. Kersting, Michel La Rue, Ian Latham, Albert Le Berrurier, Bedford Lemere, Dr K. J. H. Mackay, Erling Mandelmann, Luciana Miotto Muret, Bebbe Klatt Mooring, Richard Nickel, Vittoria Pallucchini Pelzel, Giorgio Pezzato, Marvin Rand, Caroline Rose, Nicolas Sapieha, Otto Simoner, Studio Chevojon, Laurent Sully-Jaulmes, Jean-Luc Touillon, Louli Van Wynsberghe, Paul Vonberg, Hans Wieser.

Archival sources: figures refer to illustration numbers. The prefix B denotes illustrations to biographies. Colour illustrations are referenced by page number.

A. C. L. Brussels 3.12-14, B.71; Ampliaciones y Reproducciones MAS, Barcelona 2.1, 2.14, 2.19-20, 2.25, 2.31, 2.33, 2.36; Architektursammlung der TU, Munich 7.7; Archiv AU, Prague 9.14; Archives d'Architecture Moderne, Brussels 3.1-3, 3.5-6, 3.15, 3.20-24, 3.26-29, 3.34, 7.12-13, 7.15, B.6, B.13, B.31-32, B.39-40, B.70, B.84; Arch. Phot. Paris/S.P.A.D.E.M. 4.1, B.3, B.17, B.21-22, B.25; Archivio Modulo, Florence 8.21-22, 8.24-25, B.16, B.72, B.80; Archiv I. Salvátorská ul. E.8, Prague 9.2, 9.15-18, 9.20-21, B.45; Austrian National Tourist Board, London 10.14; Bibliothèque Royale, Brussels 3.33, 7.14, 7.16-19; Bildarchiv der Österreichische Nationalbibliothek, Vienna 10.1, 10.17, 10.43, B.87; Bildarchiv Foto Marburg, Marburg 7.8-9; Bildarchiv Preussischer Kulturbesitz, Berlin 7.4-5, 7.35-37, 10.18, B.23; Chicago Historical Society 11.4-5; City Art Gallery, Manchester 1.31, B.77, B.92; Ediciones Poligrafa, Barcelona 2.3-6, 2.9, 2.11, B.20, pp. 53-54, p.71; Escuela Tecnica Superior de Arquitectura de Barcelona, Barcelona 2.2, 2.12-13, 2.15-16, 2.21-23, 2.26, 2.29-30; Freie Universität Berlin, Berlin 7.34; Glasgow School of Art, Glasgow 1.41; Mario Ghisalberti 8.26, 8.33-35; Greene and Greene Library, USC, Pasadena 11.22, 11.24-25, B.29; Haags Gemeentemuseum, The Hague 5.1-2, 5.10, 5.28-29; Horniman Museum, London B.82; Institut Belge d'Information et de Documentation, Brussels 3.4, 3.7, 3.9; Inventaire Général Lorraine, Nancy 4.2, 4.26-30, 4.32, 4.40-41, B.1, B.83, B.91, p.8, p.128; Kensington and Chelsea Borough Libraries, London 1.5; Kodak Museum, London 1.36-37, B.89; Krajské Středisko Památkové Péče a Ochrany Přírody, Brno 9.11; Mila Levi-Pistoi 8.16-17; Marc Vokaer Editeur, Brussels p.110; Luciana Miotto Muret 4.36; National Monuments Record, London 1.1, 1.3, 1.9-10, 1.14-15, 1.24-25, B.28, B.62, B.67, B.79, B.86, B.90; Ned. Doc. centrum v.d. Bouwkunst (Stichting Architectuurmuseum), Amsterdam 5.6-9, 5.11-12, 5.17, 5.19-22, 5.24-25, 5.30-43, B.9, B.11, B.15, B.18, B.47, B.88, pp.145-146; Régie Autonome des Transports Parisiens, Paris 4.11-12; Royal Commission on Ancient Monuments, Scotland frontispiece, B.53; The Royal Institute of British Architects, London 1.11-13, 5.20; Soprintendenza ai Monumenti, Florence 8.29, B.55; Spanish National Tourist Office, London 2.27, B.26; Franz Stoedtner 7.2-3; The Hague Municipality, The Hague 5.3-5; University of Glasgow, Hunterian Art Gallery 1.4; University of Glasgow, Mackintosh collection 1.38, 1.40, 7.28-29, B.51, p.176 bottom; William Morris Gallery, Walthamstow 1.16.

Other illustrations are reproduced from the following publications:
L'Architecte; Architectural Review; L'Architecture aux XXe Siècle, vols I-IV; *Der Architekt; Architektur von Olbrich* Verlag von Wasmuth, Berlin; *Architetture alla prima Esposizione Internazionale d'Arte decorativa moderna* Turin 1902; *L'Architettura Italiana; Arte Decorativa Moderna; L'Art Décoratif;* Beltrami, L., *Gaetano Moretti – Costruzioni concorse schizzi*, Milan 1912; Cresti, C., *Firenze 1895-1915. La Stagione del Liberty* Florence 1978; *Deutsche Kunst und Dekoration;* Dostál, O., Pechar, J., Procházka, V., *Moderní architektura v Ceskoslovensku* Prague 1967; Hasbrouck, W. R. (ed.), *Architectural Essays from the Chicago School from 1900 to 1909;* Koch, A., *Meister der Innenkunst: Haus eines Kunstfreundes von M. H. Baille Scott* Darmstadt 1902; Olbrich, J. M. *Ideen von Olbrich* Vienna 1900; Schönthal, O., (ed.), *Das Ehrenjahr Otto Wagners an der K. K. Akademie der bildenden Künste in Wien* Vienna 1912; Spencer, R. C. Jr., *The Work of Frank Lloyd Wright from 1893 to 1900; The Studio; Wendingen; The Western Architect.*

INDEX

Figures in italics refer to pages containing illustrations

INDEX